D0203817

WITHDRAWN

FOND DU LAC PUBLIC LIBRARY

32 SHEBOYGAN STREET

FOND DU LAC, WI 54935

OXFORD HISTORY OF MODERN EUROPE

General Editors

LORD BULLOCK *and* SIR WILLIAM DEAKIN

Oxford History of Modern Europe

THE STRUGGLE FOR MASTERY
IN EUROPE 1848–1918 *Available in paperback*
By A. J. P. TAYLOR

THE RUSSIAN EMPIRE 1801–1917
By HUGH SETON-WATSON

A HISTORY OF FRENCH PASSIONS
By THEODORE ZELDIN *Available in paperback in two volumes:*

AMBITION, LOVE , AND POLITICS
INTELLECT, TASTE, AND ANXIETY
GERMANY 1866–1945
By GORDON A. CRAIG *Available in paperback*

THE LOW COUNTRIES 1780–1940
By E. H. KOSSMANN

SPAIN 1808–1975 *Available in paperback*
By RAYMOND CARR

GERMAN HISTORY 1770–1866 *Available in paperback*
By JAMES J. SHEEHAN

THE TRANSFORMATION OF EUROPEAN
POLITICS 1763–1848
By PAUL W. SCHROEDER

RUMANIA
1866–1947

BY

KEITH HITCHINS

CLARENDON PRESS · OXFORD
1994

Oxford University Press, Walton Street, Oxford OX2 6DP
Oxford New York Toronto
Delhi Bombay Calcutta Madras Karachi
Kuala Lumpur Singapore Hong Kong Tokyo
Nairobi Dar es Salaam Cape Town
Melbourne Auckland Madrid
and associated companies in
Berlin Ibadan

Oxford is a trade mark of Oxford University Press

Published in the United States
by Oxford University Press Inc., New York

© Keith Hitchins 1994

All rights reserved. No part of this publication may be reproduced,
stored in a retrieval system, or transmitted, in any form or by any means,
without the prior permission in writing of Oxford University Press.
Within the UK, exceptions are allowed in respect of any fair dealing for the
purpose of research or private study, or criticism or review, as permitted
under the Copyright, Designs and Patents Act, 1988, or in the case of
reprographic reproduction in accordance with the terms of the licences
issued by the Copyright Licensing Agency. Enquiries concerning
reproduction outside these terms and in other countries should be
sent to the Rights Department, Oxford University Press,
at the address above

British Library Cataloguing in Publication Data
Data available

Library of Congress Cataloging in Publication Data
Hitchins, Keith, 1931–
Rumania: 1866–1947 / by Keith Hitchins.
p. cm. — (Oxford history of modern Europe)
Includes bibliographical references.
1. Rumania—History—Charles I, 1866–1914. 2. Rumania—
History—1914–1944. 3. Rumania—History—1944–1989.
I. Title. II. Title: Rumania. III. Series.
DR250.H58 1994 949.8'02—dc20 93–31575
ISBN 0–19–822126–6

1 3 5 7 9 10 8 6 4 2

Typeset by Best-set Typesetter Ltd., Hong Kong

Printed in Great Britain
on acid-free paper by
Bookcraft Ltd.
Midsomer Norton, Avon

949.8
H 637
c 1

For Thomas and Ruth Mullen

FOND DU LAC PUBLIC LIBRARY

PREFACE

This book is about modern nation-building, a process that absorbed the energies of the Rumanian political and intellectual élite between the latter half of the nineteenth century and the Second World War. It traces the efforts of that élite to form a national state encompassing all Rumanians and to provide it with modern political institutions and an economy and social structure based on industry and the city rather than on agriculture and the village. As the leaders of a lesser power they also recognized how crucial shifts in the international order were to the success of their undertakings at home. Thus, this account of nation-building keeps constantly in view Rumania's relations with the great powers. Of all these contacts, those with Western Europe were the most decisive: the West, or 'Europe', as many Rumanians referred to it, served the élite as a model of development, to be followed or avoided, but never ignored.

Political events grouped in five distinct periods—independence (1866–81), the reign of King Charles (1881–1914), the First World War (1914–18), Greater Rumania (1919–40), and the Second World War (1940–4)—provide the framework for this study of modern Rumania. But chronological boundaries have been crossed in order to follow general trends in economic and social development and to discern changes in the way Rumanians thought about themselves. A final chapter deals with the brief period between the overthrow of the wartime military dictatorship in August 1944 and the proclamation of a People's Republic by Rumanian Communists in December 1947. It traces the disintegration of modern Rumania and thus serves as an epilogue to this account of classical national-building.

I am glad to have this opportunity to thank persons who have helped me to bring this work to print. Many colleagues and friends in Rumania have aided me with ideas and suggestions. I cannot mention them all, but I would like to express my gratitude again to Pompiliu Teodor, Cornelia Bodea, Mihai C. Demetrescu,

Ioan Beju, and Mircea Păcurariu. Colleagues in the Department of History at the University of Illinois have been supportive in numerous ways. I found membership for seven years on the Joint Committee for Eastern Europe of the American Council of Learned Societies especially valuable. The exchanges with colleagues in other disciplines there expanded my understanding of both Rumania and of history. At the Oxford University Press Ivon Asquith and Anthony Morris were encouraging and patient. I am particularly indebted to Sir William Deakin, who was a stimulating critic and whose advice did much to improve the text.

K.H.

CONTENTS

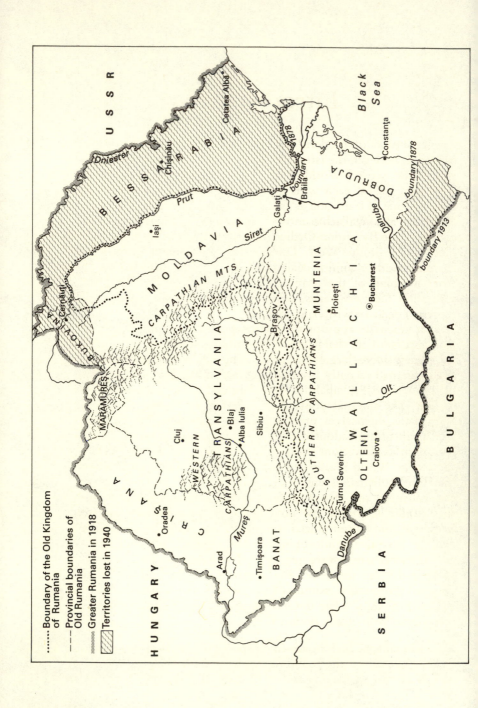

Boundary of the Old Kingdom of Rumania

Provincial boundaries of Old Rumania

Greater Rumania in 1918

Territories lost in 1940

USSR

Black Sea

BESSARABIA

Dniester

Cetarea Albă

Chişinău

Prut

BUKOVINA

Cernăuţi

Iaşi

MOLDAVIA

Siret

Galaţi

boundary 1878

Brăila

DOBRUDJA

boundary 1878

Constanţa

boundary 1913

CARPATHIAN MTS

MUNTENIA

Braşov

Ploieşti

Bucharest

Danube

MARAMUREŞ

TRANSYLVANIA

Blaj

Alba Iulia

Sibiu

SOUTHERN CARPATHIANS

WALLACHIA

Olt

Cluj

WESTERN CARPATHIANS

OLTENIA

Turnu Severin

Craiova

CRIŞANA

Oradea

Mureş

BANAT

Arad

Timişoara

Danube

HUNGARY

SERBIA

BULGARIA

Introduction

The evolution of modern Rumania took place over some two centuries, between the latter half of the eighteenth century and the end of the Second World War. Discernible in this long process were two stages, each with its own distinct characteristics. The first was one of transition as the Rumanians of the principalities of Moldavia and Wallachia moved away from the patriarchal traditions of the Byzantine-Orthodox South-east toward the dynamic innovations of the West. During the second stage currents of change already manifest coalesced, and modern Rumania, in the strict meaning of the term, came into being. The critical date separating the two stages, to the extent that a single year may represent such a division, is 1866.

That year is an appropriate starting-point for a study of modern Rumania, since its characteristic institutional framework and mental climate were largely in place. The union of Moldavia and Wallachia had recently been accomplished, and the independence of the 'United Principalities' had been assured *de facto*, if not yet *de jure*. The internal political foundations of 'Rumania', as the Rumanians themselves preferred to call their country, had been laid: a constitution adopted in 1866 would serve as the fundamental law, with modifications as circumstances required, until the eve of the Second World War; a new dynasty, the Sigmaringen branch of the Hohenzollerns, ascended the princely throne in the same year and enhanced the prospects for political stability; the principles that would determine the governance of the country—a strong executive and a centralized administration—had been codified; and the dominant philosophies of the modern state—liberalism and conservatism—were represented by political parties in the making. By this time, too, the country's political and intellectual élite had thoroughly assimilated the modern idea of nation and had accepted the duty it laid upon them to redraw political frontiers in accordance with ethnic boundaries.

The Rumanians had occupied a special place in South-eastern Europe ever since the founding of the principalities of Moldavia and Wallachia in the fourteenth century. To be sure, they were

Orthodox like the Serbs, Bulgarians, and Greeks and thus shared with them membership in the Byzantine Commonwealth. The Rumanians' links to this world were strong. Besides the ecclesiastical allegiance to Constantinople, they had used Old Slavonic as the official language of both church and state until the seventeenth century. Their cultural life and agrarian economy were also characteristic of South-eastern Europe. But at the same time significant differences separated the Rumanians from their neighbours. Most striking were their affinities to Western Europe: they spoke a language descended from Latin, and they claimed the Romans as ancestors.

During the long era of Ottoman domination of South-eastern Europe between the fourteenth and nineteenth centuries the Rumanians followed a path of development distinct from that of their neighbours south of the Danube. By treaties with the sultan, later on to be known, inaccurately, as 'capitulations', Moldavia and Wallachia maintained their political autonomy and with it their traditional social and economic structure—the boier (noble) class as the ruling élite and the large estate as the foundation of agriculture. In contrast, south of the Danube the Bulgarian and Serbian empires had been destroyed and, along with the territories inhabited by the Greeks and Albanians, had been incorporated into the Ottoman Empire as provinces administered by Turkish governors. As a consequence, local aristocracies disappeared, their lands were confiscated, and the preservation of the ethnic community was left largely to the village and the parish church.

In the seventeenth century the Rumanian principalities continued to evolve differently from the Orthodox communities to the south. By recognizing the sultan as their suzerain and by paying an annual tribute, the Rumanians avoided an occupation by Ottoman armies and the Islamization to which the South Slav lands had been subjected. Moldavian and Wallachian princes even maintained relations with foreign countries, a clear violation of their vassal status. The Orthodox Church of both principalities carried on its spiritual responsibilities at home and pursued its canonical relations with the Patriarchate of Constantinople and the other Eastern patriarchates without significant interference from Ottoman authorities. The princes and many boiers, together with the higher clergy, were deeply conscious of the special place they occupied in Eastern Christendom, which, except for Russia, had fallen under Muslim domination. They eagerly assumed responsibility for supporting the holy places in the East and for providing refuge for the numerous clergy, mainly Greek, who fled Ottoman-held territories.

The Ottoman connection over the centuries thus had the effect of reinforcing the Rumanians' cultural and spiritual ties to the Orthodox world. In foreign relations and international trade, as well as religion, the principalities were drawn to Constantinople. Although they were by no means cut off from the West, they faced East both willingly and out of necessity.

The autonomy of Moldavia and Wallachia became increasingly precarious in the eighteenth century. Ottoman officials, uncertain of the princes' loyalty as Austria and Russia pressed relentlessly against the empire's northern frontiers, tightened their political control over the principalities. The sultan treated the princes as mere Ottoman officials, to be appointed and dismissed at his pleasure. In this way the so-called Phanariot regime, which was to endure until 1821, was inaugurated. Its main characteristics were increasing interference in the domestic affairs of the principalities, and, in particular, an unprecedented drain on the economic re-sources of the principalities, as Ottoman officials raised at will the amount of the tribute and the quantities of wheat, animals, and other raw materials they purchased at fixed prices or simply requisitioned.

Rumanian boiers in the second half of the eighteenth century sought outside aid to restore political autonomy and eventually throw off Ottoman domination altogether. They turned first to Russia as a proven champion of the Orthodox peoples under Ottoman rule, and during the Russo-Turkish War of 1768–74 they addressed numerous appeals to the Empress Catherine and Russian officials urging them to liberate their fellow Orthodox from Muslim oppression. Russian policy-makers responded in the Treaty of Kuchuk Kainardji of 1774, which ended the war, by obliging the sultan to allow Russian diplomats in Constantinople to make 'representations' on behalf of the Orthodox of the Ottoman Empire. In subsequent decades this device was to prove invaluable in enabling Russia to undermine the sultan's authority in the principalities.

Russia's intervention marked the beginning of a long process by which the Rumanian principalities eventually gained the recognition of the great powers as distinct, if minor, components of the Eastern Question. Rumanian leaders were convinced that such a status was essential to the recovery of autonomy and, ultimately, the achievement of independence. Consequently, they turned all their efforts toward the internationalization of what came to be known in diplomacy after 1800 as the 'Rumanian Question'.

The Rumanians' prospects for success were not at first promising. None of the powers thought of the principalities as more than instruments for achieving their own broader objectives elsewhere in Europe and the Eastern Mediterranean. Russia was the most aggressive. In three wars against the Ottoman Empire she steadily enhanced her position in the principalities: the Treaty of Iași (1792) allowed Russia to annex the territory between the Bug and Dniester rivers and thus brought her to the frontier of Moldavia for the first time; the Treaty of Bucharest (1812) recognized Russia's annexation of Moldavia between the Dniester and the Prut rivers, known as Bessarabia; and the Treaty of Adrianople (1829) granted Russia a virtual protectorate over the principalities that was to last until the Crimean War.

Several generations of Rumanian boiers, the principal defenders of autonomy, became alarmed at Russia's aggressiveness and feared that the principalities were in danger of exchanging Ottoman for Russian suzerainty. They thus turned elsewhere for support. Austria was close at hand, but the Habsburgs had alienated many boiers through their own predatory designs on Rumanian territory, manifested by the occupation of Oltenia between 1718 and 1739 and the annexation of Bukovina in 1775. Increasingly, therefore, the boiers placed their hopes in the West. After 1830, the sons of boiers, who had studied and travelled in Europe, and a growing middle class eagerly sought to expand contacts with France and Great Britain. They admired France as the champion of the rights of man and, by extension, of oppressed nations, and they held up Britain as a model of orderly, constitutional government. They felt a special kinship with 'Latin' France and were better acquainted with French culture and language than with English.

The springtime of peoples in 1848 seemed to offer Rumanian intellectuals and politicians the opportunity they had long awaited to escape the tutelage of both Ottomans and Russians. In Moldavia the impetus for reform was short-lived, but in Wallachia between June and September 1848 liberals established a provisional government that promised extensive political and civil rights and devised an economic system that would encourage the industrial and commercial entrepreneur and at the same time render justice to the dispossessed majority—the peasants. They were also intent on asserting their nationhood. Foremost among their objectives were the abolition of the Russian protectorate and recognition of the principalities' autonomy by the sultan, both necessary preliminaries, in their view, to union and independence. Inspired by the modern idea of the ethnic nation, they also contemplated the formation of a greater Rumania that would include the Rumanians of the Habsburg and Russian empires, and to this end they promoted contacts with Rumanian intellectuals outside the principalities, especially in Transylvania.

The shaking of the old order in Vienna and the proclamation of political and civil freedoms in Buda-Pest in March 1848 impelled Rumanian intellectuals in Transylvania to mount a campaign of their own to gain recognition of their people as an autonomous nation within a liberal Hungary and, later, in a federalized Habsburg monarchy. In the absence of political institutions they relied on the Orthodox and Uniate churches to provide an infrastructure and to rally the population at large to their cause. The clergy of both churches had long before identified themselves with the fortunes of their people. The Orthodox Church represented the traditions of Eastern Christianity, whereas the Uniate Church, which had come into being in 1700 when a part of the Orthodox clergy accepted the Church Union with Rome, represented an opening to the West. But the forty-eighters in Transylvania, like their counterparts across the Carpathians, were secular in their world-view and intentions and owed their primary allegiance to the ethnic nation. They, too, contemplated the creation of a single state for all Rumanians, but, aware of political realities both at home and abroad, they left the achievement of this goal to the future. For a year, from the summer of 1848 to the following August, their energies were absorbed in a bitter struggle with Magyar liberals and nationalists to secure national autonomy and preserve ethnic identity. The attempts by forty-eighters from Wallachia in the summer of 1849 to reconcile Magyars and Rumanians in order to strengthen the defences of nationhood and liberalism against a resurgent conservative order failed.

Russia played a decisive role in bringing Rumanian national movements on both sides of the Carpathians to naught. Tsar Nicholas I had watched the spread of revolution in Central Europe in the spring and summer of 1848 with growing alarm. Then, in September he sent his troops into Wallachia. They occupied Bucharest and dispersed the provisional government, bringing to an end the brief Rumanian experiment in liberalism. Wallachia and Moldavia, which Russian troops had occupied earlier, served as staging areas for intervention in Hungary and Transylvania. In June 1849, at the request of the Court of Vienna, Russian armies crossed the frontier and in August forced the main Hungarian field army to surrender, thus dashing Rumanian hopes for autonomy in Transylvania.

The failure of revolution left two fundamental questions of Rumanian nation-building—the union of the principalities and independence—unresolved. Yet, within a decade the forty-eighters were to achieve *de facto* recognition of both by the great powers. Rumanian unionists, as the proponents of nationhood came to be known, pressed their case relentlessly, but, sobered by the experience of revolution, they exercised tact in dealing with the powers.

The crisis in international relations that led to the Crimean War offered the unionists the opening they sought. Although the powers were determined, as usual, to settle Ottoman affairs and ancillary issues as they thought best, several among them found Rumanian aspirations surprisingly in harmony with their own objectives in the region. France, in particular, was sympathetic to enhanced autonomy for the principalities primarily as a means of expanding her influence in the East. Even Russia now found it advantageous to support the union of the principalities in order to divide France from her wartime allies. Britain, too, initially approved of union as an impediment to further Russian expansion into the Ottoman Empire, but later she grew cool towards the idea because a united Rumania appeared to serve French rather than British interests. Two powers that had been consistently hostile to any significant change in the status of the principalities adamantly opposed expanded autonomy and union. The Ottoman government insisted on the maintenance of the sultan's full suzerain rights, while Austrian officials viewed any strengthening of the principalities as an obstacle to further political and economic penetration of the lower Danube and as a stimulus to nationalist activity among their empire's own large Rumanian population.

In the Treaty of Paris of 1856, which ended the Crimean War, the powers acceded to two long-standing demands of Rumanian intellectuals and politicians. First, they placed Moldavia and Wallachia under their collective protection, thereby discouraging future Russian and Ottoman intervention and requiring Austria to withdraw her army of occupation in place since 1854, and, second, they recognized the right of the Rumanians themselves to have a voice in shaping their form of government. Granted such an opportunity, the majority of Rumanians left no doubt about their desire for union and independence, and the powers (Austria and the Ottoman Empire grudgingly) responded by promulgating the so-called Convention of Paris in 1858. This document, intended to serve as a fundamental law for the principalities, outlined the way in which the Rumanians should henceforth govern themselves. It also recognized the sultan as their suzerain, but by this time all the parties to the agreement knew that what remained of his prerogatives—payment of the annual tribute and investiture of the prince—had become mere formalities.

The Convention of Paris contained one major disappointment for the Rumanians: it said nothing about the union of the principalities. But the unionists, backed by a surge of popular support, took matters into their own hands. At the beginning of 1859, exercising a right granted them by the Convention of Paris to elect their own princes, they chose the same man, Alexandru Cuza, in each principality. The powers, bowing to the inevitable and preoccupied elsewhere, acquiesced in the *fait accompli*, and Cuza himself completed the administrative union of the principalities in 1861.

During his brief reign (1859–66) Cuza, a forty-eighter and a liberal, undertook to endow 'Rumania', as the new union was now officially called, with modern political and economic institutions. But he insisted that they conform to his specifications. Impatient to get on with fundamental reforms, he dissolved an obstreperous assembly in May 1864 when it rejected the agrarian and electoral laws that formed the core of his legislative programme. Barely two weeks after his coup he submitted a constitution, the *Statut*, to a popular referendum in order to legitimize his regime. Approved overwhelmingly, the new fundamental law confirmed the prepronderance of the executive over the legislature, limited the role of the mass of citizens in the political process, and consolidated the power of the central bureaucracy at the expense of local government. Cuza thus retained parliamentary forms, but under the *Statut* the essence of Rumanian constitutionalism lay in the personal rule of the prince.

During Cuza's reign another institution gradually took form which was to infuse life into the legislature and thus raise a serious challenge to the prince's authority. Political parties, though still amorphous, had by the 1860s become identified with distinct currents of social and economic thought, and two broad groupings of intellectuals and politicians had already emerged—liberals and conservatives. Liberals generally stood for an expansion of political rights and civil liberties, supported industry, and extolled Western Europe as the model to be followed. Conservatives, on the other hand, insisted on rule by the propertied classes, who alone, they thought, could assure order and stability, giving priority to agriculture and rejecting the Western model as fundamentally incompatible with the character and needs of Rumanian society. Yet, neither liberals nor conservatives succeeded in forming united parties at this time, despite their opposition to Cuza's personal rule, because the factions among both had not yet learned the art of compromise. Rivalries among the liberals were particularly acute, as radicals, the most revolutionary of the forty-eighters and the most intransigent of the unionists and thus dubbed 'reds' by their opponents, broke with the moderates. Fierce champions of legislative supremacy, they became uncompromising foes of Cuza.

The Rumania of Cuza's time remained overwhelmingly rural. Agriculture was the foundation of the country's economy, and although acreage and production had expanded since the beginning of the century, its structure had remained essentially unchanged. As in the eighteenth century the peasant working his allotment of land had primary responsibility for production: he decided what to plant and how to cultivate the crop, and he supplied not only the labour but also the tools and the animals. The changes that had occurred over half a century—the transformation by landlords of large portions of their estates into private property free of all responsibilities to their peasants and the abolition in 1864 of obligatory labour services (clacă) owed landlords by peasants—did not alter this central fact. Reinforcing the traditional structure of agriculture were the slow pace of urbanization, which deprived producers of nearby, stable markets, and the growing reliance on exports of wheat and other products, which perpetuated extensive agriculture with all its deficiencies.

Industry in its modern form had barely made its appearance by mid-century. There were few factories, as artisan shops and manufactories continued to satisfy the bulk of consumer needs. The obstacles to industrialization were daunting: the lack of adequate foreign and domestic capital, the poverty and consequent low purchasing power of the rural masses, which discouraged the expansion of the fledgling urban industry, and a persistent weakness of the entrepreneurial spirit and resistance to long-term investment. Prospects for change during Cuza's reign were none the less encouraging. The new national government he had installed had begun to take responsibility for shaping an economic policy beneficial to Rumanians, and the gradual absorption of the country into the Western economic sphere promised to shake existing structures.

Society in Cuza's Rumania preserved the fundamental characteristics of the previous century: the peasantry continued to form the overwhelming majority of the population, while the number of urban dwellers grew only modestly. But beneath the surface far-reaching changes were already under way. Within the peasantry social differentiation was accelerating and a rural middle class forming, as a growing, if uneven, capitalist economy impinged upon the village. The other traditional class of rural society, the boiers, was also in the throes of change. The Convention of Paris and the *Statut* had deprived them of noble rank and privileges, but as great landowners they retained considerable economic and political power and stoutly defended the interests of agriculture and the great estate. But many of them were being drawn into industry and commerce and were adopting middle-class values. The process of assimilation into the middle class was even more pronounced among the former lesser boiers. But the new class, whose core of merchants, master artisans, and 'industrialists' was expanding through the addition of increasing numbers of professionals and civil servants, remained small, and its members lacked cohesion and a sense of themselves as a social class with a vocation of its own.

Intellectuals formed another social group on the rise since the early decades of the century. They belonged mainly to the liberal professions and showed no hesitation in assuming the role of critics. Their special province was social change and the adaptation of existing institutions to the 'spirit of the times'. It was they who were mainly responsible for elaborating the theory of the ethnic nation and for devising the strategies of national development. They were also the chief bearers of Western economic and political ideas, which, as they had demonstrated in 1848, they were eager to adapt to Rumanian circumstances. By Cuza's reign many had turned to politics and filled the ranks primarily of the liberals.

Of all the groups and classes composing Rumanian society at mid-century, the Orthodox clergy had suffered the most drastic change in status. Its upper ranks, once members of the highest administrative and judicial councils of state, had gradually been relieved of their secular duties, while the parish clergy had lost such civic responsibilities as the keeping of vital statistics. The church itself came under the increasing supervision of the state and suffered the intrusion of bureaucrats even into such intimate matters as the education of priests and discipline in the monasteries. Cuza's church legislation of 1864 stands as the culmination of a series of measures enacted over half a century and aimed at codifying the subordination of the church to the state. Yet, the church continued to enjoy great moral prestige as a national institution, for it had been linked to the fortunes of the principalities since their foundation and offered spiritual guidance to the overwhelming majority of Rumanians who were Orthodox and made no distinction between religion and nationality.

The controversy over the role of the Orthodox Church in society was symptomatic of a general crisis of identity caused by modern nation-building. On one side stood conservatives, the clergy, and the peasantry, who represented agrarian social and Byzantine-Orthodox cultural traditions, which had defined the national character up to the nineteenth century. Their world-view was patriarchal, and they were wary of change. Others, mainly liberals, had formulated a new image of Rumanians anchored to two ideas—nation and Europe—which, moreover, were a measure of the distance educated Rumanians had travelled since the eighteenth century. Contacts with Western Europe, which had deepened earlier notions of their 'Latin' affinities, gradually separated them from the international Orthodox community they had shared with the South Slavs and Greeks. Although they could not deny this Eastern spiritual heritage, they now gave their moral allegiance to the ethnic nation. Based on a consciousness of descent from the Roman colonizers of ancient Dacia, the new idea of nation proved to them the essential Europeanness of modern Rumania.

1
Independence, 1866–1881

PRINCE CHARLES, 1866–1876

The decade in which Rumania achieved independence began in 1866 with the overthrow of Prince Alexandru Cuza by an unlikely combination of Conservative and radical Liberal politicians. At odds with one another on almost every significant public issue, they none the less found ample reason to join forces in opposing what they claimed were Cuza's abuses of power and his intention to establish a dictatorship. A reformer who had seen the urgent need to rationalize government administration and increase the productivity of agriculture, Cuza had made the mistake of imposing his *Statut* and an agrarian reform bill, both in 1864, in such a manner as to alienate old supporters and unify his enemies. Thus isolated politically, he himself encouraged the plotters by intimating that he might abdicate. On 23 February 1866, swiftly and without public disorder or resistance from Cuza, the coalition, led by the radical Liberals Ion C. Brătianu and C. A. Rosetti, both revolutionaries of 1848, forced Cuza to abdicate and go into exile.

The leaders of the coup immediately established a provisional government. Executive power was vested in a princely lieutenancy (Locotenenţa domnească), or regency council, consisting of Nicolae Golescu, one of the members of the Wallachian provisional government in 1848 and Minister of the Interior and of War under Cuza; Lascăr Catargiu, a leader of the Conservatives; and General Nicolae Haralambie, prefect of police of Bucharest. Both Liberals and Conservatives obtained ministerial posts, and the moderate Ion Ghica, a forty-eighter and a unionist as well as an erudite economist and skilled diplomat, became Prime Minister and Minister of Foreign Affairs. They were all agreed that their most urgent task was to find a prince and to do so quickly, since the longer the interregnum lasted, the greater the instability, and, hence, the greater the likelihood of foreign intervention.

The immediate reaction of the great powers to the coup was to demand that all the treaties and other agreements affecting the principalities of Moldavia and Wallachia since 1856 to which they had been parties be respected.[1] By the Treaty of Paris of 1856 and the Convention of Paris of 1858 they had established a kind of protectorate over the principalities. Although they had acquiesced in the union of Moldavia and Wallachia in 1859 when the voters in each had elected Cuza as their prince, they continued to recognize the suzerainty of the Ottoman Sultan over them. They made no effort to restore Cuza to his throne, apparently regarding his undoing as largely his own fault. Only the Ottoman government assumed an aggressive stance. Ali pasha, the Foreign Minister, pointed out that the powers had agreed to the union of the principalities only for the duration of Cuza's reign and insisted that new elections in each principality be held under the supervision of Ottoman commissioners. But none of the other guaranteeing powers were eager to reopen the whole Rumanian question. They all had other, more pressing concerns and assigned a low priority to the principalities. France, the Rumanians' traditional patron, supported union and was willing to go along with a foreign prince, but in the spring of 1866 Napoleon III was once again exploring the possibility of Austria's ceding Venetia to Italy in exchange for the principalities. Britain was pursuing a number of contradictory goals all at the same time—the maintenance of the integrity of the Ottoman Empire, respect for the treaties, and the satisfaction of Rumanian claims, if only to avert an international crisis—and ended by following the French lead. Russia, which favoured the separation of the principalities, did not wish to appear as the opponent of the national aspirations of the Balkan Orthodox and so refused to take the initiative. Austria, which under ordinary circumstances would have joined Turkey and Russia, was at the moment seeking French support against Prussia in her contest for supremacy in Germany and reluctantly acquiesced in both the union and a foreign prince. The differences among the powers and their reluctance to act decisively brought their conference in Paris (March to June) to a standstill and left the initiative in the hands of the Rumanians.[2]

In the meantime, the provisional government had moved swiftly to fill the vacancy on the throne. The majority of Conservatives and Liberals remained committed to a foreign prince. The former

---

[1] The reaction of the powers is analysed by T. W. Riker, *The Making of Roumania* (Oxford, 1931), 507–37.

[2] Grigore Chiriţă, 'România şi Conferinţa de la Paris, februarie–iunie 1866', *Revista de istorie*, 38/10 (1985), 967–86; 11: 1075–100.

thought that only a foreign dynasty could hold liberal radicalism in check and thus guarantee their own control of the state, while moderate Liberals, who favoured a constitutional monarchy as the best way to maintain a balance between 'despotism' and 'anarchy', saw in a foreign prince an added guarantee of social and political stability. When the provisional government's first choice for prince, Philip of Flanders, the brother of the King of Belgium, declined the honour, it courted Charles of Hohenzollern-Sigmaringen. Ion Brătianu, representing the regency council, was instrumental in persuading Charles to accept the invitation and in gaining support for him in Bucharest. On 1 April, from Düsseldorf, where he had met Charles and his father, he telegraphed the provisional government that Charles had agreed to become prince, even though he had not, in fact, made a clear statement of his intentions. Brătianu returned home at once to organize a plebiscite on the question, which took place on 14–20 April and overwhelmingly endorsed the selection of Charles, 685,696 in favour out of 686,193 votes cast. Buoyed by such apparent popularity and with the encouragement of Bismarck, then Minister-President of Prussia, Charles decided to accept the invitation without the prior approval of the powers, whose representatives were then in conference in Paris (Bismarck had suggested to Charles that a *fait accompli* was the best way to handle the matter). Charles informed Brătianu of his decision on 7 May.

The new prince had only a modest knowledge of the country, whose throne he had been invited to occupy, and it was only by trial and error that he was to learn the fine points of Rumanian politics. But in other respects he came well equipped for the job. Born on 20 April 1839, he was the second son of Prince Karl Anton of Hohenzollern-Sigmaringen, the Catholic branch of the Hohenzollern family. The young prince was well connected. His father, who was to serve as Minister-President of Prussia from 1858 to 1862, a relatively liberal period before the advent of Bismarck, enabled his son to form close relations with the Prussian royal family, part of those links to Germany which were to have such an extraordinary influence on Charles's foreign policy. He was also warmly received by Napoleon III during long sojourns in France in the early 1860s. Trained as a soldier and well educated, Charles had displayed good political judgement. He was even known as something of a Liberal, but it was a Liberalism tempered by discipline and a sense of duty.

Throughout his long reign, first as prince and then, after 1881, as king until his death in 1914, Charles was the key political figure in the country. From the very beginning he assumed a paramount role in foreign and military affairs. The leaders of parliament between 1866 and 1871 allowed him a relatively free hand in these matters, even though they themselves enjoyed considerable power and prestige in the aftermath of Cuza's overthrow. They recognized the value of his connections in Germany and France, which, they thought, could be used to achieve their foreign policy goals. Moreover, Charles enjoyed considerable military prestige, because he had participated in the war waged by Prussia and Austria against Denmark in 1864 and had been an officer in an army famous for its military spirit and organization. But Charles's role in the internal political life of the country, at least initially, was limited. He lacked personal popularity and was unacquainted with both men and issues. For a time, therefore, he presided rather than ruled.

The reaction of the powers to Charles's accession was consistent with their handling of Cuza's overthrow. They were divided and took no action.[3] At the final meeting of the Paris conference on 4 June the majority opposed Ottoman projects for military intervention and occupation. The war between Austria and Prussia, which began on 17 June, brought the work of the conference abruptly to an end, and by default the powers, in effect, acquiesced in the Rumanian *fait accompli*.

The powers formally recognized Charles as prince in the latter part of 1866 and the beginning of 1867. They imposed no special conditions, but they acted only after Charles had reached an understanding with the Ottoman government. Their negotiations had dragged on throughout the summer with neither side showing an inclination to yield on the essential points defining their relationship. Charles and the Council of Ministers insisted upon the maintenance of their country's full autonomy as specified in the ancient capitulations and subsequent international treaties, and they demanded that their country be called 'Rumania', the 'United Rumanian Principalities', or the 'United Principalities', but without the addition of 'Wallachia and Moldavia', which implied that they could be separated. For their part, Ottoman officials

---

[3] An extensive collection of mainly diplomatic papers concerning the powers' views on the accession of Charles and his subsequent negotiations with the sultan to secure recognition as prince have been published by Paul Henry, *L'Abdication du Prince Cuza et l'avènement de la dynastie de Hohenzollern au trône de Roumanie* (Paris, 1930), 302–457.

demanded that the 'United Principalities' accept their status as a 'constituent part' of the Ottoman Empire and that they renounce the right to conclude treaties with other states. Finally, the uprising in Crete and unrest in Serbia, combined with the firmness of the Rumanian government, persuaded Ottoman officials to make several crucial concessions. On 19 October 1866 the grand vizir recognized Charles as hereditary prince, but he did not yield on the question of autonomy, stipulating that the United Principalities would have to remain an integral part of the Ottoman Empire. Such a status entailed, in his view, the preservation of centuries-old links between the principalities and their suzerain and respect for treaties and conventions between him and foreign countries, at least to the extent that they did not impinge upon the rights of 'Moldo-Wallachians'. The grand vizir also expressed the hope that the United Principalities would increase their annual tribute, would take all practical measures to protect Ottoman subjects engaged in trade there, and would not allow 'revolutionary elements' to assemble on their territory.[4] In his reply of 20 October Charles accepted these conditions and on the next day left for Constantinople where he received a *firman* from the sultan granting him formal recognition as prince.

While this manœuvring was going on, Conservative and Liberal leaders in Bucharest had begun work on a constitution to lay the foundations of the new political system. During the latter years of Cuza's reign the majority of both Liberals and Conservatives had favoured a constitutional monarchy and guarantees of fundamental civil liberties, but abstract principles proved too weak a bond to hold together their fragile coalition once Cuza was gone. Now, both wanted to dominate the new state in order to promote the political and economic interests of the groups they represented. The elections in April 1866 for a new Chamber of Deputies, which was to serve as a Constituent Assembly, showed how keen their rivalry had become. The Conservatives won a majority of the seats, partly because they had gained control of the administrative apparatus at the very beginning of the campaign and were thus able to exert pressure on the voters, and partly because the Liberals were weakened by serious internal divisions.

The new assembly began its work on 10 May. As the first order of business the princely lieutenancy set forth its proposals on the course it thought the country should take and then requested a

---

[4] *Aus dem Leben König Karls von Rumänien*, vol. i (Stuttgart, 1894), 132–3.

vote on the new prince, whose selection, as we have seen, had already been confirmed by a plebiscite. A majority approved, although there was lingering support for a native prince. Upon his arrival in Bucharest on 22 May Charles took the oath in the Chamber to rule in a constitutional manner, and immediately afterwards appointed a coalition government with the Conservative Lascăr Catargiu (1823–99) as Prime Minister. All sides agreed that the maintenance of the Liberal-Conservative coalition, as a manifestation of national unity, was necessary in order to hasten recognition of the new regime by the powers and gain approval of the new constitution from the country at large.

The Chamber of Deputies wasted no time in taking up the draft of a constitution prepared by the Council of State, an institution held over from Cuza's reign. Sharp differences quickly divided Conservatives and Liberals over such crucial issues as the merits of a bicameral legislature, the extent of the franchise, the powers of the prince, especially his right to veto legislation, and the status of foreigners. The Conservative point of view generally prevailed. For example, an upper house—the Senate—was approved as a restraint on the Chamber, which Conservatives thought would almost certainly be a Liberal body. Both Conservatives and Liberals favoured tax or property qualifications for voting, but they differed on amounts and on how various social classes and groups should be represented in the legislature. Once again the Conservatives prevailed. In an avowed attempt to keep the 'ignorant and inexperienced' masses from 'diluting or annihilating the votes of the intelligent and cultivated classes' a large income was made a prerequisite for voting, and voters were separated into colleges weighted in favour of education and wealth. Conservatives also succeeded in according the prince an absolute veto over legislation. The debates over the political rights to be granted foreigners, especially Jews, were passionate, and the division between Liberals and Conservatives was often blurred. Strong opposition developed against those provisions which eliminated religion as an impediment to naturalization and offered naturalized citizens full political rights. But since the economic competition from Jews and other foreigners and the extraterritorial privileges of the *sudiţi* (foreigners, mainly merchants, who enjoyed the protection of foreign consuls) were on the minds of many deputies, article 7 of the constitution allowed only foreigners of the Christian religion to become citizens and, hence, to enjoy political rights.[5]

[5] Alexandru Pencovici, *Dezbaterile Adunării constituante din anul 1866 asupra constituţiunei şi legei electorale* (Bucharest, 1883), 94–117.

This formulation remained in effect until 1879, when a grudging revision in favour of Jews was made at the demand of the Congress of Berlin. The Liberals did have one notable success—they won approval of the article stipulating that the Assembly alone, without the concurrence of the Senate, should have the right to approve the budget.

The rest of the articles passed without much ado either because there were no serious differences over them or because the special 'compromise committee' set up to reconcile divergent opinions succeeded in getting many litigious articles through with little or no discussion. The ninety-one deputies unanimously approved the constitution on 11 July, and on the following day Charles promulgated it. On 18 July the Assembly passed a new electoral law, and, its mission now completed, the prince dissolved it.

Although the Conservatives, representing mainly the large landowners, had won most of the major battles in the Constituent Assembly, the Constitution of 1866 was, paradoxically, essentially a Liberal document. It limited the powers of the prince to those of a constitutional monarch, provided for representative government, made ministers responsible for their acts, and reinforced the principle of the separation of powers. It also set down at length the rights and liberties of the citizenry, who were henceforth guaranteed equality before the law, complete freedom of conscience, of the press, and of public meetings, the right of association, and the protection of one's domicile and person against arbitrary search and arrest.[6] The exercise of these rights over time, despite occasional infringements by the authorities, brought larger numbers of people into the political process and, by assuring a free exchange of ideas, especially through the press, contributed greatly to the formation of a democratic public opinion. The constitution also guaranteed property owners full rights of possession, declaring property to be 'sacred and inviolable' and promising that the only cause of expropriation would be public utility. The main purpose of these stipulations was to protect the great estates against the encroachments of any new agrarian reform, but article 20 of the constitution also declared that the land given to the peasants by the rural law of 1864 'must never be touched'.

The parliamentary system instituted in 1866 differed in important respects from that provided for in Cuza's *Statut*. Immediately

---

[6] The most detailed analysis of the constitution is by George G. Meitani, *Studie asupra Constituțiunei Românilor*, 14 vols. (Bucharest, 1880–90).

striking is the enhanced position of the legislature, which now became an almost equal partner with the prince in making laws. To become law under the new constitution a bill required the approval of both. Both might also initiate legislation, except for bills relating to the income and expenditures of the state, which had to originate in the Chamber of Deputies. Thus, the almost exclusive law-making powers of the prince under the *Statut* were significantly reduced in favour of representatives of the electorate. The bicameral legislature of the *Statut* was maintained, but the new Senate was now an elected, not an appointed, body, and its function was no longer to pass on the constitutionality of laws, but to serve as a second legislative body equal to the Chamber. The legislature also gained the right to point out abuses of power committed by the executive branch and to question ministers and even subject them to parliamentary investigations. The legislature had to meet at least once a year, normally every 15 November (and at other times when convoked by the prince), and its sessions were open to the public, except in special cases when the president of the Chamber or Senate or ten members of either body requested that their deliberations be secret.

The other powers of the prince, besides the legislative, were also diminished. In the first place, he could exercise only those powers expressly granted to him by the constitution and, thus, rule by decree, as practised by Cuza, was no longer possible. But the prince none the less retained enormous authority, and, if he were skilful and determined, he could more often than not manipulate the political machinery in such a way as to make his will prevail. His role in the legislative process was decisive. He could submit his own bills to parliament and he could veto bills, action which could not be overridden by the legislature. He also had considerable latitude in interpreting and carrying out laws through his power to draw up regulations governing their application, even though such regulations could not modify or suspend the laws in question or excuse anyone from carrying them out. He could convoke, close, and dissolve the Assembly and the Senate, but that power was limited by the provision for annual sessions of parliament of at least three months duration and the requirement that an act of dissolution contain a call for new elections within two months and the convocation of both houses within three months. Although the prince represented the executive power, he was declared to be not responsible legally for his acts. Instead, ministers were responsible, and, consequently, no act of the prince was valid unless countersigned by a minister. The prince appointed and dismissed ministers, whom he could choose from among the members of the two houses or from outside the legislature. In any case, they answered to him, not to the parliament, but the practice gradually developed whereby the majority party or coalition in the Chamber of Deputies formed the government.

The Constitution of 1866 thus resembled liberal fundamental laws in place in Western Europe. The similarity between them was one of the main consequences of that opening of the West to Rumanian intellectuals which had begun in the 1830s and 1840s. Many sons of boiers who had studied law and political economy in France and Germany had tried upon their return home to adapt the institutions of an enlightened and prosperous Western Europe to the social and economic circumstances of their own country. The programmes of the forty-eighters and of the radical and moderate Liberals after the revolution are eloquent testimony to the strength of outside influences. It was massively present in the Constitution of 1866.

The main source from which its authors drew was the Belgian Constitution of 1831, both in form and in substance. The selection of the Belgian constitution as a model was not accidental. The first choice for prince after the overthrow of Cuza had been Philip of Flanders, precisely because the authors of the coup wanted to introduce the institutions of his country into the United Principalities and thereby on the lower Danube form a true 'Belgium of the East', as the liberal Bucharest newspaper, Steaua Dunării, put it. Even though Philip of Flanders refused their invitation, the Rumanians could think of no more suitable model for themselves than a constitution which had allowed a small nation to make such enormous progress in a little over three decades. Yet, the Rumanian Constitution of 1866 was by no means a simple imitation of the Belgian, for its authors took account of specifically Rumanian conditions, for example, in articles dealing with property, education, elections, and local government.[7]

A fundamental question arises: was the Constitution of 1866 suited to the social realities of the principalities? At first glance, it would seem not to be, for it was a middle-class document prepared for a country whose middle class formed only a thin stratum of the population. At the top of the social scale remained the

[7] Alexandre Tilman-Timon, Les Influences étrangères sur le droit constitutionel roumain (Paris, 1946), 323–9.

boiers, who were intent upon maintaining their political and economic predominance.[8] At the other end of the scale was a peasantry who composed over 80 per cent of the population and had had little political experience. An enlightened public opinion and an experienced citizenry capable of making the sophisticated political machinery outlined in the constitution function as its authors intended were largely absent. Consequently, the real world did not always accord with the written text, and high principle was often compromised in order to maintain the structures (and the fictions) of constitutionalism. Yet, despite the criticism of their motives by Conservative and Liberal intellectual currents after the fact, there is no indication in contemporary sources that those who debated and approved the constitution article by article, both Conservatives and Liberals, thought that they were dealing in abstractions. Rather, they were certain that the institutions they were creating were well attuned to existing social conditions. They were also satisfied that they had provided the new national state with a flexible legal structure within which rapid economic and cultural progress could occur. Moreover, they intended the promulgation of the constitution to be a sort of declaration of independence, for they had drawn it up and approved it without the participation of the guaranteeing powers, and they had made no mention of dependence upon the Ottoman Empire. The change of name from 'United Principalities' to 'Rumania', which the constitution made official, accurately reflected their state of mind.

In other ways the constitution did not live up to its noble intent. The electoral law, which established the norms under which the public would choose its deputies and senators, fell short of the liberal principles it proclaimed. The tax and income qualifications for voting, which were more restrictive than those of Cuza's *Statut*, and the division of the electorate into colleges, all engineered by the Conservatives in the Constituent Assembly, assured a preponderance to the possessing classes in both houses. According to the earliest complete statistical data available (for 1883, when the number of electors had increased slightly), in the two colleges for the Senate there were 2,355 and 4,524 electors, respectively, the great majority of whom were large landowners. A similar situation prevailed in the Chamber of Deputies. In the first three colleges there were 3,388, 4,814, and 15,382 electors,

---

[8] The boier ranks had been abolished in 1858, but the term 'boier' was used for a long time afterwards to refer to the landowning upper class.

respectively, while in the fourth college there were 12,657 delegates possessing a direct vote and representing 626,906 indirect voters. As a result, the 23,584 electors of colleges I, II, and III (landlords, middle-sized property owners, and elements of the urban middle class) sent 118 deputies to the Chamber, while college IV (the peasantry) elected but 30. The principle of equality of rights proclaimed in the constitution was thus gravely compromised by a suffrage which was neither equal nor direct. Moreover, the relatively small number of voters and the lack of adequate safeguards against the interference of central and local officials in the electoral process encouraged fraud. The government in power and landlords, in particular, could exert strong pressure on peasant voters, because of their economic vulnerability and lack of experience. As a result, the fourth electoral college was often referred to as the government's 'dowry' (*zestre*). Widely practised intimidation and bribery led to a growing cynicism among politicians (and the people) and enhanced the ability of the prince to manœuvre among competing political factions.

In practice, despite the provisions of the constitution, the prince gained a preponderant role in the parliamentary system, because of his right to dissolve the legislature at any time and to appoint and dismiss ministers. Thus, the cabinet, or government, was not the creature of parliament. This fact was evident in the procedure for changing governments. The process began with the resignation of the sitting government and the prince's appointment of a new Prime Minister and other ministers, after which parliament was dissolved and new elections scheduled. The new government used all available means to assure itself of a majority in the legislature, and until after the First World War it was never disappointed. The electoral system itself weighed heavily upon the legislative activity of the two houses. Since the government was a creation of the executive, not of parliament, the Chamber of Deputies and the Senate tended to become simply ratifying bodies of the government's legislative programme, and since the government never had less than an absolute majority in both houses, its practical responsibility to parliament lost any significance. The fate of government, therefore, depended primarily upon the will of the prince. He thus became the decisive force in the competition for power between parties and groups. The latter, in turn, naturally sought support not among the electorate but at the palace, where the ruler served as a kind of arbiter between rival political factions.

The system did not always work smoothly, and the powers of the prince were not so formidable as they might appear at first glance. The replacement of one government by another was not necessarily dependent upon the will of the prince alone. Sometimes a change was forced upon him by the pressure of the opposition from both inside and outside parliament. Despite the restricted franchise and the government's interference in elections, the politically active public skilfully used the almost complete freedom of the press and of meetings and public demonstrations to make its wishes known. The prince and politicians were by no means insensitive to public opinion, sometimes weighing it carefully when deciding if a particular government had outlived its usefulness. Often the press, the meetings, and the demonstrations were manipulated by the leaders of one or another of the parties, and thus, in changing governments, the prince ended up conforming to the will of significant political forces.

The parliamentary character of the political system remained intact, despite the preponderance of the executive. The Chamber and the Senate maintained their prerogatives. No bill could become law without their concurrence, and the right of their members, including the opposition, to criticize the government and ask searching questions of government ministers was respected. Deputies could also propose their own bills, but those sponsored by the government or members of the majority party could be (and often were) considered at once, while those offered by the opposition went first to committees, from which they might never emerge.

The formation of two large, dominant political parties in the decade after the adoption of the Constitution of 1866 largely completed the Rumanian political superstructure of the pre-First World War era. With the National Liberal Party (Partidul Naţional Liberal) and the Conservative Party (Partidul Conservator) in place the system sketched above came fully into operation.

At the beginning of Charles's reign the Liberals were still divided.[9] There were the radicals, led by Ion Brătianu and C. A. Rosetti; the moderates under Ion Ghica; the so-called 'Free and Independent Faction' in Iaşi grouped around Nicolae Ionescu, professor of history at the university; and small groups which followed Mihail Kogălniceanu. Kogălniceanu (1817–91) enjoyed

---

[9] Apostol Stan, *Grupări şi curente politice în România între unire şi independenţă (1859–1877)* (Bucharest, 1979), 186–208.

enormous prestige as a pioneering historian and journalist before 1848 and the author of a liberal constitution during the revolution who as Prime Minister under Cuza had taken the lead in enacting agrarian and electoral reforms. The radicals were the most dynamic and aggressive.[10] They had in Brătianu and Rosetti leaders who for the majority of Rumanians embodied the spirit of 1848, of that noble effort to create a modern society based upon the economic emancipation of the humbler classes of society and respect for fundamental civil liberties. Their personalities complemented one another: Rosetti was the ideologist, the publicist full of enthusiasm and spontaneity who believed passionately in the power of ideas to transform society; Brătianu was the politician, skilled in debate and organization, committed, like his friend, to liberal ideals, but unwilling to be dominated by ideology. Convinced that only a large, cohesive party could expect to remain in office long enough to achieve significant economic and social goals, they set about organizing a broad-based party in every *judeţ* (administrative district or county) and important city in the autumn of 1866. Under the auspices of their 'Society of the Friends of the Constitution' they dispatched representatives to every corner of the country to distribute literature and hold meetings to explain the guiding principles of the new political system (their opponents naturally saw in such feverish activity a recrudescence of the 'Jacobinism' of 1848). The radicals were especially eager to win over the urban business and professional groups and young intellectuals who had studied in Western Europe, but they pitched their message also to the poorest elements of the urban working classes. Their objective was to form a national party with support in all strata of the middle and lower classes.

The radicals achieved results quickly. An understanding with Kogălniceanu at the beginning of 1867 paved the way for the installation on 1 March of that year of a coalition Liberal government, in which Brătianu, as Minister of the Interior, was the dominant figure. He and Rosetti pressed ahead with their plans to create a nation-wide party. They gave particular attention to Moldavia, where the radicals had always been weak. They wooed Ionescu's faction, but although they made numerous concessions, including limitations on the economic activities of Jews, which had alarmed Moldavian business and financial interests, Ionescu

[10] For the spirit of radicalism during the decade 1866-76, see Marin Bucur, *C. A. Rosetti: mesianism şi donquijotism revoluţionar* (Bucharest, 1970), 236-73.

preferred to maintain the independence of his group. The radicals also encountered opposition from the Masonic lodges, which had been formed in numerous cities beginning in 1866. Brătianu and Rosetti regarded them with suspicion as political centres of Conservative opposition and planned to destroy them from within, but were unsuccessful. The radicals, or the 'reds', as they were now dubbed by their opponents, did not hesitate to manipulate the machinery of government to strengthen their party. Brătianu used his powers as Minister of the Interior to remove large numbers of functionaries, especially in the *judeţe*, and replace them with supporters of the radical cause. He acted on the advice of local committees of the radical party, which had been carefully scrutinizing the activities of all officials since 1866.

Thanks in great measure to Brătianu, the radicals had quickly succeeded in creating a powerful organization, which dominated both the Senate and the Chamber. They seemed destined for a long tenure. But within a year and a half they had been driven from office. None the less, even though out of office for most of the next decade, the radicals remained the best organized and disciplined Liberal faction, and it was they who took the lead in forming a unified, national Liberal party.[11] They formed the Liberal Union in Bucharest in 1872 and invited all politicians who shared their views to join. In parliament in 1873 and 1874 they drew closer to the Moldavians (Kogălniceanu) and the moderates (Ion Ghica) in pursuing their common goal of creating new credit institutions. In these debates the various Liberal factions discovered a close identity of views on general economic development. The parliamentary election of April 1875 enhanced the co-operation of the Liberal factions as they strove to defeat the Conservatives and encouraged them to form a National Liberal Party. Although it was a coalition of diverse elements, the strong radical organization headed by Brătianu and Rosetti gave it direction. Together they embarked upon an ambitious plan to establish local committees in every part of the country, which would serve to mobilize supporters at election time and maintain permanent organizational links between Bucharest and the *judeţe*. Their members came mainly from the middle class of the cities and a few landlords and well-to-do peasants in the countryside.

---

[11] The political turmoil of these years is amply described in V. Russu and D. Vitcu, 'Frămîntări politice interne în vremea guvernării D. Ghica-M. Kogălniceanu (1868−1870)', *Anuarul Institutului de Istorie şi Arheologie*, 7 (1970), 139−71; 8 (1971), 61−98.

The Conservatives in 1866, like the Liberals, were divided and incapable of forming a true political party.[12] The various factions were held together by their aversion to the social policies and political activities of the radicals, especially their wooing of the lower classes (the 'street', in Conservative parlance). The diverse groupings came together under the leadership of Lascăr Catargiu at the end of 1870 during a serious dynastic crisis. Catargiu persuaded other Conservative leaders to join him in a coalition by promising to maintain the political dominance of the landlord class and to pursue economic policies that would further agricultural interests. But differences of social and political ideologies and goals and rivalries for leadership prevented the transformation of this 'harmonious coalition' into a strong, cohesive party. Catargiu's authoritarian methods, which he used to keep the Conservatives in power for five years (1871–6), proved in the end to be the undoing of the coalition, as other Conservative leaders finally asserted their independence. The break-up of the coalition led to a regrouping of Conservative forces, first around the newspaper *Timpul* (Time) in 1878, and then, in 1880, around a new and more cohesive political organization. The adoption of a formal programme and party statutes on 3 February marked the birth of the Conservative Party.

Although 'Liberalism' and 'Conservatism' might appear nebulous, because of the divergences within the Liberal and Conservative coalitions, the lines between them were none the less sharply drawn. The evidence lies in their opposing views of agricultural and industrial development.[13] In agriculture the Liberals generally were eager to modernize methods of production and improve the peasants' standard of living. They treated Cuza's agrarian reform of 1864 as the starting-point for dynamic, reasoned change. The majority of Conservatives, on the other hand, looked to the past for ways of organizing agriculture. They proposed to use the law of 1864 to defend their property against further expropriation and, hence, they showed no inclination to engage in further 'experiments'. They thought that the reform had solved the 'social question' once and for all, that class contradictions had disappeared along with the old-style peasantry (the *clăcaşi*, those who were

[12] Anastasie Iordache, *Originile conservatorismului politic din România, 1821–1882* (Bucharest, 1987), 262–84.
[13] V. Russu, 'Cauzele luptelor politice dintre grupările liberale şi conservatoare în anii instabilităţii guvernamentale şi parlamentare (1866–1871)', *Cercetări istorice*, 9–10 (1978–9), 411–37.

obliged to perform *clacǎ*, compulsory labour service), and that, henceforth, landowners, the new peasant proprietors, and lease-holders (*arendaşi*) formed a more or less homogeneous social entity with identical economic interests.

The role of industry in the new state also found Liberals and Conservatives on opposite sides. Both recognized the backward condition of Rumanian industry, but only the Liberals were eager to improve it. The Liberals' concern was not solely economic, for they regarded a diversified economy as essential if Rumania was to become a 'civilized state' and was to free herself from political dependence upon other countries. They were much influenced by the ideas of Enric Winterhalder and Dionisie Pop Marţian, economists who promoted industrialization, but they also kept in mind economic realities. Acknowledging the primacy of agriculture, they urged the building of a native industry based upon 'internal resources', an industry that would complement agriculture and stimulate its productive potential. The West, with its large-scale, mechanized industry, was not, at least for the moment, their model. Instead, they advocated support for enterprises producing consumer goods for the mass market. The Conservatives, by contrast, saw little possibility of serious industrial development. Convinced that Rumania was destined to remain a 'pre-eminently agricultural country' for the foreseeable future, they found congenial the writings of Ion Strat and other agrarianists who advocated a 'natural course' of economic development. They thought that industry would 'be born' in Rumania when a surplus of capital and labour which could not be absorbed by agriculture had accumulated, and they rejected 'artificial' attempts to change the existing economic profile of the country.

Liberals and Conservatives found themselves on opposite sides again over the question of state intervention in economic affairs. The debate centred on the desirability of protection for nascent industries. Both the radical Liberals led by Brătianu and Rosetti and the more moderate elements around Kogălniceanu strove to make protectionism standard government policy as the most effective immediate aid to industry and, in the longer term, an indispensable weapon with which to overcome the country's general economic backwardness. The Conservatives, on the other hand, demanded free trade because such a policy, in their view, conformed to the 'natural', that is, the agrarian character of the Rumanian economy. They argued that since a national industry was out of the question, it offered the only way for Rumanians to obtain the foreign manufactured goods they needed. It was no coincidence that free trade also facilitated access to foreign markets for the grain and cattle that conservative landowners produced.

The continuous battles between Liberals and Conservatives were the main cause of early governmental instability. During the first five years of the new regime there were ten different governments and six dissolutions of the legislature. But party strife alone provides only a partial explanation for the political effervescence of the time. Constitutional guarantees of political and civil liberties had encouraged new and diverse elements to enter public life and to form their own groupings. Since none of these was strong enough to form a government by itself, coalitions became the order of the day. Adding to the instability was the novelty of the parliamentary system introduced by the Constitution of 1866. For this brief period parliament was its own master and was the most important element in the political life of the country. But the majority of deputies, in their inexperience, were individualistic and ambitious and little inclined to accept the discipline of others. The debates in both the Chamber and the Senate offer ample evidence of the free-wheeling nature of political life: they were dramatic, unpredictable, often unending. The prince tried to impose order on these proceedings, but failed, for as a political unknown and a foreigner, he lacked a following among the populace at large. In the absence of a dynastic sense in the country, he could rely for the time being only upon the prestige of the House of Hohenzollern (which, in fact, he used effectively on several occasions). The political situation itself prevented him from having much influence over parliament, for parties, which implied structures and hierarchies and would thus have enabled him to exercise some direction over affairs had not yet been formed.

The first elections to be held under the new electoral law took place in the autumn of 1866. They were free because the government formed by Ion Ghica in July did not interfere with them. No faction secured a majority in the Chamber (there were forty Conservatives, thirty radical Liberals, twenty-five moderate Liberals, twenty Liberal 'factionists'), and as a result, Ghica's government was beset by continuous crises. The Liberal coalition, 'Concordia', which was formed in February 1867, finally gave a certain direction to the activities of the Chamber. One of its first acts was to replace the Ghica government by a Liberal coalition dominated by the radicals, which held together long enough to install three governments between 1 March 1867 and 16 November 1868. In order to assure themselves of a sufficient majority to carry out their ambitious legislative agenda the radicals and their allies did not hesitate to apply all manner of administrative measures— 'moral influence', they called it—to win votes, thereby contributing no little to an undermining of the parliamentary system itself.

Despite their sizeable majorities in the Chamber and Senate, the radicals were forced from office in November 1868 because of sharp differences with Prince Charles and pressure from the great powers. They had aroused the prince's ire by their opposition to his plans for army reorganization and railway construction and by attempts to transform the throne into a mere instrument of their domestic policies, and they had turned most of the powers against them because of their support for the national aspirations of the Rumanians of Transylvania, their efforts to free their own country from the last vestiges of Ottoman sovereignty, their support of Bulgarian revolutionaries on Rumanian soil, and their measures to limit the economic activities of Jews. Charles was only too glad to accede to the strong foreign pressure to replace them with a moderate government. Kogălniceanu, the new Minister of the Interior, 'conducted' the elections with enough 'vigour' to diminish the power of the radicals, at least temporarily. Pushed aside, they resorted to an anti-dynastic campaign, which gained widespread support in 1870 as a result of Charles's repeated interventions to shore up shaky government coalitions, thereby giving substance to Liberal charges of 'personal rule'. The outbreak of war between France and Prussia on 19 July fuelled the opposition: the Chamber and the Senate voted resolutions supporting France, while Charles's sympathies manifestly lay with Prussia.

Relations between Charles and radical and moderate political leaders had deteriorated to such an extent by the autumn of 1870 that he contemplated abdication. In November he revealed his distress in a letter addressed to the rulers of all the protecting powers, except France. He described the difficulties he had encountered in governing, which he attributed primarily to institutions that were too liberal for the level of political experience of both politicians and the population at large. He urged the powers to consider a change in the existing governmental structure in favour of a 'firm, powerful regime' at their forthcoming conference to revise the Treaty of Paris of 1856. The changes he had in mind—the creation of a Council of State composed of his close advisers, a Senate appointed by himself, a curtailment of the powers of the Chamber, and restrictions on the right to vote and freedom of the press—would have undone representative, parliamentary government and instituted an authoritarian regime with an all-powerful prince.[14] He went even further in revealing his disenchantment with conditions in Rumania in a letter published anonymously in the *Augsburger Zeitung* on 27 January 1871. He accused the Liberals, who, he noted, had been educated abroad and had ignored conditions in their own country, of applying at home indiscriminately the political and social ideas they had picked up in Western Europe.[15] He thus fully shared the views of the Conservatives on the anomaly of bourgeois institutions in a country without a bourgeoisie. All his efforts, however, failed to bring about the changes he sought. The Liberals adamantly opposed any diminution of the role of parliament, and the powers, divided as usual, failed to act.

At the height of the anti-dynastic movement, on 22 March 1871, Charles removed the government headed by Ion Ghica on the grounds that it had failed to preserve order and was implicated in a 'republican movement'. He chose Lascăr Catargiu, whose authority among Conservatives was unassailable, to form a new government,[16] which was to remain in office for an unprecedented five years, until April 1876. The accession of the Conservatives marked the end of governmental instability, and as they settled into a regime of order the danger that the Hohenzollerns might leave the scene gradually receded. Charles himself regained confidence in his ability to rule and put aside thoughts of abdication.

The character and aims of the new government may be judged from its handling of local administration and the agrarian question. Although the Conservatives had long promised to carry out a decentralization of *judeţ* and village government, once in power they did the opposite; they worked to strengthen the control of the government bureaucracy in Bucharest over local affairs. In March 1874 they engineered passage of a new law on village administration which gave central government and *judeţ* officials the power to dismiss the mayor and the communal council, there-

[14] *Aus dem Leben König Karls von Rumänien*, ii (Stuttgart, 1894), 135–6.
[15] Démètre A. Sturdza, *Charles Ier: Roi de Roumanie*, i (Bucharest, 1899), 642–44.
[16] V. Russu and M. Timofte, 'Împrejurările şi semnificaţia instaurării guvernării conservatoare Lascăr Catargiu (martie 1871)', *Anuarul Institutului de Istorie şi Arheologie*, 16 (1979), 359–84.

by making both merely adjuncts of a centralized bureaucracy rather than representatives of local public opinion. Legislation dealing with agriculture revealed the Conservatives' intention to protect landlord interests. The agrarian law of 1872, ostensibly enacted to clarify vague sections of the reform act of 1864, served mainly to increase the constraints on peasants to fulfil the terms of their contracts with landlords and *arendaşi*. Thus, instead of addressing themselves to the plight of the mass of rural pro-prietors, the Conservatives strove to relieve large property of its heavy burden of debt. Their argument—that old debts be liquidated as a means of encouraging new investments and of increasing production—carried the day. The rural land credit insti-tution (Creditul Funciar Rural), which was approved by both houses on 29 March 1873, provided for a state subvention to back long-term loans to landowners, who were to be grouped together in associations to guarantee repayment of the sums they had borrowed. Although created by a Conservative government, the institution, paradoxically, came to be controlled by the Liberals, who used it to attract middle and smaller landowners to their party.

The Conservatives seemed destined to continue in office for the foreseeable future. When the normal period of the legislature came to an end in March 1875, elections the following month gave the Conservative coalition an overwhelming majority in parliament. Defeat convinced Liberal leaders that they could not expect to prevail against the Conservatives unless they integrated their various factions into a large, united Liberal party. In May Ion Brătianu, Rosetti, Kogălniceanu, and representatives of the free and independent faction, joined by the dissident Conservative Manolache Costache Epureanu (1824–80), a former Minister of Justice in the Catargiu cabinet, decided to form a National Liberal Party. Since they met at the home of a former English major, Stephen Lakeman, who had served in the Ottoman army under the name Mazar pasha, the new party was initially known as the 'coalition of Mazar pasha'. Although composed of diverse elements, it had a powerful radical nucleus and rested largely upon the organizations created earlier by Brătianu and Rosetti. Under radical leadership the coalition undertook a vigorous campaign in the summer of 1875 to resuscitate branch organizations in cities and towns throughout the country. They sought to attract to their ranks especially merchants, artisans, and rural landowners, includ-ing the holders of large estates and the well-to-do peasantry.

All these activities were directed at achieving a single goal—the removal of the Conservative government.

By the beginning of 1876 the once powerful Conservative coalition was in disarray. The causes were many. Catargiu's own authoritarian methods, his insistence upon defending the privileges of the great landowners at whatever the price, including the manipulation of elections, and his general drift to the right had cost him the support of the moderates in his own party. The grave financial condition of the country brought into question the ability of the cabinet to govern. On 12 April Catargiu resigned and was succeeded in 9 May by Epureanu. He, in turn, gave way on 5 August to a National Liberal government headed by Ion Brătianu, who was to remain Prime Minister, except for a two-month interruption in 1881, until 1888.

In foreign policy both Liberal and Conservative governments between 1866 and 1875 pursued the same long-term goals—security and independence—but the means they chose reflected the sharp ideological differences separating them. None the less, their country's geographical position as the place where the vital interests of three empires converged imposed a policy of caution and balance upon both Conservatives and, eventually, even the radical Liberals.

The radical Liberals at first had been anything but cautious in foreign affairs. During their brief tenure in 1867–8 they had decided to achieve independence by supporting the national liberation movements of the peoples south of the Danube. The most forceful manifestation of that policy had been aid to armed Bulgarian revolutionaries who used Rumanian territory as a staging area for raids against Ottoman positions across the river. Rosetti and Brătianu took the lead in encouraging the Bulgarians. Their objective was to hasten the break-up of the Ottoman Empire, which, they were certain, would give them the opportunity to declare Rumania's independence.[17] Their policy may also have been the last important manifestation of the revolutionary spirit of 1848, of the feeling of solidarity of oppressed peoples. But the results were quite different from what the radicals had expected. Instead of the abolition of Ottoman suzerainty, they succeeded

[17] Traian Ionescu-Nişcov, 'Unele aspecte din mişcarea de eliberare naţională a Bulgarilor în nordul Dunării între 1850–1870', in *Relaţii româno-bulgare de-a lungul veacurilor, sec. XII–XIX* , i (Bucharest, 1971), 376–88; Constantin N. Velichi, *La Roumanie et le mouvement révolutionnaire bulgare de libération nationale (1850–1878)* (Bucharest, 1979), 68–125.

only in stirring up the indignation of the great powers, who, in turn, put pressure on Prince Charles to remove the radicals from power.[18]

The radicals also carried on negotiations with Serbia and Greece for an alliance against Turkey. Relations with Serbia were especially close because of the overwhelming sentiment in both countries for independence. Charles and Prince Michael Obrenović agreed to co-operate in April 1867, and a treaty of alliance providing for joint military action to throw off Ottoman suzerainty was signed in Bucharest on 20 January 1868.[19] A similar agreement with Greece, the subject of intermittent discussions between 1866 and 1869, was never signed, in part because the Rumanians were wary of becoming too deeply involved in ambitious Greek plans for war against the Ottoman Empire.[20] In negotiations with the Serbian and Greek governments Prince Charles and Rumanian diplomats, both Conservatives and Liberals, continually urged caution on their prospective allies. They insisted that action against Turkey be carefully planned in order to avoid the intervention of the great powers, an event which might impede rather than further their strivings for independence or territorial gain. The willingness of the three countries to co-operate was by no means unconditional. Each was anxious to achieve its own national aims and thus refused to enter into binding agreements that might curtail its freedom of action. Hence, the grand alliance, which was widely discussed, never came to fruition. Limited bilateral treaties—between Greece and Serbia (1867) and Rumania and Serbia (1868)—took its place. But no important joint action followed.

A major reorientation of Rumanian foreign policy occurred after the radicals left office in 1868. The moderate and Conservative governments that followed cultivated good relations with the great powers as the surest means of achieving their goals. As a result, relations with the Balkan states became of secondary importance. The shift in direction was evident shortly after the installation of the coalition government of moderate Conservatives and Liberals headed by Dimitrie Ghica on 28 November

[18] Lothar Maier, *Rumänien auf dem Weg zur Unabhängigkeitserklärung 1866–1877* (Munich, 1989), 335–8.

[19] N. Ciachir and C. Buşe, 'Cu privire la tratatul de alianţa româno-sîrb din 1868', *Revista arhivelor*, 9/1 (1966), 189–204.

[20] Constantin Velichi, 'Les relations roumano-grecques durant la période 1866–1879', *Revue des études sud-est européennes*, 8/3 (1970), 525–48.

1868. It immediately renounced support for liberation movements south of the Danube and proclaimed its intention to honour all treaties bearing on their country's international status. The Conservatives adopted a similar stance when they came to power in 1871. The defeat of France by Prussia in 1870–1, which diminished the international role of Rumania's traditional patron, seemed to confirm the correctness of a policy of moderation and restraint. Even the radical Liberals understood the need to avoid precipitate action as the economic and political power of the Conservative monarchies—Austria-Hungary, Germany, and Russia—in Southeastern Europe grew.

The Conservative government of Lascăr Catargiu turned increasingly to Austria as the great power most likely to further the consolidation of the Rumanian state. The *rapprochement* that it now vigorously pursued had seemed a remote possibility at the beginning of Charles's reign. In 1866 and 1867 he had tried to establish a Rumanian diplomatic agency in Vienna and to conclude an advantageous commercial agreement, but the radical Liberals, who were pursuing a nationalist foreign policy, got in the way. Earlier, like Cuza, they had negotiated with Hungarian *émigrés* over joint armed action against Austria, and now they openly attacked the Austro-Hungarian Compromise of 1867, which had destroyed the hopes of the Rumanians of Transylvania for political autonomy. At the height of the crisis the Austro-Hungarian government issued a 'Red Book' in November 1868, which accused Rumania of being a 'disturber of the peace' and a 'threat to the frontiers' of the Dual Monarchy.[21] But the installation that same month of the moderate coalition government under Dimitrie Ghica, who was known for his pro-Austrian sentiments, brought a quick end to the dispute. Shortly afterwards, on 24 December, an agreement was reached establishing a Rumanian agency in Vienna. Although only semi-official, it none the less represented a major step toward the general *rapprochement* with Austria favoured by moderates and Conservatives. The degree of their reliance on Austria is suggested by the note from the Rumanian government on 19 July 1870 to Foreign Minister Julius Andrássy enquiring about what action his government might take if Russia invaded Rumania. Although relations with Russia since the accession of Charles had been friendly, Rumanian politicians

---

[21] Uta Bindreiter, *Die diplomatischen und wirtschaftlichen Beziehungen zwischen Österreich-Ungarn und Rumänien 1875–88* (Vienna, 1976), 30.

feared that the tsar might take advantage of the war between France and Prussia to denounce the Treaty of Paris of 1856 and recover southern Bessarabia, which Russia had been forced to cede to Moldavia. Andrássy replied that Gorchakov, the Russian Foreign Minister, had assured him that no Russian intervention in Rumania was contemplated, but, Andrássy promised, if such an event did take place, Austria would oppose it 'most vigorously'.

While out of office in the early 1870s the radical Liberals continued to combat the policy of reliance on Austria, partly because they were repelled by an authoritarian political system contrary to their own ideals and partly because they wished Rumania to gain independence through her own efforts, rather than be beholden to a foreign power. They thought this could be done by a reopening of the Eastern Question, in which Rumania would take an active part and thereby earn the right to share in the final settlement. But they preferred that the peoples of the region themselves take the initiative rather than the great powers because they feared the latter's aggressive political and economic designs. Mainly because of that fear, the radicals abandoned their earlier ideas about bringing down the Ottoman Empire in Europe as quickly as possible by force. They were now willing to keep it intact until the peoples of the region could settle matters to their own advantage. Thus, they reasoned, the Ottoman Empire, under the protection of Britain and France, could serve as a shield against the hostile Conservative monarchies—Austria-Hungary and Russia—who, they were certain, had no genuine interest in the political emancipation of the peoples of South-eastern Europe.

Whatever views Conservatives and Liberals may have held on the most effective strategy for achieving independence, both parties realized that Rumania by herself had little room for manœuvring. They grudgingly acknowledged the predominance of Austria-Hungary, Russia, and Germany, who, united in the Three Emperors' League, had shown no inclination to allow the peoples of the region to gain independence by themselves. Under the circumstances Prince Charles and the Conservatives saw little possibility of playing one power off against another. Instead, they devised a subtler strategy to win international support for independence by expanding diplomatic relations and by concluding commercial treaties with as many foreign states as possible without seeking the prior approval of the Ottoman government.

Discussions with Austria about a comprehensive trade agreement, which had dragged on since shortly after Charles's acces-

sion, now accelerated as both parties recognized its advantages.
The Rumanians sought the agreement primarily as a means of
advancing the cause of independence. From that standpoint the
proposed treaty was more a political than an economic document, but at the same time large landowners and commercial and
banking interests exerted strong pressure to break the remaining
economic dependence on the Ottoman Empire and to expand trade
with Western and Central Europe. For their part, the Austrians
had shown an increasing interest in developing closer ties with
Rumania, and by the time of Charles's visit to Vienna in the
summer of 1873 enough progress had been made to enable
him and Andrássy to discuss particulars. It was evident that the
latter was eager to secure the political dependence of Rumania on
Austria-Hungary, which he now intended to accomplish through
strong economic ties rather than by occupation or annexation, as
in the past. Andrássy (and his colleagues) also wished to further
Austria-Hungary's economic interests in South-eastern Europe
by assuring a ready market for manufactured goods and a convenient source of raw materials, especially grain, and by obtaining
Rumania's support for her efforts to control navigation on the
lower Danube.

The treaty was signed on 22 June 1875 and was to remain in
effect for ten years after formal ratification.[22] It provided for the
development of commerce between the two countries in accordance with the principle of free trade, but the economic advantages
clearly lay with Austria-Hungary, for she was granted the lowest
possible tariff rate on almost all goods, especially manufactures,
while her grain, flour, iron ore, and a number of other items
could be exported to Rumania duty-free. In return, Rumania was
allowed to export grain to Austria-Hungary duty-free and other
goods in accordance with the most favoured nation principle.
But these relatively modest concessions could be annulled by a
unilateral decision of Austria-Hungary to stop the importation of
any Rumanian goods which she judged to be harmful to humans,
animals, or even plants. The device was used often in the next
decade and seriously strained relations between the two countries.

When the treaty was submitted to the Rumanian Chamber
on 9 July 1875 the Liberals violently attacked it as 'anti-national'.
Foreign Minister Vasile Boerescu and other Conservatives de-

[22] Frederick Kellogg, 'Convenţia comercială din 1875, un pas către independenţă?', Studii: revistă de istorie, 25/5 (1972), 989–1003.

fended it as a political act that would aid the country significantly in gaining international recognition of its independence. In the end, it was this argument rather than the economic objections of the Liberals that carried the day. On 13 July the treaty passed the Chamber 68 to 22 and the Senate 25 to 8. The Austrian parliament approved it overwhelmingly in February 1876, and it came into effect on 1 July 1876.

As a political document, the treaty contributed to the general *rapprochement* between Rumania and Austria-Hungary, which was to culminate in the former's adherence to the German–Austro-Hungarian alliance in 1883. But economically it had the opposite effect. It harmed relations between the two parties because it allowed the Rumanian market to be flooded with Austrian manufactures, a circumstance which struck a fatal blow at local artisan production and retarded the development of a modern industry. The anti-Austrian sentiments aroused by these economic woes became a major obstacle to closer political relations, thus frustrating Andrássy's original hopes for the treaty.

Rumania also pursued closer formal relations with Russia. In 1874 a diplomatic agency was established in St Petersburg, and in May 1875 negotiations began for a treaty of commerce.[23] Since trade between the two countries was modest, the primary objective of both sides was political. The Rumanians sought additional support for their independence, while the Russians wished to counterbalance Austria's growing presence in Rumania. Although a draft was ready by August, the Russian negotiators were reluctant to sign it in the tsar's name for fear of offending the Turks and suggested that it be submitted to the Rumanian parliament for ratification under the signature of the Minister of Finance. The Rumanians immediately objected, demanding that the treaty be signed by Foreign Minister Gorchakov with the full authorization of the tsar. Otherwise, Boerescu informed the Russian consul in Bucharest, it would have no value for Rumania as a political document. The growing crisis in the Balkans, precipitated by the uprising in Bosnia and Herzegovina in July 1875, and the realization that Serbia and Montenegro might make war on the Ottoman Empire and that Russia might then have to send aid through Rumania, finally persuaded the Russians to accede to the Rumanian conditions. The treaty was signed on 27 March 1876

---

[23] Barbara Jelavich, 'Russia and the Rumanian Commercial Convention of 1876', *Rumanian Studies*, 3 (Leiden, 1976), 39–60.

and ratified in October. As with the commercial convention with Austria-Hungary, the Rumanians made economic concessions for the sake of political advantages. Thus, a second great power within a year had recognized the right of Rumania to conclude international agreements without the consent of the Ottoman government, and Rumanian political leaders were persuaded that they had gained Russia's benevolence. Yet, expectations on both sides that the treaty had inaugurated an era of good feeling and co-operation were dashed by events in the Balkans.

THE EASTERN CRISIS, 1876–1878

As it became clear to Prince Charles and Rumanian politicians in the summer of 1875 that the uprising in Bosnia and Herzegovina had ceased to be an internal Ottoman affair and had raised again the general question of the European balance of power in the region, they decided that caution was the best policy. Both Conservatives and Liberals agreed that for the time being they must avoid any act that might compromise the international guarantees Rumania enjoyed under the Treaty of Paris of 1856, and thus on 27 and 30 November 1875 the Chamber and the Senate solemnly proclaimed the country's neutrality.

Yet, at the same time the Conservative government was exploring ways of using the crisis to gain independence. On 16 January 1876 Lascăr Catargiu instructed Rumanian diplomatic agents abroad to sound out foreign governments on what Rumania's role in the crisis should be and whether they would be receptive to a unilateral declaration of Rumania's independence. He reminded them of the position long held by Rumanian political leaders and intellectuals that neither Wallachia nor Moldavia had ever been an integral part of the Ottoman Empire and that by placing themselves under the protection of the sultan they had in no way compromised their sovereignty. Thus, he urged his diplomats to bring the problem of Rumania's 'complete independence' to the immediate attention of all the powers as forcefully as possible. In the event of a general war in South-eastern Europe Catargiu was prepared to co-operate militarily with the allies against Turkey, but only if these powers would guarantee the territorial integrity of Rumania and all her 'centuries-old rights', that is, political independence. Gheorghe Costaforu, the Rumanian agent in Vienna, put matters more bluntly in conversations with the German ambassador and other diplomats, informing them that the Rumanians were determined to break their remaining links with Turkey and to proclaim themselves independent at the earliest opportunity.[24] The powers received Catargiu's initiative coolly; they did not relish the intrusion of a new element into an already dangerous situation and warned Rumanian agents that obstinacy in this matter could deprive Rumania of their support.

The negative response of the powers temporarily halted further Rumanian diplomatic initiatives on behalf of independence. In March 1876 the Foreign Minister, Ion Bălăceanu, reiterated his government's intention to observe strict neutrality. On the 20th in response to enquiries from the Serbian government about Rumania's position in the event of war with Turkey, he noted that his country's self-interest compelled her to remain only 'an observer' of events south of the Danube, despite sympathy for fellow Christians. He said essentially the same thing in a memorandum to Rumanian diplomatic agents on the 31st. But here he went on to explain that Rumania could not become directly involved in the struggles of the Slavs against the Turks because they were so different from the Rumanians in 'language, blood, and national genius'.[25] Implicit was the notion, cultivated in some intellectual circles, that Rumania, because of her unique historical and cultural ties to the West, belonged to Europe, whereas her southern neighbours fell within the cultural world of the East.

The uprising of the Bulgarians in April 1876 severely tested Rumania's policy of neutrality, for the tradition of aid to Bulgarian revolutionaries had remained strong. Despite a wave of public revulsion at the ruthless suppression of the Bulgarians by the Turks, the Rumanian government stuck to its official policy of neutrality. But it quietly allowed Bulgarian revolutionaries to continue to use Rumanian territory as a base for armed forays across the Danube.

In May 1876, as we have seen, a government headed by Manolache Epureanu replaced the Conservatives under Catargiu. Although Epureanu was himself a Conservative, the Liberals of the Mazar pasha coalition dominated the new cabinet, and it was they who would direct foreign policy. While Epureanu was assuring the powers that there would be no change in the previous

[24] *Documente privind istoria României: Războiul pentru independenţă*, vol. i, part 2 (Bucharest, 1954), 81: Costaforu to Minister of Foreign Affairs, 23 Jan. 1876.

[25] R. V. Bossy, *Politica externă a României între anii 1873−1880 privită dela agenţia diplomatică din Roma* (Bucharest, 1928), 133−4.

government's policy of neutrality, the new Foreign Minister, Kogălniceanu, had already embarked upon an aggressive campaign to force the Ottoman government to recognize Rumania's independence by threatening the very opposite—to abandon neutrality unless the desired concessions were forthcoming. On 28 June 1876 he instructed Rumanian diplomatic agents to convey the same message to the powers in the hope that they, in turn, would put pressure on the sultan to accede to Rumania's demands. But all Kogălniceanu's efforts had no effect. The powers thought Rumania of little importance, and the Turkish Foreign Minister rejected out of hand Kogălniceanu's 'ill-timed' proposals.

Undaunted, Kogălniceanu pressed on. Two events in the early summer of 1876 made a clarification of Rumania's status all the more imperative. On 30 June Serbia and on 2 July Montenegro declared war on the Ottoman Empire, thereby extending hostilities beyond the borders of two Turkish provinces and increasing the probability of great power involvement. Then the Reichstadt agreement of 8 July between Austria-Hungary and Russia on the future of Ottoman territories in Europe raised additional concern in Rumanian political circles. Although it was secret, they knew of its existence and thought that it had cleared the way for a new war between Russia and Turkey, in which Austria-Hungary would remain neutral. On 1 and 5 August Kogălniceanu, under the mounting pressure of public opinion and the army for action against Turkey, instructed his diplomatic agents to inform the powers that the Rumanian government might be compelled to abandon its neutrality and seek a 'speedy resolution' of the issues raised in his letter of 28 June.[26]

The vagaries of domestic politics brought Kogălniceanu's campaign abruptly to a halt. After their electoral victory in June 1876 the radical Liberal majority in the Chamber had sought to deliver a knockout blow to the Conservatives by bringing certain ministers of the previous government to trial on charges of having violated the constitution. Kogălniceanu and Epureanu strenuously objected and resigned. The new government, which took office on 5 August and was headed by Ion Brătianu, decided to reverse Kogălniceanu's course and again announced a policy of neutrality.

Prince Charles and Brătianu recognized, none the less, that neutrality and the diplomatic efforts to extract concessions from Turkey had been a failure. They were now bent upon bringing

---

[26] Mihail Kogălniceanu, *Documente diplomatice* (Bucharest, 1972), 133–6, 138–9.

their foreign policy into line with the decisions they assumed Austria-Hungary and Russia had made at Reichstadt. They were even prepared to co-operate with Russia, a decision based upon their belief that war between her and Turkey was inevitable. The majority of the radical Liberals supported this course, despite their distaste for the tsarist autocracy and fear of Russia's territorial ambitions. They had been disappointed by the lack of concern which Britain and France had shown for their country's welfare and were convinced that Rumania could not afford to stand alone.

Their plans, however, did not go unchallenged. A number of politicians, especially Conservatives and moderates, demanded the maintenance of strict neutrality, even in the event of a war between Russia and Turkey. They were willing to accept a temporary military occupation by Austria-Hungary, as during the Crimean War, if it would prevent their country from being over-run by Russian armies. They sought to use Austria-Hungary generally as a counterweight to Russian expansion in South-eastern Europe, which they regarded as the gravest threat to Rumania's independence. They were certain that Austria-Hungary, as Russia's 'natural' rival in the area, would not hesitate to block the latter's expansion into the Balkans. They also hoped that 'Europe', i.e. France and Britain, would pursue a similar course by giving Rumania the same kind of guarantee of perpetual neutrality enjoyed by Belgium.[27]

The initiative lay with the prince and Brătianu, whose views were to prevail during the next two years. Negotiations with Russia began in earnest in October 1876 with Brătianu's visit to Livadia in the Crimea. On the 11th the Rumanian delegation met the tsar and Foreign Minister Gorchakov. The Russians wanted to arrange for the passage of their troops across Rumania in the event of war and were willing to sign a military convention. But they did not seek the active participation of the Rumanian army in the campaign. Brătianu was disappointed. He wanted more. In return for the right of transit he insisted upon a general treaty that would not only cover military questions, but would include recognition of Rumania's independence and a guarantee of her territorial integrity. He also wanted the Rumanian army to participate in the war in order to assure his country's representation at the peace conference, and he raised the delicate question of southern

---

[27] Constantin Căzănişteanu and Mihail E. Ionescu, *Războiul neatîrnării României* (Bucharest, 1977), 75–7; Ion Ghica, 'O cugetare politică' (1877) in Ion Ghica, *Opere complete*, iv (Bucharest, 1915), 93–129.

Bessarabia, which Russia had been obliged to cede to Moldavia in 1856. Accounts vary as to whether the Russians said in so many words that they intended to take it back, but it must have been clear to the Rumanian delegation that the tsar considered the return of this territory a matter of honour.[28] When the Rumanian delegation left Livadia on 12 October no final decisions had been reached on crucial issues, but both sides had agreed in principle to the passage of Russian troops.

Neither Prince Charles nor Brătianu was yet ready to enter into a formal alliance with Russia. They had no intention of renouncing the guarantees Rumania enjoyed by virtue of inter-national agreements and thus put her fate in the hands of a power they did not trust. Neutrality, consequently, remained official government policy, and new diplomatic overtures were made to the Western powers to gain support for the neutralization of Rumania in case of a new Russo-Turkish war. The results were disappointing. France and Britain expressed concern, but made no commitments.

Negotiations with Russia were resumed with the arrival in Bucharest on 28 November of Alexander Nelidov, a political adviser to the Grand Duke Nicholas, the commander of the Russian army being assembled in Bessarabia. Brătianu raised the same questions as at Livadia, but Nelidov was unable to respond satisfactorily because he had been authorized to discuss only a military convention covering the transit of Russian troops across Rumania. None the less, these difficult negotiations resulted in drafts of both military and political accords. The latter signified a concession by Russia, for it contained a guarantee of Rumania's territorial integrity, but did not specifically mention southern Bessarabia. Charles and Brătianu put off signing the agreement in the hope that a forthcoming conference of the powers at Con-stantinople would provide a collective, and thus more certain, guarantee of Rumania's security. Nor had they entirely given up on the possibility of a direct Rumanian—Ottoman accord covering independence and neutrality.[29] Encouragement for the latter course

---

[28] The Russian ambassador to Turkey insisted that he told Brătianu of the tsar's intention to take back southern Bessarabia: N. P. Ignatiev, 'Zapiski', *Istoricheskii vestnik*, 139 (Feb. 1915), 378, 381, 391–2. On subsequent negotiations over the matter in Bucharest, see the recollections of the special Russian envoy, A. I. Nelidov, 'Souvenirs d'avant et d'après la guerre de 1877–78', *Revue des deux mondes*, 28 (15 July 1915), 245–54.

[29] *Documente privind istoria României: Războiul pentru independență*, vol. ii, part 2, 476–8: Iancu Ghica to Minister of Foreign Affairs, 25 Nov. 1876.

came from Savfet pasha, the Ottoman Foreign Minister. On the eve of the Constantinople Conference he urged the Rumanians to resist a Russian invasion and promised to supply them with everything they needed, including troops.

At the outset the prospects for the success of the Constantinople Conference seemed bright. The British had proposed it, and the Russians had quickly agreed to attend. Gorchakov welcomed the opportunity to find a solution short of war to the growing impasse in the Balkans. Although Russia had forced the Turks to conclude an armistice with Serbia on 2 November, she was reluctant to take drastic action alone, for fear that it might revive the coalition that had defeated her in the Crimean War. No one invited the Rumanians to come because the powers continued to regard their country as a dependency of the Ottoman Empire and because they thought the 'Rumanian question' a minor issue. The conference, which lasted from 12 December 1876 to 20 January 1877, proved a failure. The Ottoman government was in no mood to accept a further reduction of its powers in the Balkans and rejected all the proposals of the powers to settle the issues in dispute peacefully.

The conference led to a worsening of relations between Turkey and Rumania. In order to ward off the interference of the powers in Ottoman internal affairs the sultan had promulgated a 'reform constitution' on 23 December 1876. Whatever the motivation behind it may have been, it caused an uproar in Rumania, for it referred to Rumania as a 'privileged province' and declared it to be an integral and permanent part of the Ottoman Empire. Sharp protests came from the Council of Ministers and the Chamber of Deputies in Bucharest, who pointed out that the Rumanian principalities had always been sovereign, a 'fact' contained in the Treaty of Paris of 1856, which had recognized the validity of the 'capitulations', as agreements between the sultans and the princes of Moldavia and Wallachia in the fifteenth century were known. Explanations by the Ottoman Foreign Minister about 'erroneous interpretations' of certain articles of the constitution and assurances about the absence of any intention to impinge upon the rights of the 'United Principalities' averted an immediate rupture between the two countries, but the incident ended any hope of diplomatic or military co-operation between them.

The collapse of the Constantinople Conference had a decisive effect also on Russo-Rumanian relations. It convinced Prince Charles and Brătianu that if they wished to gain independence, they had no choice but to come to terms with Russia and to co-operate with her in the forthcoming war with Turkey. In subsequent negotiations down to April 1877 they none the less held to the position they had taken since the beginning of the Eastern crisis in 1875 that there could be no military convention without an accompanying political treaty recognizing Rumania's territorial integrity and independence. Russian negotiators finally gave in to these demands because the Grand Duke Nicholas and other commanders insisted that a military agreement be concluded as quickly as possible. The matter had become urgent. After the Ottoman government had rejected the London Protocol of 31 March, which had represented a final attempt by the powers to resolve the crisis, the tsar had decided to begin hostilities on 24 April.

On 14 April Charles presided over a meeting of the Crown Council, composed of the Prime Minister, members of the cabinet, and former Prime Ministers. The realities of the situation were clear to the majority, and they accepted the convention with Russia. Kogălniceanu, who became Foreign Minister on the 16th, signed the convention on the same day. By its terms the Rumanian government granted the Russian army the right of unhindered transit across Rumania, all the expenses of which were to be borne by the Russian ally, and the Russian government agreed to respect the 'political rights' of the Rumanian state, as stipulated in both native legislation and international treaties, and guaranteed the 'existing integrity' of Rumania.

Co-operation between the two allies got off to a shaky start. Russia declared war on Turkey on 24 April, and on the same day her troops began to cross the Prut River into Moldavia. But the Rumanian government immediately protested because the Chamber and Senate had not yet ratified the convention. It also objected strenuously to the issuance of proclamations to the Rumanian people by Russian military commanders as a usurpation of its sovereign authority. But there was, of course, no turning back. The prince had ordered mobilization on the 18th, and he left unanswered an invitation from the Ottoman government on the 24th to join it in repelling the Russian advance. The Chamber ratified the convention on the 29th and the Senate, after new elections had to be held to reduce the size of the opposition, on the 30th. On 12 May the parliament declared war on the Ottoman Empire on the grounds that a state of war in fact already existed because of the Turkish bombardment of Rumanian cities along the Danube.

Public opinion and the radical Liberal majority in the Chamber demanded that the government declare independence at once. In response to an interpellation in the Chamber on 21 May Kogălniceanu declared that the votes of the Chamber and the Senate on 29 and 30 April ratifying the convention with Russia had automatically dissolved Rumania's final links with the Ottoman Empire and that the Rumanians were thus already an independent nation. The Chamber responded immediately by passing a motion taking cognizance of the 'absolute independence' of the country. The Senate concurred on the same day. But the Rumanian initiative won no sympathy among the powers. They disapproved of it as a violation of existing treaties and a further complication of an already dangerous situation. Only Russia accepted it as a *fait accompli*, but reserved a final resolution of the question until after the war.

Before these events, as war seemed increasingly likely, the Rumanian government had taken a series of measures to place the army on a war footing. On 11 April it decided on a general mobilization, which began on the 18th and was completed by 7 May. The total force reached 120,000, of whom 58,700 represented first-line troops or the 'operational army'. But, of these, only a fifth were regular army troops, the rest being composed of the so-called 'territorial units'—the *dorobanţi* (infantry) and *călăraşi* (cavalry)—which were organized on the basis of one regiment for every four or five *judeţe*. These troops were well trained, but they lacked adequate equipment. For example, only one infantryman out of four had a modern rifle, and ammunition for all types of weapons was in short supply. Nor did the government have the funds to buy what was necessary. The situation became so critical that in September, five months after the beginning of hostilities, Kogălniceanu had to appeal to the public for contributions with which to buy rifles. Perhaps even more serious was the inability of the army quartermaster corps to keep the troops adequately supplied. Serious shortages of food and clothing regularly occurred at the front because of the failure to stockpile them and the absence of adequate transportation facilities. The Rumanian army was thus not prepared to fight a modern war. It owed its successes on the battlefield, notably at the siege of Plevna, in northern Bulgaria, in the autumn of 1877, mainly to the tenacity and endurance of its officers and men.

In the first months of the war Prince Charles and Brătianu sought to establish the ground rules for military co-operation between Rumanian and Russian armies. The prince's main objective was to gain for Rumania the status of a co-belligerent and thereby assure recognition of her independence. Accordingly, he offered the Russians the full participation of the Rumanian army in the forthcoming campaign south of the Danube, but insisted that it remain under his control. He met with the Grand Duke Nicholas, the commander-in-chief of Russian forces, at his temporary headquarters at Ploieşti, north of Bucharest, on 14 and 18 May. Nicholas seemed interested in a Rumanian military contribution and indicated that its aid in crossing the Danube would be welcome, but he did not go beyond generalities. Tsar Alexander, however, was categorically opposed to the participation of the Rumanian army. He informed the Rumanian diplomatic agent in St Petersburg, General Ion G. Ghica, that Russia did not need Rumanian troops. When he and Charles met at Ploieşti on 7 June he avoided any discussion of either the role of the Rumanian army in the war or Rumanian independence. A week later Charles told Foreign Minister Gorchakov, who had steadfastly refused to treat the Rumanians as equal partners, that he was determined to defend the territorial integrity of his country at all cost and wanted control of the mouths of the Danube. Gorchakov's reply was to demand the northern, or Chilia, channel for Russia, which meant southern Bessarabia as well.[30]

In the meantime, Rumanian and Russian armies had been assembling along the Danube. Between 19 and 27 May Russian forces had taken up positions on the north bank of the river on a broad front between the Black Sea and the Olt River. Two Rumanian divisions, which had been deployed south of Bucharest, were transferred to southern Oltenia to join two other divisions already there. Their task was to keep up pressure on Turkish troops along the Danube at Vidin, Rahova, and Nicopolis and to prevent them from crossing the river.

The Russian campaign in the Balkans began with the crossing of the Danube at two points—between Galaţi and Brăila on 22 June and then at Zimnicea (opposite Sviştov) on 27 June. To the west of Sviştov Russian forces captured Nicopolis on 16 July and moved south toward Plevna. This rapid advance appeared to confirm the expectations of the tsar and his army commanders that the war would be short and glorious. But, then, Turkish

---

[30] *Aus dem Leben König Karls von Rumänien*, iii (Stuttgart, 1897), 179–80, 185–6, 188–9.

resistance stiffened. General Gurko's forces were obliged to retreat from Stara Zagora, south of the Balkan Moutains, and General Krüdener's attacks against Plevna on 20 and 30 July were repulsed by superior Turkish forces under Osman pasha. Lacking reinforcements, Russian commanders were faced with a temporary withdrawal from much of the territory they had overrun.

At this critical moment the tsar and his advisers were obliged to reassess the value of Rumanian arms. General Krüdener now urgently requested Charles to send Rumanian units to occupy Nicopolis and take charge of 7,000 Turkish prisoners there in order to free Russian troops for action at Plevna. The prince bluntly refused because no agreement on military co-operation south of the Danube had been reached, but at the personal request of the tsar he instructed a part of the fourth Rumanian division to occupy Nicopolis. The Rumanian army thus made its first crossing of the Danube on 28 July. Charles had made a decisive military commitment without obtaining any of the guarantees he had insisted upon.

The deterioration of the Russian position at Plevna nevertheless soon brought Charles the satisfaction he sought. After the second battle of Plevna on 30 July Russian commanders realized that reinforcements were desperately needed if they were to hold their positions and prevent the enemy from undertaking a major counter-offensive. Charles agreed to their urgent request for troops, but he stipulated that his army have its own base of operations and a separate command. Hard bargaining ensued, as each side stuck essentially to the terms it had set forth in the spring. Finally, the tsar, the Grand Duke Nicholas, and Charles came to an agreement mainly on Rumanian terms. On 24 August Rumanian troops began to cross the Danube in force, and on the 28th the Russians offered Charles supreme command of the allied armies before Plevna.

Victory at Plevna was hard won. The third battle took place on 11 September. The joint Russo-Rumanian attack on the Turkish fortifications surrounding the city failed to achieve its objectives. Only one of the fourteen redoubts, Griviţa I, which Rumanian troops had captured at the cost of nearly 800 killed and 1,200 wounded, could be held. That was the main success of the day. The siege continued until 10 December, when Osman pasha attempted to fight his way out of the encirclement. The two Rumanian divisions contributed decisively to his defeat by preventing reinforcements from reaching that part of his army leading the break-out. With his forces divided and under constant attack, Osman pasha surrendered. Turkish losses were 5,000 men killed and wounded as against 2,000 Russian and Rumanian casualties.

After the victory at Plevna the Rumanian army played a more modest role in the war, as Russian armies moved deeper into the Balkans. A part of the Rumanian army was diverted to the east and north-east to Belogradjik and Vidin to protect the right flank of the Russian army as it marched south-west to Sofia, which it captured on 4 January 1878. Nor was the Turkish army able to stop the Russian advance toward the south-east, to Constantinople. With Russian troops almost at the gates of its capital, the Ottoman government accepted Russia's terms for an armistice at Adrianople on 31 January.

Both the terms of the armistice and the manner in which it had been concluded caused dismay and bitterness in Bucharest. No Rumanian had been invited to participate in the negotiations, nor had Prince Charles or Kogălniceanu been asked to submit a list of Rumanian conditions. They learned of Russian intentions only shortly before the armistice was signed. In St Petersburg Gorchakov informed Ghica that Russia intended to take back southern Bessarabia as far as the Chilia channel, but promised that Rumania would receive part of Dobrudja and the Danube delta. He justified the recovery of the Bessarabian districts as a matter of national honour and disingenuously argued that, in any case, they had been ceded to Moldavia, not Rumania, under terms of a treaty (Paris 1856) which no power respected any longer. As for the Russian guarantee of Rumania's territorial integrity in April 1877, he said simply that it had been directed at Turkey.[31] He showed no inclination to allow Rumania to participate in subsequent peace negotiations on the grounds that her independence had not yet been recognized and declared that her interests would be represented by Russia. Nicholas Ignatiev, the Russian ambassador to Turkey, conveyed the same message to Prince Charles in Bucharest on 31 January. Kogălniceanu voiced the anger felt by politicians and the public at large in dispatches to Ghica in St Petersburg in which he accused Russian officials of deception and of treating an ally like a conquered province.[32]

Relations between Russia and Rumania became even more

[31] Radu Rosetti, *Corespondenţa Generalului Iancu Ghica, 2 aprilie 1877–8 aprilie 1878* (Bucharest, 1930), 128: Ghica to Minister of Foreign Affairs, 14/26 Jan. 1878.

[32] Ibid. 129, 133–5: Kogălniceanu to Ghica, 14/26 Jan., 18/30 Jan., and 23 Jan./4 Feb. 1878.

strained when the provisions of the Treaty of San Stefano of 3 March, which formally ended the war between Russia and the Ottoman Empire, became known in Bucharest. To be sure, it recognized Rumania's independence, but it also provided for the return of southern Bessarabia to Russia in exchange for Dobrudja and the Danube delta, compensation which did little to soften the sense of betrayal felt by the Rumanians. Kogălniceanu even went so far as to draw up a memorandum on Bessarabia designed to influence governments and public opinion in the West. He not only denounced the cession of its southern districts, but called into question the legality and morality of Russia's acquisition of 'half of Moldavia' in 1812.[33] Yet, the loss of this territory could not have surprised either the prince or his ministers, for the tsar, Gorchakov, and Ignatiev had made it plain that the return of the territory 'detached' from the empire in 1856 was not negotiable. Still more unpleasantness for the Rumanians was contained in article 8, which, while allowing Russia to occupy the new, autonomous Bulgaria, provided for the maintenance of a supply route through Rumania for two years. Prince Charles and Brătianu were alarmed that a Russian presence in their country for so long a period might be transformed into a protectorate similar to that of the 1830s and 1840s.

Differences between the two former allies finally came to a head on 1 April, when Gorchakov told Ghica in St Petersburg that unless his government stopped its opposition to the territorial provisions of the Treaty of San Stefano and the right of transit for Russian troops and supplies for Bulgaria, the tsar would have the Russian army occupy Rumania and disarm the Rumanian army.[34] Charles replied that an army that had fought under the eyes of the tsar at Plevna might well be crushed, but it would never allow itself to be disarmed. Although the number of Russian troops in the country steadily increased during the first half of April, and the Rumanian government feared a coup engineered by Russia, the situation calmed perceptibly mainly because of the strong pressure exerted by the other powers on Russia to submit the peace treaty with Turkey to an international conference.

[33] Vasile Kogălniceanu, *Actes et documents extraits de la correspondance diplomatique de Michel Kogălniceano relatifs à la guerre de l'indépendance roumaine (1877–78)*, i (Bucharest, 1893), 81–2.

[34] *Aus dem Leben König Karls von Rumänien*, iv (Stuttgart, 1900), 19–23, 25–7, 34–5.

Rumanian leaders joined wholeheartedly in the demand for a revision of the Treaty of San Stefano. This time the Rumanians were in step with Austria-Hungary and the Western powers. The former and Britain, in particular, had objected strenuously to the terms of the armistice and treaty as contrary to existing international agreements and the principle of collective action by the powers. They saw in the large autonomous Bulgaria with its Russian occupation force a base for further Russian expansion into South-eastern Europe and domination of the Straits. Adamantly opposed to unilateral action in the region, and joined by Germany and France, they obliged Russia to submit the settlement she had negotiated with Turkey to a general European congress, which was scheduled to open in Berlin, with Bismarck as host, on 13 June 1878.

The immediate concern of the Rumanian government was to gain admittance to the congress. It tried to form a united front of small powers, including Serbia and Greece, and repeatedly argued its case before the powers, but to no avail. Only France showed a willingness to allow a Rumanian presence at the congress. Russia, of course, firmly opposed it, but Austria-Hungary, pursuing the policy inaugurated by Andrássy with the commercial convention of 1875 of drawing Rumania into a close political and economic relationship, showed marked sympathy for the Rumanian stance against Russia. Andrássy went so far as to assure the Rumanian agent in Vienna that the Dual Monarchy would quietly support Rumania's admittance to the congress, recognition of her independence, and even a shortening of the period during which Russia could resupply her forces in Bulgaria. But he urged the Rumanian government to yield on the question of southern Bessarabia because there was no question of the tsar's determination to retake it, and he warned that none of the powers thought the matter important enough to risk a conflict with Russia. Brătianu, who had been to Berlin and Vienna in April to drum up support for Rumania's claims, had reluctantly come to the same conclusion and decided that her best hope lay in the forthcoming congress. But the powers refused to admit Rumania as a member, on the pretext that she was not independent, and only grudgingly agreed to let Rumanian representatives appear briefly to state their case. The Serbs and Bulgarians fared no better, for the powers were determined to settle matters privately among themselves.

THE SETTLEMENT, 1878–1881

The Rumanian delegation arrived in Berlin on 10 June 1878 still hopeful that somehow the decision about southern Bessarabia could be modified. But as Brătianu and Kogălniceanu, the leaders of the delegation, made the rounds of the great power delegations, they realized that intransigence in the matter would be fruitless and even dangerous. Andrássy, who repeated his earlier assurances of support on other issues, pointed out to them how 'laughable' it was for Rumania to oppose the united will of the congress.[35]

When Brătianu and Kogălniceanu presented their case to the powers on 1 July, they did so in detail but with tact and moderation. They requested the maintenance of the 'existing territory' of Rumania, possession of the mouths of the Danube, a prohibition against the transit of Russian troops through their country to Bulgaria, payment of a war indemnity by Turkey, and the recognition of the independence and neutrality of their country. After they had departed the representatives of the powers proceeded to settle matters as they had already agreed, except for a more generous boundary in Dobrudja, a boon suggested by the French delegate, who thought Rumania had been treated 'a little harshly'.

The final treaty, which was signed on 13 July, recognized Rumania's independence, but set two conditions: the elimination of all religious restrictions on the exercise of civil and political rights contained in article 7 of the Constitution of 1866, and acceptance of the return of southern Bessarabia to Russia. As compensation Rumania was to receive the Danube delta, Serpent Island, and Dobrudja as far as a line drawn from east of Silistria on the Danube and south of Mangalia on the Black Sea. The treaty limited Russia's occupation of Bulgaria to nine months and thereby reduced the period during which supplies and reinforcements could be moved across Rumanian territory.

To the extreme disappointment of Prince Charles and his ministers the recognition of independence by all the powers and, hence, the establishment of regular diplomatic relations with them did not immediately follow the signing of the treaty. Russia recognized Rumania's independence unconditionally probably in order to assuage at least some of the ill-feeling generated during

---

[35] Ion C. Brătianu, *Acte și cuvântări*, iv (Bucharest, 1932), 70–1: Brătianu to C. A. Rosetti, 19 June 1878.

the peace negotiations and at Berlin. Austria–Hungary did the same, in keeping with her general policy of *rapprochement* with Rumania. But France, Germany, and Britain withheld recognition until 1880, when the revision of the discriminatory clauses of the constitution had been carried out and Rumania had accepted certain economic agreements, notably the settlement of the dispute with German investors over the building of railways in Rumania.

Although the terms of the Treaty of Berlin aroused vehement protests in Bucharest and other cities, by October, when parliament convened, the loss of southern Bessarabia had been grudgingly accepted, and both houses approved the necessary legislation to effect its cession to Russia. The Russians occupied the area immediately with only a minimum of friction with the departing Rumanians.

Rumania took formal possession of Dobrudja in November and December 1878 as a Rumanian civilian administration replaced Russian military authorities.[36] The task of integrating the new territory into Rumania proved complicated. Dobrudja had been under Ottoman rule since its incorporation into the empire in 1417. In the succeeding four centuries and a half it had been open to extensive immigration, particularly of Muslim Turks and Tartars and Bulgarian Christians, which changed the ethnic balance significantly, and its economy had been oriented toward Constantinople. Dobrudja suffered severe economic and population losses as a result of the war of 1877–8, and the new Rumanian administration found the country culturally and economically backward. They replaced the old Ottoman administrative structure with three *judeţe* and their subdivisions and introduced the practices of centralized control from Bucharest. Another measure introduced immediately was compulsory schooling for all children between 8 and 12 years of age in the towns, but not in the villages, because of the lack of teachers and money. The agrarian problem in this agricultural province was acute, but reformers had to take into account such complexities as the Ottoman land law of 1874 concerning property rights and had to replace old institutions carefully in order to avoid economic chaos. A start

---

[36] On the beginnings of the Rumanian administration, see Nicolae Ciachir, *Războiul pentru independenţa României în contextul european* (Bucharest, 1977), 287–97; G. Dumitraşcu, 'Aspecte ale situaţiei Dobrogei în perioada noiembrie 1878–mai 1883: Activitatea primului prefect de Constanţa, Remus N. Opreanu', *Anuarul Institutului de Istorie şi Arheologie*, 18 (1981), 293–304.

was made in 1880. All in all, Rumanian public opinion showed little enthusiasm for the acquisition of this large area (15,600 square kilometres) and thought it an unfair exchange for southern Bessarabia. Yet, in time it was to bring substantial economic benefits to Rumania as agriculture developed and as the port of Constanţa became a major commercial gateway for Rumanian exports and imports.

The Rumanian acquisition of Dobrudja raised two serious disputes with Russia. The first had to do with an extension of the nine-month period for the passage of Russian troops and supplies through Rumanian territory to Bulgaria, which was to expire in May 1879. The Russians pressed for a new agreement extending the deadline, but the Rumanian government, still aggrieved over its experiences with the Russians during the war and at Berlin, categorically refused. Thanks to support from Britain and Austria-Hungary, who sought to limit Russian influence in the Balkans, the Rumanians prevailed. On the second matter—the drawing of the frontier between Rumania and Bulgaria in Dobrudja—the Rumanians lost. They badly wanted Silistria, and in January 1879 Rumanian troops occupied Arab Tabia, a fortress dominating the city. The Russians, intent upon obtaining as much territory as possible for their client state and, this time, backed by Britain and Austria-Hungary, forced the Rumanians to withdraw. A European commission charged with determining the new boundary awarded the Rumanians Arab Tabia, but Silistria went to Bulgaria.

The Rumanian government fulfilled a final stipulation of the Treaty of Berlin with utmost reluctance. In October 1879 parliament passed a law modifying article 7 of the constitution, which had effectively prevented Jews from becoming citizens and, hence, from enjoying full civil and political rights. Opposition came as usual from those inside and outside parliament who feared the economic competition of Jews and resented their 'intrusion' into the 'life of the nation'. There was widespread opposition also from those who had no strong feelings in these matters, but who resented the interference of the great powers in the internal affairs of the country.[37] The law in question revealed the grudging nature of the Rumanians' compliance with the wishes of the powers.

---

[37] The arguments of the opponents of revision are amply set forth in *Cestiunea israelită inaintea Camerilor de Revisuire* (Bucharest, 1879). See also Barbu B. Berceanu, 'Modificarea, din 1879, a articolului 7 din Constituţie', *Studii şi materiale de istorie modernă*, 6 (1979), 67–89.

It required an individual who sought Rumanian citizenship to petition the prince. Then, after ten years' residence in the country the request might be granted by a special act of the legislature if the petitioner had shown himself to be 'useful to the country'. Those foreigners who had rendered valuable services to the country, including those who had fought in the War for Independence in 1877–8, might be exempted from the probationary period. The number of Jews who obtained citizenship under these complicated procedures before 1918 was exceedingly small.[38]

The most important result of the Congress of Berlin for Rumania was clearly the recognition of independence. It finally severed the juridical link with the Ottoman Empire which had endured some four centuries. Although Ottoman suzerainty had become largely nominal since 1829, its formal termination gave a powerful boost to national pride. In a practical way the achievement of independence allowed Rumanian politicians and intellectuals to focus their attention on nation-building. Yet, despite the enthusiasm of the moment, they remained realists. Recognizing the limitations of independence, they understood that a small country in the pursuit of even limited foreign policy objectives and the development of a prosperous national economy could afford to ignore the interests of the great powers only at its peril.

The Eastern crisis of 1875–8 caused a decisive shift in Rumanian foreign policy. Between 1866 and 1877 Prince Charles and both Liberal and Conservative politicians had followed a policy of balance between Austria-Hungary and Russia. But after 1878 they tilted toward Austria-Hungary. Bessarabia, which now joined Transylvania as an object of Rumanian irredentist aspirations, lay at the heart of Rumanian bitterness toward Russia, but the Rumanians' assessment of Russia's overall aims in the Balkans, suggested by her patronage of Bulgaria at Rumania's expense, reinforced their distrust of an erstwhile ally. Hostility toward Russia also affected Rumania's contacts with her neighbour to the south. The perception of Bulgaria as Russia's client state, added to a continuous dispute over southern Dobrudja, soured relations between the two countries down to the outbreak of the Balkan Wars.

A logical consequence of independence was the proclamation of Rumania as a kingdom and of Charles as king on 26 March 1881.

---

[38] Carol Iancu, *Les Juifs en Roumanie (1866–1919): de l'exclusion à l'émancipation* (Aix-en-Provence, 1978), 186–9.

The event seems to have taken the population of the country by surprise. The public celebrations in Bucharest following the proclamation reflected the organizing skill of local officials rather than the enthusiasm of the public, for after fifteen years Charles remained a cold, distant figure. Abroad, the powers, perhaps out of fatigue, raised no serious objections, and their recognition followed in due course.

2
Models of Development

The advent of the Hohenzollerns, the promulgation of a constitution in 1866, and the achievement of independence in 1878
brought Rumanian politicians, economists, and social thinkers
face to face with the new problem of national development. The
specific issues were many and varied, but two general directions
presented themselves. One, drawing upon the Western European
experience, would lead to industrialization and urbanization and
bring radical changes to every facet of Rumanian society; the
other was based upon Rumania's agricultural past and emphasized
the preservation of traditional social structures and cultural values.

The outlines of this dichotomy were already visible before
mid-century. In political organization emulation of the West was
evident in the reception of liberal theories of government and the
drafting of new law codes; in the economy, in calls for a modern
industry and a modern credit system; and in culture, in the wholesale reception of French literature and such projects as a French
college in Iaşi. On the opposite side, the circle around the literary
review, *Dacia literară*, in the 1840s represented a reaction to the
uncritical embrace of the West. It reminded fellow Rumanians of
their own unique national heritage and urged them to seek literary
inspiration and social goals in the native experience. The forty-
eighters as a group belonged to neither camp exclusively, but in
their search for solutions to urgent political and economic problems they drew generously upon Western experience. Yet, it was
only after the revolution of 1848 that these often disparate ideas
and tendencies were transformed into distinct ideological currents.
It was then that the 'Europeanists' and the 'traditionalists' coalesced
and inaugurated a wide-ranging national debate that was to last
until the Second World War.

In the second half of the nineteenth century advocates of one or
another course of development, whether Western or autochthonous, took a cultural or philosophical approach, or were
guided by economic theory and data. Divergence of opinion rather
than consensus was the rule. Yet, central to all the doctrines
enunciated was the role of agriculture in the new Rumania, not

just in the economy but also as the determinant of social relations and ethical values. Nor could modern industry be ignored, for everyone, staunch agrarianists and committed Westernizers, recognized its potential for transforming society.

FORM WITHOUT SUBSTANCE

The first coherent, organized criticism of the direction modern Rumanian society had taken came from a group of young men in Iaşi who had studied at universities in Western Europe and who were eager to raise Rumanian intellectual and cultural life to a European level. They argued that after the Treaty of Adrianople in 1829, which had formally ended the Ottoman commercial monopoly, the Rumanian principalities had precipitously entered the European economic and cultural world and had 'opened their doors too widely' to innovations of all kinds. Young Westernizers, they complained, borrowed and imitated, ignoring criteria of selection based upon local customs and experience. The inevitable result was, so their indictment ran, that contact with Europe touched only the surface of Rumanian society, which still lacked a foundation and substance of its own. Such ideas were to lie at the heart of traditionalist currents of thought about Rumanian development for almost three quarters of a century. But these early critics were not, in fact, traditionalists. Rather, they had been nourished on ideas which would bring Rumanians into closer communion with Europe.

Filled with optimism about the future of their nation in the years immediately following the union of the principalities and imbued with confidence in their own ability to set it on a proper course, a number of these young, Western-educated intellectuals formed a society to propagate their ideas and turn public opinion in their favour. They called it 'Junimea' (Youth). Perhaps 'community' would be an appropriate description of the group, since it did not come into being through some formal act; nor was it held together by a set of rules. Rather, Junimea owed its appearance to the personal affinity its founding members felt for one another, and it maintained itself through the common sentiments they shared about society, culture, and literature.

Junimea had its beginnings in 1863 when five young men, recently returned from studies abroad, met in Iaşi to discuss ways of presenting the results of their studies and of stimulating intellectual life in their city, which had been somewhat diminished since the departure of the prince to Bucharest. The public lectures, which were to be a regular feature of Junimea's activities for seventeen years began in 1863, and the first formal literary gathering of the society took place the following year to hear a translation of *Macbeth* by one of its members. Thereafter, it became customary after the public lecture on Sunday for the society to meet at a member's home to discuss important questions of the day or criticize new literary or scholarly work by colleagues. The lectures, which from 1866 on became annual cycles and dealt with broad themes such as 'Psychological Researches' (1868 and 1869), 'Man and Nature' (1873), and 'The Germans' (1875), gained a wide following among the educated classes of Iaşi and, in time, made the Junimea Society and 'Junimism', a potent force in the intellectual and political life of the entire country. The audiences were composed solely of intellectuals—professors, lawyers, high government officials, and students—a demanding public which imposed a rigorous adherence to high standards on the part of the lecturers. These lectures, which continued until 1881, thus became an institution, respected by many, feared by some.

The founding members of Junimea, with one notable exception, came from the highest ranks of Moldavian society. Theodor Rosetti was the brother-in-law of Prince Alexandru Cuza; Petre Carp and Vasile Pogor were the sons of wealthy boiers; and Iacob Negruzzi was the son of Costache Negruzzi, one of the masters of Moldavian prose. Only Titu Maiorescu came from the 'third estate'. His father, Ioan Maiorescu, was a professor at the National College in Craiova and had represented the Wallachian provisional government at the Frankfurt Parliament in 1848. But none of them was concerned about social class. What mattered was nobility of the mind and intellectual accomplishment. Their co-operation and friendship were thus not chance occurrences, but were based upon shared convictions and aspirations. They had studied in Germany (a few, like Pogor, in France) and had assimilated the post-revolutionary ideas predominant there and were agreed on the direction that Rumanian social and political life should take. Their views were enlightened and conservative, and their method of analysis iconoclastic.

Titu Maiorescu (1840–1917) was the dominant figure of Junimea from its inception to its effective end at the turn of the century. The decisive influence which Junimea exerted on Rumanian cultural life during this long period was owing in great measure to his intellectual leadership and superb skills as an organizer and manager. His intellectual formation was German, first at the élite college in Vienna, the Theresianum, where he spent seven years, and then at the universities of Berlin and Giessen, where he took his doctorate in philosophy in 1859 for a thesis on Johann Herbart, the nineteenth-century German philosopher noted for his application of psychology and ethics to pedagogy. The greatest influences on his thought were Schopenhauer, and through him Kant, and Feuerbach, who was the main source of his materialism and of his attempts to establish the foundations of a secular morality, one of the chief preoccupations of the period. In 1863, the same year the Junimea Society came into being, he became rector of the University of Iaşi, which had been founded in 1860. From this time on he was to be deeply involved in shaping cultural policy as teacher, writer, and public official.

As significant as Maiorescu's contributions were Junimea would have been something less than what it became, had it not been for the presence of others, who were outstanding figures in their own right. Foremost among them was Petre Carp (1837–1919). The descendant of an old Moldavian boier family, he, like Maiorescu, received his education in Germany, at a French lyceum in Berlin and then the University of Bonn, where he studied law and economics. He moved easily in aristocratic student circles, where he adopted social attitudes that were to remain with him all his life. Upon his return home in 1862 he made his presence felt immediately in the intellectual life of Iaşi. He contributed substantially to the creation of the distinctive Junimea spirit, that mixture of critical intensity, erudition, and conviviality, which cemented relations among a diverse assemblage of individuals. Carp's colleagues respected him for his political and sociological knowledge, his wide reading in European literature, and his talent as a literary critic, and they often turned to him as a final authority. But he appeared less and less frequently at meetings of the society as his political career absorbed his energies. Vasile Pogor (1833–1906) also played an exceptional role in the creation of the Junimea mystique. The son of a *răzeş* (a free peasant) who had been made a boier in 1821, he had received a French education at a pension in Iaşi and then in Paris where he studied law. He was the *enfant terrible* of the group, always ready with a joke or sardonic comment. He had an inexhaustible curiosity, which made him receptive to whatever was new. His difficulty was that he could not choose. Besides the Greek and Latin classics—he translated

Horace and felt the need to re-read Homer annually—he translated Baudelaire, who was at the time completely unknown to the Rumanian public, and lectured on such diverse subjects as the influence of the French Revolution on modern ideas, Shakespeare's plays, and Schopenhauer.

There were many others who contributed to the prestige and influence of Junimea. Joining the 'founders' was a remarkable company of scholars from all the major disciplines, among them: Alexandru D. Xenopol, history; Alexandru Lambrior, linguistics; Vasile Conta, philosophy; and Gheorghe Panu, history and, later, social reform. The intellectual and spiritual values promoted by Junimea served as a source of inspiration for the great creators of Rumanian literature in the second half of the nineteenth century: Mihai Eminescu, a Romantic and the greatest poet of the Rumanian language; Ion Creangă, the creator of an authentic, realist vision of the village; Ion Luca Caragiale, who focused attention on the urban classes in his masterpieces of the drama and short narrative fiction; and Ioan Slavici, a novelist and short story writer who excelled at the examination of character.

The Junimists owed much of their influence in intellectual and literary life to their monthly, *Convorbiri literare* (Literary Conversations). It had been Iacob Negruzzi's idea to publish a journal modelled on the *Revue des deux mondes* of Paris, and as its editor for twenty-eight years he made it the foremost Rumanian review of its time. But it was Maiorescu who set the tone. In the first issue on 1 March 1867, he announced that the review would devote itself to 'art and science' and would avoid the 'passions of politics', which he found inimical to creativity and scholarship. *Convorbiri literare* also avoided specialization. Instead, it reflected the broad interests and the striving for synthesis of its founders. The humanities predominated—literature and literary criticism, history, philosophy, and philology.

Politics, despite Maiorescu's dictum, became a major preoccupation of Junimea after 1870, when a number of members formed their own group, 'Juna dreaptă' (The Young Right), under the aegis of the Conservative Party. They tried to keep their literary and cultural activities from becoming entangled in politics, but to no avail. Politics increasingly monopolized the attention of Maiorescu, Carp, and others, and the enmities born of competing ambitions dulled the light-heartedness and camaraderie of the founders.

The heyday of Junimea, and of *Convorbiri literare*, lasted until about 1885, the year when the society moved to Bucharest. But even before this time in Iaşi it had already ceased to be what it had once been, as its leading members moved away or died and as its centre gradually shifted to Bucharest, especially after Maiorescu's move there in 1874. After 1885 the dominance of Junimea over literary and intellectual life was on the wane, too, because Rumanian literature and culture had entered a new phase, in which the theories and values espoused by the society appeared increasingly incongruous. Maiorescu himself admitted as much in 1890, when he said that the old Junimea Society of Iaşi should be spoken of as a thing past, but he rejected the notion that Junimism as a doctrine had died. For a time from his professorial chair at the University of Bucharest he succeeded in raising up a new generation of Junimists from among a singularly talented group of students. But the new youth could not dominate intellectual life and literature as their elders had done. Increasing numbers of intellectuals were drawn to aesthetic theories and a philosophical discourse deeply influenced by positivism and science or were preoccupied by the two great social issues of the time—the peasant question at home and the nationality problem in Transylvania. By the end of the first decade of the new century Junimea had in fact ceased to exist. Even politically it no longer represented a separate current, for in 1907 it had united with the Conservative Party, now headed by Petre Carp.

The most lasting influence which the Junimists exerted may have been on the way Rumanians thought about themselves. The critical attitude which they assumed toward the course of development their country had taken since the early decades of the nineteenth century ignited a debate among intellectuals and politicians that was to last until the Second World War.

The Junimists' very approach to the question proved a shock to many intellectuals. Nourished and dominated by France since the 1830s, Rumanian culture was now exposed to massive German influences.[1] German philosophy and social thought lay at the heart of Junimist ideology, and nowhere else were they felt more strongly than in the Junimist world-view. Constructed in accordance with the principles of organic social development, it drew heavily upon the historicist theories of German romantic

[1] See, e.g. Ştefan Zeletin, 'Romantismul german şi cultura critică română', *Minerva*, 1/3 (1929), 63–83; Tudor Vianu, *Influenţa lui Hegel în cultura română* (Bucharest, 1933).

philosophy. Somewhat later the evolutionist ideas of Herbert Spencer, which emphasized slow, gradual development and with which the Junimists became acquainted mainly through German commentaries, were also influential. Maiorescu and his colleagues also discovered in Henry Buckle's *History of Civilization in England* scientific confirmation of their theories about social change and the course of development which their own country should follow.[2] Thus indebted to evolutionist theories, the Junimists perceived in recent Rumanian history a fateful deviation from the principles of organic development which had created a 'paralysing antinomy' between form and substance.

In reaching their conclusions, the founders of Junimea had been greatly influenced by their studies of law. At the time the historical school had been predominant. It demanded respect for native traditions in legislation and constitutional structures, and, shunning the discontinuity caused by revolution, it praised evolution as the norm for healthy societies. These were the ideas that formed the backbone of Junimist ideology. Thus, the European Restoration, which had already run its course in the West, finally reached Rumania in the social thought of Titu Maiorescu and his colleagues. They applied to Rumania the idea that revolution (their point of reference was always France in 1789) was an 'arbitrary act' that invariably disrupted the steady, natural course of historical development and visited upon society the most dire consequences. According to this line of reasoning, revolutionaries were those who formulated and applied abstract principles of social development without taking into account the 'organic' growth of a nation's institutions. Maiorescu thought that the avoidance of revolution was especially important for a small country like Rumania, which, surrounded by 'predatory' great powers, could ill afford sudden upheavals. Revolutionaries, he warned, might know why they were starting a revolution, but they could never be certain who would gain what in the end. He and his fellow Junimists insisted that social institutions could never be the products of ideology, but had, instead, to assume their proper form gradually, over time and through experience. For them, society, like nature, was never 'created'; it was always in the process of 'becoming'.

[2] Alexandru Zub, *Junimea: Implicaţii istoriografice* (Iaşi, 1976), 254–62; Vasile Pogor, 'H. T. Buckle: Istoria civilisaţiunei în Englitera', *Convorbiri literare*, 1/6 (1867), 80–7.

From this perspective of reverence for tradition and organic development the Junimists dissected the institutions and culture of contemporary Rumania. They took to task especially the generation of 1848. They accused the young revolutionaries of having succumbed completely to modern Western culture, of having touched only its outward forms, and, thus, of having ignored the deeper historical foundations which had produced these forms and without which they could not exist. Maiorescu, in 1895 looking back over nearly a half-century, thought that the importance of the forty-eighters lay in their having awakened the national consciousness of the Rumanians and having sharpened their will to develop in harmony with Western civilization, but he found them utterly lacking in practicality. Specifically, he denounced the revolutionary programme proclaimed in June 1848 as a 'work of fantasy', a 'naïve jotting down on paper of an amalgam of nebulous ideas'.[3]

Maiorescu's immediate concern was the lamentable state of Rumanian culture. The principal vice from which it suffered was 'untruth', untruth in aspirations, politics, poetry, grammar, and every manifestation of the public spirit. In a stinging indictment, 'În contra direcţiei de astăzi în cultura romănă' (Against the Contemporary Direction in Rumanian Culture), which he published in *Convorbiri literare* in 1868, he wrote: 'Before having a political party which felt the need for a newspaper of its own and before having a public interested in learning and thus needing to read, we founded political organs and literary reviews and falsified and disdained journalism. Before having village teachers, we established schools in the villages, and before having an extensive cultural life outside the schools, we created atheneums and cultural associations and thus we cheapened the spirit of literary societies. Before having even the shadow of original scientific activity, we founded the Rumanian Academy . . . and we falsified the idea of an academy. Before having the necessary musicians, we created a music conservatory; before having a single painter of any value, we founded an École des Beaux Arts; before having a single play of any merit, we built a national theatre, and in the process we cheapened and falsified all these forms of culture.'[4] Thus,

[3] Titu Maiorescu, *Istoria contemporană a României (1866–1900)* (Bucharest, 1925), 40–1.

[4] Titu Maiorescu, 'În contra direcţiunii de astăzi a culturei romăne', *Convorbiri literare*, 2/19 (1868), 305–6.

Maiorescu concluded, in appearance, the Rumanians possessed almost the whole of Western civilization, but in reality, he admonished, the politics, the science, the academies, the newspapers, the theatre, and the constitution were all stillborn, 'phantoms without bodies', 'forms without substance'.

Maiorescu had discovered a fundamental incongruity between the institutions and the social structure of contemporary Rumania. For him, there were only two classes in Rumanian society—landlords and peasants. He denied the existence of a third class—the bourgeoisie.[5] Such a view fitted in with his own and the general Junimist conception of Rumanian society as one of form without content. Maiorescu argued that cultural and political forms had been imported and simply placed on top of the ancestral customs and patriarchal spiritual life of the great mass of the population. These forms, introduced, according to the Junimists, haphazardly and in haste, did not in the least correspond to the prevailing social conditions in Rumania; they were, rather, suited to those profound changes in the West that had brought the bourgeoisie to power. But, Maiorescu insisted, Rumania had no bourgeoisie, and that was why, in his view, the prevailing Rumanian constitutional system was ineffective—it had no reason to exist. Petre Carp went even further. He labelled the National Liberal Party, which had been founded in 1875, 'artificial' because it could not hope to represent the interests of a class—the bourgeoisie—which did not exist. The Junimists persisted in denying the existence of a middle class, even though Rumanian economic development in the last third of the century showed otherwise.

Not surprisingly, the Junimists found socialism an even greater anomaly than the bourgeoisie and denied the existence of a Rumanian proletariat. Maiorescu made their case in uncompromising terms in a public lecture in 1892 entitled, 'Condiţiunile progresului omenirii' (The Conditions for the Progress of Humanity). His argument is familiar enough. He thought that socialism in Western Europe had a function as the product of a mature society, but it could have no purpose in Rumanian society, which was still in its 'childhood'. He saw in the radicalism propounded by socialists a long-term threat to existing social structures, but he could see little immediate danger in the fledgling

[5] Titu Maiorescu, *Discursuri parlamentare*, i (Bucharest, 1897), 434: Speech in Parliament, 22 Jan. 1876.

Rumanian socialist movement and dismissed it as an 'exotic plant'.[6]

The Junimists could discern no significant incompatibility between the two classes of Rumanian society they did recognize. They thought that landlords and peasants formed a single bloc, bound by a common attachment to property. Consequently, according to this line of reasoning, they were both inherently conservative and represented a bulwark against sudden structural changes and thoughtless innovations. As a matter of conviction and public policy, the Junimists thus stood for the maintenance of private property in land and opposed all measures that threatened it with fragmentation or confiscation. They approved of the agrarian reform of 1864 because it reinforced the attachment of the mass of the peasants to property and freed their productive capabilities from centuries-old burdens. They were glad to see that government had at last recognized that the value of land ultimately depended upon peasant labour. Nevertheless, they found the law wanting in its failure to keep the new proprietors from dividing up their allotments and thereby endangering the economic viability of the small peasant holding and undermining the social stability which it assured. They consistently sought to protect the small independent producer, whom they recognized as the pillar of every agricultural country—'the only real class' of Rumanian society, Maiorescu claimed in 1868—by supporting legislation to make small rural property inalienable and indivisible. But in all their measures to improve the lot of the peasantry the Junimists opposed any agrarian reform that would diminish landlord property. In property relations, as in other social questions, they advocated a slow, gradual transition to new forms.

The Junimists believed in progress and accepted the need for Rumania to evolve toward a modern civilization on the Western model, but they were convinced that this process could take place only through moral and cultural means, while native social and economic structures were left intact. Thus, they foresaw no significant changes in the primacy of agriculture in the national economy or in the traditional roles of landlords and peasants in social relations. At first, they dismissed industry as practically non-existent, and thought that in those few places where it did exist it lacked a national character, being only the creation of

    [6] Z. Ornea, *Junimea și Junimismul* (Bucharest, 1975), 607–9. Maiorescu translated and published Herbert Spencer's 'From Freedom to Bondage' (the preface to Thomas Mackay, *A Plea for Liberty*, New York, 1891) under the title, *În contra socialismului (din libertate spre asuprire)* (Bucharest, 1893).

foreigners with foreign capital.[7] Yet, by the end of the century they had become less categorical. Some among them were even inclined to encourage industry, but only those branches which processed agricultural products. Petre Carp, however, went further. He sponsored the mining law of 1895, a major piece of legislation which laid the foundations of the modern Rumanian mining industry, and he and other Junimists favoured the unimpeded flow of foreign capital into the country as the best means of developing the national economy in the absence of sufficient local capital.

The theories of development elaborated by the founders of Junimea exerted a powerful influence upon the second generation, who adapted them to the new advances being made in the social and experimental sciences at the end of the nineteenth century. A leading member of this generation, who was to carry on the Junimist tradition in the period between the World Wars, was Constantin Rădulescu-Motru (1868–1957). He was one of a handful of professors, which included Titu Maiorescu, who were responsible for the remarkable flourishing of philosophy and psychology in Rumania between the 1870s and the early 1940s. As a student of Maiorescu's at the University of Bucharest between 1885 and 1888, he was inspired by both the ideas and the method of his teacher. He continued his studies of psychology and philosophy in Paris and then in Leipzig with Wilhelm Wundt. Upon his return to Bucharest in 1893 with a doctorate in philosophy, he published a series of articles on philosophical problems in *Convorbiri literare* and in 1897 began his long teaching career at the university.

Deeply influenced by German philosophy and sociology and following in the Junimist tradition, Rădulescu-Motru was preoccupied with problems of the philosophy of culture. From the German Romantics and more immediately from Houston Stewart Chamberlain he learned to appreciate the superiority of 'culture' over 'civilization'. He defined culture as the unique, 'organic' expression of the spirit of a community or nation, and he identified it with the 'spiritual inclinations' of a people. Thus, its components lay in creations of both the heart and the mind—religious beliefs, moral values and institutions, works of art, and the truths

[7] C. Gane, *P. P. Carp și locul său în istoria politică a Țării*, ii (Bucharest, 1936), 119–20, 329; Theodor Rosetti, 'Despre direcțiunea progresului nostru', *Convorbiri literare*, 8/1 (1874), 10–11.

of science. Civilization, on the other hand, meant material gain and technological progress, the exterior forms, the 'things' of social life. For him, the essential difference between culture and civilization was one of depth, the former fully permeating the essence of a people, the latter remaining at the surface; culture was 'lodged in the soul', while civilization was merely a 'cloak for the body'; civilization could be borrowed by one people from another quickly and easily through imitation, but a borrowed culture was inconceivable.[8]

In a small book, *Cultura română și politicianismul* (1904; Rumanian Culture and Politics for the Sake of Politics), Rădulescu-Motru applied the antinomy of culture and civilization to the modern development of Rumania. His debt to Maiorescu's conception of 'form without substance' is evident. He equated form with civilization and substance with culture. He, too, accused the generation of 1848 of having broken the continuity of Rumanian cultural development through the hasty importation of Western political forms, which were utterly foreign to the spirit of the nation. Borrowing and imitation were thus the main causes of the anomalies that had afflicted Rumanian society ever since. Western laws and institutions, he pointed out, had been produced in abundance in Rumania, but they had had no effect on the everyday life of the mass of the people. They had simply remained ideas, and beneath the bright surface of an 'external civilization' the traditional spirit of Rumanian culture remained untouched.

From the German Romantics directly, and from his Junimist forebears indirectly, Rădulescu-Motru discovered the locus of organic forms of social life, of 'natural' links among members of the community in the traditional Rumanian village, but he could perceive only cold, 'mechanical' relationships among the inhabitants of the growing urban centres. He had no doubt, therefore, that the future of the Rumanian nation lay in a strengthening of their rural way of life. His eyes were turned toward the past as he idealized the relations between the old boier class and the peasantry as harmonious and as he denied to the Rumanian people any aptitude for industry and large-scale commerce. Moreover, he regarded them as constitutionally incapable of disciplined work

---

[8] Constantin Rădulescu-Motru, *Cultura română și politicianismul* (Bucharest, 1904), in C. Rădulescu-Motru, *Personalismul energetic și alte scrieri* (Bucharest, 1984), 7–20, 39–43.

and planning, those 'superior habits', which had produced the dynamic industrial, capitalist society of Western Europe.[9]

Rădulescu-Motru's ideas thus represented a continuation of Junimism with their emphasis on the native intellectual and cultural tradition. Yet, he went further than his mentors by making the village the centre of the national tradition and the focus of social and economic development. As a result, he belongs at least as much to the agrarian currents which had come to the fore at the turn of the century as to Junimism.

For a time after the turn of the century the most dynamic of the burgeoning agrarian currents was Sămănătorism, which derived its name from *sămănător*, sower, the symbol of the movement's didactic aims. It was an amalgam of the national current of *Dacia literară* of the 1840s, the Junimist theory of 'form without substance', and the growing preoccupation with the economic and social plight of the peasantry. The new current came into being, as happened so often in Rumanian intellectual life, when likeminded individuals were drawn together around a review, in this case, *Sămănătorul*, a weekly which began publication in Bucharest on 2 December 1901. Although its editors and contributors came from diverse backgrounds, they were united in their dissatisfaction with the course of development their country had taken. They were also of one mind on the urgent need for reform, but the measures they proposed were moral and cultural, for they regarded the peasant question and national development in general as ethical issues. Like Rădulescu-Motru, they were wary of 'politics for the sake of politics' and denounced politicians who, in their view, used the anomalies of 'empty' Western constitutional forms to gain personal advantage at the expense of the mass of the population. They believed that the peasants did not so much lack land as 'light'. Hence, they formulated an extensive programme of acculturation, which would bring teachers to the village to 'enlighten' its inhabitants and would promote a 'healthy literature' capable of instilling in all a piety for their glorious past and a determination to improve the present.

In certain ways the Sămănătorists' view of Rumanian development resembled that of the Junimists. It fitted into that broad current of ideas which held that Rumania had been diverted onto a false path wholly unsuited to her historical experience. The Sămănătorists therefore denounced capitalism with special

---

[9] Ibid. 52–6.

vehemence as an 'unnatural implantation' into a traditional society subject to other economic and social laws. Since Rumanian capitalism was the work of only a handful of persons, who had no higher motive than private gain, so the argument ran, this unwholesome intrusion could easily be excised, thus enabling Rumania to avoid the 'affliction' of capitalist development.

The Sămănătorists indulged in the same harsh criticism of nineteenth-century Rumania as other anti-capitalist theorists, but, unlike them, they offered no solutions to the pressing social and economic problems of contemporary Rumania except education. Moreover, they lacked direction. They glorified the institutions of the past, but did not think they could be brought back; they lamented the disappearance of the old boier class, but accepted the process as inevitable; and they disparaged the accomplishments of the generation of 1848 and the political system created in 1866, but they did not advocate their abolition. Instead of specific economic and social reforms, the Sămănătorists stood for a general improvement of public life through a kind of moral purging to be accomplished by the dissemination of culture among the mass of the population, a culture permeated by 'true national values'. All this was to take place gradually, for, like the Junimists, they conceived of social development as an evolutionary process, which precluded outside influences and abrupt changes of direction.

As defenders of national ideals, the Sămănătorists favoured social harmony. Those currents of ideas and political movements, such as socialism, which promoted class antagonisms, were anathema to them. In their idealized rural world they discerned no fundamental incompatibility between the peasant and the landlord. Thus, they could show genuine sympathy for the cultivator of the soil and at the same time praise the historical role of the boier.

The principal animator of Sămănătorism was the historian Nicolae Iorga (1871–1940). From his voluminous writings the outlines of a doctrine emerged, which to some extent made up for the lack of a systematic philosophical or sociological exposition of Sămănătorist views. In 1904, the year he became director of *Sămănătorul* at the age of 33, Iorga had already achieved pre-eminence in Rumanian cultural life. He had taken his bachelor's degree in history at the University of Iaşi in 1889 and had spent the next four years in Europe, first in Paris at the École Pratique des Hautes Études, where he obtained his diploma for a thesis on Philippe de Mézières and the crusade of the fourteenth century, and then at the University of Leipzig, where he received his doctorate in 1893 for a dissertation on Thomas III, Marquis de

Saluces. In 1895 he was appointed professor of world history at the University of Bucharest and two years later was elected a corresponding member of the Rumanian Academy. During this period his critical attitude toward Rumanian culture had slowly taken shape. He approached the problem from his broad background of studies in Western European history and literature, a perspective which heightened the contradictions he perceived in all facets of Rumanian society. In a volume of studies published in 1899 and entitled, *La Vie intellectuelle des Roumains en 1899*, he applied Titu Maiorescu's celebrated theory of form without substance to his analysis of existing institutions, but he was more passionate and more vehement in his criticism than his older colleague.

At the heart of Iorga's theory of social development lay his belief that change, to be beneficial and enduring, must be gradual, evolutionary. His own extensive studies of world history had persuaded him that mankind, and especially the ethnic nations, had over the long course of time followed an essentially organic development. As a result, he argued, any break with tradition could only be at a nation's peril, since every people had of necessity to follow a course of development determined by the 'national spirit', which had formed slowly and through experience over many centuries. Under no circumstances, then, could a people abandon its heritage by imitating foreign models or by indulging in abstract social experiments. In his works on Rumanian history Iorga stressed the virtues of the political and social system that had prevailed in medieval Moldavia and Wallachia, in which he chose to see not the selfish domination of a small class of boiers and high churchmen over the mass of the rural population, but rather the rudimentary democracy of a patriarchal, peasant society. The contrast he drew between the American and French revolutions reflected the same evolutionary pattern of his thought. He viewed the former as a struggle to defend institutions that had grown up gradually out of the experience of many generations and were being threatened by an external force (England) that had 'set itself against the course of history'. He thought that the French Revolution, on the other hand, had been promoted by 'bourgeois intellectuals for the bourgeoisie', who in the process had destroyed an 'organism' still capable of meeting the changing needs of society and had put in its place an 'abstract structure' which had proven to be 'uninhabitable'.[10]

[10] Nicolae Iorga, *Originea și sensul democrației* (Vălenii de Munte, 1927), 50–1.

Iorga showed unrestrained sympathy for the peasantry because he thought the village was the place where the laws of social change operated in their purest form. For him, the village was by definition the preserver of a tradition built up and nurtured through the centuries where change occurred with 'full respect' for organic structures. He admired the village especially as the locus of high moral values, and he drew a sharp distinction between it and the modern industrial city, where impersonal, 'mechanical' relationships created a sterile environment. There was something in the peasant's nature, he found, which made it impossible for him to adapt to the new political and economic structures that had been created in the nineteenth century. He characterized the peasant's attitude toward the city as one of incomprehension, for he could not imagine why such a large number of people had come together in such an ugly setting, making themselves miserable in the pursuit of money.[11]

The city, for Iorga, was thus a symbol of everything that had gone wrong in the evolution of nineteenth-century Rumania. He identified it as the place where capitalist industry flourished and where the heart of the new economic and social order that was undermining the moral foundations of traditional society lay. The whole process, political as well as economic, by which modern Rumania had come into being struck him as artificial, an 'exercise in ideology' imposed arbitrarily upon a people who until then had followed a 'natural, organic evolution'. Completely odious, in his eyes, had been the attempt of the generation of 1848 to integrate Rumania into the general currents of European civilization, an act which could only compromise the morals of a patriarchal society. He accused the forty-eighters of being 'romantics' and 'naïve dreamers', who thought their people mature enough to endure any kind of social innovation. He was even harder on those who had fashioned the Constitution of 1866. He called it a 'calamity' and the work of 'ideologues' following abstract notions of state-building, which had nothing to do with the previous course of Rumanian political development. By ignoring the constitutional development of the country since 1300, he complained, they had created a state out of abstract principles borrowed from abroad and, hence, one incapable of 'true life'.

Yet, despite these fulminations, Iorga recognized the impossibi-

---

[11] Z. Ornea, *Sămănătorismul*, 2nd edn. (Bucharest, 1971), 154–5, quoting from an article by Iorga which appeared in *Sămănătorul* on 5 Dec. 1904.

lity of returning to some earlier age. In a public lecture in 1907 on the relationship of the village to the city he accepted the latter as characteristic of the modern age and even admitted that it would eventually dominate the village. As a historian he could not but recognize the inevitability of change; all he asked was that the forms of social life from the past be replaced with care by others that were neither 'false' nor 'foreign'.

None the less, Iorga envisioned a Rumania in which agriculture would remain the economic and cultural foundation of society. Although he was prepared to accept industries that were engaged in the processing of agricultural products or would develop other natural resources, he could foresee no substantial change in Rumania's condition as a pre-eminently agricultural country. He denounced the policy of industrialization being vigorously pursued by the Liberal Party as 'erroneous' because its leaders, like earlier generations of Westernizers, ignored the essential agrarian character of Rumania's development. Rumanians, he thought, should specialize in what they did best, and he rejected the notion that a concentration on agricultural pursuits doomed a country to permanent inferiority.

Iorga was the spirit of Sămănătorism. When he resigned as director of the review in 1906 in a dispute with the editors Sămănătorism as a cultural movement began a slow dissolution. By 1910 it had ceased to be a significant force in intellectual life.

Contemporary with Sămănătorism was Poporanism (Populism, in the sense of the Russian *narodnichestvo*; from *popor*, people). The Poporanists shared with the Sămănătorists certain basic assumptions about the agrarian character of Rumanian society, about the deviations that had occurred in their country's development in the nineteenth century, and about the need to return to the earlier foundations of organic growth. But, unlike the Sămănătorists, they were not satisfied merely to speculate on the relative merits of culture and civilization and to issue calls for a moral revival. Instead, they were committed to a far-reaching reform of agrarian structures and sought to achieve immediate political and economic goals.

The leading theorist of Poporanism was Constantin Stere (1865–1936). Born in Bessarabia, he shared the social concerns and suffered the consequences of political nonconformity of many young Russian intellectuals of the time. While a lyceum student he read the great critics of tsarism, among them, Chernyshevsky, Dobroliubov, and Mikhailovsky, and joined the People's Will

(Narodnaia Volia) Party, which cultivated a sense of duty on the part of intellectuals toward the common people. Because of his revolutionary activity, he was arrested in 1883 and exiled to Siberia for eight years. Upon his return home in 1891 he decided to resume his studies in Iaşi and with his family secretly crossed the border into Rumania. He quickly integrated himself into the cultural and political life of his new home: he obtained a law degree and in 1901 was appointed professor of administrative and constitutional law at the Faculty of Law in Iaşi; he became a leader of the National Liberal Party; and in 1913 he was elected rector of the University of Iaşi.

Stere's main objective throughout this period was to improve the conditions of life for the mass of the population—the peasantry. The persistence of his youthful preoccupations in Russia is evident. In 1893 he founded a student society, 'Datoria' (Obligation) in Iaşi, the purpose of which was to bring education to the poorer classes of the city suburbs and the surrounding villages. That same year he was in Bucharest at the founding congress of the Social Democratic Workers' Party of Rumania, where he tried to convince its leaders that their efforts to achieve socialism before a democratic regime had been installed and the peasants emancipated were at best premature. The next year during the second congress of the party he again put forward peasant demands, arguing that socialism could be applied only in developed, industrial countries. He had also begun to publish articles on the same themes, and in one of them in 1894 he used the term 'Poporanism' for the first time, which he defined as 'sincere love for the people, the defence of their interests, and honest work to raise them to the level of a conscious and independent social and cultural force'. In 1906 he and several colleagues founded the monthly *Viaţa românească* (Rumanian Life), which became the most prestigious cultural review of the period and the principal defender of Poporanist ideals. They wanted it to reflect the entire life of the Rumanian nation and to promote land reform for the peasant, universal suffrage, and access to education for all. They also sought to counter the efforts of the Sămănătorists to gloss over the harsh realities of contemporary peasant life and idealize the past.[12]

In Stere's writings, as in those of Iorga and the Sămănătorists, there is a strong element of nostalgia at the passing of the tradi-

---

[12] D. Micu, *Poporanismul şi 'Viaţa Românească'* (Bucharest, 1961), 115–68.

tional rural world, and he perceived as taking its place a Rumania composed of two separate countries—a small number of persons at the top and the great mass of the population (the peasantry) at the bottom. He attributed this unfortunate turn of events to the enthusiasm of the generation of 1848, who had abandoned an organic course of development, which had gradually and solidly brought into being the country's institutions, in exchange for the tempting model offered by Western Europe. He found the ultimate source of Rumania's troubles in all the anomalies thus created between the old and the new.

Despite their shared condemnation of the path contemporary Rumania had taken, Stere (and other Poporanists) and the Sămănătorists parted company over the nature of Rumania's relationship with Europe. Although Stere emphasized the unique aspects of Rumanian development and advocated an organic evolution, he refrained from xenophobic outbursts and urged closer links to Europe. Perhaps the essential difference between the Poporanists and the Sămănătorists was the former's (and Stere's) firm conviction that Rumania belonged to Europe.

Stere did not make the distinction between culture and civilization that lay at the heart of Sămănătorist and Junimist analyses of Rumania's relationship to Western Europe. Rather, the distinction he perceived was between two contemporary civilizations, one rural, the other urban. He praised the former as authentic and as an organic part of the Rumanian past and dismissed the latter as an import and, hence, artificial. But he did not advocate the preservation of rural civilization either as it stood or resurrected in some form in accordance with an idealized past. Recognizing that many aspects of rural society were backward or obsolete, he was anxious to raise it to a modern level, by finding ways of adapting to it all that was most useful in European experience.

Despite his commitment to reform and his recognition of Rumania as a part of Europe, Stere was wary of modern industrialism and sought to prevent rural society from being overwhelmed by it. He returned again and again to the theme that rural civilization was the only possible social and political form for Rumania, and he had no doubt that the human ideal was to be found in the village and that the peasant—in the new rural civilization he envisaged—was the man of the future. From this perspective, the peasant was the 'whole man' as opposed to the fragmented, specialized, and even brutalized man of modern industrial society.

Stere had few good things to say about the Rumanian constitutional system which had been inaugurated in 1866, but, unlike other critics, he did not seek to abolish it. His complaint was that the provisions of the constitution had never been fully carried out for the benefit of the mass of the population. Most objectionable, in his eyes, was the extreme centralization of political power and the almost complete neglect of the resources of local government. For him, the foundation of efficient, beneficial administration was the village, which he called a natural administrative entity. In the absence of any genuine representation of the thousands of 'little communities', the existing parliamentary system seemed to him 'suspended in mid-air'.

Stere (and the Poporanists, in general) thought of development mainly in economic terms, unlike the Junimists and Sămănătorists, who accorded pride of place to culture. Underlying his theory, which he elaborated in his famous polemic with the socialists, 'Social-democratism sau poporanism?' (Social Democracy or Populism?), a series of articles published in *Viaţa românească* in 1907 and 1908, was the rejection of the notion that every country was destined to follow the same path as Western Europe. He declared Rumania to he a country of peasants, and he conceived of its economic and social development as being linked to small, self-sufficient peasant holdings.[13]

Stere did not reject industry completely, but he was at pains to point out that large-scale industry as found in the West was neither inevitable nor even possible in a country like Rumania. The type of industry he advocated had to serve the needs of the peasantry and be in harmony with the prevailing economic and social structure. In his view, the most suitable type of industry would be that which provided work for the peasants during the slack winter months and did not take them away from their primary occupation—agriculture. Such a modest industry would thus not exceed the limits of a cottage industry; it would simply develop out of the peasant holding as an adjunct to agriculture. Equally important, in Stere's view, it would be geared to the satisfaction of domestic needs, thereby avoiding dependence on the foreign market, which, he insisted, was a major cause of the prevailing crisis in peasant agriculture. He counted on the organization of the peasants into rural industrial co-operatives to

[13] Constantin Stere, 'Social-democratism sau poporanism?', *Viaţa românească*, 2/8 (1907), 328, 9 (1907), 327–34, 10 (1907), 17–18; 3/4 (1908), 59–60.

assure the success of his plan. This type of industry, which had nothing in common with that of the West, accorded perfectly with the Poporanists' conception of an economy dominated by small, independent holdings. It could not be capitalist, they argued, because it was simply an extension of small-scale agriculture, which operated in accordance with categories and values of its own outside the sphere of capitalism.[14]

Stere acknowledged the need for a few large-scale industries to process raw materials from the countryside which could not be handled by peasant industry and to develop the country's natural resources, such as oil and lumber. Here, too, he remained wary of Western forms and proposed establishing state monopolies in order to protect the new industries from foreign capital and to keep their income from being sent abroad.

Stere and the Poporanists seemed on the verge of achieving two of their principal goals—land reform and universal suffrage—when the First World War broke out, causing the Liberal Party, which had sponsored both measures, to postpone action. Poporanism emerged from the war stronger than ever under the guise of Ţărănism (Peasantism). It offered the vision of a 'peasant state', supported by a popular, democratic political organization, the National Peasant Party. Stere was to play a crucial role in both.

The leaders of the fledgling socialist movement conceived of a Rumania fundamentally different from that advocated by the Junimists, Sămănătorists, and Poporanists. At the heart of their theories was the conviction that Rumania could not be isolated from the broader currents of European economic and social development. They were thus certain that industry, not agriculture, held the key to Rumania's future.

The pre-eminent socialist theorist of development was Constantin Dobrogeanu-Gherea (1855–1920). Born in Russia, he studied in Kharkov at the Faculty of Sciences, where he became active in narodnik (populist) circles. Because of his activities in the villages spreading revolutionary propaganda among the peasants, he was constantly pursued by the police. In 1875 he crossed the border into Rumania, establishing himself in Iaşi, where he began his career as a propagator of socialist ideas. He was active in organizing the first socialist circles in Moldavia, but his main contribution to the development of Rumanian socialism was as a theoretician. He was the author of numerous articles and books

[14] Z. Ornea, *Poporanismul* (Bucharest, 1972), 247–50.

analysing Rumanian economic and social conditions and defending the necessity and the viability of socialism in an underdeveloped country. Beginning in the 1880s he took Marxism as his frame of reference, but he understood it as a method of investigation and analysis rather than as a rigid set of laws of development. Gherea, like the Sămănătorists and Poporanists, admitted Rumania's economic backwardness, but he rejected their formulas for making the best of underdevelopment. As a Marxist, he felt a special obligation to show why Rumania was not destined to remain forever agricultural, and he was anxious to justify the need for industry and a proletariat. He by no means denied the importance of agriculture or minimized the gravity of the agrarian problem, but he had no doubt that the future of Rumania, specifically, her ability to overcome economic underdevelopment, would depend primarily upon industrialization. Yet he insisted that progress would not occur in isolation, for Rumania was inescapably a part of Europe. He argued in such works as, *Ce vor socialiştii români?* (1885–6; What Do Rumanian Socialists Want?) and *Asupra socialismului în ţările înapoiate* (1911; On Socialism in Backward Countries), that underdeveloped countries inevitably came under the influence of economically advanced countries, which, indeed, determined the former's entire course of development. He also pointed out that the prevailing form of economic organization in the highly developed countries at any given period 'imposed itself' upon their less advanced neighbours. He identified that form in the modern world as bourgeois capitalism, and he was certain that it would eventually revolutionize social and economic relations and the mental climate in Eastern Europe as it had already done in the West. Such an inevitable series of events, Gherea concluded, justified, indeed made imperative, the formation of bourgeois-liberal institutions in underdeveloped countries.[15]

This whole process, it seemed to him, was exactly what had been taking place in Rumania during the nineteenth century. As he saw it, the decisive event had been the Treaty of Adrianople, for through it Rumania had entered into rapidly increasing exchange relations with the West, which marked the beginning of the country's transformation. From this time on, he argued, Rumania had begun to be an integral part of capitalist civilization, and he perceived in all that was happening a confirmation of his thesis about the connection between advanced and underdeveloped

---

[15] Constantin Dobrogeanu-Gherea, *Neoiobăgia* (Bucharest, 1910), 35, 43.

nations: social, economic, and spiritual relations in Rumania were being 'revolutionized' as Western capitalist institutions were imposed upon her.

Gherea, unlike his Poporanist adversaries, thought that the borrowing from Western Europe which had already occurred and was still going on was a natural process. In underdeveloped countries, he pointed out, the superstructure—bourgeois-liberal political and legal institutions—developed first. Only then did the economic and social substratum develop, the reverse of what had occurred in advanced capitalist countries. In the underdeveloped countries, he reasoned, not only did the substratum come later, it was even affected by the new political and legal forms. In a sense, Gherea had turned Titu Maiorescu's dictum 'form without substance' on its head, since he argued that development in Rumania had occurred from form to substance. He was, furthermore, optimistic about the prospects for beneficial change in Rumania. By developing within the orbit of the advanced West, she could learn from its experiences and thus shorten the road to capitalism and socialism. In Rumania at the turn of the century he had already detected an acceleration of the passage to capitalism. The main task of socialists under such conditions, then, was educational: to prepare men's minds to accept the introduction of new social forms.

Gherea linked the full development of bourgeois-liberal institutions and capitalist economic forms in Rumania to the elimination of existing economic and social structures, which he dubbed 'neoiobăgia' (neoserfdom). In a work with that title published in 1910 he painstakingly analysed Rumanian social development since the middle of the nineteenth century. He sought to discover its unique features and, in so doing, identify the main obstacles to Rumania's progress. Not surprisingly, he focused his attention on agriculture.

The agrarian regime which emerges from his investigation combines semi-feudal forms of production with capitalist relations in the exploitation of labour and in the distribution of goods. Thus, he found, the dominant class derived from the old system of serfdom the 'sweet advantage' of forced labour through agricultural contracts without having to fulfil any of the obligations owed to labour under the old agrarian order, and at the same time it enjoyed, under the burgeoning capitalist system, complete freedom to exploit labour without having to endure the disadvantage of a free labour market. This is the essence of the regime he called neoserfdom, and he attributed to its operation over nearly half a century the main cause of Rumania's economic backwardness. As a way out of this developmental impasse he urged the abolition of neoserfdom. Such action, he was certain, would produce an immediate regeneration of the entire social organism and enable Rumania to acquire a modern bourgeois structure and enter upon a capitalist path of development similar to that of Western Europe.

The abolition of large landed property and its replacement by small peasant holdings was, however, not one of the measures Gherea advocated, as did the great majority of agrarian reformers. His reasoning was twofold. In practical economic terms he considered large property superior to a network of small, even self-sufficient plots, which could offer only limited possibilities for agricultural development in a country like Rumania with little industry. But theory also influenced his judgement. He reasoned that when Rumania finally abandoned neoserfdom and embarked upon the capitalist path of development, she would assume all the characteristics of the latter. Since large-scale, capitalist agricultural enterprises were features of the advanced countries of the West, he could not conceive of Rumania avoiding similar property relations.

Yet, Gherea concerned himself with agriculture only to the extent that he wished to understand Rumania's present. He was convinced that her future belonged to industry, not the rural and urban co-operatives and the modest processing plants advocated by the Poporanists, but to modern, large-scale enterprises on the Western model. Industrialization, he argued, was a 'historical task', which all Rumanian socialists should undertake, because it would open the way to a higher level of civilization. For Rumania, he concluded, it was simply a question of 'to be or not to be'.[16]

PRAGMATISM

Thought about national development was not confined to philosophers of culture and social theorists. Rumanian economists approached the problem armed with statistics and the results of field research. In the 1860s and 1870s the majority were beholden to the principles of classical nineteenth-century European economic liberalism. They were firm believers in private enterprise and,

[16] Ibid. 487–8.

with few exceptions, they advocated free trade. Thus, they opposed permanent state regulation of 'natural' economic forces. They also tended to accept the theory that Rumania was destined to remain a 'pre-eminently agricultural country' and, hence, they rejected the notion that an extensive, large-scale industry patterned after that of Western Europe was possible. None the less, on this vital question, which was to agitate intellectual circles and politicians down to the Second World War, the liberal economists were far from unanimous. A few, who held that large-scale commerce in cereals and cattle would ensure the economic prosperity of the country, rejected industry outright as injurious to the 'national economic organism'. More numerous were those who, while acknowledging the essential agrarian character of Rumania, considered industrial development in some form both possible and necessary, but opposed measures by the state to create and maintain 'artificial' industries.

Nicolae Suțu (1798–1871), an economist and statistician, had been Minister of Foreign Affairs during the reigns of princes Mihai Sturdza (1834–49) and Grigore Ghica (1849–56) of Moldavia. He was one of the earliest proponents of the idea of Rumania as a predominantly agricultural country. In *Noțiuni statistice asupra Moldovei* (1849; Statistical Data on Moldavia) he insisted that agriculture was and would continue to be the fundamental economic activity of the country and that other branches of the economy could develop only in relation to it. Twenty years later, in *Quelques observations sur la statistique de la Roumanie* (1867), he stuck to essentially the same position, arguing that it was 'undesirable' to divert the inhabitants of an agricultural country from those occupations which 'nature' had assigned to them. He thought that the 'productive capabilities' of the country could yield an optimum return only if they were linked to large estate agriculture.[17] He did not deny the importance of industry, for he considered diversity a necessary condition for general economic progress, but he rejected any role for industry beyond the services it could render agriculture.

Suțu's views on the relative importance of agriculture and industry for Rumania were conditioned by his more general ideas on how economic change occurred. A fervent economic liberal, he believed in the benefits of unfettered economic activity, though he recognized that for a time some form of central economic

[17] N. Suțu, *Opere economice* (Bucharest, 1957), 261.

direction would be necessary. But after a country had reached a certain level of 'economic maturity', he recommended that measures be taken (by whom was not specified) 'to smooth away obstacles' to the free development of production. He was a consistent advocate of free trade, which he thought necessary to maintain exports of grain at a high level and thereby ensure the prosperity of large estate agriculture, in his view, the basis of the country's economy.

Alexandru D. Moruzi (1815–78), the grandson of a prince of both Moldavia and Wallachia, belonged to the same agrarianist, free-trade economic school as Suţu. Even more categorical in his opposition to industry, he stressed the absence of native capital and saw little likelihood that foreign investors would be tempted to invest in Rumania because the opportunities for profit were so much better elsewhere. Moreover, he declared in *L'Abolition des monopoles et l'amélioration de l'état du paysan en Moldavie* (1860), Rumania could never hope to create the conditions that would attract sizeable amounts of international capital. Although he could see no sense whatever in state support for industry, he thought Rumania as an agricultural country was by no means doomed to poverty and backwardness. He perceived salvation in a policy of absolute free trade. Besides encouraging the export of cereals, which would lead to an expansion of agricultural production and increased prosperity, such a policy would, he wrote in *Progrès et liberté* (1861), transform Rumania into a commercial entrepôt, a market-place not only for Europe but for the East as well. Like many of his contemporaries, he conceived of economic exchanges among nations as an unceasing contest in which each participant used 'weapons' most suited to its 'genius'. 'Our arms', he proclaimed confidently, 'are ploughs; the markets of the world are our battlefields.'[18]

The idea that Rumania was destined to remain an agricultural country found an equally passionate advocate in Ion Strat (1836–79), a professor of economics at the University of Bucharest and Minister of Finance in 1865 and 1876. A convinced free-trader, he thought that economic activity was governed by natural factors such as population and climate and should, therefore, be free of all constraints, including those imposed by the state, even in the

[18] Alexandru D. Moruzi, *L'Abolition des monopoles et l'amélioration de l'état du paysan en Moldavie* (Galatz, 1860), in Victor Slăvescu, *Vieaţa şi opera economistului Alexandru D. Moruzi, 1815–1878* (Bucharest, 1941), 132.

interests of 'production'. Thus, for the time being he saw no possibility of industry developing in Rumania because the conditions which he deemed essential were totally lacking. A dense population, in his view, was the main determinant of industrialization, but Rumania had a relatively sparse population. Yet, in time he thought that when her population had increased sufficiently, as had happened in other European countries, agriculture would cease to be the exclusive occupation of her people for the simple reason that there would be too little land. At that point, he predicted in his *Tractat complet de economie politică* (1870; A Complete Treatise on Political Economy), the 'manufacturing industry', following a natural process of transformation, would 'be created by itself'. It followed that 'artificial means' to stimulate industry would be to no avail and might in fact upset the 'normal economic balance'.[19]

The most influential exponent of free trade and liberal economic doctrines in the second half of the nineteenth century was Ion Ghica, who had played a prominent role in the revolution of 1848 and the union of the principalities in the late 1850s. He, too, had no doubt that agriculture would continue to be the basis of the Rumanian economy in the foreseeable future, and throughout his long career in public life he insisted that this 'natural' economic path be followed as the best means of ensuring national well-being. But he did not oppose industry. Especially in his later years he came to recognize its broad social as well as economic importance. For him, it was not only a means of material progress, but, as he wrote in 1884 in *Convorbiri economice* (Economic Conversations), it was also essential for intellectual and political development: industry was the 'incubator' of art and science and the 'cradle' in which the liberties and rights of man were nurtured. He also recognized the benefits agriculture and industry could derive from each other. In *Bucureștiul industrial și politic* (1876; Industrial and Political Bucharest), noting the increasing dependence of agriculture on industry, he concluded that the former could no longer make progress without modern technology.[20] He of course had in mind the large-scale, commercial agricultural enterprise, where, in his view, the future of Rumanian agriculture lay, not the small peasant holding. Nevertheless, in analysing the structure of the

[19] Ion Strat, *Tractat complet de economie politică* (Bucharest, 1870), 214–16, 305–6.
[20] Ion Ghica, 'Bucureștiul industrial și politic', in I. Ghica, *Scrieri economice*, ii (Bucharest, 1937), 48.

Rumanian economy, he accorded industry a strictly secondary role, assigning to it the task of processing the products of agriculture or of making certain items more cheaply than could be done abroad. Nor could he suggest any way of hastening the development of industry beyond the formation of 'industrial associations'.

Ghica's analysis of the Rumanian economy and his expectations for its future were decisively influenced by the principles of free trade. For half a century he promoted the idea that absolute freedom of commerce was essential for the healthy development of the country's economy. He pointed out that Rumania had to sell her agricultural products on the international market in order to prosper and, because of her favourable geographical position, she could profitably serve as the commercial intermediary between East and West. He therefore welcomed the unimpeded flow of foreign manufactured goods into the country as a means of stimulating the local economy and even of attracting foreign investments. But he rejected state intervention in 'natural' economic processes as unnecessary and harmful. 'Laissez faire, laissez passer' was his motto.

Ion Ionescu de la Brad (1818–91), a pioneer in the study of agricultural conditions in the Rumanian village and a staunch advocate of agrarian reform both before and after the passage of the law of 1864, belongs naturally to this group of economists who believed that Rumania's future lay in the perfection of agriculture. Yet, he was one of the few who thought of agriculture mainly in terms of smallholdings rather than large estates and was primarily interested in the welfare of the independent peasant proprietor.[21] His treatment of industry as an adjunct of agriculture was typical of most of his contemporaries, but, unlike them, he favoured the active participation of government in economic affairs whenever other means of improvement failed. He was concerned especially about practical matters as they affected the day-to-day existence of the peasant. He could not understand, for example, why Rumania should export wool at one price and then import it back in the form of finished goods at five or ten times the price. The solution, he urged, was to create a Rumanian industry to clothe Rumanians.

A quite different group of economists emphatically rejected the notion that Rumania was fated to remain an agricultural country.

---

[21] Simion I. Pop, 'Concepţia social-economică şi politică a lui Ion Ionescu de la Brad', in Nicolae Ivanciu (ed.), *Din gîndirea economică progresistă românească* (Bucharest, 1968), 477–83.

They by no means ignored agriculture, but they had no doubt whatever that industrialization was the key not only to economic progress but also to the general well-being of society. They were equally certain that Rumania would follow roughly the same path of development as Western Europe and, hence, would eventually industrialize. But they were anxious to help the process along and had no intention, like the agrarianists, of letting 'natural economic forces' take their course. Instead, they urged planning and protection, and they assigned a critical role to the state, at least initially, until private entrepreneurs were able to stand on their own. Their feelings toward the West were ambivalent. On the one hand, they were afraid of becoming hopelessly dependent upon foreign capital, and, on the other, they were convinced that the Western model must be their own.

Enric Winterhalder (1808–89), an Austrian who obtained Rumanian citizenship and the principal writer on economic matters for C. A. Rosetti's radical liberal newspaper, *Românul* (The Rumanian), was a representative of those Rumanian economists who combined the principles of economic liberalism with an admiration of industry as the most advanced form of production. As he surveyed the course of European history, he interpreted the word 'progress' to mean a 'natural' evolution of the economy from primitive to agricultural to mixed agricultural-industrial-commercial forms. He had no doubt that industry was the end-product of this process and that it was destined to play the chief role in the economic life of modern nations. Every people, he reasoned, would experience the same progression, and his model was Western Europe. He was convinced that free trade was the key mechanism which had made economic progress possible. He thus rejected the arguments of both the advocates of an agricultural Rumania and those who wished to foster domestic industry through protectionist measures and other forms of state intervention. He pleaded for a national industry which could 'stand on its own feet'.

Dionisie Pop Marţian (1829–65), who received his law degree in Vienna and was director of the newly founded Central Statistical Office in Bucharest from 1860 to 1865, had as his primary objective the construction of a strong national economy. Although he reserved an important role to private entrepreneurs, he doubted that they had sufficient resources and a broad enough understanding of the national interest to be able to pursue this critical goal systematically. He thus looked to the state to serve as the chief 'economic entrepreneur', at least during the early stages of modern economic development. But he had no wish to jeopardize the creative participation of the middle class, and as it matured and the economy grew he recommended that the state gradually reduce its role in economic life.

Throughout his career Marţian advocated a strong national industry and consistently opposed all attempts to restrict economic development solely to agriculture. He feared that the absence of a modern industry threatened the very existence of the country. It would, he warned, ensure Rumania's economic dependence on the developed countries of Europe, which were now seeking to dominate their weaker neighbours through the expansion of industry and commerce rather than by force of arms.[22] On the positive side Marţian thought that a strong industry would benefit all other branches of the economy, especially agriculture. It would contribute to the expansion of the domestic market for agricultural products and thus rescue large and small producers alike from the vagaries of the international market, and it would make available large quantities of tools and other supplies at reasonable prices. Taking into account prevailing economic conditions, he proposed that attention be given first to those industries which could make use of readily available raw materials, such as food processing, forestry products, and construction, especially brickmaking. But unlike most of the economists of his day, he thought the prospects for developing heavy industry right away were also good, but he limited his purview to salt- and coal-mining.

For Marţian, state intervention was indispensable for the creation of a viable industry, because, in his view, it alone was capable of applying the protectionist measures required to defend fledgling enterprises from foreign competitors. He looked to the state to prevent a massive influx of both foreign goods and capital. Foreign investors, he warned, were interested in exploiting raw materials to suit their own, often momentary, interests and would thus give little thought to the well-being of Rumania. He preferred to create conditions favourable to the formation of an internal capital market.

Marţian recognized a close interdependence between agriculture and industry. But rather than seeing industry as an adjunct to agriculture, as the agrarians did, he made the full development

---

[22] D. P. Marţian, *Economia socială* (Bucharest, 1858), in Victor Slăvescu, *Vieaţa şi opera economistului Dionisie Pop Marţian, 1829–1865*, i (Bucharest, 1943), 441.

of industry dependent upon a modern, dynamic agriculture. Praising the agrarian reform of 1864 as an essential step in the creation of conditions favourable for industrialization, he reasoned that the emancipation of the peasants from *clacă* and the grants of land to them would lead to a reorganization of the Rumanian economy 'in accordance with the laws of free labour and free capital'. Specifically, he wanted to raise the material well-being of the peasants and give them incentives to improve their skills in order to supply his projected factories with a trained labour-force and expand the internal market for domestic manufactures. As components of a comprehensive reform of agriculture, he also urged the introduction of new varieties of seeds and modern methods of cultivation, research on soil quality, and diversification of production through the introduction of new crops such as raw silk, flax, and hemp. To accomplish these 'difficult and costly tasks', he recommended the exercise of private initiative through agricultural associations, but if they failed, he had no hesitation in turning to the state. Yet, despite his continuous preoccupation with agricultural problems, he never ceased to accord industry pride of place in the national economy.

In the last quarter of the nineteenth century Alexandru D. Xenopol (1847–1920), the noted historian and a member of the Junimea Society, was one of the most influential advocates of industrialization. A student of history, law, and economics at the University of Berlin between 1867 and 1871, he was attracted to the theories of protectionism expounded by Friedrich List. But he also studied the works of Dionisie Pop Marţian and developed his ideas further in his own principal work on economics, *Studii economice* (1879; Economic Studies). Although Xenopol classified himself as an economic liberal, he favoured protectionism and state intervention as the only means of creating a national industry and, hence, of overcoming underdevelopment. In a sense, for him, the enemy was the West, with its advanced technology, incredible productive capacity, and seemingly inexhaustible capital, all of which threatened to overwhelm an economically weak country like Rumania, but at the same time he held the West up as the only model worth following.

Like Marţian, Xenopol was convinced that industrialization was imperative if Rumania was to escape from economic and cultural backwardness. The chief 'vice' of her entire development, he complained, was her exclusive reliance on agriculture, particularly on the raising and export of grain, which had made her subject to the ups and downs of foreign markets. As a recent example he cited the 'invasion' of Rumania's traditional markets by cheaper and better quality American grains, which had caused a grave 'crisis of overproduction' in Rumania incapable of an easy solution because no other branch of the economy, notably a viable industry, could take up the slack. Dependent upon exports to foreign countries and even upon foreign imports for a whole range of goods, Rumania was, in his view, ill equipped to defend herself in the most critical contest of all in the contemporary world—economic competition.[23]

Xenopol did not for a moment doubt that the industrialization of Rumania would take place, and he devoted much of his writing on the subject to refuting the arguments of the agrarianists. He was not, for example, discouraged by the absence of 'capitalists' in Rumania. He thought adequate capital to establish factories could be accumulated through joint-stock companies and cited 'Dacia' (1871) and 'România' (1873), the first two Rumanian insurance companies, both of Bucharest, as successful examples. The relative sparseness of Rumania's population, cited by almost all the opponents of industry as an obstacle to its development, did not faze him either. If the work-force proved too small to meet the needs of agriculture and industry at the same time, then he recommended the hiring of foreign skilled workers (but only from other 'Latin' countries) in order not to take peasants away from agriculture. He dismissed as specious those arguments which held that a Rumanian industry would have no markets for its goods. There might not be foreign markets for Rumanian goods, he admitted, but he argued that the primary goal for the moment had to be to satisfy the domestic market. He was certain that local demand for Rumanian manufactures would be adequate, especially if imports were curtailed.

Despite all his optimism, Xenopol was painfully aware that the material and human resources available to create and sustain a strong national industry would be inadequate for the foreseeable future. He therefore turned to the state, whose main function would be to serve as a protector of newly formed enterprises. He rejected free trade as a grave hindrance to the growth of industry in underdeveloped countries. As long as Rumania was forced to

[23] Alexandru D. Xenopol, *Studii economice*, 2nd edn. (Craiova, 1882), in A. D. Xenopol, *Opere economice* (Bucharest, 1967), 84–9, 98–100, 116–22. For a succinct appreciation of his economic thought, see G. Zane, 'A. D. Xenopol şi ideile sale economice', in G. Zane, *Studii* (Bucharest, 1980), 462–73.

compete on an equal footing with the advanced industrial powers of Western Europe, he reasoned, she could never hope to overcome underdevelopment. The function of the state, then, was to make the contest more even by imposing duties on foreign imports until native industry could match foreign goods in both price and quality and could thus persuade the local population to buy Rumanian. But Xenopol understood protectionism in a broad sense to include all possible measures by the state to promote a healthy and diverse industry: purchases of locally produced goods by the state, even though they might not at first be as well made or as cheap as foreign products; relief from certain taxes; low interest loans from the state treasury, which would acquire the necessary funds through new taxes on other economic activities; and the construction of roads and railways to open up new sources of raw materials and to transport processed goods to markets. He realized that some of these measures would impose hardships on large segments of the population by raising taxes and increasing the cost of living, and he worried that a customs war with one or more of the great powers might break out over these protectionist measures, but he could see no alternative. The country must defend its right to be an industrial nation at all costs.

National sentiment was clearly a strong component of Xenopol's economic thought, as his change of attitude toward foreign capital reveals. At first, in the 1870s and 1880s, he welcomed it as a means of carrying out a rapid expansion of industry. He saw no particular danger in encouraging foreign investments and even advocated government concessions to foreign entrepreneurs to develop mines and other raw materials. But by the turn of the century he had come to oppose the influx of foreign capital, for as the amounts invested grew spectacularly and foreign businessmen became more aggressive, he saw the economic and political independence of the country slipping away.

Petre S. Aurelian (1833–1909), an agronomist by training and an economist by vocation, was not only a theorist of protectionism and industrialization, he was also in a position to alter the economic direction of the country as a Liberal government minister and Prime Minister (1896–97). Concern for the welfare of the Rumanian nation lay at the centre of all his work, a preoccupation he thought natural, since Rumanian society as a whole was then absorbed in self-examination and the 'critical assimilation' of Western culture. He made the modernization of the Rumanian economy his primary goal, the pursuit of which helps to explain significant shifts in his economic thinking over the course of his long career.[24] At the time of the union of the principalities, he embraced the doctrines of the liberal economists as the appropriate guide to economic development, but as the country became increasingly subject to the workings of the international market he came to the conclusion that economic backwardness could never be overcome on the basis of free trade. He reasoned that if Rumania was completely open to foreign goods, she risked becoming merely an adjunct to the economies of the advanced industrial states and would never secure control of her own destiny. In *Terra nostra*, an analysis of the Rumanian economy published in 1875, he argued that economic policy had to take into account 'objective conditions' and warned that progress at home would be impossible if principles advantageous to other countries were adopted. He therefore became a staunch advocate of protectionism, but he could, none the less, foresee a time, after industrialization had reached a certain level, when it might be to Rumania's advantage to return to free trade.

He accorded the state a major role in developing the national economy. Its primary function would be to create the necessary institutional and legal framework for the healthy growth of production and trade. He professed faith in the individual entrepreneur, but he was worried by the lack of order and continuity in economic life. Here, he thought, was precisely where state intervention could be the most beneficial: it could elaborate long-range economic projects and provide co-ordination, which would, in turn, create optimum conditions for private initiative. He emphasized that he was not advocating a rigid economic plan with precise tasks and goals, but rather a general orientation for both state institutions and individual entrepreneurs, a device that would enable the state to accelerate economic development for the benefit of all.[25]

In the 1890s the rapid industrialization of the country had become an urgent matter for Aurelian, as it had for other leaders of the Liberal Party. He perceived a sharpening of the international economic competition for markets and a feverish drive to produce more and more manufactured goods, foodstuffs, and raw materials. He likened it to a war. On one side were the great

---

[24] Radu-Dan Vlad, 'L'industrialisation de la Roumanie dans la vision de Petre S. Aurelian', *Revue roumaine d'histoire*, 23/3 (1984), 257–73.

[25] P. S. Aurelian, *Opere economice* (Bucharest, 1967), liii–lvii.

industrial powers, and, on the other, the agrarian countries. As he saw it, the former were attempting to dominate the latter through 'modern methods of conquest', notably the export of capital and the promotion of policies such as free trade. Aurelian, like Xenopol, was certain that Rumania could not compete successfully in such an economic world if she remained an agricultural country. Nor, he warned, could she expect to maintain her existence as an independent state under circumstances in which economic conquest had become the modern form of domination. The only certain defence of Rumania's independence, he concluded, was to follow the same path of development as her economic adversaries —industrialization.

This debate between economists—the agrarianists and the industrializers—and, simultaneously, between proponents of competing philosophies of culture was by no means merely an academic exercise. The polemics moved from the realm of theory to practical application when political parties adopted the arguments of one side or the other as their own. Agrarian economic interests and traditional social values were reflected in the policies of Conservative governments, while the Liberal Party, representing the rising commercial and industrial middle class, pressed forward with the building of a national economy inspired by the Western model. But the matters at issue were not resolved; they continued to generate controversy well into the twentieth century.

3
The Reign of King Charles, 1881–1914

POLITICS

The political structure of the Rumanian Kingdom between 1881 and 1914 remained essentially that of the Principality. The Constitution of 1866, modified in 1884, notably in matters affecting the franchise, provided the general framework for political activity.

The relations of the several branches of government to one another continued to be based, at least in theory, on the principle of the separation of powers and the mechanism of checks and balances. But the role of the judiciary in government was limited by its subordination in practice to the executive and legislative branches. The irremovability of judges had been left to the discretion of the legislature by the Constitution of 1866, but little by little the principle became reality, particularly as a result of legislation in 1890 and 1909. None the less, the king and the Council of Ministers decisively influenced the composition of the judiciary, and, hence, its social and political philosophy through their power of appointment. Yet, the potential power of the judiciary was immense, especially if its right to declare laws unconstitutional were recognized. The constitution contained no precise statement on the matter. Despite sporadic attempts to establish the principle of judicial review of the constitutionality of legislation in the decades following the promulgation of the Constitution of 1866, it was only in 1912 in the celebrated case of the trolley corporation of Bucharest that the Court of Cassation (Supreme Court) recognized the right of the courts to examine the constitutionality of laws.[1] It based its decision on two points—first, the principle of the separation of powers and the consequent need for the three branches of government to keep a constant check on one another, and second, the constitutional obligation of the courts to apply the laws and, hence, their need, in effect, to choose between the

---

[1] Paul Negulescu and George Alexianu, *Tratat de drept public*, ii (Bucharest, 1943), 73–4.

articles of the constitution and laws passed by the legislature. Yet, the practice of judicial review did not become a feature of Rumanian statecraft. Although the independence of the judiciary from the executive branch was frequently stated, the courts never seriously challenged the political system in the interwar period.

The Orthodox Church continued to serve as a bulwark of national consciousness, but it no longer played a direct role in political affairs. The secularization of political institutions, underway since the eighteenth century, had been completed by the legislation enacted in the latter years of Alexandru Cuza's reign and by the Constitution of 1866. Yet, there was no separation of state and church, for the constitution had declared Eastern Orthodoxy to be the dominant religion. The term 'dominant' meant that the Orthodox Church had been inextricably bound up with the historical development of the Rumanian nation and was the faith of the great majority of the population, and was, consequently, entitled to precedence over the other churches in the country. But there was no question that the interests of the state were paramount, a situation codified by the law on church government passed by the parliament in 1872. It allowed political interests to predominate in the election of metropolitans and bishops by allotting seats in the electoral college to all Orthodox deputies and senators in parliament, who thus outnumbered the clergy. The law also established the Holy Synod as the principal governing body of the 'Rumanian national church', but it seriously curtailed its freedom of action. The Synod could enact no law which might run counter to the laws of the state and could not enforce any church legislation until it had been approved by the head of state. Such stipulations followed naturally from the fact that Rumanian law traditionally had not recognized the separation of church and state. The predominance of the state was also manifest in the law on the secular clergy and the seminaries passed by parliament in 1893. It promised improvements in the material life and education of the parish clergy by instituting the regular payment of salaries to priests by the central government and the local communes and by making the curriculum in the seminaries more rigorous. But the state reserved to itself the final word in all these matters and thus weakened still further the autonomy of the church.[2]

That secular concerns were paramount in the minds of poli-

---

[2] C. G. Dissescu, *Cursul de drept public român*, ii: *Dreptul constituţional* (Bucharest, 1890), 440–2; Mircea Păcurariu, *Istoria Bisericii Ortodoxe Române*, iii (Bucharest, 1981), 129–39.

ticians in their treatment of the church is evident in their determination that the new national state be reinforced by a national church. They made their intentions known in the Constitution of 1866, which declared the Rumanian Orthodox Church 'independent of any foreign hierarchy'. The legislation of 1872 went further, proclaiming the church 'autocephalous'. But it could have no canonical validity without the assent of the Patriarch of Constantinople. The matter became the subject of long negotiations and sometimes bitter recriminations, but agreement was finally reached between the Rumanian government and the Patriarchate in 1885. The Rumanian Church was independent in the sense that it could manage its own affairs in accordance with the canons of the Eastern Church without interference from other churches, while respecting the spiritual unity of Orthodoxy.

In the political life of the Rumanian Kingdom parties were the engines that ran the complex machinery of government, but they did not always respect the spirit of the laws which they themselves had formulated. There were two major parties between 1881 and 1914—Conservative and Liberal. In general, the Conservatives continued to represent the interests of the large landowners and the Liberals those of the growing urban commercial and industrial middle class. But social and economic roles were steadily changing in the latter decades of the nineteenth century. Large landed property was passing out of the hands of the traditional landowning class, the descendants of the old boier families, into the possession of the newly wealthy middle class. Even many of those estates which their owners still possessed had been mortgaged to Creditul Funciar Rural, which was controlled by the Liberals. Differences in economic policy persisted. The great landlords (and those who leased their estates, the *arendaşi*) favoured free trade, as advocated by the Conservatives, because it would enable them to export their grain and animals more easily, while the middle class, represented by the Liberals, saw its interests best served by protective tariffs. Yet, here too, the boundaries between the two classes were far from rigid. The urban bourgeoisie, especially merchants and bankers, who left commercial and financial occupations and bought land, adopted the outlook of the old Conservative landowners, while those among the latter who had sold or lost their estates entered the ranks of the urban middle class as they assumed positions in the bureaucracy. Consequently, a growing number of landlords or former landlords joined forces with the Liberals, while a number of bankers and merchants found the Conservatives congenial partners in furthering their economic interests.

Large segments of the population were practically excluded from the political process and thus exerted little influence on the course of events. The peasants, for the most part, continued to be merely onlookers. Their voting strength was diluted by high income qualifications for the ballot, and despite several noble attempts, a viable peasant party failed to develop before the First World War. The urban working class was also grossly under-represented, but it was somewhat better off than the peasantry. After a period of crisis, a social democratic party emerged in 1910 which promised a sturdy defence of workers' economic and political interests. But a small constituency prevented the socialists from mounting a serious challenge to the major parties, and on the eve of the war they had no deputies in the Chamber.

Only a small part of the citizenry took part in political life. Besides income requirements for voting, the system of electoral colleges and government manipulation also limited participation in the electoral process. A revision of the electoral law in 1884 increased only slightly the number of voters permitted by the Constitution of 1866. There were now three electoral colleges for the Chamber of Deputies instead of four. The first two represented the well-to-do of the countryside and the cities and towns, respectively, and elected 145 deputies; the third represented the peasants, the great majority of the population, and elected only thirty-eight, eight more than under the old system of four colleges. The number of eligible voters in each college steadily increased as economic development continued and more persons were able to satisfy property and income qualifications for the franchise. In 1888, for example, the number of voters for the three colleges was 9,151, 24,750, and 25,776, respectively, or a total of 59,677; in 1905 the corresponding figures were 15,973, 34,742, and 42,907, a total of 93,622. The electoral body for the Senate was considerably smaller, because of the higher property and income qualifications. In 1905 its two colleges were composed of 10,659 and 13,912 electors, respectively, or a total of 24,571.

An analysis of the elections of 1911 suggests how representative the Chamber of Deputies and the Senate were of the general population. Of the 1,644,302 adult men, 101,339 electors were registered to vote for the Chamber (6.16 per cent) and 24,921 for the Senate (1.5 per cent). Of these, only 73,633 participated in the elections for the Chamber (74.2 per cent of those eligible) and

18,003 for the Senate (72.2 per cent). Thus, one deputy represented 402 voters, and one senator 164. Large property owners dominated the elections. For example, in college I of the Chamber 60 per cent of the electors belonged to this category, while 10 per cent were engaged in commerce and industry: in college II, composed mainly of the bourgeoisie, 27 per cent were public functionaries, 23 per cent merchants and industrialists, 14 per cent property owners, 5 per cent lawyers, and smaller percentages of other professional people; in college III, 57 per cent were landowners (mainly peasants), 10 per cent priests, 10 per cent schoolteachers, and 8 per cent small merchants. The preponderance of large landowners in the two electoral colleges for the Senate was striking— 60 and 40 per cent, respectively—with the upper bourgeoisie accounting for most of the rest.[3]

The king played a key role in determining the outcome of elections through his constitutional authority to appoint the incoming Prime Minister. By the final decades of the century the procedures for changing governments had been perfected. The process began with the resignation of the sitting government, consultations between the king and leading politicians, and the selection of one among the latter to form a new government. The first task of the newly designated Prime Minister after he had chosen his cabinet was to organize elections for a new Chamber and Senate. That was the responsibility of the Minister of the Interior, who mobilized the prefects of the *județe* and the rest of the state administrative apparatus, whose loyalty had been verified, to make certain that the opposition would be overwhelmed in the coming elections. Between 1881 and 1914, as the result of their zeal, no government designated by the king was ever disappointed at the polls. The 'rotation' of parties also became the rule during this period. It became customary for the king to alternate the two major parties—Liberals and Conservatives (including the Junimists)—in office as a means of resolving serious economic and political problems and of maintaining his own political power by balancing one party off against the other and requiring them to compete for his favour. The practice was accepted as normal and desirable, except by those parties that were excluded, because it provided an additional guarantee of political stability.

Shortcomings notwithstanding, the political system offered

---

[3] Matei Dogan, *Analiza statistică a 'democrației parlamentare' din România* (Bucharest, 1946), 10–14.

substantial protection of the civil liberties of individual citizens. Constitutional guarantees of freedom of association and of assembly were respected, as was the widest possible freedom of the press. Citizens could also sue the state, i.e. administrative bodies, for violations of rights guaranteed them in the constitution. The revised Constitution of 1884 reinforced this protection by removing such cases from the jurisdiction of administrative courts on the grounds that the existing system allowed the executive branch to pass judgement on its own acts. Legislation in 1905 strengthened this aspect of the separation of powers by establishing a third section of the Court of Cassation to hear complaints brought by individual citizens against abuses committed by the state bureaucracy. Such cases appear to have been rare.

The political system gave the majority of citizens little, if any, experience in managing their own affairs. Besides the restricted franchise, the concentration of power at the centre in Bucharest tended to discourage participation in public life. By virtue of laws enacted between 1892 and 1903 the Ministry of the Interior wielded enormous power over the affairs of *judeţe* and village communes. As the minister responsible for the general administration of the country and the maintenance of public order he had general oversight of the activities of *judeţ* and communal councils and examined and submitted for royal approval the budgets of the *judeţe* and the more important communes. It was also he who, in effect, appointed the prefect of the *judeţ*, whose role strikingly reveals the degree of control the central bureaucracy exercised over local government. The prefect was first and foremost the representative of the central government and was directly responsible to the Minister of the Interior for carrying out all his instructions. Besides 'conducting' parliamentary elections, he supervised the work of all administrative officials in the *judeţe*, was the government commissioner on the *judeţ* council and could participate in its deliberations or dissolve it, and had direct responsibility for public order. Such extensive powers suggest that virtually all the decisions of the various organs of village and *judeţ* administrations, to be valid, had to be submitted to one or another central government official for approval. The process often brought local government to a standstill, for in Bucharest differences of opinion over high policy and the lack of acquaintance with local conditions made prompt action nearly impossible. Critics at the turn of the century complained that the twin banes of the existing administration— centralization and 'functionarism'—had undone the noble principles set forth in the constitution. They urged that local persons be given more responsibility for managing local affairs in order to revive interest in public life and arouse a spirit of initiative in the villages and *județe*.[4]

The Liberals dominated political life for an unprecedented ten years after the War for Independence, from 1878 to 1888. The Prime Minister and the foremost politician of his era was Ion Brătianu. Possessed of enormous political experience dating back to 1848, he had managed with great skill the complex problems arising out of the struggle for independence and the proclamation of the kingdom. He had thus made himself indispensable to both the king and his party. But after the proclamation of the kingdom and especially during the controversy over the modification of the constitution in 1884, Brătianu became increasingly authoritarian in his dual capacity as Prime Minister and party head. He instituted a kind of personal rule over both government and party. His methods and intentions were manifest in the way the government Liberals conducted the parliamentary elections of November 1884. The prefects and the rest of the administrative apparatus at all levels left no device unused in order to ensure a government victory, and afterwards the mandates of numerous opposition deputies and senators were invalidated.

As Prime Minister Brătianu continued the centralization of the bureaucracy, concentrating more and more power in his own office.[5] Besides being chief minister, he held a number of other ministries at one time or another, notably the Ministry of the Interior between 1884 and 1887. All important directives came from him, and no ministerial, parliamentary, or important local administrative decision could be made without his approval. He frequently changed members of the cabinet, not to improve efficiency, but to settle old scores within the party. All these practices tended to isolate him from his colleagues and to discourage men of talent from taking governmental or ministerial posts. They finally led to the most painful personal break of all, when he parted company with his long-time friend, C. A. Rosetti, in 1884. For several years the radical Liberal faction led by Rosetti had found itself increasingly at odds with the government Liberals over a whole host of issues—extension of the franchise to more

[4] Paul Negulescu, *Tratat de drept administrativ român*, i, 2nd edn. (Bucharest, 1906), 229–30, 271–8, 321–4.

[5] For a highly critical estimate of Brătianu's methods, see Frédéric Damé, *J. C. Bratiano; L'ère nouvelle—la dictature*, 2nd edn. (Bucharest, 1886), 6–42.

members of the middle and lower classes and fair elections without government intervention, decentralization of the administration, further agrarian reform, and the observance of democratic procedures in the conduct of both parliamentary and party business— all contrary to the behaviour and objectives of the Liberal majority led by Brătianu. The radical Liberal group did not survive the death of Rosetti in 1885. Its members joined other groups or, like the erstwhile Junimist, Gheorghe Panu, founded small groups of their own.

Brătianu had little to fear from the members of his own party and the opposition in and out of parliament because he enjoyed the full confidence of King Charles. A congenial working relationship had developed between them based upon similar ideas about major issues of domestic and foreign policy. Brătianu had accepted Charles's pro-German orientation in foreign policy and the reorganization of the army on the Prussian model, while Charles allowed his Prime Minister a relatively free hand in carrying out his domestic policy as long as he respected the prerogatives of the crown. In a sense, Brătianu also benefited from a lack of competition. Except for the Junimists, who indeed favoured a pro-German orientation in foreign policy, but lacked any sort of popular following and, hence, could not create the parliamentary majority and the administrative apparatus necessary to keep themselves in power, there was no other political grouping capable of performing more satisfactorily than Brătianu's Liberals. Yet, the relationship between Brătianu and the king was not one of friendship. Charles judged his Prime Ministers solely on the basis of their usefulness. For him, the office was of crucial importance: a majority in the Chamber meant nothing; the man 'at the helm' was everything.

Brătianu's forceful methods were undoubtedly inspired in part by the factionalism to which the Liberals were prone and by the resulting need to enforce party discipline. The core of Brătianu's support within the party remained his faction of the radicals, but after the split with Rosetti he relied increasingly upon leading personalities in the party, among them, Eugen Carada (1836–1910), a director of the National Bank and Brătianu's chief adviser on financial matters; Dimitrie A. Sturdza (1833–1914), a future president of the Liberal Party (1892–1908) and Prime Minister four times between 1895 and 1908; and the economist Petre S. Aurelian.

Brătianu had to deal continually with dissident members of his party. Undoubtedly, one of the most troubling incidents was the defection of a group of young lawyers, the very type of party member Brătianu had always striven to recruit. Prominent among them were Take Ionescu (1858–1922), who had obtained his law degree in Paris in 1881 and was an editor of *Românul*, and Nicolae Fleva (1840–1914), a member of the coalition of Mazar pasha, a stirring orator, and mayor of Bucharest in 1884. They and their colleagues had entered parliament through Liberal support, but, beginning in 1885, they began to display their independence by criticizing the existing political system. Finally, a year later, they formally declared themselves to be in opposition and formed their own group. They drew a sharp distinction between themselves, as Liberals in the full sense of the term, and government Liberals, and in the debate over parliament's response to the message from the throne they denounced the type of Liberalism practised by Brătianu as 'debased'.[6]

The Conservative Party gave Brătianu less trouble than the dissidents within his own party. In the years immediately following the War for Independence the Conservatives were in disarray. Some had drifted away from the party altogether because they thought its policies were out of touch with the times. Others left because the party's prospects of coming to power in the near future seemed bleak. Perhaps the most notable defector was Vasile Boerescu, who as Foreign Minister in the Catargiu government had promoted the commercial convention with Austria-Hungary and who joined the Liberal government in 1879. In 1880 a number of Conservatives, led by Lascăr Catargiu, tried to infuse life into the party by forming a political club in Bucharest and by drawing up a party programme and party statutes as a means of enforcing discipline among its members. But the new organization did not prosper, and Catargiu had to resort to various political combinations in order to combat the all-powerful Liberal political machine. First, he united his party with a dissident Liberal group led by Gheorghe Vernescu in 1884 to form the so-called Conservative-Liberal Party.[7] Their collaboration had little to do with principle: it was tactical—opposition to the Brătianu government. None the less, to effect this fusion Catargiu had to adhere to certain Liberal

[6] P. Cîncea, *Viaţa politică din România în primul deceniu al independenţei de stat* (Bucharest, 1974), 198–203; Take Ionescu, *Discursuri politice*, i: *1886–1892* (Bucharest, 1897), 69–81.

[7] Ion Bulei, *Sistemul politic al României moderne: Partidul Conservator* (Bucharest, 1987), 60–6.

principles—administrative decentralization and freedom of the press—even though the Conservatives had traditionally stood for centralization and limitations on the press. The new party constituted the strongest element in the so-called 'United Opposition' against the Brătianu government, but the Conservatives proved ineffective in parliament between 1883 and 1888.

The Junimists were perhaps the most cohesive of the Conservative political groups of the period, but they remained aloof from the Catargiu wing of the party for most of the 1880s. Titu Maiorescu and Theodor Rosetti were members of the executive committee of the party in 1880 and 1881, but were out of step with the leadership. They wanted a new programme 'of practical ideas and actions', but Catargiu and his supporters continued to draw inspiration from the practices of an earlier era. The Junimists pursued their own programme and legislative agenda, which Petre Carp, their acknowledged political leader, made public in 1881 and which deviated in crucial ways from traditional Conservative objectives.[8] In a speech in the Chamber of Deputies on 30 March, which came to be known as the 'Eră Nouă' (New Era), he accepted the 'democratization' of Rumanian society as a *fait accompli*, even though the process which had brought it into being struck him as 'defective'. Adhering to Maiorescu's theory of 'form without substance', he found the process unnatural; democratization had been introduced from the top, rather than from the bottom. By this he meant that institutions had been created in accordance with abstract principles and had not had their origins in existing economic and social conditions. But, for him, the past was past, and he urged his colleagues to bend their efforts toward organizing the future. He proposed to create a 'democracy of work' (*o democraţie a muncii*) in which the three classes of society—peasants, artisans, and 'governing elements' (*guvernanţi*)—would receive the full encouragement of the state in performing their specific tasks. For the peasants, he urged the enactment of laws that would protect them economically (notably, one law on primogeniture to prevent the fragmentation of peasant holdings and another regulating taverns in the village to curtail alcoholism) and would enable them to manage their own affairs (a law recognizing the village as the 'cell' around which the whole 'social organism' had formed and abolishing the 'artificial' rural commune which had

---

[8] On the Junimists in politics in the 1880s, see Z. Ornea, *Junimea şi Junimismul* (Bucharest, 1975), 239–69.

become enmeshed in the state administrative bureaucracy). For the artisans, he proposed to guarantee them work and to protect them from unfair competition by organizing them into corporations. Finally, for the governing class, he proposed that administrators and judges be admitted to office on the basis of merit and be shielded from political influences to enable them to carry out unhindered their primary function—to increase the production of the whole society. When all these tasks had been accomplished, then, he concluded, a national government, truly representative of the country's interests and, thus, more in keeping with the requirements of a genuine parliamentary regime would be possible.[9]

Carp's programme provided a basis for short-lived co-operation between the Junimists and Brătianu. In 1883 and 1884 they worked out terms of a permanent alliance, but Brătianu judged the Junimists' pretensions to share power exaggerated, and when he reorganized his government in June and November 1884, he left the Junimists out. As a consequence, in December they reaffirmed their own programme and declared themselves to be adherents of conservatism. During the next three years they tried to rejuvenate the Conservative Party in accordance with their own political and economic principles.

Another Conservative group that followed a path different from that of Catargiu's Conservative-Liberal Party was composed of so-called 'young conservatives' headed by Nicolae Filipescu (1862–1916), the publisher of the influential newspaper, *Epoca* (The Epoch). They had as their immediate objective a reconstitution of a 'pure' Conservative Party in order to free it from the 'tutelage' of the Liberals. Only in this way, they reasoned, could the Conservatives be themselves and acquire the means of turning their ideas into laws and institutions. None the less, in 1887 they joined various dissident Liberal factions in parliament as the only effective means of combating the government.

Despite opposition from within and outside the Liberal Party, the Brătianu government carried out significant political and economic changes, which moved the country closer to modern forms. The revision of the constitution in 1884 and the reorganization of local government were milestones in the development of middle-class democracy and the centralization of public administration, and a protectionist trade policy and the promotion of industry helped to lay the foundations of a diversified national economy.

[9] P. P. Carp, *Discursuri*, i (Bucharest, 1907), 261–7.

After the War for Independence and the proclamation of the kingdom demands for a revision of the constitution, which had been heard ever since its adoption in 1866, grew more insistent. The attention of reformers was focused particularly on the electoral law, which they denounced as unfair and undemocratic. Liberals, generally, claimed that changes in the structure of the state and the rapid evolution of economic and social relations had made revision imperative, but Conservatives were just as determined to thwart any attempts to dilute their political strength by expanding the franchise. C. A. Rosetti, speaking for the radical Liberals, inaugurated a new and more vehement phase of the debate over revision on 29 August 1882 with a scathing editorial in *Românul* attacking the existing electoral law as 'corruption prescribed, imposed, and legalized by the constitution'. He and his supporters condemned the high tax qualification for voting and the unequal distribution of deputies and senators among the existing electoral colleges because they concentrated power in the hands of a few and were thus the prime causes of corruption and injustice. As the reform campaign intensified the radicals directed public attention especially at college IV of the Chamber of Deputies (where the peasantry exercised its franchise) to show how its electors were prevented from meeting and expressing their will freely, but they also found that government pressure produced similar results in the other colleges because the small number of voters made intimidation relatively easy. To eliminate corruption and strengthen democracy they demanded substantial increases in the number of electors in each college.[10]

Brătianu was the key figure in the process of reform. He favoured a revision of the constitution and an increase in the electorate, but he was unwilling to go as far as Rosetti's radicals. His motives were complex. There can be no doubt that he was anxious to meet Rosetti half-way in order to avoid an open break between the radicals and his own more moderate followers and risk the disintegration of the party. But even more important to him in the long run was his calculation that modest changes in the electoral system would strengthen the political power of the industrial and banking classes, whom he saw as the principal support of the Liberal Party in the future. His government had already taken numerous steps to encourage industry, provide credit,

---

[10] G . Chiriţă, 'Modificarea constituţiei în 1884', *Studii: revistă de istorie*, 23/4 (1970), 150–62.

and stimulate exports, all of which had enhanced the economic fortunes of the middle class and of those large landowners who had an interest in developing a native industry. These classes were already demanding a greater role in political life, for they were eager to create a suitable legal framework for the development of a national economy, which they themselves intended to direct. These goals coincided with Brătianu's. By strengthening the bourgeoisie through electoral reform, he intended to strike yet another blow at the power of the great landowners, who were the primary support of his chief antagonists, the Conservative Party.

The king also played a crucial role in the process of constitutional revision. His own objectives were straightforward. He was not interested in democratization, but wanted the constitution to reflect the changes that had occurred in Rumania's international position between 1878 and 1881 and sought increases in the civil list and the budget of the royal household. He recognized some kind of electoral reform as unavoidable, but was confident that Brătianu would keep it within 'appropriate' bounds.

Conservatives were practically unanimous in opposing constitutional revision, in particular the extension of the right to vote to the middle and lower classes, but they differed in their approach to the problem. Their main political organization, Catargiu's Conservative-Liberal coalition, stood squarely for the maintenance of the electoral law approved in 1866. The great landowners, who supported the coalition, were afraid that if broader elements of the population gained control of the legislature they would enact laws detrimental to the interests of property, notably a reform of agrarian relations in favour of the peasants and perhaps even a tax on income. The Junimists were more philosophical. They objected to an expanded franchise on the grounds that the mass of the population was illiterate and lacked civic training. As a consequence, so the argument ran, they would simply become instruments of electoral fraud and political corruption because the political principles which had guided the forty-eighters in 1866 were too sophisticated for the Rumanian peasant masses. Instead, they urged that the existing provisions of the constitution about compulsory education and the decentralization of public administration be rigorously applied so that the peasantry could be prepared to exercise the duties of citizenship.

The parliamentary elections of April 1883 were crucial to the success of constitutional revision. Brătianu once again used all the administrative levers at his disposal to prevent the Conservatives from gaining one-third of the deputies or senators, the minimum necessary to thwart a modification of the constitution. Thanks to the vigilance of the Ministry of the Interior and the prefects, the Liberals won an overwhelming victory (132 governmental and radical deputies to 13 for the opposition in the Chamber, and 51 to 11 in the Senate). From this time on the authoritarian nature of Brătianu's government became more manifest, and his opponents took to calling him 'dictator' and 'vizir'.

The struggle over the revision of the constitution in parliament lasted from May 1883 to June 1884. The Liberals were almost alone in debating the issues, since the Conservatives absented themselves on the grounds that their presence served no purpose in the face of the 'arbitrary' and 'absolutist' behaviour of the government. The only exceptions were a few Junimists, including Titu Maiorescu, who continued to oppose changes in the electoral law, but had no influence on the proceedings. The two houses concluded their work and adopted the changes in the constitution favoured by the Brătianu Liberals on 8 June 1884. Although Brătianu had thus won a notable victory, he lost the support and friendship of Rosetti, who along with a number of followers resigned from parliament on 13 June.

Although the number of voters increased somewhat, the most important result of constitutional revision was to strengthen the political influence of the middle class. Electoral colleges I and II for the Chamber of Deputies were combined into a single, larger one, which gave the upper middle class a voice in a body that had previously been dominated by the Conservative large landowners. In the new colleges II and III other elements of the middle class, especially small artisans and merchants from the cities and teachers and priests from the villages, gained the direct vote as a result of lower tax qualifications, thereby increasing the overall influence of the middle class and the number of its representatives in parliament. Of the 183 deputies to be elected to the Chamber, 75 in college I and 33 in colleges II and III—108 in all—were reserved to the middle class. The Senate was also more susceptible to middle-class influence, but it remained a Conservative stronghold. The strengthening of the industrial and banking middle class led to important changes in the way in which parliament dealt with vital economic questions. It helps to explain, for example, why a series of laws to stimulate industry and expand credit were enacted after 1884 and why the commercial convention of 1875 with Austria-Hungary was not renewed. The new electoral law, however, did little for the mass of the population. It left the peasantry without genuine representation in parliament.

Although the revised constitution thus continued to limit the expression of the popular will at the ballot box, it expanded the rights of the printed word. As a result, the newspaper press flourished. In turn, it stimulated political life by popularizing ideas among broad segments of the population and by contributing significantly to the moulding of public opinion. The main limitation on freedom of the press was the prohibition against direct criticism of the dynasty, but even several noteworthy prosecutions did not impede the general trend toward the wide-ranging public discussion of major issues.[11]

With the struggle over the revision of the constitution successfully completed, the Liberal government turned to the economy. Its overriding concern was economic independence, which, it was certain, could not be attained unless the country moved beyond its traditional reliance upon agriculture. Backed by the middle class and drawing theoretical justification from the 'industrializing' economists, it embarked upon a many-sided programme to create a viable national industry by offering entrepreneurs both protection and encouragement. On the one hand, it adopted a new general tariff in May 1886 which raised duties significantly by imposing a surtax of 30 per cent on imports from those countries which applied a similar surtax on Rumanian goods. The main intent was to protect native manufactures from foreign competition. In 1886 and 1887 the government renegotiated commercial treaties with Britain, France, and Germany in the spirit of the new protectionism. The Liberals also encouraged industry directly by providing a variety of incentives to private entrepreneurs. Their passage on 12 May 1887 of the first comprehensive law to assist national industry, reflecting the ideas of Petre S. Aurelian, set numerous precedents for later state intervention in the economy. It provided that those persons who already owned enterprises with a capital of at least 50,000 lei and employed a minimum of twenty-five workers or who wanted to establish such an enterprise would receive free one to five hectares of land, exemption from all direct taxes for fifteen years and from tariff duties on imports of necessary machinery, and significant reductions in the cost of transporting raw materials and the finished products on the railways.

[11] Dissescu, *Cursul de drept public român*, ii. 461–3; Nicolae Iorga, *Istoria presei românești* (Bucharest, 1922), 132–68.

Agriculture was clearly secondary in the economic calculations of the Liberals, but they could not afford to ignore the foundation of the country's economy. Rather than formulating a comprehensive agrarian policy, however, they dealt with specific issues as they arose. The legislation they enacted eased conditions for various categories of peasants, but their primary interest was to increase production. For this reason, they did not tamper with the prevailing structure of agriculture and did not infringe upon the property rights of landlords.

The Liberals tried to strike a balance between the two principal goals of their agricultural policy. On the one hand, they sought to strengthen the independent peasant producers as the political bulwark of the monarchy, an idea implicit in the rural law of 1864, but, on the other hand, they imposed strict work rules on the mass of the peasantry in order to ensure a high level of production. Thus, in 1878 they approved regulations, in accordance with the reform of 1864, granting land to various categories of peasants, especially newly married couples (*însurăţei*), who had received none. Subsequently, they enacted laws providing for the sale of state lands in small lots to other peasants and protecting small peasant holdings from acquisition by landlords and *arendaşi*. They also made a modest attempt to provide credit to the small peasant producer by passing the law on agricultural credit offices in 1881. Their idea was to invest state funds to get the programme underway and then gradually replace that support by capital from the members of each credit institution. The project, which illustrated the Liberals' favourite method of combining private enterprise with state intervention, languished because the idea of association was still too novel, the requirements for collateral excluded the most needy (hence, the majority of peasants), and the term of the loans—a maximum of nine months—was too short to produce the desired results. The law on agricultural contracts of 1882, pushed by Rosetti and the radicals, brought a measure of relief to the peasants by eliminating criminal penalties for non-fulfilment of their obligations to landlords and reserving two days a week for work in their own fields.

The relationship between Brătianu and the king, which had been productive and mutually satisfactory, came under increasing public attack after 1884. The United Opposition continued to denounce the Prime Minister's 'dictatorial' ways and the administrative abuses he condoned. Now the actions of the monarch himself came under close scrutiny. The press led the way. In

Lupta (The Struggle) Gheorghe Panu, the leader of a small radical faction, accused the king of abusing his prerogatives and of allowing his ministers to ignore the constitution and suggested that he abdicate. The upshot was that Panu, brought to trial in 1887, was found guilty of having slandered the king in an article entitled, 'Omul periculos' (The Dangerous Man), but by fleeing to Paris, he escaped a two-year prison sentence.[12] More restrained, but no less telling, were the criticisms by the young Conservatives in *Epoca* who accused the king of disregarding the constitution and of keeping the Brătianu government in office long after it had ceased to represent the will of the country. Despite the constant pressure to replace his Prime Minister, Charles hesitated to act because he had little confidence in the ability of the Conservatives or other members of the opposition to govern effectively. He was also reluctant to inform them about the alliance with Austria-Hungary and Germany, which he and Brătianu had concluded in 1883 and had kept secret.

The final showdown came in March 1888. In the elections in February the Liberals had won a solid victory. Although Brătianu could have continued to prevail over the most determined opposition, he and his cabinet unexpectedly resigned on 4 March. He apparently realized that he had lost the confidence of the king. Charles had indeed decided that Brătianu had been 'used up', that he was no longer capable of governing the country in a 'creative way', and that it was time to promote those elements that had been excluded from power for almost twelve years. But signs of unhappiness with Brătianu's departure from Berlin and Vienna, where he had been regarded as one of the leading exponents, along with the king, of the German orientation in foreign policy, persuaded Charles to recall him to form a government.[13] Nevertheless, the king regarded the new government as merely temporary until he could calm his foreign allies. The opposition took advantage of the ruling party's disarray to step up its attacks on the Prime Minister and now resorted to mass meetings and street demonstrations to drive home their point. Since it was generally assumed that Brătianu maintained his hold on power only with the king's support, the public clamour in effect turned into a confrontation between the United Opposition and Charles. As the

---

[12] Corneliu Mateescu, *G. Panu şi radicalismul românesc la sfîrşitul secolului al XIX-lea* (Bucharest, 1987), 66–71.

[13] U. Bindreiter, *Die diplomatischen und wirtschaftlichen Beziehungen zwischen Österreich-Ungarn und Rumänien 1875–88* (Vienna, 1976), 249–50.

opposition showed no sign of relaxing its pressure on the government Charles concluded that Brătianu had lost the support of the middle class and the landlords and feared that the maintenance of the Liberals in power might endanger the dynasty itself. He therefore requested the resignation of a minister who was no longer of use to him. On 22 March Brătianu obliged. He retired from public life, spending his final years at his estate, Florica, near Piteşti, until his death in 1891.

Brătianu's successors, Conservatives of various hues, separately and in combination, formed the governments between 1888 and 1895. Following Brătianu's resignation, Charles brought the Junimists to power, a surprising choice at first glance, since they lacked both a strong political organization and wide support among the electorate. He turned to them in part because their domestic programme accorded with his own position on major issues, especially agriculture. In his view, the Junimists had an acceptable plan to resolve the 'peasant question' through grants of land from state domains, which would lessen tension in the countryside and at the same time preserve large landlord property. Moreover, they could be counted upon to deal firmly with the peasant uprising which had just broken out. Charles was also guided by foreign policy considerations. No one was better suited to assure continued reliance upon Germany and Austria-Hungary than the Junimists, who were well known for their pro-German sympathies and had co-operated with Brătianu in formulating this policy. Charles did not ask the United Opposition to form a government mainly because he thought they lacked the cohesion and decisiveness which the circumstances required.

The Junimist government, which took office in March 1888, had as Prime Minister Theodor Rosetti, but its real leader was the chief political theorist of the Junimists, Petre Carp. Despite extraordinary ability, Carp himself had not been invited to form the government because he had deeply offended the king by blunt criticism of some of Charles's most cherished ideas and because he was at odds with Lascăr Catargiu, the leader of the Conservatives, whom the king was holding in reserve and did not wish to alienate.

Although the new government put down the peasant uprising in the spring of 1888 with dispatch, it was unable to move legislation through a parliament dominated by Liberals. On 8 September parliament was dissolved, but the king invited Rosetti to form a new government. In the ensuing election campaign the Junimists enunciated a moderate, forward-looking programme that promised an honest and efficient administration and sympathetic concern for the welfare of the economically deprived classes. Specifically, they proposed a decentralization of administration and safeguards for the general population against bureaucratic abuses; the protection of judges from political pressures and arbitrary removal; the granting of additional land to smallholders as a means of establishing a greater equity between landlords and peasants; and the protection of artisans from 'ignorance, accidents, and the infirmities of old age'. The elections, as usual, confirmed the king's choice of Prime Minister, and parliament, which opened on 1 November, had a comfortable Conservative majority. But the Junimists and their Conservative allies were far from united. Disagreements over policy and personal animosities brought down the government on 22 March 1889 before it had had a chance to act upon its ambitious election promises.

Three Conservative governments followed in rapid succession. The longest and most important (March 1889 to February 1891) was the 'concentrated' Conservative government, so called because it was composed of all the main factions of the party (Conservative-Liberals, the 'pure' or *Epoca* group led by Nicolae Filipescu, and Junimists). Headed by General Gheorghe Manu, commander of the Rumanian fourth army at Plevna in 1877, it had as one of its chief goals the unification of the Conservative Party. Since the idea of rotation in office between Liberals and Conservatives was now commonly accepted, all the Conservative factions had come to see a united party as essential if they were to compete successfully with the Liberals.

The advantages of cohesion were soon manifest. In November 1891 the 'great Conservative government', which, at least in appearance, represented a unified party and held office for four years, was installed with Lascăr Catargiu as Prime Minister. Although two separate Conservative clubs—the regular and the Junimist—continued to function, and Catargiu and Carp competed for leadership of the party, the entrance of Carp into the cabinet as Minister of Agriculture, Industry, and Commerce and of his fellow Junimist, Alexandru Marghiloman (1854—1925), as Minister of Justice laid the foundation for the co-operation of all Conservative groups.

The presence of Take Ionescu in the cabinet reveals much about the evolution of party life in the latter decades of the century. After returning home from studies in France and England, he joined the Liberal Party, but, as we have seen, disenchanted with Ion Brătianu's style of administration, he went over to the Conservative opposition in 1886. At the time it struck many observers as unusual for one whose origins and inclinations were bourgeois to join the party of the great landlords. When asked this question in the Chamber of Deputies Ionescu replied that he took the step out of conviction, out of dissatisfaction with a whole system of government.[14] This was the same route taken by other young and ambitious politicians at a time when the leadership of the Conservative Party was seeking to attract new blood. It was characteristic of the last two decades of the century that social background as a criterion for party membership had lost much of its significance. After 1900 both the Liberal and Conservative parties had energetic bourgeois and landlord wings.

The new Conservative government was strongly influenced by the Junimists. Its programme, which was drawn up on the eve of the parliamentary elections of February 1892, was a reformulation of the Junimist programme first enunciated by Petre Carp in 1881 under the title 'The New Era' and then revised in 1888. Thus, the Conservatives had achieved at least temporary unity largely on the basis of Junimist principles. The ideological leadership of the Junimists and their preponderance in the cabinet suggest that the real head of the government was Carp, not Catargiu.

The leaders of the government stood forth as advocates of order and reasoned change. In 1892 they passed laws extending the control of the central bureaucracy over the *judeţe* and its subdivisions by transferring numerous responsibilities for local government from mayors and communal councils to prefects and their aides, and in 1893 the Conservatives established the rural gendarmerie, with a post in every commune, for the purpose of preventing disorders or suppressing them as soon as they broke out. The cost of maintaining the new police force fell upon an already overtaxed rural population. The Conservatives also concerned themselves with economic development, generally in accordance with their traditional agricultural interests. A noteworthy exception was the law on mines of 1895, sponsored by Petre Carp. His purpose was to develop the petroleum resources of the country as rapidly as possible by encouraging investment by foreign capitalists and assuring their co-operation with large landowners. It was Carp's way of adapting the Rumanian economy to the needs and op-

[14] Take Ionescu, *Discursuri politice*, i. 93–100.

portunities presented by Western Europe without seriously altering the social and political structures at home.

The debates in parliament over the mining law brought to the surface the underlying antagonisms within the Conservative Party and encouraged the Liberals to try to unseat the government. They made much of the fact that the law was unconstitutional because it allowed foreigners to own landed property, a violation of article 7, which stipulated that only a Rumanian citizen could acquire rural property. The Liberals not only sought to embarrass the Conservatives, but made a point of proclaiming publicly one of the main principles of economic nationalism—that Rumanians, not foreigners, should be responsible for developing the country's natural resources and charting its economic course. This attitude foreshadowed the post-World War I Liberal economic policy expressed succinctly in the phrase, 'By ourselves' (*Prin noi înşine*). When the Liberals lost and the mining law was passed they withdrew from parliament in order to obstruct the further work of the government and oblige the king to call on them to replace the Conservatives.

Their action was by no means hasty. It was, rather, the culmination of a campaign that had been going on since June 1892, when Dimitrie Sturdza assumed leadership of the Liberal Party. He was the third person to hold that position in a little over a year. When Ion Brătianu died on 4 May 1891, his brother, Dimitrie, who had led a group of dissident Liberals, succeeded him. During his short tenure (he died on 8 June 1892) he proved incapable of holding the various factions together. Sturdza was a popular choice to succeed him. He had had a long political career, being a member of the coalition that had overthrown Alexandru Cuza and the coalition of Mazar pasha, in which he had distinguished himself by his hostility to the Hohenzollern dynasty. He had also been a minister (finance, foreign affairs, justice, and cults and public instruction) almost continuously during the long Liberal tenure between 1876 and 1888.

Sturdza's presidency of the party in 1892 signalled the beginning of a sustained effort by the Liberals to overturn the Conservative government. The next three years were by all accounts one of the most tumultuous periods in the history of Rumanian political parties between the achievement of independence and the First World War.[15] The struggle for power extended beyond the

---

[15] The most detailed account is in C. Gane, *P. P. Carp şi locul său în istoria politică a Ţării*, ii (Bucharest, 1936), 20–159.

boundaries of the kingdom, as the worsening situation of the
Rumanians of Transylvania was used by the Liberals to prove that
the Conservatives were 'anti-national'. Nor was the king spared.
A number of Liberals revived old accusations that he kept in
power a regime that he himself had forced upon the country in
total disregard of the popularity of the Liberals. But Sturdza
discouraged such open attacks on the king because he was certain
that sooner or later, in accordance with the rotation system, his
turn to form a government would come.

Sturdza was right. The political crisis largely generated by the
Liberals coincided with the end of the Conservatives' normal
legislative mandate, and the king took the opportunity to bring
the Liberals to power. Their accession seemed to politicians of
both parties a natural consequence of the rotation system and,
hence, caused little stir. Charles turned to Sturdza in part at least
because he hoped to put an end to the campaign against Austria-
Hungary on behalf of the Rumanians of Transylvania initiated by
Sturdza. Well before his appointment as Prime Minister Sturdza
had begun to soften his tone, for he realized that otherwise he
would have little chance of coming to power, because of the
king's commitment to the Central Powers and their own significant influence on domestic Rumanian political life. Thus, Sturdza
made it clear that he favoured the maintenance of the status quo in
Transylvania, which signified a declaration of loyalty to the Triple
Alliance. The elections in November 1895 followed the usual
pattern and resulted in an overwhelming victory for the new
government.

The Liberals remained in power until the spring of 1899,[16] but
their accomplishments fell short of expectations. In neither of
the two main issues that had come to absorb public opinion—
the agrarian problem and the situation of the Rumanians of
Transylvania—did the party in general distinguish itself by legislation (in the first) or leadership (in the second). There were, of
course, bright spots. Men of talent served in ministerial posts, for
example, Spiru Haret (1851-1912) in education and Ion I. C.
(Ionel) Brătianu (1864-1927), the eldest son of Ion Brătianu,
who had made his political debut in 1895 as an elected deputy
from Gorj judeţ and in 1897 became Minister of Public Works.
There were also a few notable pieces of legislation: the creation

---

[16] For a critical estimate of the Sturdza government, see Titu Maiorescu, *Istoria
contemporană a României (1866-1900)* (Bucharest, 1925), 329-408.

in 1896 of Casa Şcoalelor (The Foundation for Schools), whose purpose was to centralize all funds designated for the building and upkeep of schools, to receive donations and bequests for education, and to grant scholarships; and the law on secondary education enacted in 1897, which, among other things, reorganized the upper classes of the lyceum into three sections—science, classical, and modern—thereby allowing earlier specialization than in the previous unitary lyceum. But other bills had to be withdrawn from consideration, owing to the lack of money, and the revision of the mining law of 1895, which Liberals had denounced as a grave violation of the constitution, had to be abandoned altogether, because of two mounting crises, financial and political, in 1899. The former had been brought on by the government's spending beyond its means; the second by revelations that Sturdza had acquiesced in the Hungarian government's harsh policy toward the Rumanians of Transylvania. The obstructionist tactics of the Conservatives and other opposition deputies in parliament, which brought government to a standstill, and street demonstrations persuaded Sturdza to resign on 10 April 1899.

During the next eight years Conservative and Liberal governments, five in all, followed in easy rotation. The relatively short tenures of the governments headed by Gheorghe G. Cantacuzino, the new leader of the Conservative Party (Lascǎr Catargiu had died on 30 March 1899), between April 1899 and July 1900, and by Petre Carp (July 1900 to February 1901) were bedevilled by a severe economic and financial crisis. The main cause was the enormous debt which had accumulated partly because of enormous government public works projects—railways, highways, the development of the port of Constanţa, and large public buildings, especially in Bucharest—and partly because of a rapid growth in the number of government employees, a consequence mainly of the desire of both political parties to reward their supporters. Both Conservative governments took extraordinary measures to deal with immediate symptoms and long-term causes. To repair the damage from a persistent drought the Cantacuzino cabinet made special credits available for the purchase of hay and enacted a law granting a moratorium to those who had leased state lands and were unable to meet their payments. To overcome the worsening financial situation it floated a loan in Germany and tried to attract foreign investments by declaring an open-door policy. Even the Liberals went along, although they insisted that local capital be included in all undertakings. None of these measures, however, brought relief. The government simply mishandled some of its own programmes and, in any case, could not control economic events abroad. Like his predecessor, Carp also negotiated for foreign loans and offered favourable terms to foreign companies, notably an oil pipeline concession to Standard Oil, but he also took greater political risks than Cantacuzino by urging a cut in the government budget by 15 per cent through a reduction in the state bureaucracy and a simplification of *judeţ* and village administrations. But the issue that brought about his fall was a proposal for new taxes, especially on the production of alcohol, which struck at the mass of the peasants. It was seized upon by rivals in his own party, notably Cantacuzino and Take Ionescu, who were certain that the king would appoint one of them to succeed Carp.

Charles thought otherwise and turned once again to Dimitrie Sturdza. He had been disappointed by the continuous infighting of the Conservatives and by their inability to solve the financial crisis, all of which threatened the country with political instability and diminished its prestige, and his own, in Berlin and Vienna. He was also impressed by the Liberals' programme for economic development and welcomed Sturdza's continued willingness to co-operate with Germany and Austria-Hungary.

The Liberals succeeded in overcoming the country's immediate financial difficulties by drastic measures intended to assure a balanced budget, including reductions in salaries and the elimination of jobs in the bureaucracy. The government could now proceed to carry out an ambitious social and economic programme. A number of measures were taken under the general direction of Spiru Haret, who was once again Minister of Education, to improve the condition of the peasantry. Haret believed in self-help as a means of solving the agrarian problem and therefore sponsored legislation that would draw on the human and material resources of the rural population itself. The most important of these acts were the law on local credit banks (*băncile populare*) of 1903, which were intended to provide peasants with loans at reasonable rates of interest to improve their productivity, and the law on village co-operatives (*obştii săteşti*) of 1904, which encouraged peasants to pool their resources to lease additional land. Both laws were aimed primarily at the peasant who had already demonstrated his ability to make an adequate or even profitable living from the land and ignored the poorest strata of the peasantry. The Liberals, of course, also directed much of their attention to industry. In 1904 they introduced a new tariff designed to protect and encourage industry, but perhaps just as significant was their abolition of local excise taxes the year before, which they hoped would increase the exchange of goods between the cities and the countryside and thereby expand the market for native manufactures.

Despite respectable legislative accomplishments, the Sturdza government was brought down by dissension within its own ranks. Led by Ionel Brătianu, who had been Minister of Public Works and then Foreign Minister, younger and mainly middle-class elements of the party were eager to accelerate the economic and social development of the country. Success, in their view, would require a comprehensive solution of the agrarian problem and greater participation by the mass of the population in political life, or, translated into legislation, a new land reform and an expanded franchise, measures which could not be carried out as long as the 'old Liberals' like Sturdza remained in control of the party. The young Liberals in parliament so thoroughly undermined Sturdza's authority that he was obliged to resign on 3 January 1905.

The guiding force of the new Conservative government, which took office in January 1905, was Take Ionescu, the Minister of Finance. It was he who organized the elections in February which resulted in a compliant parliament, and who devised the party's economic and financial strategy. But a vigorous legislative pro-gramme concealed internal divisions within the Conservative Party so severe that they convinced the king that it could not lead the country out of its gravest internal crisis since independence—the great peasant revolt of 1907. In the face of growing peasant unrest and the opposition of all the diverse groups which clamoured for an amelioration of conditions on the land, Conservative leaders continued to insist that there was no 'peasant question' and that the inviolability of private property must be maintained at all cost. Take Ionescu, who represented the bourgeois wing of the party, contributed no little to the disarray and, ultimately, helped to bring about the resignation of the government through his persistent efforts to gain leadership of the party and bring his supporters—bankers, arendași, and grain exporters—to the fore.

The king turned once again to the Liberals, this time to deal with the peasant violence. With Sturdza again at the helm the government proceeded to repress with the utmost brutality what had become a country-wide revolt of the villages against unbearable economic and social relations on the land. In doing so, it had an almost united parliament behind it, for both parties sensed the gravity of the peasants' action and the danger it posed to the existing social order.

The Liberals had formed their government in March 1907 at the height of the peasant revolt. What had begun on 21 February as a purely local disturbance in the village of Flămînzi in northern Moldavia had in succeeding weeks spread across Moldavia and Muntenia to the western parts of Oltenia.[17] Assured of the support of the two major political parties, the government mobilized the army to crush the revolt. By the time the peasants had been subdued, in the middle of April, some 11,000 persons had been killed and the destruction of property was so great and so widespread that the losses could never be accurately tabulated. Under the pressure of a shocked public opinion the Liberal government undertook to 'solve' the peasant question through a variety of laws.

In the midst of this extensive legislative activity a significant change in the leadership of the Liberal Party occurred. It had been evident for some time that Sturdza, now 75 and in failing health, was no longer the leader he had once been. Party leaders finally forced him to resign. He was succeeded as Prime Minister on 22 December 1908 and as president of the party on 11 January 1909 by Ionel Brătianu. These events were to have a profound effect on Rumanian politics. Ionel Brătianu's ascendancy in the party marked the return to political prominence of the Brătianu family, which for the next twenty years would again play a decisive role in the public life of the country. It also signified the definitive triumph of the middle-class wing of the Liberal Party over its landlord elements, which Sturdza had represented. These changes at the top were to determine the party's economic and social policies until its dissolution in 1947. Those who favoured rapid industrialization dominated by native capital and who sought a modernization of the party machinery to make it more responsive to changing social needs were now in charge.

Ionel Brătianu's principal aim in domestic policy was to continue transforming the economy by promoting industry and by keeping control of it in Rumanian hands. He was not a committed political reformer, but he was prepared to make whatever changes might be necessary in the existing political system in order to gain acceptance for his vision of the country's development.[18] In foreign

---

[17] The causes and development of the revolt are described in Ch. 4.

[18] The Liberal Party's economic and political objectives after the turn of the century are set forth in Vintila I. C. Brătianu, *Scrieri și cuvântări*, i: *1899–1906* (Bucharest, 1937), 108–61, 313–35, 341–77.

policy his sympathies lay with France, but he was also practical. He was well aware of the king's preferences, and he understood the importance of Austria-Hungary and especially Germany for the economic development of Rumania. Yet, the legislative accomplishments of his nearly two years in office were modest. The Liberals failed to enact significant agrarian or electoral reforms.

In keeping with the practice of rotating parties the king turned to the Conservatives at the end of the Liberals' regular four-year legislative term. Of the two leading Conservative candidates to succeed Brătianu, the king showed no hesitation in choosing Petre Carp over Take Ionescu. Although Carp's intransigence and bluntness repelled him, Charles welcomed his unwavering support of the institution of monarchy, his pro-German leanings in foreign affairs, and his prudent domestic programme, which aimed at social stability and the preservation of large landed property. But Carp's insistence upon principle as he saw it almost cost him his appointment. At a meeting of Conservative leaders on 20 December 1910, as the Liberal parliament in its last days debated bills on the police and the electoral system, he declared that he would not assume office if they became law. It was typical of him to confront his colleagues with the dilemma of either accepting his ideas and giving up their own or 'forcing' him to give up his post and withdraw from political life. Titu Maiorescu pointed out the absurdity of Carp's stand. He reminded his long-time colleague that laws meant nothing in Rumania, only the men who applied them did. On this occasion Carp's colleagues agreed not to participate in the debates on the offending legislation. The crisis passed, and Carp assumed office on 29 December.

Carp had a far from united Conservative Party behind him. The most serious challenge to his leadership came from the ambitious Take Ionescu. At the root of their differences lay a clash of personalities and competition for office rather than ideology. The break between them had already come in 1907 when Carp excluded all but two of Ionescu's supporters from the Conservative Club in Bucharest, the main party organization. Ionescu, on vacation in France, hurried home and set about organizing a new party. Previous attempts of this sort by others had resulted only in the establishment of small factions whose life had been short and capabilities meagre. But Ionescu's party lasted for almost a decade and caused great difficulties for both the Conservatives and Liberals. In an open letter of 19 January 1908 to his Conservative colleagues Ionescu announced his intention to proceed with the 'modernization' of their party by making it more responsive to the great issues of the day and more adaptable to future trends, while at the same time preserving existing social structures. He thus clearly expressed the aims of his main constituency—the conservative middle class.

The founding congress of the new Democratic-Conservative Party was held in Bucharest on 3 February 1908. It drew support from the middle classes of the cities and villages, especially professional people, small and middle-sized property owners, and the well-to-do peasantry. A number of outstanding figures in intellectual and cultural life such as the historian Alexandru D. Xenopol and the playwright Ion Luca Caragiale also joined. The party programme concerned itself with administrative reforms; free, though non-compulsory, primary education; solutions to the peasant question; and accident and old-age insurance for workers. In 1910 Take Ionescu offered a more specific agenda.[19] He proposed to reduce the three electoral colleges to two and to make the second more representative of peasant interests by expanding the franchise and guaranteeing its independence from landlord and governmental pressures. To improve the efficiency of the bureaucracy and heighten its responsiveness to the local population he proposed to define precisely the duties of the prefects, who were to be civil servants rather than agents of the party in power. He also outlined a series of measures designed to improve conditions on the land. His primary goal was to strengthen the peasant with middle-sized holdings through the sale of public lands, the creation of model farms, and the leasing of machinery. But he drew back from any wholesale land reform or similar measure that threatened private property. In foreign affairs, in order to please the king, the new party declared its adherence to the traditional policy of co-operation with the Central Powers, but in fact Ionescu had no intention of following it. He was an ardent supporter of Rumanian national aspirations in Hungary, and he made no secret of his sympathy for France.

The Democratic-Conservative Party prospered because of its programme and the popularity of Ionescu. It steadily gained adherents and in by-elections for parliament between 1908 and 1910 it won seven out of ten contests. Although Carp dismissed these results as insignificant, he none the less undertook negotiations for

[19] Mircea Iosa and Traian Lungu, *Viaţa politică în România, 1899—1910* (Bucharest, 1977), 243–5.

a fusion of the two parties in the autumn of 1910. Since neither side was ready to make serious concessions, the talks failed. Moreover, rumours that Carp would be asked to form a government caused a violent reaction from the Democratic-Conservatives. Ionescu organized a series of public meetings in order to impress the king with his party's popularity, but Charles, as we have seen, had already decided on Carp. Although he recognized Ionescu's abilities, he had greeted the formation of the new party with reserve, preferring to retain the alternating two-party system as a guarantee of political stability.

The legislation enacted by the Carp government was far-reaching and, in general, it confronted squarely the major problems of the country's economic and social development.[20] The laws Carp proposed did not fit the old Conservative economic stereotype: rather, they encouraged industry and provided for regular government intervention in the economy. One of his first measures was to extend the law for the support of industry until 1912. During the interim a new law was drawn up which offered assistance and protection on a proportional basis to both large and small enterprises and gave priority to those which used raw materials from agriculture and exported at least one-fourth of their annual production. The chief motive behind these provisions was the recognition that agriculture was the foundation not only of the country's economy in general but, ultimately, of industry, too. Yet, despite his support of large-scale industry, Carp attempted to rejuvenate the artisan crafts, which that very industry had helped to undermine. Under his sponsorship a law was enacted in 1911 which provided for the organization of artisans in specialized guilds (*bresle*), whose purpose was to protect the economic interests of their members, and in broader-based corporations, composed of many *bresle* and at least 1,000 members each, which could offer their members aid in case of illness or disability. Carp's intentions were partly economic and partly social. On the one hand, he was eager to improve the technical efficiency and productivity of the artisan industry, and, on the other, he wanted to provide a measure of security for artisans and to avert serious labour disturbances, which might weaken the existing structure of society. The maintenance of social peace also lay behind the bill he sponsored in 1912 to enable peasants (the better off among them) to buy in lots of five hectares some 250,000 hectares of state-

[20] Gane, *P. P. Carp*, ii. 409–57.

owned land. As usual, the Conservatives, like the majority of Liberals, shied away from serious reform, which would have required the expropriation of land from the great estates.

Despite his notable legislative achievements, Carp's lack of measure and tact in pursuing his goals, his stubborn opposition to significant political and social reforms, and, in foreign policy, his attachment to the Central Powers, which ran counter to the overwhelming pro-French sentiments of the public, created instability at home at a time of growing international tension in Southeastern Europe. The king was anxious to retain the Conservatives, but sought a 'concentrated' government, one that would unite all elements of the party, including the Democratic-Conservatives. When several members of the government suggested a reconciliation with Take Ionescu, Carp, typically, wondered out loud if the king was crazy. After a short interim government headed by Titu Maiorescu (28 March–12 October 1912), during which the several Conservative factions reached an understanding, the united Conservative government desired by the king took office on 14 October.

The new government was a coalition, in which the regular Conservatives and the Democratic-Conservatives shared power. Maiorescu was Prime Minister, but Take Ionescu also wielded great influence. Besides being Minister of the Interior, he shared with Maiorescu, in accordance with the king's wishes, the conduct of foreign affairs. Charles was eager to use Ionescu's widely recognized abilities as a diplomat as a new Balkan crisis deepened, but, as in the past, he was unwilling to give Ionescu exclusive direction over matters of the highest importance, because of his manifest sympathies for the Western powers. Maiorescu also respected Ionescu's intellectual abilities, but he condemned as 'amoral' the methods he had used in his struggle for power and was, consequently, unyielding in his opposition to Ionescu as head of the Conservative Party. Maiorescu co-operated with him during the Balkan Wars of 1912 and 1913 in order to present a united front in critical diplomatic negotiations, but once these problems had been resolved, the two men went their separate ways. Ionescu held a similar view of their relationship. He regarded their co-operation as fortuitous, brought on by the international situation, and while he could foresee genuine unity at some future time, he thought the two parties would for the time being have to remain separate.

The statements of principle drawn up by Maiorescu and Ionescu in the autumn of 1913 revealed the shades of difference in their respective brands of conservatism. On the two most critical domestic issues of the day—agrarian reform and universal suffrage—Maiorescu restated the essence of conservative doctrine.[21] He continued to oppose any reform that threatened the integrity of the large estates. While acknowledging the disparity between large and small property, he declared that his party was ready to explore every means of achieving 'progress'. But, he warned, progress did not mean infringing upon private property, which his party considered a fundamental constitutional right and a guarantee of social stability. He condemned as 'utopian' and 'dangerous' the notion that every peasant ought to be endowed with land and recommended, instead, a process of 'natural selection', which would separate the ambitious and intelligent peasants, who merited state support and large holdings, from the mass of peasants, who lacked the ability to survive economically. To give all peasants land by dividing up the large estates would, so Maiorescu and other Conservatives reasoned, merely disrupt agricultural production. Maiorescu and his party also saw no pressing need for electoral reform, since, in their view, the existing system had not interfered with the development of the country. When the time came for change, they wanted it to be the result of an understanding among all the political parties, as in the case of the Constitution of 1866, rather than a project forced upon the country by a single party (they had Liberals in mind).

Take Ionescu was in a difficult position. Standing between the Conservatives and the Liberals, he had to make his own position on the major issues of the day clearly distinguishable from theirs and at the same time avoid alienating the former, since he still aspired to leadership of a united Conservative Party. He continued to favour a merging of the three electoral colleges into two in order to give more representation to the peasants, but he opposed a single electoral college on the grounds that the élite of society would be overwhelmed by the mass of ordinary voters. He also proposed to make land available to the peasants through a limited expropriation of large estates, but he insisted that the private property thus taken be paid for immediately in cash rather than in long-term bonds, a requirement that would have nullified the reform, since the peasants lacked the money to pay for the land.[22]

The coalition Conservative government had been formed in the

---

[21] *Programul Partidului Conservator* (Bucharest, 1913), 3–17.

[22] Anastasie Iordache, *Viaţa politică în România, 1910–1914* (Bucharest, 1972), 249–50.

first place to carry out specific tasks, mainly in foreign affairs, and had, on the whole, successfully met its responsibilities. It initiated no significant domestic legislation, owing in part to its concentration of the Balkan crisis and in part to the divergences between the two coalition partners.

Third parties did not fare well under the system of alternating Conservatives and Liberals in power, a practice that over time had taken on the attributes of a constitutional imperative. Perhaps the most successful of these was Ionescu's Democratic-Conservative Party, but, dominated by a single individual and never completely divorced from the Conservative Party, it retained the characteristic marks of a faction. Two notable attempts to found distinct third parties, that is, political organizations representing interests other than those of landlords and the middle class, centred on the peasantry and the urban working class.

The systematic political organization of the peasantry began with the activities of Constantin Dobrescu-Argeş (1859–1903), a young teacher from the Argeş region of western Muntenia. He was thus the initiator of political peasantism (ţărănism), which was to become a major political force in the period between the two World Wars. In the 1870s he undertook a vigorous cultural and economic programme to improve the material conditions of the peasantry and arouse them to action on their own behalf. He gave numerous public lectures, organized evening courses for adults, established libraries, and promoted village co-operatives and credit banks (bănci populare). He was also eager to create a political base for his activities on behalf of the peasants and in 1880, supported by teachers and well-to-do peasants in his own and neighbouring judeţe, he established a peasant committee (Comitet Ţărănesc), the first Rumanian peasantist organization, which put forward a series of economic and political demands aimed at improving the working conditions and living standard of its constituency. It sought to extend the right to vote directly for candidates to everyone who could read and write, to obtain respect in practice for all the civil rights granted under the constitution, to provide peasants with arable land and pastures, and to reduce taxes. The committee also began publication in 1881 of a weekly, Ţăranul (The Peasant), the first peasantist newspaper, which tried to awaken the peasants to a consciousness of their own strength and importance.

The peasant movement initiated by Dobrescu-Argeş spread rapidly as committees were organized in judeţe all across Wallachia. A measure of its success was the election to parliament of four deputies supported by the Peasant Committee from the *judeţe* of Argeş, Gorj, Dîmboviţa, and Brăila. Dobrescu-Argeş himself was elected a deputy seven times between 1883 and 1895. His organizing activities took yet another turn in 1892, when, assisted by the Bishop of Argeş, he established Societatea pentru Cultura Ţăranilor (The Society for the Culture of the Peasants), whose primary aims were to encourage education and thereby raise the self-esteem of the peasants and to urge intellectuals and politicians to study at first hand the condition of the peasantry as a prerequisite for reform. The Society had its own organ, *Gazeta ţăranilor* (The Peasants' Gazette), a weekly which Dobrescu-Argeş and his brother-in-law, Alexandru Vălescu, also a teacher, published beginning in 1892.

On these foundations Dobrescu-Argeş established in October 1895 the first formal party in Rumania which had the welfare of the peasantry as its main concern, Partida Ţărănească (The Peasant Party). Delegates from twenty-four *judeţe* meeting at the founding congress in Bucharest adopted a comprehensive programme. They placed economic justice for the peasants first on their agenda. They looked back to a seemingly simpler past, for they urged the restoration of 'ancient rights' of villages to 'two-thirds of the land of the country', an obvious reference to the provisions of earlier legislation reserving two-thirds of a landlord's estate for the use of its peasants, and the restoration of the right of peasants to pasture their animals on landlords' estates and to take firewood from the forests.[23] The leaders of the new party also demanded a diminution of the burdens imposed upon the peasantry by the existing law on agricultural contracts and a strict accounting of dues paid and labour performed by peasants. But they also recognized the economic imperatives of the new age and proposed the creation of an agricultural credit bank supported by the state to buy estates put up for sale by their owners and resell parcels of land from them to peasants, teachers, and priests who had less than five hectares. They also insisted that estates be leased only to peasant communes and not to the *arendaşi* and urged that cheap credit be made available to peasants and that the export of grain and animals be encouraged. They were clearly not revolutionaries, as is evident from the absence of any appeal for the expropriation of great estates. They seem, rather, to have been bent upon adapting

---

[23] Ion Scurtu, 'Mişcarea ţărănistă din România pînă la 1907', *Studii: revistă de istorie*, 25/3 (1972), 534–5.

peasant farming to the requirements of commercial agriculture, while at the same time strengthening the independent small producer. Dobrescu-Argeş and his colleagues also realized that if the peasant were to improve his situation he had to become an active force in the political process. They therefore repeated earlier demands for an expansion of the franchise and proposed to give the peasant necessary experience in managing his own affairs by ensuring administrative autonomy for village communes. At the end of the congress Dobrescu-Argeş and Ioan Rădoi, a lawyer, were elected chairmen of a committee of action. Although they made a strenuous effort to recruit members for the party, they preferred for the time being to rely upon the traditional political parties to enact the reforms they had enunciated.

Dobrescu-Argeş and his followers had to wage a continuous battle against both the Liberals and Conservatives, who treated the peasant movement with deep suspicion. Dobrescu-Argeş himself was arrested on trumped-up charges and gaoled for three months in 1898. He never recovered emotionally from the experience. His lieutenants tried to carry on his work and fielded a slate of candidates for the parliamentary elections of 1899, but government pressure prevented the election of even a single deputy. Dobrescu-Argeş decided to retire from politics and turned the editorship of *Gazeta ţăranilor* over to Vălescu. These acts marked the end of the Partida Ţărănească and the failure of the first attempt to establish a peasant party. Most of its members withdrew from politics. A few joined the Liberal Party, thereby strengthening its left wing, while others, like Vălescu, continued to work for the peasant cause through the press.

The peasant movement after 1900, despite the disbanding of its political party, gained rather than lost momentum. One of the main reasons was the growing public consciousness, encouraged by both politicians and intellectuals, that the 'peasant question' was an issue of overriding national importance. Influential individuals—politicians, sociologists, historians, economists, and novelists—and powerful movements such as Sămănătorism and Poporanism kept it continually before the public and the two major political parties. But the countryside itself provided the essential base of support for the movement. Here the village middle class took the lead. It was composed of a diverse grouping of peasants with middle-sized holdings (from 10 to 50 hectares), village merchants, and the majority of village priests and teachers, a number of whom had been attracted to Dobrescu-Argeş's Partida

Ţărănească. Their rise to prominence came about at least in part through the gradual development of new economic and social relations in the village. Although they shared with the mass of the peasants a common interest in opposing large landlords, they pursued political and economic objectives that diverged significantly from the aspirations of the majority of peasants. The village middle class was clearly on the rise as a result of conditions created by the gradual introduction of capitalist relations into the rural economy. Nor was it averse to taking advantage of the hardships of poorer neighbours to increase its purchases of land, to use hired labour, and to engage in money-lending. Not surprisingly, the village middle class stood for the preservation of the existing economic order as the proper framework that would allow it to achieve prosperity and political influence. Its leaders were anxious to avoid revolution and therefore supported greater political rights and economic benefits for the mass of the peasants as a means of directing their activities into legal channels.

The rural middle class was by no means totally absorbed in economic pursuits. Teachers and priests, often referred to as the village intellectuals, did much to raise the educational and moral level of the mass of the peasants and even contributed to their economic emancipation and the achievement of political rights.[24] They established a variety of cultural and co-operative organizations, which improved conditions for at least a part of the peasantry. Teachers founded and published newspapers, which did much to raise the political consciousness of all elements of the peasantry, especially the more affluent. These publications concerned themselves with matters of direct interest to the peasants. Some dealt with immediate economic problems, while others urged the peasants to establish their own political organizations.

The village intellectuals received strong support from Spiru Haret, a leader of the Liberal Party and Minister of Education in 1897–9, 1901–4, and 1907–10. He regarded the agrarian question as primarily cultural and insisted that knowledge would mean a better material life for the peasants. He therefore promoted the dissemination of useful information in the villages, using the printed word and schoolteachers as his principal instruments. He patronized a number of publications and was instrumental in founding Sămănătorul in 1901 and in choosing its first two editors,

---

[24] Such activities are alluded to in Romus Dima, Organizarea politică a ţărănimii (sfîrşitul sec. XIX-începutul sec. XX) (Bucharest, 1985), 162–93.

the noted writers Alexandru Vlahuţă and Gheorghe Coşbuc, and he mobilized schoolteachers to continue their didactic activities after school by organizing night classes for adults. But he also recognized the economic side of the peasant question and sought to bring an immediate improvement in the standard of living of the village by promoting small rural credit bands and agricultural co-operatives.[25]

Haret's activities were not an isolated phenomenon. Support came from the left wing of his party, which used the peasant movement to expand Liberal influence in the rural areas, especially among the growing village middle class. Former members of the defunct Partida Ţărănească and the so-called 'generous' faction (generoşii) of the Social Democratic Party, who had joined the Liberal Party in 1900, reinforced these efforts of the Liberal left. The wooing of the peasantry was also manifest in legislation providing for the organization of rural credit banks and the right of village communes to obtain loans from Creditul Funciar Rural.

The leaders of the peasants, heartened by Liberal support, were, none the less, on guard against all attempts by 'traditional' political parties to take over their movement. Alexandru Vălescu continued to promote the idea of a separate peasant party in the columns of Gazeta ţăranilor, and in Moldavia Vasile M. Kogălniceanu (1863—1941), the son of Mihail Kogălniceanu, had been active since the turn of the century in urging the peasants to organize. In September 1906 Kogălniceanu and Vălescu joined forces to establish Partidul Ţărănesc (The Peasant Party). They had both concluded that the peasants could expect no improvement in their condition from either the Conservatives or the Liberals.

The economic and political programme of the new party was similar to that of the earlier Partida Ţărănească. As a solution to the agrarian problem it proposed the distribution of land to all peasants who needed it, the easing of conditions imposed on the peasants by landlords and arendaşi through agricultural contracts, the expansion of credit at moderate interest rates, and, to bring peasant influence to bear directly on legislation, the enactment of universal suffrage. Kogălniceanu and Vălescu gave their programme the widest possible publicity by distributing it in thousands of copies in a brochure entitled, Către sateni (To the Villagers), which aroused great ferment in the countryside and led

---

[25] Şerban Orăscu, Spiru Haret (Bucharest, 1976), 86—112.

to a rapid increase in party membership.[26] The massive peasant uprising which erupted in March 1907 brought this promising experiment in peasant political organization to an abrupt end. In suppressing it, the Liberal government arrested numerous teachers, priests, and other 'intellectuals' whom it regarded as instigators of the uprising, including Kogălniceanu and Vălescu. Although the two men were soon released, they were unable to revive their movement, and for a time the effort to organize a peasant party languished.

The strongest and most consistent champions of the peasants during this period were the rural schoolteachers. The majority were either Poporanists or adherents of Spiru Haret's brand of Liberal social activism. By the time of the peasant uprising of 1907 they had created their own extensive professional organization and were eager to use their numbers and influence to enhance their economic and social status. In 1909 and 1910 they engaged in wide-ranging public discussions about the kind of political organization best suited to their needs. Some insisted that teachers ought to establish their own party, while others argued that they should try to achieve their goals by working through existing parties. Still another group favoured a thorough structural reform of the village as the best means of promoting social justice in the countryside.

At the national teachers congress in Bucharest in December 1913 the latter group won a substantial victory when it elected its candidate, Ion Mihalache, president of the Association of Teachers. Critical of the agrarian policies and the economic and social legislation of both the Liberals and Conservatives, he demanded reductions in the size of large estates, the distribution of land to those who tilled it, and the extension of full political rights to the peasants as a class, and, to ensure that these reforms would be carried out, he set about organizing a mass peasant party.[27] The outbreak of the First World War delayed his work. But the Partid Țărănesc, which he helped to found in 1918 and which he served as president, became the most important peasant party and the most democratic of all political parties in the interwar years.

At the end of the nineteenth century the urban working class entered organized political life with the founding of Partidul

[26] Philip G. Eidelberg, *The Great Rumanian Peasant Revolt of 1907* (Leiden, 1974), 140–4.

[27] Ion Scurtu, 'Contribuții privind mișcarea țărănistă din România în perioada 1907–1914', *Studii: revistă de istorie*, 21/3 (1968), 507.

Social-Democrat al Muncitorilor al României (The Social Democratic Party of Workers of Rumania). Its appearance was the result
both of the growth of industry and accompanying economic and
social changes and of the maturing of socialist thought, particularly of Marxism, and its application to Rumanian conditions
by a small number of committed intellectuals. But socialism as a
guide to development and social democracy as a political force
exerted only modest influence on public life during the period.[28]

The origins of socialism in Rumania may be traced back to the
decade before the Revolution of 1848 when Teodor Diamant
(1810–41), a member of the lesser nobility, and other intellectuals
became fascinated with the ideas of the French utopian socialist
Charles Fourier. Diamant met Fourier and became a devoted
follower during his studies in Paris in the 1830s. He was attracted
particularly to the idea that men could improve their moral and
material lives by combining their talents and labour in associations. When he returned home in 1834 he established at Scăieni,
north of Bucharest, a phalanstery of some sixty persons based upon
Fourier's principles, but his experiment in a model agricultural-
industrial community was terminated by the authorities in 1836.
None the less, a small number of intellectuals remained faithful to
the idea of association. It came to the fore again in 1848 under
various guises. Ion Heliade Rădulescu, who placed Fourier alongside Socrates and Martin Luther as a great social reformer, attempted to use the principle of association to harmonize the
interests of landlords and peasants. From another direction, C. A.
Rosetti, who admired Proudhon and Louis Blanc, contemplated
doing away with social inequality by eliminating large landed
estates and by reorganizing all labour on the basis of associations
and community workshops. Socialism of this type had little effect
outside narrow circles of intellectuals, in part because Rumanian
society was ill prepared to receive it and in part because its proponents failed to organize and transmit their convictions to others.

The influence of Marxian socialism among Rumanian intellectuals was at first even more modest than that of other forms.
Information about the circulation of Marx's works in Rumania is
imprecise, but it appears that *Deutsch-französische Jahrbücher* (1844)
and the Manifesto of the Communist Party (1848) (in German)

---

[28] For a survey of the Rumanian socialist and labour movement of the period,
see Keith Hitchins, 'Rumania', in Marcel van der Linden and Jürgen Rojahn (eds.),
The Formation of Labour Movements, 1870–1914, i (Leiden, 1990), 369–92.

had found their way to Bucharest shortly after publication, as had Engels's *Die Lage der arbeitenden Klasse in England* (1845). The First International, founded in 1864, and the Commune of Paris in 1870–1 seem to have stimulated an interest in Marx's ideas, but the evidence is sporadic. A few Rumanians, among them Zamfir Arbore, a journalist, and Vasile Conta, a materialist philosopher from Iaşi, were members of the International, and several newspapers in Bucharest gave prominent coverage to the rise and fall of the Commune. But the systematic reception of Marxism had to await the formation of the first socialist circles and the emergence of a working-class and socialist press in the late 1870s and 1880s.

The eclectic character of socialism began to change, and it became a cohesive set of ideas and a political movement directly related to social and economic realities in Rumania when socialists established regular links with one another and made the creation of a formal organization one of their major concerns. The earliest exponents of socialist ideas were university students at the faculties of law and medicine in Iaşi and Bucharest, who formed small discussion groups between 1875 and 1877.

The most dynamic elements of the fledgeling socialist movement were *émigrés* from Russia. Three in particular who left a strong impress on early Rumanian socialism arrived in Rumania in 1874–5: Nicolae Zubcu Codreanu (1852–78), Dr Russel (Nicolae K. Sudzilovski) (1850–1930), and Constantin Dobrogeanu-Gherea (1855–1920). All had been active in revolutionary movements in Russia and, forced to emigrate, had come to Rumania initially to organize the sending of illegal publications from the West into Russia. They soon made contact with local radical groups and began to organize socialist circles.[29]

These early socialist organizations were far from homogeneous. Their members represented a variety of occupations and ideologies, including anarchists and nihilists from Russia and Bessarabia and Rumanian students who had been influenced by various radical thinkers, especially Vasile Conta. But there were few among them with a knowledge of socialist theory and still fewer who were acquainted with Marx's writings. They were socialists by feeling rather than reflection. By far the dominant current was Populist,

---

[29] Gheorghe Haupt, *Din istoricul legăturilor revoluţionare romîno-ruse, 1849–1881* (Bucharest, 1955), 139–66, 226–47. This work reflects the ideological atmosphere of the mid-1950s and thus exaggerates Russian influence on the development of Rumanian socialism. For a corrective, see Z. Ornea, *Viaţa lui C. Dobrogeanu-Gherea* (Bucharest, 1982), 81–93, 179–223.

in the Russian sense of *narodnichestvo*, for Gherea and his colleagues had grown up in that revolutionary tradition. They regarded the peasantry as the main social force in an overwhelmingly agricultural country like Rumania and, hence, the main foundation of a revolutionary movement. Analysing agrarian conditions from the standpoint of class antagonisms, they were certain that the peasants could be roused to action by a systematic propaganda campaign in the villages directed by the newly formed socialist circles. They and their circles were nourished by a steady flow of *narodnik* books and newspapers from Russia. The works of the Russian revolutionary Nikolai G. Chernyshevsky were especially influential. But they were also acquainted with socialist movements in Western Europe. Gherea, for example, had read the works of Jules Guesde and Paul Lafargue and professed great admiration for Ferdinand Lassalle, whose writings, moreover, were immensely popular among university students and responsible for attracting many of them to socialism.

The socialist circles which were active in Bucharest, Iaşi, and the Danube port cities soon began to explore ways of co-ordinating their activities. A sign that they had achieved some degree of cohesion was the founding in Bucharest in 1877 of *Socialistul* (The Socialist), the first Rumanian socialist newspaper. Its disappearance after only four issues reveals another characteristic of the socialist movement—its chronic lack of funds. The leaders of the circles had by now concluded that an organized party independent of all other political parties was essential if they were to achieve their long-term goals, and in December 1877 Codreanu, Russel, and Gherea were ready to draw up statutes and a programme for a 'Societate Social-Democrată Română' (Rumanian Social-Democratic Society). But their work went slowly, apparently because of disagreements over tactics. Gherea, for example, thought that the socialists and their sympathizers were too few in number to be able to undertake a nation-wide organizing and propaganda campaign and recommended instead that they concentrate their efforts in Bucharest, where they could be certain of a large, sympathetic audience. Finally, fifteen delegates from socialist circles in Bucharest, Ploieşti, and Iaşi gathered in the latter city in October 1879 to discuss the future development of socialism in Rumania. At this first Rumanian socialist congress they debated the fundamental question whether conditions yet existed in Rumania for the organization and success of a revolutionary socialist party. In the end, a majority of the delegates answered in the affirmative and decided to expand their activities among both students and workers. They referred to their new organization as Partida Muncitorilor (The Party of Workers) or Partida Socialistă (The Socialist Party), but it lacked both the cohesion of a true party and a programme, undoubtedly because of continuing ideological differences within their ranks.

During the latter 1870s and early 1880s Marxism was only one of many 'socialisms' that competed for the adherence of the socialist circles. The eclectic nature of their thought is evident in Dr Russel's *Un studiu psihiatric urmat de cîteva comentarii asupra ideilor sănătoase* (1880; A Psychiatric Study Followed by a Few Commentaries on Healthy Ideas). On the one hand, he tended to equate socialism with altruism, placing Marx, Lassalle, Robert Owen, and Alexander Herzen on the same level, but, on the other hand, he urged his fellow socialists to spare no effort to organize the masses and prepare them for the seizure of power from the 'capitalist minority', without, however, shedding blood.[30] Yet, by 1883–4 it was evident that Marxism had won the adherence of numerous Rumanian socialists. In 1883 Gherea published his article, 'Răspuns domnului Prim-ministru I. C. Brătianu' (A Reply to Prime Minister I. C. Brătianu), in which he developed his ideas about the importance of collective property as a basic factor in bringing about change in traditional society, and Anton Bacalbaşa, a prolific socialist journalist, published his article, 'Capital', the first systematic attempt in Rumania to explain the contents of *Das Kapital*. The appearance of *Revista socială* (The Social Review) in 1884 as the organ of the socialist circle in Iaşi confirmed that Rumanian socialism had placed itself more firmly on a Marxist foundation. Its editor, Ioan Nădejde (1854–1928), set as its principal goal the dissemination of Marxism, and in the three years of its existence the review published a number of fundamental pieces, including Gherea's 'Karl Marx şi economiştii noştri' (1884; Karl Marx and Our Economists), the most important work of the period on Marxian economic principles.

Gherea's *Ce vor socialiştii români?* (1885–6; What Do Rumanian Socialists Want?), the first systematic programme for Rumanian socialism, signified the growing influence of Marxism among Rumanian socialists. This critical analysis of Rumanian society, subtitled, 'an exposition of scientific socialism', marked Gherea's own conversion from *narodnik* theories to Marxism, a process

[30] Dr Russel, *Un studiu psihiatric* (Iaşi, 1880), 17, 20, 31–2.

which had begun about a decade earlier, when he first became acquainted with Marx's writings. In 1885, feeling confident of his knowledge of Rumanian social and economic conditions and armed with Marxian tools of analysis, he had no hesitation in predicting the development of industry and of a proletariat in Rumania similar to that of the economically advanced countries of Western Europe. The main function of the Rumanian socialist party, as he saw it, was to hurry this process along by raising the political consciousness of the working masses and by democratizing public life. The immediate tasks of socialists, he urged, were, first, to intensify the dissemination of scientific socialism in order to prepare men's minds for the coming transformation of society, and, second, to change the situation of men by modifying the material conditions of their existence.[31] To accomplish these tasks he stressed the need to introduce general democratic political reforms such as universal suffrage, full freedom of the press, assembly, and association, free compulsory education, the election of judges by the people and justice for all without cost, and equality for women. He also proposed to hasten the transition from a feudal, 'neoserf' economy to modern capitalist forms by transferring the properties of the state and of large landowners to peasant communes and by providing credit to both peasants and urban workers in co-operatives or other associations to carry on their economic activities more profitably. This formulation of short-term, practical goals greatly influenced Rumanian socialists in the last decade of the century and lay at the heart of the programme adopted by the socialist party in 1893. Gherea's analysis of where Rumanian society was headed is significant also because for the first time in Rumania he set forth the thesis of the dictatorship of the proletariat as a necessary means of bringing a socialist society into being. But, clearly, by his own reckoning, neither was imminent.

The socialists intensified their political activities in the latter 1880s and early 1890s as they strove to achieve greater organizational cohesion and bring their ideas before a wider audience. They were particularly eager to draw closer to the working class and in 1890 founded Clubul Muncitorilor (The Workers' Club) in Iaşi with the support of members of the railway, metallurgy, and printing unions. They intended it to serve as the nucleus around which a strong workers' party would eventually coalesce, making

[31] Constantin Dobrogeanu-Gherea, Opere complete, ii (Bucharest, 1976), 60–71.

it the centre of socialism in Rumania and the vehicle for establishing permanent relations with workers' parties in other countries. A measure of their success was the election of the first two socialist members of parliament, Ioan Nădejde and Vasile G. Morţun, in 1888.

The organizational activities of the socialists culminated in the founding of the Social Democratic Party in Bucharest in 1893. The delegates to this first party congress, adhering to Gherea's earlier elaborations of Marxist theory, accepted the crucial role of the proletariat in transforming Rumanian society and urged that the industrialization of the country proceed as rapidly as possible. They also recognized the importance of agriculture and proposed a solution to the agrarian problem which called for the division of large properties among the peasants and support for peasant co-operatives, but their concern at this point was mainly with the poor peasantry, or the agricultural proletariat, as they called it, rather than with the independent peasant producer.[32] Moreover, they regarded agriculture and the peasantry as of secondary importance in bringing about social change. As for other political parties, they left the door open for limited co-operation. Although they branded all 'bourgeois' parties as hostile to the working class, they made a distinction between 'reactionary' parties and those that were 'more or less progressive'.

Despite a promising beginning, the party did not prosper. Although its membership as a whole reached 6,000 in 1897 and that of the workers' club of Bucharest grew from 575 in 1895 to 1,315 in 1897, the number of new clubs and the increase in membership, especially outside Bucharest, fell short of expectations. In the parliamentary elections of 1891, 1892, and 1895 the party elected only one deputy, Morţun, from Roman, a small city in Moldavia, and in 1899 it failed to elect any. The situation in which the party found itself led to a crisis of confidence within the leadership. The majority came to the conclusion that the prospects for the achievement of socialism in Rumania in the foreseeable future were nil, because of economic and social underdevelopment, particularly the slow pace of industrialization and the small size of the proletariat. They were intellectuals from middle-class backgrounds who favoured a gradualist approach to social change. Ioan Nădejde, a leader of the party since his membership in the socialist

---

[32] *Documente din istoria mişcării muncitoreşti din România, 1893—1900* (Bucharest, 1969), 59—60.

circle at the University of Iaşi in the late 1870s and the respected editor of the party's newspaper, *Lumea nouă* (The New World) since 1894, urged his colleagues to remain within the bounds of legality and avoid violence. A resort to revolution, he argued, would do great harm to the cause of socialism at a time when it needed to attract as many supporters as possible and to create the proper atmosphere for the installation of a 'bourgeois-capitalist' regime in Rumania, which he thought essential for the advance to socialism. Their task, in his view, was to hasten the advent of the bourgeois capitalist state by supporting full civil and political rights for all citizens rather than a revolution before its time. Nădejde and his colleagues even considered a temporary alliance with the Liberal Party.

A minority within the party leadership claimed to speak on behalf of the workers. They emphasized class struggle and objected to co-operation with the National Liberal Party and other bourgeois parties, urging, instead, strikes, street demonstrations, and other forceful means to achieve their goals. They were, however, continually outvoted by the moderates.

These differences grew and led to the resignation of Ioan Nădejde and a number of other middle-class intellectuals from the party in 1899. These were the *generoşi*, who in 1900 joined the Liberal Party, where they intended to work for the democratization of the country as a necessary precondition for the creation of a viable socialist party. A few leaders along with their supporters, mainly from the workers' club of Bucharest, decided to carry on as socialists under the name, Partidul Muncitorilor (The Party of Workers). Gherea, who had avoided becoming enmeshed in the controversy, remained the chief theoretician of Rumanian socialism.

During the next decade the recovery of the socialists and of the small number of trade unions associated with them was slow and sometimes discouraging. In 1905 Partidul Muncitorilor revived the socialists' national organ, *România muncitoare* (Working Rumania), and in 1907 helped to found Comisia Generală a Sindicatelor (The General Commission of Trade Unions), the first nation-wide trade union organization. But efforts to merge party and trade unions into a single organization, Uniunea Socialistă (The Socialist Union), were unsuccessful. Many socialists and workers wanted a separate labour organization in order to shield workers from government reprisals for engaging in political activities.

Fully engaged in the struggle to create a strong socialist and labour movement was Bulgarian-born Cristian Racovski (1873–1941), who between 1907 and the Russian Revolution of 1917 held high office in the Socialist Union and the Social Democratic Party. He was a skilled polemicist and was deeply involved in the debate over Rumania's future course of development. Although Gherea was recognized as the paramount theorist of Rumanian socialism, Racovski's analyses of the critical issues facing Rumanian Social Democracy from agrarianism to national self-determination yielded nothing in originality and sophistication to the works of his older colleague. Well travelled and with extensive contacts in Europe, Racovski was not only the chief link between Rumanian socialists and the international socialist movement, but also made significant contributions to Marxist theory, especially in his writings on the national emancipation of the Balkan peoples in conditions of economic backwardness and dependence on the great powers.

Only in 1910 did a cohesive socialist party reappear. A party congress, convoked ostensibly to consider the ramifications of the so-called Orleanu Law, which the Liberal government had passed in 1909 forbidding workers in government enterprises, including the railways, to belong to trade unions, decided to establish a new party under the name Partidul Social Democrat (Social Democratic Party), and reaffirmed its revolutionary character. They adopted a minimum programme whose main objective was to achieve universal suffrage and other reforms necessary to bring about the 'bourgeois-democratic transformation' of the country. They had little success. The trade union movement remained weak, and worker class-consciousness was fragile. Although the number of organized workers reached a high of 9,700 in 1912, they represented only a small fraction of the workers engaged in industry and transportation. In politics the party continued to be beset by a lack of funds and by apathy in many local political clubs, where members stirred themselves only at election time. 'Parliamentary struggle' brought few successes. Between 1899 and the First World War the socialists were unrepresented in parliament. In the elections of 1911, for example, the party ran eight candidates for the Chamber of Deputies on a platform calling for universal suffrage, a graduated income tax, and social security for workers. It sought votes not only from workers, but also from all who had grievances against the existing economic and political system. Yet, the party attracted few voters and failed to elect any of its candidates, obtaining only 1,459 votes out of a total of 73,633 cast.

The influence exerted by the socialists on Rumanian political life before the First World War was clearly modest. Under the prevailing party system, which favoured wealth, they could not compete with the Liberals and Conservatives. They had neither the organization nor the resources nor the voters needed to mount a successful challenge to these entrenched parties. The lack of socialist and trade union representation in parliament is striking evidence of their failure. But they were successful in other ways. The socialists obliged Liberal and Conservative politicians and a wider public to recognize that alongside the agrarian crisis their country also faced a growing industrial and labour problem as it assumed modern economic and social forms. Undoubtedly, their revelations of misery among the working class and their campaign for reform in the press and through strikes and public demonstrations were responsible at least to some degree for the enactment of legislation beneficial to the workers. Yet the passage of these bills and their provisions depended primarily upon the calculations of Liberals and Conservatives, who controlled parliament. Their primary interest in reform lay in making the existing economic and political order work more smoothly.

Perhaps the chief obstacle to the success of the socialist and trade union movements was tradition. A majority of Rumanians viewed socialism as harmful or at the very least inappropriate to their circumstances. Conceiving of Rumania as a 'pre-eminently agricultural' country, they rejected capitalism as a model of development. Even those who accepted the inevitability of Rumania's passing through a capitalist phase of development preferred the Western liberal tradition to socialist collectivism. While many intellectuals and others may thus have thought of socialism as an 'exotic plant', they were obliged in their polemics with the socialists to confront hard issues of economic development and the obvious social consequences of industrialization. The persistence of tradition limited the appeal of socialism among other classes also. The peasantry associated it with collective property and atheism, which threatened their sense of community. The suspicions thus aroused lingered among those peasants who migrated to the cities, thus making their recruitment into trade unions difficult. Yet, despite all these impediments and failures, the socialists and their allies in the trade union movement brought into being an organization which alone among political parties was fully committed to the interests of the urban working class.

The Conservative coalition government formed in the autumn of 1912 left office at the end of 1913. Rumania's military and diplomatic successes in the Balkan Wars, confirmed by the Treaty of Bucharest,[33] led Titu Maiorescu and Take Ionescu to conclude that the tasks for which their government had been formed had been accomplished and that the time had come to leave office. Aware of deep divisions among their fellow Conservatives, they were convinced that the government they had headed could not deal effectively with the two pressing domestic issues which the Liberals had brought to the fore—universal suffrage and agrarian reform. Maiorescu resigned on 31 December 1913, and the king chose Ionel Brătianu to head a new, Liberal government on 4 January 1914. The elections in early February resulted, as usual, in a victory for the government party.

The Liberals lost no time in presenting their reforms to the new parliament, and despite bitter denunciations from such diehard Conservatives as Petre Carp, by April both houses had approved a revision of the constitution, which was a necessary preliminary to the expropriation of the privately owned land to be offered to the peasants and to the enactment of universal suffrage. Elections in May for a Constituent Assembly produced a large majority in favour of both reforms. But the outbreak of the First World War in July forced the assembly to postpone action, and they were not taken up again until 1917, when the fate of the country hung in the balance.

FOREIGN POLICY

Experiences during the War for Independence and at the Congress of Berlin had impressed upon King Charles and politicians the dangers of pursuing foreign policy goals that lacked the patronage of one or more of the great powers. They were convinced that only adherence to an alliance system could further the country's foreign policy interests and offer protection from dangerous external pressures. Their decision to link their country to one of the great powers came only gradually. The creation of the Three Emperors' League in Berlin on 18 June 1881 played an important part in their calculations because it signalled an end to the relatively independent foreign policy they had been able to pursue since the reign of Alexandru Cuza. Under its terms Austria-Hungary and Russia agreed to temper their rivalries in South-eastern Europe

---

[33] See below, p. 153.

and to conduct their policies in such a way as to avoid disturbing the status quo. Although Rumanian officials did not know the provisions of the treaty, they realized that it would no longer be possible to take advantage of the differences between Austria and Russia and that the time for making binding commitments was thus at hand.

As the king and Brătianu examined the choices for a strong, durable alliance, they found one partner after another unsatisfactory. Rumania's small neighbours offered the possibility of a regional alliance, since their interests were, in general, similar. But Bulgaria was weak and could provide no effective help in an international confrontation. Besides, she had entered the Russian sphere of influence. Serbia, with whom Rumania had long had friendly relations, was also weak and, in any case, had attached herself to Austria-Hungary by treaty in 1881. Among the great powers, France was certainly the sentimental favourite of public opinion. French literature and culture enjoyed enormous prestige, and many Rumanian political leaders had studied in France. But the attitude of the French government toward Rumania at the Congress of Berlin and in the years immediately following had diminished enthusiasm for her. France had been one of the last powers to recognize Rumania's independence, and her commercial relations with Rumania were relatively modest. Even her financial markets remained closed to Rumania, French investors preferring to make loans through German banks. Perhaps decisive for the Rumanians was their perception of France as diplomatically isolated and, hence, unable to bring significant advantages to an alliance. Rumanian politicians, especially the Liberals, and the public generally considered Russia an enemy and therefore hardly a serious candidate for an alliance. But they found in the Triple Alliance of Germany, Austria-Hungary, and Italy the political and economic advantages they sought. The main attraction for them was, without question, Germany. Despite the bitterness left over from the Congress of Berlin when Germany had insisted that independence be conditional upon the grant of civil equality to Jews, both Liberals and Conservatives favoured an alliance because of her military strength and dynamic economy.

Rumania was already closely linked to the Triple Alliance economically. She sent large quantities of grain and animals to Central Europe and had become a valued customer for manufactured goods, especially from Austria-Hungary, while the German financial market had become an important source of loans for Rumania.

Liberal commercial and industrial groups, who were eager to develop and diversify the country's economy, and Conservative large agricultural producers, who sought to expand their markets, favoured closer ties with Germany and Austria-Hungary. The king's support also weighed heavily in the balance. Besides a sentimental attachment to Germany, he was convinced that the alliance would enhance Rumania's international standing and enable her more easily to achieve her foreign policy objectives in South-eastern Europe.

The possibility of an alliance with Austria-Hungary aroused considerable misgivings. Relations between the two countries after the Congress of Berlin had been severely tested by profound economic and political differences. The full effects of the commercial convention of 1875 were now being felt in Rumania. Tariff concessions had resulted in the tripling of Austro-Hungarian exports between 1876 and 1881 and a flooding of the Rumanian market with manufactures of all kinds, especially textiles and metal products. At the same time Austria-Hungary maintained first place as an importer of Rumanian goods, notably grain and cattle. Although large landowners and merchants found the arrangement eminently satisfactory, Liberal politicians and industrialists, who were anxious to build an independent national economy, and artisans, who up to this time had produced the bulk of consumer goods for the mass of the population and were now suffering high unemployment, demanded protection from the mounting flow of imports. The Rumanian government itself complained that its trading partner had not observed all the stipulations of the commercial convention, for, with the exception of the tariff-free importation of grain, Austria-Hungary had arbitrarily restricted the entry of Rumanian cattle and pigs and had gradually raised the tariff on almost all other goods.[34]

The control of navigation on the lower Danube also brought the two countries into conflict.[35] By recognizing the independence of Rumania and Serbia and the autonomy of Bulgaria, the Congress of Berlin had ended Ottoman authority over that stretch of the river which flowed along the borders of the three countries

---

[34] Hilde Mureşan, 'Date cu privire la restricţele comerciale faţă de România, impuse de guvernul austro-ungar în anii 1878—1879', *Anuarul Institutului de Istorie din Cluj*, ii (1968), 291—305.

[35] G. N. Căzan, 'La question du Danube et les relations roumano-austro-hongroises dans les années 1878—1883', *Revue roumaine d'histoire*, 18/1 (1979), 43—61.

and, at least nominally, transformed it into an international water-
way. Rumania thus gained sovereign rights to navigation and
commerce on the river and became a member of the European
Commission of the Danube, a body based in Galaţi and established in 1856 to regulate use of the river. In the spring and
summer of 1880 Austria-Hungary drafted new regulations for
navigation on the lower Danube which would in effect have given
her the decisive voice in the matter and have forced the small
riverine states to turn their trade in her direction. The vehicle for
this predominance was to be the Mixed Commission, with the
Austro-Hungarian delegate as chairman, having authority over
navigation between the Iron Gates and Galaţi. The Rumanian
government felt obliged to accept this arrangement in principle,
but insisted that all decisions by the new commission be reached
unanimously, a device to protect small states from dominance by
the great powers.

Just at this time relations between the two countries reached a
low point. The bitterness felt on the Rumanian side by Austria's
prohibitions against the importation of cattle and by her aggressive
Danube policy was vented in King Charles's address from the
throne at the opening of parliament on 27 November 1881. The
new Austro-Hungarian Foreign Minister, Count Gustav Kálnoky,
took offence at these remarks and on 2 December instructed his
minister in Bucharest to avoid all personal contacts with the
Rumanian government and limit his activities to routine, current
matters. After several weeks of tense expectation, the Rumanian
government, convinced that Kálnoky was in no mood to compromise, instructed its minister in Vienna to apologize. It appears
that Kálnoky had been concerned not just with the offending
statements by the king, but wanted to use the occasion to serve
notice that Austria-Hungary would not put up with demonstrations of self-importance from a minor state.

The situation of the Rumanians of Hungary had not yet become
a critical issue in Austro-Hungarian-Rumanian relations, but it
was on the minds of statesmen in both countries. Through the
newspaper press, particularly, the 'Rumanian question in Transylvania' was gradually intruding upon the public consciousness
in Rumania and was becoming a weapon in domestic political
struggles as one party used it to embarrass the other. For example,
in 1881 and 1882 the Conservative organ, *Timpul*, published
numerous articles on the measures taken by the Hungarian government to limit the political and cultural activities of the Rumanians

with the clear implication that the Brătianu government was ignoring the plight of fellow Rumanians.

The London Conference on the Danube of February and March 1883 did nothing to assuage Rumanian fears about Austria-Hungary's aggressive intentions. The Treaty of London of 10 March in effect endorsed the earlier Austrian project, which would allow the Mixed Commission to make decisions about navigation and commerce in Rumania's territorial waters without her consent. These provisions were never put into effect because on 15 September Austria-Hungary dropped her demands in order to smooth the way for the conclusion of the treaty of alliance with Rumania. Austro-Hungarian officials were willing to set aside the offending project because they were certain that this alliance would guarantee the maintenance of the monarchy's position on the lower Danube. The signing of the treaty in 1883 brought the matter effectively to an end, and subsequent attempts by Austria-Hungary to revive the Mixed Commission were unsuccessful.

The adherence of Rumania to the Triple Alliance owed much to the initiative of Bismarck. Although German–Rumanian relations in the aftermath of the Congress of Berlin were hardly warm, Bismarck recognized that an independent Rumania could become a useful force in South-eastern European affairs. He told the Rumanian finance minister, Dimitrie Sturdza, during his visit to Berlin in July 1879 that he wanted Rumania to be an active element in German foreign policy and thought she had every reason to seek close ties with Germany in order to prevent Russian expansion in the region. Bismarck's primary objective in gaining Rumania for his political system seems to have been to strengthen Austria-Hungary's position in the Balkans and in this way to lighten some of the burdens that Germany had assumed under the Dual Alliance.[36] But Austria-Hungary did not make his task an easy one, and in October 1880 he complained that her policies led to one dispute after another with the small countries of the region, thus thwarting his own efforts to remove them from Russian influence.

Rumania's adherence to the Dual Alliance was also discussed by Bismarck and Brătianu in Berlin in March 1880. The Rumanian prime minister expressed interest in a treaty with Germany, but Bismarck chose not to go into specifics. He suggested, instead, that if Rumania could first reach an accord with Austria-Hungary,

---

[36] Ernst Ebel, *Rumänien und die Mittelmächte* (Berlin, 1939), 25–8.

then she would also find the desired link to Germany. At about the same time the Austro-Hungarian Foreign Minister, Heinrich von Haymerle, encouraged King Charles to seek an arrangement within the framework of the Dual Alliance. He thought that the fundamental interests of their two countries were 'identical', by which he meant their need to create a barrier to the 'Slavicizing' of Eastern Europe under the aegis of Russia. None the less, strained relations over trade and the Danube stood in the way of a *rapprochement.*

Bismarck took the initiative in reviving negotiations with Rumania in August 1883, when on a visit to Vienna he raised the question whether it would be useful and possible to extend the 'league of peace' with Italy to Eastern Europe in order to 'guide' the policies of Rumania and, eventually, Serbia in a 'desirable direction'. (Italy had adhered to the German-Austro-Hungarian alliance in 1882, making it a Triple Alliance.) Bismarck chose this moment because of concern with the growing tension between Russia and Austria-Hungary in the Balkans over Bulgaria. Kálnoky was amenable to negotiations and agreed to Bismarck's proposal that he, Bismarck, prepare the general political ground with the Rumanians, while he himself took responsibility for settling the Danube question and for drafting a treaty of alliance.

A final agreement was reached in the autumn. On 7 September Bismarck and Brătianu met at Gastein.[37] Although Bismarck could not overcome his lingering distrust of Brătianu because of the latter's radical past and nationalist sentiments, on this occasion he warmly supported Rumania's alliance with the Central Powers. He viewed the matter from a general European perspective. By strengthening Austria's position in the East and thereby diminishing the likelihood of war with Russia, a treaty with Rumania would, he thought, enhance the prospects for European peace and stability. Kálnoky and Brătianu quickly produced the draft of a treaty in subsequent negotiations in Vienna between 23 and 27 September. Brătianu, who knew of Bismarck's desire for an accommodation with Russia, was particularly eager to conclude matters before the Central Powers had time to reach a new agreement with the tsar. For him (and other Rumanian leaders), the primary objective of the treaty was protection against Russia, but

---

[37] G. I. Brătianu, 'Bismarck şi Ion C. Brătianu', *Revista istorică română*, 5–6 (1935–6), 95–101; *Die Grosse Politik der Europäischen Kabinette 1871–1914*, iii (Berlin, 1922), 265–9: Bismarck to Reuss, German ambassador in Vienna, 8 and 15 Sept. 1883.

Bismarck had made it clear that the alliance would be a purely defensive one and could not be used as a cover for aggressive action against Russia.

Rumania's adherence to the Triple Alliance took the form of a bilateral treaty, dated 30 October 1883, with Austria-Hungary. The new allies agreed to come to the aid of the other if it was attacked by Russia, although the latter was not named, and they promised not to join any alliance directed against one of them. Germany adhered to the agreement on the same day by a separate act. King Charles and Brătianu insisted that the arrangement be kept secret because they knew that it would raise a storm of protest among politicians and the public, who were overwhelmingly pro-French. Thus, for good reason, the treaty was never submitted to parliament for discussion or ratification, and, hence, the execution of its provisions depended solely upon the king.

Both sides benefited from the treaty. The advantages for Austria-Hungary lay primarily in the increased security it offered on her southern and eastern frontiers. Kálnoky was confident that a united front with Germany and Rumania would deter Russia from seeking a confrontation over the two countries' conflicting interests in the Balkans. He also expected the new relationship with Rumania to diminish tension in Transylvania between the Hungarian government and the Rumanians. Although Brătianu had refused to condemn 'irredentist agitation' in the treaty, Kálnoky was certain that the Rumanian government would not allow itself to be drawn into activities that challenged the existing political system in Hungary. Austria's further economic penetration of Rumania also seemed assured through closer foreign policy co-operation between the two countries. The advantages of the treaty for Rumania were even more substantial. She achieved her main objective—an alliance with Germany, albeit indirect, and a lessening of the danger of war with Russia—and settled several outstanding differences with Austria-Hungary, notably the Danube question.

The evidence is abundant that both Austria-Hungary and Rumania valued the arrangement, despite a lack of warmth in their relations. The Rumanian government agreed to regular renewals of the treaty, and Austria-Hungary was represented in Bucharest by diplomats of the first rank, including Agenor Goluchowski (minister to Rumania, 1887−93, and Austro-Hungarian Foreign Minister, 1895−1906), Alois Aehrenthal (minister to Rumania, 1895−98, and Foreign Minister, 1906−12).

and Ottokar Czernin (minister to Rumania, 1913-16, and Foreign Minister, 1916-18). The weak link in the alliance was Rumania. Austro-Hungarian diplomats acknowledged that there was no genuine sympathy for their country in Rumania. Kálnoky had no illusions on this score, for King Charles himself had made this sentiment clear when he declared that he would not approve the treaty unless Germany was a party to it. Another significant weakness of the treaty was the secrecy which all the parties to it agreed to observe. It thus could not fulfil its main purpose—to serve as a deterrent to a Russian attack against the Central Powers and Rumania.

The alliance with the Central Powers nevertheless formed the cornerstone of Rumania's foreign policy for thirty years because the king and a handful of Liberal and Conservative politicians perceived the Central Powers to be the strongest military and economic force in Europe. But they watched closely for changes in the political atmosphere of Europe and in the balance between competing alliance systems. They were especially sensitive to any changes in the relationship between Germany and Austria-Hungary. With Germany they felt a close community of interests and were constantly troubled by the prospects of Austria-Hungary's snatching leadership of the Triple Alliance from her. The Rumanians also followed closely the evolution of the Franco-Russian alliance after 1891 and the *rapprochement* between Britain and France signalled by the Entente Cordiale of 1904.

Relations between Austria-Hungary and Rumania between 1883 and 1914 served as an accurate measure of the health of the Triple Alliance in South-eastern Europe. They were anything but smooth. Within two years of the signing of the treaty negotiations began for a renewal of the commercial convention of 1875. It proved impossible to reconcile Rumania's aspirations to achieve some measure of economic independence and to shelter her fledgeling industry from foreign competition, on the one hand, and the desire of Austria-Hungary to hold on to positions already gained and to protect her agricultural producers from Rumanian grain and cattle, on the other. The result was a bitter tariff war, which began on 1 June 1886, the day when the ten-year commercial convention expired.[38] Rumania introduced a new tariff which was designed to protect native industry and agriculture

[38] Gheorghe Cristea, 'Antecedente şi consecinţe ale războiului vamal cu Austro-Ungaria', *Studii şi materiale de istorie modernă*, 6 (1979), 91-137.

(export duties on almost all agricultural products were eliminated) and to serve as a basis for renewed negotiations with Austria-Hungary. The latter responded with restrictions of her own against Rumanian imports (all goods were subject to regular customs duties and a 30 per cent surtax; even higher duties were imposed on the main Rumanian exports, grain and cattle; and the importation of vegetables and fruit and the transit of animals was forbidden). The purpose of these drastic measures was to inflict such great economic damage on Rumania's economy that she would be forced to accept Austrian terms for a new trade treaty. Although Rumanian exports of grain and animals to Austria-Hungary were sharply reduced (grain from an annual average of 3,563,000 lei in 1876–86 to 93,000 lei in 1887–91; pigs, 7,344,000 lei to 629,000 lei) and caused temporary hardship, Austria-Hungary was the real loser. Gone were valuable markets and important sources of raw materials. Rumanian agriculture found new markets (Britain replaced Austria-Hungary as the chief importer of Rumanian grain), and Rumanian industry, supported by a new law to encourage a variety of enterprises, experienced accelerated growth. In 1891 a break in the tariff war finally came. Almost all of Rumania's commercial treaties with foreign countries expired in that year, and she was obliged to introduce lower tariffs on all imported goods, including those from Austria-Hungary. The latter responded with lower tariffs on Rumanian goods, and trade between the two countries gradually increased. Finally, in December 1893 they signed a new commercial agreement which allowed Austria–Hungary to recover most of her old markets and enabled Rumania to resume exports of grain and cattle to her neighbour, though on somewhat less favourable terms than before 1886. Perhaps the most enduring result of the tariff war was political: it reinforced the underlying hostility the majority of Rumanians felt for Austria-Hungary and thus diminished further the prospects for co-operation in foreign affairs.

Rumania's adherence to the Triple Alliance came up for renewal at a time when the ill-feeling engendered by the tariff war was still fresh. There were other difficulties as well. The Conservatives were in power in 1891, and none of their leaders had been informed of the treaty. Charles expected no co-operation from Prime Minister Lascăr Catargiu and Foreign Minister Alexandru Lahovary, who were known to favour a foreign policy of non-alignment. Rather than initiate them into the secret, the king preferred to wait until the Liberals could be brought back. Another impediment to a speedy renewal of the treaty was the increasingly difficult situation of the Rumanians of Transylvania. The magyar- ization policy pursued by the Hungarian government had put Charles in a difficult position, for hostility to Austria-Hungary over the 'nationality question' was rising among the general public and had become a frequent subject of debate in the parliament. It caused misgivings about the future of the alliance in Vienna and Berlin, too. Kálnoky had begun to doubt that Rumania would ever support the Central Powers militarily and thought the best they could hope for would be Rumania's neutrality if war broke out in Eastern Europe. The German Chancellor Leo von Caprivi wondered if even that would be possible in view of widespread Rumanian hostility to Hungary's nationality policy. Still another problem for the alliance was the Franco-Russian convention of August 1891. It encouraged Rumanian Francophiles to hope for a more active French involvement in Eastern European affairs and to see in her *rapprochement* with Russia an alternative to the Triple Alliance. But such expectations were premature. France continued to show little interest in Rumanian affairs, and her supporters in Bucharest could not overcome the ingrained fear of Russia, which made the Triple Alliance so attractive to both Conservative and Liberal policy-makers. A number of Rumanian leaders even thought that France had sacrificed Rumania's interests and would abandon the entire Balkan peninsula to Russia in order to gain the latter's backing for a war of revenge against Germany.[39]

A break in the stalemate over the renewal of the treaty with the Triple Alliance came in October 1891. Charles finally gained the support of influential Conservatives, including Catargiu and Lahovary, for the alliance and could thus bring negotiations for the treaty renewal to a speedy conclusion. Although he was the driving force on the Rumanian side for the maintenance of the alliance with the Central Powers, he had made it clear during the negotiations that he did not regard the treaty as a bilateral agreement between Rumania and Austria-Hungary, to which Germany adhered as merely a benevolent onlooker. He pointed out that the treaty had value for Rumania only because of Germany's active participation in the alliance, and he warned that no Rumanian statesman could support such a treaty under any other conditions.[40]

[39] *Die Grosse Politik*, vii (Berlin, 1923), 167: Bülow to Caprivi, 11 Aug. 1891.
[40] Ibid. 179–80: Bülow to Caprivi, 8 June 1892.

Rumania's ties with the Triple Alliance were unexpectedly strengthened by events in the Balkans a few years later. In 1895 the treaty between Austria-Hungary and Serbia expired, and the latter turned to Russia, much to the distress of Rumanian leaders. Bulgaria's ambitions in Macedonia to fulfil the ever-present dream in Sofia of a Greater Bulgaria and a warming of relations with Russia were a constant source of unease in Bucharest. Under the circumstances, Charles and those politicians who knew of the treaty were satisfied that they had chosen the right course. The alliance with Rumania also took on added importance for Austria-Hungary with the defection of Serbia. Both sides were thus in a mood to make their commitments to each other firmer and in 1896 decided to extend their treaty of alliance until 1903.

When the time for another renewal drew near, the Liberal prime minister, Dimitrie Sturdza, proposed in April 1901 that the method of Rumania's adherence to the Triple Alliance be changed. He and other Rumanian supporters of the alliance wanted to have direct treaties with each of its members, in effect, turning the Triple into a Quadruple Alliance. They sought, first, to gain equal standing for Rumania and, second, to assure themselves of full German backing against Russia and, if need be, against Bulgarian expansion south of the Danube, for they had serious doubts about the military capabilities of Austria-Hungary. The latter was agreeable to the Rumanian proposal, for there was concern in Vienna that the Rumanians might decide that more could be gained by effecting a *rapprochement* with Russia. German officials, however, rejected the Rumanian proposal in order to avoid offending Russia and becoming involved in Rumanian or Austro-Hungarian initiatives in the Balkans. Mainly because of their firmness, the treaty was renewed for five years on 17 April 1902 without significant change.

A new element now thrust itself between Rumania and the Central Powers—an aggressive Bulgaria, whose territorial ambitions, in Rumanian eyes, threatened to upset the balance of power among the states of South-eastern Europe. Rumanian anxiety rose to the surface in 1908 when Bulgaria declared independence and a war with Turkey seemed likely. The Rumanian government demanded compensation, since it expected large increases in territory for Bulgaria as a result of the war. Charles and his advisers, aware of how strong Bulgaria was militarily and how deficient in equipment and manpower their own army was, were not eager for war, but they were determined to maintain the status quo in the Balkans as the best hope of preserving Rumania's regional predominance. With this aim in mind Charles rejected overtures from both Turkey and Bulgaria for an alliance because he was certain that Rumanian support would merely encourage its new ally to launch an attack. None the less, if war did break out and the expansion of Bulgaria could not be prevented, he was determined to obtain territory in Dobrudja as compensation—specifically, a new frontier between Silistria and Varna or Rustchuk and Varna.

Charles and leading politicians were dismayed by Austria-Hungary's diplomatic manœuvrings in the Balkans. They were especially upset by their ally's refusal to support Rumania's territorial claims in Dobrudja, which they interpreted as a tilt toward Bulgaria. Austro-Hungarian diplomats were indeed eager to gain Bulgaria's adherence to the Triple Alliance as a counterweight to a hostile Serbia in the Balkans, and they tried to convince Rumanian leaders that it was in their own best interest to keep Bulgaria out of the Russian fold. But their explanations had little effect in Bucharest.

The selection of Ionel Brătianu as Prime Minister at the head of a Liberal government in January 1909 was viewed with some misgivings in Vienna and Berlin. He was less committed to the Central Powers than Liberals of the older generation like Dimitrie Sturdza. Nor did the Russian danger seem so great to him, probably because he had not experienced the crisis of 1877–8. He had made no secret of his sympathy for France, which, moreover, caused him to overestimate the strength of France's army and to doubt Germany's widely acknowledged military superiority. Yet, he was impressed by the close co-operation between Austria-Hungary and Germany and the smoothness with which the former had mobilized during the Bosnian annexation crisis in 1908.[41] Despite his leanings toward the West, then, he had no intention of abandoning the Triple Alliance, but, instead, sought the support of Rumania's treaty partners for a favourable solution of the 'Bulgarian problem'.

On a trip to Austria and Germany in the summer of 1909 Brătianu raised the question of compensation if Bulgaria gained territory in a war against Turkey. In Vienna Foreign Minister Aehrenthal urged him to seek a direct accord with Bulgaria,

---

[41] *Österreich-Ungarns Aussenpolitik von der Bosnischen Krise 1908 bis zum Kriegsausbruch 1914*, ii (Vienna, 1930), 345: Report from Bucharest, 28 May 1909.

and, if that failed, to await a general peace conference to settle Rumania's claims. He reminded Brătianu that aid in obtaining territorial compensation from Bulgaria fell outside the framework of the alliance with Rumania, but he promised that Austria-Hungary would represent Rumania's interests at all stages of the Eastern Question and would loyally fulfil all her treaty obligations. In Berlin Chancellor Bethmann-Hollweg informed Brătianu that it was premature to talk of compensation, but he expressed sympathy for Rumania's position. Brătianu thus returned home confident that both Austria-Hungary and Germany would support Rumania by diplomatic means, but now he could have no illusions that they would join her in hostilities against Bulgaria.

The status of the Rumanians in Transylvania was a growing cause of tension between Rumania and Austria-Hungary. Although Brătianu thought that Balkan problems were for the moment the most urgent, he wanted to keep the Rumanian question in Transylvania before the great powers for the time when it would be a useful bargaining tool. During his visit to Vienna and Berlin in order to gain support for his compensation policy in the Balkans he alluded to Russia's offer of Transylvania as an inducement to join the Franco-Russian Entente. Neither his German nor his Austrian hosts took the gambit seriously, but they were made uneasy by the obvious effects of Hungary's nationality policy on King Charles's commitment to the alliance. Charles had repeatedly warned officials in Berlin and Vienna that the Hungarian government's policy of assimilation was undermining what modest support there was for the Triple Alliance in Rumania. For a time after the signing of the treaty in 1883 he had thought that Hungarian politicians would see the wisdom of moderating their policy, but after the trial and imprisonment of the leaders of the Rumanian National Party in the early 1890s he seems to have given up hope of voluntary action on their part. Although he never supported irredentism, he could not escape the influence of the national movement. He repeatedly urged those Rumanian leaders from across the Carpathians who came to see him to be patient and to stay within legal bounds, but, if we may believe Take Ionescu and other politicians, he seems to have concluded that the Dual Monarchy would eventually collapse and that the union of Transylvania with Rumania would 'inevitably' follow.[42]

[42] *Documents diplomatiques françaises*, 2nd series, 3 (Paris, 1931), 494–5: Henry to Delcassé, 29 July 1903; 563: Henry to Delcassé, 4 Sept. 1903.

Even Petre Carp, who was originally outspoken in his support of the Central Powers, found it prudent as head of the Conservative government in 1911–12 to refrain from public comments on the situation in Transylvania, because of the sensitiveness of the issue.

Before the outbreak of the first Balkan War in the autumn of 1912 France and Russia made only modest attempts to take advantage of Rumania's growing disenchantment with Austria-Hungary. After Serghei Sazonov became Russian Foreign Minister in 1910 he instructed his minister in Bucharest to cultivate friendly, but discreet, relations with influential Rumanian politicians and the Rumanian government, but he wisely avoided public initiatives because he realized that the majority of Rumanians had not forgotten the events of 1877–8 and were ever on guard against 'Pan-Slavism'. Russian strategy, therefore, was to leave the task of wooing the Rumanians mainly to the French. Yet, beyond a sentimental attachment to France on the part of many Rumanians, a feeling, moreover, that was not reciprocated, a strong political basis for close relations did not exist. Successive French governments had done little to win Rumanian support for their alliance system because they had assumed as late as 1911 that Rumania was 'enfeoffed' to the Central Powers. Nor did economic relations offer an incentive for closer political ties. In the decade before the First World War France remained in seventh place in both exports to and imports from Rumania, and the Rumanian government found it impossible to borrow funds in France, where banks preferred, as late as 1913, to make loans through German credit institutions. The coming to power at the beginning of 1911 of a Conservative government with Petre Carp as Prime Minister, Titu Maiorescu as Foreign Minister, and Alexandru Marghiloman as Minister of the Interior, all Germanophiles, removed the possibility of any serious initiative from the Rumanian side to improve official relations with France.

The two Balkan Wars put Rumania's alliance with Austria-Hungary to its severest test yet and provided an opening for France to draw Rumania closer to the Triple Entente.[43] Rumania's shift towards neutrality between the two alliance systems owed as much to the ineptness of Austrian diplomats as to French (and Russian) inducements, but Rumania's alienation from the Central

[43] The deterioration of Rumanian-Austro-Hungarian relations is described in Ebel, *Rumänien und die Mittelmächte*, 136–207; On French and Russian wooing of Rumania, see Vasile Vesa, *România şi Franţa la începutul secolului al XX-lea, 1900–1916* (Cluj-Napoca, 1975), 27–60.

Powers was mainly a consequence of forces inherent in the strivings of the Rumanians themselves to achieve their national aspirations.

Rumanian leaders chose not to become involved in the first Balkan War. On 16 October 1912, as the Balkan allies (Bulgaria, Serbia, Greece, and Montenegro) moved toward war with Turkey, the newly installed coalition Conservative government, headed by Titu Maiorescu and Take Ionescu, and the king decided not to order mobilization, but to negotiate a settlement of the boundary question in Dobrudja directly with Bulgaria and, if that failed, to seek the aid of both Russia and Austria. As usual in foreign policy, the king's views carried the day. He chose to remain neutral, despite advice from some politicians that more could be gained by immediate intervention, because he doubted that the Balkan allies could win an easy victory over the Turkish army. Rather, he foresaw a long period of changing military fortunes, which would eventually require the intervention of the powers to restore peace and stability. He reasoned that at the peace conference where the powers would again decide the fate of the Balkan peoples Rumania, because of her neutrality, would be seen as a force for order in the region and would be invited to participate as a full partner. Charles and many Rumanian politicians thus had in mind an elevated foreign policy that would distinguish Rumania from her smaller neighbours and give her pre-eminence in the Balkans.

The rapid, stunning victories by the Bulgarians and Serbs in late October and early November 1912 were an unpleasant surprise for King Charles and his advisers. At first, Charles contemplated occupying a strategic line in the Bulgarian Dobrudja as a guarantee of compensation, but both Germany and Austria-Hungary cautioned against rash acts, promising that they would look after Rumania's interests at the proper time. Although Charles postponed intervention, he had no intention of standing by as events took their course. He turned to Russia for aid in persuading a reluctant Bulgaria to be more receptive to Rumanian proposals. Sazonov replied favourably on 2 November, but made no specific commitments. Ionel Brătianu, speaking for the majority of Liberals, urged an activist policy in the Balkans. He demanded immediate mobilization and participation in the war as the surest means of maintaining Rumania's position in the region.

Between the autumn of 1912 and the following spring the exasperation of both Liberals and Conservatives and the king with

Austria's Bulgarian policy intensified. The chief architect of that policy, Foreign Minister Leopold von Berchthold, was eager to win Bulgaria over to the Triple Alliance as a counterweight to Serbia. Thus, instead of giving unqualified support to Rumanian demands on Bulgaria, he tried to effect a peaceful compromise of their differences. But the Rumanians thought that he was simply reneging on earlier promises of support and chose to ignore repeated protestations of good will from Vienna.

The visit to Bucharest of Franz Conrad von Hötzendorf, Chief of the Austrian General Staff, at the end of November 1912 did little to reassure the king and the Conservative government of Austria's full support in the Bulgarian question, despite Conrad's promises to represent Rumania's interests 'vigorously' during the present crisis. Nevertheless, he received assurances from Charles that in the event of a European war Rumania would honour her obligations as a 'faithful ally' of Austria, and he and General Alexandru Averescu, Chief of the Rumanian General Staff, approved plans for a common deployment of troops against Russia and Serbia. Conrad left Bucharest certain that Austria could rely upon the existing government, but he had grave doubts about the attitude of Brătianu and Take Ionescu toward Austria and the Triple Alliance.

The success of Conrad's mission to strengthen the ties between Rumania and the Central Powers depended not upon his own promises but upon the forcefulness with which Austria supported Rumania's territorial claims against Bulgaria. Negotiations in London in December 1912 and January 1913 between Bulgarian and Rumanian representatives, which paralleled the peace negotiations between the Balkan allies and Turkey, came to naught. The Rumanians' demand for a boundary in Dobrudja of Silistria-Balchik as a minimum and Turtucaia-Balchik as a maximum was completely unacceptable to the Bulgarians. As it became evident that the Bulgarians were intent upon dragging out negotiations until a general peace in the Balkans had been concluded (when, presumably, Bulgaria would be able to deal with the Rumanians at full strength), King Charles threatened military action. Berchthold found himself in the middle. On the one hand, he sought to demonstrate Austria's fidelity to Rumania by urging Bulgaria to increase the pace of negotiations, but, on the other, he tried to win Bulgaria's adherence to the Triple Alliance and therefore cautioned the Rumanians against a military solution to the boundary problem in Dobrudja. His argument that an attack on Bulgaria would strengthen the Balkan alliance and thereby further tip the balance against Rumania merely heightened mistrust of Austria in Bucharest.

At this critical juncture Rumania and Austria-Hungary renewed their alliance on 5 February 1913 for a period of seven years. But the speed with which it was accomplished belied the precarious state of relations between the two countries. King Charles knew that the treaty lacked the support of the public and a large number of politicians in both parties and was thus at more pains than usual to maintain secrecy. He was under enormous pressure from the war party in Bucharest, which demanded immediate intervention against Bulgaria, and he appealed to his Austrian partner to make a strong public declaration of support for Rumania as a means of counteracting anti-Austrian feeling. Yet, the fragile state of the alliance was plain to both, for it would soon be the Liberals' turn to form a government, and Brătianu had made clear his preference for the Entente.

The impasse between Rumania and Bulgaria, which threatened to become an armed conflict and involve the great powers on opposite sides, led to the convening of a conference of ambassadors at St Petersburg. In May they approved a compromise which awarded Silistria and a three-kilometre zone around the city to Rumania, but made no further changes in the frontier. Confronted by such rare unanimity on the part of the powers, the Rumanian and Bulgarian governments yielded, but both held fast to their original claims. As bilateral negotiations failed to resolve their differences, the likelihood of Rumania's involvement in the Balkan conflict grew. Relations between Rumania and Austria-Hungary also hardened, as Rumanian politicians faulted Austrian representatives at the St Petersburg conference for having shown too much solicitude for Bulgaria.[44]

In late May and June Rumania and Austria-Hungary drew farther apart as their conflicting interests in the Balkans brought to the surface all the underlying sources of hostility. The estrangement of the Balkan allies over the division of the spoils after their defeat of Turkey offered the Rumanian government an opportunity to increase its pressure on Bulgaria. But Serbian and Greek proposals for an alliance against Bulgaria brought forth a

---

[44] *Die Grosse Politik*, xxxiv, part 2 (Berlin, 1926), 690–1: Tschirschky, German ambassador in Vienna, to Foreign Ministry, 13 April 1913: *Österreich-Ungarns Aussenpolitik*, vi (Vienna, 1930), 320–1: Report from Austrian minister in Bucharest, 2 May 1913.

warning from Berchthold that in the event of a war between Bulgaria and Serbia, Austria-Hungary would be compelled to act against Serbia, by armed force, if necessary. He admonished the Rumanian government to avoid any alliance with Serbia or Greece, for such commitments would place Rumania at odds with the policy of the Triple Alliance in the region. These threats, instead of intimidating the Rumanians, convinced the king and the leaders of both parties to pursue an independent policy toward Bulgaria, a decision that loosened ties to the Triple Alliance still further.

By the end of June Rumanian leaders had thus achieved a remarkable unanimity of views on the need for military intervention, if Bulgaria attacked her former allies. This was the king's position, and Titu Maiorescu informed the Bulgarian government that Rumania 'would act' in the event of war. Ionel Brătianu also urged the king to take energetic action in order to prevent a modification of the 'Balkan equilibrium'. On 3 July, three days after Bulgarian armies had attacked Serbian and Greek positions, Charles ordered mobilization, which was met by patriotic enthusiasm and demonstrations against Austria-Hungary. A week later Rumania declared war on Bulgaria. Her army met no serious opposition, as the main Bulgarian force was engaged against Serbian, Greek, and Turkish forces in the south. On 22 July, as Bulgarian resistance disintegrated on all fronts, the Rumanian government agreed to an armistice, for Charles and Liberal and Conservative politicians had not gone to war to destroy Bulgaria. Their objective had been, rather, to maintain the balance of power in the Balkans and to assert Rumania's role as its guarantor.

The making of a general peace in the Balkans took little time, for Bulgaria had been thoroughly defeated. By the terms of the Treaty of Bucharest, signed on 10 August, Bulgaria was obliged to give up most of the territory she had acquired in the first Balkan War and ceded southern Dobrudja to Rumania, recognizing the line Turtucaia-Balchik as the new frontier between the two countries. Rumania emerged from the peace conference not only with more territory but with enhanced prestige and a new feeling of self-confidence, which would make it less likely than before that politicians and public opinion would acquiesce in Austrian tutelage.

The Balkan crisis of 1912–13 completed the alienation of Rumania from Austria-Hungary and the Triple Alliance. Ottokar Czernin, the Austro-Hungarian minister to Rumania, offered a melancholy appraisal of the situation in December 1913. He warned that a restoration of the old relationship with Rumania was extremely remote and urged a drastic change in the nationality policy of the Hungarian government as the only means by which Rumania could be kept from joining the Entente.[45] Czernin's reading of the mood in Bucharest was accurate. Liberals and many Conservatives were now determined to achieve long-cherished national goals and to shape foreign policy accordingly. Their attention naturally focused on Transylvania and Bukovina. The advent of Ionel Brătianu and the Liberals in January 1914 signalled the reorientation of Rumanian foreign policy. Although King Charles, who had been profoundly disappointed by Austria-Hungary's policy in the Balkans, did not oppose the new course, he continued to believe that a Germanophile policy was in the long run best for Rumania.

A *rapprochement* with the Entente was well underway by the spring of 1914. Official relations between France and Rumania warmed perceptibly, as French diplomats had given full support to Rumania during the second Balkan War and had approved the terms of the Treaty of Bucharest. They co-ordinated their policy with Russia's assiduous courting of Rumania under Sazonov's direction. The visit of the tsar to Constanţa on 14 June 1914 marked the beginning of a new era in relations between the two countries. They agreed to maintain the Treaty of Bucharest and to work together to protect their respective commercial interests in the Black Sea, but Brătianu refused to commit his country to the Triple Entente. He was eager to continue the *rapprochement* with Russia, but he had no desire to increase tensions with Austria-Hungary and respected the military and economic power of Germany. He intended to take the same cautious approach in threading his way between competing great powers that his father had followed at the onset of the Eastern Crisis of 1875–8. His policy was to risk nothing that had already been won and thus to draw closer to France and Russia without precipitating an open break with Austria-Hungary and Germany.

---

[45] *Österreich-Ungarns Aussenpolitik*, vii (Vienna, 1930), 609–14: Report of 5 Dec. 1913.

4
Society and the Economy

The second half of the nineteenth century down to the outbreak of the First World War was decisive for the social and economic development of Rumania. In many areas she moved toward modern forms. Population grew steadily and became more urban, industrialization gained momentum, and the infrastructure of an advanced economy began to fill out. The Liberal and Conservative parties encouraged private enterprise, but the role of the state as an entrepreneur and regulator proved indispensable for economic progress. At the same time many characteristics of an underdeveloped country persisted. Agriculture remained the foundation of the economy, and the great majority of the population continued to live in the countryside. Despite an increase in production and agrarian reform legislation, agriculture in 1914 remained essentially what it had been structurally about mid-century, and rural inhabitants generally did not share in the benefits of economic progress. Poverty was widespread, and the death rate remained high, because of inadequate diet, sanitation, and health care. Industrialization, despite impressive gains, was uneven, as key industries and a mutually beneficial relationship with agriculture were slow to develop. Rumania's economic ties to Europe increased in complexity, but the relationship was not one of equals. Foreign markets for agricultural products, foreign suppliers of manufactured goods for both industry and the mass consumer market, and foreign capital became indispensable for Rumania's economic health, thereby increasing her dependence upon the great powers of Western Europe.

POPULATION AND SOCIAL STRUCTURE

The population of Rumania increased steadily in the second half of the nineteenth century. In 1861 the two principalities together had 3,969,675 inhabitants. Of these, 2,400,921 'souls', according to the statistics assembled by Dionisie Pop Marţian in 1859 and 1860, lived in Wallachia. Another census, this one prepared by Ion

Ionescu de la Brad for Moldavia in 1859, set the number of inhabitants of that principality at 1,403,927. By 1899 the total population of the country had risen to 5,956,690. Growth had not been uninterrupted. For a time, in the early 1870s, it had been reversed, mainly because of a severe drought and poor harvests in 1873 and 1874. The countryside suffered more severely than urban areas from these natural calamities, but epidemics of cholera and smallpox during the decade took a heavy toll in urban areas. Then, in the 1880s a rapid increase occurred, followed by a levelling off in the 1890s and steady, if undramatic growth in the two decades preceding the outbreak of the First World War.[1]

The increase of population was not everywhere uniform. For example, the population of Moldavia rose by only 40 per cent between 1859 and 1899, while that of the country as a whole grew by 54 per cent. This regional slowdown, which reversed the trend of the first half of the century, was caused by the migration of Moldavians to other parts of the country, especially to Bucharest, after the union of principalities, by a decrease in the number of immigrants from Galicia and Bukovina, and by a higher mortality rate than in Muntenia (that part of Wallachia east of the Olt River). Urban centres experienced dramatic fluctuations in population until the end of the century. Between 1870 and 1874 the total population of cities declined by 28,000, mainly because of epidemics. Then between 1886 and 1899 it increased at annual rates that fluctuated between 4.2 and 18.6 per cent, after which a measure of stability in growth rates was achieved. In the rural areas generally, unlike the cities, there were no sudden changes, but rather a permanent increase of population, although rates varied from one half-decade to the next. For example, between 1870 and 1874, as in the cities, annual average population growth slowed considerably from 40,015 to 3,893, and then between 1896 and 1899 it rose from 60,318 to 78,024 a year.

The increase of population between 1859 and 1914 was due to a high birth rate combined with a modest decrease in the mortality rate. The rural areas were primarily responsible for maintaining the growth of population. Between 1859 and 1889 births exceeded deaths by slightly over a million, but in the cities during the same period births exceeded deaths by only 6,228. Thus, the natural

---

[1] On demographic development in the latter part of the nineteenth century, see Radu Vasile, 'L'Évolution démographique en Roumanie au cours des trois dernières décennies du XIXe siècle', *Revue roumaine d'histoire*, 19/2–3 (1980), 333–52; 20/1 (1981), 65–89.

increase in the countryside was almost 100 per cent, but in the cities only 0.56 per cent during the period.[2] The high mortality rate continued to be a serious check on the growth of population down to the First World War, especially among children. For example, in 1892 of a total of 96,062 deaths in the whole country between January and June, 44,092 were children under the age of 5, almost half the total number of deaths. The main cause was the lack of proper care they received (inadequate nutrition, sanitation, and health facilities).[3]

As the figures cited above suggest, the majority of Rumanians lived in the countryside. In 1859, 85 per cent of the population was rural, and shortly before the First World War, in 1912, about 82 per cent. These figures also reflect the growth of cities and towns. Between 1859 and 1899 the urban population increased from 552,000 to 1,050,000, or 90 per cent, and continued at approximately the same pace until the First World War. The position of Bucharest as the country's major population centre was reinforced as it grew from 122,000 inhabitants in 1859 to 381,000 in 1916.

The growth of urban population was largely due to immigration from the countryside, for, as we have seen, natural increase was practically nil. Between 1859 and 1889, for example, some 300,000 persons moved from the rural areas to the cities. In the decade before the First World War that migration was directed particularly toward those cities with the most dynamic pace of economic development—Bucharest, the leading industrial centre; the two great ports on the Danube, Galaţi and Brăila; Ploieşti, the centre of the new oil industry; and Craiova, the principal economic and financial centre in Oltenia.[4]

Social structure at the turn of the century preserved the broad outlines visible in 1850, but significant changes, as the growth of cities suggest, were already underway. Immediately striking was the formal disappearance of the old boier class at the beginning of the period. Alexandru Cuza's *Statut* of 1864 abolished all privileges of class and, by extension, eliminated the boier ranks, action confirmed by the Constitution of 1866. But this legislation was hardly revolutionary. It simply recognized a state of things that already existed, for the boier hierarchy had been steadily undermined by economic change and the rise of the new, dynamic

[2] *Buletin statistic general al României*, i (1892) (Bucharest, 1893), 150.
[3] Ibid. 304–10.
[4] Ibid. 12/36–7 (1915) (Bucharest, 1915), 431–3.

middle class. Yet, the large landowning class (*moşierime*) remained a powerful economic force in the countryside, and it retained a key place in the country's economy as a whole. Some 2,000 large landowners (possessing over 500 hectares) held a total of three million hectares, roughly 38 per cent of all arable land.[5]

The majority of great landowners maintained a style of life already evident in the first half of the nineteenth century.[6] They took no direct part in managing their estates or concerned themselves with technological advances. Instead, they preferred to live in Bucharest or some other city, or they spent much of their time abroad, in France, Italy, or Switzerland. They leased their estates in return for a fixed sum, which they spent on everything except agriculture. They thus lost contact with the village and its inhabitants. Their neglect, even abandonment, of agriculture, their traditional source of income and the basis of their political and social position, accelerated the dissolution of their class. The majority were in severe financial difficulty. By 1900 many estates had been mortgaged to Creditul Funciar Rural, and other sources of credit were sharply restricted. Landlords did not have access to the National Bank, which was a Liberal stronghold used to promote the economic and social policies of the Liberal Party, while Banca Agricolă (The Agricultural Bank), created in 1894 for the express purpose of shoring up large properties, failed to carry out its responsibilities.

The place of the large landowners in the countryside was taken not by the urban bourgeoisie, but by the *arendaşi* (leaseholders), who formed a thin stratum between the great landowners and the peasantry. The typical *arendaş* was rural in origin, but had little to do directly with agriculture. He was originally a money-lender or a small shopkeeper or a grain broker who had accumulated capital and had invested it in land. Through his primary occupations and

---

[5] Radu Rosetti, *Pentru ce s-au răsculat ţăranii* (Bucharest, 1908), 577–80. On landholding in general after the turn of the century, see Mircea Iosa, 'Relaţiile agrare din România în deceniul premergător primului război mondial', *Revista de istorie*, 35/2 (1982), 205–27.

[6] The evolution of the large landowning class is viewed from different perspectives in Paraschiva Câncea, 'Situaţia moşierimii din secolul al XIX-lea reflectată în literatura epocii', *Revista de istorie*, 39/6 (1986), 542–56, and Vasile Liveanu and Irina Gavrilă, 'Calculator electronic şi informaţii nenumerice: Despre evoluţia clasei marilor proprietari funciari în România (1857–1918)', *Revista de istorie*, 40/2 (1987), 134–46.

temperament and lack of respect for rural traditions he was the chief ally of the bourgeoisie in the countryside.[7]

As the role of the landlord diminished, the prominence of the *arendaş* grew, owing to the rapid expansion of leasing in the latter decades of the nineteenth century. By 1900 over half the land of estates over 500 hectares and three-quarters of the land of estates over 3,000 hectares was leased. The median amount of arable land leased by an *arendaş* was 700 hectares. But in some parts of the country large-scale, commercial leasing was common, notably in northern Moldavia, where the Fischer Trust, formed in the 1890s, leased land in ten *judeţe* amounting to 237,863 hectares. A number of *arendaşi* were Austrian Jews, like the Fischer family, who had ready access to Austrian bank capital and were not only able to control land, but also organized the storage and transportation of grain to market. They thus dominated the entire process of production and distribution and brought the peasant cultivators face to face with the practices and mentality of capitalism on a large scale. Many *arendaşi* favoured the Conservative Party, especially the Junimist wing, because it defended the large leasing trusts as economically efficient.

The peasantry not only formed the largest segment of the rural population, but remained the most numerous class in Rumanian society as a whole. It was far from homogeneous.[8] Several strata, distinguished from one another by their occupations and standard of living, stand out. Among the poorest peasants were those without land who worked as hired hands. In 1913 they numbered about 200,000, or 14 per cent of all persons active in agriculture. They constituted an agricultural proletariat. If some 100,000 heads of family who had no land of their own, but were forced to rent land in return for payment of a tithe, are taken into account, the size of the agricultural proletariat rises to about 300,000. Although this figure remained roughly constant during the decade before the First World War, it should not imply that a degree of economic stability on the land had been achieved. Many peasants continued to fall into the ranks of the landless, but they were no longer

[7] G. Maior, *România agricolă* (Bucharest, 1911), 156. For an extended discussion of the role of the *arendaşi* in rural society, see P. G. Eidelberg, *The Great Rumanian Peasant Revolt of 1907* (Leiden, 1974). On leasing, see G. D. Creangă, *Grundbesitzverteilung und Bauernfrage in Rumänien* (Leipzig, 1907), 136–55.

[8] *Relaţii agrare şi mişcări ţărăneşti în România, 1908–1921* (Bucharest, 1967), 48–74: Creangă *Grundbesitzverteilung*, 97–122.

included in agricultural statistics because they had been drawn into industry and transportation.

Still other categories of peasants led precarious existences. Notable among them were those who possessed less than 5 hectares, the minimum necessary to support a family of five. Numbering about 750,000 and representing over half the peasant holdings over 50 hectares, they were obliged to supplement their meagre incomes with labour for landlords, *arendaşi*, and wealthier neighbours. Even the so-called middle-sized peasants (*mijlocaşi*), who usually had enough land, sometimes had to hire themselves out to nearby estates to make ends meet. Possessing 5 to 10 hectares each, they formed a thin stratum of about 176,000 households or 14 per cent of the total number of peasant households. A poor harvest or an increase in taxes might be enough to push them into the ranks of the agricultural poor.

There were also well-off peasants, those who possessed 10 to 50 hectares and whose holdings provided for a relatively comfortable living. Although they numbered only 36,000, they were economically powerful, controlling 696,000 hectares, or 18 per cent of all peasant property. They formed the core of the village agricultural middle class, whose ranks were swelled by other social groups, notably small merchants, priests, and schoolteachers. Although these groups rarely owned more than 10 hectares of land, their salaries and other income gave them a standard of living equivalent to that of the wealthier peasants. They also shared similar social and political aspirations.

The urban middle class rose to economic and political prominence in the half-century before the First World War. Composed of merchants and industrialists, civil servants, and professionals, especially lawyers and teachers, it was primarily a Rumanian bourgeoisie and thus replaced the heterogeneous and largely foreign commercial and money-lending class of the eighteenth and early nineteenth century. The expansion of the administrative system and the consequent growth of its personnel and the affirmation of a national economic policy after the union of the principalities in 1859 encouraged the growth of the Rumanian bourgeoisie. Of particular importance was the creation of the National Bank of Rumania (Banca Naţională a României) by the Brătianu government in 1880. It gave impetus to the development of the bourgeoisie, particularly its upper strata, because it laid the foundation for the entire banking system, which Liberal financial circles used to gain a dominant position in the national economy.

Eager to develop all its branches, they used their political influence to ensure the enactment of laws that accelerated the modernization of the economy and, not least of all, consolidated their own position in banking, industry, and commerce. This Liberal bourgeoisie invariably thought in terms of nation and identified its interests with their own. As we have seen, they advocated protectionism, a policy they thought essential for the creation of a national industry, and they opposed the free flow of foreign capital into the country in order to prevent the subordination of its economic and political interests to the 'caprices' of the great powers (and, no less important, to assure their own predominance).

The upper bourgeoisie came into its own in the latter two decades of the nineteenth century. The protectionist tariff of 1886 and the law to encourage a national industry of 1887, which accorded special advantages to Rumanian entrepreneurs, marked the emergence of an aggressive industrial bourgeoisie. They were joined by a number of large landowners who invested extensively in industry. Large banking families also belonged to the upper bourgeoisie and were closely associated with the industrialists. They were grouped around the National Bank, which the Brătianus and other Liberals used to further their own economic interests. The number of large bankers, though small, grew steadily, and in the last decade of the nineteenth century alone fifteen new banks were founded with a total capital of 74 million lei.[9]

The middle-sized bourgeoisie was far more numerous than the great bankers and industrialists. They were the owners of modest 'industrial' establishments, such as small flour mills and food-processing plants. In the industrial survey of 1901–2 these were designated as 'special industries' and represented some 7,000 businesses out of a total of 54,000 'medium and small enterprises'.[10] In the same social category were merchants who engaged in local or regional commerce, white-collar workers in industry and banking, and the majority of professional people. The precise number of persons in each category is difficult to determine because of the absence of detailed statistics. None the less, records of those persons subject to payment of the *patentă* (as of 1896, a

---

[9] N. I. Păianu, *Industria mare, 1866–1906* (Bucharest, 1906), 80–95; Victor Slăvescu, *Istoricul Băncii Naționale a României (1880–1924)* (Bucharest, 1925), 108–10, 142–4, 204–6.

[10] *Ancheta industrială din 1901–1902*, i (Bucharest, 1904), 6; *Statistica profesiunilor supuse impozitului de patentă în anul 1903–1904* (Bucharest, 1905), 197–204.

tax of 4 per cent on business) for 1903–4 indicate 10,364 'entre-preneurs', 1,325 lawyers, 151 engineers, and 42 bankers.

In the latter decades of the nineteenth century another segment of the urban population—the civil service—steadily expanded as the central government and its branches in the *judeţe* assumed new responsibilities. In 1901 there were 102,560 government em-ployees, or roughly 2 per cent of the total population of the country. Civil servants did not form a homogeneous stratum, but the majority had lives of privation in common. Nearly half had salaries of less than 50 lei per month, which placed them at about the level of a salaried worker, while less than 1 per cent received a salary sufficient to allow a middle-class standard of living.[11]

The artisans of the cities and towns still formed a distinct and important segment of society. At the turn of the century there were approximately 166,000, according to one set of statistics, and 98,000, according to another. Such large numbers suggest the continued dependence of the mass of consumers for necessities on small, individually owned workshops. Yet, the craft industry was in the throes of an economic crisis, from which it would never recover. The number of artisans had been declining since the middle 1870s. The pressure on traditional artisan production did not come primarily from local industry, which was still relatively little developed, but from the continuous importation of cheap manufactured goods for the mass market, especially from Austria-Hungary under the terms of the commercial convention of 1875. Later on, as Rumania's international trade became more diversified and native industry expanded the artisan faced insurmountable competition. The general economic and financial crisis of 1899–1903 hastened his ruin. The law enacted in 1902 by the Liberals regulating the organization of artisans and promising government aid failed to reverse the decline, for after 1900 the domestic manu-facturing industry steadily encroached upon markets that had typically sustained the artisan. Many masters had ceased to be independent, and journeymen had lost hope of ever becoming masters themselves and had fallen into the ranks of wage labourers.

Wage labourers indeed had become a significant component of urban society by the turn of the century. They were employed in food-processing and other consumer-oriented industries, coal mining, oil production, and transportation. Their numbers had been increasing steadily since 1860 when Dionisie Pop Marţian

---

[11] *Anuarul statistic al României, 1904* (Bucharest, 1904), 137.

estimated that there were 28,000 'workers' employed mainly in mills and distilleries and other small enterprises in both villages and towns. By the outbreak of the First World War the working class numbered about 200,000, or 10 per cent of the active population. Their concentration in large enterprises was well underway, for, according to the industrial survey of 1901–2, over half of all industrial workers were employed in enterprises of at least 100 workers. The process was well advanced in and around Bucharest, the Prahova Valley, north of Bucharest, with its oil refineries, and the ports of Galaţi and Brăila, where food-processing and the transport of grain had attracted many workers.[12]

The new urban working class was formed from diverse elements. The majority came from the countryside, where overpopulation had become a critical economic and social problem. The newcomers found work in factories, transportation, and commerce, but almost always at the bottom as unskilled labour. They usually preserved their links to the village and continued to obtain a part of their income from agriculture. Other workers came from the growing reservoir of impoverished artisans, whose skills were eagerly sought by industry. Yet, despite steady expansion in the latter decades of the century, industry and other urban enterprises were still too little developed to accommodate all who sought work. The consequence was a persistent oversupply, particularly of unskilled labour, which, in turn, kept wages depressed and living conditions for many unbearable.

Working conditions in urban shops and factories were by all accounts abominable.[13] They were crowded and unhealthy, and workers had no protection against the exploitation of their employers. No comprehensive law regulated the hours of labour. The average workday was twelve to fourteen hours and in some industries it might go as high as sixteen. The median wage for a man was $1\frac{1}{2}$ lei per day, but for highly skilled workers in certain industries it might be as much as 3 or 4 lei. Even relatively good wages were often inadequate to cover a worker's basic needs for food and housing. Food prices in Bucharest at the turn of the

---

[12] On the growth and composition of the working class between the 1870s and 1914, see N. N. Constantinescu (ed.), *Din istoricul formării şi dezvoltării clasei muncitoare din România* (Bucharest, 1959), 204–32, 330–65.

[13] M. Iosa, 'Despre dezvoltarea industriei în România la sfîrşitul secolului al XIX-lea şi începutul secolului al XX-lea (1880–1914)', *Studii şi materiale de istorie modernă*, iii (Bucharest, 1963), 412–25; G. Zane, *L'Industrie roumaine au cours de la seconde moitié du XIXe siècle* (Bucharest, 1973), 249–57.

century suggest that the standard of living for the average worker must have been low, since the prices for staples such as bread were on the rise, while wages remained more or less constant. Industries of all kinds were eager to hire women and children because they could be paid lower wages (20 to 50 per cent less than men) for the same number of hours as men and presented fewer discipline problems. The availability of women and children tended to keep wages low and hours long. So did the general overpopulation of cities and towns. Around 1900 for the first time in Rumania there was an overabundance of urban labour, mainly because of continuous migration from the countryside. An inexhaustible supply of labour often meant widespread unemployment, particularly during periods of economic crisis, as in 1899–1903.

From an ethnic and religious standpoint the population of Rumania between the middle of the nineteenth century and 1914 was remarkably homogeneous. In 1899, out of a total population of 5,956,690, there were 5,489,296 Rumanians, or 92.1 per cent. By religion, Orthodox constituted 91.5 per cent, the overwhelming majority being Rumanian (there were small numbers of Greeks, Bulgarians, Russians, and Serbs).

Jews formed the only significant minority in Rumania during the period.[14] Their numbers grew steadily in the second half of the century, mainly because of immigration from Russia and the Habsburg Monarchy. In 1912 they numbered 240,000, or 3.3 per cent of the population. They resided mainly in cities and towns and in the same year constituted 14.6 per cent of all urban dwellers. This concentration was especially striking in Moldavia, where Jews formed almost 32 per cent of the urban population. In Iași 42 per cent of the inhabitants were Jews, and in thirteen other cities they represented more than 30 per cent of the population. Outside Moldavia in only two cities did Jews exceed 10 per cent of the population: Brăila (14 per cent) and Bucharest (13 per cent).

The growth of the Jewish population and its concentration in cities and towns and the consequent economic and social competition they represented in the eyes of native Rumanians brought forth a series of restrictions on their activities. Throughout the second half of the nineteenth century Jews were considered for-

---

[14] *Buletinul statistic al României*, 12/40 (1915) (Bucharest, 1915), 703–4, 710–13, 728–30; Anastase N. Hâciu, *Evreii în Țările Românești* (Bucharest, 1943), 286–304; Carol Iancu, *Les Juifs en Roumanie, 1866–1919, de l'exclusion à l'émancipation* (Aix-en-Provence, 1978), 142–3.

eigners, but during the reign of Alexandru Cuza several measures were adopted which suggested that the process of their emancipation had begun. These were, to be sure, modest steps: the new civil code of 1862 allowed individual naturalization by the Council of State ten years after the submission of a petition to the prince; it was even suggested that they be granted civil rights in the localities in which they lived, if they could 'prove their Rumanian sentiments'. In 1865 Cuza went so far as to announce a project for the 'gradual emancipation of inhabitants of the Mosaic cult'.

After Cuza's overthrow in 1866 a decisive change of attitude toward Jews took place. It was immediately manifest in article 7 of the new constitution, which denied citizenship to non-Christians. Perhaps the change of attitude can be attributed to the weakening of Romantic liberalism after 1848 and the replacement of the cosmopolitan approach to social problems by a narrow nationalism that demanded a Rumania solely for ethnic Rumanians. The matter was already put in stark terms in 1862 in Iaşi by a committee charged with beautifying the city which demanded that the 'colonization' of Iaşi by Jews be ended at once because the city had been inundated by 'these foreigners [who] had no connection at all with the country'. After 1866 Liberals took the lead in tightening restrictions on Jews. In 1867, for example, Ion Brătianu, as Minister of the Interior, instructed prefects to enforce strictly the regulations concerning 'Jewish vagabonds', by which he intended to limit their immigration and settlement, particularly in villages. The Conservatives followed similar policies when they came to power. In 1873, for example, the Catargiu government introduced a new law on the sale of alcoholic beverages which attempted to undo the monopoly which the Jews had in effect established. Jews in Rumania protested and gained the support of Jewish organizations abroad, notably the Alliance Israélite Universelle in Paris, which through sympathetic Western European politicians brought pressure to bear on the Rumanian government to modify its legislation. Such pressure culminated in the requirement imposed on Rumania at the Congress of Berlin in 1878 to revise article 7 of the constitution to enable Jews to obtain civil and political rights.

From 1879 down to the First World War the treatment of Jews as foreigners did not change significantly. Only a small number, probably no more than 1,000, succeeded in obtaining citizenship under the new procedures outlined in the constitution. Rumanian legislation, particularly in economic matters and during Liberal governments, discriminated against foreigners, and, hence, against Jews, in favour of native Rumanians. For example, the law on chambers of commerce of 1881 and the commercial code of 1887 stipulated that certain offices could be held only by Rumanian citizens. In the midst of what critics have called the 'era of legal persecution' a substantial emigration of Jews took place. Some 52,000 left the country between 1899 and 1907. The main cause seems to have been economic and connected with the crisis of 1899–1903, especially with the decline of the craft industry, since many of the emigrants were small artisans.[15] In 1908 and 1909 the tide of emigration subsided, apparently because of the country's economic recovery. On the eve of the First World War the juridical status of the Jews remained essentially what it had been in 1879.

AGRICULTURE

Agriculture continued to form the basis of the Rumanian economy in the second half of the nineteenth century down to the First World War. The great majority of the population resided on the land and depended upon agriculture for a livelihood. As late as 1900 agriculture accounted for two-thirds of the gross national product and supplied over three-quarters of the country's exports. Yet, despite advances in industry and banking, the strengthening of the infrastructure, and an increase in agricultural production itself, no significant changes occurred in the organization of agriculture. The direct responsibility for production remained in the hands of peasants, who owned most of the animals and tools and followed traditional ways of working the land. Agrarian relations also changed but little. Despite several notable attempts at reform, the majority of peasants remained subject to the will of landlords or middlemen, the arendaşi.

The effects of the agrarian reform of 1864 fell far short of expectations. Although peasants were granted property rights to the land they had worked for their landlords and had gained their personal freedom, a prosperous class of small, independent peasant proprietors forming the economic and social backbone of a constitutional monarchy failed to develop. Instead, large numbers of peasants remained dependent upon their former land-

---

[15] Iancu, Les Juifs en Roumanie, 256–64.

lords. After the reform large landholders, together with the state, retained about 70 per cent of the agricultural land of the country, while peasant property (that of the former *clăcaşi* and of the free peasants, the *răzeşi* and *moşneni*) accounted for the rest. The majority of peasants had too little arable land and pasture to be economically independent. They were thus obliged to turn again to their former landlords, who were more than willing to rent land in return for labour services. As a result, a new system of dependency, aptly dubbed 'neo-serfdom' by Constantin Dobrogeanu-Gherea, gradually came into existence.

In the two decades after the agrarian reform the majority of those peasants who had received land suffered a diminution of their holdings or lost them altogether.[16] In 1864, out of 445,000 *clăcaşi*, 406,000 received land of some sort from the state and private landlords. But at least 100,000 *clăcaşi* received no land at all for cultivation, only a house and a garden plot, and another 150,000 obtained plots too small to support a family of four. These groups constituted the poorest segment of the peasantry. Yet, by the end of the 1880s it had become evident that even broader elements of the peasantry could not survive as independent producers. Many had lost the land they had been granted under the reform. They had been obliged to sell all or a part of it to landlords or more prosperous neighbours, contrary to the provisions of the agrarian law, because they lacked enough land or land of good quality to make their holdings economically viable. Even those whose plots were otherwise adequate often lacked the know-how or the means (tools, fertilizers, credit) to make agriculture profitable. All peasants were subject to the pernicious effects of the continuous fragmentation of holdings, for in the absence of a law of primogeniture, fathers followed tradition by dividing even dwarf holdings among their sons. They, in turn, out of desperation, sold or mortgaged them for a pittance. The chief beneficiaries were landlords and wealthier peasants and merchants in the village. It is no coincidence that in this period (1864–88) the *arendaşi* established themselves as an important element of rural society.

The agrarian reform and the peasants' continued need for land created a complex situation in the village, which was to determine

---

[16] A comprehensive analysis of the condition of agriculture during the period has been made by Gheorghe Cristea, 'Probleme ale modernizării agriculturii României (1864–1877)', *Studii şi materiale de istorie modernă*, 7 (1983), 147–203.

the evolution of agrarian relations for the next forty years. Land-lords continued to control nearly six million hectares of arable land, hayfields, pasture, and forest, but they lacked the animals and tools and the labour-force necessary to work their estates. They thus had every reason to satisfy the peasants' need for land. Because of the severe droughts that swept the country in 1865 and 1866, they were able to impose rents and other conditions highly advantageous to themselves. The agreement between the two parties took the form of a written contract by which the peasant agreed to perform a certain amount of labour, or, in some cases, provide a share of the crop, in return for the use of a specified amount of land. But the landlords were not satisfied with this tra-ditional arrangement. They demanded guarantees that the peasants would in fact perform all the labour they had promised.

The government responded to the concerns of landlords (and *arendaşi*) with a law on agricultural contracts in 1866.[17] It required peasants who received arable land or pasture to pay rent in the form of money, produce, or labour services or some combina-tion of these. In addition, they were obliged to work a specified amount of land for the landlord or *arendaş* and to offer them certain 'gifts' (*plocoane*) in produce. These obligations were not at first unduly burdensome, since landlords and *arendaşi* were desperate for peasant labour and could not afford to alienate prospective hands by imposing harsh terms. But the enforcement of the contracts was especially onerous for the peasants. Com-munal authorities, who were often under the influence of land-lords, had the power to force peasants to comply with the terms of their contract and to exact severe penalties if they failed to do so, including the summoning of armed force (the *dorobanţi*) and the immediate sale of the offender's animals and other property. Peasant appeals to the courts and the central bureaucracy were rarely successful, since these bodies were satisfied to leave matters in the hands of local officials. Onerous, too, for the peasants was collective responsibility. The majority of contracts, which were concluded with an entire village, stipulated that all its inhabitants were responsible for the failure of any one of them to fulfil his obligations to the landlord or *arendaşi*, no matter what the cause might be.

The deteriorating economic condition of the peasants and the use of force against those who failed to carry out the terms of their contracts led to mounting violence in the countryside.

---

[17] Gheorghe Cristea, *Contribuţii la istoria problemei agrare în România: Învoielile agricole (1866–1882)* (Bucharest, 1977), 47–103.

Liberals who were committed to further agrarian reform and others who recognized the economic shortcomings of the existing system finally forced through parliament a general modification of the law on agricultural contracts in 1882. It redressed the balance slightly in favour of the peasants by forbidding the use of force against them and by abolishing collective responsibility for the non-fulfilment of contracts. It also made more precise the kinds of work they had to perform, how they would perform it, and over what period of time, and it required the landlord to collect the tithe within ten days of the harvest in order to prevent him from demanding more later on the grounds that the harvest had been larger than it actually was. None the less, the peasant remained subject to severe penalties for failure to carry out the terms of his contract, while landlords and *arendaşi* could ignore their obligations to peasants with impunity.

Landlords and *arendaşi* were by no means alone in seeking to take economic advantage of a nearly defenceless peasantry. The tax collector often treated the rural population not as a source of public revenues but of personal income. The fiscal agents of the commune, *judeţ*, and central government sometimes collected more than the law stipulated or they abruptly confiscated and sold the property of those who had fallen behind in their payments. Such practices were actually encouraged by a new law on the collection of taxes passed in 1882, which gave fiscal agents 3–9 per cent of the sums they collected in place of a salary.

Officials at all levels could generally violate the rights of the peasants with impunity because the latter, owing to the limited franchise, remained outside the political process and were, in any case, unaccustomed to exercising the rights of citizenship. They were politically isolated, for no party truly represented their interests.

Peasant distress deepened at a time when agriculture was experiencing an unprecedented expansion. Agricultural production increased steadily in the quarter-century after the agrarian reform, as the amount of land devoted to the raising of grain steadily expanded. Yet, the volume of production grew at a less rapid rate than the amount of land under cultivation would suggest because techniques and tools in most places belonged to an earlier era.[18]

---

[18] For an overview, touching especially the nineteenth century, see Valer Butură, *Etnografia poporului român* (Cluj-Napoca, 1978), 130–63. A broad sociological approach by Henri H. Stahl, *Contribuţii la studiul satelor devălmaşe româneşti*, i (Bucharest, 1958), 223–332, puts the nineteenth and twentieth centuries in a historical perspective.

Yields were everywhere reduced by the failure of all but a few peasants to manure their fields regularly and to let fields lie fallow for a time or plant crops other than wheat or corn to restore their fertility. The majority of peasants still used a primitive plough, which failed to work the ground adequately. Many had no plough at all, but had to share one with neighbours. Heavier and more modern ploughs were limited almost exclusively to large estates and, occasionally, to the holdings of wealthier peasants. Machines were slowly becoming more common, but their number was woefully inadequate for the amount of land under cultivation. Many peasants also lacked animals. In 1900, the only year for which detailed statistics on animal ownership are available, 472,000 peasant households (about 40 per cent of the total) had no draught animals at all. The poverty of many peasants obliged them to get along without new tools and other improvements and prevented them from keeping animals, which were indispensable for successful farming.

Production on the land was adversely affected also by the peasant's way of life. A survey of many villages in the plains of Wallachia made just after the turn of the century catalogues inadequate housing, clothing, and nourishment.[19] Particularly damaging to the health of the peasant was a monotonous diet lacking in meat and milk products and based upon *mămăligă*, a kind of polenta made from corn. As a result, the peasants' resistance to illness and disease was substantially weakened and their capacity for work reduced. The situation did not improve. For example, the incidence of pellagra, caused by the consumption of spoiled corn, rose between 1888 and 1906 from 10,626 reported cases to 100,000. The most striking evidence of poor diet and the lack of proper health care was the high death rate among children.

A serious obstacle to economic progress among the peasants was widespread illiteracy, which kept them tied to tradition and made it difficult for them to benefit from advances in technology and participate in social and political life beyond the village.[20] Significant improvements began to take place only when the government decided to devote more attention and more money to rural education. In 1893 public education was substantially re-

[19] Constantin Corbu, *Ţărănimea din România între 1864 şi 1888* (Bucharest, 1970), 64–73.

[20] On literacy rates in the rural areas and cities, see *Buletinul statistic general al României*, 1 (1892), 178; 12/40 (1914), 669–75. On elementary education, Ibid. 1: 252–4; 12: 686–98.

organized, attendance began to be systematically enforced, and the recruitment and training of teachers was improved through the establishment of normal schools. Between 1890 and 1913 both the number of schools and teachers increased substantially, and the number of registered pupils rose from 144,000 to 532,000. The results were reflected in the rise of the literacy rate of the rural population over 8 years of age from 15 per cent in 1899 to 33 per cent in 1912. By comparison, the literacy rate in urban areas exceeded that in the countryside by a considerable margin, at least in part because of more extensive opportunities for instruction and more stringently enforced attendance. In 1912 two-thirds of urban inhabitants over 8 years of age could read and write (75 per cent of men, 55 per cent of women).

Improved schooling served not only the practical economic needs of the peasants. It was essential in instilling in them a consciousness that they belonged to a national community beyond the village, enjoying the benefits as well as shouldering the burdens of citizenship. Such a sense of mutual responsibility, or what might be called national feeling, was often weak or even non-existent, for, to many peasants, the state, represented by its bureaucracy and by urban dwellers in general, was predatory and oppressive. The process of turning peasants into Rumanians was thus far from over.

Agriculture took on an increasingly commercial character during this period, as the production of grain became ever more closely linked to the demands of the international market.[21] The completion of the first railway lines between 1869 and 1875 had decisively affected this trade, for they reduced the costs of transporting grain to the Danube ports and made possible its export overland directly to the industrial centres of Central Europe. No other branch of economic activity showed such rapid growth in so short a time as the export of grain. At the end of the century grain production accounted for nearly 85 per cent of the total value of Rumanian exports. In certain years almost the entire grain crop was exported, as in 1890 when 92 per cent was exported. Wheat was the main component of this trade, followed by corn. In the second decade of the twentieth century Rumania ranked fourth in the world as an exporter of wheat and third as an exporter of

---

[21] Ibid. 12: 750–1; Mircea Iosa, 'Comerțul cerealier și piața de cereale din România la sfîrșitul secolului al XIX-lea și începutul secolului al XX-lea', *Revista de istorie*, 42/3 (1989), 247–59.

corn. Not only was the great landowner inextricably linked to the international market, but, because of the organization of Rumanian agriculture, the small peasant producer was directly affected by fluctuations in world prices and demand. Thus, whenever the demand for Rumanian grain slackened, as in the 1880s, when its quality was suspect or when the competition from American exports became acute, a crisis occurred on the land and made more precarious the existence of large numbers of peasants.

Burdened by debt to landlords and *arendaşi* and always on the edge of poverty, abused by officials and ignored by politicians, who considered them less than fully-fledged citizens, peasants in the later 1880s resorted to violence to gain a redress of grievances. They seized land and occasionally killed a landlord or an *arendaş*, or they took flight, crossing the Danube to settle in Bulgaria. Their desperation reached breaking-point in the summer of 1887 and the following winter. A severe drought that summer destroyed the grain crop and dried up the pastures. Many peasants were forced to pawn or sell animals to meet interest payments on their debts, or they simply lost those they had pawned earlier. In many *judeţe*, especially in Moldavia, peasants were driven to the verge of starvation. The Liberal government appropriated a substantial sum of money with which to buy corn for distribution among peasants, but amounts made available fell short of needs.

Desperation caused by fear that they would not receive corn from the government led peasants in several villages in Ialomiţa *judeţ*, east of Bucharest, to attack local authorities on 20 March 1888.[22] Their example was quickly followed in neighbouring *judeţe* and within two months clashes of greater or lesser dimensions between peasants and local authorities, landlords, and *arendaşi* had broken out in twenty-seven of the country's thirty-two *judeţe*. Violence was most concentrated in five *judeţe* around Bucharest, where the revolt encompassed some 300 villages at one time or another. Only in September was the last of the local uprisings suppressed. By then about 1,000 peasants had been killed and some 3,000 arrested. Poor peasants and those with middle-sized holdings had been the driving force behind the movement. The causes of their discontent were everywhere manifest: they demanded food and land, a softening of the terms of agricultural contracts, and an end to arbitrary treatment by local officials,

[22] The immediate causes of the uprising are discussed in N. Adăniloaie, *Răscoala ţăranilor din 1888* (Bucharest, 1988), 111–37.

landlords, and *arendaşi*. In the end, they failed to gain their objectives because their uprisings had been spontaneous. They were isolated from one another and their actions were unco-ordinated, and thus they could not match the resources mobilized against them by the Junimist government.

The uprising had one positive result: it brought the plight of the peasant forcefully to the attention of both Liberal and Conservative politicians. Persuaded, at least temporarily, that decisive action was necessary, a broad coalition favoured a bill proposed by the Junimist government to sell state lands to the peasants in lots of 5, 10, and 25 hectares. Its supporters won the approval of parliament on 6 April 1889 as a means of ending the ferment in the countryside, but as Petre Carp openly admitted, many of them were equally anxious to preserve the great estates. The majority of Conservatives insisted, therefore, that the sale of state lands was an 'exceptional case', which should not be used as a precedent for making similar grants of land in the future. They rejected the notion that the peasants had an inherent right to land and insisted that they be made to understand that the only way for them to obtain it was by working harder, by saving, by planning for the future, and by buying and selling among themselves and with other private landowners. These Conservatives were intent upon staving off any attempt by reformers to solve the agrarian problem by expropriating private property. Yet they also sought to strengthen the village bourgeoisie—hence, the provision in the law for the sale of relatively large lots which only the more substantial elements of the peasantry could afford—as a support for the existing political and social order.

Later Conservative and Liberal governments continued to seek solutions to the agrarian problem in the same spirit. They created a number of new institutions in the countryside to aid the independent peasant producer, but they refrained from tampering with existing economic and social structures.

Agrarian reformers focused their attention on providing peasants with credit at reasonable interest rates. Ion Ionescu de la Brad was one of the most enthusiastic proponents of 'rural banks', which would primarily serve the peasants. In 1868 he pointed out one of the main shortcomings of the agrarian law of 1864: it had given the peasant land, but had withheld from him money, without which he could never complete his emancipation. Ionescu de la Brad conceived of a country-wide network of small credit banks based upon the German model of credit co-operatives. But he was reluctant to leave the initiative to the peasants themselves because of what he saw as their inveterate lack of enterprise, and he placed his hopes for success in the intervention of the state. He was certain that the resistance of the local possessing classes, who feared any diminution of their hold over the rural population, and the lack of private capital could not be overcome without the support of the central government. But he and other advocates of rural credit had little success until after the War for Independence when the Liberals came to power and were finally in a position to carry out their projects for economic modernization. In 1876 in his famous brochure, *Creditul Rural* (Rural Credit) Ionescu de la Brad restated his case in simple, moving terms.[23] He pointed out that after the peasants had been emancipated from their 'slavery' to land they had fallen into slavery to money and were worse off than they had been before 1864.

The Liberal government established Credit Agricol (Agricultural Credit Society) in 1881 in order to improve the productivity of agriculture by offering cheap loans to peasants. Capital came from the state and from private sources through the sale of shares. A branch of the society was established in every *judeţ* and was authorized to make loans for up to nine months' duration at no more than 7 per cent interest. Yet, it soon became evident that the original intent of the law was being ignored. Designed to help the smallholder, the institution was gradually taken over by large landowners and *arendaşi*, who obtained the lion's share of loans. The requirement that the peasant put up a part of his crop and tools as collateral and have two co-signers to guarantee the loan, created conditions which few peasants could fulfil. Nevertheless, later governments recognized the value of the programme, and in 1892 the Conservatives reorganized Credit Agricol to ensure greater participation by peasants. Yet, even though it loaned an average of 50 million lei annually, the majority of peasants were too poor to qualify for help.

Of crucial importance in expanding credit opportunities in the rural areas were 'popular banks' (*băncile populare*). Their appearance was spontaneous and their growth unregulated by law. The first was founded in 1891, and by 1902 their number had risen to 700 with almost 60,000 members. They owed their success chiefly

---

[23] C. I. Băicoianu, *Istoria politicei noastre monetare şi a Băncii Naţionale, 1880–1914*, ii, part 1 (Bucharest, 1932), 170–81; Ion Ionescu de la Brad, *Opere*, ii (Bucharest, 1943), 255–62.

to their closeness, physically and psychologically, to those they served. They were run by local people who were well acquainted with both local economic conditions and the applicants for loans and could reach quicker and more accurate decisions on credit-worthiness than the more remote officials who administered the Agricultural Credit Society.

The success of the popular banks owed much to Spiru Haret, who as Liberal Minister of Education in 1897–9 and 1901–4 actively promoted them in the villages. It is no coincidence that their numbers increased rapidly at this time. In 1902 Haret decided that the time had come to regulate these banks and co-ordinate their activities with the general plans of the Liberals for the development of a modern national economy. In 1903 he intro-duced a bill in parliament, drafted by Constantin Stere and Emil Costinescu, the Minister of Finance, which granted the banks a juridical personality, made them subject to the commercial code, and established the criteria for their formation. But it also took away their independence and subordinated them to the Agricul-tural Credit Society.

The popular banks continued their impressive growth down to the First World War. By 1913 they numbered 2,900, almost all of them based on the German Schulze-Delitzsche system. They were thus profit-oriented and paid dividends and succeeded in attracting capital, but they necessarily appealed to the well-off peasant rather than the poorer majority of rural inhabitants. The bulk of the capi-tal accumulated by these banks was controlled by the burgeoning village middle class—prosperous peasants, teachers, priests, and small merchants. The popular banks fell short of fulfilling their original purpose of improving the productivity of the smallholder and transforming the organization of agriculture. Although they made numerous loans, most of them (80 to 90 per cent) were non-productive, that is, they amounted to less than 300 lei and were, therefore, not invested in animals or equipment, but were used to cover current living expenses.[24]

The Liberals attempted to bring order and prosperity to the village through yet another comprehensive rural law. In 1904 they enacted legislation giving legal status to co-operatives (obştii săteşti) and specifying the procedures for their establishment. The main purpose of the law was to enable peasants to form an association for the purpose of renting a landlord's estate or other land, but, as

---

[24] *Buletinul statistic al României*, 12/32–3 (1914), 211–32.

with the law on popular banks of the previous year, the Liberals were concerned primarily with the well-off, productive peasant, not his poorer, unsuccessful neighbours. The co-operative movement which they thus set in motion continued to grow until the First World War. By 1913 there were 495 co-operatives with almost 77,000 members, but all together they leased only a modest amount of land, about one-sixth of that leased by *arendaşi*.

The popular banks, the co-operatives, and the sales of state lands touched only a small percentage of the peasants. The ineffectiveness of these measures was dramatically revealed by the massive peasant uprising which swept the country in the spring of 1907. The underlying causes of this unprecedented violence were the harsh conditions under which the majority of peasants—and by no means only the poorest—lived. On the eve of the uprising 424,000 peasants possessed too little land with which to make ends meet (less than three hectares), and 300,000 had no land at all. Large numbers of these and other peasants were economically defenceless before landlords and *arendaşi*, who could impose almost at will whatever terms they wished as rent for small grants of land. Equally ruinous were the exactions of money-lenders. Peasants were often forced to mortgage all their possessions or future years' crops in return for loans at high rates of interest. They also found themselves compelled by poverty to sell their produce immediately after the harvest to speculators for less than its market value, and then in the winter and spring they were obliged to buy it back at inflated prices. Added to these private burdens were state taxes, which in some parts of the country amounted to 80 per cent of the peasants' total annual production. Under these circumstances natural calamities like the cruel droughts of 1899 and 1904 brought vast numbers of peasants to the brink of starvation.

The uprising grew out of a minor dispute on 21 February 1907 between the peasants of Flămînzi, a village in Botoşani *judeţ* in northern Moldavia, and the manager of an estate leased to the great Fischer Trust. News of the trouble spread quickly to neighbouring villages and *judeţe*, where mass meetings were held and petitions drawn up demanding lower rents for leased land. At first, the peasants carried on their demonstrations peacefully, but on 13 March they began to occupy the estates of landlords and entered a number of market-towns, destroying the houses of landlords and *arendaşi* and the storehouses of merchants. On the 16th the first clashes between the peasants and the army took place. By this time the uprising had spread to all of northern Moldavia.[25] As the violence took its course many Jewish *arendaşi* and money-lenders were attacked, but the uprising was not an anti-Semitic outbreak. Its causes were broadly social and economic, and no distinction was made between Christian and Jewish 'oppressors'. If many Jews were attacked, it was because in northern Moldavia they controlled most of the leased properties. Nor was the violence solely an act of desperation by the poverty-stricken. The poorer peasants were indeed the first to revolt, but they were soon joined by their better-off neighbours. To the extent that the actions of the peasants had any direction, it was supplied by village intellectuals and, especially in Wallachia, by reserve army non-commissioned officers.

By the latter part of March the uprising had spread to Wallachia, where it gained an even higher degree of intensity than in Moldavia. Here, too, peasant violence was a response to the lack of land and to the harsh terms imposed in leasing contracts by landlords and *arendaşi*. The uprising was less spontaneous than it had been in the neighbouring province. The activities of Vasile Kogălniceanu and the village intellectuals—priests and teachers—had created an atmosphere of expectation and had prepared the peasants for action. Beginning in 1906, through brochures and the newspaper, *Gazeta ţăranilor*, wide-ranging discussions of the 'peasant question' had penetrated the villages, where their inhabitants were urged to unite as the only way to improve conditions. Kogălniceanu's brochure, *Către săteni*, distributed in 1906 and early 1907, had a powerful effect on the peasants. It began and ended with the call, 'Vrem pămînt' (We want land), and gave the peasants to understand that their right to rise up against injustice had been endorsed by the queen. A further stimulus to action were the inflamatory accounts in *Gazeta ţăranilor* and other newspapers about the uprisings in Moldavia.

The uprising was more intense in Wallachia than in Moldavia. The event which set the peasants in motion in many *judeţe* was the call-up on 21 March of army reservists to put down the violence in Moldavia. Disturbances broke out precisely in those *judeţe* where reservists refused to join their regiments, and soon the uprising had spread to every corner of the country. It reached its

---

[25] The extensive literature on the uprising is noted in the Bibliographical Essay. An original analysis of the spread of the violence has been done by Vasile Liveanu, Irina Gavrilă, and Constanţa Moţei, 'Statistica matematică şi istoria: Despre ordinea declanşării mişcărilor ţărăneşti în 1907', *Revista de istorie*, 33/9 (1980), 1697–736.

greatest intensity between 25 and 28 March in Oltenia, where massive encounters between peasants and the army took place and where the loss of lives was correspondingly great.

The Conservatives under Prime Minister Cantacuzino were slow to react, but the Liberals, who replaced them at the end of March, undertook a vigorous campaign of suppression. The army, under the command of General Alexandru Averescu, resorted to the most ruthless measures, even the bombardment of villages by artillery, to regain control of the countryside. After an enormous loss of life—some 11,000 persons killed—and a wholesale destruction of property an uneasy calm had been restored by the middle of April.

The uprising made a profound impression on all political parties. Both the right and the left viewed the event as a national tragedy, and they hastened to put forward proposals to remove what a few among them had come to see as a moral wrong and the majority as a barrier to economic and political development.

The majority of Conservatives were determined to defend the integrity of private property at all cost, but they realized that an expropriation of land was unavoidable if social peace was to be maintained in the countryside. The more thoughtful among them were even persuaded that a partial expropriation of large estates might work to their benefit. They thought the use of hired labour would be more efficient than the prevailing exploitation of labour by contract. One of their number, Constantin Garoflid, recommended the expropriation of 500,000 hectares from private estates (about 15 per cent of the total) and an equal amount of land belonging to institutions and the state. But he insisted that no holding be reduced to fewer than 500 hectares, which he considered the minimum necessary for an estate to remain economically viable. Like many of his contemporaries, both Liberals and Conservatives, he thought that the modernization and prosperity of agriculture depended upon the maintenance of large property.[26] But the leaders of the Conservative Party would not yield on the question of expropriation and proclaimed again the 'sanctity' of private property. The Liberals, who were now in power, also drew back from an expropriation of the large estates. The majority shared the views contained in Spiru Haret's influential *Chestia ţărănească* (The Peasant Question), published in 1905 and republished in 1907 after the peasant uprising. In it he called for an

---

[26] C. Garoflid, *Problema agrară şi deslegarea ei* (Bucharest, 1908), 96.

improvement of the peasants' condition through village banks and co-operatives, which in turn would assist the peasant in buying and leasing estates directly from their owners. Finally, on the left of the political spectrum, the Poporanists denounced the prevailing 'unjust' division of land and its 'evil' consequences and demanded the immediate granting of land to the peasants. Constantin Stere, while condemning peasant uprisings, supported the expropriation of landlord estates (with at least partial compensation) as the only practical way of obtaining the necessary land for redistribution.[27]

The new Liberal government, headed by Dimitrie Sturdza, with Ionel Brătianu as Minister of the Interior and General Alexandru Averescu as Minister of War, took office on 25 March 1907 at the height of the uprising. Although it stopped short of advocating the expropriation of private property, it was prepared to enact a series of reforms that would bring relief to at least a part of the peasantry. On the very day it took office it issued a manifesto to the nation promising to reduce the land taxes paid by peasants to the state, facilitate the leasing of public lands directly to peasants, lighten the terms of agricultural contracts, establish a rural credit bank (Casa Rurală) to enable peasants to lease and buy land more easily, and abolish leasing trusts.

Beginning with the parliamentary session of the autumn of 1907 the Liberal Party pushed through an impressive array of measures designed to carry out the promises contained in the manifesto of 25 March and, in the words of Ionel Brătianu, preserve the 'social credit' of the governing parties with the mass of the population.[28] The most important of the reform laws dealt with three fundamental problems: agricultural contracts, credit, and leasing. The law on agricultural contracts of 23 December 1907 sought to limit the degree to which landlords and arendaşi could exploit peasants who rented or leased land from them. It set maximum prices for leases of arable land and pastures and minimum wages for peasants who worked estates with their own inventory. The law establishing Casa Rurală of 5 March 1908 provided for the creation of a fund of 10 million lei, half from the state and half from private sources, to enable individual peasants to buy lots of five hectares (up to a total of twenty-five hectares) from estates volun-

[27] Ioan Căpreanu, Eseul unei restituiri: C. Stere (Iaşi, 1988), 182–4; C. Stere, Scrieri (Bucharest, 1979), 469–94, 526–40.
[28] On the agrarian laws enacted and the accompanying parliamentary debates, see Istoria parlamentului şi a vieţii parlamentare din România pînă la 1918 (Bucharest, 1983), 386–421.

tarily put on the market by their owners. This law was supplemented by legislation in 1908 and 1909 authorizing the central popular bank to make loans to village co-operatives to enable them to lease entire estates and then sublease small parcels from them to individual peasants. Finally, parliament passed a law on 12 April 1908 forbidding any person or organization to lease more than 4,000 hectares of arable land at one time.

This body of legislation had little or no effect on the majority of peasants partly because many of its provisions were not enforced and partly because it was designed primarily to assist the well-off peasant. For a time landlords abided by regulations on rents and wages. Yet, since there were few officials to enforce the law, the old abuses soon reappeared. Many peasants who could not qualify for loans from the popular banks and could not afford to join village co-operatives were desperate for land and had no choice but to accept the conditions set down by landlords. Only a relatively small amount of land was made available to peasants under the auspices of Casa Rurală. Nor did the reform legislation affect the fundamental character of agricultural production. The Liberals had made no serious attempt to change the direction of agriculture away from a concentration on the production of grain, which in 1914 accounted for about 84 per cent of the total agricultural production. The dependence of agriculture on grain production was reinforced by the favourable international market. Between 1901 and 1915 an average of 45 per cent of grain production was exported annually, a quantity which placed Rumania first among the exporters of corn and second among the exporters of wheat in Europe.

Agrarian relations also remained much as they had been before 1907. Large numbers of peasants, perhaps as many as 725,000 households, lacked the minimum of five hectares considered necessary to maintain a family of five. Especially serious was the lack of adequate pastureland. Although peasants owned about 90 per cent of the cattle in 1910, they possessed only 30 per cent of the pastures. The sales of some 178,000 hectares of pastureland by large landowners for the purpose of creating communal grazing lands, in accordance with the law on agricultural contracts of 1907, fell short of meeting the demand, and, hence, the peasants still had to turn to landlords and *arendaşi* to satisfy their needs.

Several changes in the organization of production on large properties were none the less discernible. The reforms of 1907 had reduced the supply of contract peasants, who were gradually replaced by wage labourers. Between 1906 and 1913 the portion of the estate worked by hired hands rose from 25 to 35 per cent. Agricultural machinery was also slowly displacing traditional peasant labour. Yet, its use was spotty. Steam-driven machines had an insignificant role in field work. For example, in 1915 there were only 300 steam-driven ploughs in operation. The only activity where machinery predominated was threshing, from which the traditional oxen had practically been eliminated. Thus, on the eve of the First World War few estates were well endowed with machinery, and their owners or *arendaşi* were seldom able to dispense with peasant animals and tools. Needless to say, the use of machinery on peasant holdings was extremely rare.

The separation of the peasant from agriculture itself continued a steady, if undramatic, course. Many peasants who had been forced off the land found work in non-agricultural occupations in the countryside in the mining, forestry, and oil industries and on the railways. Still others, especially women, turned to a new form of the cottage industry—sewing and weaving—operated by small entrepreneurs from nearby cities or better-off peasants in the villages. Many peasants, with skills and without, moved to cities to seek work in artisan shops, transportation, and factories. It is difficult to measure the extent of these processes, for statistics show that the number of poor, landless peasants in the countryside remained stationary between 1905 and 1913 at 300,000. None the less, since the rural population grew significantly in these years, it is clear that the proletarianization of the peasantry was unrelenting.

The slow pace of industrialization and urbanization had profound effects on agriculture and the standard of living of the peasant. Underdevelopment helped to keep the domestic market for agricultural products from expanding and offered little stimulus for a diversification of crops. Even though the standard of living in the cities was higher than that of the countryside, the demand for agricultural products in the cities remained modest, since the urban population itself represented only 17 per cent of the total population in 1910. Demand from peasants who did not raise their own food and from mills, which in 1913 took about 30 per cent of the wheat produced, was not strong enough to alter the organization of agriculture.

One of the most encouraging signs of a fundamental change in the organization of agriculture was the rapid growth of peasant leasing co-operatives (*obştii de arendare*) after 1907.[29] As a result of Liberal legislation in 1908 and 1909 a significant amount of land from the great estates passed into the hands of peasants. The latter were attracted to the co-operatives because they were thus able to escape the domination of the despised middlemen, the *arendaşi*. Between 1907 and 1914 the number of co-operatives increased from 103 to 605 and the amount of land they leased from 73,000 hectares to 475,000. The majority of the participants were prosperous peasants, and, consequently, the poorer strata were not directly affected by the movement. Sympathetic observers noted the general efficiency and receptivity to innovation which characterized the co-operatives and were certain that if the First World War had not broken out the gradual transfer in this fashion of large property to those who worked it might have provided a 'natural' solution to the agrarian problem.

Persistent problems on the land and the failure of the agrarian economy to move forward, despite the post-1907 legislation, convinced many Liberals that a new and more comprehensive agrarian reform was needed. Immediately after the second Balkan War, at the end of 1913, Ionel Brătianu proposed a partial expropriation of private large estates in order to provide additional land to the peasants. In a series of articles published in 1914 Vintilă Brătianu, the party's chief economic theorist and the brother of the prime minister, pointed out how closely the new reforms corresponded to the broad economic and social goals of the Liberals.[30] He argued that the proposed measures would allow landlords to adopt intensive forms of agriculture, which were more efficient and productive than the extensive agriculture they were currently practising, and he urged that the compensation payments be used to modernize their estates. Brătianu and the Liberals were also intent upon strengthening the successful peasant, whom they considered a pillar of the existing economic and social system. By enhancing the prosperity of the most dynamic element of the peasantry, they hoped to expand the domestic market for manufactures and thereby contribute to the development of Rumanian industry and commerce. This 'worthy' segment of the peasantry, therefore, was favoured in their reform projects. Reserved to it was the bulk of the land to be expropriated. The Liberals gave little thought to

[29] Gheorghe Cristea, 'Amploarea mişcării cooperative în România după răscoala din 1907', *Revista de istorie*, 38/9 (1983), 865–78.
[30] Vintilă I. C. Brătianu, *Scrieri şi cuvântări*, iii (Bucharest, 1940), 403–4, 411–15.

the poor peasantry, except to express the conviction that a growing industry would draw off surplus population from the countryside into the cities, thereby alleviating the problems caused by
overpopulation. The outbreak of the First World War brought the
consideration of all these matters to a halt.

INDUSTRY

The structure of industry underwent significant, if uneven, changes
during the period. The final disintegration of the old guild system
occurred, and the undermining of the artisan craft industry ran its
inexorable course in both the countryside and the city. The causes
must be sought in the steady growth of large-scale processing and
manufacturing at home and Rumania's further integration into
the Western European economic system, which opened the gates
wide to foreign manufactured goods and capital. Through legislation and regulatory agencies the state placed itself on the side
of modern industry at the expense of traditional methods of
production. Although by 1914 Rumanian industry as a whole
had achieved notable progress, significant gaps remained. Key
elements of a modern industrial base, such as metallurgy and
machine-building, were still practically non-existent, and industry
remained closely linked to agriculture, as the processing of raw
materials—foodstuffs, forestry products, and oil—predominated.

In 1850 the peasant cottage industry was the chief, and often the
only, means by which the peasant could obtain the finished goods
he needed. The range of articles thus produced was almost infinite,
from bricks for building houses and tools for agriculture to clothes
and every sort of household item. Individual households tended to
specialize in one or two types of articles, and in some regions
whole villages became famous for a particular product or for
wood-working or cloth-making. But by the end of the century
these thriving industries had become merely a secondary source of
consumer goods and in many parts of the country, particularly in
the plains, they had disappeared altogether.

The causes of the decline of this traditional component of the
village economy lay in the fundamental changes taking place in
agriculture and in the economy as a whole in the second half of
the nineteenth century. Social differentiation within the peasantry
itself, which was accelerated after the agrarian reform of 1864,
tended to undermine the family-based cottage industry. Only the

middle-sized peasant household kept up the tradition. It possessed a modest holding, which was sufficient to cover basic needs, but did not permit family members to buy consumer goods on the market. Rather, they were obliged to make many items for themselves, and, in any case, they found it more advantageous to process rather than sell the products they raised. It was the well-to-do and the poor peasants who no longer made goods at home. The former could afford to buy what they needed from specialized artisans or from the mass production of the new factories. They were the first to give up the family crafts. The poor also bought manufactured goods, but for different reasons. They lacked the land, the animals, and even the rudimentary tools necessary for craftwork and, hence, had to rely upon cheap consumer goods produced elsewhere to satisfy their modest needs. In places where peasant holdings had become miniscule or where large properties predominated, crafts suffered because peasants had been drawn into the labour-force that worked the estate and no longer had time to honour household traditions.

Those peasants who still practised their crafts faced two critical problems. First of all, they found it increasingly difficult to obtain adequate supplies of raw materials—wood, animals, and textile plants. As the concentration of Rumanian agriculture on grain intensified, forests were diminished and the price of wood increased; the number of animals, which supplied wool, skins, and furs, declined between 1860 and 1900, or grew too slowly to meet the needs of the mass of the peasants; and the amount of land sown in flax and hemp, traditionally used for cloth-making at home, had diminished to such an extent that by 1900 weaving by women in many places had ceased altogether. To obtain the needed raw materials those peasants who could afford to do so turned to the market, especially for cloth. They were able to take advantage of the large quantities of imports, especially of cheap cotton cloth, which inundated the country in the last three decades of the nineteenth century. The second and most formidable threat to the family craftsman was the competition from manufactured goods, especially clothing, shoes, cloth, leather products, and agricultural implements. Besides the surge of foreign imports, the quantity of goods being turned out by domestic large-scale industry became overwhelming in the last decade of the century. As a consequence, by 1900 the family craftsman's share of production had declined dramatically. Even where traditional crafts were still practised, their old, patriarchal character had been undermined by new market conditions. Many Rumanian politicians and economists lamented the passing of the traditional crafts, and some, like Petre Aurelian, sought (in vain, as it turned out) to revive them as a means of improving rural living standards.

Peasant family crafts themselves contributed significantly to the development of modern industry by creating a skilled work-force capable of going directly into the factory. It was not simply coincidence that industrial enterprises tended to be established in those regions which had had strong traditions of peasant craftsmanship, for example, in Prahova and Dîmbovița *judeţe* in Wallachia, and in Bacău and Neamţ in Moldavia.

The organized artisan industries in towns and cities underwent a process of decline similar to that of the peasant crafts. In the middle of the nineteenth century artisan production was the most important branch of Rumanian industry. Except for textiles and certain wood products, it supplied most of the needs of the mass of the population in the urban centres and the surrounding rural areas (the wealthy had recourse to imports). The organization of this production did not differ in essentials from what it had been a half-century earlier. The hierarchy of master artisan, journeyman, and apprentice preserved its essential features, although in the typical workshop the proprietor usually worked alongside those he employed. The ordinary shop had one to three craftsmen, although many were larger. The master artisan rarely became as wealthy as the banker or merchant, but generally he could assure himself of a comfortable living. The position of the journeymen at this time also seemed secure, for they were eagerly sought by masters.

The crafts were organized into guilds, or corporations, as they were now called, much as they had been in 1800 and for the same purpose—to assure the welfare of their members. But they no longer exercised the same degree of control over their members as they once had. Legislation embodying the widely proclaimed principle of free trade gradually whittled away at their monopolistic practices. The final step in deregulation was taken in 1873 when the government abolished the remaining corporations. The act drew no serious protest, for it simply recognized a state of things that already existed.

In the last four decades of the century the artisan crafts suffered drastic changes as the capitalist mentality and business practices infiltrated the economy. The most striking feature of the new regime was the general absence of regulations in all those aspects of production where they had existed earlier. Restrictions on the right to practise a trade, on the number of journeymen and apprentices, on the acquisition of raw materials, and on the quality and price of goods were a thing of the past, as the artisan was cast into the whirlpool of competition. The struggle was far from equal. Inexorably, the smaller artisans, who formed the overwhelming majority and lived a precarious existence, were slowly forced into the ranks of the factory workers, or left the profession altogether, while a few great artisans not only survived but managed to re-establish a quasi-monopoly in those branches which were of little interest to the large-scale capitalist entrepreneur.

By the turn of the century economic competition and government neglect, compounded by the general economic crisis of 1899–1903, had brought the master artisans to the point of desperation. Their public agitation throughout the country forced the Liberal government, which counted upon their political support, to act. In 1902 it passed the Missir Law, named for the minister who sponsored it, which provided for a restoration of the corporations, thereby arousing the hopes of the master artisans that they could somehow return to the conditions of an earlier, more prosperous era. Although the law revived some of the old restrictive privileges of the guilds, it did nothing to protect them from the destructive competition of the burgeoning factory system. Nor could the law reverse a half-century of economic and social change, and, in the end, it proved completely ineffective. In 1908–11 the number of small workshops declined by 11 per cent and their work-force by 30 per cent. Of the 36,678 'master artisans' officially registered in 1911, some 30,000 were merely wage earners who worked at home and were paid by the piece by commercial entrepreneurs who supplied them with the raw materials and marketed the finished product.[31]

The prospects for the growth of a large-scale, modern industry had appeared dim at mid-century. Essential elements were lacking: adequate investment capital, skilled labour, and a large domestic market for manufactured goods, shortcomings caused in part by the underdevelopment of agriculture and the low standard of living of the mass of the population. The remedies for these deficiencies— the institutions and the mentality of modern capitalism—had barely made their appearance.

[31] Virgil Madgearu, *Ocrotirea muncitorilor în România* (Bucharest, 1915), 6; Virgil Madgearu, *Zur industriellen Entwickelung Rumäniens* (Weida, 1911), 102–12.

A formidable obstacle to the development of large-scale industry was the mounting flow of foreign goods and the absence of protective tariffs. Before the union of the principalities the volume of imports had been moderate, but in the following quarter-century, particularly after the commercial convention of 1875 with Austria-Hungary, they threatened to engulf the Rumanian market. Before 1860 imports were mainly 'luxury' items—silks and fine cloth, clothing, carriages, glassware, and spices—and their chief purchasers were the upper classes. They were too expensive for the population at large and, hence, did not seriously impinge upon the markets of local industry and the artisan crafts. Peasants bought almost nothing of the imports, except cotton goods. After 1860 imports assumed a strikingly different character. Large quantities of cheap goods intended for mass consumption, even by the poor, flooded the country. This change reflected the immense capacity of Western European industry to satisfy the needs and tastes of a foreign public. It also revealed both the increased capacity of the Rumanian market to absorb these goods, because of accelerated agricultural production, and the defence-lessness of the Rumanian market. The continued functioning of Ottoman commercial norms was undoubtedly decisive in keeping the Rumanian market open to foreign goods. Even after the union of the principalities economic concessions granted by Turkey to various European powers continued to be applied to Rumania. In Rumania itself the free-trade theories of economists and politicians, which were prevalent in the 1860s and 1870s, militated against the imposition of protective tariffs. According to them, the only purpose served by customs duties was to raise revenue. In 1874 the Rumanian government finally decided to introduce on its own a new tariff structure, protective in nature, but it abandoned the project when the commercial convention with Austria-Hungary was signed the following year.

Significant changes took place in the 1870s and 1880s which encouraged the development of large-scale industry. The abolition of Ottoman suzerainty removed the remaining political impediments to international trade and enabled the Rumanian government to pursue a commercial policy designed to promote national economic development. An immediate consequence was the rapid growth of foreign trade, which, in turn, stimulated economic activity and attracted foreign investments. In the same two decades a modern infrastructure began to take form: private commercial banks and a national bank were founded to assure adequate credit and provide a measure of financial co-ordination and stability; a national monetary system was introduced; uniform weights and measures based upon the decimal system were adopted; commercial stock exchanges where the prices of goods and interest rates could be determined in free market conditions were established; comprehensive commercial and civil legislation which offered both Rumanian and foreign businessmen the necessary legal framework within which to carry on their activities was passed; and transportation facilities, notably railways, were expanded and improved.

Two other elements were also essential to bring about economic change: a new spirit of business enterprise based upon credit and adequate investment capital. Between the 1840s and the 1860s a number of economists, notably Ion Ghica and Dionisie Pop Marţian, had extolled the virtues of a modern credit system. Although to transform ideas into institutions proved difficult, as Prince Grigore Ghica's failure to establish the National Bank of Moldavia in 1856 attests, they and numerous supporters helped to prepare the way for a general change in business mentality. At about the same time investment capital began to accumulate from a variety of internal sources: the more intensive exploitation of agricultural lands, the sums created by compensation payments for lands expropriated in 1864, the increased leasing of estates, foreign and domestic commerce, and the sale of supplies to the army and public institutions. Opportunities for individual enrichment thus multiplied, and a growing number of persons began to invest in industry, at first in food-processing and then in a variety of other enterprises. In the 1860s they formed the nucleus of the new industrial bourgeoisie, which by the 1880s was to exert a decisive influence on the economic policies of the state.

Foreign capital played a crucial role in the development of heavy industry and of the economy in general.[32] It began to flow into Rumania in substantial amounts after the War for Independence, and, besides industry, it was invested in banks, commerce, and insurance. In industry, by the First World War, foreign capital had become predominant in gas and electricity (95.5 per cent), oil (94 per cent), sugar (94 per cent), metallurgy (74 per cent), chemicals (72.3 per cent), and forestry products (69 per cent). Its greatest concentration was in the production of raw materials.

[32] Victor Axenciuc, 'Penetraţia capitalului străin în România pînă la primul război mondial', Revista de istorie, 34/5 (1981), 821–51.

Anglo-Dutch and Franco-Belgian capital together held about 57 per cent of the capital invested in industry. Foreign capital was also a massive presence in banking after 1880, as a national system of credit institutions became fully functional. On the eve of the First World War the five largest banks controlled by foreign capital had resources of 500,000,000 lei, as compared to 325,000,000 lei for the four largest Rumanian-controlled banks. Loans to the Rumanian government were another avenue through which foreign capital entered the country. Between 1866 and 1914 they amounted to 4,000 million lei, which were used for an ambitious programme of public works, particularly the construction of railways and government buildings. Rumania attracted foreign capital because of the relatively high return, usually between 4.25 and 5.6 per cent. Such investments were essential to the development of a modern economy, but they also served as a means by which foreign individuals and governments could influence Rumanian government policy.

The processing of agricultural products was the leading industry of the period. Milling, in particular, showed steady growth and was one of the first industries to undergo a technological transformation. The appearance on the European market of plentiful and cheap American grain caused a dramatic decline in Rumanian exports to numerous countries (in 1860, 16 per cent of Rumanian grain exports went to Britain and France; in 1874, only 1.4 per cent), but such competition stimulated domestic food-processing by forcing Rumanian landlords to expand existing facilities and establish new branches of the industry. One of the most profitable of these was sugar refining, which began to receive modest encouragement from the state in 1873. Tobacco also was among the crops which attracted attention, and in 1872 two factories were established, one in Bucharest and the other in Iaşi, which together employed 1,000 workers. It now became normal for large landowners and arendaşi to join industrialists in seeking subsidies and other benefits from both Liberal and Conservative governments for industries which used their agricultural and forestry products.

Industry benefited enormously from the patronage of the Liberal Party beginning in the 1860s. As we have seen, the Liberals were sympathetic to protectionist ideas, but they had been prevented from applying them by existing treaties, notably the commercial convention with Austria-Hungary. Their brand of protectionism took form only gradually. At first, they lacked a comprehensive economic strategy, and thus their legislation dealt only with individual industries and was intended primarily to stimulate the use of local raw materials (e.g. the law of 1881 to promote the paper industry by guaranteeing regular state purchases). Nor did the Liberals immediately grasp the importance of heavy industry. Much of the legislation they enacted before 1887 to stimulate industry was concerned with the improvement of the artisan crafts. Even the comprehensive law presented to parliament in 1882 by Petre Aurelian was based on the premiss that the development of a modern industry had to begin with the encouragement of the artisan crafts and the improvement of technical and professional education. It said nothing about founding industrial production on large-scale enterprises. A decade later, in 1895, Aurelian's views had not changed substantially. While arguing that protective tariffs were essential for the creation of industry and, hence, of a flourishing economy, he urged that attention be given first to the cottage and artisan industries as a necessary preliminary to the establishment of a factory system.[33] He recognized the value of large-scale industry, but for the time being relegated it to 'accessory' status. None the less, the encouragement of large-scale industry was becoming an important component of Liberal economic theory, and major legislation began to be passed in the mid-1880s.

Beginning in 1886 the Liberals put in place an industrial policy based upon protective tariffs and direct state support for medium-sized and large enterprises. The long-range goal of these and all the measures which followed was the creation of a modern capitalist industry patterned after that of Western Europe, a policy which meant more competition for peasant and artisan forms of industry. The first important act of the new industrial policy was the general tariff law of 1886, which, as we have seen, was enacted after the expiration of the commercial convention with Austria-Hungary. Import duties were applied to some 600 articles and represented roughly 10–15 per cent of their value. In comparison with the practices of other countries, these tariffs offered only a modest degree of protection. They were designed to shield from foreign competition, first of all, those industries already in existence, mainly food-processing and other light consumer goods industries, and thus they represented the initial phase of protec-

[33] P. S. Aurelian, 'Industria zahărului', *Economia națională*, 19/9 (1895), 193–8. For an earlier elaboration of his ideas, see P. S. Aurelian, *Cum se poate fonda industria în România și industria română față cu libertatea comerciului de importațiune*, in P. S. Aurelian, *Opere economice* (Bucharest, 1967), 185–218.

tionism, which aimed at expanding the use of raw materials from Rumanian agriculture and forests. But the act also looked to the future and offered modest support for other types of industries which its authors were certain would eventually be established. The tariff law was substantially revised in 1904 and 1906 in order to take into account the country's industrial progress and the increased pressure of foreign manufactured goods. The new duties ranged from 10 to 25 per cent of the value of the goods and were high on those items which competed with the products of local industry and low on machinery and items needed to develop that industry.

Many businessmen and bankers found the tariff laws too indirect a means of promoting industry. They favoured, instead, an expansion of direct government assistance, and in 1887 were instrumental in gaining the approval of parliament for a comprehensive programme to sustain industrial growth. The new law for the encouragement of industry provided exemptions from all taxes and tariff duties on imported machinery and raw materials for a period of fifteen years, a reduction of transport costs on the railways, and the granting by the state of building sites free of charge for ninety years to all Rumanian and foreign citizens who would establish industrial enterprises with a capital of at least 50,000 lei or employing a minimum of twenty-five workers. It also allowed the unlimited investment of foreign capital in the new industries, a recognition by the Liberals, despite their rhetoric about native initiative, that they did not possess sufficient financial resources to carry out their ambitious economic plans.

The law of 1887 remained in force for a quarter-century. The support it offered large industry was extended in 1912 to include artisans employing at least four workers or artisan co-operatives with at least twenty members. The new law also provided that goods furnished the state by all these enterprises could be priced up to 5 per cent higher than similar products available from foreign countries. Both laws contributed substantially to the progress of large-scale industry. If between 1866 and 1886 only an average of eight enterprises were founded each year, there were sixty-three per year in 1906–11, after the tariff of 1906 went into effect. Of some 1,150 enterprises functioning in 1915, 837 received support from the state. Capital invested in large-scale industry increased significantly from 247 million lei in 1901 to 329 million lei in 1915 (the latter figure includes only those industries encouraged by the state).

On the eve of the First World War the dominant industries were oil and lumber, which together represented 36.2 per cent of production, and food-processing, 32.3 per cent. Other industries accounted for the remaining one-third, including textiles (8.3 per cent) and metallurgy (7.8 per cent). The gaps in the structure of Rumanian industry are evident. The absence of an iron and steel industry and of a machine-building capability and the rudimentary nature of the chemical industry were among the indicators that the level of industrialization lagged well behind that of Western Europe. Moreover, industry accounted for only 17 per cent of the national income.

The accelerated expansion of Rumanian industry from the 1890s on was accompanied by a concentration of capital and production in a relatively small number of enterprises. At the beginning of the twentieth century, 4 per cent of the large enterprises (those with over 2 million lei fixed capital) held 46 per cent of all capital invested in industry. In 1913 six joint-stock companies held 40 per cent of the capital of all such companies. Banks contributed to the process. Here, too, a concentration of capital was taking place, and in 1913 seven banks, 4 per cent of all commercial banks, controlled 58 per cent of the banking capital. Banks steadily increased their holdings in industry, gaining control of some and taking the initiative in founding others.[34]

The most dynamic branch of Rumanian industry was oil. But it became so only after 1895. In the previous half-century exploration and production had proceeded slowly and with rudimentary methods and equipment. The first company, the Wallachian Petroleum Company, was founded in 1864 with a capital of 4 million francs by an Englishman, Jackson Brown. Three years later a group of Rumanian economists and politicians established Compania Anonimă Romănă pentru Explorări şi Comerţul cu Păcura (The Rumanian Enterprise for the Production and Sale of Petroleum). In this and subsequent modest undertakings Rumanian capital predominated, but both Liberals and Conservatives recognized that native resources were inadequate to develop the industry. The mining law of 1895, which marked a dramatic turn in the size and character of the Rumanian oil industry, was an attempt to remedy the situation. Soon foreign capital began to flow into oil exploration and production in ever-increasing

---

[34] G. M. Dobrovici, *Istoricul dezvoltării economice şi financiare a României şi impru-muturile contractate, 1823–1933* (Bucharest, 1934), 263–71.

amounts. Between 1903 and 1914 many of the major trusts were founded which were to dominate the Rumanian oil industry until the Second World War: Steaua Română, acquired by German capital in 1903, Româno-Americană (Standard Oil, 1904), and Astra Română (Royal Dutch-Shell, 1910). By 1914 the Rumanian oil industry had been thoroughly internationalized: German capital controlled 35 per cent, followed by British (25 per cent), Dutch (13 per cent), French (10 per cent), and American (5.5 per cent).[35] Rumanian capital represented only 5.5 per cent. The effects of massive foreign investments may be measured by a dramatic growth in production, stimulated, of course, by the rapidly increasing world demand for oil: 250,000 tons in 1900 and 1,885,000 in 1913. During the period as a whole more than 50 per cent of this production was exported, while internal consumption did not in general exceed 40 per cent, much of it in the form of kerosene and lubricating oil. The state became one of the largest consumers, especially after the replacement of coal by oil in railway engines at the end of the nineteenth century.

Despite impressive growth in oil refining, food-processing, and forestry products, which together accounted for 74 per cent of the value of production by large-scale enterprises on the eve of the First World War, several fundamental branches of a modern industry barely existed. Most serious was the failure of the metallurgical industry to develop. The industrial inquiry of 1901–2 revealed the existence of only seventy-five such enterprises, some of them merely ordinary workshops. A machine-building industry was non-existent. Thus, Rumanian industry generally remained dependent in these vital sectors upon foreign imports. It was the same with coal. Consumption was 610,993 tons in 1913–14, but production was only 230,431 tons, too little to meet the needs of an expanding industry.

Foreign trade had a decisive effect on the development of Rumanian industry and the economy as a whole. It expanded greatly in the half-century before the First World War. For a time, it followed traditional forms and routes. Rumania exported grain, mainly wheat and corn, and other agricultural products, and imported manufactures, primarily consumer goods. During this period both Conservative and Liberal governments kept the export taxes on grain low in order to encourage sales abroad and

---

[35] Gheorghe Buzatu, *România și trusturile petroliere internaționale pînă la 1929* (Iași, 1981), 34–5: Maurice Pearton, *Oil and the Romanian State* (Oxford, 1971), 22–34.

thereby increase state revenues and stimulate economic development. Besides Austria-Hungary, Rumania signed commercial agreements with other major powers. A trade and navigation treaty with Russia, concluded in March 1876, was based upon the principle of most favoured nation. The Western European states at first refused to conclude tariff conventions with Rumania in order not to offend the Ottoman government. But in November 1876 agreements with France, Britain, and Italy, and in 1877 with Germany, using the convention with Austria-Hungary as a model, were signed.

The effects of these treaties on Rumanian economic development were mixed. On the one hand, trade increased dramatically. Between 1872 and 1911 the total value of exports rose from nearly 840 million to 2,700 million lei, and imports from 600 million to 2,200 million lei. During the same period Rumania enjoyed a favourable balance of trade except for the period 1877–99 and the years 1904 and 1908. The trade surpluses were owing primarily to an increase in the export of grain, especially wheat, and after 1900 to the export of oil and wood products. Deficits were caused between 1876 and 1885 by the unfavourable terms of the commercial convention with Austria-Hungary and after 1887 by the policy of heavy investments in industry. Important also was the growth of the domestic market at a time when industry at home was not sufficiently developed to satisfy the demand and when the artisan crafts were disintegrating. The importation of consumer goods thus grew substantially. For example, in 1882 textiles accounted for 33 per cent of all imports, but by 1902 that figure had risen to 48 per cent.

The relative openness of the Rumanian market to imports in the decade 1876–85 dealt severe blows to all branches of local industry. The foreign goods easily replaced local products, mainly because they were cheaper. Foreign manufacturers had reduced their costs by mass production, the use of raw materials of inferior quality, especially for textiles and household goods, and advanced marketing techniques, all of which overwhelmed native producers. The competition for Rumanian markets among entrepreneurs of various countries also helped to keep prices low. Local consumers undoubtedly benefited, but local industry, particularly textiles, suffered. The old forms of production practised by artisans and peasants, who lost their position as the main suppliers of industrial goods to the general population, underwent a radical transformation. In some regions they survived on a reduced scale, but elsewhere such trades as cloth-weaving disappeared entirely. In almost all branches of the craft industry imports sharply reduced the living standard of artisans, causing many to abandon their profession altogether. In a sense, these imports left a void in the native economy. They created no new industrial organization to take the place of traditional craft structures. A few artisan industries survived by using imported raw materials and semi-finished goods, but they became appendages of Western industry and led a precarious existence of dependence upon the technology and marketing strategies of Western entrepreneurs.

Several significant changes occurred in the direction of Rumanian trade after the War for Independence. As for exports, the Ottoman Empire had been Rumania's best customer during the 1860s, but afterwards, as Rumanian commerce shifted westward away from traditional Eastern markets, Austria-Hungary assumed first place between 1876 and 1880. Then, mainly as a result of the tariff war, she yielded that position to Britain, who was Rumania's best customer for agricultural products until the early 1890s. Among the suppliers of goods to Rumania, Germany took over first place in the early 1890s, followed by Austria-Hungary. On the eve of the First World War (1912) these two countries provided Rumania with 60 per cent of all her imported goods.[36] In the same year Austria-Hungary was also an important purchaser of Rumanian products (she took 14.8 per cent of all Rumanian exports, and Germany 6.6 per cent). The Western powers remained well behind. Britain and France together supplied about 20 per cent of Rumania's imports and took about 15 per cent of her exports. Trade with the East (the Ottoman Empire and Russia) was negligible.

BANKING AND TRANSPORTATION

The expansion of industry and of business generally and the growing volume of foreign trade in the second half of the nineteenth century sharply increased the demand for capital and brought fundamental changes to Rumania's financial system. Large, modern banks, both state and private, replaced the money-lenders and the commercial houses which had flourished before

---

[36] A detailed analysis of Rumania's foreign trade after 1900 is in Mircea Iosa, 'Comerţul exterior al României în primul deceniu al secolului al XX-lea', *Revista de istorie*, 41/2 (1988), 171–90; 3: 299–312.

the middle of the century. Rumanian banks now became associated with major European financial institutions, and it was through them that foreign capital flowed into the country in record amounts. The new banks were the engines of important economic undertakings—the establishment of modern industries, the exploitation of natural resources, and the building of railways and other transportation facilities. At the same time more modest financial institutions, such as credit co-operatives and the popular banks, increased rapidly in number after the turn of the century in order to meet the needs of small borrowers.

Of crucial importance in creating a national economy was the adoption of a national monetary system. As late as the 1860s a bewildering variety of currencies, sometimes as many as seventy-five at one time, continued to circulate in the United Principalities, impeding the development of the economy in general and commerce in particular. Prince Alexandru Cuza had attempted to solve the problem in 1860 when he proposed that a national currency, the *romanat*, having the same value as the French franc, be established. But, because of opposition from the Ottoman government and the lack of financial resources, the project had to be abandoned. It was revived and enacted into law in 1867 under the impulse of a new national confidence. The monetary unit was called the *leu* (lion), taking its name from the *Löwenthaler*, which had been minted in the Netherlands in the latter part of the sixteenth century and had circulated in the Rumanian principalities until the second half of the eighteenth century. At the same time Rumania adopted the monetary, decimal, and metric systems of the Latin Monetary Union, which was composed of France, Italy, Belgium, Switzerland, and now Rumania. The first Rumanian coins, of copper, were minted in Britain in 1867, and the first silver coins in 1870 at the mint established that year in Bucharest. The first paper money—mortgage banknotes, backed by the lands and other property of the state—was issued in June 1877 to cover the expenses of the War for Independence. The new standard currency brought monetary order and contributed no little to the encouragement of foreign investment.

Between the latter years of Alexandru Cuza's reign and the War for Independence a variety of financial institutions came into being. The old money exchange offices, which made short-term loans in return for mortgages on property suffered an eclipse after the introduction of the new monetary system. Their place was taken by private banks such as Marmorosch, Blank, and Company and Chrissoveloni, which specialized in commercial transactions. But the latter could not satisfy the growing need for a safe, stable supply of capital. Cuza took the initiative in providing such a source in 1864 when he established Casa de Depuneri și Consemnațiuni (Savings and Loan Bank), which received deposits from various state and local agencies and private individuals. It also made loans to the state, thereby enabling successive governments to cover deficits, which were a regular feature of public finances down to the War for Independence. In order to strengthen the financial capabilities of the state Cuza also granted to a consortium of English, French, and Austrian financiers the right to establish a discount bank, Banca României (The Bank of Rumania), in Bucharest in 1865. A commercial bank, it funnelled foreign capital into the Rumanian market and influenced export and import operations. In 1873 landlords, who were burdened by enormous debt, despite the compensation payments they had received in 1864, created Creditul Funciar Rural (The Rural Land Credit Bank) with state aid. Its main purpose was to make loans to its members at interest rates considerably lower than those charged by traditional money-lenders or the new commercial banks. It proved to be a successful device for easing landlord debts and encouraged the owners of large urban properties to establish their own Creditul Urban București (The Bucharest Urban Credit Bank) in 1874.

None of these institutions, alone or collectively, could meet the rising demand for credit after the War for Independence. Banca României, in 1879 still the most important financial institution in the country, was unable to supply industrial and commercial entrepreneurs with the financing they needed to take advantage of expanding opportunities. Private banks such as Marmorosch, Blank, and Company had sufficient resources to loan money for sewer construction in Bucharest and to participate in railway construction, but it could not perform the functions of a state credit institution. There was also pressure for expanded, cheap credit facilities from modest borrowers, especially in rural areas, where rates of interest charged by money-lenders reached 50 per cent between 1878 and 1880 (interest rates were lower in the cities, where credit was more easily obtainable than in the villages, usually 10–12 per cent). Businessmen and large landowners, Liberals and Conservatives, supported greater accessibility to credit, which they regarded as critical to the success of their respective enterprises.

To satisfy these needs and to ensure financial stability Banca Naţională a României (The National Bank of Rumania) was founded in 1880. The initiative came from Ion Brătianu and the Liberals, who devised a plan whereby they could assure their own control of this key institution.[37] In accordance with the principle of native control of the national economy which they had enunciated, their bill provided that Rumanian capital alone could be used to create the bank, two-thirds of which would come from private sources and one-third from the state. The Liberals made no secret of their intention to subordinate the activities of the National Bank to their party's interests, and when the shares allocated to private investors were put on sale, they were snapped up in a few hours, mainly by party leaders. The partnership between the state and private stockholders lasted until 1901. Thereafter the National Bank continued its operations as a private institution under the same name, enjoying special privileges from the state, notably the exclusive right to issue banknotes. It also functioned as a central commercial bank and in this capacity played a crucial role in creating the modern Rumanian banking system. Until the First World War the National Bank was the main source of native Rumanian credit and helped to mobilize inactive financial capital and to channel it into productive industrial and commercial enterprises. The value of its loans rose from 66 million lei in 1891 to 1,073 million in 1914, figures which reflect the expansion of credit and of economic activity in general.

On the eve of the First World War the Rumanian banking system had been fully formed and was capable of satisfying the credit needs of industry, commerce, and large landowners. The total number of banks had increased rapidly, from thirty in 1901 to 215 in 1914. The majority were modest-sized institutions which catered to small merchants and industrialists, prosperous peasants, and medium-sized landowners. But by this time the entire financial system had come to be dominated by nine great banks, four of which were controlled by foreign capital. In 1913 they possessed 70 per cent of the total resources held by all commercial banks, while 188 small and medium-sized banks had 30 per cent.

The transportation network also expanded to accommodate the increased industrial activity and the growth of foreign trade. The most immediate problem was to get agricultural products and oil

---

[37] Mircea Iosa, 'Aspecte ale politicii economice liberale după cucerirea independenţei', *Revista de istorie*, 39/1 (1986), 34–7.

to markets as quickly and cheaply as possible. Rail transportation seemed to offer the best solution.

Railway building in Rumania began in 1865 when Alexandru Cuza granted a concession to an English company headed by John Trevor-Barkley to build a line from Bucharest to Giurgiu, a distance of 70 kilometres. The concession was confirmed by Prince Charles in 1867, and the line opened in October 1869, enabling the products of the Rumanian plains to be brought with ease and in large quantities to the Danube ports and from there to the Black Sea and Western markets. This promising beginning was followed by the completion in northern Moldavia between 1869 and 1871 of a series of lines by an Anglo-Austrian consortium, headed by the Austrian industrialist Victor von Ofenheim. By linking up with the Lemberg–Cernăuţi–Suceava line, the new network enhanced the access of Austrian industrialists and merchants to the Rumanian market.

An even more ambitious programme of railway construction, designed to link Bucharest with all parts of the country, had already been inaugurated by Prince Charles. In 1868 he persuaded the government to grant a ninety-year concession to build and operate some 915 kilometres of railway to a Prussian consortium headed by the financier Henri Bethel Strussberg. While construction was underway the consortium went bankrupt in 1871, and its rights and obligations were acquired by a Prussian banking consortium headed by Gerson Bleichröder and backed by Bismarck.[38] Between 1872, when the Roman–Galaţi–Bucharest–Piteşti line was opened, and 1880, when the Ploieşti–Predeal line was completed, the basic Rumanian railway network became operational and was connected at Predeal with the Hungarian rail system. In 1874 it had already been linked to the Russian railway system when a Rumanian entrepreneur built a short line between Iaşi and Ungheni, on the Russian border. It proved to be of enormous strategic importance in 1877, when it was used to transport Russian troops to the Danube. Thus, from 173 kilometres of rail in 1869 the Rumanian network grew to 1,300 kilometres in 1880. From then until 1914 an additional 2,250 kilometres were built.

As in so many areas of economic development, the Rumanian state assumed responsibility for the operation of the entire railway

---

[38] The intricacies of Rumanian railway building during the period have been sorted out by Lothar Maier, *Rumänien auf dem Weg zur Unabhängigkeitserklärung, 1866–1877* (Munich, 1989), 170–262.

system. By 1889 it had become a state monopoly through the acquisition of the lines built by the Strussberg and Ofenheim consortia and smaller lines, including the one linking Cernavoda, on the Danube, with Constanţa, which had been built by Barkley in 1860 when Dobrudja was part of the Ottoman Empire. The entire system was administered by an autonomous state agency, Direcţiunea Generală a Căilor Ferate Române (The General Directorate of Rumanian Railways), which had been created in 1880 and was also responsible for the planning and construction of new lines.

Railways stimulated the economy. First of all, they facilitated exports and imports. Between 1880 and 1914 the quantity of goods they carried tripled from three million to nearly nine million tons a year. Railways also contributed directly to the growth of industry, for they were the main consumers of domestic coal, accounting for nearly 90 per cent of annual production, and of imported coal, and were the chief customers for locomotives, freight and passenger cars, and rails. From its very beginnings, therefore, the country's metallurgical industry was closely connected with the construction and maintenance of rail lines, bridges, and rolling stock. Because of its diverse and far-flung activities, the General Directorate of Railways was the largest industrial enterprise in the country with over 1,000 million lei invested and 23,000 employees.

The expansion of the road and highway network kept pace with railway construction. In 1861 there were only 309 kilometres of paved or maintained roads in the country. A decade later these had increased to a modest 1,800 kilometres. The great era of road-building began in the latter 1870s and ended about 1900, by which time there were 24,800 kilometres of paved or otherwise improved roads. Efficient management and the sacrifices of the population in taxes and labour were mainly responsible for this success. Legislation in 1868, the first to deal comprehensively with the matter, laid the foundations for a modern network of national and local roads. Amended several times, the law provided for state funding of major highways, but left the responsibility of building and maintaining judeţ and communal roads mainly to the local population. A state agency, Direcţiunea Generală de Poduri şi Şosele (The General Directorate of Bridges and Highways), established by parliament in 1906, assumed ultimate responsibility for the maintenance of highways and bridges in every judeţ. The expanded network of roads complemented the economic services of the railways. They were not used for the long-distance transport of bulk goods, but they made travel between the countryside and nearby towns and cities easier and thus stimulated the exchange of rural agricultural produce and urban processed goods.

Improvements in the transport of goods by water proceeded more slowly than those affecting railways and highways. Only after the War for Independence was serious attention given to the creation of a Rumanian river and maritime fleet. Among its most ardent champions was Petre Aurelian, who in a series of articles in the latter 1880s touted the solid economic benefits of a national merchant marine. Parliament voted to create a river fleet in 1888, and a modest sum was made available the following year to buy a tug and four barges. In 1890 the government established Serviciul de Navigație Fluvială Română (The Rumanian River Navigation Service). The small fleet slowly expanded and was used to transport grain, oil, salt, and lumber on the Danube as far as Budapest, Vienna, and Regensburg. The venture proved successful, as the amount of cargo and the number of passengers continued to grow until the First World War. International shipping was inaugurated in 1895 when the government established Serviciul Maritim Român (The Rumanian Maritime Service), and the first ships plied routes between Constanța and Brăila and Constantinople. In 1897 a line was opened between Brăila and Rotterdam, which was served by five Rumanian cargo ships, each of 3,500 tons. International shipping also attracted private capital. In 1913 eight banks formed Societatea Română (The Rumanian Company), which began operations with four cargo ships of 6,500 tons each. However, both the state and the private Rumanian maritime companies proved too small to be able to compete with the major international shipping firms. In 1911, for example, Rumanian ships carried only 11 per cent of all goods imported by sea and less than 3 per cent of the country's exports. Rumania's participation in the First World War brought about the destruction of both the river and maritime fleets.

The structures thus in place by 1914 offered Rumanian politicians, economists, and social theorists of the most diverse aims and opinions hope of continued economic and social advances. The First World War was to subject them and their fellow-countrymen to the supreme test of national endurance and cohesiveness, and, having passed it, the creation of Greater Rumania in 1918 and 1919 raised expectations of unprecedented growth and well-being.

5
The Rumanians Outside Rumania

Many Rumanians in the second half of the nineteenth century continued to live outside the borders of the United Principalities and the Rumanian Kingdom. As of 1900, there were approximately 2,785,000 in Hungary (the historical principality of Transylvania and the adjoining regions of the Banat, Crişana, and Maramureş), 230,000 in Bukovina, and 1,092,000 in Bessarabia. In some ways their course of development under Hungarian, Austrian, and Russian administration, respectively, was similar. They were unable to participate in political life as distinct ethnic communities, and their cultural life was under constant pressure from an unsympathetic government bureaucracy. Of the three communities, the Rumanians of Transylvania put up the strongest defence of their national existence. They were conscious of their nation's historical rights in Transylvania and had behind them a long period of common struggle which had drawn the community together. They also benefited from two vigorous national institutions—the Orthodox and Uniate churches with strong political and cultural centres at Sibiu and Blaj, respectively—and from increasingly close relations with politicians in the Rumanian Kingdom, beginning in the latter decades of the nineteenth century. The Rumanians of Bukovina and Bessarabia were less fortunate. Cut off abruptly from their Moldavian homeland in 1774 and 1812, respectively, and subject immediately to the centralizing tendencies of two absolutist empires, they suffered from the lack of strong native institutions and a distinct political and social identity in the states of which they were now a part.

TRANSYLVANIA

The main goal of Rumanian leaders in Transylvania in the second half of the nineteenth century was political autonomy. It had been their rallying cry during the Revolution of 1848 when they demanded that all the Rumanians of the Habsburg Monarchy be united in a Rumanian 'duchy' with the Emperor in Vienna as its Grand Duke. The suppression of the revolution in 1849 and the imposition of a centralized regime in the following decade dashed such hopes, but the idea of autonomy remained a vital, cohesive force in Rumanian political circles. In the early 1860s success seemed finally at hand as the Court of Vienna sought the aid of the Rumanians and Slavs to counteract the 'centrifugal tendencies' of the Magyars and experimented with constitutional forms. In Transylvania the Court of Vienna allowed a diet to be convoked with a large representation of Rumanians. Together with Saxon (German) deputies, and benefiting from a boycott of the diet by Magyars, they enacted legislation recognizing the political equality of the Rumanians with the other peoples of Transylvania and according the Rumanian language official status alongside Magyar and German. The majority of Rumanian leaders were reluctant to tamper with fundamental political structures, for they were convinced that an autonomous Transylvania provided the indispensable constitutional framework within which their newly won national equality could be transformed into national autonomy. But they were not masters of their own destiny. By 1865 the political currents in Vienna had shifted. The aim of the Court now was to strengthen the Empire by reaching an accommodation with the Magyars through direct negotiation.

The Compromise of 1867, which was the result of these negotiations, divided the governance of the Habsburg Monarchy between Austria and Hungary and dashed the hopes of the Rumanians of Transylvania for autonomy. They had made the preservation of a Transylvanian crown land their primary defence against the mounting pressure of Magyar nationalism, but now, as a result of the pact setting up the Dual Monarchy, Transylvania had ceased to exist as a separate political entity and the Rumanians themselves had been transformed from the majority population in the former principality into one of several minorities in Greater Hungary.

Lacking a political organization and weakened by conflict between the so-called passivists, who opposed participation in the new political order, and activists, who urged a defence of national interests on all fronts, the Rumanians could do little else but offer up protests. The most important of these was the so-called *Pronunciament*, a succinct statement of principles drawn up in 1868. In it Rumanian intellectuals restated their commitment to the cause of Transylvanian autonomy. They also demanded the revival of the laws passed by the Transylvanian diet in 1863 and 1864 recognizing the Rumanians as a constituent nation of Transylvania and guaranteeing the equality of their language and churches, and they denied to the Hungarian parliament the power to legislate for Transylvania. Such ideas accurately reflected Rumanian public opinion, but they were not new. What was new was the reaction of the Hungarian government, which accused the authors and the editor of *Gazeta Transilvaniei*, a leading Rumanian newspaper in Transylvania where the *Pronunciament* had been published, of disturbing public order. The matter went no further, but it was a harbinger of many *causes célèbres* to come which would envenom relations between the government and the Rumanians.

The so-called Law of Nationalities, which the Hungarian parliament passed on 5 December 1868, found little favour with the majority of Rumanian political leaders. Although it specified a number of rights which the non-Magyar minorities would enjoy, it made no provision for their separate political organization. Rather, it reflected the ideas of those Hungarian leaders who favoured a centralized Magyar national state. On 6 December Francis Joseph gave them a double victory by sanctioning article 44, the Law of Nationalities, and article 43, which set forth the conditions regulating the union of Transylvania with Hungary.

The Rumanians took their places in the dual system unwillingly and, so they thought, only temporarily. They were certain that the compromise between Germans and Magyars would fail and that Vienna would turn again to the other nationalities, as it had in 1848 and 1860, for help in governing the empire.

In the twenty years following the union of Transylvania with Hungary Rumanian passivists made the restoration of the principality's autonomy their principal objective. They were convinced that it alone could provide their nation with the necessary constitutional protection for free political and cultural development. Transylvania's autonomy was thus a central issue at all Rumanian political conferences between 1869 and 1890. Their linking of autonomy and national rights was an essentially historicist view of the question, which reinforced traditional Rumanian attitudes toward the Magyars.

At first, the Rumanians lacked unity of purpose and an organization capable of mobilizing public opinion. Moreover, the Rumanians of Hungary proper (Maramureş, Crişana, the Banat) had their own political agenda, and, rejecting passivism, they regularly sent deputies to the Hungarian parliament. Rumanian leaders in both Transylvania and Hungary tried to remedy the situation in 1881 by founding the Rumanian National Party as the sole political representative of all the Rumanians of Hungary, a position not seriously challenged until the end of the Monarchy. Its leaders voted to remain passivist, except in Hungary proper, where participation in the Hungarian parliament, they thought, might benefit the national cause, and they placed the restoration of Transylvania's autonomy first on their agenda.

They justified their demand, as earlier generations of national leaders had, on historical and constitutional grounds. In various published statements of their position they were at pains to show that the Rumanians had formed a nation equal to the Magyars from the very beginning of Transylvania's political existence and, hence, ought to enjoy the same rights in the nineteenth century. To prove their point they cited passages from the works of medieval Hungarian chroniclers such as the Anonymous Notary of King Béla III and the diplomas of King Andrew II of 1211 and 1222 to the Teutonic Knights. Then they explained, as had Rumanian historians of the late eighteenth and early nineteenth century, how the development of new political and social relations and the religious struggles of the fifteenth and sixteenth centuries had excluded the Rumanians from political life. They showed how the new state of things had been sanctioned by the Diploma Leopoldinum of 1691, in which the Habsburg rulers recognized the constitution of the principality and the privileges of the Magyar, Szekler, and Saxon nations, and then they described the union of Transylvania with Hungary in 1848, denying its validity on the grounds that the Rumanians had not been represented in the decision-making process. They also denounced the Law of Nationalities and article 43 of 1868 regulating the union of Transylvania with Hungary because neither, in their view, offered adequate protection to the non-Magyar nationalities.

Despite worsening relations with the Hungarian government, many Rumanian political leaders continued to believe that Magyars and Rumanians must eventually come to some sort of understanding. The idea of a *rapprochement* remained an important aspect of Rumanian political thought until the 1880s. It was rooted in history. Influential Rumanians who looked back over the development of Transylvania since medieval times were convinced that destiny had linked the two peoples and that they must share responsibility for the future of the principality. This sense of community was reinforced for these same Rumanians by the certainty that the two peoples were 'natural allies' in a struggle for survival against the Slavs. Pointing to the ethnographic map of Eastern Europe, they compared the Rumanians and Magyars to 'two islands in a Slavic sea', which threatened 'to engulf them'. If this were so, the Rumanians concluded, then their very existence was at stake, and since neither they nor the Magyars had a strong empire abroad to which they could turn, they did not doubt that they would have to rely upon one another for protection. A number of Rumanians were even moved to observe that they had never been the enemies of Hungary and the Magyars because they had recognized in Hungary an indispensable barrier to 'Slavism' and, hence, regarded her welfare as of paramount importance for their own future development.

A typical and persistent advocate of a Rumanian–Magyar *rapprochement* in the 1870s and 1880s was Vincenţiu Babeş, a deputy in the Hungarian parliament from the Banat for many years and a leader of the Rumanian National Party. He urged upon his fellow delegates to the party's national conference in 1881 a kind of Rumanian–Magyar dualism in Transylvania. Even as he recommended a continuation of passivism, he called for solidarity with the Magyars, 'with whose fortunes ours are so closely bound'. To enthusiastic applause he exclaimed, 'As brothers . . . what progress, what happiness we could achieve for all the nationalities'. But on other occasions he took Magyar political leaders to task for their failure to comprehend the 'mortal danger' which Russian-sponsored Pan-Slavism posed for both Magyars and Rumanians and for their folly in pursuing policies which merely widened the breach between two natural allies. At the national conference in 1884 Babeş repeated a favourite dictum that the Rumanians and Magyars had been fated to stand between the 'two great rivals' in South-eastern Europe—Germany and Russia—and added that had it not been for these two peoples, Russia would surely have gained control of the Balkans. The historical mission of the Rumanians and Magyars, then, was to preserve the independence of Central Europe, and if they could not grasp that fact, he had no doubt that they would perish.[1]

The legislation and the administrative acts of successive Hungarian governments, however, gradually destroyed the hopes

---

[1] Teodor V. Păcăţian, *Cartea de aur, sau luptele politice-naţionale ale Românilor de sub coroana ungară*, iv (Sibiu, 1906), 355.

of even the most sanguine Rumanian political leaders that co-operation between Magyars and Rumanians was possible. 1879 marked a watershed in their relations. In that year the Hungarian parliament passed a law which made the teaching of Magyar obligatory in Rumanian Orthodox and Uniate church elementary schools. It was the first of a series of laws designed to bring the education of Rumanians (and other nationalities) into harmony with the idea of Hungary as a Magyar national state. It was followed in 1883 by a similar law affecting non-Magyar-language middle schools and in 1891 by a law requiring the use of Magyar in non-Magyar kindergartens. There was legislation also which was intended to undermine the autonomy of the Rumanian Orthodox and Uniate churches, particularly the law of 1893, which provided for the payment by the state of the salaries of teachers in Rumanian church schools, and the law of 1899, which offered state supplements to the salaries of Rumanian priests. The object of both was to extend the government's control over Rumanian teachers and priests, whom it regarded as the fomenters of resistance to its assimilation policies.

The Hungarian government also used its considerable administrative powers to curtail Rumanian political activity. For example, in 1894 it brought the executive committee of the National Party to trial on charges of agitating against the security of the state for having published and distributed the Memorandum, a protest against the government's nationality policy. The trial resulted in the conviction and imprisonment for up to a year of the majority of the committee. In 1894 also the Minister of the Interior dissolved the National Party, although it continued to function as an electoral committee. Such acts all but destroyed the remaining hopes of a Rumanian–Magyar *rapprochement* of the sort advocated in the 1870s and 1880s. As a result, Rumanian politicians sought solutions to national problems elsewhere.

As their situation deteriorated Rumanian politicians and intellectuals decided to bring their case before a wider public and to make the 'Rumanian question', as they now called it, a matter of general European concern. They did so in two detailed public manifestos. The first of these was the *Replică* (Rejoinder). It was drawn up in 1891 by a group of Rumanian university students to refute a defence of Hungarian nationality policy published in that year by Magyar university students in Budapest, who claimed that the rights of the political nation—the Magyars—superseded the rights claimed by the ethnic minorities—the Rumanians and the Slavs. The principal author of the *Replică* was Aurel C. Popovici (1863–1917), a medical student in Graz who later achieved fame as the author of *Die Vereinigten Staaten von Gross-Österreich* (1906), a widely read book on the federalization of the Habsburg Monarchy. In the *Replică* he was concerned with two questions—national autonomy and federalism—which, in his view, could not be separated. He gave much space to an indictment of the Hungarian government's treatment of the Rumanians, which had made them 'outcasts' in their own country, and he concluded that the Rumanians could become a free nation equal to the Magyars only if the two peoples were separated politically and the Rumanians gained their own national territory within the Habsburg Monarchy.[2] He said nothing about Transylvanian autonomy. Nor did historical and constitutional arguments figure prominently in his defence of national rights.

The other major Rumanian declaration of the period was the Memorandum, a protest addressed to the Emperor Francis Joseph by the National Party against the Hungarian government's treatment of the Rumanians under dualism. It represented the views of the traditional Rumanian political leadership and, unlike the *Replică*, it sought a solution to the Rumanian question through the intervention of the emperor. But the Memorandum was no less forceful in defending national rights, which, its authors claimed, had been violated so systematically that the Rumanians had become 'foreigners' in their own land. The consequence of such a policy, they argued, was greater disharmony than ever before among the peoples of Hungary, clear proof, in their view, that the attempt to govern Hungary by a single people—the Magyars—had failed. In place of the existing centralized structure they urged the emperor to undertake the federalization of the empire by creating an 'internal association of peoples gathered around the throne'.[3] They obviously had in mind national autonomy. In brief references to the earlier history of Transylvania they pointed out that ever since the eighteenth century the Rumanians had continuously asserted their 'national individuality'. They cited as the culmination of these efforts the autonomy fashioned at the Transylvanian diet in 1863 and 1864, and they declared such

---

[2] *Cestiunea română în Transilvania și Ungaria; Replica junimii academice române din Transilvania și Ungaria la 'Răspunsul' dat de junimea academică maghiară 'Memoriului' studenților universitari din România* (Sibiu, 1892), 144, 151.

[3] *Memorandul Românilor din Transilvania și Ungaria cătră Maiestatea Sa Imperială și Regală Apostolică Francisc Iosif I* (Sibiu, 1892), 22–3.

autonomy to be the only certain guarantee of their existence as a nation. Like Popovici in the *Replică*, they said nothing about the restoration of Transylvania's autonomy. Their idea of nation, though nourished by history, had outgrown the narrow limits imposed by historical tradition.

The *Replică* and the Memorandum represented a significant change in Rumanian political attitudes. It is evident from their contents that Rumanian leaders had come to see the relationship between Rumanians and Magyars in a new light. They now set forth a vision of the future Hungary sharply at variance with the idea of the Magyar national state and even their own long-cherished dream of a restored Transylvanian principality.

A new attitude of the Rumanians toward the Slavs was a striking manifestation of their emphasis upon national, as opposed to Transylvanian, autonomy. They now perceived the Slovaks, Serbs, and Croats as political allies against the Hungarian government, whose own nationality policy had blurred historical distinctions between them and had drawn them together in self-defence. Aurel Popovici, among others, thought that the Slavs were destined to play a major role in bringing about a solution to the nationality problem in Hungary. He rejected the old idea of a Rumanian–Magyar compromise, which had ignored the Slavs. Although he was concerned about the danger to the peoples of Central Europe of Russian Pan-Slavism, he thought that a federalized Hungary, based on the Swiss model, would enhance the sense of 'national individuality' of each Slavic people and, by thus separating them from the Russians, would create a sense of community with the Rumanians and even the Magyars.[4]

Popovici and younger members of the Rumanian National Party grouped around *Tribuna*, the party newspaper, favoured some sort of formal understanding with the Slavs. Pressure from the 'Tribunists' finally caused party leaders to take the initiative in forming an alliance with the Slovaks and Serbs (the Croats showed no interest), which culminated in the holding of a so-called Congress of Nationalities in Budapest on 10 August 1895. Here their representatives made clear that their primary goal was national autonomy, which they justified by appeals not to history or imperial diplomas, but to 'natural law' and the material contributions they made to the general welfare of Hungary.

[4] Aurel C. Popovici, *Cestiunea naţionalităţilor şi modurile soluţiunii sale în Ungaria* (Sibiu, 1894), 44–5.

Rumanian delegates to a preparatory meeting in Novi Sad on 21 July had put the matter succinctly: 'We're not asking how long we've been here or if the Magyars were here ahead of us. We act as we do because we are citizens of Hungary, because we support it with our blood and our goods, and because we form a majority of her citizens. And so we have the right to give this country the form of government we desire.'[5]

At the congress itself the three nationalities urged a political restructuring of Hungary on a 'natural basis'. They meant national autonomy and they proposed to achieve it by making local political boundaries conform to language boundaries. Consequently, in counties, municipalities, and rural areas where, for example, the majority of the population was Rumanian, officials would be Rumanian as would the language of administration and the courts. Since the Rumanians formed compact masses of population in many parts of Transylvania, a large separate Rumanian territory, with perhaps small Magyar enclaves here and there was an obvious, if unexpressed, goal of the 'natural' redistricting of Hungary.

The 'alliance' which the three nationalities formed was short-lived and ineffective. Yet, it was further evidence of a fundamental change of attitude on the part of the Rumanians toward historical Transylvania.

The causes of this change were complex. Of paramount importance was a new idea of nation which rendered Transylvanian autonomy obsolete as a means of satisfying national aspirations. Aurel Popovici gave the most eloquent exposition of this idea in a series of brochures which he published in the early 1890s. He drew from a variety of Western European sources and was the first Rumanian to apply the evolutionary theories of the Social Darwinists to an analysis of the national movement. His approach was deterministic: he saw the triumph of the 'principle of nationality' as the inevitable result of the operation of 'natural law'. For him, the dominant creative force in modern Europe was the idea of nationality, which he interpreted as the striving of every people to develop in accordance with its own distinctive character. He treated it as a 'more advanced phase' of the 'natural evolution of the ideas of liberty and equality' which had emerged in the latter part of the eighteenth century.

Popovici believed that the one compelling force which bound

<hr>

[5] *Tribuna* (Sibiu), 18/30 July 1895.

the members of a social group together and distinguished it from all others was national consciousness. In reaching this conclusion, he eliminated one by one those attributes which were frequently cited as the distinctive marks of a nationality. Language, he admitted, was important but not decisive: after all, the Irish had not ceased to be a separate nationality, even though they had adopted English, the language of their oppressors. Political unity, in his view, was not crucial either, and he cited the Jews as an example of a viable nationality that had no state of its own. He raised similar objections to racial uniformity, religion, and customs. When all was said and done it seemed to him that the specific character of a people was determined primarily by the awareness it had that some or all of these attributes together formed the basis of its existence as a distinct community.[6] This awareness is what he meant by national consciousness. It was this intangible element that raised a people to the height of its aspirations; without it, he warned, neither nationality nor national rights could exist.

Popovici argued that once a people had become conscious of itself, as the Rumanians had, it took on all the attributes of a living organism and was endowed by nature with the inherent right of survival and freedom to develop. But if a nation was to grow and prosper, he suggested, it must, like any organism, have a suitable environment. It required living space, and, eventually, all its parts would have to function as a unit. A people conscious of itself must, he concluded, inevitably establish an independent or autonomous state of its own and, if it chose, unite with other states on the basis of nationality. He characterized these two tendencies—the establishment of national states and the political union of 'dismembered' nations—as natural laws and, hence, he viewed their fulfilment as inevitable.

Popovici did not believe that the principle of nationality was necessarily centrifugal, and he pointed to the example of Switzerland where Germans, French, and Italians lived together in harmony, even though they were surrounded by three powerful national states that could have exercised a strong attractive power over them. In Switzerland, he argued, these three nationalities were equal before the law and enjoyed perfect freedom to develop as they chose. But in Hungary, he complained, the condition of the non-Magyar peoples, and especially the Rumanians, was strikingly different. There, because of the policies of the Hun-

[6] Aurel C. Popovici, *Principiul de naţionalitate* (Bucharest, 1894), 12.

garian government, the principle of nationality did indeed act as a strong centrifugal force. Voicing the alienation felt by large numbers of Rumanian politicians and intellectuals, he accused the Magyars of having declared war on the non-Magyar peoples of Hungary and of having mobilized the parliament, the ministries, the courts, and the county administrations to destroy their national consciousness and stifle their political, cultural, and spiritual development. Although he could see little hope of reconciliation between the Rumanians and Magyars, he stopped short of advocating the outright destruction of Hungary and its division into small independent national states. He proposed, instead, a reorganization of the Habsburg Monarchy as a whole into a federation based upon ethnic rather than historico-political principles. Such a restructuring, he was certain, would allow all the peoples of the Monarchy to develop freely and at the same time would protect them from what he viewed as the greatest danger of all—Russian expansion into Central Europe.

Popovici's theory found practical expression in the demand for national autonomy. Already formulated in the *Replică* and Memorandum, it became the centre-piece of all subsequent Rumanian plans for political development until the First World War.

The Kingdom of Rumania occupied an important place in the political calculations of the Transylvanian Rumanians. The ethnic and cultural affinities which Rumanians on both sides of the Carpathians felt for each other were, of course, not new, but in the 1890s the Transylvanian Rumanians looked increasingly to Bucharest for support in their struggle for national rights. They sought to use the close ties between the Rumanian government and the Triple Alliance (the exact nature of which they could only surmise, since the treaty of 1883 had been kept secret) as a means of forcing the Hungarian government to modify its nationality policy.

The Rumanian government, for its part, provided generous financial support for Rumanian churches and schools in Hungary. Regular payments seem to have begun about 1860 when Prince Alexandru Cuza agreed to give the Orthodox Church schools of Braşov 58,500 lei annually. The sums made available for all cultural purposes grew steadily thereafter, and during the period 1892–5 the Rumanian government paid 723,900 lei to Rumanian churches and schools in Hungary out of a total of 2 million lei set aside for Rumanian institutions abroad. Additional funds not recorded in the state budget were supplied by, among others,

Take Ionescu, the Conservative Minister of Education (1891–5). Undoubtedly, some of this money was used for political purposes. Moral support was also forthcoming. Politicians of various persuasions spoke warmly in defence of national rights in parliament and at public gatherings,[7] and intellectuals founded cultural societies to promote solidarity with their 'oppressed' brothers across the Carpathians. The most famous of these organizations was Liga pentru Unitatea Culturală a tuturor Românilor (The League for the Cultural Unity of All Rumanians), which was founded in Bucharest in 1891. The Cultural League, as it was generally known, enjoyed the backing of many prominent political figures and intellectuals and was especially active in Western Europe.

Political contacts between the National Party and government officials in Bucharest intensified during the drawing up of the Memorandum. Rumanian leaders from Hungary were intent upon publicizing their grievances against the Hungarian government in Western Europe and made frequent visits to Bucharest. In May 1890 Iuliu Coroianu, the principal author of the Memorandum, took the manuscript to Bucharest, where he met Dimitrie Sturdza, a leader of the Liberal Party, and King Charles, among others. In January 1892 Ioan Rațiu, the president of the Rumanian National Party, and Coroianu, who were in Bucharest to discuss the final text of the petition, received advice on the most opportune time for its presentation and information on the political climate in Vienna and Europe generally. As a result of these contacts the text of the Memorandum seems to have been modified significantly by the elimination of the long historical introduction in favour of a sustained indictment of the current nationality policies and administrative abuses of the Hungarian government.

However beneficial the intervention by Bucharest on behalf of the Rumanian cause in Hungary may have been, the actions of the Rumanian government represented at the same time a serious challenge to the autonomy of the national movement. Strong support by Rumania in Vienna and Berlin must have been a tempting prospect for leaders of the National Party, whose position after the Memorandum trial had become desperate. Yet it was clear to them that in return for this aid their cause would

---

[7] Aurelia Bunea, 'Parlamentul României pentru o politică externă favorabilă unirii Transilvaniei cu România (1892–1899)', *Acta Musei Napocensis*, 7 (1970), 329–53.

become subordinate to the vagaries of both international relations and the domestic politics of foreign states. The decision reached by the majority of Rumanian leaders to avoid such entanglements reveals much about the nature of the national movement and their commitment to it.

There is little doubt that the leaders of both the Conservative and Liberal parties in Rumania regarded the nationality problem in Hungary as a tactical weapon of domestic politics useful for arousing popular support and embarrassing the opposition. They were concerned chiefly about gaining or holding onto political power and achieving the country's foreign policy goals, and they had no intention of permitting the nationality problem to interfere with the maintenance of friendly relations with Austria-Hungary, which, in the 1890s, was the pivot of Rumanian foreign policy. King Charles and Conservative politicians made clear to Austro-Hungarian diplomats that they wished to solve the nationality problem in such a way as to avoid 'difficulties' with Austria-Hungary and preferred quiet negotiation to public petitions like the Memorandum and demonstrations.[8]

The most striking case of the use of the nationality problem to achieve other goals is provided by Dimitrie Sturdza, who, as we have seen, became head of the Liberal Party in 1892. In the following year he launched an all-out campaign to topple the Conservatives from power. In a series of speeches in parliament and at public gatherings he denounced the Conservatives for standing idly by in the hope of gaining tariff concessions from the Dual Monarchy while the 'tyrannical' Hungarian government Magyarized three million Rumanian brothers. In an especially partisan speech on 7 October 1894 he revealed for the first time the amounts given by the Conservative government to Rumanian churches and schools in Hungary and named the persons who had received them, among whom were National Party leaders. Since the Hungarian government had had prior knowledge of the payments (though not all the details), Sturdza went on to accuse the Conservatives of working hand in glove with the Magyars to use the money to manipulate the national movement for their own purposes.

When Sturdza finally came to power in October 1895 he did a

[8] Keith Hitchins, 'Austria-Hungary, Rumania, and the Memorandum, 1894', *Rumanian Studies*, 3 (1976), 108–48, and 'Austria-Hungary, Rumania, and the Nationality Problem in Transylvania, 1894–1897', *Rumanian Studies*, 4 (1979), 75–126.

complete about-face: he declared the nationality problem across the Carpathians to be a strictly internal affair of Austria-Hungary. Although he seemed to be abandoning the Rumanian cause in Hungary, his actions were none the less consistent with his overall assessment of international relations in Central and South-eastern Europe. For many years he had been convinced that adherence to the Triple Alliance and, hence, good relations with Austria-Hungary were essential if Rumania was to preserve her independence from Russia. Like many leaders of the Rumanian National Party in Hungary, he regarded the Dual Monarchy as the indispensable protector of the small nations of South-eastern Europe from Russian Pan-Slavism. In spite of his own demagogic appeals to popular emotion, he had become genuinely alarmed over the virulence of the nationality conflict in Hungary since the Memorandum of 1892. He feared that a continuation of this state of affairs could only harm Rumania by undermining her relations with the Dual Monarchy and her adherence to the Triple Alliance.

Sturdza was determined now to use the nationality problem in Hungary to achieve his foreign policy objectives. In 1895 he attempted to gain control of the Rumanian National Party. By thus eliminating the causes of friction between Rumania and Austria-Hungary, he hoped to strengthen his country's ties with the Triple Alliance. In the end, he failed because the leaders of the National Party refused to become tools of the politicians in Bucharest or pawns in international relations. Sturdza (and many others in Rumania) failed to understand the nature of the national movement or appreciate the dedication of its leaders.

The agitation of the Transylvanian Rumanians and the growing concern of the Rumanian government and especially of King Charles about their fate were not lost on statesmen in Vienna. The Austro-Hungarian joint Minister of Foreign Affairs, Gustav Kálnoky (1881–95), and the Minister to Rumania, Agenor Goluchowski (1887–94), who would be Kálnoky's successor, feared that the Hungarian government's heavy-handed treatment of the Transylvanian Rumanians would alienate Rumania from the Triple Alliance. They repeatedly warned Hungarian leaders of the 'fateful' military and diplomatic consequences of their actions and urged moderation, but to no avail.

All the pressure coming from the Transylvanian Rumanians (and the other non-Magyar nationalities) and from Bucharest and Vienna had no significant effect on the Hungarian government. Minister-Presidents Sándor Wekerle (1892–5) and Dezsö

Bánffy (1895–9) showed little understanding of the international implications of their Magyarization policies. They insisted that the Rumanian movement in Transylvania was the work of 'agitators' and 'malcontents' supported from 'abroad' (by which they meant Rumania). Bánffy, a champion of the unitary Magyar national state and of the forcible assimilation of the minorities, rejected the whole idea of national equality as merely the first step in the dissolution of historical Hungary.[9]

By the end of the century new ideas about the nature and destiny of the ethnic nation, the aggressive nationality policy of the Hungarian government, and significant changes in the international situation which enhanced the role of the Rumanian Kingdom had caused Rumanian political leaders in Transylvania to re-examine passivism[10]. Calls for an activist policy came from many quarters. The Tribunists, who had been the driving force behind both the Memorandum of 1892 and the Congress of Nationalities in 1895, led the campaign to abandon passivity and resume full participation in the political life of Hungary. Eugen Brote (1850–1912), who had had a prominent role in all their activities, gave clear expression to their ideas. Passivity, he argued, had achieved nothing. Rather, after the Memorandum it had led to 'stagnation' and 'disorientation'. The only way out of the impasse and the only way the Rumanians could hope to achieve their objectives, he insisted, was 'constitutional struggle', which meant the creation of a strong party capable of sending as many deputies to parliament as possible.

The proponents of activism in effect abandoned the goal of a restoration of Transylvania's autonomy, which had been the central goal of passivism. Characteristic supporters of the new course were the lawyers and other young professionals from the small city of Orăştie who founded a newspaper, *Libertatea* (Liberty), to promote their ideas. They created a sensation in 1902 by publishing an open letter from Ioan Mihu, a Rumanian lawyer and large landowner, who bluntly demanded an overhaul of the national programme adopted in 1881. He urged the National Party to renounce passivism as a political tactic and to disavow the programme's first article, which had committed

---

[9] Dezsö Bánffy, *Magyar nemzetiségi politika* (Budapest, 1903), 29–31, 62, 69–70, 117, 121, 124.

[10] Lucian Boia, 'Contribuţii privind criza Partidului Naţional Român şi trecerea de la pasivism la activism (1893–1905)', *Studii: revistă de istorie*, 24/5 (1971), 963–84.

the party to do nothing that would compromise the autonomy of Transylvania. These changes were needed, he argued, because political circumstances and men's minds had changed drastically since the early years of dualism.[11] He, along with the Tribunists, advocated 'realism'. Shortly afterwards, in 1903, the activists achieved success when Aurel Vlad, a lawyer from Orăştie, was elected to parliament running on a platform which renounced passivism and the restoration of Transylvania's autonomy.

A formal end to passivism in Rumanian political life came at the National Party conference in 1905. The majority of the delegates voted to participate in the upcoming elections to the Hungarian parliament and to use every constitutional means available to achieve their goals. These they formulated in demands for the recognition of the Rumanians as a 'political individuality' and for legal guarantees of their 'ethnic and constitutional development'. Thus, they had replaced the historical principality of Transylvania with national autonomy for all the areas inhabited by Rumanians where, they demanded, they should be administered, judged, and educated by Rumanians in the Rumanian language.

The advocates of national autonomy agreed that federalism was the proper constitutional framework for its development. The best known Rumanian plan was Aurel Popovici's book, *Die Vereinigten Staaten von Gross-Österreich*, which he published in 1906. By that time the federalization of the Habsburg Monarchy had become a commonplace for Rumanian politicians. Iuliu Maniu, a leader of the National Party and a deputy in parliament, spoke for the party leadership when he declared in parliament in 1906 that every nationality had a right to develop in accordance with its own inherent qualities. He urged a political restructuring of Austria-Hungary to provide the necessary environment of justice and liberty, but he also hinted where the idea of national autonomy might eventually lead. He proposed that the Rumanians of Hungary bring their political struggles into harmony with those of Rumanians everywhere, since they all served a single idea—Românismul (Rumanianism). That idea, he was certain, could never be altered by political and geographical boundaries.[12] Significantly, he made no mention of Transylvanian autonomy.

At this time the Rumanians formed the largest ethnic minority in Hungary. According to the census of 1900, they numbered

---

[11] *Libertatea*, 23 Feb./8 Mar. 1902.
[12] Iuliu Maniu, *Discursuri parlamentare* (*29 maiu–31 iulie 1906*) (Blaj, 1906), 76–7; *Revista politică şi literară*, 1/1 (Sept. 1906), 3–4.

2,784,726 of 16.7 per cent of the total population of Hungary, not including Croatia, and by 1910 the figure had reached 2,932, 773, or 16.2 per cent. In certain counties in Transylvania the Rumanians lived in compact masses: in 1900, 90.2 per cent of the inhabitants of Făgăraş and 84.7 per cent of the inhabitants of Hunedoara were Rumanian.

Rumanian society from the middle of the nineteenth century to the outbreak of the First World War remained overwhelmingly rural. In 1900 87.4 per cent and in 1910 85.9 per cent of the Rumanians of Hungary derived their income mainly from agriculture. Of these, smallholders formed the great majority: 55 per cent possessed between 5 and 20 *Joch* and 23.1 per cent had less than 5 *Joch* (1 *Joch* = approximately $\frac{1}{2}$ hectare). In general, their productivity was poor and their standard of living correspondingly low, because of inadequate plots of land, outmoded agricultural methods, and the lack of credit. Overpopulation was also a serious problem because industrialization and urbanization were too little developed to provide employment for the excess labour in the countryside. One solution for many in agriculture was emigration, which became large-scale after 1904. Between 1908 and 1913, 87,000 Rumanians, or 19 per cent of the total number of emigrants from Hungary, left the country. The majority were agricultural labourers, and their main destination was the United States, although a significant number also went to Rumania. Emigration, however, had little effect on overpopulation and the development of agriculture. At the other end of the scale the number of Rumanian landowners with holdings of over 50 hectares was small—no more than 1,200 at the turn of the century. A survey of eighteen counties in Transylvania and Hungary with a substantial Rumanian population found 876 Rumanian estates of over 50 hectares, compared to 4,854 non-Rumanian estates in the same category. The latter, moreover, were generally much larger than the Rumanian holdings.[13] Although the amount of land coming into the possession of Rumanian peasants and middle-sized landowners increased, primarily at the expense of Magyar middle-sized landowners who were obliged to sell their land because of debt, the fundamental pattern of landholding in Transylvania did not change. A Rumanian large landowning class did not exist.

[13] Acaţiu Egyed, 'Structura proprietăţii funciare în Transilvania la sfîrşitul veacului al XIX-lea', *Anuarul Institutului de Istorie şi Arheologie Cluj-Napoca*, 17 (1974), 136–53.

The Rumanian urban population was small. Although it increased from 82,000 (3.4 per cent of all Rumanians in Hungary) in 1880 to 134,000 (4.5 per cent) in 1910, it is clear that the movement from the countryside to the city in that thirty-year span was modest. Few peasants were drawn to the cities, partly because they lacked marketable skills and partly because industry was relatively little developed in areas inhabited by Rumanians. As of 1910 the Rumanian population of the major cities of Transylvania remained small: Braşov (28.7 per cent), Sibiu (26.3 per cent), and Cluj (12.4 per cent).[14]

The Rumanian middle class formed a thin social stratum. Only 3.6 per cent of the Rumanians of Hungary were engaged in industry, transportation, and commerce in 1910. The majority were small entrepreneurs or individual artisans and shop-owners, who were dependent upon the local market. A Rumanian industrial bourgeoisie worthy of the name did not exist. For example, in Hungary in 1904 there were 6,411 German and Hungarian medium and large entrepreneurs and industrialists employing more than five persons and 338 of other nationalities, but among the latter there were only thirty-eight Rumanians. Rumanians employed in the professions and public service, often referred to as 'intellectuals', though small, formed the leading stratum within Rumanian society. Their total number increased slowly from 9,972 in 1890 to 11,538 in 1910. In the latter year the largest categories were priests (3,979), elementary schoolteachers (3,117), and 1,394 persons employed in local administration. In addition, there were 370 lawyers and 314 doctors. All together they represented about 3 per cent of the Rumanian population of Hungary, and it was from among them that the leaders of the Rumanian National Party were recruited.

The accelerated economic development which Hungary experienced, beginning in the 1870s, had relatively little effect on Rumanian-inhabited areas. Industrial and agricultural development in Transylvania lagged behind that of the western parts of Hungary. The Rumanian areas were stuck in the mould of a traditional economy. Only at the turn of the century was there a significant move toward modern forms of production, which was marked by the expansion of the iron and coal industries in Hunedoara and the infusion of large amounts of Austro-Hungarian, German, and other European capital. Yet there was

[14] *Magyar statisztikai közlemények*, NS 27 (1909), 121, 129; 64 (1924), 130–3.

too little time before the outbreak of the First World War for the effects of these changes to be felt on the structure of Rumanian society.

The absence of a great bourgeoisie and the insignificance of the large landowners as a social category left Rumanian society with relatively little class antagonism. Rather, the main antagonists of the Rumanian peasantry and petty bourgeoisie were the Magyar great bourgeoisie and landlords. The Rumanian middle class stood relatively close to the Rumanian peasant, for many of its members were only a generation or two removed from the village. In a sense, then, all Rumanians could stand united against the 'foreigner'.

Besides politics, Rumanian leaders devoted much attention to economic development. They were chagrined by the backwardness they observed in every area of Rumanian economic activity, for they had no doubt that failure to make economic progress would stifle political and cultural development and relegate the Rumanians to a condition of perpetual inferiority *vis-à-vis* the Magyars and Germans. Persuaded that a viable economy could be organized only on a national basis, they sought to create a Rumanian agriculture, a Rumanian industry, and Rumanian banks.

The majority of Rumanian leaders recognized agriculture as the foundation of their national economic life. A few even thought that the Rumanians were a pre-eminently agricultural people and were destined to remain so. But all were agreed on the generally deplorable condition of Rumanian agriculture. They found multiple causes: overpopulation on the land, the fragmentation of peasant holdings, the lack of cheap credit, widespread illiteracy, and the absence of any sort of organization among the peasants. The solutions they proposed were in keeping with their middle-class respect for law and private property. They urged improved education in the villages with emphasis upon practical agricultural instruction and promoted credit co-operatives and agricultural self-help associations. But they drew back from advocating radical reform such as the break-up of large estates, even Magyar ones, and the distribution of the land to those who had little or none. They feared a disruption of production and social disorder, and, besides, their ideal was the independent medium-sized producer who would form the backbone of the national movement. Yet, they could not escape the fact that the land question was also a national question because most of the medium and large holdings were in the hands of Magyars.

While recognizing the primacy of agriculture as an immediate fact of life, the majority of Rumanian leaders were convinced that in the long run industrialization and urbanization were the keys to the development of the Rumanian nation. They perceived the root cause of Rumanian economic backwardness to be the absence of industry in Rumanian-inhabited areas and increasingly saw in industrialization the solution to the agrarian problem and the foundation of a strong national movement. For the time being they set modest goals for themselves. They decided to build on Rumanian strengths and therefore concentrated their energies on developing the artisan crafts. At the turn of the century, rejecting Sămănătorist ideas from Rumania about the unfortunate social influence of capitalism and the city, they made the creation of a strong Rumanian middle class, 'the most dynamic class of modern society', and the Rumanianization of Transylvanian cities their most urgent economic tasks.

Up to the outbreak of the First World War Rumanian leaders made only moderate progress in martialling the economic resources of their people. They were most successful in banking and credit. Between the founding of Albina, the first important Rumanian bank, in 1872 and the First World War 274 banks were established. The majority were small and limited their activities to agriculture: the buying and selling of land and the granting of credit to peasants and other owners of medium-sized holdings. They helped Rumanians acquire land from Magyar estates when these were put up for sale and they contributed to numerous Rumanian cultural undertakings, but at the same time their directors insisted that banks were businesses and thus could not devote their resources solely to good works and the support of the national cause, a stand which angered Rumanian politicians and intellectuals. In any case, the role of Rumanian banks in the general financial life of Hungary was exceedingly modest. In 1900, of 1,030 banks in Rumanian-inhabited areas, only eighty-one were owned by Rumanians, and the financial transactions of Rumanian banks amounted to only 1.2 per cent of those of all banks in Hungary.[15]

The effort to place Rumanian agriculture on a strong institutional foundation was for the most part unsuccessful. A number of intellectuals established associations to improve agriculture and tried to involve the peasants in their activities. The first important

---

[15] Nicolae N. Petra, *Băncile româneşti din Ardeal şi Banat* (Sibiu, 1936), 26–59, 98–100.

such organization was Reuniunea Română de Agricultură (The Rumanian Agricultural Society), which was founded in Sibiu in 1888. From an initial membership of 84 it grew to 1,119 by 1914. It disseminated publications about new agricultural methods, supplied high quality seeds and breeding animals, sponsored lectures and special courses on agricultural subjects, and helped to organize credit co-operatives. The main beneficiaries of all these activities were the better-off peasants. The vast majority of peasants had neither the education nor the material resources to participate. Many intellectuals also put their hopes in co-operatives as the most immediate, practical solution to agrarian problems. Besides credit co-operatives, other forms of associations were also tried, particularly consumer and producer co-operatives after 1900. But their numbers remained insignificant, mainly because their promoters lacked entrepreneurial skills and could not inspire others with the co-operative spirit.

The Orthodox and Uniate churches remained important bastions of the national movement, despite the assumption of its leadership by the middle class and intellectuals. They were, in a sense, the only national institutions the Rumanians possessed and under the provisions of the Law of Nationalities of 1868 and other legislation enacted early in the dualist period they preserved a large measure of administrative autonomy and control over Rumanian education through church elementary and secondary schools. But the era of Andrei Şaguna, the powerful bishop-national leader between the Revolution of 1848 and the Compromise of 1867, was past. The intensification of the Hungarian government's assimilationist policies in the 1880s and 1890s put the clergies of both churches on the defensive. They could no longer count upon the intervention of Vienna on their behalf, and the laws on schools and government supplements for the salaries of priests in particular made them increasingly dependent upon the state bureaucracy. Yet, the influence of the churches remained strong in the villages, and many priests were as devoted to the national movement as to their religious vocation. In 1910 church membership was 1,798,669 Orthodox and 1,333,512 Uniates.

The nationality policy pursued by successive Hungarian governments between the 1880s and 1914 fell far short of the goal they had set—the assimilation of the Rumanians. The Rumanians proved extraordinarily resistant to integration into the broader strata of Hungarian society. Religion was one obstacle. They were Orthodox or Uniate, and thus their historical and cultural traditions were different from those of the Magyars. They were overwhelmingly agrarian and had maintained largely intact the traditional customs and beliefs of the village. They were thus protected from the assimilative power of the cities in the central industrial regions, which served as 'foundries of Magyarization' for those who came from less developed regions. The high rate of illiteracy among Rumanian peasants also proved to be an impediment to assimilation, for their contacts with a more cosmopolitan culture were sharply reduced. These 'natural' barriers, in a sense, isolated the Rumanians from the larger Hungarian community. The Rumanian bourgeoisie and industrial working class, the social strata most susceptible to assimilation, were small and did not have extensive contacts with corresponding Magyar classes. The majority of the Rumanian banking and professional classes, who dealt regularly with Magyar businesses and government authorities, used Magyar in the conduct of their affairs, but remained committed to the national movement. Of enormous importance in enabling the Rumanians to resist Magyarization was their success in preserving relatively intact the autonomy of their churches and schools. They thus had their own elementary and middle schools, teacher-training institutes, and seminaries, all of which were staffed by Rumanians and used Rumanian as the sole or chief language of instruction. None the less, the Magyar language was making modest headway among the Rumanians. For example, the number of Rumanians who knew it rose from 5.7 per cent in 1880 to 12.7 per cent in 1910. But the official policy of Magyarization must be judged a failure.

Despite decades of suspicion and hostility engendered by the government's nationality policy, there were still Rumanians and Magyars who believed that some kind of accommodation between the National Party and the Hungarian government was not only possible but desirable. The advent of a new government in 1910 offered an opportunity for negotiation. István Tisza (1861–1918), the head of the National Party of Work, which had won an impressive victory in the June elections, and Prime Minister from 1913 to 1917, thought that the moment had come for a comprehensive settlement of the Rumanian question (and the nationality problem in Hungary in general). His chief aim, however, was to strengthen the Hungarian state, not to satisfy the minorities. In his view, the future of Hungary as a sovereign state depended upon the continued viability of the dualist system and the maintenance of Austria-Hungary as a major European power.

It seemed axiomatic to him that a *modus vivendi* between the Hungarian government and the Rumanians and Slavs would promote these ends by ensuring internal tranquillity and by consolidating existing constitutional structures. Then, too, such a demonstration of the inner strength and cohesiveness of the state would discourage irredentist tendencies among the Rumanian and Serb minorities and convince the neighbouring Rumanian and Serbian kingdoms just how fanciful their hopes were of satisfying their territorial ambitions at the expense of Hungary. Finally, as he saw the process unfold, a strong Austria-Hungary would enhance the prestige of the Triple Alliance and would draw Rumania and Serbia out of the Russian and into the Austrian orbit once and for all.

Although Tisza's aim was a general peace with all the nationalities, he decided to concentrate his efforts on the Rumanians because he regarded them as the key to any enduring settlement. They impressed him as better organized politically than the Serbs and more resistant to assimilation than the Slovaks. They were, moreover, the largest minority in Hungary. Hence, if they could be brought into the mainstream of public life, he was convinced that they could play a crucial role in the development of Hungary. But if they remained alienated, then, he feared, their role could have only 'negative consequences'. It was precisely the failure of the Rumanians to participate fully in Hungarian political and social life that most disturbed him. In his view, they presented special obstacles to assimilation: their Orthodox and Uniate faiths kept them apart and prevented the 'normal' influences of Hungarian Roman Catholicism from working as it had on the Slovaks; and the great mass of the population was agricultural and rural, while the commercial and industrial middle class, urban dwellers most exposed to cosmopolitan influences, remained small and parochial. Tisza was also disturbed by the relations of the National Party with politicians in Bucharest and by the strong sense of national solidarity that united Rumanians on both sides of the border, all, he thought, potential threats to the territorial integrity of Hungary. Yet, he discerned a special bond between Magyars and Rumanians. He regarded the two peoples as natural allies who over the centuries had been drawn together to defend each other against the 'Slavic threat', especially Russian 'Pan-Slavic designs'. Although the alleged Russian menace to Eastern Europe was a convenient ploy that both sides were to use to try to gain concessions, the idea of the Magyars and Rumanians as 'an island in a Slavic sea', as we have seen, had had a long and not unimportant history in the nineteenth century.

For Tisza, then, the main tasks at hand were to reverse the trend of alienation and to integrate the leading elements of Rumanian society into the structure of Hungarian social and political life. He turned his attention to the business and professional classes and the higher clergy, for he judged that they were far more susceptible to the attractions of modern society than the compact, patriarchal rural masses. He was certain that once the educated had been won over, the peasantry would quickly fall into line, since, given the largely undifferentiated nature of Rumanian society, class antagonisms hardly existed. He was no less aware than Rumanian leaders of the fact that when class antagonism manifested itself, it usually pitted Rumanian peasantry and petty bourgeoisie against Magyar landlords and great bourgeoisie, thereby reinforcing national antagonism.

To accomplish his goals Tisza intended to listen to Rumanian grievances and to grant modest concessions. But he never wavered in his adherence to the fundamental principles that had guided all his predecessors. His devotion to the idea of Hungary as a Magyar national state and his determination to maintain Magyar political supremacy as the guarantee of the unity of that state are the keys to an understanding of his handling of the Rumanian question (and the nationality problem in general).

Rumanian leaders were willing to enter into a dialogue with Tisza, but they were extremely sceptical about the possibility of a genuine *rapprochement*, since their own objectives were diametrically opposed to Tisza's efforts to strengthen the Magyar character of Hungary. The Rumanians' chief spokesman was Iuliu Maniu (1873–1953), who owed his position of leadership in the National Party to his stubborn defence of Rumanian aspirations to autonomy and his commitment to political democracy. His own goal (and that of most of his colleagues on the executive committee of the National Party) was national autonomy, and he thought that the federalization of the Habsburg Monarchy was the best way to achieve it. But he also went beyond questions of political organization to urge changes in the very political and social structure of Hungary. He found it wanting and in need of drastic reform. He thought, first of all, that the introduction of universal suffrage was essential. The right of all citizens to vote freely seemed to him the key to a solution of the nationality question in general because it would assure each ethnic group proportional representation in parliament and even enable each to organize itself on an autonomous basis in those areas where it formed a majority of the population.[16]

In September 1910 the leaders of the National Party set forth their negotiating position in a memorandum to Prime Minister Károly Khuen-Hederváry and Tisza. Echoing Maniu's ideas, they focused on a single goal—national autonomy. Absent was a long preamble containing historical and legal justifications for their demands as in previous documents of this sort. Rather, its authors went directly to the heart of the matter. They demanded: (1) political autonomy—the right to organize and manage a political party on the same basis as all other parties in the country; the introduction of universal suffrage, or if that was not possible at once, an end to electoral abuses and a broadening of the franchise; and the creation of fifty Rumanian electoral districts; (2) administrative autonomy—the appointment of Rumanian functionaries in Rumanian-inhabited areas, and the use of Rumanian in all administrative and judicial bodies having direct contact with the citizenry; (3) autonomy for the Orthodox and Uniate churches—the management of internal affairs in accordance with norms guaranteed by civil and church law, and state financial support in the same proportion as that accorded Protestant churches; (4) educational autonomy—the right of churches and communities to establish and maintain elementary schools; the use of Rumanian as the language of instruction in all elementary schools that served Rumanian pupils; the construction at state expense of three middle schools in Rumanian-inhabited areas with Rumanian as the language of instruction; and the establishment of a Rumanian section in the Ministry of Education and Cults; and (5) economic autonomy—the granting of regular state subsidies to develop Rumanian-inhabited areas.[17]

This round of negotiations did not go further. Although Tisza agreed to state support for Rumanian churches, schools, and economic enterprises he refused to recognize the Rumanians as a distinct political entity entitled to proportional representation at all levels of government. He also rejected universal suffrage and insisted that the language of administration and the courts be Magyar, although he agreed that Rumanian could be used as a supplement at the local level. He even seemed willing in principle

---

[16] 'Declaraţiuni asupra chestiunilor actuale politice: un interviev cu dl. Dr. Iuliu Maniu', *Revista politică şi literară*, 3/4–6 (1910), 112.

[17] Ioan Mihu, *Spicuiri din gândurile mele* (Sibiu, 1938), 159–64.

to let the Rumanians have their own political organization, but he made no mention of a role for the National Party. The Rumanians judged Tisza's reply unsatisfactory. Adopting Maniu's position, they decided in November 1910 to suspend negotiations until a 'substantial change' in the government's attitude toward the Rumanians had occurred and it had granted them 'institutional guarantees' of their national existence.

A new round of negotiations began in January 1913 and lasted, with interruptions, until February 1914. At the first meeting between leaders of the Rumanian National Party and Tisza on 21 January they reviewed Tisza's ideas on the future of Magyar–Rumanian relations. Tisza raised again the notion that the two peoples were natural allies and that they must stand together with the Germans to prevent the expansion of Russia. It followed, so he reasoned, that a strong Magyar national state was the best guarantee not only of the free cultural and economic development of the Rumanians of Hungary but also of the independence of the Rumanian Kingdom. Although his manner was thus conciliatory, he offered his listeners few practical inducements to abandon their reserve. He rejected as groundless the accusation that the government was pursuing a policy of Magyarization, admitting only that occasional abuses had been committed and would be corrected. Although he expressed a willingness to work with the National Party to achieve mutually beneficial aims, he intimated that as soon as the demands of the Rumanians had been satisfied its reason for being would have ceased. In parting, he asked the Rumanians to give him a new list of their desiderata in writing.

Two days later, on the 23rd, Maniu and Vasile Goldiş (1862–1934), a respected social theorist with extensive contacts among Magyar intellectuals, presented an eleven-point memorandum to Tisza. It went over familiar ground, but it sharpened the idea of autonomy: the language of instruction for Rumanian pupils in both state and church schools at all levels was to be Rumanian; in areas inhabited by 'compact masses' of Rumanians the language of administration and the administrators were to be Rumanian; and the political influence of the Rumanians was to be guaranteed by direct, secret universal suffrage and by the assignment to them of one-sixth of the seats in the lower house of parliament, a number corresponding to the percentage of Rumanians in the population of Hungary.[18]

[18] Biblioteca Academiei Române, Bucharest. Arhiva Valeriu Branişte, III, 2 a–c.

Tisza replied on 7 February. He rejected out of hand the administrative division of the country on the basis of nationality and the notion that Rumanians should be administered and judged by Rumanians. His position on the language of administration was similar. To diminish the role of the Magyar language in the life of the state struck him as 'incompatible' with the evolution of Hungary during the preceding forty years. As for electoral reform, he hinted that a 'rounding-off' of electoral districts in favour of the Rumanians would be possible, but only within the context of a general agreement. Matters were thus at an impasse, and by mutual consent the discussions were adjourned on 16 February.

In the autumn of 1913 new elements had entered the peace process as the Rumanian question in Hungary assumed growing importance in international relations. Primarily from Vienna and Bucharest strong pressure was brought to bear on Tisza and the Rumanian National Party to settle their differences in the interest of regional peace and stability. On the Austrian side, Archduke Franz Ferdinand, the heir to the throne, and his associates, especially the Austro-Hungarian Minister to Rumania, Count Ottokar Czernin, used all their influence to preserve Rumania's links with the monarchy and the Triple Alliance. Both men were convinced that one of the main obstacles to good relations between the two countries was the abiding discontent of the Rumanian minority in Hungary. Czernin served the cause of a *rapprochement* between the Rumanians and the Hungarian government with great skill. Upon his arrival in Bucharest he had been shocked to discover the extent of the hostility which public opinion harboured toward the Dual Monarchy. The effect of widespread public indignation at the alleged mistreatment of the Rumanians of Hungary on Rumanian government policy had, in his view, been nothing short of disastrous for Austria. Even King Charles, who had remained firm in his attachment to the alliance with the Central Powers, and a number of leading pro-German politicians, could no longer afford openly to pursue a policy of friendship with Austria-Hungary. To defuse this hostility and suspicion and to restore friendly relations between the Dual Monarchy and Rumania he urged that no effort be spared to placate the Rumanians of Hungary. The matter was urgent. He feared that delay would merely encourage the expansion of an irredentist movement on both sides of the Carpathians that would make any discussion of a *rapprochement* academic. As matters stood, he reported in December 1913, the alliance between Rumania and Austria-Hungary was 'not worth the paper it was written on', and in the event of a crisis the monarchy could not count upon the military support of Rumania.[19]

Czernin kept Franz Ferdinand regularly informed about the situation in Bucharest and pleaded for his personal intervention both in Vienna to counteract opposition to a Magyar–Rumanian agreement and in Bucharest, where he enjoyed some influence, to persuade the government to discourage intransigence on the part of the National Party. Franz Ferdinand's efforts may have had some effect in Bucharest, since an agreement between Tisza and the National Party fitted in with the foreign policy objectives of both the king and (for the moment) the Liberal opposition. The Archduke even seems to have influenced policy in Budapest where he persuaded Tisza (through the monarchy's Foreign Minister Berchthold) to increase the number of electoral districts to be assigned to the Rumanians from twenty-four to twenty-seven.

Negotiations between Tisza and the National Party came to an end in February 1914. The task of explaining his party's rejection of Tisza's proposals fell to Iuliu Maniu. As he saw it, the immediate cause of the collapse of the negotiations had been Tisza's insistence upon maintaining the Magyar national character of the Hungarian state. In the final analysis, Maniu complained, he had failed to reconcile the legitimate interests of a unitary state with the equally legitimate strivings of diverse ethnic groups to preserve their national character and further their political, economic, and cultural development. His refusal to admit that Hungary was a multinational state and his recognition of the Magyars as the sole creators and sustainers of the state, who could not be 'degraded' to the level of the other nationalities, had emptied his concessions of any real substance. In a state where the constitution placed one people above all the others there could be no genuine equality of nationalities; there could be only concessions to individual citizens and groups, such as language rights, in exceptional circumstances and at the pleasure of the government in power. Consequently, Maniu argued, throughout the negotiations Tisza had made no attempt to alter the existing constitutional structure and provide the political and judicial institutions necessary to guarantee the rights of the minorities in perpetuity. Under these circumstances, he concluded, the National Party could not accept Tisza's offer,

[19] *Österreich-Ungarns Aussenpolitik*, vii (Vienna, 1930), 611–12, 628.

could not change its programme, and could not acquiesce in the passive role he had reserved for it.[20]

The negotiations between Tisza and the Rumanian National Party were symptomatic of the impasse that had arisen between the 'master nations' and the minorities of Austria-Hungary after 1890. In both halves of the Dual Monarchy, whether in Cisleithania in the Austro-Italian or Austro-Czech relationship, or in Transleithania in the Magyar–Croat or Magyar–Rumanian relationship, a similar irreconcilability is discernible between the efforts of one side to enhance the powers of the central authority and those of the other to stretch that authority to the limit in the interest of national self-determination.

The issue between Tisza and the Rumanians, at one level, was clearly centralism versus federalism. Had the dispute remained strictly constitutional, a workable solution might have been found. Maniu and his colleagues were, after all, not revolutionaries who sought to overthrow the existing social and political order in Hungary. Rather, as their dealings with Tisza showed, they stood for gradual change through the extension of democratic political and economic institutions. Nor can they be described as irredentists. As long as the hope of a federalization of the monarchy existed, Maniu and company were prepared to accept a solution to national aspirations within existing frontiers. Tisza himself was not averse to compromise; he went farther than any of his predecessors in putting together a combination of concessions that might weave the Rumanians (and, later, the other minorities) into the general fabric of Hungarian society.

In the final analysis, the negotiations between Tisza and Rumanian leaders failed because both parties had become convinced that theirs was no ordinary political give and take or constitutional touching-up, but that national survival itself was at stake. For Tisza, the supreme goal was to complete the process of Magyar nation-state building; for the Rumanians, it was to ensure the free expression of the national genius. At this level compromise became unthinkable. Neither side could subordinate its 'being' to the other, still less to the 'simpler' concerns of Vienna and Bucharest. Consequently, as Tisza and the Rumanians pursued the ideal of the national state, the middle ground between assimilation of the minorities and dissolution of historical Hungary gradually disappeared.

[20] *Românul*, 6/19 Feb. 1914.

BUKOVINA

The social structure and economic preoccupations of the Rumanians of Bukovina, which Austria had seized from Moldavia in 1774, were similar to those of the Rumanians of Transylvania. Agriculture lay at the foundation of both. But the artisan crafts, commerce, and banking showed comparatively little development, and the middle class and intellectuals were fewer in number and less cohesive than their counterparts in Transylvania.

Between 1880 and the First World War the Rumanian population grew at an average rate of 10 per cent per decade. In 1880 it numbered 190,005, or 33 per cent of the total population of the province, and in 1910, 273,254 (34 per cent). In these three decades the Rumanians ceased to be the most numerous people of the province, having been overtaken by the Ruthenians. The overwhelming majority of Rumanians (88 per cent in 1910) depended upon agriculture for their livelihood. Practically all of them were smallholders possessing less than 5 hectares. Although they had received title to the land they worked in 1848 and, hence, no longer had to pay the tithe or perform labour services for a landlord, they were otherwise ill prepared for an independent economic life, and by the end of the century many holdings had been forfeited or were burdened by debt. The majority of households scraped by on plots of less than 5 hectares, considered the minimum necessary to satisfy the modest needs of a family of five. Traditional and generally unproductive agricultural methods offered them little expectation of improving their lot. Bukovina was also a land of large property: 63 landowners (3 per cent of the total) had estates of over 2,000 hectares (30.2 per cent of all agricultural land).[21] But only a fraction of these, some 300,000 hectares, were still in the hands of the descendants of Moldavian boiers.

The Rumanian urban population was small and the middle class correspondingly weak. Only about 12 per cent of Rumanians lived in cities and the important market towns, but after 1900 this percentage gradually increased. The figures for Cernăuți, the capital, are instructive: in 1900 the Rumanians constituted 14.3 per cent of the population (9,400 out of 65,767), and in 1910, 15.7 per

---

[21] I. E. Torouţiu, *Poporaţia şi clasele sociale din Bucovina* (Bucharest, 1916), 414–16; V. M. Botushans'kii, *Stanovishche i klasova borot'ba selianstva Pivnichnoi Bukovini v period imperializmu* (Kiev, 1975), 52–73.

cent (13,440 out of 85,458).[22] But in both Cernăuţi and the province as a whole the Rumanians formed a very small percentage of those engaged in typical urban occupations. In 1910, only 3.82 per cent were active in industry and business (out of 10.41 per cent for the entire population), 2.23 per cent in commerce and transportation (9.38 per cent), and 2.86 per cent in the civil service and the professions (4.29 per cent). In all these categories the Rumanians generally occupied the lower rungs. In numbers they were exceeded by Germans and Jews. In the province as a whole in 1910, for example, there were 444 Rumanian merchants as opposed to 8,642 Jews and 1,226 of other nationalities, and 737 Rumanian artisans (5,091 Jews and 3,494 of other nationalities). In Cernăuţi there were only 12 Rumanian merchants (1,269 Jews and 121 of other nationalities) and 44 artisans (1,481 Jews and 615 of other nationalities). The figures for almost all other cities were similar. In the professions Rumanians were numerous in elementary and secondary education: there were 850 Rumanian teachers out of a total of 2,248. But there were only 11 Rumanian lawyers (136 Jews and 14 of other nationalities) and 14 Rumanian physicians (136 Jews and 28 of other nationalities).[23]

Rumanian politicians and intellectuals were anxious to end what they regarded as their people's economic stagnation. They were guided in part by a perceived need to create a middle class which, as the most dynamic force in society, in their view, would lead the Rumanians into the modern world. They established a few banks, artisan associations, and retail shops, but such enterprises had little success, mainly because of the lack of experienced Rumanian personnel and the overwhelming competition from well-established businesses run by the other nationalities. The number of credit co-operatives increased after 1900, but they had few members and only modest amounts of money to lend. Societatea Meseriaşilor Români din Cernăuţi şi Suburbii (The Society of Rumanian Artisans of Cernăuţi and Suburbs), founded in 1907 for the purpose of encouraging young Rumanians to take up trades, seems to have increased by only a few the number of Rumanian artisans. The retail co-operative, Prăvălia Română (The Rumanian Shop), founded in 1905 to keep Rumanian consumer spending in Rumanian hands, and sawmills established by

---

[22] Österreichische Statistik, 63/1 (1902), 124; Torouţiu, Poporaţia şi clasele sociale din Bucovina, 61.

[23] Österreichische Statistik, NS, 3/1 (1916), 160–2; 3/10 (1916), 223–7. Torouţiu, Poporaţia şi clasele sociale din Bucovina, 142–68, 190–3, 237, 302, 311–16, 393.

Rumanian politicians to enable Rumanians to profit from the thriving Bukovina forest industry, failed for want of efficient management.

Political activity among the Rumanians of Bukovina never achieved the same cohesion and intensity as in Transylvania.[24] There was no equivalent, except in name, to the National Party in the latter province. Two main political currents were discernible in the 1860s and 1870s. The first, the so-called Centralists, favoured the amalgamation of the disparate lands of the Habsburg Monarchy into a unified state based essentially upon Enlightenment principles espoused by Joseph II. Led by the Hurmuzaki brothers, who had played a prominent role in the Rumanian movement in 1848, the Centralists included the majority of Rumanian boiers and many intellectuals, but since they stood for the equality of Rumanians, Ruthenians, and Germans in the civil administration, church affairs, and education, they were unpopular with Rumanian nationalists. The second current, the Federalists, or Autonomists, on the other hand, was composed of those nobles and intellectuals who emphasized the historical Rumanian character of Bukovina and wanted to maintain its separate identity. For a time they prevailed in local politics, but after the German Liberals came to power in Austria in the latter 1860s the Centralists, in league with the Bukovina German liberals, usually won local and provincial elections. Neither the Centralists nor the Federalists formed a political party. Distrustful of the mass of the peasantry and the nascent middle class and showing little interest in their problems, both groups preferred to deal directly with provincial authorities. Unlike Transylvania where Hungarian authorities discouraged Rumanian participation in the administration, in Bukovina the civil service was open to Rumanians at the highest level. For example, Eudoxiu Hurmuzaki, a supporter of the Austrian state idea, was *Landeshauptmann* from 1864 to 1874, and Alexandru Petrino, a large landowner and a leader of the Centralists, was Minister of Agriculture in the provincial government in 1870–1.

The last two decades of the century witnessed various attempts to establish a viable political organization. A significant advance was the founding of 'Concordia' in 1885 by Ioan Bumbac, professor of Rumanian language and literature at the gymnasium, or

[24] Teodor Bălan, *Procesul Arboroasei 1875–1878* (Cernăuți, 1937); Constantin Loghin, *Istoria literaturii române din Bucovina 1775–1918* (Cernăuți, 1926), 144–63, 205–11; Erich Prokopowitsch, *Die rumänische Nationalbewegung in der Bukowina und der Dako-Romanismus* (Graz, 1965), 59–75.

high school, in Cernăuţi. Dissatisfied with the domination of
Rumanian affairs by 'aristocrats', as he called the Hurmuzakis, he
and a few supporters looked to a new, middle-class association to
awaken an interest among a broader public in national politics and
instil in them a concern for the common good. Their goal was
national harmony, to be achieved by reconciling boier and peasant,
and priest and intellectual. They had the support of *Revista politică*
(The Political Review), which was published twice a month between 1886 and 1891 in Suceava and was the first Rumanian
political newspaper to appear since the authorities shut down
Bucovina in the aftermath of the Revolution of 1848. Its editors
represented a new force in Rumanian politics—the intellectuals—
who belonged to the rural and urban middle class. Although they
did not join any party, their alarm over the political apathy of the
Rumanians combined with their opposition to Austrian centralism
brought them into communion with the founders of 'Concordia'.
In 1892 disparate political elements—members of 'Concordia',
centralists, and a few remaining federalists—proclaimed the
national solidarity of all Rumanians in Bukovina and organized
themselves into a National Party. The new organization stood for
the maintenance of Bukovina's autonomy and its 'historical and
political individuality' and called for the strengthening of the
Rumanian component through the rapid expansion of Rumanian
schools and the introduction of Rumanian into the civil administration and the courts. *Gazeta Bucovinei* (The Gazette of
Bukovina), which Concordia had founded in Cernăuţi in 1891,
became the organ of the new party. But reconciliation and unity
were short-lived. Younger men, fervent nationalists led by Iancu
Flondor (1865–1924), a large landowner, took over leadership of
the party. They set the party on a new course by giving more
attention to the needs of the peasants and by speaking to them in a
language they could understand. This attempt to rally all elements
of society to the national cause was pursued in the party's new
organ, *Patria* (1897–1900; The Fatherland), which was edited by
the Transylvanian Valeriu Branişte. Another element was added
to political life in 1900 when Aurel Onciul, a lawyer and official in the Austrian civil service, founded Partidul Democrat
(The Democratic Party). Although he urged a strong defence
of Rumanian national interests, he was concerned mainly about
social questions. He himself had investigated the living conditions
of the peasants and now encouraged them to make social and
economic demands, and he tried to organize schoolteachers.

Co-operation with other nationalities seemed to him essential if genuine social reform was to occur, and he therefore allied himself with Ruthenians and Jews in a kind of peasant-liberal coalition. His cultivation of good relations with all ethnic groups and his loyalty to Austria inevitably brought him into conflict with the National Party. Several other political groupings also emerged after the turn of the century. Partidul Social-Democrat Român din Bucovina (The Rumanian Social Democratic Party of Bukovina), founded in 1906 and led by George Grigorovici (1871–1950), a deputy in the Austrian parliament from 1907 to 1918 and the editor of the party organ, *Lupta* (1906–10; The Struggle), had only a small constituency upon which to draw and pursued a moderate social and political policy. Iancu Flondor, continually in search of new vehicles for his strong nationalist sentiments, presided over Partidul Creştin Social Român (The Rumanian Social Christian Party) from 1908 to 1910. Its primary reason for being was to co-ordinate the activities of those nationalists who regarded the Jews as the chief threat to the Rumanian character of the province.

The Orthodox Church, which was raised to the rank of a Metropolitanate in 1873, made a significant contribution to Rumanian cultural life through its support of schools and teachers and its faculty of theology at the University of Cernăuţi, which had been founded in 1875. But because of its multinational character the church could not serve the Rumanian national movement as faithfully as it did in Transylvania. The Ruthenians demanded positions in the church administration and a share of church revenues commensurate with their numbers. The Rumanians, on the other hand, strove to preserve the Rumanian national character of the church, but with diminishing success in the face of demographic change and the inclination of the Court of Vienna to effect a compromise.[25] The intentions of the Court were made clear in 1912 when it brought about the appointment of a Ruthenian episcopal vicar, traditionally the successor to the Metropolitan. The First World War halted the process of accommodation.

Rumanian education made steady, if slow, progress from the 1860s on. The number of Rumanian schools, at least at the elementary level, and the number of Rumanian students in all types of schools grew, and the literacy rate improved. But the school in Bukovina was not the bulwark of nationality that it was

---

[25] Ion Nistor, *Istoria Besericii din Bucovina* (Bucharest, 1916), 161–97.

in Transylvania. In the first place, the Orthodox Church had much less influence over education than the Orthodox and Uniate churches in Transylvania. Although the Orthodox Church in Bukovina obtained the right to supervise Rumanian education in 1850, when Galicia and Bukovina were separated administratively, the government of Bukovina took over the direction of primary education in 1869. Language also worked against the maintenance of an exclusively Rumanian school system. The pervasiveness of German at all levels of education, especially in the secondary schools, the university, and a large number of 'mixed' schools (German–Rumanian and Ruthenian–Rumanian) significantly diluted the national content of the instruction received by Rumanian students. German owed its preponderance in education and cultural life to its status as the official language of the province, but the spectacular growth of the German population from 8 to 22 per cent of the total between 1857 and 1900 provided a solid demographic base for its widespread use.

Rumanian education was most promising at the elementary level. In 1900, out of 312 primary schools, 115, or 37 per cent, were Rumanian (137 were Ruthenian, 28 German-Rumanian, 6 German-Ruthenian, and 23 German). By 1908 the number of such schools had risen to 492, with 169 (34 per cent) Rumanian, 199 Ruthenian, 82 German, and the rest mixed. The situation at the secondary and university level was far less encouraging for the Rumanians. Of the four gymnasia operating in 1899, none was Rumanian. Only the gymnasium in Suceava, which had been founded in 1860 with the financial support of the Orthodox Church Fund, had parallel Rumänian and German sections. Of a total of 2,152 gymnasium students, 576, or 27 per cent, were Rumanian. The Rumanians failed to keep pace with the expansion of secondary education after the turn of the century. In 1908 the 844 Rumanian gymnasium students constituted only 22 per cent of all gymnasium students (3,853), even though a Rumanian gymnasium had finally been established in 1906 in Cernăuţi. In two of the most important professional schools of the province, the Rumanian presence was negligible. In 1908 there were no Rumanians among the 123 students at the Kaufmännische Fortbildungschule in Cernăuţi and only one out of 111 students at the Staatsgewerbeschule in the same city. But at the third, the Fachschule für Holzarbeitung, which was largely run by Rumanians, 58 of the 66 students were Rumanian. The most important Rumanian institution of higher learning continued to be the Orthodox Theological Seminary, which in 1875 had been incorporated into the newly founded university in Cernăuţi as the faculty of theology, but the language of instruction was German, except for courses in practical theology, for which Rumanian and Ruthenian could be used. Later, a chair for the history of the Rumanian language was established, and courses in the history of the Rumanians were offered as electives. In 1903, 125 Rumanians, 23 per cent of the student body and the majority enrolled in the faculty of theology, attended the university.[26] All these data gave little comfort to those Rumanian leaders who sought to awaken and fortify national consciousness among the broader elements of the population and to create a vigorous middle class. They complained bitterly about Germanization, but in fact the Rumanian school in Bukovina was less threatened by government action than in Transylvania.

Rumanian politicians and intellectuals strove to mobilize literary and cultural resources to further the development of a self-conscious nation.[27] Their most important organization was Societatea pentru Literatura şi Cultura Română în Bucovina (The Society for Rumanian Literature and Culture in Bucovina). Beginning its activities in 1865, it pursued a variety of goals: it published house organs, *Foaia* (The Journal; 1865–9) and *Aurora Română* (The Rumanian Dawn; 1881–4), in order to encourage the creation of a modern literature and promote a standard national language, 'the eternal symbol of the Rumanian people's individuality'; it provided scholarships for Rumanian students to the gymnasia in Cernăuţi and Suceava and the universities of Vienna and Lemberg; it supported the establishment of a chair of Rumanian language and literature at the University of Cernăuţi; and it used the printing press which it acquired in 1897 to publish books in Rumanian in all domains of knowledge, including school textbooks, newspapers, and journals. Beyond these specific undertakings the society served as a rallying point for Rumanian intellectuals, its annual meetings becoming a national forum where all issues affecting the Rumanians of Bukovina could be aired.[28] The

---

[26] *Österreichische Statistik*, 3/2 (1884), p. xxi; 62/1 (1902), 38–9, and part 2 (1903), pp. xxii–xlvi, 38–40: 91/2 (1910), 44–5, 110–11, 122–3, 148–9, 214–27.

[27] There is much on the cultural activities of the Rumanians of Bukovina with useful bibliographical references in Ionel Dîrdală, 'Relaţiile culturale ale Bucovinei cu celelalte provincii româneşti', *Anuarul Institutului de Istorie şi Arheologie*, 18 (1981), 281–91.

[28] Vasile Curticăpeanu, *Die rumänische Kulturbewegung in der Österreichisch-Ungarischen Monarchie* (Bucharest, 1966), 40–6.

society's work was seconded by student organizations, the most important of which was Arboroasa (The Beach Grove), the association of Rumanian students at the University of Cernăuţi. It was nationalist, and when its members took part in political activities it was dissolved in 1877, only two years after its founding. Its successor, Junimea (Youth), which drew its name and inspiration from the prestigious society of the same name in Iaşi and engaged in similar activities, had a longer life, 1878 to 1914. From 1903 to the First World War its members published the influential review, *Junimea literară* (Literary Youth), which followed the progamme of *Sămănătorul* in Bucharest. Besides defending the traditional cultural heritage of the Rumanians, they held up the peasant as the preserver of Rumanian individuality, and in prose and poetry they made him a special object of their sympathy.[29]

Two issues in particular stirred Rumanian nationalists between the 1890s and the First World War. The most urgent was the so-called Ruthenian question, which caused them to fear the 'submersion' of the Rumanians in 'our own province'. The danger was all too apparent in the population figures. Until the 1870s the Rumanians had been more numerous than the Ruthenians, but by the 1880 census they had fallen behind 239,690 to 190,005, a situation which prevailed until the First World War. The number of Ruthenians increased primarily because of steady immigration from Austrian Galicia. Rumanian nationalists claimed that the Rumanians were the only autochthonous inhabitants of Bukovina and accused Austrian authorities of encouraging Ruthenians to emigrate and favouring them over Rumanians in order to weaken the ties between the province and Rumania.[30]

The other major issue was irredentism. Since the 1890s many Rumanians had felt themselves on the defensive—in the church against the Ruthenians, in education and the civil service against the Germans, and in economic life against the Jews—and they held the Austrian government responsible for their precarious situation. They accused it of playing one nationality off against another in order to maintain the political dominance of the Germans. Yet, the evidence of a policy of divide and conquer is inconclusive. It is perhaps more accurate to see Austrian officials

[29] Teodor Bălan, *Suprimarea mişcărilor naţionale din Bucovina pe timpul războiului mondial, 1914–1918* (Cernăuţi, 1923), 168–9; Loghin, *Istoria literaturii române*, 216–21.

[30] *Rutenisarea Bucovinei şi causele desnaţionalisării poporului român*, de un Bucovinean (Bucharest, 1904), 330–73.

as mediators between the contending nationalities. On the eve of the First World War there were in fact few Rumanian irredentists, despite the activities of the Ligă Culturală and various individuals in Rumania such as Nicolae Iorga, who enthusiastically championed the political unity of all Rumanians. The absence of a strong irredentist movement must be attributed in great measure to the relative efficiency and integrity of the bureaucracy, especially at elections, and to its recognition, however lukewarm and uneven, of the individuality and aspirations of the various nationalities. Important also was the willingness of the latter, despite sharp differences among them, to compromise. This state of things contrasts sharply with the treatment of the national minorities in Hungary during the same period.[31]

BESSARABIA

Following the annexation of Moldavia between the Prut and the Dniester rivers, or Bessarabia, in 1812 Russian authorities had as their long-term goal the merging of the province into the general administrative structure of the empire. Although they left intact its institutions and laws for a time and allowed Moldavian boiers to participate in running its affairs, a governor, as the representative of the tsar, had full discretionary powers. The period of 'autonomy' ended in 1828, when Bessarabia was attached to the Novorossiisk general government and the civil and judicial institutions and tax system characteristic of the administration of Russian *gubernii* were introduced and Russian became the official language. This administration, based upon Russian models, ignored native traditions and discouraged local, Moldavian initiative until 1917. Periodic attempts at administrative reform, as during the reign of Alexander II (1855–81), did not alter the basic assumptions of the regime. The introduction of the *zemstva* in the 1860s, for example, simply furthered the integration of Bessarabia into the general administrative structure of the empire. Designed to increase local participation in civic affairs, in Bessarabia they were in practice run by Russian and other non-Moldavian functionaries brought in from other parts of the empire.

Moldavian resistance to Russian predominance was sporadic and ineffective. Leadership should have come from the boiers, but

---

[31] Prokopowitsch, *Die rumänische Nationalbewegung*, 130–53.

at the time of the annexation and during the period of autonomy they were pro-Russian. Eventually, they became uneasy as 'old customs and laws' were ignored and they themselves were excluded from the administration or treated as mere functionaries. They protested, but they were too few in number and too disorganized to make an impression on the Russian bureaucracy. As Russian rule was consolidated the old boier community itself slowly dissolved as new nobles were created and as lands in Bessarabia were granted to nobles from outside the province. By 1911, of 468 noble families in Bessarabia, only 138 were Moldavian. In any case, in the second half of the nineteenth century the latter had in large measure been integrated into Russian society, and in customs, attitude, and even language the majority did not differ in essentials from the nobility of the empire as a whole.

The mass of the rural population had much less direct contact with government functionaries than did the nobility and urban dwellers. The village tended to manage its own affairs in accordance with traditional rules and practices. Its elders even retained responsibility for allocating and collecting taxes and for deciding how other instructions from government authorities should be carried out. In administering justice, the villagers usually avoided the regular courts, where non-Moldavians presided as judges and Russian rather than Moldavian law supplied the procedural norms. They settled inheritances and other civil cases informally in accordance with long-established custom and in their own language.

The annexation of Bessarabia profoundly affected the composition of the population. Most striking during the century of Russian rule was the steady decrease in the percentage of Moldavians. According to the census of 1817, 86 per cent of the inhabitants (419,420 out of 482,630) were Moldavians, while 6.5 per cent (30,000) were Ukrainians and 4.2 per cent (19,130) were Jews. By 1856, Moldavians had fallen to 74 per cent (736,000 out of 990,000), while Ukrainians and Jews had risen to 12 and 8 per cent, respectively. In 1897, 56 per cent (1,092,000 out of 1,935,412) were Moldavian, 18.9 per cent Ukrainians and Russians, and 11.7 per cent Jews. These changes were primarily the result of immigration from neighbouring provinces promoted by Russian authorities. Moldavians formed an overwhelming majority in the central part of the province, but in the far northern and southern districts other ethnic groups together outnumbered them.[32] For example, in Hotin *uezd* in the north 53.3 per cent of the population were Ukrainian and only 23.8 per cent Moldavian, and in Akkerman *uezd* in the south 26.7 per cent were Ukrainian, 9.7 per cent Russian, and 16.4 per cent Moldavian. In the centre the countryside belonged to the Moldavians, whereas the cities took on an increasingly cosmopolitan character.

The great majority of Moldavians (and of the population generally) were rural and depended upon agriculture for their livelihood. Peasants constituted the largest class of Moldavian society, and of these the majority were, like their counterparts in the Rumanian principalities, economically dependent upon landlords before the emancipation of the 1860s. They did not possess their own land, but rather worked plots obtained under a kind of hereditary lease from monasteries and lay landlords in return for the payment of *obrok* (rent) and the rendering of *barshchina* (labour services). Unlike Russian serfs, however, they were personally free, and their right to move was repeatedly upheld by legislation in the first half of the nineteenth century. None the less, the power and influence of landlords often circumscribed the exercise of this and other rights. *Răzeşi* (free peasants) formed another significant category of the Moldavian peasantry. On the eve of the emancipation of the serfs in 1861 they represented about 12 per cent of the rural population in central Bessarabia. The majority were still independent smallholders, but their property had been under attack from boiers and merchants for half a century. By 1861 boiers and the middle class had brought 90,000 *desiatiny* of land (1 *desiatin* = 2.7 acres), or 40 per cent of all *răzeş* property, under their control. Thus, about one-third of the *răzeşi* had lost their land and had fallen to the level of dependent peasants, and the average *răzeş* holding had shrunk from ten to less than three *desiatiny*.

Land reform in the 1860s in Bessarabia took a somewhat different course from that in Russia proper. The decree of emancipation of 19 February 1861 had little effect in Bessarabia, for there were only 12,000 serfs, the majority of whom had been brought from Russia and were engaged in non-agricultural pursuits. Far more important was the statute of 14 July 1868, the main agrarian

---

[32] Ion Nistor, *Istoria Basarabiei* (Cernăuţi, 1923), 288–9, 299–300, 303–4; Iakim S. Grosul and Ilya G. Budak, *Ocherki istorii narodnogo khoziaistvo Bessarabii (1861–1905 gg.)* (Kishinev, 1972), 42–51.

reform act for Bessarabia, which dealt with the structure of land-holding and the redemption of allotments. Unlike the procedure followed in Russia, land was granted to individual families, not to the commune, and peasants were allowed to transfer their allotments to others. As a result, the more prosperous peasants became the chief beneficiaries of the law.[33]

The long-term consequences of these private property relations were greater social stratification in the village and a more rapid development of commercial relations in agriculture than in Russia, where the commune remained intact. In Bessarabia, small peasant holdings became smaller and less numerous, while large peasant holdings grew larger. For example, in 1877 holdings of less than five *desiatiny* constituted 37.6 per cent of all holdings, but by 1905 they amounted to 56.9 per cent, a sign that large numbers of peasants were losing at least a part of their land. During the same period the number of peasant holdings of 15–20 *desiatiny* increased from 5,395 to 11,493, and by 1905 there were 7,101 holdings between 20 and 300 *desiatiny*, whereas in 1877 there had been none. Disparities in the size of land holdings were sometimes striking. At one extreme were the estates of nobles, which still accounted for over half of all property in private hands at the turn of the century. The average size of an estate was 600 *desiatiny*, but the largest, such as that belonging to the Sturdza family in Bel'tskii *uezd* in central Bessarabia, encompassed 20,000 *desiatiny*. At the other end of the scale, by 1905, 23 per cent of all the peasants of Bessarabia had no land at all. The continued commercialization of agriculture and the agrarian laws introduced by Prime Minister Peter Stolypin between 1906 and 1911 accelerated these trends.[34]

The urban population of Bessarabia remained small throughout the nineteenth century down to the First World War. In 1912 only 14.7 per cent of the population lived in cities. The largest city was Kishinev, the chief administrative and industrial centre, whose population rose from 87,000 in 1861 to 128,000 in 1915. Other cities such as Akkerman, Bendery, and Izmail owed their growth during the period primarily to commerce and to their functions as local administrative centres, rather than to industry. The urban

---

[33] *Istoriia narodnogo khoziaistva Moldavskoi SSR (1812–1917 gg.)* (Kishinev, 1977), 107–14.

[34] *Istoriia Moldavskoi SSR,* i (Kishinev, 1965), 475–6, 486–97; Dmitrii E. Shemiakov, *Ocherki ekonomicheskii istorii Bessarabii epokhi imperializma* (Kishinev, 1980), 56–78.

population was largely non-Moldavian. In 1912, 37.2 per cent were Jewish, 24.4 per cent Russian, 15.8 per cent Ukrainian, and only 14.2 per cent Moldavian. In Kishinev (100,500 inhabitants in 1897) Moldavians made up only 17 per cent of the population, and in the next two largest cities, Bendery (31,800) and Akkerman (28,200), they were 8 and 0.8 per cent of the population, respectively.[35] The modest presence of Moldavians in the urban artisan crafts, commerce, the professions, and the bureaucracy accounts for such a low percentage. The general cause of this situation lay in the slow pace of industrialization and the persistent non-Moldavian character of the cities, both of which tended to discourage the migration of large numbers of Moldavian peasants to urban areas.

Industry as late as 1914 remained for the most part within traditional bounds. The mechanization and consolidation of enterprises had made little progress, and the great majority of workers were employed in small factories and workshops. Small-scale artisan production maintained its vitality mainly because of the ample supplies of agricultural raw materials and abundant and cheap labour, and because of poor transportation facilities, which tended to discourage competition from the more distant (and developed) Russian industry. Food-processing was the largest branch of industry. In 1897 it employed 73 per cent of all workers and accounted for 86.8 per cent of the value of all industrial production. Wine-making and beer-brewing were a distant second. The total number of workers employed in industry at the turn of the century was about 30,000. Many were local peasants who had too little land to make ends meet or none at all. Still others were artisans, but a surprisingly large number, especially skilled workers, were from outside Bessarabia. As of 1902, 49.3 per cent of the workers in enterprises employing 6 to 50 persons and 74.8 per cent in enterprises with 50 to 500 persons were from the Russian and Ukrainian *oblasti*.

The Orthodox Church was the one native institution that remained to the Moldavians after the Russian annexation. But as the Russian political administration consolidated itself and as the integration of the new province into the general fabric of the empire became its goal the church could not become the centre of Moldavian national sentiment. The annexation severed the church's links with the Metropolitanate of Moldavia. It was placed

---

[35] Viktor I. Zhukov, *Goroda Bessarabii (1861–1900)* (Kishinev, 1975), 32–53.

under the jurisdiction of the Holy Synod in St Petersburg, which in 1813 created out of most of Bessarabia the Eparchy of Kishinev. Although the church in Bessarabia did not fulfil the same national role as the church in Transylvania, it was, none the less, a focal point for Moldavian religious and cultural activities at the parish level throughout the nineteenth century, which prepared the way for broader social movements during the period of crisis after 1900.

For almost a century, down to the First World War, the church in Bessarabia was subject to relentless centralization and Russification. All the archbishops after 1821 strove to bring the administration of the eparchy into conformity with the regulations and practices of the Russian Church. Characteristic were the activities of Archbishop Irinarh Popov (1844–58), who faithfully carried out the programme of Nicholas I to promote Orthodox conservatism, loyalty to absolute monarchy, and Russian nationalism. He took no account of the Moldavians as a separate nationality, but expected them to conform to the Russian model like all the other Orthodox peoples of the empire, and he reserved decisions in all church matters to himself as the chief representative of the Holy Synod in St Petersburg. Under him a greater effort than ever before was made to introduce the Russian clergy into the Bessarabian church. Candidates for all the higher posts in the administration, rectors and professors in the seminary, protopopes, and priests in the larger, especially the urban, parishes were brought from Russia because they were familiar with the norms in the Russian Church and knew Russian and thus would be more likely than Moldavians to carry out official policy. In the rural parishes, where the great majority of the Moldavian faithful lived, native priests continued to serve, and religious life followed tradition. Popov would have introduced graduates of Russian seminaries here, too, but he recognized the futility of appointing Russian-speaking priests in parishes where only Moldavian was understood. He was thus confronted by one of the great contradictions of official policy in Bessarabia: Russian was promoted in order to bind the province securely to the empire, but such zeal entailed the neglect of the native language, which alone could serve as an instrument of that policy among the mass of the population. The era of reform under Alexander II brought no essential changes. Archbishop Pavel Lebedev (1871–82) continued the same policies as his predecessors. He introduced large numbers of clergy and administrators from outside Bessarabia, made a knowledge of Russian a prerequisite for candidacy to the priest-hood, and instructed priests to keep church registers, including vital statistics, in Russian. One important concession which church authorities made to the spirit of reform of the period was the inauguration, in 1868, of eparchial congresses of the clergy. Al-though purely consultative, they served as a forum where priests from all over Bessarabia could discuss common problems and out of which a sense of solidarity slowly developed. The effects of Popov's and Lebedev's activities were mixed. There was greater order than before in the administration, but the majority of both the clergy and faithful in the countryside became increasingly isolated from the church leadership and were little touched by its efforts at reform.

Centralization and Russification, so evident in the church's administrative practices, also governed its educational and cultural policies. At the theological seminary in Kishinev from 1840 on all subjects were taught in Russian. Not surprisingly, the seminary did not prosper. Parish priests sent few students, in part because they viewed it as a foreign institution and in part simply because few Moldavians knew Russian.

Church-sponsored primary education in the villages foundered for the same reasons. As its contribution to the reforms of Alexander II's reign the Russian Orthodox Church embarked upon an ambitious programme to establish schools in every parish. In Bessarabia some 400 schools with 7,000 pupils were functioning in rural parishes in the mid-1860s, but by 1880 only 23 remained. The main cause of such a catastrophe seems to have been the insistence by church authorities that instruction be done in Russian, a senseless requirement, inasmuch as neither priests, who in most villages served as teachers, nor pupils knew the language. An effort to revive the programme in 1884 failed for the same reasons and for lack of adequate funds.[36] The eparchial congress of the clergy in 1894 came up with the first viable solution to the problems of primary education. It requested the eparchy's school council to undertake the printing of appropriate textbooks in bilingual Russian and Moldavian editions. Although no imme-diate action was taken, the debate itself in the congress was sig-nificant because it was the first time since the early decades of the century that Moldavian had been seriously considered as a

---

[36] Nicolae Popovschi, *Istoria Bisericii din Basarabia în veacul al XIX-lea subt Ruşi* (Chişinău, 1931), 174–5.

language of instruction in the schools. This novel idea was eventually taken up by church authorities, who grudgingly recognized that they could extend their influence among the mass of the rural population only by using the language of the parishes.

Other cultural initiatives by church administrators during this period showed a singular disregard of local needs. The eparchial printing press, which had been founded in 1814 for the purpose of supplying the Moldavians with church books and other useful publications in their own language, functioned fitfully. By the 1860s the number of church books it published had fallen drastically. An *Antologhion* appeared in 1861 and an *Octoih* in 1862, both based upon texts printed earlier at the Monastery of Neamţ in Moldavia, but the imprimatur was given only after they had been compared with Russian texts to make certain that they contained no doctrinal errors. In any case, the publication of books in Moldavian ran counter to the official policy on nationality, and in 1882 Archbishop Serghei Liapidevski (1882–91) closed the press and sold off its equipment.[37]

Ecclesiastical authorities recognized that the best interests of the church required an increased use of Moldavian, and in the process they stirred the cultural life of the province. In 1867 they founded *Kishinevskie eparkhialnye vedomosti* (The Kishinev Eparchial Gazette) in order to relay official information to the general population and to disseminate practical advice on pastoral duties and interpretations of Scripture among the parish clergy in both Moldavian and Russian. But the Gazette also devoted considerable space to local church history, village monographs, and folklore. Toward the end of the century it began to carry articles on contemporary issues, especially schismatic movements within the church. Church authorities showed their concern for the moral and religious upbringing of the mass of the population by founding a missionary society, the Frăţime (Brotherhood), 'Naşterea lui Hristos' (The Birth of Christ), in 1899. It received permission to publish brochures with a religious and cultural content in Moldavian with or without parallel Russian texts, and by 1903 the annual number of copies printed reached 195,000. The eparchy also sponsored Societatea Istorico-Arheologică Bisericească din Basarabia (The Historical-Archeological Society of Bessarabia),

---

[37] On the drastic reduction in the number and significance of publications in Rumanian between 1862 and 1905, see Paul Mihailovici, *Tipărituri româneşti în Basarabia dela 1812 până la 1918* (Bucharest, 1941), 119–78. He lists no publications between 1879 and 1894.

which began to function in 1904 and whose primary task was to investigate the history of the church in Bessarabia.

The revolution of 1905 and the political concessions which followed affected the Orthodox Church throughout Russia. In Bessarabia church authorities yielded to the spirit of the time by allowing a decentralization of administration, which enhanced the role of the clergy and promised to transform the advisory congress of priests into a permanent administrative body. The church leadership also accorded greater scope to the Moldavian language in everyday religious life, and the clergy, now that the Moldavian majority was in a position to act, decided at its congress in 1905 that village priests should preach in Moldavian, that Moldavian should be added as a subject of study at the seminary, and that the eparchial printing press should be re-established to publish religious literature and a newspaper for the mass of believers.[38] Church authorities approved these proposals because they recognized the value of Moldavian in carrying out their spiritual mission and, especially, in combating revolutionary propaganda in the rural areas.

These liberalizing tendencies proved to be short-lived. As in political life after the first flush of parliamentary activity a reaction set in in the Russian Church. It was reflected in the Eparchy of Kishinev by a reassertion of episcopal authority. Archbishop Serafim Chichagov (1908–14) was alarmed by what he saw as nationalist tendencies within the church in Bessarabia and decided to concentrate the direction of its affairs in his own hands. In particular, he sought to relegate the congress of the clergy to a purely advisory role, but he found that its mediation had become indispensable in dealing with the parish clergy and faithful.

One of the most serious challenges to the official church came from a fundamentalist religious movement known as Inochentism, which originated at the monastery of Balta in Podolia, across the border from Bessarabia. There between 1909 and 1911 a young Moldavian monk, Inochentie, became famous for his preaching in Moldavian and for his ministrations to the sick. Soon Balta became a place of pilgrimage for thousands of Moldavians from all over Bessarabia, and disciples of Inochentie took up his mission at other monasteries. Inochentie's message was simple and stark: the age of anti-Christ had come, and the end of the world and the day of judgement were at hand, and it behoved all who wished to

[38] Popovschi, *Istoria Bisericii din Basarabia*, 369–70.

avoid eternal damnation to return to the strict morality of early Christianity.[39] Church authorities, alarmed by the commotion Inochentie had aroused among the rural faithful, exiled him to an island in the White Sea. By the time of his death in 1917 his movement had petered out, but the excitement it had aroused reveals much about the mentality of the rural world. The response to Inochentie was a spontaneous expression by the Moldavian peasants of their alienation from the official church, which had failed to minister to their spiritual needs.

Moldavian intellectual and cultural life during most of the period of Russian rule did not flourish. Besides the absence of strong church patronage, the cause must be sought in the deliberate neglect of all aspects of Moldavian culture by the Russian bureaucracy. The teaching of Moldavian as a subject in state elementary and secondary schools ceased in the 1860s and 1870s, and the last school grammar of Moldavian, Ioan Doncev's *Curs primitiv de limba română* (An Elementary Course in Rumanian), was published in 1865. In the half-century before the First World War Russian was the language of instruction in all state schools. The foreign character of public education helps to account for the high rate of illiteracy among Moldavians. In 1897, only 10.5 per cent of men and 1.7 per cent of women could read and write, figures which did not change significantly until after 1918.

In such circumstances Moldavian literature stagnated. At first, in the decade immediately following the Russian annexation intellectuals in Bessarabia maintained regular contact with Iaşi and Bucharest and thus continued to participate in Rumanian cultural life. There were several outstanding figures: Alexandru Hăşdeu (1811–72), a polymath who was attracted to Moldavian folk poetry and wrote short stories based upon historical themes, and Constantin Stamati (1786–1869), a poet and translator who combined classical literary tastes with the patriotic spirit of *Dacia literară* in Iaşi. Teodor Vîrnav (1801–60), a lesser boier, wrote a charming autobiography, *Istoria vieţii mele* (The Story of My Life), the first volume of memoirs in Rumanian literature. Completed in 1845, it was composed in a simple, direct prose abounding in the archaic expressions and Russian words which dotted the writing of Bessarabian boiers of the time. In the second half of the century down to the First World War little in the way of *belles-lettres*

---

[39] Ibid. 441–56.

appeared. Literary links with Rumania all but ceased, and in Bessarabia one cannot speak of literary currents or schools of criticism.

A Moldavian national political movement, or even a political party, did not exist before 1905, but in that year of revolution in Russia several disparate groups of boiers and intellectuals were spurred to action. Two main currents emerged. The moderates, who were led by Pavel Dicescu, a large landowner, established Societatea pentru Cultura Naţională (The Society for National Culture). They advocated the introduction of Moldavian as the language of instruction and a subject of study in state schools, but they were firmly opposed to reforms which might upset existing social relations and diminish their own wealth and influence. Their one success was to persuade the *zemstvo* of the *guberniia*, on which Dicescu sat, to pass a resolution urging the teaching of Moldavian in the primary schools.

The 'radicals' wanted to go much further. They were mainly university students who had organized discussion groups at various Russian universities to promote the Moldavian language and, in general, reinforce a sense of national consciousness among their fellow Moldavian students. In 1905 they returned to Bessarabia to take advantage of the new opportunities to press their cause through political action. Influenced by various Russian radical currents, notably the Socialist Revolutionaries and Social Democrats, they sought not only national rights but also social justice. They used the newly liberalized press laws to found *Basarabia*, which began publication on 24 May 1906 under the direction of an editorial committee headed by Constantin Stere, who had hastened to Chişinău to support the reformers against tsarism. In its pages they called for the recognition of the special status of the Moldavians as the predominant nationality and the granting of autonomy to Bessarabia in accordance with 'its traditional historical character'. In particular, they sought the introduction of the Moldavian language into public administration and the schools and insisted that Moldavians be allowed to form associations to promote their language and culture unhindered by the authorities. But at the same time they made clear that they did not seek separation from the Russian Empire, but were in fact prepared to work in common with all its peoples to establish a democratic regime and to obtain full political and civil rights for all citizens without regard to nationality or religion. Thus united, they thought, the peoples of Bessarabia could then proceed to deal with crucial social and economic problems, notably the agrarian question, which they placed at the top of their agenda.[40]

The national democrats, as the main body of intellectuals grouped around *Basarabia* began to call themselves, accomplished little, because of the reaction which set in in 1906 and 1907. The elections to the second Duma in February 1907 resulted in a total victory for the candidates of the extreme right, who opposed both social reform and concessions to the national minorities. The new conservative administration subjected *Basarabia*, which was unequivocally national and democratic, to repeated confiscations until it finally closed after nine months of publication. This event signalled the end of organized Moldavian political action. Thereafter, until 1917, the national movement languished. It lacked money, organization, and a significant number of persons willing to make sacrifices for a cause which seemed all but hopeless.

[40] P. Cazacu, *Moldova dintre Prut şi Nistru, 1812–1918* (Iaşi, n.d.), 165–74; Nistor, *Istoria Basarabiei*, 392–400.

6
The First World War

NEUTRALITY, 1914–1916

In the weeks following the assassination of Archduke Franz Ferdinand on 28 June 1914 King Charles and Liberal and Conservative politicians watched the deteriorating international situation with increasing anxiety. They had good reason to fear war, for Rumania's geographical position made it inevitable that she would find herself in the middle of an expanding, European conflict. The country faced the crisis far from united. There were serious political divisions between the king and a small group of Germanophiles, on one side, and the majority of politicians and public opinion, on the other, which favoured the Entente. Yet both sides could agree on the urgent need to avoid war. The lack of preparedness of the Rumanian army and the aggressive behaviour of Austria-Hungary toward Serbia gave everyone pause. Convinced that Serbia wished to settle the crisis peacefully and fearful that otherwise Russia would support Serbia militarily and a general war would break out, the king and Prime Minister Brătianu urged both parties to settle their differences through negotiation. They became thoroughly alarmed when Austria-Hungary presented a drastic ultimatum to Serbia on 24 July. War now seemed to them inevitable, since Serbia, in their view, could not possibly accept all its terms.

As July passed it became evident that the Rumanian government would remain neutral. Charles would have preferred to honour Rumania's treaty commitments to the Central Powers, but as he confessed to Czernin on 24 July, so many things had happened in the preceding year that such a course had little chance of being adopted. But he assured Czernin that he would do everything possible to honour Rumania's commitments to the Central Powers. He also insisted that if internal conditions made such a course of action impossible, then Rumania would adhere to a policy of strict neutrality. The majority of Austro-Hungarian officials expected nothing more. Field Marshal Conrad von Hötzendorf, the chief of the general staff of the Austro-Hungarian army, spoke for many of them when he confessed that he had no illusions about where Rumanian sympathies lay. Rumania, he thought, had been 'lost' because Rumanians were eager to create a unified national state by annexing Transylvania and Bukovina and in the present circumstances would act in a manner calculated to achieve that goal.

As the crisis deepened Rumanian leaders became as much concerned about the Balkans as with Central Europe. The Treaty of Bucharest had not put an end to the rivalry between Rumania and Bulgaria. On 27 July, one day before the Austro-Hungarian declaration of war on Serbia, Czernin met with Brătianu to extract a clear statement of his intentions. Brătianu informed him that Rumania would pursue a policy of watching and waiting, but if Bulgaria became involved in the conflict and if there were sigificant changes in the balance of power among the states of South-eastern Europe, then Rumania's situation would become 'critical'. Although Brătianu had no doubt that Austria-Hungary would defeat Serbia, he opposed any change in Serbia's frontiers. But if that happened and Bulgaria was the beneficiary, then he declared his intention to seek a corresponding increase in Rumania's territory.[1]

The Rumanian government formally decided on a policy of neutrality at a meeting of the Crown Council on 3 August. Presided over by the king and attended by members of the government, former Prime Ministers, and the heads of major political parties, it weighed two choices. The first—an immediate entrance into the war on the side of the Central Powers—was championed by Charles, who expressed his certainty of a German victory and appealed to his listeners' sense of honour to uphold treaty commitments to Germany and Austria-Hungary. But he stood alone, except for Petre Carp, the Conservative leader, who dismissed the overwhelming public sentiment in favour of the Entente as irrelevant and expressed a lack of interest in the situation of the Rumanians of Transylvania. But these were precisely the questions uppermost in the minds of everyone else. Italy's decision to remain neutral also influenced their thinking. Brătianu's moralizing was also welcome: he argued that Rumania had been relieved of her treaty obligation to come to the aid of Austria-Hungary by the latter's failure to consult the Rumanian government before

---

[1] *Documents diplomatiques concernant les rapports entre l'Autriche-Hongrie et la Roumanie (22 juillet 1914–27 août 1916)* (Vienna, 1916), 3: Berchtold to Czernin, 26 July 1914.

delivering its ultimatum to Serbia and by the character of the ultimatum itself, which, Brătianu thought, had been formulated in such a way as to force war upon Serbia. Confronted by the overwhelming sentiment for neutrality of party leaders, who declared that they could not assume responsibility for a government which embarked upon war alongside the Central Powers, the king, emphasizing his role as a constitutional monarch, acquiesced in their decision.

The Central Powers were bitter at the refusal of Rumania to join their war effort, but they decided to interpret her action in the best possible light. On 5 August their ministers in Bucharest informed Brătianu that they judged the action of the Crown Council as fully in accord with their traditional friendly relations and that they would continue to regard Rumania as an ally. Yet, both countries kept up the pressure on Rumania to join the war on their side. Germany took a different approach from her ally by advocating concessions to Rumania, in particular on the nationality problem in Transylvania. Both countries overestimated Charles's influence, and when he died on 10 October they feared a sharp turn in Rumania's policy away from the Central Powers under his successor, his nephew Ferdinand. Czernin was in an especially gloomy mood. He was certain that if the Central Powers were checked on the battlefield, no power on earth could prevent Rumania from attacking Austria-Hungary. Yet, as events would show, neither Ferdinand nor Brătianu had any intention of abandoning neutrality until the course of the war had become clear. For the moment the most noticeable change in their policy was an end to the easy access which the representatives of the Central Powers had had with King Charles and the openness of their discussions.

During the first months of the war the Brătianu government sought to shore up its international position by intense diplomatic activity. It concluded advantageous agreements with Italy and Russia. The understanding between Rumania and Italy, signed in Bucharest on 23 September, reflected their common interests toward Austria-Hungary. Although allied with her, both coveted territory inhabited by their respective co-nationals. They now agreed to inform one another of any contemplated policy changes and promised not to renounce neutrality without prior consultation.[2]

[2] Glenn E. Torrey, 'The Rumanian–Italian Agreement of 23 September 1914', *Slavonic and East European Review*, 44/103 (1966), 403–20.

The accord with Russia had a longer history. Negotiations had been underway even before the Rumanian declaration of neutrality. On 5 August the Russian Foreign Minister, Sazonov, presented the draft of a convention to the Rumanian minister in Petrograd. Its main provision called for military co-operation against Austria-Hungary as soon as the treaty came into force. Russia agreed to continue fighting until all the territory of Austria-Hungary inhabited by Rumanians had been united with Rumania, and Rumania undertook not to make peace without the consent of Russia. Furthermore, Russia offered to guarantee Rumania's frontiers against an attack by Bulgaria. However attractive the territorial arrangements were, Brătianu had no intention of being drawn into the conflict at this early stage. Nor had the Rumanians' distrust of Russia's intentions in South-eastern Europe been noticeably assuaged. Moreover, France and Britain, with whom the Rumanians' sympathies lay, had been sceptical about the Russian initiative, because of King Charles's well-known Germanophile sentiments and Rumania's close economic and political ties with the Central Powers. They also thought that a bilateral agreement between Russia and Rumania might upset the delicate balance in the Balkans by inducing Bulgaria and Turkey to attack Serbia and Greece. Sazonov was sensitive to Rumanian reservations and on 26 September made a new proposal, which required only Rumania's benevolent neutrality in exchange for Russian recognition of Rumania's territorial claims on Austria-Hungary. In so doing, he ignored the concerns expressed by some of his colleagues that the enlargement of Rumania in accordance with ethnic principles might well raise the matter of Bessarabia. When the question was put to the Rumanian minister, Constantin Diamandy, he avoided a direct answer. He told Sazonov that the cause of the differences which had divided their two countries in 1877–8 had been Gorchakov's high-handed treatment of Rumania, and he expressed the hope that Sazonov's policy would lead to 'mutual confidence'.[3] The agreement was concluded on 1 October, when letters were exchanged between Sazonov and Diamandy. Brătianu had made the treaty with the king's authorization. Charles seems still to have believed that Germany would be victorious, but after the Battle of the Marne, which halted the German advance in

[3] On the negotiations for a treaty, see Anastasie Iordache, 'Încheierea acordului româno-rus din 18 septembrie/1 octombrie 1914: însemnătatea şi consecinţele sale', *Revista de istorie*, 29/1 (1976), 49–62.

France, he decided that an agreement to ensure Russia's neutrality would be of great strategic value to Rumania.

Negotiations between Russia and Rumania for a more formal treaty of alliance continued intermittently throughout 1915 and the beginning of 1916. Brătianu, who was clearly in charge of foreign policy after the death of King Charles, made the stakes high for Rumania's entrance into the war. He had great respect for Germany's military and economic power and was determined not to join the conflict prematurely. Foremost among his conditions was a written guarantee that Rumania would receive Transylvania, Bukovina, and the Banat as a reward for services rendered. He and the majority of Rumanian politicians thought this demand perfectly justified by the history and ethnic character of these territories. With the campaign of 1877–8 undoubtedly on his mind, Brătianu also insisted upon a separate military convention with Russia setting forth the conditions under which the two armies would co-operate and limiting the freedom of movement of the Russian army on Rumanian territory. He was also acutely aware of his country's geographic isolation from the Western Allies and sought guarantees from them of a continuous flow of armaments and supplies, which could come only through Russia. The ill-fated Dardanelles campaign of April–December 1915 and the failure of the British and French expeditionary force at Salonika to accomplish anything in the autumn of that year could hardly have reassured him. At the same time Sazonov was reluctant to make far-reaching political commitments, and Russian military commanders could not make up their minds whether the opening of the Rumanian battlefront would help or hinder their cause.

Britain and France favoured Rumania's immediate entrance into the conflict, but they had grave doubts about the capacity of the Rumanian army to wage a sustained war against the Central Powers. British leaders also had reservations about Rumania's territorial claims on Austria-Hungary. They had not yet decided on the break-up of the Dual Monarchy, for they wished to maintain a strong state in East Central Europe to balance the power of Russia. Moreover, they had no intention of sacrificing Serbian interests in the Banat to satisfy 'exaggerated' Rumanian claims. As for the kinds of military action Brătianu demanded as a condition for joining the Entente, British policy-makers showed little interest in mounting an Allied offensive on the Salonika front, on the grounds that precious resources could be better expended elsewhere. Yet, despite their reservations, they generally supported the French initiative to bring Rumania into the war.

During the first year of the war Rumania's political relations with the Central Powers became increasingly strained over Brătianu's refusal to modify his neutral stance. To win him over Vienna and Berlin tried various inducements. They put heavy pressure on István Tisza, the Hungarian Prime Minister, to make concessions to the Rumanians of Transylvania or even to allow the Rumanian army to occupy a part of the province on the pretext of defending it from a Russian invasion. But Tisza would have none of it. To all such entreaties he replied that the more the Rumanians were given the more they would demand. Instead of concessions, he recommended toughness toward Rumania as a far more effective policy.[4]

The Central Powers also tried to play the 'Bulgarian card' again. Their representatives continually raised with Brătianu the possibility of Bulgaria's adherence to the Triple Alliance and the latter's willingness to satisfy her territorial ambitions, including the recovery of southern Dobrudja. For his part, Czernin, convinced that Brătianu was too thoroughly committed to the Entente to be won over by either blandishments or threats, worked to install a Conservative government headed by Alexandru Marghiloman or another pro-German politician in place of the Liberals. But nothing worked. Brătianu refused to budge, citing his inability to govern 'against the country', which, all sides recognized, was overwhelmingly sympathetic to France and Britain. Nor could the king, who did not fully approve of Brătianu's actions, be persuaded to change Prime Ministers. Ferdinand, clearly influenced by Brătianu, expressed doubts that the Central Powers could win the war. In any case, Brătianu, not he, had effective control of the government. The only alternative to the Liberals—the Conservatives—were now but a mere remnant of the once powerful party which under Charles would have replaced their rivals at such a critical time.

The course of domestic politics during the two years of neutrality was dominated by the war. Within both major parties significant differences of opinion emerged on the question of neutrality or intervention. The Conservatives failed to maintain even a semblance of cohesion. One group, led by Alexandru

---

[4] István Tisza, Összes munkái, ii (Budapest, 1924), 126: Tisza to Czernin, 7 Sept. 1914.

Marghiloman and Titu Maiorescu and traditionally pro-German, favoured neutrality, but wanted to maintain good relations with the Central Powers. Another, smaller group, gathered around Nicolae Filipescu, demanded Rumania's immediate entrance into the war on the side of the Entente and was thus close to Take Ionescu's Democratic Conservatives, who were also eager for immediate action against Austria-Hungary. Although both groups recognized the dangers of precipitate action, they were driven by the urge to 'liberate' Transylvania and achieve national unity. At the opposite pole stood Petre Carp and a handful of his supporters. They continued to insist that the government honour its treaty commitments to the Central Powers, but were ignored. A final break between the Marghiloman and Filipescu wings occurred at the party congress on 18 May 1915. The causes were deep-seated: rivalry for leadership of the party and acute differences over foreign policy.[5] Subsequent efforts to heal the breach and reconstitute a strong, united Conservative Party failed. The most promising initiative—the 'fusion' in 1916 of the Filipescu wing and Take Ionescu's party—lacked substance and failed utterly to revive Conservative fortunes.

The Liberal Party had remained more or less united. The majority supported the government policy of 'expectant neutrality'. Brătianu avoided making public statements on foreign policy, and while he did not prevent others from airing their own, often emotional, opinions in parliament, he himself refused to take a stand. The general European situation seemed to justify his caution. The failure of the Central Powers to gain a quick victory on the Western front and the need to obtain firm commitments from the Allies to support Rumania's territorial claims before decisive action could be taken buttressed his policy of non-involvement and shielded him from critics.

The small Social-Democratic Party voted against entrance into the war at an extraordinary congress on 23 August 1914, but it approved mobilization to defend the territorial integrity of the country. During the next two years the majority of socialists continued to favour strict neutrality, but a few urged greater understanding for national aspirations. Constantin Dobrogeanu-Gherea provided the theoretical justification for the socialists' stand on neutrality. He favoured the peaceful solution of international

---

[5] I. Căpreanu, 'Criza din anul 1915 a Partidului Conservator', *Anuarul Institutului de Istorie și Arheologie*, 10 (1973), 255–65.

disputes as a general rule, but he made an exception in the case of wars of national liberation which represented the culmination of a long period of struggle. He therefore thought the First Balkan War justified, in part at least, because its origins went back to 'tragic events 500 years earlier', but he condemned the Second Balkan War as merely the expression of the rivalries among the 'exploiting classes' of the several Balkan countries. He put the new European-wide conflict in the same category, denouncing it as a classic imperialist war being fought for the economic domination of the world. The only policy for Rumania to follow was, therefore, strict neutrality, since small nations could participate in such a conflagration only as pawns of the great powers or objects of compensation among them.[6]

Neutrality could not protect the Rumanian economy from the war. Every branch was affected. Industry was slowly geared to military needs, as the Brătianu government strove to prepare the army for combat. But the low level of industrialization, especially of the metallurgical and related industries, and the shortage of skilled labour were acutely felt. The Liberals, therefore, were forced to order urgently needed military equipment from abroad.

Agriculture was adversely affected by the disruption of traditional markets abroad and by preparations for war at home. Mobilization, which accelerated after April 1915, caused hardship particularly on smallholdings, for they were deprived of their main source of labour at a time when the additional burden of state requisitions of animals and foodstuffs fell mainly upon them. As a result, many peasants could not pay their state taxes or their private debts and lost their land.

To deal with the growing economic crisis the government intensified its intervention in economic affairs.[7] Its immediate concern was to ensure sufficient supplies of food for home consumption, cover the needs of the army, and secure necessary raw materials for industry. A series of decrees in 1914 and 1915 restricted the export of a long list of items and imposed heavy new export duties payable in gold on some, but, because of pressure from large producers and exporters, corn, the basic food of the majority of the population, was not protected, and in 1915 earlier prohibitions on the export of other grains were lifted.

---

[6] For a discussion of Dobrogeanu-Gherea's attitude toward the war, see D. Hurezeanu, C. *Dobrogeanu-Gherea: studiu social-istoric* (Bucharest, 1973), 314–30.

[7] Ema Nastovici, 'Măsuri de reglementare a situaţiei economice interne în anii 1914–1916 şi urmările lor', *Revista de istorie*, 31/8 (1978), 1373–90.

As reserves of foodstuffs dwindled, export restrictions were re-imposed at the beginning of 1916. The government had also to deal with the financial effects of the war, which were felt almost immediately. The availability of credit became severely limited, as foreign banks withdrew large amounts of capital, and new foreign investment all but ceased. Domestic sources of credit proved insufficient to meet normal economic needs and to cover the additional costs of armaments. The government, in desperation and in secret, turned to Italy and Britain for loans. The latter granted two loans of five and seven million pounds in 1915 for the purpose of buying military equipment from British firms, credits which were obviously intended to draw Rumania closer to the Entente. The government also took measures to increase supplies of weapons and ammunition. In 1915 it created Comisia Tehnică Industrială (The Technical Industrial Commission) to oversee the production of military equipment and Direcţia Generală a Muniţiilor (The General Directorate of Munitions) to obtain the raw materials necessary for the manufacture of shells, cartridges, and grenades. The results were encouraging, but, as events would show, production fell far short of what was required to fight a modern, large-scale campaign.

The war caused a general reorientation of Rumanian foreign trade. Until the summer of 1914 80 per cent of Rumania's exports had passed through the mouths of the Danube, the Black Sea, and the Straits, but Turkey's closing of the Straits seriously disrupted normal trading patterns. Rumania's commercial relations with Britain, France, Belgium, and The Netherlands, in particular, were thus severely restricted, a situation which led to increased trade with the Central Powers.[8] Germany and Austria-Hungary, which already supplied Rumania with 60 per cent of her imports and took 20 per cent of her exports, reinforced their position in the Rumanian market. Between 1914 and 1916 Germany's share of Rumania's foreign trade increased from 23 to 29.4 per cent and Austria-Hungary's from 18.5 to 47.9 per cent. Rumania exported large quantities of grain and oil to both countries, and it is evident that she figured prominently in the war plans of the Central Powers as a supplier of foodstuffs and raw materials. In return, the Rumanian government sought to purchase military equipment from both Germany and Austria-Hungary, but both, conscious of

---

[8] Ema Nastovici, *România şi Puterile Centrale în anii 1914–1916* (Bucharest, 1979), 162–87.

where Rumanian sentiments lay, provided only a small part of the items requested and insisted upon immediate payment for all goods shipped.

As the war dragged on the diplomatic pressure on Brătianu to abandon neutrality intensified. In the spring of 1916 France and Russia pulled out all the stops to gain Rumania's adherence to the Entente in time to coincide with the general Allied offensive planned on both the Eastern and Western fronts. On 16 June the French minister in Bucharest, Camille Blondel, bluntly informed Brătianu that the time for decision had come. Brătianu asked for more time, but he now realized that a policy of neutrality could no longer be sustained. Yet, to abandon it was to expose his country to incalculable danger, for nothing that had happened since the summer of 1914 had persuaded him that the Allies could provide adequate aid to his country. He was also painfully aware of how exposed Rumania's southern frontier was since Bulgaria's entrance into the war on the side of the Central Powers in October 1915. He therefore demanded the fulfilment of a series of conditions intended to protect his country militarily and to guarantee the achievement of her territorial ambitions. He wanted: a joint guarantee by Russia and Italy to supply 300 tons of munitions per day for the duration of the war; a general Allied offensive on all fronts to coincide with the Rumanian attack on Austria-Hungary; a Russian offensive in Bukovina and Galicia to defend Rumania's northern flank; and the dispatch of Russian troops to Dobrudja to protect southern Rumania from a Bulgarian attack, or, if this were not possible, then a joint Franco-British offensive against Bulgaria from Salonika. Brătianu also insisted upon the conclusion of a political treaty with the Allies guaranteeing the union of Transylvania and Bukovina with Rumania in accordance with the boundaries he had indicated in negotiations with Russia in 1915. When he presented his terms to Blondel on 4 July he assured the Allies that if they were accepted, Rumania would begin military operations shortly after 1 August.[9]

Although negotiations were to last another six weeks, Brătianu's proposals brought an effective end to two years of uncertainty. He did not take this step lightly, and as late as the end of June he still hesitated to make a final commitment to the Allies. His underlying motive was now, as it had been in 1914 and 1915, to use the war to achieve national unity by acquiring Transylvania and Bukovina

[9] Glenn E. Torrey, 'Rumania's Decision to Intervene: Brătianu and the Entente, June–July 1916', *Rumanian Studies*, 2 (1973), 3–29.

from Austria-Hungary. His decision to act had been influenced by the intensification of the fighting and, paradoxically, by what he perceived to be the improved prospects for peace. The Russian offensive in Galicia, begun in early June by General Brusilov, had been a critical element in Brătianu's calculations because it had revealed the military weakness of Austria-Hungary and, coupled with rumours about peace-feelers from the Central Powers, it suggested that a general peace might be near. Brătianu was afraid that if the belligerents reached a settlement before Rumania had entered the war and had thus 'earned' a right to share in the spoils, the opportunity to create a Greater Rumania would be lost. He also knew that if he was to gain territory from Austria-Hungary, he would need the support of France and Britain at the peace conference and could not, therefore, afford to disappoint them at this critical moment, as he had done in 1915 when he had drawn back from joining the Entente.

All these considerations coincided with a determined Allied diplomatic offensive at the end of June. France and Russia used all their powers of persuasion to force Brătianu to enter the war immediately, issuing, in effect, an ultimatum that unless he acceded to their demands, he could not expect to achieve his territorial goals. Yet, Russia was reluctant to satisfy all Brătianu's demands, a circumstance which blocked an agreement until the beginning of August. By then Russian field commanders had come around to the idea that the support of the Rumanian army against Austria-Hungary would be advantageous, but Russian politicians continued to judge Brătianu's terms 'exaggerated'. The intervention of France, supported by Britain and Italy, finally overcame Russian reluctance. The French offered a flexible formula, whereby Russia would grant, on paper for the time being, everything Brătianu wanted, even equality with the other Allies at the peace conference, but if at the end of the war it turned out that all Rumania's conditions could not be met, then the French proposed that the principal Allies would simply force Rumania to accept less than what had been promised. Finally, on 17 August 1915, Brătianu and the diplomatic representatives of France, Britain, Russia, and Italy in Bucharest signed political and military conventions stipulating the conditions of Rumania's entrance into the war. Of immediate importance were the provisions for an attack on Austria-Hungary to commence not later than 28 August and the recognition of the right of the Rumanians of Austria-Hungary to self-determination and to union with the Kingdom of Rumania.

The Rumanian Crown Council formally approved the treaties and declared war on Austria-Hungary on 27 August. On the following day Germany declared war on Rumania. Turkey followed suit on 30 August and Bulgaria on 1 September.

WAR, 1916–1918

On the eve of the most important campaign it had fought since 1877–8 the Rumanian army had almost doubled in size from what it had been three years earlier. It had grown from 10,600 officers, 460,000 men, and 150,000 horses in 1913 to 19,843 officers, 813,758 men, and 281,210 horses in 1916. But mobilization had aggravated long-standing deficiencies in equipment and supplies. Rumanian industry by itself was capable of meeting only a small portion of the army's needs. For example, it could provide only two shells for every cannon and one cartridge for every rifle per day. Despite Brătianu's efforts to increase armaments production, the army had had to rely upon purchases of weapons and munitions of all kinds from abroad. In the pre-war years Germany and Austria-Hungary had been the chief suppliers of military equipment, but after the war began and as his government moved closer to the Entente, Brătianu sought to lessen the army's dependence upon the Central Powers. The first of a series of new purchase agreements had been made with France on 21 March 1915. But the transport of goods from the West to Rumania proved difficult. The only feasible route was through Salonika to Turnu Severin on the Danube. But that supply line was cut by the Bulgarian attack on Serbia in October 1915. Afterwards, until November 1917, supplies had to come by a long, circuitous route through the Russian ports of Archangel on the White Sea and Vladivostok on the Pacific.

The Rumanian army thus entered the war inadequately equipped and uncertain of its sources of supplies. The most serious deficiencies were in heavy artillery, machine-guns, and airplanes. While a Rumanian division averaged three to four field artillery pieces and one to two heavy machine-guns per battalion, a German or Austro-Hungarian division had six to seven field artillery pieces and six to eight heavy machine-guns, along with twelve light machine-guns, which Rumanian forces lacked entirely. The Rumanian air force consisted of twenty-eight planes, all of them old and none capable of a speed in excess of 80 kilometres per hour. There were other shortcomings, too. The rail network was ill designed to move troops and supplies to the battlefront, and the number of engines and carriages was too small to handle military and civilian traffic at the same time. The rapid build-up of the army had left many officers and soldiers with only rudimentary training. The lack of enough experienced, well-trained officers was especially critical. These were problems of long standing, and both Conservative and Liberal governments bore the responsibility, since they had paid little attention to such matters after the achievement of independence. Now, on the battlefield, these deficiencies manifested themselves with fateful consequences.

The primary objectives assigned to the Rumanian army were ambitious and, as events soon showed, unrealistic. The high command sought, first, to clear Transylvania of enemy forces and then proposed to drive on to the Tisza and Danube valleys in order to deprive the Austro-Hungarian army of its main source of foodstuffs. It assigned three-quarters of its available forces, or some 420,000 men, to these operations. In the south it stationed an army of 142,000 men to defend the frontier against a Bulgarian-German attack and to cover the landing of Russian troops in Dobrudja. Once the latter were in place, Rumanian and Russian armies were to take the offensive in north-eastern Bulgaria and establish a permanent defence line from Ruschuk to Varna.

The first phase of this grand design began on the night of 27–8 August when Rumanian troops crossed the frontier into Transylvania. Meeting only light resistance, they occupied Braşov on the 30th, and by 2 September they had secured the main Carpathian passes. In the next few days they entered Făgăraş, Miercurea Ciuc, and Odorhei and advanced to the vicinity of Sibiu and Sighişoara. Then, on 8 September, the high command suddenly ordered a halt to the offensive. Despite initial successes, the campaign had not been pursued vigorously enough to take full advantage of the enemy's lack of preparation. The average day's advance had been only two or three kilometres, a pace which allowed German and Austro-Hungarian armies to be reinforced and regrouped for a counter-offensive.

The main reason for halting the offensive in Transylvania was the alarming turn of events in the south. The Bulgarian army, supported by German forces, all commanded by Field Marshal August von Mackensen, had gone on the offensive on 31 August and had captured Turtucaia on 6 September and Silistra on the 8th. In the face of the steady enemy advance the Rumanian high command decided to reinforce the Dobrudja front by transferring reserves from Transylvania. The tactic worked, and Rumanian resistance stiffened. Although Bulgarian and German forces continued to advance northward in Dobrudja, they were finally stopped south of Constanţa on 19 September. General Alexandru Averescu, the new commander of the Rumanian third army in the south, devised a bold plan for a counter-attack behind the Bulgarian–German line from across the Danube combined with a frontal assault in Dobrudja. This was the so-called Flămînda operation, named after the small port east of Giurgiu on the Danube where the campaign began. Both Rumanian public opinion and the troops at the front had high expectations of a decisive victory, for Averescu, who had commanded one of the thrusts into Transylvania, was enormously popular. Rumanian forces crossed the river on 1 October and achieved their initial objectives. But the operation was abruptly halted and the troops pulled back across the Danube on 4 and 5 October in order to make possible the reinforcement of the Transylvanian front where a dangerous Austro-German counter-offensive was gathering momentum.

In Transylvania the Rumanian army held firm on all fronts between the end of September and the end of October once it had fallen back to the Carpathians and had established strong defensive positions in the passes. But the enemy counter-offensive recovered almost all the territory lost to the Rumanians in the first two weeks of the campaign. On the western end of the front after the battle for Sibiu on 26–8 September the Rumanians were forced to retreat south along the Olt River, and in the east they evacuated Braşov on 8 October. But until the end of the month the Rumanian army, now under the command of Averescu, retained control of the passes, which barred the route to Bucharest and the Wallachian plain.

The main objective of Erich von Falkenhayn, who had assumed command of German and Austro-Hungarian armies in Transylvania on 30 September, was to force the passes of Bran and Predeal, south of Braşov, for a rapid advance on Bucharest, which, he expected, would divide Rumanian armies in Moldavia from those in Wallachia and force Rumania to capitulate. To the north Falkenhayn's troops attempted to invade Moldavia through the broad Oituz River valley, but they were pushed back across the frontier in a series of hard-fought battles between 18 and 27 October. On the western end of the Carpathian front German efforts to break through the mountains along the Jiu River, between 23 and 28 October, were also thwarted by stubborn Rumanian resistance.

Falkenhayn quickly assembled a new and more powerful force on the Jiu River consisting of four infantry and two cavalry divisions, and on 11 November he launched a powerful offensive which turned out to be the beginning of a military catastrophe for Rumania. Opposed by only one Rumanian division, the Germans broke through, taking Tîrgu Jiu on 17 November and Craiova on the 21st. Rumanian troops withdrew to the Olt River, but a defence line here could not be maintained, because of the enemy's superiority in men and fire-power. The decisive battle took place further east on the Argeş and Neajlov rivers between 30 November and 3 December. The defeat of the Rumanian army here led to a general retreat eastward, and on 6 December German troops entered Bucharest. The Rumanian army established a series of temporary defence lines further east until the front finally stabilized on 10 January 1917 along the Danube and Siret rivers in southern Moldavia and, further north, west of the Siret. The campaign which had begun auspiciously with the Rumanian invasion of Transylvania a little over four months earlier had thus come to a disastrous conclusion. The Rumanians had suffered heavy losses in manpower—some 250,000 soldiers killed, wounded, and prisoners, or nearly one-third the force mobilized in August 1916— and in equipment—two-thirds of the weapons of individual soldiers, half the army's machine-guns, and a quarter of its cannon. Over half the country, in which its most important agricultural regions and industrial centres were located, was occupied by the enemy.

The main causes of the defeat of the Rumanian army were the industrial underdevelopment of the country and the lack of adequate equipment for the army. In addition, the Rumanian general staff had not prepared a sufficiently comprehensive and detailed plan of operations, which was essential for the co-ordination of forces dispersed over such a far-flung battlefront. As events showed, the improvised shifting of units from one front to another weakened the offensive and defensive capabilities of the army as a whole. The shortage of officers and the insufficient training of the majority of the front-line troops made these problems worse. Finally, the Rumanian army had to confront a far stronger concentration of enemy forces than expected, because of the failure of the Russian offensive in Galicia and the absence of a sustained Allied attack on the Salonika and Italian fronts.

One of Brătianu's first acts after the evacuation of the king and his ministers from Bucharest to Iaşi was to form a government of national unity on 24 December 1916. Take Ionescu and a number of other Democratic Conservatives closed ranks with the Liberals, but the Conservatives remained aloof. Fully aware of the low morale among the rank and file of the army, because of the defeat it had suffered, and fearing widespread social unrest, caused by the extreme hardship which all segments of the population were experiencing, Brătianu made agrarian and electoral reform the main domestic goal of the coalition government.

The Russian revolution of March 1917 gave impetus to reform. The possible repercussions of the revolution on Rumanian soldiers and peasants caused genuine alarm in government circles. Many politicians feared that the 'contagion' would quickly spread from Russia across the Prut to Moldavia. Under the pressure of these events the king issued a proclamation to his troops on 5 April 1917 promising them land and the right to vote as soon as the war had ended. His gesture was supported by both Liberals and Conservatives and seems to have had the desired effect on army morale.

In the Chamber of Deputies on 6 May Brătianu proposed the enactment of new agrarian and electoral laws. The bills which his government introduced were designed to modify articles of the constitution which prohibited the expropriation of private property for any reason except public utility (national defence or roads and railways) and which restricted the right to vote in such a way that the peasant majority was in effect disenfranchised. The proposed agrarian reform broadened the notion of public utility to include increasing the size of peasant holdings and allowed the expropriation of land owned by the crown, public and private institutions, foreigners, absentee landlords, and an additional two million hectares belonging to private landlords. Finally, it specified that within six months after the end of the war the legislature would enact a law embodying these general principles and setting forth in detail the means by which they would be carried out. As for electoral reform, the government proposed to introduce universal suffrage for all males over 21 immediately after the war.

The most significant opposition to the coalition government came from the newly formed Partidul Muncii (The Party of Labour) which had been formed on 1 May by a few parliamentary deputies headed by George Diamandy and Dr Nicolae Lupu and a number of intellectuals, all of whom belonged to the left wing of the Liberal Party. They wished to go further and faster with electoral and agrarian reform than Brătianu. They not only urged the immediate enactment of universal suffrage and the granting of five hectares of land to all peasants who had none (with compensation for private landowners), but they also advocated a broad programme of social reform, which included the nationalization of mineral wealth and the National Bank, a progressive income tax, and labour legislation permitting strikes and authorizing collective contracts between workers and employers.[10] Brătianu refused to allow the party to publish its programme on the grounds that the grave circumstances in which the country found itself made any appeal to social conflict unthinkable. Partidul Muncii was unsuccessful in gaining support for its programme and disbanded in December 1918. Its leaders joined other parties, notably the newly formed Partid Ţărănesc (Peasant Party).

The Liberal majority pushed its legislation quickly through the two houses of parliament, a haste which suggests how urgent the need had become to placate the mass of the population. The Chamber of Deputies adopted the government's project for a revision of the constitution on 14 June, 130 to 14, and the Senate followed suit on 20 June, 79 to 5. On 19 July the king gave his final sanction in a decree amending articles 19, 57, and 67 of the constitution.

In foreign affairs, in the meantime, Brătianu worked feverishly to establish close relations with the Provisional Government in Petrograd in order to bolster Rumanian–Russian military co-operation on the Moldavian front and maintain the flow of supplies from the Western allies through Russian ports. He spent a week (5–12 May) in Petrograd acquainting himself with the new Russian leaders. He came away from meetings with the Minister of War, Alexander Guchkov, and the Foreign Minister, Paul Miliukov, satisfied that supplies would continue to flow to the Rumanian army. But he recognized the precarious situation in which the Provisional Government found itself and was clearly worried by the lack of co-operation between it and the 'Committee', as he called the Soviet of Workers and Soldiers in Petrograd, which, he noted, was gaining strength and influence.[11]

The reorganization of the Rumanian army had been completed

---

[10] Eufrosina Popescu, 'Crearea Partidului Muncii şi activitatea sa în parlamentul din Iaşi (mai–iunie 1917)', *Studii: revistă de istorie*, 25/5 (1972), 1017–33.

[11] *România în primul război mondial* (Bucharest, 1979), 309.

by June 1917 under the most difficult conditions. The effects of a hard winter and a typhus epidemic, the heavy losses of horses, which affected both the transport of supplies and the size of the cavalry, and the lack of weapons of all kinds had to be surmounted before the army could again hope to take the field. Fortunately, the winter and the exhaustion of both sides limited the fighting during this period to indecisive local skirmishes. The French military mission headed by General Henri Berthelot, who had arrived in Rumania in October 1916, contributed significantly to the work of reorganization. Consisting of some 1,500 men, including nearly 300 officers, it provided expert instruction in the use of new weapons and tactics, particularly the conduct of a war of position. Berthelot himself gained the confidence of the king and Rumanian officials and exerted considerable influence on military policy. Through the call-up of new recruits the army reached 700,000 men, approximately 460,000 of whom were organized in regular combat units. Large quantities of weapons arrived— machine-guns, heavy and light artillery, and grenades—mainly from France, which added significantly to the army's fire-power. Every platoon was supplied with two light machine-guns, and every battalion now had eight heavy machine-guns. Communications were also improved through the establishment of telegraph links between command centres and units in the field, a network which had been almost totally lacking in 1916.

In July and August 1917 hostilities resumed on the Moldavian front. The Rumanian army, under the command of Averescu, took the offensive on 22 July against Austro-Hungarian forces near Mărăşti. The attack was planned as part of an overall Allied effort on both the Western and Eastern fronts to drive the Central Powers from the war. The objective in Moldavia was to keep German and Austro-Hungarian troops pinned down and prevent their being moved to other fronts. The immediate goal of the Rumanian attack at Mărăşti was to seize the Putna Valley ten kilometres to the west in order to pre-empt an expected enemy offensive. Although the Rumanian 2nd Army reached the valley, its commander, General Averescu, halted his advance, because of the deteriorating situation in Galicia where German and Austro-Hungarian troops had taken Tarnopol from the Russians on 25 July. The shift of Russian reinforcements from Moldavia to the north and the collapse of morale and discipline in many Russian units convinced Rumanian commanders of the need for caution.

None the less, the action at Mărăşti caused Marshal Mackensen, who commanded the German 9th Army to the south, to postpone his own offensive and shift the focus of his operations to less favourable terrain in order to counter the threat posed by the Rumanian advance.

Mackensen decided upon a two-pronged offensive, the first moving from south to north along the Siret Valley and the second from west to east centred on the Oituz Valley. The two armies were to meet in the vicinity of Adjud. The objective of the operation was to deliver a knockout blow to Rumanian and Russian forces that would drive Rumania from the war and open the way to Odessa. German commanders counted upon the continuing deficiencies of the Rumanian army which they had encountered in 1916 and upon the demoralization of the Russian army to make victory possible at as little cost as possible.

The attack began on 6 August near Mărăşeşti. The fighting, which yielded nothing in ferocity to the battles of attrition on the Western front, reached a climax on the 19th, when Rumanian forces effectively halted the German advance. Thereafter, until 3 September, when Mackensen ordered an end to the offensive, action was limited to local skirmishes. The German army had been able to push forward 6–7 kilometres along a 30-kilometre front, but at great cost and without achieving any major objectives. Its losses in killed, wounded, and missing were about 60,000 men as against 27,000 for the Rumanian army. The Rumanians could thus claim victory in the most important battle they were to fight in 1917. The second, Oituz offensive, which began on 8 August, also brought only modest territorial gains for the Germans. Mackensen halted the attack on 3 September in order to transfer troops to the Italian front. His action effectively ended the major fighting for 1917 on the Moldavian front. Subsequent battles, on a much smaller scale, brought few changes to the battle line. The Rumanians had thus survived the all-out effort of the Central Powers to force their capitulation.

A new danger now arose. By the end of the summer of 1917 revolutionary events in Russia had created a volatile situation along the battle line and threatened to disrupt political and social stability in Moldavia. The abdication of the tsar in the previous March and the liberal pronouncements of the new Provisional Government had aroused enormous enthusiasm among Russian troops in Moldavia. Weary of war, they interpreted these events as a sign that peace and a better life were near at hand. In April they began to hold massive public meetings and to organize street demonstrations in many places near their camps, and they urged Rumanian soldiers and civilians to join them. Events in Bacău and Tîrgu Ocna, both close to the front, were typical. At mass meetings Russian officers and enlisted men passed resolutions calling for the immediate conclusion of peace and proclaimed their support of democrats and liberals at home. Here and throughout Moldavia councils of soldiers deputies on the model of the Petrograd Soviet sprang up.

The sense of expectation brought a revival of political activity among Rumanian Social Democrats. Small groups of Socialists had followed the course of events in Russia closely and had debated their significance for Rumania with evident anticipation. In Iaşi, their main centre of activity in 1917, they reopened the party offices and began to publish a newspaper, *Social-Democraţia*. Militants came immediately to the fore and sought to use the war-weariness and hopes for peace of the common people to advance their cause. In the middle of April they staged their first important anti-war demonstration in Iaşi. Speakers denounced the war as a capitalist undertaking and completely foreign to the interests of the working class. But they had only praise for the revolution in Russia as an event of universal importance, and they urged their audience to extend its 'beneficent' influences to Rumania.

An important turning-point in the development of radical Rumanian Social Democracy was the flight of a number of militants to Odessa in May and June 1917 to escape arrest by the Rumanian government. Here they came more directly under the influence of the revolution in Russia. Cristian Racovski, a Bulgarian-born leader of the Rumanian Social Democratic Party, and several associates established the Rumanian Committee of Social Democratic Action for the purpose of revitalizing the party and organizing a revolution in Rumania on the Russian model. They kept up a steady propaganda campaign, demanding the overthrow of 'Rumanian tsarism' as a prerequisite for democratic government and agrarian reform. Yet the revolution they had in mind was the bourgeois-democratic one. They said nothing about a socialist revolution because they judged economic and social conditions in Rumania too little developed to ensure its success. But the Bolshevik seizure of power in November changed all that. A number of militants now expected the outbreak and triumph of the socialist revolution at home much sooner than they had dared hope, and they redoubled their propaganda efforts among workers and soldiers in Moldavia.[12]

The situation across the Prut River in Bessarabia complicated further the Rumanian government's relations with the Russian Provisional Government. The March Revolution had set Moldavians of all social classes in motion. In April they held public meetings in every part of the province to voice their dissatisfaction with the old order. Village co-operatives stood in the forefront of the protest movement. Their representatives, meeting on 19 and 20 April, demanded the administrative, cultural, and economic autonomy of Bessarabia and the convocation of a national assembly to enact the necessary legislation. A far more numerous gathering of some 10,000 Moldavian officers and soldiers in Odessa on 1 May also demanded political autonomy for Bessarabia and, in addition, announced the formation of separate Moldavian army units (*cohortele moldoveneşti*) to maintain public order. A committee chosen by the assembly requested General Dmitri Shcherbachev, the commander of Russian forces on the Rumanian front, to increase the number of Moldavian units and to withdraw all Russian troops from Bessarabia. A few days later, on 2 and 3 May, a congress of Bessarabian priests met in Chişinău to voice similar national concerns. Besides political autonomy and the establishment of an Înalt Sfat (High Council) with executive and legislative powers, the majority demanded a Moldavian Metropolitan as the head of the Bessarabian Church. At almost the same moment representatives of Moldavian teachers were holding their own congress in Chişinău to demand the 'Moldavianization' of education and the replacement of the Cyrillic alphabet by the Latin in textbooks. Perhaps the most important of all these April and May meetings brought together leaders of the liberal intellectuals and conservative boiers. Putting aside past differences, they founded Partidul Naţional Moldovenesc (The Moldavian National Party), which proclaimed as its main goal the establishment of an autonomous, Rumanian Bessarabia. In addition to these formal, urban gatherings, powerful social movements were underway in the countryside. In April peasants began to occupy lands belonging to large estates and to form committees to oversee the division and distribution of such lands. Serious agrarian disorders and a breakdown of rural administration followed.

---

[12] On the activities of Rumanian militant socialists, see Keith Hitchins, 'The Russian Revolution and the Rumanian Socialist Movement, 1917–1918', *Slavic Review*, 27/2 (1968), 271–5.

In the summer of 1917 Bessarabia was thus in turmoil. The National Party and various Moldavian professional and economic organizations strove to give the movement for autonomy coherence and to defend their cause against Ukrainian nationalists, who demanded the integration of Bessarabia into an independent Ukraine, on the one side, and, on the other, the Bolsheviks, who denounced nationalism of any kind and sought to win the province for the proletarian revolution. Moldavian army officers now took matters in hand. On 29 July several members of the Central Army Committee, which had been formed in April, decided to convoke a general assembly of the province, a Sfat al Ţării, to draw up a plan for the 'national and territorial autonomy' of Bessarabia. As a preliminary they held a 'military congress' in Chişinău on 5–9 November, at the moment of the Bolshevik seizure of power in Petrograd. The nearly 900 delegates, representing Moldavian officers and soldiers from units of the former Russian army, by an overwhelming majority proclaimed the autonomy of the province and decided to convoke the Sfat al Ţării as soon as possible in order to ratify their action. Because of the general tumult the election of delegates had to be carried out indirectly through worker and peasant committees, various professional corporations, and local administrative bodies. The result was an assembly of 138 members representing a wide spectrum of economic and social interests and ethnic groups (70 per cent were Moldavian and the rest were divided among Russians, Bulgarians, Germans, and Jews).

The Sfat al Ţării convened on 4 December, and from the beginning the Moldavian majority dominated the proceedings. They chose as president Ion Inculeţ, a liberal and nationalist and a member of an old Moldavian family who had been a lecturer at the University of Petrograd when the March Revolution broke out. On 15 December, after long and often heated debates, the Council proclaimed the establishment of a 'Moldavian Democratic Federated Republic' between the Prut and Dniester rivers with Inculeţ as president and a Council of Directors, composed of Moldavian nationalists, acting as an executive committee.

To survive, the fledgling republic needed outside support. The Council of Directors recognized the precariousness of their situation, and on 21 December it dispatched a delegation to Iaşi to request the Rumanian government to assist it in 'restoring order'. Because of the critical situation on its own battlefront, however, the Rumanian government at first declined to send troops. The situation of the new republic across the Prut became increasingly desperate, and on 17 January 1918 Bolshevik forces occupied Chişinău and dispersed the Sfat al Ţării. The latter's Moldavian members met secretly on the same day and decided to send a new appeal to Iaşi for aid. This time the Rumanian government responded with a division of troops, which drove the Bolsheviks out of Chişinău on 26 January and restored the Sfat al Ţării to power. When on 6 February the Sfat declared the Moldavian Republic independent, the majority of its members considered this act merely a prelude to union with Rumania.[13]

The Rumanian government could take little immediate comfort from the pending acquisition of Bessarabia. The overthrow of the Russian Provisional Government and seizure of power by the Bolsheviks on 7 November and their intention to seek peace with the Central Powers jeopardized the very existence of the Rumanian state. Russia's withdrawal from the war would leave the Rumanian army standing alone against a far superior enemy on the Moldavian front and would effectively cut off all military supplies from the West. The Crown Council voted on 2 December to continue the war, even if the Russian army concluded an armistice with the enemy. But when on the following day General Shcherbachev informed Mackensen of his willingness to negotiate an armistice, the Rumanian cabinet decided that it had no choice but to participate. The armistice between Russia and the Central Powers signed on 5 December at Brest-Litovsk sealed the fate of Rumania.

Peace, none the less, came slowly to that remnant of the Rumanian Kingdom that had escaped German occupation. Negotiations between Rumania and the Central Powers at Focşani between 7 and 9 December resulted in a cease-fire, which required opposing armies to remain in place. But the Brătianu government was in no hurry to reach a definitive peace settlement, and its procrastination finally led an exasperated Mackensen to issue an ultimatum at the beginning of February 1918 to decide on war or peace within four days. The cabinet was far from united on a precise course of action, although all its members favoured a continuation of the war. The four Democratic Conservative ministers demanded an immediate denunciation of the armistice and the resumption of the war, while Brătianu and his Liberal colleagues

---

[13] Ştefan Ciobanu, *Unirea Basarabiei: Studiu şi documente* (Bucharest, 1929), 148–51.

favoured a continuation of the armistice and further peace talks with the Germans in order to gain time for a withdrawal of the army to the Ukraine. When the Democratic Conservatives decided to leave the cabinet, thereby dissolving the coalition government, Brătianu and the Liberals resigned. Neither party was eager to make peace with the enemy. The king therefore entrusted the formation of a new government to General Averescu, who could see no alternative to a separate peace with the Central Powers. He undertook negotiations at once and arranged a meeting between the king and Czernin, now Austro-Hungarian Foreign Minister, near the front on 27 February. The peace terms Czernin offered were harsh: large cessions of territory, including Dobrudja and the passes in the Carpathians; German and Austro-Hungarian control of the Danube; the disbanding of the Rumanian army; the right of passage for German troops across Rumanian territory to Russia; and effective control of Rumanian oil production until the end of the century. Under the impress of a new ultimatum from the Central Powers, the Rumanian government signed a preliminary peace, on Czernin's terms, at Buftea, outside Bucharest, on 5 March. The Peace of Brest-Litovsk between Russia and the Central Powers on 3 March, which deprived Rumania of all Russian support and effectively cut her off from the West, weighed heavily in the decision to sign the peace of Buftea. But Brătianu and the Liberals stubbornly opposed the conclusion of a final peace with the Central Powers. Because of the impasse, Averescu resigned on 12 March. He was replaced by the Conservative Alexandru Marghiloman, who owed his appointment primarily to the expectation that as a pro-German who had remained in Bucharest after the removal of the government to Iaşi he would be able to soften the terms of peace.

Marghiloman gained no concessions whatever from the Central Powers, who were intent upon punishing Rumania and subordinating her economy to their war effort. The terms of the final peace, the Treaty of Bucharest of 7 May, therefore, left Rumania in a state of political and economic dependence upon Germany and Austria-Hungary. Rumania lost territory along the old Austro-Hungarian–Rumanian frontier which included strategic passes in the mountains and 130 villages with a population of about 725,000. The bulk of the army had to be demobilized and its equipment handed over to the victors. Germany took over Rumania's economy. She was to receive immense quantities of grain at favourable prices, acquired a monopoly of the Rumanian oil industry for ninety years, and assumed the control of navigation on the Danube, Rumanian river ports, and shipyards. Finally, Rumania remained divided. Dobrudja and Wallachia up to the Siret remained under enemy occupation, an area of roughly 100,000 square kilometres (out of a pre-war territory of 131,000 square kilometres) with 72 per cent of the pre-war population. Moldavia, which remained more or less independent with its own administration, was cut off almost completely from the occupied zone.

Marghiloman, who had assumed office on 18 March, set about at once to prepare for new parliamentary elections in order to confer legitimacy upon his government and assure himself of a majority.[14] He chose to conduct the elections in accordance with the old system of colleges and a franchise narrowed by tax and property qualifications, which, as in the past, favoured the Conservatives. Prospects of success were enhanced by the decision of Liberal leaders to abstain from the contest. They declared their intention to remain faithful to the policy they had followed since August 1916 and to take no action that would signify approval of the Marghiloman government. But they were also anxious to avoid giving the Central Powers a pretext for still harsher measures against the country by staging a spirited election campaign, which, they feared, might lead to disorders. Other political groups, however, felt no such restraints. Liga Poporului (The League of the People), which General Averescu and a few former members of the Conservative Party had founded in April, decided to run candidates. Although it put forward plans for political and agrarian reform, it was unable to capitalize on Averescu's personal popularity. To no one's surprise, the government won the elections, but Liga Poporului and Partidul Muncii were also represented in the new parliament, which opened on 17 June.

Secure in his majority, Marghiloman pressed forward with a programme which won him little popularity with the country at large. He obtained the ratification of the peace treaty with the Central Powers by a large majority, but he could not persuade the king to sign it. Ferdinand's obstinacy under existing conditions had no practical effect, but it symbolized a widespread feeling of revulsion at the humiliating peace terms and a determination to resist, if only passively.

[14] An outline of the Marghiloman government's activities is contained in Mircea Muşat and Ion Ardeleanu, *Viaţa politică în România, 1918–1921* (Bucharest, 1976), 70–7.

The main domestic issue which preoccupied the government was agrarian reform. During the election campaign Marghiloman had made clear that he opposed the expropriation of large estates as the primary means of improving the lot of the peasantry. Nor did he think that all peasants should receive land. Like many politicians who had accepted the inevitability of agrarian reform, Liberals as well as Conservatives, he wanted to create a class of medium-sized rural proprietors out of the 'hard-working' and 'worthy' peasants, who would take responsibility for agricultural production and form the backbone of a moderate constitutional political system. His Minister of Agriculture, Constantin Garoflid, tried valiantly to put these ideas into practice. He introduced obligatory leases of land to communes and groups of peasants by estates over 100 hectares, a temporary measure which he thought would prepare the way for systematic land reform when the war ended and normalcy returned. But events soon overtook him and Marghiloman.

On the Bessarabian question the Marghiloman government continued the policy of the Liberals. The situation there, despite the presence of Rumanian troops, remained in flux as the diverse ethnic and social groups strove to achieve conflicting ambitions. A threat to the Moldavian Republic also came from the Ukrainian Republic, which had been proclaimed on 20 November 1917 and had raised the question of Bessarabia's future with the Central Powers in March 1918. Pointing out that large, compact Ukrainian populations inhabited the northern and southern parts of the province and that the entire province was linked economically to Odessa, the Ukrainians demanded to be represented at peace negotiations between Rumania and the Central Powers and to have a say in any changes in the boundaries between Russia and Rumania. The Moldavians naturally looked to Rumania, where support for union by both Liberals and Conservatives, including Marghiloman and members of his government, was strong. Thus, when Inculeţ and his prime minister, Daniil Ciugureanu, came to Iaşi on 20 March with the intention of proceeding to Bucharest to participate in peace negotiations, Marghiloman urged them first of all to submit the question of union to the Sfat al Ţării. On 23 March Inculeţ and Ciugureanu returned to Chişinău accompanied by Constantin Stere, who represented the Rumanian government. The debates in the Sfat were spirited, but the Moldavian bloc, which favoured union and formed the majority, prevailed. On 27 March it approved the resolution on the union in accordance with 'historical right and ethnic right and the principle that peoples should determine their own fate'. The final vote was 86 in favour, 3 against, and 36 abstentions, mainly from among the German, Bulgarian, and Ukrainian deputies. But the Moldavian majority also set down a number of conditions to union, which would allow them to preserve the autonomy of the province. Most important were the provisions that Bessarabia would continue to have its own diet (Sfat al Ţării) with the power to approve local budgets and to appoint all organs of local government, and that the province would be represented in the Rumanian parliament in proportion to its population. The Sfat also insisted upon political and social reforms: that elections in Bessarabia at all levels of government and for the provincial diet and the central parliament be held on the basis of universal suffrage; that civil liberties, including freedom of speech, assembly, association, and the press, be guaranteed by the constitution; and that the rights of minorities be respected.[15] These demands signified a repudiation of the tsarist political system and the cultural policy of Russification and a determination to set the province on a new, democratic course. They also reflected a certain unease with the practice of politics in the Rumanian Kingdom. The new relationship with Rumania, as the Moldavians saw it, was to be based upon federalist principles.

The Moldavians proceeded quickly with the organization of their government. On 3 April the Sfat al Ţării elected Stere as its president and designated Inculeţ and Ciugureanu as ministers without portfolio in the Marghiloman cabinet. It also chose an executive committee, Consiliul de Directori Generali (The Council of General Directors), to carry out a comprehensive economic and social programme, which called for the re-establishment of public order based upon respect for law and the rights of citizens, tax reform, the reintegration of the Bessarabian eparchy into the Rumanian Orthodox Church, the 'de-Russification' of education in accordance with the spirit and the history of the peoples of the province, and full support for agriculture, as the basis of Bessarabia's economy, until agrarian reform could be carried out. Yet, despite the best efforts of the Council, it could not control the course of events in the province. In the spring and summer the economy steadily deteriorated, and the process of the union with Rumania proved cumbersome.

In foreign affairs the Marghiloman government pursued a policy

---

[15] P. Cazacu, *Moldova dintre Prut şi Nistru, 1812–1918* (Iaşi, n.d.), 319–21.

of neutrality. Surrounded on all sides by enemy forces, it had little choice but to seek closer relations with the Central Powers. In so doing, it hoped eventually to obtain a softening of the terms of the Treaty of Bucharest. Yet, it also maintained diplomatic relations with the Entente and rejected demands of the Central Powers to join the war against the Western Allies. Marghiloman already had abundant proof of how unpopular such a move would be from the grudging attitude with which the bureaucracy and the public at large were carrying out the terms of the Treaty of Bucharest.

Decisive encounters on the battlefield swiftly changed Rumania's fortunes. The failure of the German offensive of July 1918 on the Western front and the subsequent steady Allied advance toward Germany, coupled with a successful Italian offensive against Austro-Hungarian forces in northern Italy signalled the collapse of the Central Powers. In the Balkans an Allied drive northward from Salonika, which began on 15 September, forced Bulgaria to sign an armistice on 30 September and Turkey on 30 October. The so-called Army of the Danube, composed of three Allied divisions under the command of General Berthelot, who had left Rumania with his staff in March after the conclusion of the Peace of Buftea, was preparing to cross the river at Giurgiu. On 3 November Austria-Hungary accepted Allied terms for a cease-fire.

Under the impress of these events Brătianu and the Liberals and other pro-Entente politicians hastened to rejoin the war on the Allied side. The Marghiloman government, an encumbrance and an embarrassment, was forced to resign on 6 November, and the king, with the backing of the Liberals, appointed General Constantin Coandă, who had represented the Rumanian high command at Russian army headquarters in 1916 and 1917, to head a transition government. It annulled all the acts of the Marghiloman government, took steps to carry out the electoral and agrarian reforms which had been inscribed in the constitution in the summer of 1917, and prepared the army for a resumption of hostilities.

King Ferdinand ordered his army to re-enter the war on 10 November, the same day Allied troops crossed the Danube at Giurgiu. The mobilization of the army had proved unusually difficult, because of the lack of horses and equipment and the dispersal of officers and men who had been demobilized at the beginning of the year, but by the middle of November a force of

90,000 was ready for action. By this time Rumanian army units had already begun to advance into Muntenia, Dobrudja, and Transylvania. The German army began to withdraw from occupied Rumania on 10 and 11 November, and by 1 December the last German detachments had crossed the Carpathians. On that day King Ferdinand entered Bucharest at the head of his army.

GREATER RUMANIA

Greater Rumania came rapidly into being. As the Austro-Hungarian monarchy disintegrated, first, the Rumanians of Bukovina on 28 November and then those of Transylvania on 1 December declared for union with the 'motherland'. Ten days later the Sfat al Ţării in Bessarabia removed all the conditions to union it had set in March.

In Bukovina during the four years of war Rumanian nationalist activity had been modest. Until 1916 the majority of Rumanian soldiers and the civilian population, including the peasantry, had remained loyal to Austria. Cases of co-operation with the Russian occupation authorities were rare, and only a few intellectuals emigrated to Rumania to carry on anti-Austrian activities. In Bukovina their propaganda had some influence among intellectuals, who became more susceptible to visions of a Greater Rumania after Rumania entered the war. The harsh measures taken by Austro-Hungarian military authorities against Rumanian civilians suspected of subversive activities did much to promote irredentism. None the less, Rumanian deputies in the Austrian parliament remained loyal until the session of 22 October 1918, the last time the representatives of Bukovina addressed that body. Afterwards, as the old imperial institutions disintegrated, the Rumanians and the other nationalities of Bukovina assumed responsibility for their own affairs through newly formed national councils.

Rumanian political leaders in Bukovina took decisive action to ensure that the province would become a part of Rumania by convoking a constituent assembly in Cernăuţi on 27 October. Composed of deputies to the Austrian parliament and the Bukovina provincial diet, local politicians, and individuals prominent in economic and intellectual life, the assembly approved a resolution expressing its intention to unite the province with Rumania and creating a national council of fifty members to manage its affairs until the union took place. The council, with Iancu Flondor, a former deputy in the Austrian parliament as its president, left no doubt that it would oppose any division of the country along ethnic lines. This stance brought it into bitter conflict with the Ukrainian National Council, which in late October had taken control of the districts inhabited by Ukrainians (Ruthenians) and of Cernăuţi. At this point, on 4 November, Aurel Onciul, another former deputy in the Austrian parliament who was working to keep Bukovina within an Austrian federalized state, concluded an agreement with the Ukrainian National Council for a division of the province into separate Rumanian and Ukrainian (Ruthenian) districts, and, together, they forced the Austrian governor to yield power to a joint Rumanian-Ukrainian provisional government in Cernăuţi. The Rumanian National Council immediately denounced the agreement and on 7 November appealed to the Rumanian government in Iaşi to send troops. The response was immediate. On the 11th Rumanian troops entered Cernăuţi, and Ukrainian forces withdrew to Galicia without offering resistance. The Rumanian National Council thereupon created its own provisional government with Flondor as President of the Council of Ministers. But its independence lasted only two weeks, for the sentiment in favour of union with Rumania was overwhelming. On 28 November the National Council convoked a Rumanian congress, which unanimously voted for union. The Rumanian government approved the act on 19 December by decree.

In Transylvania events took a similar course. After the breakdown of formal negotiations between Prime Minister István Tisza and the Rumanian National Party in 1914 no compromise solution to the nationality problem was possible. The National Party ceased its activities in August 1914. As in Bukovina, the majority of Rumanian soldiers and civilians performed their duties loyally, although a small, if steady, stream of intellectuals and others continued to cross the frontier into Rumania, where they swelled the ranks of those working for the union of the province with Rumania. After Rumania's entrance into the war and her invasion of Transylvania the Hungarian government took severe measures to limit the political and cultural activities of the Rumanians. Most notable was its creation of a 'cultural zone' along the frontier with Rumania, which was designed to stifle Rumanian national sentiment once and for all. In 1917 and 1918 the government introduced a series of measures placing Orthodox and Uniate elementary and secondary schools under state control, action which signified Magyarization and which, in effect, was intended to bring to a conclusion the campaign that had begun in 1879 with the enactment of the first comprehensive law curtailing the activities of non-Magyar church schools.[16]

Although the National Party decided to resume activity in December 1917, it remained discreet until the autumn of 1918. On 12 October party leaders declared themselves in favour of self-determination for the 'Rumanian nation of Hungary and Transylvania' and announced their intention to convoke a national assembly to decide the fate of Transylvania. Alexandru Vaida, a deputy in the Hungarian parliament, read a statement to this effect in the Chamber of Deputies in a memorable session on 18 October. As the existing administrative apparatus in Transylvania unravelled, the National Party and the small Rumanian Social Democratic Party established a Rumanian National Council on 31 October. The Council, composed of six members from each party, took on the attributes of a Rumanian provisional government, and on 9 November it informed the Hungarian government that it was assuming control of all the areas of Hungary and Transylvania inhabited by Rumanians. Its negotiations in Arad on 12–14 November with Oszkár Jászi, the Minister of Nationalities in the new Hungarian government headed by Michael Károlyi, which had assumed office on 31 October, came to nothing. Jászi proposed a system of cantonal autonomy based on the Swiss model, but the Rumanians insisted upon the full right of self-determination.[17] Accordingly, the National Party convoked a Grand National Assembly, which met at Alba Iulia on 1 December. Attended by some 100,000 persons from all parts of Transylvania, it overwhelmingly approved union with Rumania. But it set conditions: Transylvania was to remain autonomous until a constituent assembly for a united Rumania could be elected and the new national state organized in accordance with liberal and democratic principles. The assembly placed executive power in the hands of a Consiliu Dirigent (Directing Council) with headquarters in Sibiu. The Rumanian government recognized the union by decree on 11 December.

While the constituent parts of the expanded Rumanian national state were thus coming together, Brătianu was making feverish

---

[16] Lazăr Triteanu, *Şcoala noastră 1850–1916: 'Zona Culturală'* (Sibiu, 1919), 61–156.

[17] Oszkár Jászi, *Visszaemlékezés a román nemzeti komitéval folytatott Aradi targyalásaimra* (Cluj-Kolozsvár, 1921).

preparations for the struggle he was sure would come at the general peace conference. But he was, none the less, taken aback by the hostility he had already encountered from the Western Allies. French and British politicians interpreted Rumania's separate peace with the Central Powers as an abrogation of the treaty of 1916, and thus they considered themselves relieved of any responsibility for fulfilling the promises they had made to gain Rumania's entrance into the war.

Brătianu arrived in Paris on 13 January 1919 with his own conception of what Rumania's place at the peace conference should be. Underlying all his activities was his insistence that the treaty of 1916 with the Entente remained valid and that, consequently, Rumania was entitled to receive everything promised and to be treated as a full Allied partner. He adamantly rejected the counterarguments that Rumania herself had abrogated the treaty by concluding a separate peace with the enemy. He was also determined to obtain Allied recognition of the acquisition of Bessarabia, which, of course, had not figured in the original treaty.

The treatment which Rumania received at the conference proved a rude shock to Brătianu. In the first place, the Big Four, which together with Japan constituted the Supreme Council, had decided that Rumania must be punished for her capitulation in 1918. Since they had reserved the final decisions to themselves anyway, they had no intention of allowing Rumania to take part in the peacemaking as an equal. The Supreme Council made its position toward Rumania clear by allowing her only two representatives to the peace conference, while granting Serbia, which had never surrendered, three. But even then the Council consulted these representatives (and those of the other smaller Allies) only when questions of direct interest to their respective countries were being considered, and sometimes not even then. The great powers gave Rumania seats on seven of the many commissions charged with investigating specific issues and preparing reports on them for use by the decision-makers, but, perhaps to avoid unwanted obstruction, they excluded Rumanian representatives from two commissions, those dealing with territorial boundaries and minorities, matters which Brătianu and the great majority of Rumanians regarded as crucial to their country's future.

In the face of these blows, Brătianu pressed Rumania's case all the more forcefully and, in so doing, made himself obnoxious to the major Allies. Two appearances before the Supreme Council during its consideration of territorial questions revealed the depth of his commitment to the idea of Greater Rumania. On 31 January 1919 he flatly rejected any compromise on Rumanian territorial claims. He demanded the cession of the entire Banat in accordance with the terms of the treaty of 1916, citing history (the ancestors of the Rumanians were the first to settle the region) and ethnic statistics (the Rumanians were the largest nationality in the region as a whole) to justify his claim. He opposed partition, even though the eastern third of the Banat had a Serbian majority, on the grounds that such action would disrupt the region's 'economic and political integrity'.[18] His listeners were unimpressed, even when he pleaded that the death of 335,000 Rumanian soldiers in the war ought by itself to justify Rumania's claim. On 1 February he continued his exposition, arguing this time that Rumania should receive all the territory she had been promised in 1916 as a just reward for supporting the Entente. He angrily rejected suggestions from the Supreme Council that impartial plebiscites in disputed territories (Bukovina, Transylvania, and Bessarabia) would offer a more reliable gauge of public opinion than the national assemblies which had voted union the previous autumn. In Transylvania, he admitted, the Magyars had not voted for union and would not because they were unwilling to accept minority status under a people they had dominated for a thousand years. He pointed out that, in any case, the war had settled the issue, but promised that the Rumanian state would grant the minorities the fullest possible political freedom. If Rumania's territorial aspirations were satisfied and if the Allies granted permission to advance further westward into Hungary, then, Brătianu promised, his army would destroy Bolshevism, 'a serious and contagious disease', which was spreading rapidly from Russia to Hungary and Central Europe. The response of the Council fell far short of Brătianu's expectations. It voted simply to establish a Rumanian Territorial Commission, whose task would be to judge the legitimacy of Rumania's territorial claims.

Brătianu recognized that alone he would have little success in challenging the authority of the great powers. In May, exasperated by the second-class status accorded Rumania and himself, he therefore tried to form a united front of the small East European 'victors' (Poland, Czechoslovakia, Serbia, Greece, and Rumania) in order to obtain a more sympathetic hearing for their grievances.

[18] *Papers relating to the Foreign Relations of the United States: The Paris Peace Conference, 1919*, iii (Washington, DC, 1943), 830–4.

The issue he chose for a test of strength was the peace treaty with Austria. He and his colleagues were upset by the fact that they were not to see the text of the treaty before it was submitted to Austria and, hence, they would have no opportunity to propose changes. Although Brătianu and his colleagues managed, in the end, to see the treaty, they had no influence on its final form.

The most important territorial issue for Brătianu (and for all Rumanians) was Transylvania. Brătianu was determined to get every square inch of the province and, if possible, to extend the frontier with Hungary as far west as the Tisza River. But his pursuit of territory became entangled in other issues: the determination of the Big Four to create a peace for Europe which accorded with their own interests; their concern for minority rights in the successor states in general and in Rumania in particular; and the perceived threat of Bolshevism in Central Europe.

The demarcation line between Hungarian and Rumanian forces drawn on 13 November 1918 by General Louis Franchet d'Esperey, the commander-in-chief of Allied forces in South-eastern Europe, along the Mureş River in central Transylvania did not hold. Rumanian troops continued to advance, despite the prohibition issued by the Supreme Council on 25 January 1919 against the seizure of territory without its authorization. By this time the Rumanian army had already advanced along a wide front to positions roughly half-way between Cluj and Oradea. The Inter-Allied War Council at Versailles sought to bring hostilities in Transylvania finally to an end on 25 February by establishing a new demarcation line along the railway running from Satu Mare through Oradea to Arad, which the Supreme Council on the 26th recognized as the absolute limit of the Rumanian occupation. The three cities themselves remained outside the Rumanian zone and continued to be garrisoned by French troops. In order to prevent further hostilities the Council created a neutral zone between Rumanian and Hungarian armies to the west of the demarcation line. When on 20 March Lt.-Col. Fernand Vix, of the Allied military mission in Budapest, informed the Hungarian government of this decision Károlyi objected strenuously on the grounds that the zone would deprive Hungary of an extensive area inhabited mainly by Magyars. A political crisis ensued. Károlyi resigned, and a new government composed of Communists and leftist socialists proclaimed a Soviet Republic on 21 March.

Brătianu was well aware of the Allies' concern about the spread of Bolshevism from Russia to Central Europe and sought to take advantage of the turn of events in Budapest to further his own cause. At a luncheon with Lloyd George on 25 March he urged solidarity on the part of all the Allies in the face of the 'Bolshevik menace' and proposed the immediate dispatch of Allied military aid to the Poles and Rumanians to enable them to stem the tide.[19] Brătianu was confident that the political uncertainty in Hungary would strengthen his position at the peace conference, since only Rumania had forces readily available to take action against the Soviet Republic. He had already been engaged in a strenuous lobbying campaign against Hungary and Bolshevism and was eager to undertake a military campaign with the authorization of the Allies in order to penetrate more deeply into Hungary, overthrow the offending regime, and in the process strengthen Rumania's territorial claims. But his hopes were dashed when the Supreme Council decided on 1 April to send General Jan Christian Smuts to Budapest to try to reach an understanding with Béla Kun, the head of the new Hungarian government. Brătianu was afraid that if Kun were conciliatory, the Supreme Council would recognize his regime and invite him to send a delegation to Paris, events which might cost Rumania dearly in territory. But his fears proved unfounded. Kun was anything but conciliatory at his meeting with Smuts. He rejected the authority of the Supreme Council to enforce its own boundary on Hungary and demanded that the demarcation line along the Mureş River of 13 November 1918 be reinstated and that, as a result, the Rumanian army be obliged to withdraw to the east of the river. Smuts had no choice but to return to Paris on 12 April, leaving the Rumanian–Hungarian conflict unresolved.

Brătianu and the Council of Ministers in Bucharest had by this time decided to take matters into their own hands by sending the Rumanian army further westward. They planned to begin their offensive on 16 April. A Hungarian attack in the region of Munţii Apuseni on the night of 15–16 April gave the Rumanian campaign the appearance of a counter-attack and was used to mollify the Allies, whose frustration with Brătianu's behaviour had reached breaking-point.

The Rumanian offensive was successful and drove the enemy steadily back into eastern Hungary. Brătianu followed the advance of his army anxiously, for he was convinced that Rumania's

---

[19] Gheorghe I. Brătianu, *Acţiunea politică şi militară a României în 1919* (Bucharest, 1940), 59–60.

future boundaries depended upon the outcome of this campaign. On 25 April he informed his colleagues in Bucharest that he was prepared to press on to the Tisza River and would not allow 'political difficulties', a reference to expected objections from the Allies, to stand in the way. He was also eager to co-ordinate a joint military occupation of Ruthenia and southern Galicia with the Polish army in order to prevent a link-up of 'Russian and Hungarian Bolsheviks'.

By the beginning of May the Rumanian army had advanced well into eastern Hungary, and no serious obstacles lay in the way of a march on Budapest. But now the Allies in Paris intervened firmly to halt the Rumanian advance toward the Tisza. Brătianu himself was having second thoughts about the wisdom of pushing deeper into Hungary, for he had no wish to bring about the overthrow of the Soviet Republic and its replacement by a conservative and nationalist Hungarian government, which, with Allied support, would certainly resist Rumania's territorial demands. At the beginning of May, therefore, the Rumanian advance stopped at the Tisza.

In June relations between the Supreme Council and Brătianu reached a new low. On the 10th the Council castigated him for having ignored Franchet d'Esperey's demarcation line and thus for having precipitated the crisis which had led to Károlyi's resignation and the coming to power of the Bolsheviks. The Council's anger had been stoked by the Hungarian army's campaign on the Czechoslovak front, which had begun on 30 May and had achieved notable successes. But Béla Kun had responded in a conciliatory manner to an ultimatum from the Council to halt the advance of the Red Army, and the Council hoped to use the occasion to bring about a peaceful settlement also of the Hungarian–Rumanian territorial dispute. The Allies now demanded that Brătianu withdraw his troops from the Tisza back to the demarcation line drawn by the Inter-Allied War Council in February. Brătianu refused. When he pointed out that he was not responsible for social conditions in Hungary and insisted that the Tisza was the only practical defence line for his army, the Council threatened to cut off all military supplies and other aid to Rumania unless he complied with its terms immediately. The impasse between the Allies and Brătianu over frontiers was compounded by a bitter dispute over Rumania's minority policy. Convinced that he could accomplish nothing more in Paris, at least for the time being, Brătianu left for home on 2 July.

Within a month Rumanian troops were in Budapest. They had simply remained on the Tisza, an act which showed once again that the Allies would take no serious action to back up their threats against Rumania. The Hungarian army, which had taken advantage of the lull in the fighting to regroup, launched an attack across the Tisza on 20 July. But after an initial advance it was thrown back by a powerful Rumanian counter-offensive, which began on the 24th. On the 29th the Rumanians crossed the Tisza and moved rapidly toward Budapest. On 1 August Kun and his government resigned, and on the 4th the Rumanian army entered the capital. Brătianu's main objective in occupying the city was to install a government willing to make peace on terms favourable to Rumania. For the time being, the Rumanians imposed severe armistice terms on the new Hungarian government: a reduction of the Hungarian army to 15,000 men, who could be used only for the preservation of public order; the confiscation of all military equipment not needed by this force; and the payment of the total cost of maintaining the Rumanian occupation force west of the Tisza River. The Rumanian occupation authorities also confiscated large quantities of industrial equipment, locomotives, and other movable goods, action which they justified as reparations for the losses Rumania had suffered during the German and Austro–Hungarian occupation of 1917–18.

While the contest over the Rumanian–Hungarian frontier was being played out Brătianu had become embroiled in a dispute with the Allies over minority rights. The matter at issue was essentially the same as that which had caused such bitterness between Rumania and the Western powers at the Congress of Berlin in 1878: the civil status of Rumanian Jews. The method applied by the great powers in dealing with the problem was also reminiscent of the earlier peace conference. They inserted in the proposed treaty with Austria guarantees of equal rights and a commitment to take other measures on behalf of Jews which they might deem necessary later on. All such rights were to be set down in detail in a separate minorities treaty, which the Allies would draw up and Rumania would be obliged to sign. Influential Jewish organizations in Western Europe had brought the matter before the great powers and pressed for a solution which would provide international guarantees of any commitments the Rumanian government might make.

Brătianu was not only deeply offended personally, but he also worried that Jewish groups, which had close connections with

Western European and American financial interests and liberal politicians, could cause enormous difficulties for Rumania at the very moment she desperately needed Allied help to achieve her national aspirations. He therefore promised the Allies on 31 May that Rumania would assure 'absolute equality' and broad political liberties for all ethnic minorities, but he refused to accept a diminution of his country's sovereignty by allowing other states to dictate government policy. His adamant refusal to go further led to new strains with the Allies, which helped to precipitate his departure from Paris on 2 July.[20]

Brătianu continued to oppose the Austrian treaty from Bucharest. A mission to Bucharest in early September by Sir George Clerk on behalf of the Supreme Council increased the tension, for Clerk carried a note from the Council accusing Brătianu of blatantly defying its will in the pursuit of his own objectives in Hungary. Under the circumstances it is not surprising that the Allies rejected Brătianu's proposal that Rumania adhere to the treaty, but not be obliged to carry out the offending provisions. With matters thus at an impasse no Rumanian delegates were present for the signing of the Treaty of St Germain with Austria on 10 September. Two days later Brătianu and his government resigned, citing as reasons the Supreme Council's disregard of the treaty of alliance of 1916 and its imposition of conditions incompatible with the country's sovereignty. Brătianu was succeeded on 29 September by his Minister of War, General Arthur Văitoianu, but no one doubted who remained the real power in the government.

The Supreme Council finally resolved matters with Rumania on 15 November when it issued an ultimatum to the Văitoianu government requiring it within eight days to withdraw the Rumanian army from Hungary to the frontier designated by the peace conference; receive an inter-Allied commission which would estimate the value of the goods requisitioned by the Rumanian occupation forces in Hungary; stop further requisitions; and sign the Austrian and minorities treaties. The Council threatened severe penalties for failure to comply. The Văitoianu government, none the less, refused and then resigned on 30 November. Its successor, the so-called parliamentary bloc government headed by Alexandru Vaida, decided to accept the Council's terms in order not to jeopardize the gains already made and to re-establish good relations with the West, which the majority of Rumanian politicians considered essential for the country's post-war development. Vaida agreed in principle to settle differences over Hungary and dispatched General Coandă to Paris, where he signed the Austrian and minorities treaties on 9 December.

The disposition of the Banat was settled with relative ease. Brătianu had sought the incorporation of the entire region into Rumania on the basis of population (600,000 Rumanians to 400,000 Swabians and 300,000 Serbs) and the economic and geographical unity of the region, but the Supreme Council drew the frontier between Rumania and the new Yugoslavia along rough ethnic boundaries: the Rumanians received about two-thirds of the area, the Serbs one-third. The Serbian army, which had occupied most of the Banat, relinquished that part which was to go to Rumania to the French, who then turned it over to the Rumanian army in July 1920.

Formal Allied approval of Rumania's acquisition of Bessarabia was another matter. It came slowly and grudgingly and put Brătianu's powers of persuasion to a severe test. He pointed out that over 70 per cent of the population was Rumanian and insisted that the union with Rumania had been carried out freely by a legally constituted assembly, the Sfat al Țării. In an appearance before the Rumanian Territorial Commission on 22 February 1919 he also warned that the Rumanian nation could not exist without the Dniester River as its eastern boundary: 'Bessarabia is the door to our house; in the hands of others it would endanger the hearth itself.' But the Allies were not easily swayed. The Americans seem to have been the most obstinate. Secretary of State Robert Lansing, unabashedly sceptical about the way Rumania had acquired the territory, asked if Brătianu would agree to a plebiscite in Bessarabia. Brătianu thought not. He professed to have no doubts about the outcome, but he would not agree to a withdrawal of the army, which, he was certain, would expose the population to 'Bolshevik anarchy'.

The whole matter, which became entangled in other issues outstanding between the Allies and Rumania, dragged on for most of 1920. At the beginning of that year Alexandru Vaida, the prime minister, went to Paris and reached an agreement with the Allies on the evacuation of Hungary. By the end of March it had been completed, but the Council of Ambassadors, which had taken the place of the Peace Conference, would not sign the treaty it had drawn up on Bessarabia until Rumania had concluded a definitive peace with Hungary. That condition was finally met when Rumania signed the Treaty of Trianon on 4 June 1920, which awarded Rumania all of Transylvania and part of eastern Hungary, including the cities of Oradea and Arad. Yet, it was not until 28 October that the Council of Ambassadors presented Take Ionescu, foreign minister in a new government headed by General Averescu, with a treaty on the union of Bessarabia with Rumania. It recognized Rumanian sovereignty over the territory and specified the Dniester River as the boundary between Rumania and Russia, but it also provided that Russia should adhere to the treaty when a government came to power with which the Allies could do business and that all matters in dispute over the details of the treaty should be settled then through arbitration by the Council of the League of Nations. But the actual negotiations for a settlement were to be left to Rumania and Russia. The latter's refusal to acknowledge Rumanian sovereignty over the territory proved a major obstacle to the normalization of relations between the two countries throughout the inter-war period.

The peace conference settled the boundaries of Dobrudja between Rumania and Bulgaria with comparative ease. The Treaty of Neuilly of 27 November 1919 left intact the frontier established by the Peace of Bucharest in 1913.

By the autumn of 1920, then, all the new territorial acquisitions of Rumania had received international sanction. They added 156,000 square kilometres (in 1919 Rumania thus encompassed 296,000 square kilometres) and $8\frac{1}{2}$ million inhabitants (in 1919: 16,250,000) to the pre-war kingdom. The number of Rumanians living outside the boundaries of the enlarged national state had, consequently, been reduced to about 600,000: 250,000 in the Soviet Union, 230,000 in Yugoslavia, 60,000 in Bulgaria, and only 24,000 in Hungary. But in the process of fulfilling long-cherished national aspirations the Rumanians had acquired substantial minorities. In 1920 roughly 30 per cent of the population was non-Rumanian, as opposed to 8 per cent before the war, according to the census of 1912. The most important minorities in the new Rumania were Magyars (9.3 per cent of the total population), Jews (5.3 per cent), Ukrainians (4.7 per cent), and Germans (4.3 per cent). The new provinces also added greatly to the productive capacity of Rumania. For example, the industrial potential of the country in 1919 was 235 per cent of what it had been in 1916, an increase for which Transylvania and the Banat were mainly responsible.

These gains in territory, population, and economic capacity

must, however, be weighed against the enormous human and material losses caused by the war. When the number of soldiers killed, approximately 300,000, is added to civilian deaths, Rumania is estimated to have lost one-tenth of her pre-war population. The total destruction suffered by industry, agriculture, and other branches of the economy and by private property has been estimated at 72,000 million gold lei. Industry suffered the most. Of 845 enterprises receiving government support in 1915, only 217 were operating in 1917–18, and production in all branches by 1918 had been drastically reduced from what it had been in 1913–14: oil to 47 per cent, coal to 41 per cent, and metallurgy to 19.4 per cent. Rail transport had been almost completely disrupted: of 910 locomotives in 1914, only 265 were in service in 1919, and the number of freight carriages had been reduced from 53,576 to 3,511. Agriculture was in a similar state. Because of the lack of adequate manpower, draught animals, and machinery and tools, production had declined to such levels that in 1919 Rumania, traditionally an exporter of grain, had to import grain and other foodstuffs in order to meet the urgent needs of the population. In 1919–20 only 8,300,000 hectares were sown compared to 13,700,000 hectares in 1911–15, and grain production during the same period fell 35 per cent.[21]

Daunting tasks lay ahead. The damage of war had first to be repaired, and then the new provinces and new citizens had to be integrated into existing structures and the institutions of a modern national state refined. As in the previous century, intellectuals provided the blueprints.

---

[21] Emil Răcilă, *Contribuţii privind lupta Românilor pentru apărarea patriei în primul război mondial, 1916–1918* (Bucharest, 1981), 288–94: Muşat and Ardeleanu, *Viaţa politică 1918–1921*, 26–30.

7
The Great Debate

In the period between the two World Wars Rumanian intellectuals of the most diverse ideological commitments engaged in spirited polemics about the course of development their country should follow. With the Great War and the struggle for political unification behind them and with the task of organizing the new Rumania immediately ahead they were compelled to re-examine old values and seek new definitions of national character. The enhanced opportunities for political and cultural integration into Western Europe gave added urgency to their task.

The responses they gave to these fundamental questions defied consensus. Yet, however diverse the issues they raised, two broad groupings of intellectuals are discernible which may be designated as Europeanists and traditionalists. The former treated Rumania as a part of Europe and insisted that she had no other choice but to follow the path of economic and social development already taken by the urbanized and industrialized West. The traditionalists, on the other hand, emphasized Rumania's agrarian character and sought models of development based upon her own unique social and cultural heritage. The affinities of both groups with pre-war currents of thought are striking, but not surprising, for they drew copiously upon the earlier agrarian and industrial visions of the future Rumania. Yet, their thought yielded nothing in originality to their intellectual forebears as they reinterpreted Rumania's place in Europe in the light of their own experience and their expectations of the new century.

THE EUROPEANISTS

The Europeanists, though approaching development from diverse perspectives, none the less shared a similar view of Rumania's modern history and of her place as a part of Europe. Two figures stand out: the literary critic Eugen Lovinescu and the economist and sociologist Ştefan Zeletin. For the first time in scholarly literature they undertook a comprehensive investigation of the causes that lay behind the development of modern Rumania.

They both linked the process to the introduction of Western-style capitalism in the Rumanian principalities and treated the revolution of 1848 and the Constitution of 1866 as landmarks in assuring its survival. But Lovinescu found the motive force of change in ideas, whereas Zeletin emphasized economic and social causes. None the less, they agreed that 'Westernization' was a necessary historical stage through which every country was fated to pass, and they had no doubt that outside, European influences, rather than internal forces, had been the main catalyst for the development of modern Rumania.

Eugen Lovinescu (1881–1943) was the most influential literary critic of the time. Besides Rumanian, French literature and thought were paramount influences on his intellectual development (he received a doctorate from the Sorbonne in 1909), and, taking a European perspective from his earliest critical writings, he opposed the ideological and aesthetic notions of those like the Sămănătorists who sought creative inspiration in an idealized rural world and insisted upon a primarily social function for art. His most sustained criticism of the agrarian and traditionalist currents came in his sweeping analysis of the formation of modern Rumania, *Istoria civilizaţiei române moderne* (3 vols., 1924–6; The History of Modern Rumanian Civilization). He traced the origins of modern Rumania back to the first half of the nineteenth century, to the beginnings of massive intellectual and cultural contacts with Western Europe, and he thus treated the encounter as a struggle between Western and native systems of ideas. The former triumphed, he argued, because the élites in the principalities of Moldavia and Wallachia judged Europe to be superior to the East. These élites thus undertook to close the enormous gap they perceived between themselves and the West by adopting the latter's institutions, ethics, and methods, in accordance with what Lovinescu called 'synchronism'. For him, this 'law' was the key to understanding the relationship between agricultural, patriarchal Rumania, on the one hand, and the industrial, urban West, on the other. Accordingly, the inferior imitated the superior—the underdeveloped peoples the more advanced, and the village the city. At first, the imitation was complete; it was superficial and unselective, but then, as maturity set in, it was transformed into the adaptation of what was consciously judged to be necessary and superior, a stage, in Lovinescu's view, that Rumania had reached in the 1920s. But, he insisted, synchronism was not merely imitation; it was also integration. He was certain that all Europe was drawing closer together as a result of the expansion of modern means of communication, and he pointed out that the most diverse societies were becoming 'homogenized' more rapidly than ever before. As an example, he cited the speed with which a new art-form became internationalized, how rapidly impressionism, cubism, expressionism, and dadaism spread across Europe. It was thus obvious, he thought, that Rumania could not help becoming part of this integral, cosmopolitan civilization.[1]

Civilization, then, for Lovinescu meant the West with its industry, urban centres, and liberal political and economic institutions, and he noted how in every way Rumania was rapidly becoming more like the West. He viewed the historical evolution of modern Europe as a contest between the innovative, democratic ideas propounded by its urban classes, on the one side, and the patriarchal, reactionary ideas fostered by the agrarian classes, on the other. A staunch believer in the idea of progress, he had no doubt which party would triumph. He denounced as 'romantic' and 'reactionary' the efforts of the Sămănătorists and similar agrarian currents to find in the Rumanian feudal past the necessary elements of an indigenous civilization. To claim, as they did, that the ideas of the French Revolution, which had had so much influence on the Rumanians of 1848, had somehow thwarted the organic, natural development of Rumanian society, to exalt rural primitivism, and to idealize the Middle Ages as the foundations of a vital and creative civilization in the modern age struck him as simply absurd. Since he admired the city of the West as representing the highest stage of social development and since the law of synchronism presupposed an alignment of the Rumanians with these great centres, he assigned to the Rumanian urban classes the primary responsibility for creating a modern Rumanian civilization. He praised the urban classes, by which he meant the bourgeoisie and intellectuals, as the bearers of the highest gifts of civilization who alone were capable of introducing all the elements of world civilization to the Rumanians and of breaking down the resistance of the 'passive' and 'inert' peasant masses.[2]

Ştefan Zeletin (1882–1934) had studied in Germany (1909–12) and had taken a doctorate at the University of Erlangen for a

[1] Eugen Lovinescu, *Istoria civilizaţiei române moderne*, iii (Bucharest, 1926), 43–51, 63–103, 187–91.
[2] His position is evident from his criticism of agrarianist, traditionalist currents in literature: Eugen Lovinescu, *Istoria literaturii române contemporane, 1900–1937* (Bucharest, 1937), 18–21, 29–32, 51–4.

dissertation on the Hegelian origins of English pragmatism. A European and a materialist, he insisted that Rumania's fate was inextricably linked to the fortunes of Western capitalism.[3] His most influential work, *Burghezia română: Origina şi rolul ei istoric* (1925; The Rumanian Bourgeoisie: Its Origin and Historical Role), offered an economic interpretation of Rumania's 'Westernization' complementing and balancing Lovinescu's analysis of the intellectual and cultural phases of the process. He tried to show that modern Rumania was the product of fundamental economic changes brought about by the introduction of Western European capital after the Treaty of Adrianople (1829), which had freed the Rumanian principalities from the stifling effects of the Ottoman commercial monopoly. The process of Europeanization, in his view, had been rapid, and he was convinced that Rumania had definitively entered the Western European economic sphere after the Crimean War, an event which caused an economic revolution in the principalities. Thus, in the next half-century the old agrarian state had slowly dissolved as the country adapted itself to the processes and demands of capitalism.[4] Economic transformation, he pointed out, brought in its wake political innovation, as old feudal institutions gave way to those of Western, middle-class democracy. He showed how a native bourgeoisie emerged out of these processes, the class that was to guide the country through all the successive stages of modernization.

Like Lovinescu, Zeletin was a determinist who saw the future as belonging to the industrial, urban classes. He relegated the 'backward' and 'apathetic' peasants to a minor role in the transformation of the country, and although he expected their situation to improve as capitalism progressed, he thought their suffering a natural, if unfortunate, consequence of the process of modernization. The notion that Rumania was destined to remain a predominantly agricultural country, so dear to agrarianists, struck him as contrary to the laws of social evolution. He could foresee no other course for Rumania except industrialization and a continued accommodation to the technological advances of the West, if she hoped to escape a permanent condition of inferiority.

The majority of writers grouped around *Viaţa românească* may also be classed as Europeanists, but they gave far more attention

---

[3] On Zeletin's career, see Cezar Papacostea, 'Ştefan Zeletin: însemnări privitoare la viaţa şi opera lui', *Revista de filosofie*, 20/3 (1935), 201–62.

[4] Ştefan Zeletin, *Burghezia română: Origina şi rolul ei istoric* (Bucharest, 1925), 34–166, 252–5.

to native realities than Lovinescu and Zeletin. In the first place, they retained something of their pre-war Poporanist outlook, which is especially evident in their opposition to wholesale industrialization. They were convinced, as late as 1935, that a modern, Western-style industry had little chance of success and would continue to be 'parasitical' because, in their view, at least two more centuries would be necessary before enough native capital could be accumulated to support industrialization. Opposition to capitalist industry is also manifest in their views on political organization; they advocated a 'rural democracy', which would give priority to the needs and aspirations of the peasantry.

Yet, leading figures of the *Viaţa românească* circle such as the literary critic Garabet Ibrăileanu (1871–1936) and the sociologist Mihai Ralea (1896–1964), the director of the review after 1930, were careful to separate themselves from radical agrarianists, especially those traditionalist currents which idealized the peasant's way of life and were satisfied to leave him in a state of economic and cultural backwardness. They stood for the triumph in Rumania of the great principles of European liberalism—liberty and equal justice for all—and the dissemination of humanist learning and technology from the more advanced West. Thus, they advocated electoral and agrarian reform and 'Europeanization', which they understood as a raising of living standards and a democratization of institutions. They regarded contact with the West as essential for the development of Rumanian civilization and thus rejected the narrow cultural exclusivism of many traditionalists. But at the same time they disapproved of Lovinescu's unabashed cosmopolitanism and preferred to base Rumanian creativity upon autochthonous sources rather than upon the 'integral imitation' of Western forms.[5]

Mihail Manoilescu (1891–1950) may be classed among the Europeanists, despite his repudiation of 'old-style' liberalism and his embrace of corporatism in the 1930s. As for Rumania's development, he had no doubt that it must follow the Western path of industrialization, which he saw as the solution to economic backwardness in general and the agrarian problem in particular and the means by which Rumania's dependence upon the economically advanced countries of Europe could be ended. He dismissed as

[5] Ovid S. Crohmălniceanu, *Literatura română între cele două războaie mondiale*, i (Bucharest, 1972), 114–36; Klaus Heitman, 'Das "rumänische Phänomen"', *Südost-Forschungen*, 29 (1970), 203–14.

fanciful the goal of the Poporanists and other agrarianists to build a prosperous, modern economy based upon agriculture. In his major work on international economic relations, *Théorie du protectionnisme et de l'échange international* (1929), he argued that industry enjoyed an intrinsic superiority over agriculture. From his own analysis he concluded that the productivity of labour in industry was greater than in agriculture. He showed how the disparity in value thus created accounted for the immense advantage in trade and the economic and political dominance that Western Europe had gained over agricultural Eastern Europe.[6]

Like Zeletin, Manoilescu accorded a key role to the bourgeoisie in the development of capitalism in Rumania in the nineteenth century. But he discerned a growing crisis in the Rumanian bourgeoisie and urged fundamental changes in its structure if it was to fulfil its tasks in the twentieth century. He pronounced the creative period of the old bourgeoisie, which had assumed leadership of Rumania's capitalist development after 1829 (his account of its origins was essentially the same as Zeletin's), at an end and prophesied that it faced a revolt of major proportions on the part of the mass of the population, whom it had exploited mercilessly. In *Rostul şi destinul burgheziei româneşti* (1942: The Role and Destiny of the Rumanian Bourgeoisie) he argued that the bourgeoisie must be 'purified' through a complete reconstruction of its political, economic, and social organization, a process he perceived already underway in Nazi Germany and Fascist Italy. In Rumania, too, he foresaw that the bourgeoisie would continue to organize and direct the economy, but it would no longer be burdened by the 'deadweight' of capitalism and liberalism. Instead of remaining dominant, it would be integrated into the state through a single, all-encompassing political party, and its economic motivation would be 'de-materialized' through corporatism. As a result, the Rumanian bourgeoisie would be composed of persons eager to produce and to serve society as a whole, but it would remain a bourgeoisie because the individual ownership of the means of production would be maintained.[7]

---

[6] Mihail Manoilescu, 'Le Triangle économique et social des pays agricoles: la ville, le village, l'étranger', *Internationale Agrar Rundschau*, 6 (1940), 16–26; Mihail Manoilescu, *Forţele naţionale productive şi comerţul exterior* (Bucharest, 1986), Introduction, 26–8.

[7] Mihail Manoilescu, *Rostul şi destinul burgheziei româneşti* (Bucharest, 1942), 322–48, 380–98; I. Didilescu, 'Burghezia văzută de un economist român', *Ethos*, 1/1 (1944), 107–25.

THE TRADITIONALISTS

Opposed to the Europeanists were groups and individuals who sought models for Rumania's development in the native past, real or imagined. 'Traditionalist' accurately describes them, but they were by no means unanimous about what constituted the Rumanian tradition. In general, they shared a belief in the predominantly rural character of Rumanian historical development and staunchly opposed 'inorganic' cultural and institutional 'imports' from the West. They all drew from currents of ideas that had come to the fore in European intellectual life in the latter half of the nineteenth century and the beginning of the twentieth. It is perhaps paradoxical that they should have been so indebted to Western European thought, for they tended to reject Western political and economic institutions. The influence of Germany was paramount. The German Romantics taught Rumanian traditionalists to appreciate the superiority of 'culture' (defined as a unique, 'organic' expression of the spirit of community or nation) over 'civilization' (conceived of mainly as material or technological progress). Later on, German sociologists reinforced the traditionalists' belief in the village as the chief moulder and protector of the national character. Of particular importance was Ferdinand Tönnies's *Gemeinschaft und Gesellschaft* (1887), which exalted 'community', based as it was upon tradition and 'natural' links among its members, as the primary, organic form of social life, and rejected 'society', which was seen as composed of individuals joined together merely by 'exterior' and 'mechanical' relationships. For Tönnies (and his Rumanian admirers), the embodiment of community was the village, while 'society' manifested itself in the great urban centres. Such ideas, as we have seen, had nurtured in varying degrees the autochthonism of the Junimists, Sămănătorists, and Poporanists.

In the years immediately after the First World War the insistence upon Rumania's unique agrarian character and the search for authentic Rumanian values in the countryside were overlaid by more general, European currents of thought opposed to the rationalism and scientific positivism of the latter half of the nineteenth century. The crisis of the European consciousness of the 1890s, which signalled a geological shift in patterns of thought and artistic expression and came to be known as 'modernism', was fully shared by Rumanian intellectuals in the 1920s. Many rejected the values which had held sway for much of the nineteenth century.

The war was partly responsible. Its cruelty and destructiveness had discredited reason and undermined the prestige of Western civilization. Moved by these experiences, Rumanian intellectuals rejected the rationalism represented by Kant and his successors, who struck them as hopelessly out of touch with the real world. They turned for guidance to others: to Nietzsche, whose anti-rationalism fascinated them: to Dilthey and Einstein, whose relativism converted them from Darwin's determinism; to Spengler, whose theories about the inevitable decline of civilizations, especially of the West, provided them with new analytical tools; to Ludwig Klages, who exposed the opposition between the soul and the mind; to Heidegger and his praise of nothingness as the only reality; and to Freud, who revealed to them the vast creative domain of the unconscious. Thus, everything appeared to these Rumanian intellectuals to be in flux, to be temporary and unstable.

In their search for new values they eagerly embraced all things Eastern. A veritable wave of irrationalist and mystical ideas seemed to break across Rumanian intellectual life. They came from Asia, especially India, but from Europe, too. Alongside Buddhism and Yoga, Christian and mystical philosophy, as expounded by the Fathers of the Church, Kierkegaard, and Berdyaev, exercised a profound influence on Rumanian thought.

For many intellectuals, the fascination with the philosophy of the East reinforced their admiration for the Rumanian village. They discovered striking analogies between the religious sensibilities and mental structures of these two seemingly diverse worlds. Their immersion in both cultures was not unlike a return to the Rousseauist vision of the healthy man of nature, uncorrupted by the vices of a cosmopolitan, rationalist civilization. At home they discovered in Eastern Orthodoxy the chief bulwark of this simple, unspoiled way of life. Through this original fusion of Eastern Christian spirituality and the Rumanian rural world they laid the foundations of a characteristic expression of Rumanian identity in the 1920s—Orthodoxism.

Of all the traditionalist currents of the inter-war period, none had greater influence on intellectual and cultural life or contributed more to the debate on Rumanian national development than that nurtured by the founders of the literary review, *Gîndirea* (Thought). They were very much in the mainstream of Rumanian intellectual life of the post-war era, and they conceived of *Gîndirea* as a vehicle for their own ideas about the Rumanian 'phenomenon'. They were traditionalists in a broad sense who wanted to plumb the depths of the native spirit and explore those regions that had hitherto been neglected. Like the majority of Rumanian intellectuals of the time, they were anxious to preserve specific Rumanian values in literature and art, which, it seemed to them, had been endangered by easy concessions to the predominant 'cosmopolitan spirit' of the age. The 'Gîndirists', as they came to be known, were attracted to speculative thought, mystical and religious experiences, and the primitive spirituality of folklore, and they were anxious to communicate their own ideas in a wholly modern idiom. These preoccupations rather than a specific ideology gave the *Gîndirea* circle its cohesiveness.

Two main currents, or wings, are discernible within the *Gîndirea* circle during its most creative period, the 1920s and early 1930s. Representative of the right wing was Nichifor Crainic (1889–1972), the editor of the review from 1926 until its demise in 1944 and the chief theorist of Orthodoxism. Alarmed by what he and many others perceived as the steady moral and spiritual decay of Rumanian society since the nineteenth century, he sought to reverse the trend by leading a return to the 'authentic values' of the Rumanian spirit, that is, to the teachings of Eastern Orthodoxy. His emphasis upon Orthodox spirituality helped to differentiate his brand of autochthonism from Sămănătorism and Poporanism, which had emphasized, respectively, cultural and economic means to a national regeneration. Crainic's theories were the soul of 'Gîndirism'. But another tendency within the circle, the left, created the 'Gîndirea style' and was responsible for the review's enormous literary prestige. These poets and novelists looked beyond Eastern Orthodoxy in their search for the deeper sources of the native tradition and the proper path of national development. While acknowledging the contribution Orthodoxy had made to Rumanian spiritual and cultural life in the past, they extended their investigations to the popular psyche as revealed in folklore and mythology, to Oriental religions, and to contemporary philosophical and social currents in Western Europe. Their leading representative was the poet and philosopher Lucian Blaga.

Nichifor Crainic initially studied for the priesthood, but he was gradually drawn to literature and journalism. By the time he joined *Gîndirea* in 1921 he was already the author of two volumes of patriotic, bucolic poetry and had acquired considerable editorial experience. He retained a deep interest in theology and accorded religion a decisive role in ethnic spiritual and cultural development. He elaborated his philosophy of culture and the aesthetic theories which laid the foundation for Orthodoxism in a series of articles in *Gîndirea* between 1922 and 1929. But his attempts to translate theory into practice after he became editor of *Gîndirea* were not notably successful. Despite his dogmatism, Crainic was tolerant—at least until the late 1930s—of colleagues who ignored his injunctions. His friendship with Lucian Blaga and respect for his philosophical works, which strayed far from the Orthodoxist ideal, is a case in point.

The central theme of Crainic's articles was the lack of originality and genuine spirituality in contemporary Rumanian culture. Artists and writers and intellectuals generally, he claimed, instead of drawing upon the rich heritage of Rumanian folk culture, had turned to foreign, especially French, models as a source of inspiration. The unhappy result had been to isolate the educated élite from the peasantry, that is, from the wellspring of ethnic spirituality. Here, Crainic assured his readers, was the main cause of the superficiality of contemporary Rumanian culture and of the absence of the 'dough of religious thought', which he judged essential to fruitful intellectual labour.[8]

Crainic's assessment of Rumanian culture and his hopes for its future development rested upon a Christian philosophy of history. Drawing upon the Fathers of the Church and such modern theologians as Vladimir Soloviev, Sergei Bulgakov, and Nikolai Berdyaev, Crainic saw history as the unfolding of a divine plan to restore man to his original place in creation through the intermediary of Jesus Christ, a process that would end with the establishment of the Kingdom of God on earth. For Crainic, the birth of Christ marked the great turning-point in human history, and Christian culture, accordingly, represented the highest development of the human spirit. The Byzantine style, a synthesis of the splendour of antiquity and the richness of Christian spirituality, represented for him the apogee of the Christian cultural tradition.

Pursuing an analysis of Rumanian realities from this perspective, Crainic made the rural world the focus of his attention. He regarded the Rumanian peasant masses (like all agricultural peoples) as eminently religious, and he cited the products of folk literature to prove his point. He felt that the *bocete* (laments) and *colinde* (Christmas carols) showed that Eastern Christianity was peculiarly suited to the Rumanian people and was somehow local

---

[8] Nichifor Crainic, 'Isus în ţara mea', *Gîndirea*, 2/11–12 (1923), 119.

and intimately fused with popular customs and beliefs. Crainic went so far as to claim that all Rumanian historical culture had developed from the church and was permeated by the 'creative force' of the Orthodox religion and the Byzantine conception of the transcendental and phenomenal worlds. He saw the East as a symbol of the many centuries of isolation of Rumanian society from the Western bourgeois, urbanized world. According to this idea, Byzantine Orthodoxy had been indispensable for the differentiation of the patriarchal mentality ('a block of raw elements in the face of history') from the currents of European civilization and had protected the native genius from assimilation by the more sophisticated West.[9]

Yet it was apparent to Crainic that modern Rumanian intellectual and cultural development had taken a path quite different from the one it should have followed, had it remained faithful to its primordial Eastern heritage. He thought this deviation was a result of massive, unthinking Westernization. It had begun with the intellectuals of 1848, whom Crainic accused of diverting the Rumanian people from their 'preordained course of development' by replacing institutions that had evolved through the ages in response to specific Rumanian conditions with random imports from the West. He likened their work to the Europeanization imposed upon Russia by Peter the Great. In Rumania (as in Russia) the spirit of the West, exemplified by a cosmopolitan, urban civilization, undermined the organic spirit of the patriarchal village. Both the Rumanian forty-eighters and Peter were thus guilty of 'denaturing' the spiritual, almost magical, content of the autochthonous culture by turning religion into an ethical and social problem.

Crainic considered the forty-eighters and their descendants responsible for the subversion of the Rumanian Orthodox Church and, consequently, blamed them for the failure of the church to infuse a genuine religious spirit into contemporary Rumanian culture. In their zeal to mould Rumanian society into a Western European pattern, these lay intellectuals had gradually subjugated the Orthodox Church to the state. They had confused Orthodoxy with Catholicism, even though it had not been 'guilty of the crimes of Catholicism'. For example, the Orthodox Church had never challenged the authority of the state, nor had it created an Inquisition to stifle learning and progress. Yet the lay intellectuals

[9] Nichifor Crainic, 'Parsifal', *Gîndirea*, 3/8–10 (1924), 184–6.

had reduced the church to impotence. Once a 'creator of spiritual values', it had become a mere creature of the state fit only to deal with such trifling matters as clerical salaries and remarriage. Under such circumstances, it was only natural for the church to become excessively concerned with outward form and (like the intellectuals) divorce itself from the soul of the people, abdicating its responsibility to guide spiritual and cultural life. How else, Crainic wondered, could the 'random borrowings' from a foreign civilization be explained? He found the ceremonials of the church especially wanting. He argued that religious ritualism in essence differed little from the ceremonies of witchcraft: both promoted spiritual passivity and both did nothing to raise the people from their present condition.

The unfortunate effects of the laicization of Rumanian society could be found in those manifestations of the Rumanian national spirit of which Crainic otherwise approved. For example, he spoke admiringly of the writers who had grouped themselves around *Sămănătorul* and especially of their leader, Nicolae Iorga. Crainic praised the 'national tendency' they represented and, in particular, approved of their part in rallying the nation behind the goal of political unification in the decade before the First World War. Yet, in the final analysis, he found the Sămănătorist movement deficient. It erred in placing man in the centre of the rural world and in portraying him merely as an 'eruption of elemental forces'; it ignored entirely what was to Crainic the most important aspect of rural life: the profound religious consciousness of the peasantry. Sămănătorism, according to Crainic, merely offered a stereotyped peasant hero of popular ballads adapted to present-day requirements—'an apology for primitive instincts' performing against a background of 'bright colours' regarded as the suitable decoration for these instincts. The Sămănătorists were too absorbed by the material side of human existence, and Crainic was eager to cast a 'metaphysical light' on their traditionalism. As he put it, Sămănătorism had a grand vision of the Rumanian earth, but it had ignored the clear sky of Rumanian spirituality; above the Rumanian earth they all loved was the 'arching cover' of Eastern spirituality.[10]

Crainic found a justification for his hostility toward the West in the writings of contemporary German philosophers of culture, notably Oswald Spengler, whose *Decline of the West* had been

---

[10] Nichifor Crainic, 'Sensul tradiţiei', *Gîndirea*, 9/1–2 (1929), 6–7, 9–10.

enthusiastically received by the Gîndirists. Crainic's theories read like a commentary on Spengler. Like Spengler, he viewed the West in terms of the antinomy between civilization and culture and considered the West a civilization in an advanced state of decay. Its salient feature was the 'world city'—for example, Berlin or New York—which was a place of 'unrelieved materialism' and 'colourless internationalism' where all the higher spiritual aspirations of man had been smothered. Civilization, Crainic argued, was the old age of a culture, a period the West had entered in the nineteenth century with its wholehearted embrace of materialism and scientism. To civilization he opposed culture, which he defined as the expression of the organic, primarily spiritual values of a people. According to his definition, culture was precisely that spiritualized traditionalism of the Rumanian rural world which must be preserved at all cost from contamination by the West.

Like Spengler, Crainic saw no hope for the West, but Rumania could avoid ruin if she would commit herself to the cultivation of higher spiritual values, namely those set forth in the gospel as interpreted by the Eastern Orthodox Church and those in the deeper layers of folk culture. In other words, Rumania would have to cleave to tradition and avoid the levelling and uniformity of civilization, which was being pressed upon the new generation by Westernizers like Eugen Lovinescu with his theory of synchronism. Using the theory of cultural style, Crainic attempted to demonstrate the organic nature of culture and the sterility of imitation. In an essay entitled, *A doua neatîrnare* (The Second Independence), he used the example of the Gothic style of architecture in medieval Western Europe to show that cultural boundaries were not determined by 'integral imitation', as Lovinescu claimed, but by a specific religious sensibility 'disciplined by a central commandment: dogma'. The Gothic style was nothing more nor less than an expression in stone of Roman Catholic dogma. Beyond its boundaries lay a world governed by Orthodox dogma and the Byzantine style. Over the centuries, the Gothic and Byzantine styles developed differently in response to the distinctive character and sensibility of the nations which adopted and moulded them. Crainic called the lengthy process of shaping, the 'discipline of tradition'. He was certain that if the Rumanians adhered to it, they could achieve a second independence—that of the spirit—to complement the political independence won in 1877.

Crainic was careful to point out that tradition did not signify a stagnation of cultural development. On the contrary, the tradition to which he referred was a living, dynamic force operating in accordance with 'national distinctiveness'; it was the element that differentiated peoples from one another and saved the collective personality of a nation from the dissolution of civilization; it was the 'internal discipline' which accompanied the organic growth of any culture. 'Internal discipline' for the Rumanians, Crainic insisted, meant Orthodoxism and to ignore it, he warned, would be tantamount to abandoning any higher sense of history and would lead to isolation from the original sources of the creative spirit.

After 1930 Crainic became increasingly absorbed in his journalistic activities. His main ambition became the establishment of a political system that would both reflect and promote his view of tradition. As might be expected, he disapproved of democracy as a political philosophy appropriate for Rumania because he associated it with Western bourgeois civilization. When he used the terms 'democracy' in a positive sense, he intended it as a synonym for love of the people in the evangelical sense. He rejected the idea of a Rumania divided into mutually exclusive social classes, claiming that the privileges of class were completely foreign to the Orthodox mentality. He professed to see no significant differences among capitalism, socialism, and communism and condemned them all as emanations of the rationalism of the Renaissance and the French Revolution, which had introduced the destructive processes of laicization into European culture by replacing the City of God with the world city.[11]

Lucian Blaga (1895–1961) took a broader, more European approach to the problem of national character and paths of development than Crainic, his colleague on *Gîndirea* for nearly twenty years. Blaga is a singular figure in the history of Rumanian poetry and philosophy. In neither domain can he be incorporated with ease into any particular school. He seems to have inspired no disciples in philosophy, though his admirers were many; in poetry, on the other hand, his influence was more creative, as may be seen in the activities of his young followers in Cercul Literar (The Literary Circle) of Sibiu during and immediately after the Second World War. As a poet Blaga experimented with a multitude of

---

[11] Nichifor Crainic, 'Pacifism', *Gîndirea*, 10/4 (1930), 105–6, and 'George Coşbuc, poetul rasei noastre', in N. Crainic, *Puncte cardinale în haos* (Bucharest, 1936), 187–8.

forms, and for his themes he drew upon the most varied sources, from Rumanian folklore and his childhood memories of village life to German expressionism and his own very personal world-view. In philosophy he created his own system, which had at its centre the idea of 'mystery'. He praised the irrational, the illogical, and the unconscious, making them the instruments for penetrating the hidden essences of the universe. He conceived of rationality as an isolating factor rather than a point of contact between man and the 'Great Anonymous One', as he called the universal first principle. His greatest debt was to German philosophy, notably Kant, Schopenhauer, and Nietzsche, and to German psychology, and his work as a whole represents the second wave of intense German influence in Rumanian thought following that promoted by Junimism in the latter half of the nineteenth century. Blaga had enormous admiration for German culture, ascribing to it a major role in the development of Rumanian letters since 1800. He called German influence 'catalytic' because it stimulated native creativity, but did not intrude upon it, in contrast to French cultural influence, which he dubbed 'modelling' because it sought to remake the foreigner's culture in its own image.[12] Moreover, he eagerly entered a realm of speculation and synthesis much in vogue in Germany at the time, but hitherto little practised in Rumania—the philosophy of culture.

Blaga was drawn to the *Gîndirea* circle by a mutual preoccupation with broad philosophical questions and the search for the sources of the Rumanian national character. He also shared with his colleagues a sense of general spiritual malaise in Rumania and Europe as a whole. Like them, he was repelled by modern mechanized society and its chief symbol—the cosmopolitan city—and as a reaction to them he clung almost desperately to rural life as the ultimate place of refuge for the oppressed human spirit. He shared the disillusionment of twentieth-century intellectuals with positivism in history and relativism and scepticism in ethics and aesthetics; he sought 'permanent values', not in an accumulation of 'positive facts' or in the rationalization of the human condition but in the intuitive apprehension of absolute spiritual structures. Blaga found within the *Gîndirea* circle an atmosphere conducive to this search and his own creativity. Yet he does not fit comfortably into the *Gîndirea* mould. Despite certain similarities of ideas, he

---

[12] Lucian Blaga, *Spaţiul mioritic* (1936), in L. Blaga, *Trilogia culturii* (Bucharest, 1944), 319–20.

differs from Crainic and other representatives of the right wing in his more profound theoretical orientation. Blaga was not interested in politics, nor did he seek ways of applying his ideas to the solution of social problems. He took up such questions as autochthonism and the Rumanian village from an ontological perspective, and he was concerned less with the outward aspect of things than with the realities that lay behind them.

From the very beginning of his career as a poet and dramatist Blaga was involved in the historical controversy over the ethnic make-up of the Rumanian people. He set himself against the dominant Latinist view by pushing back the origins of Rumanian ethnic evolution to the remote Thracian world before the Roman conquest of Dacia. This biological absolute appealed to his metaphysical bent of mind, while the poet in him was irresistibly attracted to the overflowing vitality and cosmic vision of the Thracian world, which he portrayed with such force and originality in his 'pagan drama', *Zamolxe* (1921). Blaga argued that the Rumanians were much more than Latins with their rationality and balance; they possessed also a vital Slav-Thracian heritage, which from time to time erupted like a 'violent storm from the metaphysical depths of the Rumanian soul', upsetting the Latin sense of symmetry and harmony, a storm he characterized as the 'revolt of our non-Latin sources'. As always in matters of ethnicity, Blaga maintained a sense of proportion and shunned artificial restraints on creativity. Thracianism never imposed itself upon his own work, and when an aggressive, narrow 'Thracomania' gained momentum in the late 1920s and 1930s he disassociated himself from it.

Fundamental to Blaga's understanding of autochthonism is his concept of 'style', which he set forth in a more or less definitive form in *Orizont și stil* (1935; Horizon and Style). By style he meant the sum total of categories that differentiated historical periods, works of art, and ethnic communities from one another. He discovered the sources of style in the unconscious categories of the mind, which he proposed as the primordial determinants of the originality of cultures. The unconscious, moreover, provides the key to his whole philosophy of culture, for, in his view, style grew out of the collective ethnic psychology. Unlike Freud and the psychoanalytic school, Blaga did not regard the unconscious as a 'chaos', as merely the source of animal instincts, but endowed it with a host of primary and secondary categories, which, grouped together, he called the 'stylistic matrix' and which in myriad combinations ultimately determined style. He attributed to the unconscious such primary categories as spatial and temporal 'horizons', an axiological 'accent', 'attitudes' of advance or withdrawal, and 'aspirations' to form and order, and secondary categories such as preferences for movement or calm, for sobriety or the picturesque, and for the massive or the delicate. The unconscious, then, was the zone of true creative impulses. Blaga did not deny the contribution of human reason and will, but he insisted that the fundamental stylistic direction was determined by forces beyond the control of the conscious. His debt to psychoanalysis, despite his criticism of Freud, is evident and helps to explain why he placed little confidence in rationalism and why 'mystery' (or the unknown) became the 'supreme angle of vision' from which he viewed the world. He also owed much to the theories of Jung about the collective unconscious, for the stylistic matrix represented the sythesis of thousands of years in the life of the group, a complex fusion of all that was characteristic of the collectivity and of the individuals who composed it.[13] In Blaga's view, consequently, the stylistic matrix was continually evolving as new elements were slowly incorporated; it was in this sense a product of history, and its evolution helped to explain the variations in styles from region to region and at different periods. In elaborating his theory of style, then, Blaga attempted to establish traditionalism on a new foundation rooted in the obscure, archaic, biological depths of the race.

Blaga's theory of style was greatly influenced also by the German exponents of the morphology of culture, notably Leo Frobenius, an ethnologist and authority on prehistoric art, and Spengler. An early admirer of the *Decline of the West*, Blaga described its author as a 'Copernicus of history', because of his substitution of morphology for chronology in the treatment of human development and his seeking after the 'archetypal phenomena' behind historical facts. Blaga placed him alongside Kant and Einstein as revolutionizers of thought. Among other things, Blaga borrowed from him the technique of the comparative study of civilizations and the antinomy between culture and civilization, but he found Spengler's approach essentially deficient. It reduced the phenomena of culture to form, despite the fact that they encompassed many other elements; it limited itself to description,

---

[13] Lucian Blaga, *Orizont și stil* (1935), in L. Blaga, *Trilogia culturii*, 21–40, 141–55.

when the phenomena of culture required explanation; and it made
the intuition of space the determining factor of style and treated it
as a creative act of the conscious sensibility rather than the product
of the unconscious categories as Blaga had proposed.

Blaga moved from the abstract to an application of his theories
on style in *Spaţiul mioritic* (1936; Mioritic Space), the most important philosophical investigation of Rumanian traditionalism
undertaken in the inter-war period. By 'mioritic space' Blaga was
referring to the *plai* (the ridge or slope of a hill usually covered
with meadows) of Rumanian folk ballads, especially *Mioriţa* (The
Little Lamb). But the *plai* represented more to Blaga than topo-
graphy; it was the spatial horizon specific to Rumanian culture,
the 'infinitely undulating horizon' of hill and valley, which formed
the 'spiritual substratum' of the anonymous creations of Rumanian
popular culture. From this particular unconscious horizon of the
stylistic matrix Blaga derived the 'massive' preference of Rumanian
popular poets for the alternation of accented and unaccented syllables and the unique arrangement of Rumanian peasant houses
which were separated from one another by green spaces, the
'unaccented syllables between the houses'. To demonstrate the
effect of this unconscious spatial horizon he pointed to the fact
that the Saxons of Transylvania, who had lived side-by-side with
the Rumanians for seven centuries, built their homes quite differently, in a fashion corresponding to the German unconscious
spatial horizon. Blaga emphasized that the landscape did not determine the psychic state of the individual or of the ethnic collectivity. This relationship was more profound and went back to a
much earlier era. The Rumanian, for example, had the sense of
dwelling in the mioritic space, even though he might actually be
living on the great Baragan plain of Wallachia, where the folk-
song took the place of the *plai*, while the Saxon, who inhabited
the same landscape as the Rumanian, was still dominated by
the spirit of 'Gothic space' (*spaţiul gotic*), inherited from remote
ancestors in Germany.

In his search for the co-ordinates of the Rumanian cultural style
Blaga focused his attention on the rural world, where, he thought,
the constituent elements of Rumanian spirituality lay. At first
glance, he seemed to adopt Crainic's approach to the problem in
his warm appreciation of Orthodoxy, to which he accorded an
'organic' place in the national psyche. Yet, he was uninterested in
religious dogma. When he spoke of Orthodoxy he meant rather
an ethnic-geographical area separate from Roman Catholic and

Protestant Europe. Moreover, to him, the elements that distinguished the three branches of Christianity from one another came from early 'spiritual infiltrations' of the 'local genius' into the universal Christian doctrine as it spread over various lands. This fusion endowed Roman Catholicism with the categories of 'authority' (a 'will to power'; 'a subtle juridical spirit'), Protestantism with those of 'liberty' ('independence of judgement'; 'conceptualization of problems'; 'duty'), and Orthodoxy with those of the 'organic' ('life', 'the earth', 'nature'). These differences were, then, the result of style rather than of doctrine, a point which Blaga illustrated with examples of how each regarded the church, the nation, and culture. Catholicism conceived of the church as a universal state, Protestantism as a community which embodied liberty, and Orthodoxy as an organism, a unity of the whole in which each member was responsible for the deeds of others. Toward the nation, Catholicism was almost disdainful, since it pursued universal goals; Protestantism considered membership in the nation the result of a deliberate choice of the individual who was responding to a sense of duty; Orthodoxy saw the nation as a destiny, which it enthusiastically embraced. Finally, in regard to culture, Catholicism promoted multi-dimensional movements like the Romanesque, the Gothic, and the Baroque, which served an idea; Protestantism favoured individual creations of great originality; and Orthodoxy inspired works that were 'spontaneous, anonymous, and folkloric'. Blaga thought that Catholicism and Protestantism fostered the growth of cities, while Orthodoxy was peculiarly suited to the development of the village. The villages in the West, consequently, seemed to him to be miniature cities that had lost their rural character and creative originality. Conversely, the city in Eastern Europe resembled an oversized village, while the village itself had retained its primitive creative power, even where it had been touched by outside cultural influences.[14]

Blaga used the term Orthodox in a cultural rather than a religious sense. He made it clear that the originality of the Rumanian spirit was not to be sought in Orthodox dogma at all, but in the 'derogations' of it brought about by the 'spirit of heresy', that is, in the semi-pagan folklore preserved in sacred legends, *bocete*, and *colinde*. It seemed to him that Orthodox doctrine itself had had a levelling effect on the peoples of South-eastern Europe. Con-

---

[14] Lucian Blaga, *Spaţiul mioritic*, in L. Blaga, *Trilogia culturii*, 184–90, 194–7.

sequently, the stylistic elements that differentiated Rumanians from their Bulgarian and Serbian co-religionists manifested themselves most strongly in the productions of folk poets and artists. Behind the 'mask' of Orthodoxy the Rumanians had preserved their ancient, pre-Christian beliefs and customs, especially their specific way of understanding and feeling existence, which, in Blaga's view, went back to pagan Thracian times. Peculiar to the Rumanian was a view of the world that fused nature with the transcendental, or, as Blaga expressed it, that saw the world as a receptacle of the unseen. This 'sophianic perspective' caused the earth to be suffused by a heavenly light in the same way in which, for example, all nature is transformed into a church in the ballad, *Miorița*. This way of regarding the transcendental he judged the most important stylistic determinant of Orthodoxy.

For Blaga, Rumanian spirituality, which primarily determined national character, had been preserved best in the rural world. He himself had been born in a small Transylvanian village, and the memories of his childhood remained a strong influence on his thought throughout his life. He conceived of the Rumanian village as the locale of the organic, eminently human mode of existence. The creative life of the village was what he meant by 'culture', and it was this culture that he contrasted with 'civilization'. The city was the embodiment of civilization, of the mechanized, bourgeois world, whose imminent collapse Blaga, like many of his Rumanian and West European contemporaries foresaw. His early poetry in particular is filled with the expressionist anxiety that European man was living at the end of an age, a sentiment he revealed in stark, apocalyptic visions of the modern city and 'machinism'. The city (civilization), according to Blaga, was characterized by 'non-creative' preoccupations such as the accumulation of positive knowledge and the formulation of rationalist conceptions; it was a place where man lost his 'cosmic sentiment', his attachment to a uniquely human mode of existence. The scientific spirit, which was one of the hallmarks of modern European civilization, seemed to Blaga to dissolve the 'concrete phenomena' of existence and to isolate the world from man. Such a view followed naturally from Blaga's conception of the world as essentially anti-rational and therefore intractable to the reasoned structures of science. The village, on the other hand, pre-eminently the region of myth and magic thought, assimilated concrete appearances and brought man into a creative relationship with existence. Blaga's praise of magic thought reveals his general tendency to exalt the primitive mentality at the expense of the civilized. Magic thought, he pointed out, did not have as its goal the establishment of universally valid relationships, but rather it sought to organize individual human experience in close connection with specific temporal and spatial data. This type of thought, he argued, was truly creative, for it established bold relationships between very different things. Thanks to this 'magic perspective', then, the peasant was endowed with the special gift of organizing his experience in accordance with his vital interests.[15]

Blaga's affection for the village led him in *Geneza metaforei şi sensul culturii* (1937; The Genesis of Metaphor and the Sense of Culture) to extend the antinomy between the rural world and the city into a theory of 'minor cultures' and 'major cultures'. The former, represented by the village, were in no way inferior in their structures to the latter, that is, civilization. They did not represent merely a retarded stage in the historical evolution of society; they were independent realities which expressed a mode of existence apart, classified by Blaga as 'naïve' and 'childlike'. In a later article he went further, likening minor cultures to prehistory, which for him was a form of 'permanent life' that did not evolve, but rather maintained itself parallel to history.[16] This idea represented Blaga's view of the evolution of Rumanian history. Using the Roman evacuation of the province of Dacia in the third century as his starting-point, he demonstrated that the beginnings of the Rumanian people coincided with their 'withdrawal from history' into an ahistorical world. Here they led an organic existence with a rhythm all its own with one or two brief interruptions until the middle of the nineteenth century. During this long 'boycott of history' peasant art, village architecture, and folk poetry and music experienced a rich development quite apart from the broader European cultural currents. Blaga thus offered a metaphysical explanation of Rumanian uniqueness so dear to the traditionalists.

Blaga's relationship to *Gîndirea* was ambiguous and for the Gîndirists often uncomfortable. On the one hand, there were similarities of ideas and of intellectual tendencies. The main link between Blaga and the theorists of Orthodoxism was undoubtedly autochthonism. They shared a profound dissatisfaction with the existing state of Rumanian spiritual life. They were attracted to

---

[15] Lucian Blaga, *Despre gândirea magică* (Bucharest, 1941), 135–57.
[16] Lucian Blaga, 'Despre permanenţa preistoriei', *Saeculum*, 1/5 (1943), 3–17.

the rural world and its folklore as the source of native spirituality, and, conversely, they were repelled by the mechanical, 'inorganic' spirit of urban society. Yet, in the final analysis, these are mainly surface resemblances. Blaga's traditionalism is the more complex and rests on a superior theoretical foundation. Whereas, for example, Crainic's hostility to the city and praise of the village were nationalistic, Blaga's attitudes were philosophic. Whereas Crainic shunned Western intellectual wares, Blaga's orientation was broadly European. Blaga was untroubled by cultural borrowings from abroad because he believed that the stylistic matrix would ultimately ensure the national character of literature and art and even philosophical and scientific theories. Reviewing his own work, he declared ethnicity his destiny, which he had no power to control; it was not a programme devised rationally, for he felt himself linked irrevocably to the ethnic by all the patterning categories of the stylistic matrix. Although he was in fact very national in spirit and sources of inspiration, he never allowed his own work to be dominated by narrow artistic formulas. Rejecting the Orthodoxism propagated by Crainic, he denied that a work of art became national through the facile additions of folklore and of a native landscape. He himself was attracted to folklore not as a folklorist but as a philosopher intent upon exploring its inner stylistic impulses. He judged his own poetry, admittedly modernist, to be in certain respects more traditionalist than that of the usual tradition because it re-established contact with the primitive spiritual sources of the race. In his poetry nature was never an aesthetic object, a decoration, but rather a text to be read in the attempt to decipher 'mystery'. A poem or a piece of sculpture was Rumanian for him by virtue of its inner rhythm and its way of interpreting reality. His own preference in 'national' art was best represented by the sculpture of Constantin Brîncuși, which blended the most archaic native sources with modern artistic structures and which conformed to Blaga's own expressed ideal of 'metaphysical traditionalism'.

Because of Blaga's use of the myths of Rumanian folklore and his love of the Rumanian village, his traditionalism was sometimes confused with Gîndirism. Yet, unlike Crainic and some other traditionalists, Blaga did not wish to make the past permanent. He sought contact with the past in order to discover the 'original phenomena' of human existence, an understanding which would, he believed, break obsolete patterns of behaviour and inaugurate a new age of spirituality. He sought in the ancestral world of the village the forgotten secrets of the age of innocence before the sin of knowledge had alienated man from nature and his true self.

The stand taken by the *Gîndirea* circle, particularly by Crainic and his adherents, on national character and national development provoked a spirited response from the Europeanists. Eugen Lovinescu called Orthodoxy an obscurantist religion, constrained in rigid formulas that had imposed a foreign liturgical language on the Rumanians and had cast them into the great mass of Slavs who had nearly engulfed them. He reiterated his conviction that the 'emancipation' of the Rumanian national spirit had occurred in the early nineteenth century when young Rumanians came into direct contact with the intellectual and material world of the West, which freed them from the 'slavery' of Eastern cultural forms. Mihai Ralea joined Lovinescu in condemning those who pressed upon the Rumanians instinct and mysticism which could not but cut them off from any possibility of achieving enlightenment and civilization. He thought that Orthodoxism was simply an impediment to the definition of the national character and the creation of a native spirituality, because of its 'obscurantism' and its essentially Byzantine-Slavic character. Other Europeanists, like the literary critic Pompiliu Constantinescu (1901–46), went so far as to deny altogether the religious sensibility of the Rumanian people. Constantinescu held that religion for the Rumanians had always been *lege* (law), that is, a contract between the believer and God. He also argued that the wide diffusion of superstitions among the masses demonstrated an absence of mystical, religious 'aptitude', because of the pragmatism and immediacy of these folk beliefs.

Crainic and the Gîndirists also had their defenders. The most important was the philosopher Nae Ionescu (1888–1940), the theorist of Trăirism (*trăire*, experience), a Rumanian variant of existentialism. The ideas he set forth in the newspaper, *Cuvîntul* (The Word) beginning in 1926 coalesced into a coherent philosophy of culture in the following decade and won him an extraordinary following among the younger generation of intellectuals, which included Mircea Eliade and Emil Cioran.

Like Crainic (and Blaga), Ionescu sensed the advent of a new age of spirituality, which, for him, had had its origins in the revolt against positivism in the 1890s and was approaching maturity in post-war Europe. Everywhere Ionescu saw man struggling to achieve a new 'spiritual equilibrium', to 'return to God' in order to escape the 'frightening emptiness' of scientism and tech-

nology and of the remote supreme being of the rationalists. For a
decade he had observed this great ferment of the human soul, as
he called it, with a critical eye until at last, in 1931, he declared
himself certain that a genuine spiritual revolution was underway
in Europe; it manifested itself in every field of human activity, but
exerted particular force in its opposition to the mental outlook
defined by Cartesian rationalism, the spirit of social and political
democracy, the bourgeois capitalist economic system, and Protestantism. All these hallmarks of the modern age were, to
Ionescu's evident satisfaction, suffering through an acute crisis. He
singled out Protestantism as the chief villain in the undermining
of European religious thought since the Renaissance. For him,
Protestantism meant: the rationalization of religion, that is, the
need to understand and explain the decisions of God; the fitting of
God into the categories of human logic as though there was but
one plane of reality—that of reason—in which man and God were
merely quantitatively different; and 'errant individualism' in the
interpretation of the word of God. Ionescu found all this utterly
foreign to the Orthodox spirit. In Orthodoxy, that is, true
Christianity, the believer recognized the opposition between the
mind and faith and accepted the 'painful sacrifice' of the intellect
when he proclaimed: 'I believe because it is absurd.'[17]

Ionescu identified the Rumanian aspect of the crisis of the
European soul as a search for the true sources of native spirituality.
As a philosopher his main preoccupation had been with the problem of being, at first in a general human sense, but increasingly
later on as an exploration of the specific nature of the Rumanian
soul. The definition of Rumanianness for him, as for Blaga,
was primarily ontological rather than historical and depended
upon spiritual rather than material elements. In Ionescu's mind,
Orthodoxy and Rumanian spirituality were interchangeable con-
cepts. His voluminous writings on the subject abound in such
phrases as, 'To be Rumanian means to be Orthodox,' or 'We
are Orthodox because we are Rumanian, and we are Rumanian
because we are Orthodox.' He argued that the influence of
Orthodoxy had been felt throughout the process of formation of
the Rumanian nation. This intimate association of religion and
ethnicity accounted for the peculiarly folk nature of Rumanian
Orthodoxy. In Ionescu's view, Orthodoxy had descended to the
level of everyday life, contributing to the creation of a specifically

---

[17] Nae Ionescu, *Roza vînturilor* (Bucharest, 1937), 7, 9, 24–7, 67, 74, 257–8.

Rumanian religion that manifested itself not in abstract doctrines but in the unique creations of Rumanian folklore. Like Blaga and Crainic, he identified authentic Rumanian spirituality with the rural world and spoke approvingly of 'our peasantist Orthodoxy'.

The bond between Rumanianness and Orthodoxy was, indeed, so strong that no act of will could, in Ionescu's view, sever it. Ionescu's argument is not unlike Blaga's, though understandably he shunned the authority of Freud and Jung. In a series of articles on Catholic proselytism in Rumania he argued that Catholicism and Orthodoxy were not only two different confessions with different doctrines and cultures, but, even more important, they were two fundamentally different modes of existence. In other words, each had been conditioned in the course of its development by prevailing local conditions; Catholicism, therefore, reflected the spiritual structure and historical development peculiar to south-western Europe, while Orthodoxy had accommodated itself to conditions prevailing in south-eastern Europe. Ionescu concluded that Catholicism could not hope to penetrate the Orthodox world, nor could Orthodoxy proselytize successfully outside its own spiritual zone. Catholicism and Orthodoxy were mutually impenetrable. As organic forms of spiritual life, they could not be transmitted or imposed; a Rumanian could not become a Catholic, even though he might learn the catechism by heart and declare himself a Catholic with all the fervour of a convert because, simply, he was not a product of those conditions that had given rise to Catholicism.

The inescapability, one might almost say, of Orthodox spirituality for the Rumanian goes far toward explaining Ionescu's views on contemporary Rumanian cultural and political forms. As he saw it, Rumanian higher culture of the preceding one hundred years had been anything but authentic. At fault were Westernized intellectuals beginning with the generation of 1848. Ignoring fundamental structural differences between the Orthodox East and the Catholic-Protestant West, they had endeavoured to transpose Western culture into Rumanian realities, action which created conditions of 'gross falseness' and 'artificiality'. The same men were responsible for laying the foundations of the modern Rumanian state, a political form, in Ionescu's view, utterly foreign to the character of Rumanian society as it had been evolving for centuries before 1848. The formal apparatus of the modern Rumanian state, with its parliamentarism and egalitarian democracy and urban social and political life, represented, in his view, a thin, mainly French, veneer obscuring the broad, authentic life of the nation just beneath it.

Ionescu thus perceived a fundamental incompatibility between Rumania and Western Europe. The idea that Rumania could ever be integrated into Europe struck him as absurd in the light of the dichotomy between the Orthodox and the Catholic-Protestant worlds which he had been at such pains to reveal. Consequently, the future development of Rumania would have to be based upon prevailing 'organic realities', by which he meant the social and economic categories of the village and agriculture and the spiritual glue of Orthodoxy. He rejected the city as 'too abstract' and modern industry as 'too rational', too little suited to a people who were contemplative and unused to the discipline of capitalism. Rather, he discerned a perfect fusion between the peasant and Orthodoxy and made Orthodox spirituality the foundation of the 'harmonious [Rumanian] community of thought and deed'.[18]

In the latter 1920s a number of intellectuals, who styled themselves 'the young generation' and were deeply influenced by Nae Ionescu, sought to escape the 'frightening emptiness' of positivism and modern technology and to achieve a new 'spiritual equilibrium'. Nichifor Crainic discerned in their restlessness confirmation of a 'new orientation' in Rumanian intellectual life and a 'return to religion', and he opened the pages of Gîndirea to them. But this generation had its own agenda. Intent upon discovering the true co-ordinates of Rumanian spirituality and eager to set Rumanian culture on a new course, they did not join the Gîndirea circle, but, instead, formed a loose association called Criterion. Its members included Mircea Eliade (1907–86), who was to become a renowned historian of religion; Emil Cioran (b. 1911), the later philosopher of man's tragic destiny; and Mircea Vulcănescu (1904–52), philosopher and sociologist.[19]

The Criterionists enthusiastically embraced Ionescu's exhortations to experience life rather than reduce it to abstract formulas. Mircea Eliade, Emil Cioran, and others harboured no doubts that they were thus the missionaries of a new spirituality and the founders of new laws and customs. They read Swedenborg, Kierkegaard, Shestov, Heidegger, Unamuno, and Berdyaev; they were interested in orphism, theosophy, Eastern mysticism, and

---

[18] Nae Ionescu, 'Naționalism și Ortodoxie', Predania, 8–9 (1937), 3.

[19] The fullest account of its goals and activities is Liviu Antonesei, 'Le Moment Criterion—un modèle d'action culturelle', in Alexandru Zub (ed.), Culture and Society (Iași, 1985), 189–206.

archaic religions; they spoke about the providential mission of their generation: and they decried the mediocrity of bourgeois existence and denounced materialism in all its forms. Their mission, as Mircea Vulcănescu defined it, was to 'assure the unity of the Romanian soul', that is, to bring about the spiritual reconstruction of Rumania, just as the preceding generation had accomplished the task of political unity.[20]

Like Crainic and Ionescu, the Criterionists were drawn to the village as the locus of Rumanian spirituality, and they spoke approvingly of the role Orthodoxy had had in shaping the national experience. But they were not Orthodoxists. In their revulsion at the positivism and materialism bequeathed by the nineteenth century they turned to mysticism, but not to Orthodox doctrine. It seemed to them axiomatic that mystical exaltation rather than faith was the foundation of human sensibility. Mircea Eliade's experience was characteristic. In a small book of essays about the spiritual quest of his generation published in 1927 and entitled, *Itinerariu spiritual* (Spiritual Itinerary), he at first thought that Orthodoxy could provide the young generation with an all-encompassing conception of existence and could become 'a new phenomenon in the history of modern Romanian culture'.[21] But he admitted that his understanding of Orthodoxy was superficial, and later, as his intellectual horizons and experience of life broadened, particularly during a stay in India, where he became fascinated by Hinduism, Orthodoxy henceforth occupied only a modest place in his sweeping comparative studies of religion. Emil Cioran strayed even farther afield. He became preoccupied with the tragedy of individual existence and put his hope in Protestant mysticism of the Kierkegaard variety. When he wrote about the spiritual crisis of inter-war Rumania he indeed paid homage to Orthodoxy for having shielded the Rumanian character through the centuries from assimilation by more dynamic societies, but he saw ultimate salvation only in Rumania's integration into urban, cosmopolitan Europe.[22] Mircea Vulcănescu also recognized the formative influence of Orthodoxy on Rumanian spiritual life, but, unlike Eliade and Cioran, he sought the salvation of his and future generations in the village. It was only here, he thought, that an organic style of Rumanian life had survived and

---

[20] Mircea Vulcănescu, 'Generaţie', *Criterion*, 1/3–4 (1934), 6.
[21] Mac Linscott Ricketts, *Mircea Eliade: The Romanian Roots, 1907–1945*, i (Boulder, Colo., 1988), 245–79.
[22] Emil Cioran, *Schimbarea la faţă a României* (Bucharest, 1936), 75–7, 106–9.

that the Rumanian soul would have to meet the challenge to it posed by the 'massive invasion' of the West.[23] Yet, these disciples of Nae Ionescu formed the cosmopolitan generation which Eugen Lovinescu had predicted would cease to be imitators and would begin to create original, Rumanian spiritual values.

THE THIRD WAY

Between the two World Wars the Peasantists (Țărăniști; from țăran, peasant) were the most consistent and effective advocates of a Rumania in harmony with its 'pre-eminently agricultural character'. They stood for the elaboration of economic and social policies and the creation of a state that would correspond to the interests and needs of the peasantry, who formed the overwhelming majority of the population. They were convinced of the uniqueness of Rumania's historical evolution, which they attributed to an agricultural system rooted in the independent family holding. Their aim throughout the inter-war period was thus to strengthen this nucleus of agricultural production, which they made the foundation of Rumania's future social and political development. They did not deny that capitalism was possible in Rumania and even recognized that modern industry had come to stay and could benefit agriculture. But they wanted to exclude capitalism from the organization of agriculture because they thought it incompatible with the character of Rumanian agriculture as it had developed over the centuries. They were certain that capitalism and everything which came in its wake would destroy what was exceptional and genuine in the Rumanian way of life. They had no doubt that their defence would be successful because peasant agriculture, in their view, was strong and was by its very nature non-capitalist. As proof they cited economic analyses of the family holding as a distinct production unit and the 'psychological incompatibility' between the peasant and capitalist ways.

In constructing their own theory of development, the Peasantists drew extensively from both Western and Eastern European scholarly literature, especially the writings of German economists and sociologists and of Russian agricultural economists. But the Rumanians were by no means simply borrowing foreign models and dealing in abstractions. Rather, they were concerned with the most urgent economic and social realities confronting Greater

[23] Mircea Vulcănescu, *Tendințele tinerei generații* (Bucharest, 1934), 15–16.

Rumania after the First World War—agricultural stagnation and peasant poverty. The remedies they proposed fitted in with those indigenous currents of thought which since the middle of the nineteenth century had emphasized the agrarian character of Rumanian society and had put forth strategies of development that promised to nurture 'healthy tradition' and the 'national genius'.

Of all these currents, the Peasantists stood closest to the Poporanists and were, in a sense, their successors. Both they and the Poporanists advocated an agrarian economic and social order whose foundations they sought to ground in native traditions and institutions, and both were suspicious of bourgeois, industrial society and the city. Yet Peasantism was not just an extension of Poporanism. Although its advocates borrowed generously from their intellectual forebears, they were also deeply influenced by the advances in sociological and economic thought of the inter-war period. Their most original contribution to Rumanian social thought was perhaps the systematic elaboration of the doctrine of agrarian Rumania as a third world situated between capitalist individualism to the West and socialist collectivism to the East. This doctrine, in turn, rested upon two fundamental assumptions: first, that the family holding was a distinct mode of production and formed the very foundation of the national economy, and second, that the 'peasant state', a political entity administered by and responsible to the majority of the population, must replace the existing order.

The elaboration of the economic principles of Peasantism was mainly the work of Virgil Madgearu (1887–1940), who in the 1920s and 1930s published a steady stream of books and articles on agriculture and general economic problems. In them he defined the special character of Rumania's past economic and social development and offered an assessment of its future prospects. His ideas were strongly influenced by his studies of economic theory in Germany, where he took his doctorate at the University of Leipzig in 1911, and by subsequent studies of the classical English economists and practical experience in financial management in London. After the First World War he became the principal theorist of the National Peasant Party and a minister in several National Peasant governments between 1929 and 1933. After 1933 he devoted most of his time to teaching and research. In November 1940 he was assassinated by the Iron Guard, the Rumanian fascist organization.

Madgearu was initially preoccupied with industry, which he thought was essential for the healthy development of every country. His own investigation of Rumania's economic development in the nineteenth century, which formed the basis of his doctoral dissertation of 1911, *Zur industriellen Entwicklung Rumäniens*, persuaded him that Rumania was by no means destined to remain an exclusively agricultural country. But he was already concerned that the forms which industry assumed in Rumania be suited to the character and needs of the country. In an essay on the artisan crafts written in 1912 he found the underlying cause of their decline in the 'process of Westernization', which had introduced alien institutions into the Rumanian social fabric without regard to their compatibility with 'our national being'. He attributed to this 'abrupt break' with the past the cause of the many 'contradictions' between Rumania's 'spiritual foundations' and 'foreign forms', which lay at the heart of 'all our problems'.

By the end of the First World War Madgearu had decided that the fundamental task for Rumanian intellectuals was to bring the political institutions of the country into harmony with prevailing economic and social conditions. He thought that the founders of modern Rumania in the nineteenth century had committed an egregious error in ignoring substance in the interest of form. Madgearu and his Peasantist colleagues now proposed to reverse the procedure. They intended to make the peasantry and agriculture the principal object of government.

Madgearu's own effort to explain the true nature of Rumania's social and economic development focused upon the unique qualities of the small peasant holding. In formulating his theory, he was indebted to the Poporanists, especially Constantin Stere, for fundamental ideas about peasant agriculture. But he also drew extensively upon the writings of the Russian agricultural economist, Alexander Chayanov, especially his *Die Lehre von der bäuerlichen Wirtschaft* (1923), which provided the theoretical foundation for Madgearu's analysis of the Rumanian family holding. He was attracted particularly to Chayanov's arguments about the qualitative differences existing between peasant agriculture, on the one hand, and the large-scale, capitalist agricultural enterprise, on the other.

Madgearu was at pains to demonstrate the viability of the small peasant holding, for upon it rested not only the validity of Peasantist economic and social theory but also the political doctrine of the peasant state. He admitted, along with Chayanov, that the large-scale enterprise had certain advantages over the smallholding, but these, he insisted, were technological and would eventually reach their natural economic limit, at which point the large enterprise would become 'irrational' and would, accordingly, break down. He argued that peasant holdings, despite their technological inferiority to the capitalist farm, had not only not disappeared, but had, in fact, become stronger. The key to that strength he discerned in a special quality of the peasant holding—production by the family. That economic activity, he insisted, was governed by laws of its own, especially a different conception of gain and a different economic psychology from those of the capitalist enterprise.[24] He had to admit that capitalism dominated the contemporary world economy, but beside it and separate from it, he claimed, existed an agriculture with its own distinctive mode of production and its own idea of gain, a conception which calls to mind Lucian Blaga's theory of major and minor cultures.

In his analysis of the economic activity of the family holding Madgearu showed how its size and level of production were determined mainly by 'natural, organic forces', how, for example, the number of members in the family, their ages, and their ability to work a given amount of land set the physical limits of the holding itself. He also pointed out that the total amount produced depended, in turn, upon the number of workers and consumers on the holding, since the chief incentive for its economic activity was the satisfaction of the needs of its members, not profit.

As Madgearu surveyed the condition of Rumanian agriculture after the post-war agrarian reforms, he was certain that the peasantry stood on the threshold of a new era. He thought that the moment had come at last for the creation of a peasant third way between capitalism and socialism. For him, Rumanian agriculture had been 'peasantized', by which he meant that most of the arable land was now composed of smallholdings. Statistics supported this view. As a result of the reforms, some 6 million hectares had been expropriated from large holdings, and by 1934 3.5 million hectares had become peasant property with about 1.5 million persons receiving land. As of that year small property made up almost 90 per cent of all arable land as opposed to roughly 52 per cent before the reforms.[25]

[24] Virgil Madgearu, 'Teoria economiei ţărăneşti', in V. Madgearu, Agrarianism. Capitalism. Imperialism (Bucharest, 1936), 60.
[25] Virgil Madgearu, 'Revoluţia agrară şi evoluţia clasei ţărăneşti', in V. Madgearu, Agrarianism. Capitalism. Imperialism, 40–1. D. Şandru, 'Considérations

In the wake of these 'revolutionary' changes in landholding Madgearu, in the 1920s, was certain that the family holding would endure. First of all, its unique character struck him as a major source of strength. He drew a sharp distinction between agricultural and industrial production. The former, he declared, could never assume the mode of the latter. Although agriculture, like industry, required the use of labour and capital, the former remained tied to nature, to the vagaries of the weather and the quality of the soil. Nor, in his view, was the concentration of productive forces into large enterprises feasible in agriculture. Such a process, he thought, was applicable only to capitalist industry, because of inherent differences between agricultural and industrial production. Calling the former 'organic' and the latter 'mechanical', he, in effect, accepted the philosophical-cultural dichotomy of 'culture' and 'civilization' as the cause of the incompatibility between Western economic theory and Rumanian economic reality. That fundamental incompatibility persuaded him that Rumanian agriculture could never be geared to the capitalist system, nor, consequently, could Rumanian economic development in general follow the Western European pattern.

Madgearu backed up his claim about the superiority of the small peasant holding to the large agricultural enterprise by demonstrating the former's great profitability. He cited, for example, the reduced expenses of production per surface unit, made possible by the family's ability to perform a multiplicity of tasks by itself without specialized personnel or hired labour and without large investments of capital. Such a degree of self-sufficiency had the additional merit, in his view, of protecting the small proprietor from entanglement in the capitalist system. Accordingly, he argued that the family holding had amply demonstrated the superiority of small, non-capitalist agriculture during the world economic depression of 1929–33. He pointed out that the smallholder had been better able than the large capitalist farmer to withstand the crisis because he could reduce expenses to an absolute minimum, could live off his own production without having to purchase food, and could withhold his own produce from the market until prices rose.

Madgearu was equally sanguine about the durability of the small family holding. He was so certain that the future of

Rumanian agriculture belonged to the peasant producer that he refused to consider such obvious contradictions as the increasing social differentiation within the peasantry as anything more than temporary aberrations. He confidently predicted in 1924 that the dominant peasant category was destined to be the small proprietor, working the land with the aid of his family and enjoying economic autonomy.[26]

In the 1920s Madgearu firmly opposed the expansion of the capitalist system and of large-scale industry in Rumania. He thought both were fundamentally at odds with her agrarian character. In a speech before the Chamber of Deputies in 1927 he went so far as to claim that Rumania could never become an industrial state and urged that such an 'illusion', which the Liberal Party and its middle-class supporters were promoting, be abandoned once and for all.

Madgearu's opposition to capitalism rested upon his analysis of its development in nineteenth-century Rumania as 'abnormal'. He argued that it did not evolve naturally out of economic and social conditions in Rumania, but owed its growth primarily to foreign interest in her foodstuffs and raw materials after 1829, when these goods came onto the international market in large quantities. Madgearu admitted that great amounts of Western capital flowed into Rumania from that time on, but he denied that it brought fundamental changes to her essentially 'agrarian feudal' economic structure or revolutionized the mode of production, for European investors had no interest in doing so: they had only one concern— to assure themselves of raw materials for their own needs. Nor did he find that native capital exerted any greater influence upon the organization of Rumania's economy: it served merely as an 'annexe' to foreign capital. He therefore concluded that a true bourgeoisie, in the Western European sense, did not develop in Rumania. Rather, her leading class was a political and economic oligarchy, which, instead of abolishing agrarian feudalism and thereby releasing the productive forces of agriculture, chose to maintain existing economic and social structures and to create, alongside it, a new source of income—national industry. That industry, he found, was artificial, for the oligarchy had 'forced' it by providing tariff protection and other encouragements, and the West had supported it by exporting technology and capital. None the less, the oligarchy proceeded to create a political and legal

[26] Virgil Madgearu, 'Doctrina ţărănistă', in *Doctrinele partidelor politice* (Bucharest, 1924), 72.

framework which it deemed appropriate for a modern state, but which, in fact, had little relation to economic and social reality.

Madgearu credited the Rumanian Social Democratic theorist, Constantin Dobrogeanu-Gherea, with having discerned the fundamental contradiction in the organization of Rumanian society at the beginning of twentieth century—political and legal institutions suitable for Western bourgeois society overlaying a backward agrarian economic structure characteristic of pre-modern times—a system he called *neoiobăgia* (neo-serfdom). For Madgearu, that was the supreme contrast between form and substance.

Other Peasantists held views on peasant proprietorship similar to Madgearu's. Ion Mihalache (1882–1963), one of the founders of the Peasant Party in 1918 and a leading political figure in the inter-war period, attempted to harmonize Peasantist theory with day-to-day problems of economic organization and political competition. Writing in 1925, he took a more radical approach to the land question than his more scholarly colleague, Madgearu. Under the 'new agrarian regime' that he foresaw in Rumania, large property would no longer exist, except as model farms and other necessary supports for small-scale agriculture. In any case, it would no longer be the foundation of a social class that exploited other workers in agriculture. Mihalache's ideas on the lack of significant social differentiation among the peasantry also resembled Madgearu's, but once again he was more categorical, if less profound: there would be neither a middle-sized peasantry (since its land would be expropriated for the benefit of the small family holding) nor an agricultural proletariat (since only those persons would remain in agriculture who were needed to do the work). Like other Peasantists, he relegated industry to a supporting role for agriculture.

The foundation of Mihalache's new agrarian regime was the small, independent holding. He defined small property as the amount of arable land a peasant and his family could work efficiently with occasional help from his peers, but without exploiting the labour of other social categories. This type of property, he argued, would assure a maximum of production, if the new agrarian order could guarantee the peasant proprietor all the rewards of his labour.[27] He had no doubt that this was the direction modern Rumanian economic development was destined to take.

---

[27] Ion Mihalache, *Noul regim agrar* (n.p., 1925), 6–8.

Such was the Peasantist economic and social ideal. But the actual state of small peasant agriculture in the 1920s and especially the 1930s deviated strikingly from the vision entertained by Madgearu and Mihalache. Conditions prevailing in the countryside were such as to call into question the whole theory about the strength and durability of the small family holding. A large number of peasant households, perhaps one-third, had incomes inadequate to meet even bare necessities. The consequences of such poverty were housing, nourishment, and sanitation well below minimum standards, which, in turn, contributed to an abnormally high mortality rate and seriously diminished the working capacity of a large segment of the rural population. The way out of poverty was blocked by endemic overpopulation, holdings too small and too scattered to be economically viable, and backward methods of farming, all, in turn, reinforcing the chronic low level of productivity.

Madgearu was painfully aware of the poverty and shortcomings in production among the peasantry, and he was determined to make fundamental changes in the way agriculture was organized. In seeking solutions, he remained by and large faithful to Peasantist doctrine and decided that the co-operative system was the best means of modernizing Rumania's agriculture without jeopardizing her non-capitalist economic and social structure. He thought of the co-operative as an association based upon mutual aid and income from labour and excluding the idea of profit. He characterized it as non-capitalist and peculiarly suited to the nature of peasant agriculture, ideals given form in the new law on co-operatives enacted by the National Peasant government in 1929.

Madgearu thought that co-operatives could serve many purposes, but none more vital than protecting the family holding from 'contamination' and eventual dissolution by capitalist forms. Although he was thus certain that the production methods of the family holding could be made immune to capitalism, he recognized that in time capitalist structures could come to dominate agriculture through the control of credit and the distribution of goods. He warned that through its relations with the market every small peasant holding became a part of the world economy and subject to its dictation about what could be produced and what price could be charged. Although he saw no evidence that capitalism as a world economic system had as yet penetrated the mass of peasant holdings through a restructuring of production on a capitalist basis, he was genuinely alarmed by the control which the capitalist market already exercised over peasant production through its 'commercial apparatus'. The main purpose of co-operatives, as he saw it, was to enable peasants to get control of all the links, notably commerce and credit, between themselves and the world market. In this way, he predicted, the devices of capitalist exploitation would become simply the technical instruments by which the peasant family holding would become stronger. He therefore gave full support to co-operatives of all kinds—credit, producer, and consumer—as the best means of saving the family holding from extinction and of placing the entire organization of agricultural production on a rational, yet natural, basis.

Madgearu was profoundly dissatisfied with the existing state of the co-operative movement. Despite impressive growth statistics, he realized that it had failed to achieve its potential. The situation in the credit co-operatives was particularly disappointing. Although they were prospering and steadily increasing in number, they were not, Madgearu complained, governed by the true spirit of co-operation, but were, rather, capitalist enterprises dominated by the village bourgeoisie and, occasionally, landlords, whose main concern was to obtain as high dividends as possible for themselves and other shareholders. Production co-operatives had also failed to achieve their goals. Their founders had assigned them a variety of tasks deemed essential for the rationalization and intensification of agricultural production—the acquisition of tools, machinery, and seeds, the organization of work in common, and the marketing of produce—but they had simply not prospered. Faced with such discouraging results, Madgearu repeatedly demanded an overhaul of the entire co-operative system: otherwise, he had little hope that the obstacles to a healthy agriculture could be overcome.

Yet, there were limits to the degree of co-operation Madgearu would allow. He was, for example, firmly opposed to a bill introduced in 1931 by Gheorghe Ionescu-Şişeşti, the Minister of Agriculture in the short-lived government headed by Nicolae Iorga, which provided for the organization of a new type of producer co-operative that would combine all the holdings of various categories of peasants into a single economic unit. Ionescu-Şişeşti, a specialist in agrarian problems, was persuaded that such large complexes would benefit all concerned because they would reduce expenses and increase both the quantity and quality of the produce. But Madgearu was of a different opinion. It struck him as extremely risky to tamper with small property and the system of production based upon it, and, anyway, he doubted that such associations of producers would work, because of the ingrained individualist psychology of the peasant. He evidently had in mind the peasant's demonstrated attachment to his own piece of land, but Madgearu's ideological commitment to the family holding as the basis for the organization of agriculture also made him wary of any plan that smacked of collectivization. In any case, Madgearu seems to have been correct in his assessment of the peasant reaction to the scheme. Although various financial incentives were offered these co-operatives, such as low-interest credit, only about a hundred were established, and most of these were short-lived.

Madgearu could see little possibility, at least in the 1920s, of a strong industry developing in Rumania. Besides the standard arguments about the pre-eminently agricultural character of the country, he cited the absence of a strong domestic market for Rumanian manufactures, which was caused by the low standard of living and the lack of purchasing power of the majority of the peasantry. He continued to oppose 'artificial' industries because, in the long run, such enterprises adversely affected the national economy by diverting scarce resources away from the development of the 'natural factors' of the economy, that is, from agriculture.[28] Yet, he looked forward to the time when a 'healthy industry' serving the needs of the peasantry would come into being. He thought that the initiative would have to come from the countryside itself as the success of the family holding enhanced productivity and improved standards of living. The growing prosperity in the countryside would, in turn, create new needs and expand the domestic market for processed goods. Madgearu was certain that the urban classes would benefit greatly, and, as their standard of living rose, they would naturally increase their purchases of products from the countryside. This, he argued, was the 'real' foundation of a national industry.

As the political foundation of Peasantism, Madgearu sought to create a new type of state which would satisfy once and for all the needs and aspirations of the great mass of the population and would at the same time recognize the fact that the social and economic development of Rumania was destined to remain different from that of the capitalist West. Implicit was his assumption

[28] Virgil Madgearu, *Ţărănismul* (Bucharest, 1921), 24, 57–8.

that the peasantry formed a separate class, distinct both economically and psychologically from the bourgeoisie and the urban
proletariat, and that, consequently, the state which represented the
peasantry must also differ from bourgeois and socialist political
structures. He called the new entity the peasant state.

At the heart of his doctrine of the peasant state was the certainty
that the peasantry had become the decisive force in Rumanian
political development as a result of the reforms enacted after the
First World War. He thought the time had at last come for the
creation of a strong peasant political organization as a means of
bringing to fruition Peasantist economic and social goals. He
dismissed as nonsense the claims of Liberal and Social Democrat
leaders that the peasantry was incapable of sustaining a party of its
own or even of formulating a distinct programme because, somehow, it lacked class consciousness and 'political instinct'. Madgearu
saw no reason for the peasantry always to follow in the wake of
one or another of the established parties, and he declared Peasantism
to be the beginning of a 'political renaissance' that would completely transform the social and political structure of the country.

As for the political forms that would be most advantageous to
his constituency, Madgearu unhesitatingly opted for parliamentary
democracy. Throughout the inter-war period, especially in the
1930s as the drift to the right gained mometum, he stood forth
as a champion of government for and by the people. Unlike
many pro-peasant intellectuals who rejected not only bourgeois
industrial society but also its political forms as imports unsuited to
Rumanian conditions, he never wavered in his commitment to
'genuine democracy'. By that term he meant a system of government based upon the freely expressed will of the majority and a
truly representative legislature capable of preventing the 'industrial
and financial oligarchy' from using democratic processes for its
own selfish ends.

Madgearu was enough of a realist to know that for his brand
of democracy to work the mass of the peasants had to acquire
political experience. And that, he was certain, could happen only
if the administrative system were opened sufficiently to allow for
broad citizen participation in public affairs. As a first step he
proposed a reform of village and district government that would
replace administrators appointed by and responsible to the central
government by locally elected officials and representatives who
would henceforth manage local affairs. In any case, he rejected
abrupt change or violence as merely the prelude to 'social catas-

trophe'. Change, to be beneficial and enduring, must, he warned, be 'organic', a gradual process rooted in the national experience.[29]

Madgearu's idea of change helps to explain his reserve toward Western European political institutions. In politics as in economic development he made a sharp distinction between the Eastern and Western experience. This comparative approach persuaded him that his brand of peasant democracy would in the long run prove superior to the 'bourgeois' form that had evolved in Western Europe. The economic crisis of the early 1930s had crystallized his thought on the subject. Certain that the 'bourgeois-liberal social order' was in decline, he perceived as the main cause of this phenomenon a striking contradiction in Western society, which had been exacerbated by the recent depression. He saw an infrastructure based upon economic and social inequality, on the one hand, and, on the other, a democratic superstructure based upon equality before the law and universal suffrage. This contradiction, in Madgearu's view, was inherent in bourgeois, individualist democracy and, therefore, could never be resolved. But he by no means despaired of democracy itself. Nor, as his strictures on both the Nazi and Soviet dictatorships showed, did he seek an alternative in some form of authoritarianism.

Nevertheless, he was determined to avoid the 'pitfalls' of Western democracy, which, in his view, came down to an exaggerated emphasis upon individual rights and an almost complete disregard of individual responsibilities toward society. This style of democracy, which proclaimed liberty as an inalienable right, but ignored the principles of equal opportunity and social justice, was based, Madgearu concluded, upon legal abstractions and had failed to keep pace with the general evolution of society.

By contrast, the rural democracy which he recommended so enthusiastically had arisen out of specific Rumanian conditions and, hence, could respond more effectively than bourgeois democracy to the prevailing needs of Rumanian society. By combining parliamentary democracy with social responsibility, Rumanian rural democracy would, he had no doubt, prove superior to its Western counterpart.

Other Peasantists besides Madgearu speculated on the nature of the peasant state and its role in national development. Constantin Rădulescu-Motru approached the idea of the peasant state from a

---

[29] Virgil Madgearu, 'Tendinţele de renovare ale democraţiei', *Viaţa românească*, 28/5–6 (1935), 13.

philosophical-cultural standpoint. Unlike Madgearu, who emphasized a restructuring of economic and political institutions, Rădulescu-Motru conceived of the peasant state as the foundation of a spiritual renewal of the Rumanian nation. He by no means ignored the importance of economic and political reforms, but since the turn of the century he had treated social problems primarily as moral issues and, hence, as susceptible to moral solutions. His hostility to the 'bourgeois state', evident in *Cultura română şi politicianismul* in 1904, did not abate in the inter-war period. He disdained the political system 'sanctioned' by the Constitution of 1923 as 'contractual' and 'unorganic' because it had placed the state on bourgeois foundations and had ignored the contribution of the peasantry to the development of the nation. To take the place of the old liberal, bourgeois state he proposed a type of political organization that would re-establish the 'natural' relationship between the interests of the many, whose destinies were linked to the land, and the interests of the few, who were engaged in industry and commerce. Rădulescu-Motru called such a formula a policy of 'realities', for it took into account the contributions to the nation and the aspirations of the overwhelming majority of the population. Although he assigned numerous specific social and economic tasks to the peasant state, he thought its primary mission should be a spiritual one. He had in mind nothing less than a national regeneration, which was to be brought about by re-establishing continuity with traditional institutions. In his view, the whole process had to begin with the village. Lamenting the passing of the old rural political and social structures, he called for a 'return to the village' as offering an enduring solution to the 'contradictions' of modern Rumania.[30]

The world economic crisis of the early 1930s, which caused havoc with the economies of agricultural countries like Rumania, profoundly affected Peasantist thought. Madgearu was obliged to modify his stand on industrialization. He had been influenced particularly by the inability of Rumania and other East European countries to gain tariff concessions for their agricultural products from the industrialized states of Western Europe. The failure of one international economic conference after another to reach an understanding led Madgearu to conclude that the only recourse for agricultural countries was to diversify their economies. He had

---

[30] Constantin Rădulescu-Motru, *Românismul: catehismul unei noi spiritualităţi*, 2nd edn. (Bucharest, 1939), 169–77.

been especially alarmed by the tendencies of the industrialized states of Western Europe to achieve self-sufficiency by intensifying their own agricultural production, action, he feared, that might permanently reduce their purchases from Eastern Europe. He was also on guard against what seemed to him by 1938 to be Germany's expansionist plans aimed at drawing the agrarian economies of South-eastern Europe into her autarkic economic zone.

At first Madgearu thought that a policy of industrialization geared toward the processing of agricultural products and the country's principal raw materials, which would relieve rural over-population and increase peasant income, would be enough. He still opposed 'parasitical' industries, that is, those which could not stand by themselves, but 'drained' the state budget and 'preyed upon' the consumer. But the 'reagrarianization' of the industrialized West, notably Germany, had finally convinced him that forced industrialization, even though it was contrary to the prevailing 'natural conditions' in Rumania, was the only way to expand the domestic market for agricultural products and to lessen the country's dependence on the international market.

By the mid-1930s, as Rumania experienced a gradual economic recovery, Madgearu was praising industrialization as a 'natural phenomenon' and as an aspect of the 'general process' of the economic evolution of peoples. Recognizing the close connection between agriculture and industry, he perceived various advantages for underdeveloped countries in industrialization, such as the introduction of new and more efficient methods of production, a reduction in costs and prices and a general increase in purchasing power, and an expansion of markets. He also thought that the industrialization of agricultural countries would strengthen rather than harm economic exchanges with the West because the growing prosperity and purchasing power of the former would create a demand for new products from the latter. He cited as evidence German trade with Czechoslovakia, which was more extensive than with the underdeveloped agrarian states of Eastern Europe. Madgearu's reappraisal of industrialization had wide support among Peasantists, and in 1935 the National Peasant Party fully endorsed his point of view.

As Madgearu contemplated the many facets of agrarian reform and industrialization and the equally daunting task of managing a complex economy, he assigned the key role of co-ordinator to the state. This was not a new idea for him. He had envisaged an active role for the state in the national economy early in his career, but the general economic crisis of the 1930s had convinced him that the age of economic liberalism in Europe had passed once and for all. Although he did not share the assumptions of some of his Peasantist colleagues about the imminent demise of Western capitalism, he was unwilling to leave the economic initiative solely in private hands. He proposed instead state planning and co-ordination, which he called *dirijism*. The early successes of the New Deal or, as he called it, the 'Roosevelt Revolution', in reviving and reconstructing the American economy encouraged him to think that state intervention might have similar beneficial results in his own country.[31]

Madgearu thought that *dirijism* would function best in a socialist setting, but he stopped short of advocating a socialist transformation of the Rumanian economy, in part at least because of his commitment to private peasant holdings and his conception of peasant individualism. None the less, he thought that Rumania, because of her unique agrarian structure, might be able to adapt the principles of *dirijism* to her particular needs. He entertained no illusions about the complexity of the task. There was, first of all, the difficulty in rationalizing the agricultural organization and production of thousands of small, scattered holdings. No less formidable an obstacle was the psychology of the peasant, who, Madgearu claimed, farmed in accordance with his own needs and temperament and had little concern for the market or national economic goals.

In his last major work, *Evoluția economiei românești după războiul mondial* (The Evolution of the Rumanian Economy after the World War), published in 1940, Madgearu reviewed the economic and social developments of the inter-war period. He could dis-cern no fundamental change in the structure of the Rumanian economy: the capitalist sector in general was still small, since capitalism as a mode of production had touched only a few branches of industry in a significant way and agriculture main-tained its predominance. He concluded that there was still no possibility that the Rumanian economy could be integrated into the world capitalist system, for its structure continued to be determined by several million peasant holdings, which formed an economic network governed by values qualitatively different from those of a capitalist economy. Nevertheless, he could not ignore

---

[31] Virgil Madgearu, 'Revoluția Roosevelt', *Viața românească*, 26/9 (1934), 3–20.

the fact that capitalism exerted a powerful influence over Rumanian agriculture. Although he continued to deny that it had transformed the mode of production of peasant holdings, he had to admit that it had penetrated the mechanism of distribution and, as a consequence, had subordinated the 'whole essence' of the peasant holding to the capitalist market.[32]

All the participants in the debate over national character and paths of development agreed at least on one point: that Rumania had experienced rapid and significant change in the preceding century. Behind the rhetoric they also recognized that their country had become more like Western Europe. But they disagreed on whether the process of Europeanization had been good or bad, how deeply it had affected the structure of Rumanian society, and whether it should continue. The Europeanists stressed fundamental structural changes and insisted that there was no alternative to further cultural and economic integration into Europe, whereas the traditionalists treated Europeanization as merely a veneer of civilization which had not affected the inner, spiritual resources of the community and could be scraped away. The Peasantists sought a third way of development which would reconcile the political democracy and technology of the West with unique indigenous agrarian structures. The internal economic and political crises and the unsettled state of international relations in the interwar period provided a stern test of these visions of Rumania's future.

[32] Virgil Madgearu, *Evoluţia economiei româneşti după războiul mondial* (Bucharest, 1940), 358.

8
Society and the Economy, 1919–1940

Between the World Wars Rumania presented striking contrasts between entrenched underdevelopment and burgeoning, if uneven, industrialization and urbanization. On the one hand, her economic and social structure preserved in broad outline its prewar configuration. Agriculture remained the foundation of the country's economy, and its organization changed but little, despite an extensive land reform. The great majority of the population continued to live in the countryside and to draw its income primarily from agriculture. In international relations Rumania remained dependent on the West as a market for her agricultural products and raw materials and as a source of many kinds of manufactured goods and investment capital. Yet, signs of change were evident.

Industry grew and became increasingly capable of satisfying the needs of consumers, and imports of raw materials and semi-processed goods rose at a faster rate than manufactured items. The urban population expanded as cities enhanced their role in the organization and direction of the economy. Even agriculture gave evidence of change as the traditional reliance on grain production shifted slightly in favour of vegetable and industrial crops. In all branches of the economy the state assumed an increasingly commanding role. Although it respected the private ownership of land and the means of production and granted private capital, domestic and foreign, numerous advantages, it arrogated to itself the responsibility for the planning and management of what came to be regularly called the 'national economy'.

POPULATION

The population of Rumania in 1930, when the only complete census in the inter-war period was taken, was 18,052,896, a figure which represented a growth of about 2.5 million over

the estimated population in 1920. In 1939 the population was
19,933,802. Thus, it grew by nearly four million during the inter-
war period. The density of population also increased, from an
estimated 55.2 inhabitants per square kilometre on the eve of the
First World War for the territories that would later compose
Greater Rumania to 67.6 in 1939. The rate of increase was greater
than that of Europe as a whole. Between 1930 and 1933, for
example, the median density in Europe grew by 1.1 inhabitants
per square kilometre, in Rumania by 2.5.[1]

The population remained overwhelmingly rural, and the percentage of rural over urban inhabitants increased steadily throughout
the inter-war period. In 1920 the rural population was 12,087,612
(77.8 per cent) and the urban 3,453,812 (22.2 per cent); by 1939
the figures were, respectively, 16,312,136 (81.8 per cent) and
3,621,666 (18.2 per cent). Thus, the total increase of rural inhabitants for the period was 4,234,524, while the population of
cities grew by only 167,854. In 1930 significant differences in the
proportion of urban dwellers existed from province to province.
Muntenia was the most urbanized (27.1 per cent of the population), and Bessarabia the least (12.9 per cent). But in the latter
province the *sat-tîrguri*, village-market towns, which were not
included in the urban statistics, were numerous. They served as
indispensable local economic centres and, to a limited extent, took
the place of true cities.

Population growth was the result of a high birth rate, almost
double that of Western and Northern Europe, and a modest
decline in the death rate. Yet, in the inter-war period the birth rate
was significantly lower than it had been in the years immediately
before the First World War and continued to decline from 39.4
births per thousand inhabitants in 1921 to 28.3 in 1939. The
decline was most pronounced in the countryside, from 44.2 births
per thousand inhabitants in 1921 to 29.9 in 1939. In the urban
centres the rate remained steady, but was much smaller than in the
rural areas (22.7 in 1921; 20.9 in 1939). There were significant
variations from region to region. In the Old Kingdom (Wallachia
and Moldavia) and Bessarabia the birth rate remained high, well
above the European average, but in Transylvania and the Banat

---

[1] D. C. Georgescu, 'Populaţia satelor româneşti', *Sociologie românească*, 2/2–3
(1937), 68; Sabin Manuila and D. C. Georgescu, *Populaţia României* (Bucharest,
1937), 9.

the rate declined markedly, in the latter reaching a level barely half that of the Old Kingdom.[2]

Other aspects of the demographic processes of inter-war Rumania present a generally somber picture. The Rumanian statistician, Sabin Manuila, in an unpublished study, *Spre 20 milioane de locuitori* (Toward 20 Million Inhabitants), comparing the situation in his own country with the industrialized states of Europe, observed that in none of them was life expectancy so low and the chances of survival of the newborn so bleak as in Rumania. The death rate remained alarmingly high, especially for children under 1 year. Little progress in lowering infant mortality was made during the period. Between 1871 and 1891 the average was 19.2 deaths per hundred, and in 1935 it was still 19.2, the highest rate in Europe. On the average, in the inter-war period, 120,000 children died every year before they reached their first birthday. The main causes were poor diet and lack of care of the mother, who suffered especially from overwork during pregnancy. The death rate for children between 1 and 4 years was also high, caused in the first instance by bronchial ailments, pneumonia, and various gastric illnesses resulting from a poor diet. Health studies of preschool children, aged 3–7, showed that about half were below normal weight and height, a condition attributed mainly to malnutrition. Among the population as a whole the death rate also remained the highest in Europe. Besides an inadequate diet, poor sanitation, and often substandard housing, medical services were woefully deficient, especially in the countryside. Here doctors were few and medicines, even when available, were expensive. According to various estimates, at least one-third of those who died in the rural areas had never seen a doctor and had never taken any sort of medicine. As late as 1935 the death rate for the general population was 21.1 per thousand before falling to 18.6 in 1939. However disturbing these figures may be, they none the less represent a significant decline from the immediate pre-war years, when, for example, in 1910 there were 25.1 deaths per thousand. Life expectancy was also improving. In 1912–13 it was about 40.8 years, and in 1940, 48–50 years.[3]

The movement of people into and out of the country had little effect on population growth. The most massive emigration took

---

[2] Manuila and Georgescu, *Populaţia României*, 79–88; Sabin Manuila, *Structure et évolution de la population rurale* (Bucharest, 1940), 39–54.

[3] D. Şandru, *Populaţia rurală a României între cele două războaie mondiale* (Iaşi, 1980), 18–27.

place in the years immediately after the First World War when some 200,000 Magyars left Transylvania for Hungary. Many had been employed in public administration or were business and professional men who were being replaced by Rumanians. The second largest contingent of emigrants were the 42,000 Turks, who left Dobrudja for Turkey. Emigration to the United States was relatively modest: 67,646 between 1921 and 1930, and only 3,871 in the following decade. Of these, over half were Jews. Immigration to Rumania was modest. The two most significant movements of population occurred between 1918 and 1921 from Soviet Russia, when 22,000 Jews crossed into Bessarabia, and in the 1920s when some 20,000 Rumanians returned to Transylvania and Bukovina from the United States, usually to buy land and settle in the village they had left before the First World War.

Ethnically, the Rumanians formed a substantial majority of the population. In 1930 they composed 71.9 per cent of the total (12,981,324), while the largest minority, the Magyars, represented 7.2 per cent (1,415,507), followed by the Germans, 4.1 per cent (745,421), Jews 4 per cent (728,115), and Ukrainians 3.2 per cent (582,115). But these proportions varied significantly from region to region. For example, the Magyars formed 29 per cent of the population in Transylvania and 23 per cent in Crişana and Maramureş, while Germans made up 24 per cent of the inhabitants of the Banat, and 8 per cent in Transylvania. Jews were most numerous in Bukovina (10.8 per cent of the population) and Bessarabia (7 per cent). The minorities constituted a significant proportion of the urban population. Jews were 30 per cent of the urban population in Bukovina, 27 per cent in Bessarabia, and 23 per cent in Moldavia. In Transylvania between 1910 and 1930, despite the boundary changes, the proportion of non-Rumanians living in cities increased, even though the Rumanian urban population more than doubled. In 1930, 27 per cent of Magyars, 23 per cent of Saxons, and 10.1 per cent of Rumanians (as compared to 10.6 per cent in 1910) lived in cities.[4]

THE RURAL WORLD

Agriculture remained the chief occupation of Rumania's rural inhabitants, and landholding to a great extent continued to deter-

---

[4] Manuila and Georgescu, *Populaţia României*, 50–9.

mine their social relations. According to the census of 1930, 90.4 per cent of the rural active population had agriculture—crop, animal husbandry, wine-making, and orchards—as its primary source of income. Significant economic and social differences divided this population into distinct strata.[5] Broadly speaking, those who had less than five hectares were classified as 'peasant households', while those holdings over 500 hectares were known as 'factories', for they usually produced grain for the foreign market and belonged to members of the upper bourgeoisie or the former boier class. In between were estates (*moşii*), which were divided up and rented out to peasants in return for a tithe, and 'farms' (*ferme*), commercialized holdings owned by city-dwellers. The social differences between the owners of *moşii* and *ferme* were not great, no matter what the precise size of the holding was, for they usually had other sources of income and, in any case, shared the same urban life style.

Among peasant holders social differences were more sharply defined. A few hectares more or less might place one in a different category. At the top of this particular social hierarchy were the *chiaburi* (rich peasants) with holdings of 50–500 hectares, who employed hired hands and lived in a style similar to that of the village intellectuals. They possessed enough land, animals, and machines and tools to satisfy all their needs from agriculture. Next came the *ţărani cu stare* (well-off peasants), who had holdings of 10–50 hectares and who followed the typical, limited peasant life style, working alongside their hired help. They have sometimes been described as the 'dynamic mass' of the Rumanian peasantry and represented 5–20 per cent of the inhabitants of every village. They had enough land to cover their limited needs, but they usually added to their incomes by engaging in non-agricultural pursuits. Yet, for them, such supplements were of relatively little importance. The *mici gospodari* (smallholders), with 3–10 hectares, maintained their independence and usually had sufficient draft animals and tools, but they were rarely able to engage hired labour. *Gospodari dependenţi* (dependent smallholders), possessing 1–3 hectares, lacked sufficient animals and tools and to a much greater extent than the independent smallholders they needed employment outside agriculture in order to

---

[5] For an analysis of rural social structure, see Anton Golopenţia, 'Starea culturală şi economică a populaţiei rurale din România', *Revista de igiena socială*, 10/1–6 (1940), 240–6.

make ends meet. Such sources of income were critical for the *muncitori agricoli cu pămînt* (agricultural workers with land), who possessed less than 1 hectare. They had no choice but to work for rich and well-to-do peasants and even migrated to other regions or to cities to find work, leaving the small plot of land in the care of their wives. The yields of such smallholdings were incapable of supporting a family adequately. At the bottom of the social scale came agricultural labourers without land. It is difficult to estimate how many there were, because of the variety of terms used to describe them in official statistics, but the census of 1930 indicates that there were over 500,000. The middlemen of the rural world, the *arendaşi*, were still active, but they had lost their pre-war prominence in village life, owing in large measure to the agrarian reform. A variety of persons, none the less, continued to be engaged in the leasing of lands of every category, but few derived their income solely from this source, and, in any case, the great pre-war leasing trusts had disappeared.

Peasants who had less than 10 hectares of land and who felt obliged to find other sources of income in order to maintain their standard of living often rented additional land in return for payment of a tithe or a money rent. Other, especially poor, peasants hired themselves out as day labourers, usually during the height of the harvest season, moving from place to place as the demand for labour required. The opportunities were better in some regions than in others. In Muntenia and Moldavia, for example, where *moşii* were numerous and where labour was abundant and the competition for additional land intense, landowners could often impose extravagant terms. The condition of many peasants here, therefore, did not differ markedly from what it had been before the agrarian reform. Still other peasants, especially in Muntenia and Transylvania, supplemented their incomes by practising a trade at home or by carrying on a modest retail trade between their home village or district and a large city. A few practised the traditional village artisan crafts of carpentry and blacksmithing to meet local needs, but such opportunities were fewer than before the war. In some areas, notably the Banat, smallholders who had difficulty making ends meet had no other choice but to limit the size of their families. When all else failed many heads of households were simply obliged to take to the road in search of work in another village, *judeţ*, or even province. If they were artisans, they might be away from home for much of the year. The search for additional sources of income thus kept a large part of the rural population constantly mobile. Often a simple postcard home that work had been found was enough to set people in motion. But such mobility, though an economic necessity, had dire consequences for rural society: family life was disrupted, and the health of all its members put at risk.

Roughly 10 per cent of the active rural population depended upon activities other than agriculture as their main source of income. They were employed in some form of industry as artisans, miners, or factory hands, or they were engaged in commerce, often as peddlers, or in transportation, especially as labourers on the railway.

The great majority of peasants led a precarious material existence. A survey of 303 peasant households carried out in 1935 revealed that 35 per cent of gross income came from the growing of grain, vegetables, and industrial crops, 22 per cent from the raising of animals, and 42 per cent from non-agricultural occupations. Another survey of 424 peasant holdings of 2.5–15 hectares between 1930 and 1934 shows that they were not economically viable, for their gross incomes covered only the current expenses of working the holding, the labour of others outside the family, and the amortization of capital invested in the holding. There was nothing left over for anything else; the consequence was a substandard level of existence. Agriculture, the primary source of peasant income, did not even cover the cost of food. A study done in 1933–4 of the budgets of 159 holdings between 2.5 and 15 hectares reveals that for those peasants who had less than 10 hectares expenditures on food exceeded agricultural income. If the return from non-agricultural employment is taken into account, then the total income for holdings of 3–5 and 5–10 hectares was adequate to keep the family supplied with food. But this was not true for holdings under 3 hectares. Moreover, in none of these categories did income reach a level necessary to meet the combined costs of food, clothing, and such expenses as church, school, and health, not to mention taxes. To survive households had to limit their consumption of food and be satisfied with inadequate clothing and substandard housing, conditions which often led to serious illness and even death, or they could borrow money or sell their land and animals, acts of desperation which in the long run reduced the income of the holding still further. The economic predicament in which these families found themselves was not caused by wasteful spending. Food was the most important item in the family budget: on holdings of under 3 hectares it represented six-sevenths of all expenditures; of 3–10 hectares, three-quarters; and over 10 hectares, two-thirds. There was thus little left over to 'splurge' on clothing and other 'luxuries'.[6]

The diet of the majority of peasants was in every respect inadequate to maintain good health and a high level of productivity. It lacked variety. In almost every part of Rumania corn (*porumb*) was the basic food. In the Old Kingdom it constituted 70–95 per cent of the total of grains consumed, while elsewhere—Bukovina and Transylvania, for example—the proportion was somewhat less, perhaps 50 per cent, being partially replaced by wheat or rye. Corn was consumed especially in the form of *mămăligă*. A diet dependent upon a single food was unhealthy, particularly so in the case of corn, because it was an incomplete food and did not provide a mix of nutrients necessary for growth and protection against disease. The peasants' consumption of foods other than grains was generally low. Milk was one of these, and its absence from the diet had a debilitating effect on the intellectual and physical development of children. The main cause of low milk consumption was simply the absence of cows. Of 3.5 million rural families in 1935, some 2 million had no cows. Meat was also a rarity for the majority of peasant households. The relative scarcity of cows naturally affected meat consumption, but there were also 1.5 million rural families who kept no pigs. Studies made between 1930 and 1939 in certain parts of Moldavia, for example, reveal that the consumption of meat was only 4–8 kilograms per person per year. Although elsewhere figures varied widely, the conclusion that emerges for the country as a whole was that meat consumption by Rumanian peasants was much lower than that of peasants in other European countries. Potatoes were the most widely used vegetable, especially in Transylvania and Bukovina and the mountainous regions of the other provinces.[7]

The level of consumption by the rural population naturally depended upon the material circumstances of individual families, but the nourishment available to the rural poor was always insufficient. The latter were the least able to adjust to bad harvests or other crises. Since the poor peasant usually consumed more than half of what he produced, when hard times came he and his family simply ate less in order to have enough grain or vegetables for sale to meet the family's tax obligations and other fixed expenses. The peasant diet was also limited by custom, for the

---

[6] Ibid. 235–40.
[7] Şandru, *Populaţia rurală*, 137–59.

majority of peasant households tended to consume only what they themselves raised and, consequently, bought little on the market. Improvements in the diet of the rural population could only begin with an increase and diversification of agricultural production and a more substantial return to the peasant for his labour. These improvements, in turn, would depend upon how great a commitment the state was prepared to make to agriculture.

The mass of the rural population suffered from chronic poor health, because of an inadequate diet, rudimentary housing, and ignorance of elementary hygiene. Government measures brought only a slight improvement in these conditions. Although infectious diseases such as scarlet fever and measles were brought under control in the 1930s, social diseases increased during the same period. The most serious were syphilis, tuberculosis, and pellagra. The number of cases between 1930 and 1937 nearly doubled from 341,000 to 609,000. The incidence of pellagra was especially grave because it was the characteristic disease of poverty and after tuberculosis and cancer was the leading cause of death. It was widespread in regions where the cultivation of corn was most intense and where large quantities *mămăligă* formed the main item in the diet. A striking parallel exists between the extension of cropland devoted to corn and the increase in the incidence of pellagra. As the amount of land planted in corn in the inter-war period grew from 3,295,000 hectares to about 5 million, and as consumption rose from 15,700,000 quintals to 35,800,000 quintals between 1927 and 1937, the cases of pellagra almost doubled to 68,500 (the number of cases reported in 1937 fell drastically to 8,894 for unknown reasons).

Throughout the inter-war period strong forces militated against change in the village. Traditional culture retained its hold in such critical areas of rural life as diet, hygiene, and health care. These were the domains of women and the elderly, who rarely left the village and who read less than other groups. But there was also little progress in improving the methods of agriculture, the raising of animals, or the marketing of the crop. Nor did the experience of men in the army or of those engaged in seasonal labour far from home seem to have much effect on the life of their home village.

Rural education, in which agrarian reformers put great store as a force for change, made less of an impact than they had expected.[8]

[8] Anton Golopenția, 'Gradul de modernizare al regiunilor rurale ale României', *Sociologie românească*, 4/4–6 (1939), 209–17.

Although the number of persons who could read and write had grown steadily since the turn of the century, as of 1930, 48.5 per cent of the rural population over 7 years of age were still illiterate. The largest group continued to be women, who made up 61 per cent of all rural illiterates, a situation owing at least in part to the persistent notion that girls had no need of schooling. The overwhelming majority of rural children (94 per cent) received their only formal education in the primary school. As of 1930 only 2 per cent had attended secondary school, 0.7 per cent had had some sort of professional training, and 0.2 per cent, or roughly 20,000, had attended a university.

The primary school thus played a key role in opening up the village to the outside world, but for many reasons it failed to do its job properly. Although primary education was obligatory and free for all children between 7 and 14, large numbers (as many as 400,000 out of 2,800,000) were not even enrolled and many others who were did not attend school. In the school year 1931–2, for example, only about 70 per cent of those enrolled actually went to school. In a number of rural areas there were shortages of teachers, and schools, located in a village or town, could not easily be reached by many, isolated families. But the main reasons for poor attendance were often simply the lack of adequate clothing in the winter and the need for children to work on the family holding, especially during the spring planting and the autumn harvesting.

It is evident that the ability to read was not a panacea for what ailed rural society. A comprehensive survey of sixty villages carried out by Rumanian sociologists in the 1930s turned up public libraries in twenty-nine villages with a total of 50,000 inhabitants. Between 2,300 and 4,200 borrowers frequented these libraries every year, reading an average of two or three books a year. Most of these books were literary or religious; few were concerned with technical, economic, or health matters. The number of subscribers to newspapers and magazines, vehicles through which the rural population could learn about a wider world, was small, mainly because of widespread poverty; peasants, as we have seen, had more pressing needs than reading matter.

Despite the persistence of tradition in the rural world, what might be called a cultural interregnum prevailed in many areas. Because of the broad social changes taking place, traditional values were being undermined. Older people and women, especially, still cherished them, but the majority of men and the young viewed them with ambivalent feelings. The young were reluctant or even ashamed to follow old practices and beliefs, but they had not yet assimilated the elements of the new, essentially urban civilization. In only a few places by the end of the 1930s had a balance been established between traditional rural culture and middle-class values of the city.

URBAN DEVELOPMENT

Urban dwellers accounted for about 20 per cent of the total population in 1930. Their concentration in a small number of cities is striking. Of the 172 localities classified as cities, the twenty largest were home to more than half the urban population. The explanation lies in the fact that 53 per cent of all commercial, industrial, and transportation enterprises were located in these same cities. The great majority of other cities were simple urban agglomerations that served social and cultural needs and were local administrative centres and market-places for the exchange of agricultural and artisan goods. All these circumstances suggest that urbanization had as yet made only modest progress. Yet, in the 1930s its rhythm intensified. Between 1930 and 1941 the population of cities grew over 14 per cent. The increase was due almost exclusively to immigration from the countryside, which, as we have seen, had also been the major source of urban population before the First World War.[9] So great had this influx been in the previous sixty or seventy years that the population of cities had changed almost completely. Only 2–3 per cent belonged to a third or fourth urban generation. Bucharest provides a striking example: in 1930 only 15 per cent of its inhabitants had been born in the city; the rest were from the countryside or other cities. A large proportion of the newcomers seem to have been attracted by the opportunities for employment and the better wages offered by industry, but precise data are lacking. Many peasants were also drawn to the cities by commerce, transportation, and even the artisan crafts. The link between industrial growth and migration to the cities was especially evident during the economic crisis of the early 1930s, when both processes slowed simultaneously. To

[9] D. Şandru, 'The Growth of Romania's Urban Population between the Two World Wars through Peasant Immigration', *Nouvelles études d'histoire*, 6/1 (1980), 167–77.

some extent local authorities impeded the flow of people from the countryside during these years at the behest of the Ministry of Labour, Health, and Social Welfare, which was desperately seeking ways to alleviate urban unemployment and associated problems. When industry recovered and the impediments to migration were lifted in 1937 the influx into the cities resumed with even greater intensity than before.

Bucharest had a place apart in the urbanization process. As a complex administrative, economic, and cultural centre it grew at a rate and exercised an influence in public affairs far greater than any other city. Its population grew from 382,000 in 1918 to 631,000 in 1930 and approximately 870,000 in 1939, the most sustained growth in the city's history. By contrast, the second largest city (in 1930), Chişinău, had only 117,000 inhabitants. Bucharest owed its dramatic growth in part to its role as the capital of Greater Rumania, which required new and larger administrative institutions and an expanded bureaucracy. But the main reason was economic. Nowhere else in the country did industry expand so rapidly.[10] Many new factories were established and old ones enlarged. No other place offered the entrepreneur so many advantages: a large, cheap labour supply, a large consumer market, and proximity to major credit facilities and, most critical, to the government bureaux which dispensed ample economic favours. In the inter-war period, then, Bucharest became a true industrial centre, producing almost every type of manufactured goods. It was the home of several large industrial conglomerates such as the Malaxa Works, which produced, among other things, diesel engines, locomotives, and steel. By 1938 the city's industrial production accounted for 17 per cent of the country's total (22 per cent if a 20-mile radius around the city is counted). The financial, economic, and social life of the entire country was decisively influenced by its industry.

The economic development of Bucharest also affected nearby communities and led to the growth of numerous industrial suburbs. The evolution of Colentina-Fundeni, in 1899 a small rural commune of about 1,000 inhabitants, is typical.[11] What is immediately striking is the steady increase of population from 1,970 in 1912 and 5,950 in 1930 to 14,128 in 1939. The movement

---

[10] Constantin C. Giurescu, *Istoria Bucureştilor* (Bucharest, 1966), 181–5.
[11] Petru Onică, 'Evoluţia comunei suburbane Colentina-Fundeni', *Analele Institutului Statistic al României*, 1 (1942), 165–210.

of population to Colentina-Fundeni was mainly from Bucharest rather than from the surrounding countryside and was caused especially by an extraordinary increase in rents and lack of inexpensive housing in the capital in the inter-war period. In 1939 the majority of the inhabitants were artisans and skilled workers; few belonged to the professional middle class. A great variety of small industrial enterprises (slaughterhouses, tanneries, machine shops) and retail stores sprang up to serve the needs of the growing local population and even inhabitants of Bucharest, who came there to shop. A tramway line provided a regular link between the city and the suburb. Despite the growth of population and the intensification of economic activity, Colentina-Fundeni retained many characteristics of a rural commune, especially its housing, which tended to be small, one-storey, modestly built structures. But in the 1930s the amenities of urban life began to be introduced, notably electricity and drinking-water piped from Bucharest, and house construction (location, size, and materials to be used) became subject to the same regulations as those applied in Bucharest.

AGRICULTURE

The Agrarian Reforms, promised in 1917, were introduced between 1918 and 1921.[12] They differed in detail from province to province, thus reflecting the specific economic and social conditions under which each province had evolved. For example, the legislation in Transylvania and Bessarabia was more radical than that in the Old Kingdom and Bukovina, perhaps because in the former the revolutionary mood in 1917 and 1918 had been intense and landholding and national differences could not be separated. None the less, all these laws had as their primary goal the distribution of land to the peasants and were motivated more by social than strictly economic concerns.

In the Old Kingdom the Brătianu government moved swiftly to carry out agrarian reform. On 15 December 1918 a decree-law called for the full expropriation of all lands held by the crown,

---

[12] For the agrarian reform legislation in the Old Kingdom, Transylvania, and Bukovina, see D. Şandru, *Reforma agrară din 1921 în România* (Bucharest, 1975), 42–79; for Bessarabia, see Ion Nistor, *Istoria Basarabiei* (Cernăuţi, 1923), 315–19, and Constantinescu, *L'Évolution de la propriété rurale et la réforme agrare en Roumanie* (Bucharest, 1925), 418–22.

public and private institutions, absentee owners, and foreigners, and private property over 500 hectares. But the owners of multiple estates were protected by the provision that expropriation would be based upon separate properties rather than total holdings. The former owners were to be compensated by bonds bearing 5 per cent interest and redeemable in fifty years. Peasants who received land were responsible for paying about two-thirds of the compensation and the state one-third.

Political changes prevented the implementation of the law. Brătianu's resignation on 27 September 1919 to protest Rumania's treatment at the Paris peace conference led to a defeat of the Liberals at the polls and their replacement by the so-called parliamentary bloc, which sponsored a more radical agrarian law drafted by the new Minister of Agriculture, Ion Mihalache, a leader of the recently formed Peasant Party. Unlike the proposals of 1917 and 1918, which were in essence political acts designed by landlords to stave off a feared massive peasant uprising, Mihalache's bill expressed a peasant point of view and was clearly influenced by the more drastic agrarian reform introduced in Bessarabia. It provided for the expropriation of all private arable land over 100 hectares, to be based on the landowner's total holdings, except for commercial farms of 250–500 hectares, and limited the use of lands that remained to their owners by prohibiting their leasing, except to peasant co-operatives. Mihalache could not get such a bill through parliament. The strong landlord lobby, supported by Liberal political and economic interests, persuaded King Ferdinand to dismiss the parliamentary bloc government, even though it commanded a substantial majority in the Chamber of Deputies.

A more conservative government, headed by General Averescu, which assumed office in March 1920, took responsibility for agrarian reform. Averescu's Minister of Agriculture, Constantin Garoflid, had opposed earlier reform measures, especially the provisions which would have completely replaced large estates by smallholdings, because he thought that such action would completely disrupt agricultural production. A new Land Reform Law, which he drew up, was promulgated on 17 July 1921. It did not differ in essentials from the original law, despite Garoflid's objections to it. Indeed, the peasants benefited, for now the allocation of land to them was to take greater account of terrain (hills or plains) and individual needs than the earlier law. Garoflid assumed that 5 hectares was the desirable size of a viable peasant holding, and thus he proposed that the land expropriated be distributed in 5-hectare lots or as smaller 'supplements' to bring existing holdings up to the 5-hectare limit. He also tried to solve two fundamental problems of Rumanian agriculture: scattered peasant strips and the continued fragmentation of smallholdings. As for the first, he promised to introduce specific legislation to rationalize the division of cultivated fields, but he took no action, mainly because those who wielded power showed no interest in the idea and because the majority of peasants were utterly opposed to tampering with time-honoured practices. But the agrarian law itself did try to curb the fragmentation of peasant plots by preventing the subdivision of holdings obtained under its provisions to less than 2 hectares in the plains and 1 hectare in hilly regions. The prohibition had little effect.

In the final analysis, land reform was enacted because all classes, even the landowners, had finally come to recognize the futility, and the danger, of trying to maintain the old agrarian system. Many conservatives, accepting the inevitable, hoped to use the occasion to impose a new organization on agriculture which would improve efficiency and productivity. For their part, Liberals stood for agrarian reform in principle, but many wanted to be certain that agriculture continued to serve the needs of industry. Agrarianists, on the other hand, saw the reform as a giant step toward the 'peasantizing' of agriculture and the creation of a peasant state, a view which in time proved to be too sanguine. Undoubtedly, all these groups were stirred to action in the immediate post-war years by the spectre of social upheaval from below and the need to maintain national solidarity in order to defend the newly acquired territories from aggrieved neighbours.

The agrarian reform laws in the new provinces, which had as their primary aim the granting of land to peasants who had none or too little, followed principles similar to those applied in the Old Kingdom: they proposed to accomplish reform by expropriating public, institutional, and private land on the grounds of public necessity; they offered compensation to the owners of land and thus respected the rights of private property; and they were in the first instance pieces of social legislation intended to satisfy the peasants' demand for land rather than economic measures designed to reorganize agriculture.

The agrarian reform laws for the new provinces were not drawn up primarily with a view to undermining the status of the minorities, but, because of the nature of social and economic conditions in Transylvania, for example, changes in landholding could not but adversely affect the Magyars and, to a lesser extent, the Saxons.

In Transylvania the Rumanians were almost all peasants, small-holders or landless, while large properties were mainly in the hands of Magyars. Although statistics on landholding by ethnic groups are incomplete, it appears that Magyar landlords held about 90 per cent of all properties over 100 cadastral yokes (1 yoke = 0.58 hectares), while Rumanians may have held as much as 20 per cent of all arable land and pastures, primarily in the form of small properties. The Consiliu Dirigent approved a land reform law on 12 September 1919, which provided for the total expropriation of the estates of foreigners, of specified public and private institutions, and of all properties over 500 cadastral yokes. The law treated all the holdings of a single proprietor as a unit for purposes of expropriation. Properties between 200 and 500 yokes were subject to partial expropriation and properties under 200 yokes could be expropriated if the land was needed to carry out the reform in their district. Peasants who had served in the war headed the long list of those entitled to land, while peasants with more than 5 hectares could receive land only after the needs of all those with less than that amount had been satisfied. Unlike the reforms in the other provinces and the Old Kingdom before 1924, the Transylvanian reform provided for the expropriation of forests for the purpose of creating common pastures. Of 5,258,000 yokes of all types of land in Transylvania (the Banat, Crişana, and Maramureş), 2,746,000 yokes had been expropriated by 1924. Approximately 177,000 Rumanian peasants received land (or about 73 per cent of all recipients), while 26 per cent of the recipients were Magyars, Saxons, and Swabians. The Magyar large land-owning class and numerous Magyar institutions, notably churches, suffered a drastic reduction in their landholdings and, hence, in their economic power and social and cultural activities.

Bessarabia also experienced a radical agrarian reform. It was carried out by the peasants themselves during the year following the March 1917 revolution. By April 1918, when the Sfat al Ţării voted for union with Rumania, nearly two-thirds of the property belonging to large estates had come into peasant hands. Although the Sfat stipulated that the Bessarabian land reform be respected, subsequent legislation by the Rumanian parliament in 1920 and administrative acts by the Rumanian government benefited land-lords at the expense of the peasants. Notable changes were a raising of the maximum amount of property exempt from expropriation from 50 to 100 hectares and the setting of the redemption payments at 800 lei per hectare, a sum which drew vehement protests from peasants, who claimed that they had obtained their land through revolution and thus owed nothing. None the less, smallholdings now accounted for about 90 per cent of the arable land in the province.

Land reform in Bukovina did not differ in general from that in the Old Kingdom. About 75,000 hectares were expropriated. Smallholdings grew by 28 per cent at the expense of large estates, which the reform reduced to a limit of 250 hectares of arable land. But as elsewhere, the reform could not solve the fundamental problems of agriculture. Most striking was the continued paucity of arable land in relation to the density of population and the retention by large landowners, who survived the reform, of large areas of forest, thus reducing the availability to the peasants of this critical economic resource and of the pastures which could have been created out of forestland.

Whatever their shortcomings, the agrarian reform laws brought about a massive transfer of land from large landowners to small-holders. About 6 million hectares of land were expropriated for distribution to peasants, and some 1,400,000 peasants received land. The most striking and obvious result was thus a decrease in the number and extent of large properties in favour of medium and small holdings. The trend continued between 1930 and 1941, as the amount of arable land in holdings of over 100 hectares fell from about 25 per cent of all arable land to 13 per cent, while the amount of land possesseed by small peasant proprietors with holdings of 1–5 hectares grew from 48 to 62 per cent. But the change did not bring prosperity to agriculture, for many holdings were too small to be economically viable and continued to be subdivided through inheritance. At the other end of the scale, large properties continued to exist. Although estates of thousands of hectares were rare in the inter-war period, many landlords none the less succeeded in preserving sizeable properties. Not only did they take advantage of the provision of the reform that reserved to the landowner a maximum of 500 hectares, but they were also able to retain an even larger proportion of their pasturelands and forests. Since these had played a crucial role in the peasant economy, failure to include them fully in the expropriations had an adverse effect on many peasant households. Although articles in the final reform laws of 1921 provided for the establishment of communal pastures as a means of alleviating one of the most pressing needs of the majority of peasants, the results proved disappointing. By 1927 the amount of land distributed for use as common pastures represented only 23 per cent of the total area of natural pastures and meadows of the country. As for forests, at first, only the reform law for Transylvania mandated their expropriation and the establishment of communal forests, but in 1924 the provision was extended to the whole country. Yet no government assumed responsibility for enforcing it, and, as a result, only about 12 per cent of the total forestlands were distributed to peasants.

The implementation of the land reform left many peasants dissatisfied. A large number, between 30 and 35 per cent of the 2,300,000 peasants entitled to land in 1921, received none at all, mainly because there was not enough land in all parts of the country to go around. These peasants either swelled the ranks of the rural proletariat or were forced to rent land from landlords in return for payment of money or of a tithe on produce. But even those peasants who benefited from the reform had to endure long and sometimes costly delays before they obtained their allotment. The technical work of reform—the measuring of the land subject to expropriation and the marking out of the parcels to be given to individual peasants—progressed with excruciating slowness. By 1927 only about half the land from estates subject to expropriation had been measured, and only a relatively small portion of this land, roughly 1,100,000 hectares, had been divided into parcels for distribution. Often, to relieve the frustration of the peasants, provisional grants of land were made, but such practices had unfortunate economic consequences. Production suffered because peasants had little incentive to improve the land they worked so long as there were doubts about its final disposition. For the same reason—uncertain possession—peasants found it difficult to obtain loans. They were also subject to the so-called 'forced lease' (*arendă forțată*), a sum which they had to pay the government until they gained full title to their allotment and which, until 1931, did not count toward their redemption payments.

Land continued to change hands during the 1930s, in part because of the continued distribution of expropriated land to peasants. But the operations of the market, the activities of peasant associations, and the world economic depression at the beginning of the decade had an even greater influence on the structure of landholding in the decade before the Second World War. Rural land-purchasing associations, usually dominated by prosperous peasants, bought considerable amounts of land from the remaining large landowners. At the other end of the social scale poor peasants and other smallholders who were unable to make ends meet, especially because of the depression, sold out to better-off neighbours. Much of this land had originally come into peasant hands through the agrarian reforms. A survey of selected villages in 1938 found that in the plains peasants who had received such allotments in the 1920s lost, as a whole, between 30 and 40 per cent of their lands. Land reform and supplementary legislation thus did not interrupt the processes of social stratification in the countryside. Between 1930 and 1941 the number of holdings between 10 and 100 hectares decreased from 7.6 to 6.4 per cent of all holdings, but the amount of land they encompassed rose from 14 to 24 per cent of all arable land.

The effects of the agrarian reform laws on the organization of agriculture are difficult to measure, but they do not seem to have changed existing structures significantly. The remaining large landlords made greater use of machinery and hired hands in order to compensate for the loss of peasant labour, and, at least in the first few years after the enactment of the reform, many peasants showed a reluctance to enter into contracts with landlords, and those who did preferred to pay rent in money rather than in tithes for the land they worked. But in time there was a partial return to pre-reform—some critics called them 'neoiobăgist'—conditions, as increasing numbers of peasants were compelled to rent land from landlords to supplement what they had received from the expropriated estates and thus fell back into a condition of economic dependency. But the blame for continued shortcomings in agriculture cannot be laid solely upon the land reform. There were forces at work determining the economic and social development of Greater Rumania which had little to do with the legislation of 1918–21, notably a rapidly growing population, the uninterrupted fragmentation of peasant holdings through inheritance and partial sales, the vagaries of the international market, the slow development of industry, and the Rumanian government's own economic priorities. Nor did the reform laws drastically affect the reliance of Rumanian agriculture upon grain production, even though a tendency on the part of various categories of peasants to diversify their crops was evident. Nevertheless, in 1939 grains occupied 83.5 per cent of all arable land, compared to 84.7 per cent in 1927.

Agrarian reform did not improve the standard of living of the majority of peasants. In the first place, it did not satisfy their need for land. Many, in fact, remained landless, but even those who received allotments often did not get enough to bring their holdings up to the promised level of 5 hectares. Moreover, the reform laws were concerned only with the distribution of land. They did not provide the peasant with animals, tools, and credit, all essential if he was to work his holding with some prospect of success. The so-called village middle class, those peasants with between 10 and 50 hectares, was strengthened, as its members increased their holdings of arable land and became politically more active and influential. But generally the peasant with a holding of less than 3 hectares could not make ends meet if working the land was his sole source of income.[13]

The inability of various categories of peasants to improve their living standards was due in part to government fiscal and economic policies, which weighed heavily upon the ordinary peasant. He was subject to multiple local and national taxes, which diminished his net income. According to an investigation of sixty villages carried out in 1938, taxes on holdings of under 3 hectares amounted to 2 per cent of annual expenditures for the operation and maintenance of the holding in Bukovina, 9 per cent in Wallachia, 10 per cent in Moldavia, and 17 per cent in Bessarabia. The larger the property the heavier the tax burden became. Restrictions on the export of agricultural products and high export duties (these were abolished in 1931) adversely affected the peasant household. They kept prices for such products on the domestic market low and contributed to the increasing gap between the prices of agricultural products and processed goods needed by the peasant. According to various estimates, the real prices of industrial goods rose to three times those of agricultural produce between 1913 and 1940. For a peasant to be able to buy twenty-six selected, essential manufactured items in 1913 he had to produce 264 kilograms of wheat or 407 kilograms of corn, but in 1939 those figures were 689 kilograms and 918 kilograms, respectively. The consequences were detrimental to both the peasant and industry. The former did without and suffered a decline in his standard of living, while many enterprises lost part of their market.

The agrarian reforms did benefit certain segments of the peasantry and thus had favourable consequences for the economic and social life of the village and of the country as a whole. An increase

[13] Vasile Bozga, *Criza agrară în România dintre cele două războaie mondiale* (Bucharest, 1975), 72–4.

in the per capita consumption of certain foods, an improvement in the construction of peasant houses and other buildings, and a rise in literacy may be linked to the reforms. Particularly striking is the gradual transformation of the pre-reform patriarchal village, which had striven for self-sufficiency, into a regular consumer of processed goods. Industry thus found an expanding market in the countryside for its goods which cities, because of their relatively small populations, could not offer. Producers of mass consumption goods benefited particularly, and certain industries, such as agricultural implements, grew. In 1937, according to some estimates, agriculture consumed as much as 20–5 per cent of the country's industrial output.

The agrarian reforms had a favourable effect on economic activity generally, even though they did not alter the economic structure of the country. For example, the peasant household which acquired sufficient land and was thus able to raise its standard of living tended to become a regular purchaser of processed goods, a practice which encouraged certain industries to increase production and to hire additional workers from the countryside. A few industries, as we have seen, even produced specifically for the agricultural sector. Yet, the fact remains that the peasantry as a whole still purchased relatively few manufactured goods. After the economic crisis of 1929–33, for example, peasant consumption of goods obtained in the market-place declined, at least temporarily, as many households were obliged to fall back on their own production.

After the agrarian reforms Rumanian agriculture passed through three stages. The first, up to 1928, was one of slow recovery from the devastation of war and occupation. The situation was particularly desperate between 1919 and 1921, at precisely the time when extensive land reform was being prepared. The amount of land under cultivation (taking into account post-war boundary changes) decreased about 40 per cent, from 13,700,000 hectares, the median between 1911 and 1915, to 8,300,000 hectares in 1919–20, with a resulting drastic fall in production. For the five principal grains (wheat, corn, rye, barley, and oats) production in 1922 was only about two-thirds of what the average had been in 1911–15. There was also a severe decrease in the number of animals. In 1919 there were 1,860,000 head of horned cattle, down from 2,940,000 in 1916. Although by 1921 their number was on the increase, the shortage of draft animals remained critical and slowed the recovery of agriculture. The economy as a whole suffered, for agriculture could not contribute its customary lion's share of the country's exports, and, in a reversal of pre-war conditions, in 1919, 220,000,000 tons of grain had to be imported. Even by 1921, three years after the end of the war, the country's exports had reached only three-fifths of the pre-war level.

Agricultural recovery remained uneven throughout the 1920s. To be sure, the amount of land under cultivation increased from about 10,400,000 hectares to 12,750,000 hectares, but yields of grain per hectare remained below the pre-war amounts: 8 quintals per hectare in 1928 compared to nearly 14 in 1914. The number of draft animals even declined by over a million during the period. The large number of oxen in use is an indication of the extensive character of agriculture, while the increase of horses on small-holdings, where agricultural incomes were low, shows the tendency of their proprietors to engage in non-farming activities, especially carting, to supplement their incomes. The quantity of agricultural machines and tools increased, but their distribution was uneven. The mass of poor peasants, as usual, had to make do with old-fashioned implements or none at all. But even on larger properties the number of modern machines such as tractors was far short of the number needed. In 1927 on holdings of over 50 hectares there was only one tractor for every 863 hectares of arable land. Many peasants simply abandoned agriculture because the continued fragmentation of holdings and the tight credit and high interest rates had destroyed the economic viability of their holdings.

The recovery of agriculture in the late 1920s was cut short by the world economic depression, which began to affect Rumania in 1929 by causing a steady fall in grain prices until their low point in 1934. Thereafter agricultural prices rose, even surpassing the level of 1930, but they did not represent the same level of purchasing power. Yet the total amount of land under cultivation during the agrarian crisis rose above the annual median for the period 1925–9.[14] The main exception was wheat; acreage declined significantly because it was the main export grain and was thus particularly sensitive to international market conditions. But the cultivation of corn expanded because it was grown by peasant smallholders, who were desperately trying to compensate for the fall of prices on the domestic market by increasing the production of the main item of their diet. These peasants were also primarily responsible

[14] Ibid. 99–109.

for a modest increase in acreage devoted to hemp and flax because they had turned again to their household crafts in order to supply themselves with clothes and other items they could not afford to buy.

The depression compounded the crisis in agriculture by striking at Rumanian industry and thereby reducing its use of raw materials. Its effects suggest how increasingly dependent city and countryside had become upon one another. The slackening of demand for raw materials in the milling, alcohol, sugar, vegetable oil, textile, and hide-processing industries brought a drastic reduction in peasant income. Falling industrial production and factory closings, in time, proved disastrous for thousands of peasant households, which had depended upon factory work as a means of supplementing meagre agricultural incomes. Urban unemployment also affected the countryside by curtailing the demand for foodstuffs.

The very nature of Rumania's agrarian structure—peasant agriculture, that is, agriculture carried on by peasant families on their own smallholdings—was a fundamental cause of the crisis on the land. It was uneconomical in organizaion, primitive in methods, and burdened by overpopulation and debt. Sooner or later all reformers discovered that these shortcomings were so tightly interconnected that they could not separate causes from effects.

Peasant agriculture was extensive and was based upon the growing of grain, mainly corn and wheat. Grain production for the market on peasant holdings, characteristic of Rumanian agriculture since the first half of the nineteenth century, had been reinforced by the post-war agrarian reforms. But it was apparent to many observers that the concentration on grains was unsuited to the smallholding. In the first place, it interfered with the development of vegetable gardening and the raising of industrial crops, which required large quantities of nutrients from the soil, because it discouraged the raising of animals, the main source of fertilizers in peasant agriculture. Grain production also impeded crop diversification, which would have led to a more intensive use of labour and thus would have eased the burden of overpopulation on the land.

A seemingly intractable problem in agriculture was the underemployment of available labour.[15] For example, the working

---

[15] D. Şandru, 'Consideraţii privitoare la problema suprapopulaţiei agricole din România între cele două războaie mondiale', *Anuarul Institutului de Istorie şi Arheologie*, 15 (1978), 79–91.

population in agriculture between 1927 and 1932, which numbered about 9.9 million persons, was capable of performing
1,865,100,000 working days of labour, but in fact performed only
814,400,000 days, or 44 per cent of its potential. If the days used
for other tasks on the peasant holding such as carting and walking
to and from fields are counted, the total energy expended probably
did not exceed 55 per cent of what was available. The relationship
between the agricultural population and the amount of arable land
offers another striking example of the continuing pressure of
population: in 1930 the density of population was 112 inhabitants
per square kilometre, very high by European standards, but typical
of the less developed areas of Eastern Europe. The situation grew
worse as the 1930s progressed, reaching 116 inhabitants per square
kilometre in 1938. The continued fragmentation of peasant properties exacerbated the problems of overpopulation by reducing
the capacity of these smaller and smaller plots to support their
households.

The productivity of peasant agriculture remained low. The yield
for wheat between 1928 and 1932 was 9.5 quintals per hectare, the
lowest of all the countries of South-eastern Europe except Greece.
The yield for corn was somewhat better, but also low when
compared to other countries in the region. The situation did not
improve in the 1930s, as the production of wheat, corn, barley,
and oats per hectare was less in 1934–8 than it had been in
1906–10. The causes were many. Perhaps most important were
the primitive methods of farming: sowing by hand, shallow
ploughing, lack of fertilizers and poor crop rotation, which
exhausted the soil, and the failure to weed and hoe once the crop
was in the ground. The inadequate tools available to the smallholder were part of the problem. But so was the quality of draft
animals, which deteriorated in the inter-war period as poor feed,
bad housing, and overwork took their toll. Strip farming, which
the reforms had ignored, was particularly wasteful of both land
and human energy. The agricultural census of 1941 revealed the
average size of all holdings to be 4.5 hectares and the average
number of separate plots per holding to be 5. The plots were
sometimes 400 or 500 feet long and only 15 or 20 feet wide.
Such a configuration prevented the peasant from using modern
machinery, even if he could have afforded it, and obliged him to
walk long distances between plots and to maintain necessary but
wasteful paths between the numerous strips.

The advantages of intensive over extensive agriculture are

immediately apparent when production in Ţara Bîrsei, the region around Braşov, is compared with that in Dobrudja and Bessarabia.[16] In the latter the production of grains predominated, and in 1936 they covered 83 per cent of the arable land in Dobrudja and 86 per cent in Bessarabia. Production per hectare was, in general, below the level for the country as a whole. Ţara Bîrsei, by contrast, was home to the most varied agriculture in Rumania, which included the raising of industrial plants, sugar beets, greenhouse crops, and animals, but devoted relatively little space to grains. Here agriculture was at its most productive. In 1935 17.9 quintals of wheat and 16.6 quintals of corn per hectare were raised as opposed to 7.6 and 10.4 quintals, respectively, for the country as a whole. Such yields reflected a high level of capital investment. At least in part because of the intensive nature of agriculture, overpopulation and associated problems on the land were minimal.

INDUSTRY

The war had inflicted enormous destruction in industry and had almost totally disrupted production, but its recovery in the 1920s was none the less rapid and substantial. It owed much to the Liberals, who were in office for most of the decade and who put their considerable political and economic power in the service of industrialization. The accession of the new provinces, especially Transylvania and the Banat, added significantly to the productive capacity of the Old Kingdom, the former in the ceramics, forestry, electrical, and matallurgical industries, the latter in the metallurgical and textile industries. The dynamism of the 1920s is suggested by the growth in the number of enterprises of all kinds from 86,000 in 1918 to 273,000 in 1930 and by the growth of production between 1924 and 1928 in mining of 189 per cent and in manufacturing of 188 per cent. The development of the oil industry, which was stimulated by substantial investments of capital, especially foreign, was spectacular. Production rose from 968,000 tons in 1918 to 5,800,000 tons in 1930, giving Rumania sixth place among the world's producers. The metallurgical industry also showed impressive growth, as steel production increased from 38,000 tons in 1925 to 144,000 tons in 1928. Large industrial

[16] V. Madgearu, *Evoluţia economiei româneşti după razboiul mondial* (Bucharest, 1940), 54–8.

conglomerates, provided with advanced technology and capable of producing an enormous variety of goods now came into being. The Malaxa Works in Bucharest, which specialized in steel-making, munitions, motors, precision instruments, and numerous other manufactures, and Industria Aeronautică Română (Rumanian Aeronautical Industry) in Braşov, which produced all the components of airplanes, are examples of the type of manufacturing complexes that had come into existence since the war. The state, that is, the Liberals, gave special attention to the metallurgical industry, granting it massive financing and continuous protection from foreign competition.

The economic crisis of the early 1930s temporarily halted the promising growth of industry. Between 1929 and 1932 the number of large-scale manufacturing enterprises, the amount of capital invested in them, and the number of workers they employed all fell, and production in nearly every branch of industry suffered a drastic decline.

Once industry had overcome the effects of the depression, it reached new levels of productivity between 1934 and 1938.[17] The overall value of large-scale industrial production almost doubled from 34,900 million lei to 64,600 million. The metallurgical industry expanded, as the amount of iron ore mined and steel produced increased steadily. Coal production also grew in response to the demands of heavy industry and the railways, but it failed to reach its full potential because large amounts of capital were diverted to oil, which offered a greater return. Oil production reached its peak in 1936—8.7 million tons—before falling to 6.6 million tons in 1938. The decrease was caused by the gradual depletion of known reserves and, between 1934 and 1937, a slackening of domestic consumption.

Accompanying the growth of industry was a concentration of control in fewer and fewer hands, as cartels and holding companies multiplied. By 1937, 57 per cent of the total capital of all industrial corporations (societăţi anonime) was held by 3 per cent of them. In the same year a number of cartels, which allocated markets among member companies and fixed prices, had gained control of at least 90 per cent of capital invested and production in the metallurgy, cement, paper, and sugar refining industries and a

[17] I. Puia, 'Le Développement de l'industrie roumaine dans les années qui ont précédé la Seconde Guerre Mondiale', Revue roumaine d'histoire, 10/3 (1971), 483–504.

50 per cent control of the oil, chemical, and glass industries. The role of these and other monopolies in the economic and political life of the country in 1934–8 marked a significant change quantitatively and qualitatively from the situation at the turn of the century. The concentration of capital, productive capacity, and distribution proceeded with the support of the Liberals, who accepted the argument that monopoly meant the rationalization of industry, the reduction of costs, and, thus, of the price charged the consumer, and an end to unnecessary competition at a time when Rumanian industry was struggling to confirm its role as an independent, profitable branch of the national economy. The growth of monopoly in industry in the 1930s was accompanied by a more intensive participation by banks in industrial enterprises, a process which accelerated the concentration of capital in both industry and banking.

Under the aegis of the Liberals and benefiting from the increasing intervention of the state in economic life, the Rumanian financial bourgeoisie was engaged in a struggle to gain for itself control over the domestic wholesale and retail market, the investment of capital, and the exploitation of the country's natural resources and thus free itself from the tutelage of foreign capital. It was at least partially successful. By 1938 about 60 per cent of the capital of industrial enterprises was in its hands (especially, in transportation, foreign and domestic commerce, agriculture, and various small industries), but foreign capital continued to predominate in oil, coal, and sugar-refining and maintained a strong position in forest products and chemicals. Throughout the inter-war period Rumania continued to be an importer of capital and, thus, remained dependent upon Western European investments to propel the economy forward.[18]

Many branches of industry had progressed sufficiently by the end of the 1930s to be able to satisfy almost all domestic needs for food, textiles, and chemicals. But Rumanian industry could not supply enough of the machines and other equipment needed for

[18] For an analysis of the share of foreign capital in the various branches of Rumanian industry, see Constanța Bogdan and Adrian Platon, *Capitalul străin în societățile anonime din România în perioada interbelică* (Bucharest, 1981), 39–100; in the economy as a whole, Ilie Puia, 'Capitalul străin în economia României în deceniul premergător celui de al doilea război mondial', *Revista de istorie*, 34/8 (1981) 1405–21; and in agriculture, D. Șandru, 'Capitalul străin în agricultura României în anii crizei economice', *Anuarul Institutului de Istorie și Arheologie*, 19 (1982), 431–45.

its own further growth. These still had to be imported, a situation which indicates continuing industrial underdevelopment. In technology the majority of Rumanian plants were behind those of the West. In heavy industry only the Malaxa and Reşiţa iron and steel works were up to the level of the best in Western Europe, but textile plants also were, in general, equipped with modern machinery.

The effects of industrialization were felt throughout the economy. Transportation improved markedly. The railway network, for example, was upgraded, owing in large measure to the development of the metallurgical industry. High quality engines, wagons, and rails could now be produced domestically. Industrialization also speeded the processes of urbanization by drawing people to the cities to work in the new or expanded enterprises. The newcomers were not only factory hands but also office personnel. New opportunities for employment opened up in the public service sector and the government bureaucracies, both of which expanded in order to take care of a growing population.

Despite impressive growth in many branches of industry, the fundamental economic structure of the country did not change significantly. As of 1939, 78 per cent of the active population continued to rely on agriculture for its main source of income, while only 10 per cent were similarly engaged in industry. Rumania was still dependent upon foreign imports to equip her industry and to provide consumers with a broad range of goods.

A critical weakness of Rumanian industry persisted: the inability of the domestic market to absorb its products. The growth of industry was not, therefore, determined primarily by the growth of consumer demand but rather by government intervention in the form of protective tariffs and other restrictions on imports. For its part, the domestic market was slow to expand, because of the low standard of living of the mass of the population—the peasantry, in the first instance—which lacked the wherewithal to buy domestic manufactures. In 1937, for example, agriculture took only 25 per cent of the industrial production of the country, although almost 80 per cent of the country's population, as we have seen, was agricultural. The high prices of locally processed goods also discouraged purchases. As a result, the consumption of iron, cement, paper, glass, textiles, petroleum, and sugar in Rumania was the lowest in Europe in the 1930s. The budget of the typical peasant household is revealing. It allocated only a small percentage of income for the purchase of articles that could not be produced at home, such as salt, tobacco, and matches. The rate of consumption in the cities was more encouraging than in the villages, but the majority of potential consumers were still to be found in the rural areas. Some researchers have suggested that this very situation was an impediment to commercial transactions between the city and the countryside and, hence, to the development of both industry and agriculture. They have pointed to the peasant mentality, which in many villages still regarded the exchange of goods between inhabitants of the same village not as a source of income or an opporturnity to rise in the economic hierarchy, but as a mutual provisioning of necessities and an act of social solidarity. Thus, so long as such an attitude toward commerce prevailed, they argued, exchanges between the urban centres and the countryside could not take place on an equal, mutually beneficial basis.[19]

Commercial exchanges between urban areas and the countryside did, of course, take place, but, compared to Western Europe, they were on a modest scale. Surprisingly, the bulk of the exchanges between industry and agriculture did not take place directly but rather through foreign countries. Rumanian agriculture had too little variety to offer the city and thus was unable to maintain a thriving market at home for its products. The countryside was thus forced to send its large surpluses of grain abroad in order to obtain necessary manufactures by using the income it received to buy the products of Rumanian industry. But since, as we have seen, the majority of peasants could buy few such products, Rumanian industry also had to rely upon exports to maintain its productive capacity. The Rumanian oil and forestry industries, for example, could not otherwise have achieved their existing level of development. Foreign consumers took 82 per cent of the production of the former and 70 per cent of the latter.

Rumania's foreign trade during the inter-war period, in general, followed pre-war patterns. Exports tended to remain those of a predominantly agricultural country, as grain, animals, and wood, together with oil, made up over 90 per cent of Rumania's exports. But over time there were notable shifts in the importance of specific articles. Grain, for example, which constituted over 50 per cent of total exports up to 1927, after the world depression

[19] Paul Sterian, 'Problema debuşeelor interioare', *Sociologie românească*, 3/10–12 (1938), 464–5, and 'Comerţul interior în România', *Sociologie românească*, 3/4–6 (1938), 158–69.

averaged 25 per cent per year in 1934–8. Its place was taken by oil, which in the same period accounted for about 46 per cent of annual exports. During the depression the Rumanian government encouraged the export of petroleum products in order to compensate for the loss of grain markets caused by the imposition of high tariff barriers by Rumania's traditional customers as a means of protecting their own agricultural interests. As for imports, after 1933 a shift away from a preponderance of manufactured articles toward semi-processed goods and raw materials took place. In 1930, about 10 per cent of Rumanian imports were raw materials, but by 1939 they had risen to 34 per cent, while imports of manufactured goods during the same period fell from 65 to 33 per cent. These figures reflect progress in industrialization and in the ability of industry to satisfy the needs of consumers. Yet, as in the case of capital, Rumania continued to be dependent upon the industrialized states of the West for a variety of industrial goods. As an agricultural state she was at a distinct disadvantage, for she was obliged to export raw materials at relatively low prices and import industrial goods at high prices. As a result, in 1928, for example, for one ton of imported goods Rumania had to export 6.5 tons. The importation of large amounts of capital also contributed to dependence. By 1939 Rumania had amassed an enormous foreign public debt of 69,000 million lei. Service on this debt alone required the export of huge quantities of raw materials. Perhaps the most striking evidence of dependence is to be found in the economic relationship which developed between Rumania and Germany in the 1930s. By 1939 Germany had become Rumania's best customer, taking 32 per cent of her exports, and was her principal supplier of goods, accounting for 39 per cent of all Rumania's imports. Germany's predominance appears all the more impressive in light of the fact that her trade with Rumania constituted less than 1 per cent of her total foreign trade.[20]

ECONOMIC POLICY

In the 1920s the economic fortunes of Rumania were in the hands of the Liberals. The ideas of politicians on fundamental issues of development were much influenced by the great theorist of

---

[20] I. Puia, *Relaţiile economice externe ale României în perioada interbelică* (Bucharest, 1982), 123–35.

Rumanian liberalism, Ştefan Zeletin. Like him, they assigned to the bourgeoisie, that is, to themselves, the leading role in transforming Rumania into a modern European nation. Vintilă Brătianu, the Minister of Finance in the Liberal governments of 1922–8, served as the chief interpreter of Zeletin's theories. He pursued not only economic goals, but was intent upon consolidating the Rumanian national state. He was confident that under the leadership of the bourgeoisie (and the Liberals) class differences would gradually disappear as the economy grew and became modern, and he foresaw that eventually a broad middle-class society devoid of social conflict would emerge.[21] He and his colleagues relied heavily upon the intervention of the state to achieve these ambitious economic and social goals. Theirs was the so-called doctrine of neoliberalism, as formulated by Zeletin, which held that the era of economic liberty, which had served useful purposes in the nineteenth century, had run its course and must now give way to systematic organization and direction and the pursuit of well-defined goals. They took the Constitution of 1923 as their starting-point, interpreting its provisions as justifying state intervention in the economy and attributing a social function to individual freedoms, thereby subjecting them to regulation by the state. Such ideas provided the theoretical underpinnings of Liberal economic legislation throughout the inter-war years.

The Liberals, as economic nationalists, were determined to share as little power as possible with foreigners. Although they recognized the need to maintain good relations with the industrialized states of Europe for the simple reason that they dominated international commerce and the financial markets, the Liberals wanted to avoid economic subordination to the West. They insisted that the infrastructure and the main industries be in Rumanian, that is, their own, hands. Under the motto, 'Prin noi înşine' (By ourselves), they even toyed with the notion of financing their ambitious economic programme with native capital alone.[22]

The Liberals were convinced that industry offered the best hope of bringing Rumania into the modern world and of enabling her to become a regional power whose co-operation would be indispensable to the great powers as they pursued their own interests in

---

[21] Vintilă I. Brătianu, 'Burghezimea de ieri şi de mîine', *Democraţia* (1922), nos. 1–2, 1–6.

[22] Ioan Saizu, 'Dimensiunile, caracterul şi structura concepţiei "prin noi înşine" în perioada 1922–1928', *Revista de istorie*, 32/12 (1979), 2319–39.

Eastern Europe. They devoted their limited investment capital to the development of heavy industry, the improvement of transportation, and the expanded production of raw materials.[23] As their predecessors had done before the First World War, they also allowed favoured enterprises to purchase state land for development at low prices, relieved them of duties on imported equipment, and granted them reduced rates for transportation and fuel.

To assure Rumanian control of industry and mines the Liberals passed a series of laws in 1924 limiting foreign participation in key enterprises. The Law of Mines confirmed the property rights of the state over all the country's mineral resources and allowed the state to develop them directly or indirectly through concessions to private companies. But the law specified that three-fifths of the capital and two-thirds of the boards of directors and certain officers had to be Rumanian. After 1925, because of heavy pressure from foreign governments and financial circles, mandatory Rumanian control was reduced to 50 per cent. But the law on the commercialization and control of state economic enterprises, which included the maritime service and energy companies and which the Liberals enacted in 1924, still required that two-thirds of their boards of directors be Rumanian. The law made no concessions to foreign capital. Rather, it represented an attempt by the Liberal Party to gain control of major branches of the economy through the device of nationalization. The procedure it intended to follow was, first, to nationalize sources of raw materials and various enterprises and, then, once under state control, lease them to businessmen who could be counted upon to support the government. The Liberals justified the leasing of the new state enterprises on the grounds that they could not otherwise be operated efficiently and would thus add huge deficits to the state budget, as the railway and postal service monopolies had done. Typical of the Liberal approach was a special law on energy, which offered numerous inducements to those who would invest in companies producing electricity, but reserved a quarter of the energy produced to the state.[24]

The Liberals justified their restrictions on foreign capital by pointing out, correctly, that economic penetration was frequently

[23] Ion I. C. Brătianu, *Activitatea corpurilor legiuitoare și a guvernului de la ianuarie 1922 până la 27 martie 1926* (Bucharest, 1926), 217–35.

[24] I. Saizu, 'Rolul statului în economia națională (1922–1928)', *Anuarul Institutului de Istorie și Arheologie*, 14 (1977), 211–24.

accompanied by political pressure on the part of foreign governments to gain still greater advantages. Compared with similar laws enacted by other European states, the Rumanian legislation was, in fact, moderate. But it none the less hindered economic development because it reduced the flow of investments from abroad, which were indispensable, owing to the lack of native capital. After a few years the Liberals themselves recognized the need for flexibility and loosened their controls on foreign capital investments in order to accelerate economic growth.

To some extent the Liberal government overcame the shortage of private investment capital at home by direct state financing of industry. In 1923 it created Societatea Naţională de Credit Industrial (The National Corporation for Industrial Credit), which was to play a major role in accelerating the rate of industrial growth. In 1924 the new agency financed a modest 6 per cent of large manufacturing enterprises, but by 1928 the figure had risen to 12 per cent, which, moreover, represented 31 per cent of the value of production of all such enterprises. The National Bank was similarly active.

The Liberals also promoted native industry by a series of high protective tariffs enacted between 1924 and 1927. The National Peasant government of 1928–30 and its immediate successors retained the Liberal protectionist policy. Between 1929 and 1938 tariff duties on imports rose 845 per cent, but raw materials, machinery, and other items needed by Rumanian industry were, in general, lightly taxed. Protectionism produced mixed results. On the one hand, it allowed certain large native industrial enterprises to create a near monopoly over many types of manufactured goods, thus keeping consumer prices high. Yet, there can be no doubt that protectionism stimulated production. The Liberals also imposed heavy duties on exports, particularly agricultural products. The main reason for such measures was to ensure an abundant supply of cheap raw materials for industry at home and to keep the cost of living low, especially in the cities. But Liberal and opposition governments had other motives as well: they depended upon these duties for revenue and as a means of turning the commerce of Transylvania and Bessarabia away from Austria and Hungary and Russia, respectively, and toward the interior market. Although during the mid-1920s export duties brought in more revenue than tariffs on imports, they impeded the development of agriculture and placed additional burdens on the peasantry by keeping domestic prices for agricultural produce low and discouraging agricultural exports, which were an indispensable source of foreign hard currency.

The efforts of the Liberals to retain the key segments of the economy in Rumanian hands were only partially successful. Before the First World War foreign capital represented about 80 per cent of all the capital invested in Rumanian industry (one-third of it was Austrian and German). Native capital tended to flow toward enterprises which promised a quick return—land, transportation, and banks. As a result of Liberal government policies in the 1920s native investments became more diversified, but no dramatic change in the relation of foreign to native capital occurred in that decade. Pre-war Austrian and German capital was simply replaced by English, French, and Belgian, and the most important positions in the economy remained in the hands of foreigners. Although native investments continued to grow, 65 per cent of the capital of industrial joint-stock companies and 25 per cent of that of banks between 1925 and 1928 was foreign.

The Liberals treated agriculture as something of a stepchild and preferred to channel scarce domestic capital into industry, thereby leaving the small peasant to the mercy of tradition and the village money-lender. The legislation which the Liberals enacted on behalf of agriculture dealt with specific ills, such as the safeguarding of peasant holdings by making their sale more difficult and the establishing of chambers of agriculture, modelled on business and industrial chambers of commerce and designed to co-ordinate efforts at reform and to represent agricultural interests at all levels of government. The Liberals also tried to provide the peasants with specialized training by increasing the number of professional agronomists in each *judeţ* and by establishing model farms to offer practical demonstrations of the benefits of new methods of cultivation and modern technology. None of these measures produced the desired results because both funding and moral support were lacking. The Liberals counted upon industrialization to alleviate the crisis in agriculture. Convinced that there would never be enough land to satisfy all the peasants who needed it, they hoped to reduce rural overpopulation by attracting surplus labour to the new industrial centres. But here, too, success eluded them.

The National Peasants, who were swept into office by a stunning electoral victory in 1928, pursued economic goals in appearance markedly different from those of the Liberals. They had great expectations. Their primary concern was, of course, agriculture, but they also recognized the importance of a modern infrastructure and sound finances. To carry out their ambitious plans they encouraged investments from abroad in accordance with a policy that came to be known as 'Porţi deschise capitalului străin' ('Doors open to foreign capital'). They were motivated in part by the realization that native sources of capital were insufficient, but they were also loath to pass up the opportunity to strike a blow at the immense economic power which the Liberal financial and industrial oligarchy had accumulated.

The National Peasants introduced a variety of measures to improve agriculture. In 1929 they increased the amount of credit available in the rural areas and set up new lending institutions to distribute it. But the law proved ineffective because the depression quickly dried up funding for the project. Yet, even if it had continued, it is doubtful that the average peasant would have benefited, since under the provisions of the law he lacked the necessary collateral to qualify for a loan. The National Peasants also sought to assist agriculture by introducing a new tariff law on 1 August 1929, which was designed to encourage international trade and, specifically, to reduce import duties on agricultural machinery and certain mass consumer goods, modifications of Liberal protectionism which aided certain elements of the peasantry. Once again the main beneficiaries of such legislation were the wealthier peasants, who had the wherewithal to take advantage of these concessions, rather than the average peasant who lived at a subsistence level. The National Peasants maintained tariffs on the importation of numerous manufactured goods in order to protect Rumanian industry, but now the tests for such measures were the prospects for development of the protected industry and the cost of producing the items in question at home compared to the overall cost to the national economy of their importation.

Much of the National Peasants' agrarian legislation was intended to strengthen the 'worthy peasant', that is, the one who had already demonstrated his ability to work his holding efficiently. The law of 20 August 1929 on the alienation of holdings obtained through the agrarian reforms, for example, removed certain limitations on the sale and transfer of such lands to enable the more productive peasants to extend their holdings at the expense of those who appeared unable to adapt to the demands of modern agriculture. Yet the law retained the provisions of earlier Liberal legislation restricting the sale of land to persons who would actually cultivate it and to Rumanian citizens who had less than 25 hectares. Despite such safeguards, the law, in practice, enabled wealthier peasants to acquire more land and helped reduce their poorer neighbours to the status of a landless proletariat. The law on the organization of co-operatives of 28 March 1929 also offered few benefits to the mass of peasants. Although designed to encourage the free association of peasants and to limit the control exercised over co-operatives by the government, in practice it tended to restrict participation in the co-operatives to well-to-do peasants, since they alone could make the contributions required for membership. Neither land-leasing co-operatives nor those designed to encourage peasants to group their holdings into single economic units and to work their land together, all valiant attempts to rationalize agriculture, were successful. Besides a lack of adequate financing and its appeal primarily to the upper strata of the peasantry, the co-operative movement failed to achieve the objectives of its proponents because neither they nor the state prepared the peasants for it. As a result, the peasants, among whom the spirit of co-operation was, in any case, weak, tended to regard the initiatives of the state with suspicion as attempts to regiment them and even deprive them of the lands they had acquired through the agrarian reforms.[25]

The National Peasants' agrarian programme, in the end, failed to correct the fundamental deficiencies of Rumanian agriculture. The world economic crisis, which struck agricultural states with unusual severity, was to some extent responsible for their failure by depriving them of the funds needed to carry out their ambitious projects. But some of the blame is theirs, for they neglected critical aspects of the agrarian problem. For example, their party programme of 1926 called for the expropriation of all holdings over 100 hectares, but once in power they made no effort to carry it out. The depression persuaded them that the break-up of the remaining large properties would exacerbate already desperate economic conditions by disorganizing production. Nor did they undertake to consolidate peasant strips, action that would have gone far toward rationalizing agriculture. They decided that this measure, too, would be disruptive, since it lacked support among the peasantry.

The National Peasants devoted relatively little attention to industry. Curtailing the broad state support provided by the

[25] A. G. Galan, *Patruzeci de ani de experiențe cooperative în România, 1893–1934* (Bucharest, 1935), 21–67; Ion Mihalache, M. Gormsen, and Ion Răducanu, *Problema cooperației romane* (Bucharest, 1940), 39–205.

Liberals, they encouraged with appropriate legislation those industries they considered viable, such as the construction of rail
engines and cars. But they did not hesitate to withdraw support
from industries they judged to be 'artificial'. For example, doubting
the capacity of the native armaments industry to supply the army
with high quality weapons and munitions, they turned to Czech
and French firms. They also recognized the need to improve the
transportation and communications networks. In 1929, therefore,
they sponsored an ambitious railway repair and highway-building
programme, and in 1930 they authorized the International Telephone and Telegraph Company to set up a nation-wide telephone
system.

The world economic depression undid all the economic calculations of the National Peasants. As early as 1928 signs of a crisis in
Rumanian agriculture were evident, and by the following year the
economic spurt of the preceding half-dozen years had slowed to a
halt. One of the earliest indications of trouble was the sharp fall of
prices on the Bucharest stock exchange between October 1928
and October 1929. The Rumanian economy was thus already
weakened when the effects of the world depression began to
be felt. From the beginning of 1930, when all branches of the
Rumanian economy were affected by it, until 1932 the depression
ran its course largely unchecked.[26] Agricultural prices fell to
roughly two-fifths of their 1929 level: between 1929 and 1931 the
price of corn in various parts of the country dropped from 10.40
lei per kilogram to 1.30 lei and beans from 32 to 2.40 lei per
kilogram. In response, peasant smallholders reduced significantly
their purchases of goods on the market. The output of factories
and mines, as we have seen, suffered a precipitous drop. The
only important exception was oil production, which rose from
4,200,000 tons in 1928 to 7,400,000 tons in 1933. The main reason
for such a large increase was the desire of foreign companies,
which dominated the Rumanian petroleum industry, to assure a
high level of income, despite the sharp decline in oil prices during
the period. These companies also took drastic measures to reduce
their costs of production by laying off large numbers of workers.
As a result, by 1933 the cost of producing a ton of crude oil
had fallen to only one-fifth of what it had been in 1929. Other
industries were not so fortunate. Bankruptcies of large and, particularly, small companies tripled between 1929 and 1931. Still

---

[26] On the consequences of the depression, see Puia, *Relaţiile economice*, 93–101.

other companies, among them the most important in the country, reduced their work schedules to two or three days a week. The result was massive unemployment. Nor were state enterprises spared, as the railway monopoly, one of the country's largest employers, reduced its personnel by one-third. The salaries for skilled factory and white-collar workers in all industries fell 37 per cent between 1929 and 1933. A corresponding decrease in purchasing power deepened the crisis in industry.

The depression thus struck Rumania with particular force, mainly because of her predominantly agricultural economy. The lack of diversification diminished her capacity to respond to the crisis. Dependent upon the export of grain, she was at the mercy of the international market. Not only falling agricultural prices in the West but new, high tariffs on Rumanian agricultural products imposed by the industrialized states to protect their own farmers jeopardized Rumania's economic and financial stability. The Rumanian government could do little to influence the great powers. Retaliation against their manufactured goods was out of the question because they were indispensable, and, in any case, the government had to avoid antagonizing the West, which was its only source of loans and other financial aid. This very dependence upon foreign capital exacerbated the crisis. Foreign investors withdrew large amounts of capital in search of a safer, higher return elsewhere, an exodus which merely added to the number of failed commercial and industrial enterprises and banks. The collapse of the Kredit Anstalt in Vienna in May 1931 practically cut Rumania off from foreign capital, a blow which undermined the government's efforts to cope with its own financial crisis. In its eagerness to obtain new loans it subordinated the economy of the country still further to foreign capital, a situation reflected in more moderate import duties than those levied by the Liberals in the 1920s.

The National Peasant government up to 1931 and its short-lived successors tried a variety of measures to combat the effects of the depression. Of immediate concern was peasant indebtedness. Since the onset of the crisis the government had pursued an almost draconian policy of collecting all taxes owed it by peasant proprietors, going so far as to auction off the property of delinquent taxpayers. The main reason for such drastic action was the government's own desperate shortage of money, which for months at a time between 1929 and 1933 obliged it to halt the payment of salaries to many of its own employees. The deepening crisis in agriculture and the accompanying social unrest at last forced the government to reduce taxes, but the law of 21 October 1932 relieved the peasant of only a small portion of his heavy financial burden.

Private debt proved to be the undoing of far more peasants than state taxes. The majority of those in debt had contracted loans when agricultural prices were high and the prospects of repayment were bright. Yet, even then, in the 1920s peasants had had great difficulty obtaining loans on favourable terms. In an era of expanding credit, which characterized the 1920s, investments flowed into industry and commerce, which promised high returns, rather than into a less profitable and more risky agriculture. Since official credit agencies such as the *bănci populare* had only limited resources, many peasants turned to private lenders, who normally granted short-term loans at high rates of interest. The total agricultural debt quickly reached staggering proportions. The burden fell heaviest on the poorer peasants, and by 1932 two-thirds of those with less than 10 hectares defaulted on their loans. At first, the government tried to deal with the situation piecemeal, but finally on 18 December 1931 it suspended the forced collection of debts on rural property and undertook a massive programme of debt conversion. Four laws dealing with agricultural debts were enacted between 1932 and 1934 and left no doubt as to the gravity of the situation and the eagerness of many in high places to put an end to peasant agitation, which, they feared, threatened the existing social order. But they found a solution to the debt crisis which benefited the financial oligarchy at the expense of the mass of taxpayers, who would ultimately pay the lion's share of the cost of debt conversion.[27]

To reopen markets for agricultural products in Western Europe the Rumanian government took the lead in mobilizing the agrarian states of Eastern Europe for collective action. Their immediate goals were to lift restrictions imposed by the industrialized states on agricultural imports and to overcome the competition for markets from across the Atlantic. The first conference of East European agricultural states was held in Warsaw on 28–30 August 1930, but here and at subsequent meetings during the next two years they accomplished little. The great powers were unwilling to modify their economic policies toward Eastern Europe and could ignore the agricultural states with impunity.

[27] Bozga, *Criza agrară*, 145–70.

The depression had a profound and lasting influence on the economic thought of Rumanian politicians of both the Liberal and National Peasant parties. The dependence of their country on the great industrial powers, which was starkly revealed during the depression by their restrictions on imports of Rumanian agricultural products and their refusal to consider the unique problems of agrarian states, persuaded the leaders of both parties to support a policy of accelerated industrialization. Virgil Madgearu's reaction was typical. Previously opposed to large-scale industrialization, he now urged the development of a strong industry in order to assure both the economic and political independence of the country.

The Liberals, who were in power between 1934 and 1937, made industrialization the centrepiece of their domestic programme. They emphasized heavy industry, which they planned to make the foundation of a modern national economy. All their activities reveal a pattern of increasing state intervention in and control of the economy. They were convinced that state encouragement and protection of industry were indispensable because private means had proved inadequate. But they were not alone. It had become evident to politicians of other parties and ideological persuasions that the problems of industry and of the economy generally could be solved only by firm direction from above.

Support for industry by the state took many forms. It supplied capital directly through its own budget, a policy that resulted in, among other things, an almost threefold increase of imports of machinery between 1927 and 1937. It also made large amounts of capital available through new official lending agencies and the National Bank and aided selected industries through regular purchases of their products, especially military supplies, including uniforms and reinforced concrete for fortifications. The sums involved were substantial. In the 1938/9 fiscal year, for example, the ministries of National Defence, Air, and the Navy were allocated 21 per cent of the state budget, and they and other state agencies on the eve of the Second World War were absorbing 70 per cent of the production of the metallurgical industry and 80 per cent of coal production. The government also offered special inducements to companies to produce goods not already made in the country, especially those incorporating advanced technology or capable of promoting the industrialization of the country. In order to enable certain industries to survive the government legalized cartels on 10 May 1937. The new law carried previous legislation to encourage industry one step further by providing for a permanent monopoly or quasi-monopoly over the production of certain goods under the supervision of the appropriate government ministry. The sanctioning of monopolies was intended to protect the 'interests of the state' in supporting those industries judged to be vital to the national economy and too important to be left to the 'vagaries' of private enterprise. Inherent also in the Liberals' economic policy of the 1930s, as earlier, was protectionism, and between 1932 and 1938 it increased fourfold the tariffs on a large number of imported manufactured goods. The major exceptions continued to be items such as machinery and electric motors, which were not produced in Rumania and were judged indispensable for further industrialization.[28]

Foreign capital continued to be an important source of financing for industry in the 1930s. In certain industries—coal mining, oil, and chemicals—it retained a dominant place. Yet the decade between 1929 and 1939 also witnessed a decline of foreign participation in heavy industry from 70 to 40 per cent and in the economy in general from 65 to 38 per cent. French and English capital predominated. Germany attempted to recover something of her pre-war position, especially in oil and mining (bauxite and chromium), because of their military uses, but she had little success in penetrating these branches of the Rumanian economy until after September 1940.

As in the 1920s, the Liberals lacked a coherent agricultural policy and carried out industrialization at the expense of agriculture, diverting the bulk of investment capital into favoured industries. Consequently, they left the existing organization of agriculture intact and did little to enhance productivity or improve the living standard of the majority of peasants. Rather, they continued to encourage the raising of wheat for export in order to obtain the foreign exchange necessary to expand industry. Such a policy perpetuated extensive agriculture, which remained a fundamental cause of the unrelenting agrarian crisis. None the less, the Liberals took modest steps to diversify production by introducing new crops, notably soybeans. A new company was formed with the help of the I. G. Farben Company of Germany to import soybean plants, distribute them to producers, and then buy the entire crop and export it to Germany. Plantings before 1935 were

---

[28] Marcela Felicia Iovanelli, *Industria românească, 1934–1938* (Bucharest, 1975), 50–86.

insignificant, but within two years the amount of land devoted to soybeans increased from 20,000 to 95,000 hectares.

The royal dictatorship of Carol II between 1938 and 1940 pursued the same economic policies as the Liberals. State intervention became more pronounced as projects for industrialization were accelerated with particular emphasis upon the needs of national defence. In agriculture the middle-sized and well-to-do peasants were favoured over the majority, who had holdings of less than 5 hectares. The government made new credit available to the worthy peasant and undertook to rationalize and intensify agricultural production in accordance with a master five-year plan drawn up in March 1940. It offered solutions to those problems of Rumanian agriculture which had eluded previous governments: a freeing of the peasants from their dependence upon grain production through a reduction in the amount of land planted in wheat by 800,000 hectares and in corn by 500,000 hectares; the diversification of crops through incentives to raise vegetables and industrial plants; and a closing of the price gap between agricultural and industrial products. To accomplish these ambitious goals an appropriation of 600 million lei a year was to be included in the state budget, but the political crisis and the loss of territory in the summer and autumn of 1940 cut short all these initiatives.

9
Politics, 1919–1940

The main issue in Rumanian political life in the inter-war period was the contest between democracy and authoritarianism. The prospects for the consolidation of a parliamentary system based upon Western European practice seemed bright in the early 1920s. The enactment of universal manhood suffrage held out the hope that government by oligarchy would soon be a relic of the past. The leaders of the Rumanian National Party of Transylvania and the Peasant Party of the Old Kingdom, which had broad support, were committed to the full participation of all citizens in the political process and to genuine consultations with the voters through fair elections. Both the Peasantists, who were otherwise wary of following Western models, and the Europeanists, who were certain that Rumania was destined to follow the Western path of development, were committed to parliamentary government. Among the general population, too, there was at least latent support for a democratic political experiment. When given the opportunity to express their preferences freely, as in the election of 1928, they voted overwhelmingly for those parties which stood for democracy.

Formidable obstacles stood in the way of political change. First of all were the habits of a half-century. The apathy and inexperience of the mass of the peasants, caused mainly by their almost total exclusion from the political process, were never entirely overcome, and, as a result, the impact of universal suffrage was diminished. Changes were also needed in the spirit in which politics was carried on. But politics for the sake of politics for short-term tactical advantage, instead of high principle, against which Constantin Rădulescu-Motru and many others had railed, not only was not eradicated, but intensified. The Liberal Party, the strongest political organization of the 1920s, interfered but little with custom. In theory committed to the parliamentary system, it preferred to 'conduct' elections in the time-honoured fashion and to rule in an authoritarian manner through a small financial and industrial oligarchy. Outside regular party politics were many groups and individuals who opposed everything that modern Europe represented—urbanism, industry, rationalism, and, not least of all, democratic political institutions. Thus, the followers of Nichifor Crainic and Nae Ionescu, among others, fostered a climate of opinion favourable to extreme nationalist and authoritarian political movements.

The 1930s was the decade of crisis for Rumanian democracy. The world depression exacerbated existing economic problems and social tensions and thus gave impetus to all those forces that sought to undermine parliamentary government. The gathering crisis enhanced the appeal of anti-Semitism among certain elements of society, who used it to rally support for their particular brands of nationalism. Foremost among the several organizations that made anti-Semitism the ideological core of their new Rumania was the Iron Guard, which reached the height of its popularity in the mid-1930s. The accession of Carol II to the throne in 1930 also boded ill for democracy, as he made no secret of his disdain for parliamentary institutions and of his intention to make himself the undisputed source of power in the state. Nor can shifts in the European balance of power be ignored. The rise of Nazi Germany and the aggressive behaviour of fascist Italy combined with the policy of appeasement adopted by the Western democracies encouraged both the opponents of democracy and the hesitant in Rumania to conclude that the future belonged to authoritarianism. The leading democratic parties seemed to have lost much of their *élan* of the preceding decade. They proved incapable of withstanding the assault from both within and outside the country and acquiesced in the establishment of Carol's dictatorship in 1938, an event which marked the end of the democratic experiment in Rumania.

FORM AND SUBSTANCE

As in the reign of Charles I, the king was the key element in political life. Under the new Constitution of 1923 he retained considerable powers. He could choose his ministers even from outside parliament, and he could dismiss them as he thought best, but custom obliged him to take into account the wishes of the majority party in parliament. The Prime Minister and the other members of the cabinet were expected to work with parliament, and, if they could not retain its confidence, custom required them to resign. The king then appointed their successors. The old

system of rotation in office also continued to operate. Although
the machinery was not as well oiled as before the war, no government was ever overturned by parliament. The constitution also
granted the king extensive legislative powers. He had the authority to sanction all laws, but he never exercised his right to
veto a bill passed by parliament. Thus, in practice, legislation
was solely the prerogative of parliament. But the king exercised
broad discretionary powers in interpreting the laws through his
right to issue 'regulations'. These *regulamente* were intended, in the
first instance, to expand upon laws already in force by providing
officials with detailed instructions as to their execution. They
could not change or suspend laws, and the ministers, who usually
drew them up, were in theory prevented from abusing their
power by the courts, which were empowered to hear all challenges to the legality of the regulation in question. But such
challenges were rare, as the occasions permitted by the law for
forcing administrative officials, including ministers, to assume
responsibility for their acts were narrowly defined. The king
could also issue regulations unrelated to a specific law, a power
limited only by the provision of the constitution that such acts
could not restrict individual liberty or impose a burden, such
as a new tax, on the citizenry. The king had the authority to
negotiate and conclude treaties of alliance, but they were not
valid until ratified by parliament, and only parliament had the
right to declare war and make peace. All the limitations on the
royal powers were respected under a constitutional monarch such
as Ferdinand. They were ineffective in curbing the appetite for
power of a Carol II.

   The political system in Rumania in the inter-war period was a
parliamentary democracy in form, but it worked in ways that
reflected the current social and economic conditions in the country
and its political evolution during the preceding century. As before
the First World War, although elections were usually held when
a government left office and the campaigns were spirited, the
party chosen by the king to form the new government had an
enormous advantage over all the others because it 'conducted' the
elections. By using time-honoured methods it assured itself of a
powerful majority in parliament. Thus, unlike parliamentarism in
Western Europe, where the government was a creation of the
legislature, in Rumania parliament continued to be an extension
of the government. An examination of election results reveals
how crucial the management of the elections was to the party in

power. The fortunes of the Liberal Party in the elections of 1922, 1926, and 1927 are instructive: in 1922, the Liberals, who conducted the elections, won 222 seats in the Chamber of Deputies to 147 for all other parties: in 1926, when they were out of office, they elected only sixteen deputies with 7.34 per cent of the popular vote; back in power the following year, they won 318 seats with 61.7 per cent of the vote.

Elections, which produced overwhelming majorities for the government party and left the opposition impotent, tended to transform the work of parliament into a purely governmental activity. Legislative initiative thus belonged to the government. Of the 4,574 bills introduced in the Chamber of Deputies between 1919 and 1940, 71 per cent emanated from the government. The 29 per cent that originated in parliament itself usually dealt with questions of minor importance. The power of the government majority may be judged from the fact that only one bill out of 3,225 presented to the Chamber by the government in a period of twenty-one years was rejected. Huge majorities also accounted for the general lack of control exercised by parliament over the government. The number of questions addressed to ministers in the Chamber were relatively few. During the inter-war period there were some 2,500 questions, but only 220 of them were developed in any depth, most of them by a small number of opposition deputies. In any case, no government ever fell and no minister was ever forced to resign because of an interpellation. The government majority unfailingly gave a vote of confidence to the cabinet or the individual minister.[1]

The judiciary, which, according to the Constitution of 1923, was a co-ordinate but separate branch of government, continued to act only as a modest check on the actions of the executive and legislative branches. Although judges could not be removed from office, except by the decision of a duly constituted disciplinary commission, they were to a greater or lesser degree dependent upon the party in power because advancement in the system was difficult without its support. The constitution offered judges great potential power, for it allowed for the judicial review of acts of the executive, especially the administrative bureaucracy, and of the legislature. A private citizen who believed that his constitutional rights had been violated could bring his claim before the

[1] Matei Dogan, *Analiza statistică a 'democraţiei parlamentare' din România* (Bucharest, 1946), 65–8, 101–8.

Court of Appeal in his district, and the court might find his grievance justified and declare the act in question illegal. But such cases were rare because a challenge to authority in the name of individual rights, besides being a difficult and expensive under-taking, was contrary to long-established custom. The Constitu-tion of 1923 gave the Court of Cassation, the highest court in the land, the sole authority to determine the constitutionality of laws. But it limited the court's decision to the case under review, and, hence, deprived it of the power to legislate by judicial fiat. Moreover, the Court of Cassation used its review powers spar-ingly: between 1923 and 1932 it declared only nine pieces of legislation contrary to the constitution.[2]

The methods and spirit of government administration tended to discourage broad participation in public affairs and to impede any significant change in the traditional servant-master relationship between the majority of the citizenry and the bureaucracy. Most influential in maintaining the status quo was the continued cen-tralization of authority in Bucharest. The first comprehensive post-war law on the organization of local government, which was enacted in 1925, was fully in accord with the Constitution of 1923. It endorsed the principle of the unitary national state and thus gave the organs of the central government and its represen-tatives enormous power and influence over local affairs. These officials could, for example, dissolve communal and *judeţ* councils and suspend or dismiss the mayors of communes. The law re-inforced the position of the prefect of the *judeţ* as the key figure in local government. As before the First World War, he was ap-pointed by the Minister of the Interior and exercised the powers of the central government as its chosen representative in his district. Although he headed the *judeţ* administration, he was responsible to Bucharest not to the local citizens. When the Na-tional Peasant Party came to power in 1928 it experimented with a partial decentralization by making the communal and *judeţ* administrations more responsive to local needs and by giving local authorities significant decision-making power. But the law which it enacted in 1929 did not produce the desired results mainly because local authorities and organizations lacked the experience and the material means to make a complicated and unwieldy administrative system operate efficiently. After the Liberals re-

---

[2] H. Lévy-Ullman and B. Mirkine-Guetzévitch (eds.), *Roumanie* (La Vie juridique des peuples, 4) (Paris, 1933), 19–21.

turned to power in 1933 they replaced the National Peasants' law with their own, which greatly reduced local autonomy and once again placed the final decisions in the hands of the central government and its representatives. The installation of the royal dictatorship in 1938 simply reinforced the centre at the expense of local administration.[3]

In many ways political life after the First World War promised to be different from what both politicians and the public had known before 1914. Fundamental constitutional changes between 1918 and 1921 held out the prospect of greater diversity of political expression and of increased activism on the part of the general public. The formation of a unified national state brought new Rumanian political parties and traditions from Transylvania, Bukovina, and Bessarabia and significant Magyar and German minority parties from Transylvania. The introduction of universal suffrage in November 1918 opened political life to greater numbers of citizens than ever before. Such a substantial increase in the active electorate suggested that politics could no longer be carried on in traditional ways by the few at the expense of the many. New opportunities thus opened up to such groups as the middle-sized peasantry and the urban working class.

There were, none the less, significant limits to participation in political life. The majority of the peasantry, mainly the lower strata, remained apathetic. The causes were of long standing. The peasants' social and economic life had usually been confined to the village, and thus they lacked the necessary experience with all the mechanisms of the political system that would have enabled them to use their numbers to best advantage. Political parties were also responsible for the passivity of the countryside. Even those that were nominally peasant failed to draw the mass of the rural population into the political process. The social composition of the Chamber and the Senate reflects their lack of interest. In the legislatures elected between 1922 and 1937 roughly 40 per cent of the total membership of the two houses were lawyers, 15–18 per cent large landowners, 11.2 per cent elementary and secondary schoolteachers, 8.7 per cent clergy, 6.5 per cent university professors, and 3.7 per cent doctors. Although peasants composed roughly 80 per cent of the population during this period, they obtained only 1 per cent of the seats.[4]

---

[3] Erast Diti Tarangul, *Tratat de drept administrativ român* (Cernăuţi, 1944), 146–53.
[4] Dogan, *Analiza statistică*, 55–61.

A significant regrouping of political forces occurred in the years immediately after the war. The traditional two-party rivalry between the Liberals, representing, in general, the middle class, and the Conservatives, the party of large landowners, dissolved, as the Conservative Party, already in serious decline before the war, collapsed following the agrarian reforms of 1918—21, which undermined the economic power of the large landowners. As a consequence, the fortunes of the upper bourgeoisie, grouped mainly in a rejuvenated Liberal Party, never seemed brighter. As its economic and political power steadily grew, it established itself as the dominant social class. But its ascendancy was short-lived, as it faced a determined challenge from an alliance of the Peasant Party, which had been founded in 1918, and the venerable Rumanian National Party of Transylvania. Their fusion in 1926 to form the National Peasant Party (Partidul Naţional-Ţărănesc) restored to some extent the old two-party balance in Rumanian politics, as the new party gathered together broad elements of the centre to oppose the Liberals. Support for a return to the two-party rotation system of the pre-war decades was, in any case, widespread. King Ferdinand and a number of politicians, among them Nicolae Iorga, were anxious to create a counterweight to the all-powerful Liberals, and even some Liberals preferred a single, large target for their attacks to the welter of small parties. For many persons in and out of politics the two-party system held out the promise of political stability in an era of social change and economic crisis.

The new rotation system, however, never operated smoothly, mainly because of the great diversity of parties and the lack of cohesion within the Liberal and National Peasant parties. In the first decade after the war the trend was toward fewer parties, as the disappearance of the Conservative and the fusion of the Peasant and National parties suggest, but that trend was reversed in the 1930s, as a multitude of small parties came into being, primarily in response to the unsettled economic situation and the eagerness of diverse groups to use the political process for their own, often limited, ends. Many parties formed during this period were little more than factions grouped around strong personalities which had split away from the main party. The National Peasant Party is a good example of the absence of internal cohesion during the inter-war years. A hybrid, it never succeeded in bringing its two main wings together into a smooth-working partnership. Numerous smaller groups within it retained their separate identities: on the right were the former Conservatives who had followed Take Ionescu and were now led by George Mironescu, who in the 1930s favoured a royal dictatorship, and the group headed by Alexandru Vaida, which also favoured an authoritarian government; on the left were the supporters of Dr Nicolae Lupu, who advocated further agrarian reform and social legislation to benefit the urban working class; and occupying the broad centre were the followers of Iuliu Maniu, who represented the official position of the party on social and economic issues and opposed all attempts to limit or subvert parliamentary democracy. The Liberal Party presented a similar picture. There were the so-called old Liberals, who constituted the official party and opposed Carol II's attempts at authoritarian rule and various fascist currents in the 1930s; the young Liberals, led by Gheorghe Tătărescu, who supported Carol's plans for a dictatorship; and the dissidents grouped around Gheorghe Brătianu, who favoured the maintenance of the parliamentary system and opposed Carol's political ambitions, but in foreign affairs favoured close co-operation with Germany as the most effective way of ensuring Rumania's territorial integrity. The small parties, simply because they were small or represented narrow interests, were generally more successful in maintaining their unity.

The Liberals sought to deal with the political uncertainties occasioned by the multiplicity of parties and groupings by introducing a new electoral law in 1926 which rewarded the party obtaining at least 40 per cent of the vote in parliamentary elections with a 'premium' in the form of 50 per cent of the seats in the Chamber of Deputies. But the winning party gained not only half of the seats; it also shared proportionally in the other half and thus might, in the end, have at its disposal 70 per cent or more of the seats in the Chamber. The Liberals, who were confident of their ability to control the political process, thus seemed bent upon assuring themselves of as complete a mastery of the legislature as they had of the bureaucracy.

The increased citizen participation in elections, the diversity of parties, and the spirit of political activism changed the character of elections for parliament after the war. They became true electoral campaigns which set in motion millions of voters. Even though it was still difficult for the opposition to overcome the advantages of incumbency, notably to gain 60 per cent of the vote, they never entered the campaign burdened with the thought that they had already lost. The combined opposition did well in numerous elections, garnering, for example, 52.5 per cent of the vote in 1931, 59.7 per cent in 1932, and, to the surprise of all concerned, 63.6 per cent in 1937.

In the 1920s political parties retained a key role in the selection of new governments. As before the war, upon the resignation of the government the king entered into consultations with the leaders of various parties, after which he entrusted the formation of a cabinet to one among them. The immediate task of the new government was to organize elections for the Chamber and Senate. The process of selecting a new prime minister usually went smoothly, for the king chose him from only a limited number of parties. Excluded were the leftist parties, the parties of the national minorities, and, almost always, the small parties. The leaders of the two largest parties—the Liberals and the National Peasants— therefore had the greatest influence on the king's decision.

Yet this method of forming new governments gradually changed the role of parties in the political process. In the 1920s the Liberals and, later, the National Peasants had exercised much influence at the palace, influence which often seriously limited the monarch's decision-making power. But in the 1930s Carol succeeded in freeing himself from these constraints by playing the major parties off against one another. Before he became king it had been customary for parties to come to power not through their potential strength at the polls but as a result of influence exerted at the palace. Yet, in competing for the king's favour, they, in effect, weakened one another. Under Carol the rivalry among the parties took an acute form, as many party leaders put all their political capital at his disposal, and every party took care to have among its leaders one or more with good connections at the palace who could be counted upon to protect the party's interests.

Other political forces besides the parties came to the fore in the 1930s. The camarilla—the favourites at the palace—acquired an extraordinary position under Carol. He used it effectively in his unrelenting campaign to undermine the political parties, which he had come to see as the main support of the parliamentary system he was intent upon destroying. Thus, unlike King Charles, who had sought to consolidate the power of the throne by balancing the two major parties off against each other, and King Ferdinand, who had linked the dynasty's fortunes to the powerful Liberal Party, Carol transformed the Crown into an instrument for destroying the political parties. Another element he relied upon were the great industrialists and bankers, both inside and outside the camarilla, such as Nicolae Malaxa, the owner of a large metal-lurgical complex, Max Auschnitt, a director of numerous industrial enterprises and a leading figure in various organizations of industrialists, and Aristide Blank, the head of a leading private banking house, who were especially favoured. They were linked to no political party, although they maintained close contacts with diverse individual politicians, and they were in sharp competition with the leaders of the Liberals and National Peasants for influence at the palace.

PARTIES

The Conservative Party did not survive the end of the war. Two factions struggled to carry on Conservative principles, but they, too, disappeared from the scene. Traditional Conservative leaders strove desperately to adapt to changing political and economic circumstances. Alexandru Marghiloman announced the formation of the Progressive Conservative Party (Partidul Conservator-Progresist) in December 1918 and promised to carry out agrarian and electoral reforms, but his proposals fell short of what the general public expected and what other parties were prepared to do. Marghiloman's efforts to arrange alliances with other parties failed. There was no interest in a party whose total vote for members of the Chamber of Deputies slipped from 3.98 per cent in 1919 to 2.82 per cent in 1920. After the elections of 1922, in which his party won no seats, Marghiloman resigned as its head on the grounds that it had ceased to be a factor in political life. After his death in 1925 its remaining members joined General Alexandru Averescu's People's Party. The other Conservative party was Take Ionescu's Democratic Conservative Party, which had been strengthened by a fusion with Nicolae Filipescu's wing of the Conservative Party in 1916. It attempted to bring together the few remaining large landlords and those elements of the bourgeoisie with links to foreign capital. Ionescu had returned from the Paris peace conference in the summer of 1919 with high hopes of achieving the political power he had long sought, but Ionel Brătianu was the man upon whom the king continued to rely, and Averescu was the popular hero. Ionescu tried to adapt to the new post-war circumstances. He changed the name of his party to Democrat-Unionist and revised its programme to appeal to a broad spectrum of the population, but all to no avail. When he was appointed Prime Minister, following the resignation of the first Avercscu government in December 1921, he was unable to put together a viable coalition and, losing a vote of confidence in parliament in January 1922, he resigned. This event signified the end of his own political career and the disappearance once and for all of the Conservatives as a political force. After Ionescu's death in June 1922 his remaining adherents joined the Rumanian National Party.[5]

The fortunes of the Liberal Party never seemed brighter than in the inter-war years, as it became one of the two major political formations of the period and controlled the government for long periods, notably in 1922—6. The dominant element within the Liberal Party was the 'financial oligarchy' grouped around Banca Românească, where a small group of great banking and industrial families, headed by the Brătianu family, held sway. In the years immediately after the First World War the oligarchy and the Liberal Party formed essentially a single entity, over which Ionel Brătianu presided as, to use Nicolae Iorga's characterization, 'the feared uncrowned king of the country'. At this time the oligarchy was relatively homogeneous, and its economic potential had no rivals within Rumanian capitalism. The Liberals had laid the foundations of their economic power by taking advantage of significant changes in Rumanian banking before the war, particularly the concentration of bank capital and its investment in industry. Of the 556 banks operating in 1912, twenty-one large banks (3 per cent of the total) held 44.6 per cent of the capital of all banks. Banks had also become the major financiers of industry. Before the war they had usually invested their capital in commerce and agriculture, but in the inter-war period there was hardly a bank, large or small, which did not have at least one industrial enterprise of its own. Thus, the Brătianu group within the party controlled numerous manufacturing and other industrial concerns through its multiple connections with the main bastions of Rumanian finance. For example, Vintilă Brătianu, who was the Minister of Finance in his brother's government in 1922—6 and Prime Minister himself in 1927—8, controlled Banca Românească, which in turn in 1919 dominated twenty-eight other banks and industrial enterprises along with their numerous subsidiaries and

---

[5] A succinct account of the demise of Conservative parties is in Mihail Rusenescu and Ioan Saizu, *Viaţa politică în România, 1922–1928* (Bucharest, 1979), 40–7.

branches. He and his brother, Constantin (Dinu), influenced the policies of numerous other banks and industrial concerns through membership on their boards of directors.

The intertwining of banking, industry, and political power on such a grand scale was simply a consequence of the state's having assumed the chief role in promoting economic development. Thus, there was an intermingling of business and financial interests with the political leadership and state bureaucracy, and the control of industry, banks, and government inevitably fell into the hands of the same people. Since industry depended heavily upon state financial support, such a relationship tended to eliminate competition and decrease efficiency, as political alliances and friendships rather than merit and experience determined the awarding of subsidies and contracts.[6]

The financial and industrial oligarchy maintained its dominant position in the Liberal Party throughout the inter-war period. Yet, the general membership of the party was continually shifting in response to the general economic and political development of the country. At the beginning of the period those social groups which had traditionally supported the party, such as the heads of popular banks and rural co-operatives, mainly teachers and priests, left the Liberals to found the Peasant Party, taking large numbers of peasants with them. But the Liberals found new sources of support. To achieve their goal of becoming a truly national party they courted diverse groups, which gradually altered the composition of the party and diluted the power of the Brătianu group. After 1918 the party made a determined effort to attract the business and financial interests of the new provinces, but the oligarchy could not always control the newcomers. The new entrepreneurs swelled the ranks of the party, and the Liberal economic élite thus expanded, but in the process it lost some of its homogeneity. Faced with the uncertainties posed by universal suffrage, the Liberals also attempted to increase their strength at the polls by adding whole parties and political groups, such as the remnants of the old Conservative Party and dissident elements of the Rumanian national parties of Transylvania, Bukovina, and Bessarabia. Thus, a growing number of individuals entered the Liberal apparatus, particularly at the provincial level, who had only tenuous links with the oligarchy.

In the 1920s certain Liberal theoreticians, notably Ştefan Zeletin

---

[6] Mircea Muşat and Ion Ardeleanu, *România după Marea Unire*, ii, part 1: *1918–1933* (Bucharest, 1986), 55–70.

and Dimitrie Drăghicescu, tried to gain general acceptance for the idea that the Liberal Party, because of its dominant place in economic and political life, represented the whole nation. Liberal leaders themselves presented their party as being above classes and as promoting measures benefiting all elements of society. They supported these claims by pointing to the fact that their party had initiated agrarian and electoral reforms and had made national unity a reality by creating Greater Rumania. In 1923 Ion G. Duca (1879–1933), at the time Minister of Foreign Affairs in the Brătianu government and later prime minister, claimed that the party was guided by the idea of progress, which it fostered not by violence and sudden leaps forward but through gradual, organized activity within the bounds of private property, social harmony, democracy, and national consciousness. Ionel Brătianu agreed. He argued that the Liberals took into account the needs and interests of all social groups and strove to harmonize them. Since theirs was the 'party of the nation', Brătianu and his colleagues denounced parties based upon class as 'foreign to the Rumanian spirit'. In their view, both the Peasant Party and the Socialist Party represented a danger to Greater Rumania, for, by promoting narrow class interests, they threatened to destroy the very foundations of the national state.

In the early 1920s the Liberal Party seemed to have assured itself of a long tenure in office. As late as 1926 no strong political rival had emerged, a situation which relieved the party of outside pressure and thus made inner tensions seem less acute. Moreover, Brătianu and King Ferdinand had achieved a generally harmonious working relationship. But these favourable circumstances abruptly changed; the formation of the National Peasant Party in 1926 presented the Liberals at last with a formidable adversary; the unexpected death of Ionel Brătianu in 1927 deprived the party of dynamic, if authoritarian, leadership; and the defeat in the elections of 1928 led to sharp, divisive conflicts within the party. But most of all, perhaps, the accession of Carol II in 1930 and his manifest hostility to the major political parties, especially his encouragement of dissident movements within them, weakened the Liberal Party and made it increasingly dependent upon the palace. A case in point was Carol's support of the 'young' Liberals, who became the most vehement opponents of the 'old', Brătianu party leadership. The conflict here was not of generations but between the oligarchy, on the one hand, and, on the other, professional people, small entrepreneurs from the provinces, and even large-scale capitalist interests which had been temporarily attracted to the Liberal Party by expectations of power and profit, but had made no commitment to the Brătianu brand of liberalism. The struggle between the two powerful wings of the party slowly turned in favour of the young Liberals. Thanks to the support of the king, and over the objections of the official leadership of the party, they were raised to the highest positions in the state. The differences between the two factions in time became insurmountable; they were like two separate parties that had not yet separated.

The liberalism practised by the Liberal Party differed substantially from the Western European variety. In politics the Liberals used whatever means they had to in order to assure victory at the polls: they mobilized the police, the civil service, and the all-powerful prefects to further their own ends and discourage the opposition. They ran the economy in a similar authoritarian way. Without hesitation they organized cartels, set tariffs, and distributed subsidies and other financial favours to achieve their primary goals—industrialization and the creation of a modern infrastructure based upon Western models. Such policies benefited the financial and industrial oligarchy, but left other groups and classes dissatisfied.

The obvious contradictions between the theory and practice of liberalism in inter-war Rumania went deeper than the political and economic ambitions of the Brătianu family and its supporters. The source of these contradictions may be traced back to the very beginnings of Rumanian liberalism. In the decade preceding the revolution of 1848 and especially during the revolution itself liberal and national goals were inextricably linked. The forty-eighters and their Liberal successors down to the inter-war period strove to create a modern state strong enough to defend the Rumanian nation and preserve its ethnic identity. The advanced states of Western Europe were their model, and, as liberalism prospered in France and England, Rumanian Liberals were certain that it could serve as the ideological underpinning of their own nation-state as well. But Rumania lacked the liberal, urban bourgeoisie which had carried out the economic and social transformation of Western Europe. Even though a Rumanian bourgeoisie emerged in the second half of the nineteenth century, it was too weak to perform a similar task. Instead, the state took its place as the promoter of economic and political development.[7]

[7] Henry L. Roberts, *Rumania: Political Problems of an Agrarian State* (New Haven, Conn., 1951), 108–9.

The National Peasant Party, the other major party of the inter-war period, was formed in 1926 when the Peasant Party of the Old Kingdom united with the National Party of Transylvania. Although both parties shared certain fundamental ideals—each stood for the extension of democratic political institutions and civil liberties to all classes of the population—their leaders initially judged their respective programmes incompatible and, hence, an insurmountable obstacle to fusion. In the immediate post-war years the Peasant Party aimed at radical agrarian reform, while the National Party, though drawing substantial support from Rumanian peasants in Transylvania, was essentially middle class in its outlook and more nationalist than peasant in its ideology. The union of the two parties, consequently, surprised contemporaries.

The Peasant Party was founded in Bucharest on 18 December 1918 at a meeting of some 160 teachers, priests, and well-to-do peasants.[8] Their action was the culmination of months of discussion at the local level about the importance of a separate party to defend the interests of the peasants. The initiative for the establishment of the new party belonged to Ion Mihalache (1882–1963), the President of the General Association of Elementary Schoolteachers. As a teacher in rural areas he had become acquainted at first-hand with the mentality and aspirations of the peasants and remained committed to their welfare and to democracy throughout his long career.

The mass support for the new party came primarily from the peasantry of Moldavia and Wallachia, from all strata, not just the well-to-do. But Mihalache and other leaders, despite their dedication to peasant interests, claimed that they had no intention of excluding merchants, manufacturers, and artisans from the new organization. At the second party congress in 1922 a new statute was adopted which opened membership to any citizen regardless of his previous party affiliation, and in the years following the party experienced the most spectacular growth of any political party of the period. But a serious drawback to open membership soon manifested itself: the party became more heterogeneous and, as a result, internal dissension increased. The majority of the new peasant members came from Wallachia. Outside the Old Kingdom the party was less successful in its recruiting. In Transylvania, for example, peasants continued to support the

---

[8] Ioan Scurtu, *Din viaţa politică a României, 1918–1926* (Bucharest, 1975), 11–18.

National Party. As for the leadership of the Peasant Party, it came initially from the heads of popular banks and village co-operatives, but, increasingly, intellectuals, who were attracted to the new party by its commitment to political democracy and social reform, assumed positions of leadership. Prominent among them were Dimitrie Gusti, the well-known social anthropologist, and the members of his Institutul Social Român (Rumanian Social Institute), which he founded in Bucharest in 1921; Virgil Madgearu, an economist who was to become the leading theorist of Peasantism; and the novelist Cezar Petrescu, who became a contributor to the party's official organs, *Ţara nouă* (1919–21; The New Country) and *Aurora* (1921–6; The Dawn).

The Peasant Party minced no words in setting forth its objectives and the means it intended to use to achieve them.[9] At its first general congress in November 1921 the delegates adopted a programme which declared class struggle to be a decisive force in the evolution of society, acknowledged the party as the representative of the peasant class, and declared its opposition to all other parties. Yet it denied any intention of seeking to destroy these parties and proposed co-operation with all those classes which had productive roles in society. Clearly, the party understood class struggle as a movement for reform rather than as a revolutionary overthrow of the existing social order, for it proclaimed its devotion to democratic principles. The agrarian problem was foremost among its concerns, and the solutions it proposed reflected the ideas of Constantin Stere and the principles of Peasantism elaborated in the 1920s by Virgil Madgearu: the peasant who worked the land should control the means of production; the organization of agriculture should be based upon the small independent holding; and the co-operative movement should provide the framework for production. The party programme also left room for a 'peasant industry', as a means of enhancing the productivity of agriculture and improving the standard of living of the peasant. The party had as its chief political goal the transformation of the peasant into a citizen by bringing him fully into the political process. It proposed to do this by assuring the peasant equality before the law and by decentralizing government administration in the village and the *judeţ*, a reform which would place the responsibility for local

[9] *Proiectul de program al Partidului Ţărănesc din România aprobat de congresul general din 20–21 noiembrie 1921* (Bucharest, 1921), 4–25.

affairs in the hands of local citizens. As time passed, especially after the fusion with the National Party and the influx of intellectuals and professional people, the Peasant Party lost some of its radical enthusiasm—the idea of class struggle receded into the background—but it never abandoned its commitment to democratic parliamentary government.

The National Party of Transylvania represented all elements of the Rumanian population of Transylvania, as it had done before the First World War. Although its leadership remained middle class, it continued to have the same broad social base as the party that had defended Rumanian national rights in pre-war Hungary. The mass of the peasants clearly supported it. So did the intellectuals and the small professional class of the cities. It also represented the banking and industrial bourgeoisie, which after 1918 felt threatened by the Liberal financial oligarchy in the Old Kingdom. Indeed, the party became a declared foe of the Liberals. The latter were not slow to take up the challenge, because they regarded this new force in the political life of Greater Rumania as a grave threat to their predominance.

Before the war the leaders of the National Party had succeeded in keeping social and political differences among themselves in check in their desperate defence of national rights. But after the achievement of union in 1918 the diversity of party life and the possibility of new political combinations put a heavy strain on the old coalition. Two strong tendencies now manifested themselves. One, which included Vasile Goldiş, one of the party's principal theorists, insisted upon maintaining the regional character of the party. He was certain that in this way the party could gain a decisive voice in whatever government might be formed because, he thought, Rumania could not be governed without the political participation of Transylvania. Consequently, he and his colleagues flatly opposed alliances with other parties. A second group, led by Iuliu Maniu, advocated just the opposite strategy—the abandonment of regionalism. Maniu, the chief spokesman for Rumanian democracy in the inter-war period, and his associates were convinced that if their party was to grow and prosper, it must expand its base of support, a task, they reasoned, which could be accomplished only through fusions and alliances with other parties. They were certain, too, that they could not overcome the economic and political power of the Liberals by themselves. Maniu received encouragement from King Ferdinand to gather together 'sufficient political forces' to enable him to form a government when the time came to replace the Liberals. The king clearly had in mind the revival of the old rotation system as a means of gaining leverage in his own relations with the Liberals. In the years immediately after the war, then, middle-class elements in the National Party tried to create close links with like-minded elements in parties from the other provinces, but in Bucharest their political and economic programme aroused only modest interest. Thus, for the time being, the party retained its provincial character.

The Maniu wing of the party carried on long and sometimes acrimonious negotiations with the Peasant Party until the spring of 1926.[10] The coming to power of Alexandru Averescu, the head of the People's Party, in March shocked both sides. It finally convinced them that separately they would never be strong enough to replace the Liberals. Their accord, worked out by Maniu and Mihalache, called for a single, united party, rather than an alliance in which each partner would retain its separate identity. They accepted the existing constitutional system, but pledged to add to the constitution explicit guarantees of civil liberties and political rights. to assure the integrity of elections, and to carry out a decentralization of the state administration and expand the powers of local government. Both sides were also eager to promote economic development. They emphasized the vital importance of agriculture to the welfare of the country and agreed that industry ought to be encouraged but not at the expense of agriculture. The two partners warmly endorsed the Peasant Party's efforts to promote the co-operative movement and to strengthen peasant smallholders and the National Party's policy of industrial development by giving equal treatment to foreign and domestic capital and by removing burdensome protective tariffs. A united congress of the two parties ratified the agreement in October 1926. Maniu became president, with Mihalache, Alexandru Vaida, a leader of the party's nationalist wing, and the maverick Dr Nicolae Lupu vice-presidents, and Virgil Madgearu secretary-general and head of the Bucharest party organization.

The fusion was by no means smooth. It led to defections from both partners. The most important occurred in the Peasant Party in 1927 when Dr Lupu and his supporters split off from the main party and formed their own Peasant Party (Partidul Ţărănesc).

[10] I. Ciupercă, 'Formarea Partidului Naţional Ţărănesc', *Anuarul Institutului de Istorie şi Arheologie*, 14 (1977), 245–60; 16 (1979), 385–403; 17 (1980), 513–31.

Lupu and his faction were convinced that the new, united party would be less devoted to peasant interests than the old Peasant Party and were angry that the Peasantists had received lesser posts in the new party. But Lupu's programme did not differ in essentials from that of the National Peasant Party, and, though there is no reason to doubt the sincerity of his concern for the peasants, the offer of co-operation from Brătianu and the Liberals was an important cause of his defection at this time. Lupu had little success in promoting his brand of Peasantism and rejoined the National Peasant Party in 1934.[11]

Another organization which represented peasant interests was the Ploughmen's Front (Frontul Plugarilor). Founded in 1933 in Hunedoara *judeţ* in Transylvania and headed by Petru Groza, a wealthy lawyer and landowner from Deva, the new party appealed especially to the poorer peasantry. To Groza and other founders it appeared that the National Peasant Party and government, in general, had deliberately ignored the interests of these peasants during the agricultural crisis, and thus they demanded a drastic reduction of peasant debt, the increased taxation of great wealth, and the exemption from taxation and the assurance of free medical and legal assistance for peasants with less than 5 hectares of land.[12] Despite such an attractive programme, the Front remained a purely regional party. It had little success in the parliamentary elections of December 1933, winning only 0.27 per cent of the vote. Groza, who had been a member of Averescu's conservative People's Party, but had been disappointed in his political ambitions, tried to enhance his party's standing by concluding agreements in 1935 for common action with the Union of Hungarian Workers of Rumania (Romániai Magyar Dolgozók Szövetsége) and a small faction of the Rumanian Socialist Party, but to no avail. His party won but 0.23 per cent of the vote in 1937 and thereafter had little influence until it allied itself with the Communist Party after the Second World War.

For a time in the 1920s the People's Party (Partidul Poporului) seemed destined to become the principal challenger of the Liberals' political supremacy. But it was more a union of like-minded groups and individuals than a unified party, a condition suggested by its original name, League of the People (Liga Poporului).

---

[11] Ioan Scurtu, 'Întemeierea şi activitatea Partidului Ţărănesc—Dr N. Lupu (1927–1934)', *Revista de istorie*, 29/5 (1976), 697–711.

[12] Vasile Puşcaş, *Dr. Petru Groza: pentru o 'lume nouă'* (Cluj-Napoca, 1985), 5–62: G. Micle, *Răscoala pământului* (Bucharest, 1945), 330–51.

Membership came from the defunct Conservative Party, large landowners, and army officers, that is, from those who were fearful of violent or rapid social change and wanted to preserve 'order', but who none the less recognized the need for moderate agrarian reform and an extension of the franchise. They wanted all these matters to be placed in 'strong hands' and were certain that General Alexandru Averescu was their man. They also wanted to use Averescu, who enjoyed wide popularity as a war hero, to combat the Liberals and prevent them from reasserting their pre-war dominance. Averescu, who was a political conservative and had close ties with Take Ionescu, was the heart and soul of the party.

The People's Party formally came into being on 14 April 1918. It proclaimed honest and efficient government, to be achieved by strict adherence to the Constitution, as its watchword, and had as its immediate objectives agrarian reform, to be carried out through the transfer of land from the great estates to the *obşti sătești*, and electoral reform, to be accomplished through the introduction of universal suffrage. Averescu limited his own pronouncements to broad general principles, which would not commit him to any particular course of action, a strategem he thought would be effective in creating a truly national party. But it was clear that he disdained the democratic political process, especially the parliamentary system, which he deemed 'unsuitable' for Rumania; he preferred to be brought to power on a wave of popular enthusiasm. Such ideas were behind the party's boycott of the parliamentary elections of October 1919. Averescu was then at the height of his popularity, and his expectation was that a boycott would discredit the whole process and, as a reaction, the country would turn to him and his party as its saviours. But his hopes were dashed; others—the so-called parliamentary bloc—received the call instead.

Averescu and his associates soon became convinced that the road to power lay in an understanding with the Liberals.[13] Such an accommodation also fitted in with the short-term plans of Ionel Brătianu, who wanted to use the People's Party, first, to destroy the parliamentary bloc government and then, when it came to power, to give the Liberals time to regroup. Hence, when the parliamentary bloc was forced from office he urged the king to

---

[13] G. I. Florescu, 'Evoluţia Partidului Poporului în anii 1920–1921', *Cercetări istorice*, 8 (1977), 427–41.

appoint an Averescu government, which held office from March 1920 to December 1921. Even after it left office the People's Party remained an important political force, but its popularity steadily diminished, and a part of its constituency—the peasantry and the lower middle class—joined the Peasant Party. But a more important cause of its decline was its lack of organization, as Averescu himself was its main cohesive force. Increasingly, the party became subordinate to the Liberals, a position which made possible its brief return to power in 1926–7. After the elections of 1926, when it received 53 per cent of the vote, and its departure from office the following year it was weakened by numerous defections and ceased to be a significant force in political life.

A party, or rather, a grouping, which enjoyed a prestige far beyond its political importance was the Democratic Nationalist Party (Partidul Naţionalist-Democrat). This was Nicolae Iorga's party, which he and Alexandru C. Cuza had founded in 1910. After he and Cuza parted company in 1920 Iorga remained leader of the party, which operated under several names until its dissolution in 1938. Iorga's supporters came mainly from among intellectuals, who were attracted by his scholarly reputation, and from the lower middle class, who found his brand of nationalism and his social and economic programme to their liking. Iorga stood for the full implementation of the post-war agrarian and electoral reforms and free, open elections. None the less, the principle underlying the party's activities harked back to Iorga's association with Sămănătorul—that moral and spiritual, not material, forces determined the course of society's development.

Iorga's overall political objective was to create another government party, one which would alternate in office with the Liberals. For a year, in 1925–6, he merged his party with the National Party, but the union was not a happy one because both he and Maniu wanted to lead. When the National Party made its historic agreement with the Peasant Party Iorga, citing the 'radical' character of the latter, resumed independent political activity. He became Prime Minister in 1931–2, mainly because of Carol's support, but his party, now known as the National Party (Partidul Naţional), was small and insignificant and remained so for the rest of its existence.

Parties on the left, which drew support from the urban working class and sought to represent its interests, had little direct influence on political life in the inter-war period. Their ineffectiveness was owing to the smallness of their constituency—the proletariat remained a small percentage of the active population—to their neglect of national and religious traditions, and, at least in the case of the Communists, to vigorous persecution by the government. Neither the Socialists nor the Communists were able to attract a mass following or to achieve more than a token representation in parliament.

The Social Democratic Party emerged from the war badly divided between moderates, who followed the Western socialist tradition, and radicals, who took as their model the Bolsheviks of Russia. The success of the October Revolution of 1917 had led to the creation of various small Rumanian revolutionary organizations in Russia, especially in Odessa and Moscow, which served as links between the Russian Bolshevik Party and the so-called maximalists in Rumania. In Bucharest by the summer of 1918 impatient militants had organized themselves into the 'Maximalist Federation of Rumania', through which they intended to gain control of the Social Democratic Party and then use it to transform Rumania into a Communist state and society. But they lacked both numbers in their own party and support among the working class and were thus unable to take advantage of the revolutionary situation which arose briefly in Bucharest and other parts of the country after the withdrawal of German occupation troops in November and December 1918.

The formation of the Communist International in March 1919 decisively altered the course of socialism in Rumania. The maximalists, who were now calling themselves Communists, demanded immediate affiliation with the Comintern. They were led by Alexandru Dobrogeanu-Gherea, the son of Constantin, and Boris Ştefanov, a Bulgarian from Dobrudja, and included among its new members a few intellectuals like Lucreţiu Pătrăşcanu (1900—54), lawyer and sociologist, who became a leading Marxist interpreter of Rumania's social and economic development. But at a party congress held in May the moderates prevailed and secured the adoption of a party programme which reflected the gradualism characteristic of Western socialism. Although the party declared its goals to be the abolition of all forms of exploitation and the transfer of all the means of production from private entrepreneurs to society as a whole, it proposed to work within the existing political and economic system to hasten the development of the conditions necessary for the transition to socialism. This programme, a compromise, left the Communists unreconciled to an evolutionary course. But a resort to direct action on their part failed, as the general strike they called in October 1920 was suppressed by the government. A permanent break between Communists and Socialists, as the more moderate party elements called themselves, was precipitated by the outcome of the Comintern meeting in Moscow in November. A six-member Rumanian delegation composed of both maximalists and moderates was sharply criticized by Bukharin and Zinoviev for the failure of their party to be more revolutionary. The reply of the Rumanian delegation to a series of questions posed by the Russians, which accepted the standpoint of the Comintern, appears to have been signed only by Dobrogeanu-Gherea and David Fabian, the editor of the party organ, *Socialismul*. They and other Communists also promised to bring the entire party into the Comintern and to pattern its organization and discipline after the norms of the Bolshevik Party.

Affiliation with the Comintern and the transformation of the Social Democratic Party into a Communist Party were the main issues at the general socialist party congress held in Bucharest on 8–12 May 1921. The debates and the manœuvring of the various factions, often unclear and confusing, came to an abrupt halt on the 12th when the police broke up the congress and arrested many delegates. Those who escaped arrest, mainly Communists under the leadership of younger intellectuals, including Marcel Pauker, an official in the Comintern responsible for Rumanian party affairs in the 1920s and early 1930s, assumed control of the party organization and publications. As a result, the congress came to be known as the first congress of the Rumanian Communist Party. But it was only at the second congress, held in Ploieşti on 3–4 October 1922, that the foundations of the new party were laid. The delegates adopted a new name, 'Communist Party of Rumania, Section of the Communist International', chose a central committee, and approved statutes which mandated a secret organization.[14]

For various reasons the party did not prosper. The government declared it illegal on 11 April 1924, and, henceforth, until the end of the Second World War, it was obliged to carry on its activities underground or through front organizations. Neither mode was conducive to the recruitment of a mass following or the con-

---

[14] Vasile Liveanu, 'Date privind pregătirea şi desfăşurarea Congresului I al Partidului Comunist din România', in *Studii şi materiale de istorie contemporană*, 2 (1962), 163–97.

duct of party business in democratic ways. Government persecution reinforced the authoritarian tendencies present in the party from its beginnings. Congresses had to be held in secret and outside Rumania—the third in Vienna (1924), the fourth in Kharkov (1928), and the fifth and final pre-war congress in Moscow (1931)—and participation was limited to a few leaders and selected activists.

The underground character of the party increased its dependence on the Soviet Communist Party, which through the Comintern arrogated to itself the right to choose party leaders and determine their policies. Subordination to the Soviet party forced Rumanian Communists to take positions on critical national issues that ran counter to the sentiments of the overwhelming majority of the population, including the working class. Thus, at the party congresses in 1924 and 1928 the Rumanian party was obliged to accept the principle of self-determination for the national minorities in Rumania and to approve the secession of Bukovina and Dobrudja from Greater Rumania. Naturally, the Rumanian party dared not recognize the union of Bessarabia with Rumania. Both congresses installed non-Rumanians as secretary-generals of the party—in 1924 Elek Köblös, a Hungarian worker from Transylvania, and in 1928 Vitali Holostenko, a member of the Ukrainian Communist Party—thereby reinforcing the widely held view in Rumania that the party was a foreign organization which put the interests of the Soviet Union ahead of those of Rumania. Soviet domination of the party was enhanced by the presence in Moscow in the 1930s of numerous Rumanian Communists who formed the Rumanian Communist 'bureau', in effect, simply a branch of the Soviet Communist Party.

The membership of the party remained small, probably reaching its high point in 1936 with 5,000. But the party exercised greater influence than this figure would suggest through various front organizations. The most important of these was Blocul Muncitoresc-Ţărănesc (The Worker-Peasant Bloc), which the Communist Party founded in 1925 as a legal mass organization.[15] The Bloc gained between 32,000 and 39,000 votes in the parliamentary elections of 1926, 1927, and 1928, and a high of 74,000 votes and five seats in parliament in 1931. But afterwards its fortunes at the polls declined, and in 1933 the government ordered

---

[15] Florea Dragne, 'Blocul muncitoresc-ţărănesc', in *Organizaţii de masă legale şi ilegale, conduse sau influenţate de P.C.R.*, i (Bucharest, 1970), 258–310.

it and other front organizations of the Communist Party dissolved. The Communist Party did not become an important force in political life until 1944 when the Soviet army occupied Rumania.

Many of those socialists who had rejected affiliation with the Communist International at the May 1921 congress met in June to establish a new socialist organization. The Federation of Socialist Parties of Rumania (Federaţia Partidelor Socialiste din România) was a loose association of the Social Democratic Party of the Old Kingdom (after 1922, the Socialist Party of Rumania) and the socialist parties of Transylvania, the Banat, and Bukovina. They all stood for the transformation of Rumania from its 'semi-feudal' form into a capitalist and, then a socialist society in accordance with the ideas elaborated by Constantin Dobrogeanu-Gherea in *Socialismul in ţările inapoiate*. The heart and soul of the federation was the Socialist Party of Rumania (Partidul Socialist din România), which was formed by centrists led by Constantin Titel Petrescu (1888–1957), the leading figure of Rumanian democratic socialism in the inter-war period, and his close associate, Ilie Moscovici (1885–1943). They opposed a social revolution on the grounds that conditions for it did not yet exist, because of the economic backwardness of the country and the low level of workers' class consciousness. Consequently, they emphasized the need for the further development of capitalism and intensive organizational activity among the workers.

A new Social Democratic Party, uniting all the regional parties into a single political organization, was established in 1927 by Petrescu and others to take the place of the Federation, which had proved too unwieldy to serve as the core of a strong socialist and working-class movement. It pledged to replace the existing financial and political oligarchy with a democratic society based upon the principle of the civil equality of all citizens and the socialization of the means of production. The new party was at pains to differentiate itself from the Communists by insisting that the reforms it demanded should be carried out through the processes of parliamentary democracy rather than by a revolutionary seizure of power. This programme remained the basic document of Rumanian Social Democracy until after the Second World War.

The successes of the Social Democrats in the rough-and-tumble of inter-war electoral politics fell far short of their leaders' expectations. In 1928 the party allied itself with the National Peasant Party in order to defeat the Liberals and thereby strengthen democratic political institutions. The effort was successful, as the National Peasants won a stunning victory, gaining 329 seats in the Chamber of Deputies. The Social Democrats won nine seats, but they were disappointed by the failure of the National Peasants to proceed rapidly with social and political reforms. In subsequent elections the Social Democratic Party ran separate slates of candidates, but saw its share of the vote decline from a high of 101,068 (3.4 per cent) and seven deputies in 1932 to only 37,672 votes (1.3 per cent) and no deputies in 1933. The party was not to be represented in parliament again until 1946. The decline in socialist political fortunes, which was also marked by a drop in party membership, was caused mainly by discouragement over the failure of the party to bring about any significant improvement in the condition of the working class.

Political formations on the right were relatively insignificant in the 1920s. Various attempts in the early years of the decade to establish a Rumanian fascist movement modelled on that in Mussolini's Italy failed to attract more than a handful of members. Nor did experiments with national socialism fare any better.[16] Until the end of the decade their slogans about radical economic and social change had little appeal, mainly because the economy was relatively stable and the majority of the population was still confident that political democracy would succeed in solving pressing economic and social problems.

One issue, none the less, continued to nurture rightist movements—anti-Semitism. By no means a post-war phenomenon, it could in its modern form be traced back at least to the early decades of the nineteenth century when Jewish immigration into the principalities assumed massive proportions. At first, many Rumanians regarded Jewish economic competition as the main threat to national development, but in the second half of the century anti-Semitism took on cultural and racial overtones. Typical expressions of its more virulent forms during the inter-war period came from Nicolae C. Paulescu (1869–1931), professor of physiology at the University of Bucharest, and Alexandru C. Cuza (1857–1947), professor of political economy at the University of Iaşi. The former was convinced that the Jews of Rumania, who, he insisted, already dominated trade and industry, would not be satisfied until they had completely subjugated the native

[16] Armin Heinen, *Die Legion 'Erzengel Michael' in Rumänien* (Munich, 1986), 115–18.

population and had turned the country into a new Palestine. Like Paulescu, Cuza thought that the Jews could never be assimilated and must, because of their 'parasitical' way of life, their religion, and 'degraded racial mixing', be expelled from the country.

After the First World War Cuza and Paulescu attempted to give an organized form to growing anti-Semitism in the universities by forming the National Christian Union (Uniunea Naţională Creştină), whose goal was to defend 'the economic, political, and cultural interests of the Rumanians against the Jews by all legal means'. In the same year, 1922, a group of students at the University of Iaşi led by Corneliu Zelea-Codreanu (1899–1938) formed, with Cuza's blessing, the Association of Christian Students (Asociaţia Studenţilor Creştini), which sought to limit the number of Jews admitted to the university. But neither organization had the tight structure which Codreanu and his militant followers among the students thought necessary to achieve their ends, and they prevailed upon Cuza to establish a formal party capable of mobilizing public opinion and exerting influence in high places. In 1923 Cuza formed the League of National Christian Defence (Liga Apărării Naţional-Creştin), which had as its primary goals the expulsion of the Jews from all areas of economic and cultural life and the education of young people in a Christian and nationalist spirit. Yet fundamental differences between the Cuza and Codreanu wings of the party persisted. The former conceived of the League not as a party at all but as the focus of a broad national movement standing above political parties, and he advocated legal methods of struggle and a change in the popular consciousness through education as the means of attaining his goals. Codreanu, on the other hand, was eager to have at his disposal a tightly organized party dedicated to an aggressive anti-Semitic campaign and ready to use any means necessary to achieve its ends. These differences eventually led to an open break between the two men, and Codreanu and his followers formed their own organization, the Legion of the Archangel Michael (Legiunea Arhanghelului Mihail), in 1927.

Cuza continued to pursue his brand of anti-Semitism and nationalism through the press, public meetings, and the parliament. The League had modest success in the elections of 1931 (3.89 per cent of the vote and 8 seats), 1932 (5.32 per cent and 11 seats), and 1933 (4.47 per cent and 9 seats). To enhance his party's fortunes Cuza agreed to a fusion with the National Agrarian Party (Partidul Naţional-Agrar), which the poet Octavian Goga had founded in 1932 after a massive defection from Averescu's People's Party. The new party, which took form in 1935 and was known as the National Christian Party (Partidul Naţional-Creştin), had its base of support in the small businessmen of Moldavia, Bessarabia, and Transylvania, who felt overwhelmed by the competition from the Liberal financial and industrial oligarchy, and in the petty bourgeoisie of cities and villages who felt abandoned by the other parties. Goga and Cuza agreed on the need for a strong monarchy and an authoritarian political system, the *numerus clausus* for minorities in all institutions and enterprises, and limitations on rights of citizenship granted Jews after 1918.[17]

In the 1930s it was the organization headed by Codreanu that achieved ascendancy on the right. He himself had a strong sense of mission and, convinced that God had chosen him to lead the Rumanian people in a 'healthier direction', he seems never to have doubted the rightness of the path he had chosen. He took no positions on specific political or social issues, but limited himself to vague generalizations about duty and the need for a moral regeneration of society. Evident in all his utterances was a disdain for 'programmes' and an insistence upon the need for a 'new man', a man of action to take over the direction of the country's affairs. But the motive force behind his messianism was anti-Semitism. It was not something borrowed from German National Socialism, but grew out of specific Rumanian conditions. As Codreanu himself explained, he was against Jews before he had ever heard of Hitler because he was convinced that they were the cause of the crisis that permeated all areas of Rumanian life.[18]

Codreanu established a military wing of the League in 1930, which he called the Iron Guard (Garda de Fier) and which became the common designation for the entire organization. As it assumed its characteristic form the Guard resembled German and Italian fascism with its uniforms and salutes and its glorification of the leader—the Căpitan—but all this was merely form. The substance of Rumanian fascism—the anti-Semitism, the Orthodox Christianity (in a distorted form), and the cult of the peasant as the embodiment of natural unspoiled man—came from native sources. Here the traditionalist hostility to cosmopolitanism, rationalism, and industrialization found a crude expression. But lacking was an ideology. Guard leaders ignored Mihail Manoilescu's proposals

[17] Gheorghe T. Pop, *Caracterul antinaţional şi antipopular al activităţii Partidului Naţional Creştin* (Cluj-Napoca, 1978), 121–66.
[18] C. Zelea-Codreanu, *Pentru legionari* (Madrid, 1968), 412–24.

for a Rumanian corporate state on the grounds that the appearance of the new man must precede the adoption of programmes, for, otherwise, institutions would simply reinforce the existing 'corrupt' society.

Between the elections of 1931 and 1937 the Iron Guard became a mass movement, rising from 1 to 15.58 per cent of the popular vote. Its strongest constituency was young and urban, but it cut across class boundaries, appealing at the same time to peasants and rural clergy, elements of the urban working class and the bourgeoisie, and the periphery of society. The leadership of the Guard at this time, its heyday, was formed by the university-educated middle class, but its nationalism appealed to all those who felt alienated by a political and social system which seemed to them to have been created outside and at the expense of 'Rumanian realities'.

THE DEMOCRATIC EXPERIMENT,
1919–1930

Political instability marked the three years following the end of the First World War as a succession of governments wrestled with grave economic and political problems caused or postponed by the war and by the integration of the new provinces into the enlarged national state. After the return of the king and the bureaucracy to Bucharest following the withdrawal of German forces a Liberal government, headed by Ionel Brătianu, was installed at the end of November 1918. The choice of the Liberals to guide post-war Rumania reflected their immense economic power and influence at the palace. It was, on the whole, a popular choice. All those elements of the population who were anxious to preserve 'order' welcomed it because at that moment the Liberals were the strongest and most stable political force in the country and, hence, the most capable of dealing with what was widely perceived as a growing revolutionary situation. Liberal politicians shared this view of their mission, and almost immediately upon assuming office the party enacted the electoral and agrarian reforms which had been promised during the war.

Despite their apparent determination to press forward quickly with fundamental change, Liberal leaders regarded both the electoral and agrarian reforms with mixed feelings. On the one hand, they rejoiced that the extension of the franchise would undermine support for their Conservative rivals, but, on the other, they worried that electoral reform would strengthen old parties and encourage the formation of new ones, which would in all likelihood weaken the Liberal Party's influence in the Old Kingdom and impede its organizational activities in the new provinces. Such considerations may also explain why they continued to postpone elections. As for agrarian reform, they made it clear that they would proceed cautiously with expropriation and the distribution of land to the peasants, for, although they welcomed the opportunity to destroy the economic power of Conservative landlords, they were determined to defend private property.

By the summer of 1919 Brătianu and his colleagues realized that parliamentary elections could no longer be put off as the restlessness of the public and the pressure from other political parties mounted. They also thought that a strong showing by the government in the elections might impress the Allies at the peace conference and persuade them to hasten recognition of the unitary Rumanian state. Their plan was to yield the government temporarily to a shadow administration, which would conduct the elections in the traditional manner, but on behalf of the Liberals, while they themselves kept the entire Liberal political apparatus in place. Then, with the Liberals victorious in the elections the caretakers would turn the government back to them, thereby giving the appearance that the Liberal Party had been swept into office by popular acclaim. With such a mandate Brătianu and company were certain that they could overcome any opposition and proceed to carry out their programme unimpeded.

The Liberals miscalculated. They did not take into account the strength of regional and peasant parties. The Rumanian National Party, which controlled the Consiliu Dirigent, the interim administration in Transylvania, was all-powerful in that province. The Peasant Party was energetic in building its organization in the Old Kingdom and cut deeply into peasant support for the Liberals. The elections in November 1919 were thus a rude shock for the Liberals. Their party received only 22 per cent of the vote and 103 deputies out of 568. All its seats, moreover, were from the Old Kingdom. This was the first time that the government's administrative apparatus had failed to deliver an absolute majority to the party running the elections. The Rumanian National Party won the largest number of seats, 169, while the Peasant Party gained 61. The elections showed the effects of universal suffrage on the traditional balance of political forces and served notice on all parties, especially the Liberals, that they must have a strong organization in all the provinces. The voters also used the occasion to express both dissatisfaction with the old parties and the hope that the new National and Peasant parties would somehow find just solutions to pressing economic and social problems.

A coalition of parties, led by the Rumanian National Party, the Peasant Party, and the Bessarabian Peasant Party, formed a government of the so-called 'Parliamentary Bloc' (Blocul Parlamentar) in December 1919, with Alexandru Vaida, of the National Party, as Prime Minister. The Bloc's political and economic programme was democratic and represented a clear break with the past.[19] The legislation proposed by Ion Mihalache, the Minister of Agriculture, to fulfil the promise of agrarian reform went beyond the Liberal decree of 1918. Nicolae Lupu followed with a bill to limit the role of the gendarmerie in the rural areas and then another to modify the law on rental housing in urban centres in favour of the renter, both, as he put it, in keeping with the 'democratic spirit of the time'. Still other bills planned by the Bloc would eliminate excise taxes on consumer necessities, introduce a progressive income tax, and institute a minimum wage and an eight-hour workday. All these measures, particularly the agrarian bill, aroused a storm of protest from outside the Bloc and even from within, from elements opposed to 'exaggerated' reforms. The Bloc, a coalition without a single set of principles and a unified organization, lacked the discipline necessary to carry out such an ambitious and controversial programme. The combined opposition of the palace, the king, and Averescu, who was at the height of his popularity and was eager to assume power, paralysed the government, which finally resigned in March 1920. Brătianu, working behind the scenes, persuaded the king to summon a 'strong' government, that is, one capable of preventing the enactment of radical reforms like those proposed by the Peasant Party. Since he and the Liberals were not prepared to form a government, the king gave the mandate to Averescu.

Averescu assumed office promising 'order' and 'social harmony'. Eager to form a truly national government, he drew the members of his cabinet from all the provinces and from among persons representing the middle classes and a few who were sympathetic

---

[19] G. Buzatu, 'Un capitol de istorie politică—constituirea, guvernarea şi dispariţia "Blocului parlamentar" (1919–1920)', *Anuarul Institutului de Istorie şi Arheologie*, 13 (1976), 133–46.

to the peasantry. To assure himself of victory in the upcoming elections he made electoral pacts with Take Ionescu's Conservatives and the Liberal Party and thus succeeded in creating an alignment of forces opposed to rapid and significant social and political change. The elections in May, in which the government pulled out all the stops to secure victory, gave the People's Party 206 seats. The next largest number of seats went to the National Party (27) and the Peasant Party (25).

The most difficult issue facing the new government was agrarian reform. Averescu found himself in a dilemma. On the one hand, he recognized the need to shore up his popularity among the peasants by a generous distribution of land, but, on the other, he had to demonstrate his commitment to 'order' to the Liberals and Conservatives, who were his principal supporters. He therefore moved slowly at first, but a mounting clamour from an impatient peasantry obliged the government in March 1921 to submit to parliament the first of a series of laws carrying out a definitive agrarian reform. The government's bill encountered stiff opposition from Peasant Party deputies, because it fell far short of the provisions of their own bills, but it finally passed in the form desired by the government in July.

Other pressing economic problems also confronted Averescu. To assist the recovery from the war his government established by decree a joint-stock company, 'Reconstrucţia' (Reconstruction), with 40 per cent of the capital coming from the state. Averescu thus signalled his intention to follow the Liberals' policy of state initiative in economic development. Another cornerstone of his government's economic policy was financial stability, which politicians both in and outside the government recognized as the foundation of industrial and agricultural growth. In order to overcome the disastrous effects of huge deficits in the annual budget, a rising foreign debt, and such palliatives as increasing the amount of money in circulation the Minister of Finance, Nicolae Titulescu, proposed the most comprehensive fiscal reform in Rumania up to that time. His plan, which rested upon a large increase in taxes, was approved by parliament in June 1921. But it did not have the desired effects. The Liberals opposed it because it required financial sacrifices on the part of their supporters among the middle class, and the international financial and economic crises of the 1920s upset the assumptions upon which it was based.

Although Averescu had come to power with the acquiescence of the Liberal Party, he had shown little concern for Liberal

economic interests, as Titulescu's fiscal measures had demonstrated, and was obviously planning for a long stay in office. The
Liberals retaliated by orchestrating a frontal assault in public on
Averescu's policies and by undertaking a subtle campaign behind
the scenes to undermine his credibility at the palace. These
manœuvres, combined with dissension within his own party,
persuaded Averescu to resign in December 1921.[20]

The next seven years were a period of relative political stability.
It was dominated by the Liberals, who were in power until
November 1928, except between March 1926 and June 1927,
when Averescu briefly returned. Ionel Brătianu, who became
Prime Minister in January 1922, controlled the Liberal Party and,
through it, the country, and exerted enormous influence at the
palace. But his party, because of its authoritarian ways of governing
and its solicitude for industry and foreign trade, lacked broad
popular support. It retained power by manipulating elections and
taking advantage of the disunity of the opposition. The parliamentary elections of March 1922 provide a typical example of its
behaviour. The Liberals won a decisive victory —222 seats (out of
369) to 40 for the Peasant Party, 26 for the National Party, and
only 13 for the People's Party. The striking disparity in the vote
totals between this election and the one two years earlier, when
the People's Party won 206 seats and the Liberals only 16, suggests
that the Liberals conducted the election with all the traditional
efficiency of the party in power. But the election of 1922 was
different in at least one respect from the preceding ones because
the Liberal Party had announced that it would consider the new
parliament a constituent assembly whose main task would be to
draft a new constitution. The election campaign, therefore, was
more spirited than usual, since all the parties were anxious to have
as great a share as possible in shaping the new fundamental law.
But the Liberals and their allies won enough seats—more than
two-thirds—to assure passage of a constitution to their liking.

The Brătianu government presented its draft of a constitution to
the Chamber of Deputies on 5 March 1923. For the next sixteen
days a bitter debate raged over key provisions. The Liberals and
their supporters were determined to maintain and strengthen the
unitary, centralized state and to limit the ability of individuals and
associations to challenge its authority. The National Party and,

especially, the Peasant Party fought to expand individual rights and liberties and to open the political process to all citizens on an equal basis.[21]

The Liberals prevailed. Their draft, essentially unchanged, was approved by the Chamber of Deputies on 26 March and the Senate on the following day and was promulgated by royal decree on the 28th. The new constitution, in a sense, extended the provisions of the Constitution of 1866 to the new provinces. The fundamental principles underlying both were similar. The Constitution of 1923 promised extensive civil liberties and political rights to all citizens, but it left the details of precisely how these liberties and rights were to be exercised to the legislature. The idea of administrative centralization was reaffirmed, the powers of local governmental bodies were narrowly circumscribed, and the Crown and the bureaucracy retained considerable discretion in their interpretation and execution of the provisions of the constitution.[22]

During their four years in office the Liberals directed their attention to the development of the economy, particularly of industry. Much of their legislation was forward-looking, such as the law enacted in 1924 providing for the development of water power in order to increase the energy available for a growing industry. Continuing pre-war policies, they also introduced numerous measures to encourage industry directly and to improve the transportation system. Yet, in all these undertakings they made certain that they and their friends benefited and that they would still control the economy after they had been forced from office. Two measures, especially, reflected their attitude and aims. In 1924 the government announced its intention to nationalize the mineral wealth of the country, in particular, oil. The Liberals were motivated by the desire to assure native capital control of one of the country's most important natural resources and to reduce the participation of foreign companies, already dominant, in the oil industry. In the same year the Liberals sponsored legislation to 'commercialize' state-run economic enterprises. Here the aim was twofold: first, to oblige these companies to pay their own way by taking management out of the hands of government

---

[21] The disputes over the provisions of the new constitution are analysed by I. Ciupercă, 'Relații între partidele politice burgheze în timpul elaborării constituției din 1923', *Anuarul Institutului de Istorie și Arheologie*, 10 (1973), 335–59.

[22] Angela Banciu, *Rolul Constituției din 1923 în consolidarea unității naționale* (Bucharest, 1988), 76–102.

bureaucrats and entrusting it to financial and economic specialists, and second, to allow private capital to participate in the exploitation of state properties, a measure which would open the doors wide to the Liberals and their supporters.

Toward the end of their tenure the Liberals faced a delicate issue: the 'problem of Carol'. Because of the Crown Prince's refusal to give up his mistress, Elena Lupescu, and return home from Paris, Brătianu, in December 1925, with the support of King Ferdinand, forced Carol to renounce his privileges as a member of the royal family, including his rights to the throne. But Carol's private moral conduct appears to have been only a pretext for removing him from the succession. He had stubbornly refused to accept the tutelage of the Liberals, and Brătianu was certain that Carol would try to rein in the Liberals and make himself the primary factor in political life when Ferdinand, who was ill, died. Brătianu had thus decided to move first. The majority of political leaders now considered the matter settled and were eager, as Iuliu Maniu put it, to get on with more important matters. But the problem would not go away, partly because Carol's ambition could not be deflected so easily and partly because the opponents of the Liberals were unwilling to relinquish such an advantageous political weapon.

By the beginning of 1926 it had become apparent to Liberal leaders that their popularity in the country at large had waned. In the communal and *judeţ* elections in February, despite their usual vigilance, they had received only one-third of the votes. These and other signs persuaded them that they were 'used up' and that the time had come to relinquish office, temporarily.

The king gave General Averescu the mandate to form a new government in March 1926. The choice of Averescu had been Brătianu's because the People's Party was weak and would, he thought, be a docile instrument in the hands of the Liberals, and because Averescu's commitment to continue Liberal policies would allow a future Liberal government to pick up where it had left off. The king had preferred a Maniu–Mihalache–Averescu government, which would have consolidated the opposition that had coalesced in recent local elections and would have provided a strong counterweight to the Liberals, but Brătianu had warned against the 'revolutionary proclivities' of the National and Peasant parties and the possibility of a return of Carol in the absence of a strong, united government.

The elections in May took place under a state of siege, which allowed the army and the gendarmerie an almost free hand in interfering with the activities of the opposition parties. To no one's surprise, the People's Party took 53 per cent of the vote. With the 'premium' in effect since the enactment of the new electoral law in March 1926, it gained an overwhelming 75 per cent of the seats (292 out of 387) in the Chamber. The National and Peasant parties, which had joined together in an electoral 'cartel' to combat the Liberal Party, obtained 27.7 per cent of the vote and 69 seats, a remarkable performance under adverse circumstances which indicated a solid base of support.

The Liberals remained the directing force in the new government, even though they had only sixteen seats in the Chamber. Their control of the finances and of the economy in general remained intact, but Averescu was determined to assert his independence by carrying out an ambitious legislative programme that would undermine the economic position of the Liberals. Differences over tariff policy in particular brought the antagonism between the two parties into the open. The agrarian current in the People's Party, led by the economist Constantin Garoflid, urged a reduction of taxes on imports and agricultural exports, while the Liberals were intent upon promoting industry and protecting it from foreign competition.

As Averescu's relations with the Liberals deteriorated he desperately sought some formula that would enable him to remain in office. He made contact with Carol abroad, asking him to return on the condition that he, Averescu, remain as the head of the government, but Carol refused. Then, Averescu contemplated setting up a personal dictatorship. These manœuvres thoroughly alarmed Brătianu, who, in effect, forced Averescu to resign on 4 June 1927. Averescu had accomplished little during his short tenure. Symptomatic of the paralysis of his government was its lack of initiative in dealing with the most serious of all the country's problems—agriculture and the plight of the peasantry. His dispute with the Liberals and his resignation marked the end of his role as a significant force in political life.

Brătianu formed a new government at the end of June. Only fifteen days were needed to create a parliamentary majority. In the elections of 7 July the Liberal Party won nearly 62 per cent of the votes and 318 seats out of 387 in the Chamber. The new National Peasant Party gained 22 per cent of the vote and 54 seats, and the People's Party 1.9 per cent and no seats. This election was significant for several reasons. Both the extreme right and the left revealed their weakness. On the right, Cuza's League of National Christian Defence gained only 1.9 per cent and Codreanu's Legion of the Archangel Michael only 0.4 per cent of the vote, while on the left the Social Democratic Party had 1.9 per cent and the Worker-Peasant Bloc 1.2 per cent. None, because of the 2 per cent requirement of the electoral law of 1926, obtained any seats in the Chamber. Also noteworthy was the relatively small number of eligible voters who went to the polls. Of the 3,586,086 registered voters, only 823,307 (22.6 per cent) cast ballots, a figure which suggests that universal suffrage had made less of an impact on political life than both its advocates and opponents had thought.

Back in office, the Liberals took up where they had left off in 1926. But all did not go well for them, despite their overwhelming majority in parliament. The death of King Ferdinand on 20 July 1927 removed a consistent source of support for Liberal policies. Even though Brătianu had selected the members of the Regency (Prince Nicolae, Carol's brother; Miron Cristea, the Patriarch of the Rumanian Orthodox Church; and Gheorghe Buzdugan, President of the Court of Cassation), which acted in the name of the new king, Michael, Carol's son and a minor, Carol's own accession to the throne became a serious political issue. A second death—that of Ionel Brătianu on 24 November 1927 at the age of 63—was even more devastating for the Liberals, for it deprived them of the indispensable leader who had held the party together and given it direction. He was succeeded as head of the party and Prime Minister by his brother Vintilă. As the architect of the party's economic policy since the early years of the century he had played a key role in Liberal politics, but he lacked the authority and the political acumen of his brother. Nor could any of his successors hold together all the diverse factions of the party and dominate the political life of the country as had Ionel Brătianu.

Under relentless pressure from the National Peasant Party, which accused the Liberal government of unconstitutional practices and organized mass meetings throughout the country to take advantage of the widespread dissatisfaction with the Liberals' authoritarian administration and sectarian economic policies, Vintilă Brătianu resigned in November 1928. The immediate cause seems to have been the failure of the government to obtain a desperately needed foreign loan, but the real causes went deeper. The Liberals had failed to win the confidence of the peasantry— the mass of the voters—and they had failed to put the economy of the country on a solid foundation, though the responsibility was not theirs alone. After several unsuccessful attempts by the leaders of other parties to form a government the Regency finally entrusted Iuliu Maniu with the task.

The elections of December 1928 were the most democratic in Rumanian history, and for the first time the decision of the monarch (the Regency) and the choice of the electorate coincided. To be sure, Maniu took the usual pre-election measures. He appointed new prefects in the *judeţe* from among the leaders of his party's local organizations and replaced many communal councils with interim bodies composed of National Peasant supporters. But at the same time, on 19 November, he abolished censorship on all publications and limited the interference of administrative personnel and the police in the voting. The National Peasants were swept into power by an enthusiastic electorate convinced that a new era had begun in the history of their country and that the rights and liberties long promised would finally become a reality. No party had enjoyed such popularity since the founding of the kingdom. The National Peasants won 77.76 per cent of the vote and 348 seats (out of 387); the Liberals came in second with 6.55 per cent and 13 seats.

The National Peasants, full of enthusiasm, were determined to change the way in which the country had been governed and its citizens had been treated. They undertook to decentralize government administration and to assure civil and political rights to all citizens. They were also intent upon bringing economic policy into harmony with economic realities, a goal they sought to achieve by encouraging free enterprise and developing the full potential of agriculture.

The National Peasants were convinced that democratic government could succeed if citizens were allowed to take a regular part in political life and could thus gain experience in managing their own affairs. Legislation, drafted mainly by Constantin Stere, was enacted in July 1929 giving local inhabitants a greater voice in their own affairs and curtailing the intervention of the central bureaucracy in local government. Stere's and Maniu's aim was to change the prevailing mentality, according to which the citizen was the servant of the functionary, rather than vice versa.

The National Peasants placed agriculture at the centre of their economic policy, although they also saw the value of encouraging 'necessary' industries. In their relatively short time in office they were unable to solve the agrarian problem or to bring about other lasting improvements in the economy which they and their supporters had confidently expected. Their failures were caused in part by circumstances over which they had no control, notably the world economic depression. But the National Peasants themselves must share the responsibility for continued distress in the countryside. Although their concern for the peasant was genuine, they tended to put political goals ahead of economic ones. They were particularly eager to strengthen democratic political institutions as an essential precondition for a free and prosperous economy, and they were certain that the peasant would, in the end, be the beneficiary. Yet, they did not make the peasant's immediate needs the cornerstone of their economic policy. This situation arose from the dual nature of the party: Ion Mihalache and his wing had a peasant programme and strove to create a peasant state, while the Maniu, or National Party, wing, whose policies generally prevailed, was middle class in its aims and outlook.

The National Peasant government left office for reasons other than economic ones. What to do about Carol precipitated a political crisis. Sentiment in favour of his return had been growing in many quarters, and even Maniu accepted the idea under certain conditions. When Carol made his dramatic return to Bucharest by air on 6 June 1930, Maniu argued against his immediate proclamation as king and insisted that Elena Lupescu not be allowed to return to Rumania. When Carol rejected these conditions Maniu resigned on the 7th.[23] George Mironescu succeeded him at the head of a National Peasant government, whose initial task was to arrange for Carol's restoration. The legal obstacles were quickly disposed of, and on 8 June the parliament restored to Carol all his rights and privileges as a member of the royal family and proclaimed him king by a vote of 485 to 1. After some hesitation Maniu agreed to head a new government, but the political and personal differences between him and the new king were irreconcilable and precluded long-term co-operation. The immediate cause of their open break was the return of Madame Lupescu to Rumania in August. Maniu accused Carol not only of going back on his promise to effect a reconciliation with his wife but also, in effect, of trying to impose his will on the government, an act Maniu characterized as a violation of the constitution. No reconciliation was possible, and Maniu resigned on 8 October. His

[23] Ioan Scurtu, *Din viața politică a României, 1926–1947* (Bucharest, 1983), 165–72.

withdrawal was a reaffirmation of his own integrity, but the king's personal morality was not the issue upon which to test Carol's commitment to constitutional government.

Maniu's resignation coincided with the beginning of the decline of the National Peasant Party and the weakening of parliamentary institutions. But his act was a symbol, not a cause, of dashed hopes for genuine political democracy.

THE EBBING OF DEMOCRACY, 1930–1940

Political life in the 1930s was overshadowed by a general decline of democratic institutions. The Liberals and the National Peasants, who had provided the superstructure of parliamentary government, lost much of the *élan* they had exhibited in the preceding decade. Rent by factionalism, they seemed incapable of decisive action. The effects of the world economic depression continued to be felt throughout the decade, especially among the peasants and the humbler classes of the cities, even though a recovery was underway by 1934. Persistent economic hardships, in turn, weakened support for the traditional parties and led many to question the efficacy of parliamentary democracy. King Carol encouraged these trends by openly manifesting his disdain for the party system and democracy and by intensifying his efforts to establish his personal rule. The other chief beneficiaries of widespread dissatisfaction with existing political institutions were not leftist parties and labour organizations, which were weak, but the extreme right, notably the Iron Guard.

A period of governmental instability followed Maniu's resignation. The short-lived National Peasant government, headed by Mironescu, gave way in April 1931 to a so-called government of national union, composed of the Liberal Party and a number of small parties, with Nicolae Iorga, the leader of an insignificant grouping of his adherents called the Democratic Nationalist Party (Partidul Naţionalist-Democrat), as Prime Minister. The Liberals had lent their electoral strength to the union as a way of re-establishing good relations with the palace. This type of government, composed of technocrats, suited the king's purposes admirably. He could thus avoid reliance upon the traditional parties and could bring forward new talent free of party loyalties and devoted to him. In the June elections the national union won 47.5 per cent of the vote (the Liberal Party alone provided 32.5 per cent) and, benefiting from the premium, obtained 289 seats in the Chamber to just 30 for the National Peasant Party, the next largest party. For the first time since it had been declared illegal the Communist Party was represented in parliament through the Worker-Peasant Bloc, which won five seats (parliament later invalidated the mandates of these deputies). Such a heterogeneous government proved incapable of dealing with the mounting economic problems caused by the depression and was forced by the king to resign in June 1932.

Carol recalled the National Peasants with Alexandru Vaida as Prime Minister. But he resigned in October in disputes, first, with Nicolae Titulescu, who headed the Rumanian delegation in negotiations concerning a non-agression pact with the Soviet Union, over policy toward the Soviet Union, and, then, with Maniu over the control of government policy. Maniu succeeded him as Prime Minister, serving until January 1933, when he resigned, because of differences with Carol. Vaida returned, but by now the National Peasant Party was deeply divided. Vaida and his supporters, who formed the party's right wing, were acting more like Liberals than Peasantists. They crushed strikes by oil workers in Ploieşti and by railway workers in Bucharest in February 1933, dissolved Communist Party front organizations and all other 'anti-state' organizations, and proclaimed martial law in a number of cities. Vaida also sympathized with the nationalist goals of the Iron Guard and sought to enlist it in the struggle against the Communists and their supporters. Such acts alienated the democratic majority of the party, and Vaida thus failed to gain its approval for the introduction of a *numerus Valachicus*, by which he intended to limit the number of Jews and other minorities in government, the professions, and the universities. He finally resigned as Prime Minister in November 1933, mainly, it appears, because Carol was dissatisfied with his lack of firmness in dealing with the Iron Guard.

Carol turned to the Liberals. Now under the firm leadership of Ion G. Duca, who had become head of the party in 1930 upon the death of Vintilă Brătianu, the Liberal Party presented itself as the party of experience and order. In the elections in December the party received 51 per cent of the votes, owing mainly to its efficient electoral machine. But its economic programme and its stand against the Iron Guard won it support among many who usually voted for centre candidates. Duca was determined to take drastic action against the 'forces of subversion' and during the election campaign, one of the most violent in Rumanian history, the government dissolved the Iron Guard. Members of the Guard took revenge by assassinating Duca on 29 December. He was succeeded as Prime Minister by Gheorghe Tătărescu (1886–1957), Under-Secretary of State for Internal Affairs in several Liberal governments of the 1920s and a leader of the young Liberals. The Liberal Party, despite appearances, was no longer the political steamroller it had been in the 1920s. It was badly split. The Tătărescu government of 1934–7 differed markedly from the views and objectives of the traditional party leadership, for the ministries were run by the young Liberals, while the party apparatus was dominated by the old Liberals. The latter remained true to the principles that had guided the party in the 1920s. They opposed the extreme right and remained hostile to foreign capital, while Tătărescu and his associates tolerated the Iron Guard, within certain limits, and opened the door wide to Western conglomerates.

The mid-1930s were marked by a steady movement to the right in politics. Although the government continued to outlaw the Iron Guard, it none the less allowed it to function under a new name—Totul pentru Ţară (All for the Fatherland). Nor did Carol, who opposed the Guard, wish at this time to eliminate it. Rather, both he and Tătărescu sought to use it for their own purposes as a means of gaining support from the growing nationalist segments of the electorate. They themselves were, after all, inclined toward authoritarian government. Tătărescu sought the power to legislate by decree when parliament was not in session, and Carol slowly put together the components of a personal rule such as the royal youth movement, Straja Ţării (The Guard of the Country), which he founded in 1934. Both men were sensitive to changes in the international situation. They observed with apprehension the rise of the authoritarian states, particularly Germany, at the expense of Britain and France. Nor were the implications of the mounting German economic influence in Rumania, which encouraged growth and stirred the audacity of the extreme right, lost on them. At the same time democratic elements, particularly the National Peasant Party, were in disarray and could offer no effective opposition to royal or other authoritarian aspirations.

The elections of 1937 provided a critical test of strength between democracy and authoritarianism.[24] When the Liberal government

[24] C. Enescu, 'Semnificaţia alegerilor din decemvrie 1937 în evoluţia politică a neamului românesc', *Sociologie românească*, 2/11–12 (1937), 512–26.

reached the end of its term of office in November it resigned, and Carol invited Ion Mihalache to form a National Peasant government. But Mihalache opposed the inclusion of Vaida in the government and refused the mandate, whereupon Carol turned again to Tătărescu. As the election campaign got underway Maniu assumed leadership of the opposition. His primary goal was to overturn the Tătărescu government, and, to that end, he signed an electoral pact with Codreanu, the leader of the Iron Guard, and Gheorghe Brătianu, the head of a dissident Liberal faction. Maniu, of course, had no sympathy for the Iron Guard or dictatorship, but he thought that the Guard could help discourage the government's traditional use of strong-arm tactics during the election. The National Peasant Party and the Guard did not draw up common lists of candidates; they simply agreed to support free elections. Nevertheless, the pact gave the Guard a measure of respectability, which enabled it to expand its appeal among the electorate.[25] The results of the vote were shocking: the Liberal Party indeed won a plurality (35.9 per cent) and had the most seats (152), but it did not obtain the 40 per cent of the vote necessary to receive the premium and with it a majority in the Chamber. For the first time in the history of Rumanian parliamentarism a government had fallen in an election. The extreme right made important gains. The Iron Guard, through its Totul pentru Ţară party, won 15.58 per cent of the vote and 66 seats, becoming the third largest party in parliament behind the National Peasants, who won 20.4 per cent of the vote and 86 seats. The recently formed National Christian Party also did well. Nationalist and anti-Semitic, it gained 9.2 per cent of the vote and 39 seats. The rightist parties owed much of their success to their concentration on immediate social and economic issues, which had aroused important elements of the electorate. They strove to create the impression that they were young and innovative parties and would find solutions to problems that had eluded the Liberals and National Peasants. If nothing else, the election thoroughly awakened the leaders of the Liberal and National Peasant parties and Carol to the imminent danger of a Guardist dictatorship.

Tătărescu resigned on 28 December 1937, and on the same day Carol invited Octavian Goga, the head of the National Christian Party, to form a government. The coalition he put together seemed fated to dissolve from the beginning, for he included in it members

<hr />

[25] Heinen, *Die Legion*, 346–52.

of the National Peasant Party. The members of Goga's own party aimed at the destruction of the parliamentary system and the transformation of the country into a corporatist state, and in foreign affairs they favoured close relations with Germany and Italy. But the four centrists from the National Peasant Party firmly opposed these objectives. Their leader, Armand Călinescu (1893–1939), who became the Minister of the Interior, attacked fascist groups at home, while in foreign affairs he advocated strengthened ties with Britain and France rather than with Germany and Italy, whose growing presence in South-eastern Europe he regarded as a threat to the territorial integrity and independence of Rumania. Although the National Peasant ministers were a minority in the cabinet, they held the key ministries of the interior, justice, and foreign affairs, which enabled them to impede implementation of the government's domestic and foreign policies. Carol welcomed the opportunity to further his own aims. By bringing to power a party which had obtained less than 10 per cent of the vote and by approving a weak, divided government, he intended to show that the elections, which had been as much a defeat for him as for the Liberals, had not really changed the way things were done and that it was, after all, his will that counted. In any case, he had no wish to install a strong government, since he thought the time had come to establish a royal dictatorship.[26]

Intense political manœuvring took place in January 1938. Goga was prepared for a long stay in office and before holding elections he sought to expand the base of his government beyond his own party and the centrist National Peasants. Employing General Ion Antonescu, Minister of National Defence, as an intermediary, he reached a tentative agreement with Codreanu on co-operation. At the same time Carol was busy fashioning an alliance of his own. Both he and Liberal and National Peasant leaders were anxious to prevent the establishment of a fascist dictatorship, which Goga was obviously contemplating. Constantin Brătianu, the leader of the old Liberals, urged, and Carol accepted, the creation of a government composed of leading political figures and technical experts, appointed by the king, which would temporarily suspend constitutional rights and govern by decree until political life had been restored to normal. For his part, Maniu, who refused to

[26] Florea Nedelcu, *De la restaurație la dictatura regală* (Cluj-Napoca, 1981), 248–62.

participate in such a government, agreed not to 'cause difficulties' when the National Peasants were not called upon to form a government. All three men wanted to prevent a fascist coup, which, they were certain, would subordinate the country to Germany. But Carol had ambitions of his own, and it was soon evident that he intended to make the suspension of constitutional guarantees permanent. In this way he succeeded in introducing his authoritarian regime under a constitutional cover. The royal dictatorship came into being quickly and quietly on 10 and 11 February 1938, when Carol simply replaced the Goga government with an 'advisory government' headed by the Patriarch Miron Cristea and including seven former Prime Ministers and Ion Antonescu as Minister of National Defence.

Carol moved swiftly to consolidate his power by sweeping away the institutions of the parliamentary system. On 20 February he abolished the Constitution of 1923, replacing it with a new one based upon corporatist principles and concentrating power in the hands of the king. The constitution made clear that the functions which political parties had fulfilled under the old parliamentary regime were incompatible with the new order.[27] Accordingly, on 30 March Carol decreed the dissolution of all political parties and groups, but promised that after a period of 'calm' and 'adaptation to the new circumstances' a law would be drawn up setting forth the conditions under which political 'associations' could be formed and could operate. But a series of decree-laws issued between April and September, which imposed severe penalties on any opposition to the new order, showed that Carol had no intention of restoring the old party system.

Carol took drastic action against the Iron Guard, which he regarded as his chief enemy. He instructed Armand Călinescu, the Minister of the Interior and the strongman in the new cabinet, to destroy it by whatever means, legal or illegal, he thought necessary. The campaign began with the promulgation on 15 April 1938 of a law on the 'maintenance of order'. On the 18th the leaders of the Guard were arrested and given long terms in prison, and Codreanu was sentenced to ten years' hard labour for high treason. Large numbers of Guard members and sympathizers were rounded up and interned in concentration camps established for this purpose. The severity of the repression is surprising because Codreanu and other Guard leaders had done everything possible

[27] Alexandru G. Savu, *Dictatura regală* (Bucharest, 1970), 171–96.

to avoid a clash with the king. Yet their inaction did not signify an acceptance of the new regime but rather a realization that for the moment they were too weak to seize power. Codreanu recognized the need for time to enable the Guard to prepare for a coup, and for this reason he urged his followers to do nothing that would provoke reprisals from the regime. He seems also to have hoped that Germany would apply pressure on the king to accept a Codreanu cabinet. In fact, the vigour and brutality of the measures Carol took against the Guard in 1938 and later seems to have been motivated in the first instance not by open opposition or Carol's overestimation of the Guard's strength but by his perception of it as an agent of Germany. The evidence for such a view is persuasive. The government began the massive arrest of Guardists shortly after the Anschluss between Germany and Austria in March 1938, and the killing of Codreanu and thirteen other Guardists 'while trying to escape' in November occurred immediately after Carol's visit to Germany, during which Hitler had urged the freeing of the Guardists and the formation of a Codreanu cabinet. In any case, the king's campaign destroyed the Guard as a political movement, for its mass following disappeared. Only a nucleus remained, which operated as a clandestine organization engaging in disparate acts of sabotage and assassination, notably that of Armand Călinescu in September 1939.

The Liberal and National Peasant parties fared better. Immediately after the promulgation of the decree of 30 March Maniu and Constantin Brătianu declared that their parties would carry on their activities as before and suggested that all parties and groups draw up a memorandum of protest challenging the constitutionality of the act. The protest went no further, but Maniu's and Brătianu's firm response to Carol produced results. Carol took their warning seriously and treated the two parties with great care. Party leaders continued to communicate with their provincial organizations unhindered, and their newspapers continued to appear, censorship rarely being imposed upon them. The relationship between the two great parties and Carol resembled an armistice, as each side reinforced its position for the time when hostilities would resume and a final showdown took place.

Almost all the other, smaller parties ceased to exist. Those that supported the royal dictatorship such as the Tătărescu Liberals and the centre National Peasants, which had welcomed the removal of the regular party organizations from political life, had nothing to lose from the dissolution decree of 30 March, for the highest offices in the state were open to them. Paradoxically, the extreme right parties did not prosper. Friction between the Goga and Cuza wings of the National Christian Party led to its disintegration, and Mihail Manoilescu's Corporatist League (Liga Corporatistă) remained a party on paper. On the left, socialist party and workers' organizations were abolished, and Communists and their sympathizers were relentlessly pursued, the gaols being filled with them, especially in 1940. The small German and Hungarian minority parties, on the other hand, were treated with the utmost care because Carol was anxious not to exacerbate revisionist sentiments in Germany and Hungary.

Carol and his advisors recognized the need for a new political organization to take the place of the old parties and to strengthen the royal dictatorship. Tătărescu and Vaida submitted proposals, but Carol rejected them in favour of a project drawn up by Armand Călinescu in October 1938 urging the creation of a single party as an instrument for mobilizing and channelling mass support for the new regime. Călinescu argued that the royal dictatorship could not survive if it remained merely a cabinet of functionaries. It had to have an instrument by which it could involve the mass of the population in government. Otherwise, it would become isolated and would allow other political forces to channel the interests of the people in directions favourable to themselves. Thus, Călinescu concluded, the time had come to initiate a popular movement, but he wished to avoid the old-style political party. Rather, he had in mind an intellectual or spiritual movement, which would offer the people lofty goals to be achieved through common, selfless action, something of the order of Junimea.[28]

The Front of National Renaissance (Frontul Renaşterii Naţionale), as the new organization was known, was inaugurated on 16 December 1938. The principle which underlay its activities was bureaucratic centralism. Decisions about policy and personnel were made at the top and then passed down to the local units of the Front. There was no opportunity, at lower levels, for approval or even discussion. Nor did the members of the Front have the right to elect or be elected to positions of leadership at any level. Although the Front alone had the right to run candidates in

[28] Alexandru G. Savu, *Sistemul partidelor politice din România, 1919–1940* (Bucharest, 1976), 154–8.

parliamentary and other elections, it lacked an official programme or doctrine, but such general notions as 'social harmony' and 'national solidarity' received great attention in its propaganda campaigns. In these slogans, surprisingly, traditional, and sometimes aggressive, nationalism was subordinated to the idea of peaceful coexistence with the Christian minorities and to efforts to limit overt manifestations of anti-Semitism. The Front gave urgent attention to internal solidarity as a means of bracing the country against the mounting threat of revisionism from its neighbours and against economic and political subservience to Germany. Perhaps most striking about the organization and functioning of the Front was the failure of Carol and his advisors to formulate an overall conception of the type of regime they wanted. The whole experiment was thus characterized by improvisation and haste.

By the end of 1939 Carol himself tacitly admitted that his attempt to rally mass support for the royal dictatorship through the Front had failed. In his New Year's message he invited the old political parties to set aside past differences and unite around the king in order to defend the nation against the growing international dangers. It was evident from his other public statements that he particularly wanted to bring about a reconciliation with the Liberals and National Peasants and to unite them with the non-fascist supporters of the dictatorship. His new rallying cry of 'grave national danger' was not without effect. The leaders of the old parties were anxious to defend the territorial integrity of the country. They were keenly aware of the threat posed by Germany to the Versailles settlement and of the intentions of the Soviet Union toward Bessarabia, especially after the Nazi–Soviet pact of August 1939, the provisions of which in general outline were known in Bucharest. Carol took the first step in creating a genuine national front when he appointed Tătărescu as Prime Minister in November 1939. He evidently hoped to use Tătărescu's wide contacts among all political parties of the right and centre to forge a new political alliance. But Tătărescu was only partially successful. Maniu and Brătianu refused to join the new government, but they pledged not to seek its downfall by taking advantage of its momentary internal and foreign difficulties. Neither could know that the drive for national reconciliation would lead to a further drift of the royal dictatorship to the right.

The Iron Guard enjoyed a resurgence. Both the group led by Horia Sima, who had taken refuge in Germany early in 1939 to escape Carol's persecution, and the remnants of the leadership in Rumania, the majority of whom were in concentration camps, agreed to renounce all subversive activities and work with the government. But both groups still sought power, the first through direct intervention by Germany, and the second by infiltrating the political structure and taking over from within at the proper time. On 18 April 1940 Carol completed a reconciliation with the Guard by receiving its leaders at a special audience. The Guard now resumed full political activity, unhindered by the authorities, but it was no longer the organization it had been before 1938. Because of Carol's persecution, it had been reduced from a mass movement to a party composed of leaders and bureaucrats.

Dramatic changes in the international situation vitiated Carol's efforts to maintain control over political forces at home. His inability to form a broad coalition of parties under the Front of National Renaissance had forced him to work with the Tătărescu Liberals and the Călinescu National Peasants, on the one side, and their sworn enemies, the Iron Guard, on the other. At the same time he tried desperately to keep foreign policy in the hands of pro-Western politicians, while satisfying German economic and political interests in Rumania. The fall of France in June 1940 finally undid all his calculations: it forced him even further to the right. He decreed the establishment of the Party of the Nation (Partidul Națiunii), a single, 'totalitarian' party whose task, under the supreme leadership of the king, would be to 'direct the entire moral and material life of the nation'. The new party was of little importance, as international events, rather than Carol's will, determined the political evolution of the country.

10

Foreign Policy, 1919–1940

THE VERSAILLES SYSTEM

The primary objective of Rumania's foreign policy throughout the inter-war period was to maintain the frontiers drawn at the end of the First World War. All Rumanian political parties, except the Communist, were consistent supporters of the Versailles system, a stance which dictated the choice of allies and provided continuity with the foreign policy pursued in the years immediately before the outbreak of the war. Rumanian politicians regarded France and, to a lesser extent, Britain as the chief guarantors of the peace settlement and relied upon them to counter threats to the territorial status quo in Eastern Europe from the Soviet Union, Germany, and the lesser revisionist states, Hungary and Bulgaria. Rumanian governments also sought to preserve the Versailles system by other means. They championed collective security and thus supported efforts to make the League of Nations a reliable defender of European peace and stability, and they promoted regional alliances, such as the Little Entente and the Balkan Entente, in order to discourage revisionism in Eastern Europe. On all these fundamental issues the Liberals, National Peasants, and even Carol II were in general agreement. They all recognized that the frontiers of Greater Rumania would be secure only so long as the political equilibrium established in the region in 1919 was not disturbed, and, hence, they sought to prevent both Germany and the Soviet Union from gaining dominance in regional affairs.

Relations with France and Britain after the peace conference took a course few Rumanian leaders could have foreseen. The Commission on Reparations, which had been established at Versailles to handle this complicated matter and was controlled by the major allies, gave Rumanian claims unexpectedly short shrift. First of all, the Commission granted Rumania the status of a country with only 'limited interests' and did not allow a Rumanian delegation to take part in its deliberations. Then, it set the value of the damage suffered by Rumania in the war at some 31,000 million gold lei and decided that Rumania would receive 1 per cent of the German reparations and 10.55 per cent of those of Hungary, Austria, Bulgaria, and Turkey. Rumania was thus to receive roughly 5,300 million lei, far less than the losses she had sustained, according to the Commission's own estimate. Insult was added to injury when the major allies obliged Rumania to pay a share of the 'quota of liberation'. At the peace conference Lloyd George had pointed out that the Allies had spent enormous sums in freeing a number of peoples, and he had expressed the opinion that the latter ought, therefore, to make a contribution. In 1924 the major allies put Rumania's share at 235,140,000 gold francs out of a total quota of 1,400 million gold francs.[1] The ill-feeling which such a demand aroused in Rumania was only partially allayed by subsequent negotiations. Although the general settlement of reparations payments worked out in the so-called Young Plan in 1930 excused Rumania from paying any part of this sum, international agreements on reparations deprived her of badly needed financial resources. The Hoover moratorium in 1931 and the termination of the whole system of reparations approved at the Conference of Lausanne in 1932 were severe blows to the Rumanian government, which had counted upon these payments to help solve its own severe financial problems at the height of the depression.

Despite the coolness engendered by the reparations and related fiscal disputes, Rumanian leaders continued to rely upon France to counter any threat to the Versailles system. But French political interest in Rumania remained lukewarm until the latter 1930s, even though she was a member of the French-supported alliance system in Eastern Europe. French lack of interest is suggested by the fact that a formal treaty of alliance between the two countries was not concluded until eight years after the war. Even then, the Rumanians took the initiative. They proposed a guarantee of the territorial status quo and a promise by each side to come to the aid of the other in case of an unprovoked attack. But the French government was not interested in a military alliance with Rumania because it considered the latter's army incapable of undertaking a serious military campaign. A compromise was finally reached when the two sides agreed that their general staffs would consult one another in the event of aggression. Although the treaty that was signed on 10 June 1926 did not commit France to come to the aid of Rumania, Rumanian leaders considered it of great political

[1] Emilian Bold, *De la Versailles la Lausanne (1919–1932)* (Iaşi, 1976), 12–43.

value because they assumed that it expressed the strong community of interest between the two countries. The French government accorded the treaty little importance, regarding it simply as one means among many of maintaining French influence in South-eastern Europe.[2] Renewed in 1936, it offered few practical ways of implementing symbols and assumptions.

Political relations between Rumania and Great Britain were low key. The latter did not have a well-defined political strategy in South-eastern Europe for most of the inter-war period, and only in May 1938 did the Foreign Office contemplate political and economic commitments to Rumania in response to the growing German threat. In any case, the government regarded Rumania as wholly within the French orbit and not worth cultivating. But Britain's economic interest in Rumania was intense. The size of her investments made her role in the development of the Rumanian economy second only to that of Germany. Oil was the main attraction. British investments in the Rumanian oil industry were the largest of any foreign country, representing over half the total capital in that industry and one-quarter of the total foreign capital invested in Rumania. Between 1929 and 1933 Britain imported more oil from Rumania than any other country, and for the remainder of the decade her imports were nearly equal to those of Germany. Britain's overall trade with Rumania placed her second (10 per cent of Rumania's exports and imports) to Germany (25 per cent). Yet, when Britain's world-wide interests are taken into account, these financial and commercial activities were of only modest importance.[3]

Rumanian governments, regardless of their domestic policies and ideological preferences, turned repeatedly to the League of Nations to maintain the Versailles settlement. They supported those initiatives of the League which were intended to enhance collective security and protect existing national boundaries against revision. Thus, Rumanian delegates were willing to adhere to the so-called Protocol of Geneva of 1924, which qualified aggressive war as an international crime and established procedures for identifying the aggressor and imposing obligatory arbitration by a permanent international court of justice. But ever wary of national rivalries, they offered an amendment to exempt disputes over national boundaries from the protocol in order to prevent the revisionist states, Hungary and Bulgaria, from using it for their own purposes. In any case, the protocol was not approved, because of disputes among the major powers. Later, the Rumanian government adhered to other international agreements such as the Kellogg-Briand Pact of 1928, which outlawed war as a means of settling disputes between nations; the convention on the definition of aggression signed in London in 1933, which Rumanian officials interpreted as reinforcing their country's territorial integrity; and the pact of non-aggression and conciliation signed at Rio de Janeiro in 1933, which condemned wars of aggression and territorial acquisitions resulting from them, and imposed upon all signatories the obligation to settle their differences by peaceful means.

At the disarmament conference in Geneva between 1932 and 1934 sponsored by the League Rumania supported the general principle of disarmament and stood with France and Britain, but her representatives insisted that any formula for reducing armies and armaments be applied equally to all states, that the League strictly enforce compliance, and that provision be made for mutual aid in case of violations. The Rumanian delegates also insisted that any agreement reached take into account the economic resources and geographical position of each signatory, since it feared that arbitrary, general limits on the size of armies and military budgets might prevent their country from defending itself. But Rumania's opinions carried little weight. The major powers determined the course of the disarmament talks, and when the conference ended in failure in June 1934 the responsibility was theirs.

In those critical challenges to collective security which came before the League in the mid-1930s Rumania invariably sided with the Western powers. In 1935 her representatives supported economic sanctions against Italy to protest against the latter's invasion of Ethiopia and endorsed an initial British proposal for an embargo on all exports to Italy. But the Rumanians asked League members to show their solidarity by buying goods from those countries—Rumania, in particular—which would suffer economic hardship if trade with Italy were halted. Following the decision of the League to invoke sanctions against Italy, the Rumanian government on 19 October forbade all loans to and all commerce in armaments and other war materials with Italy.[4] But, because of the half-hearted application of sanctions by the great powers, the

---

[4] Petre Bărbulescu, *România la Societatea Națiunilor* (Bucharest, 1975), 302–13.

contribution of Rumania and other small powers had no effect on the course of events. Rumania supported France and Britain again in 1935, when Germany denounced the clauses of the Treaty of Versailles limiting German military forces, and in 1936 when Germany denounced the Locarno pacts and reoccupied the Rhineland. Rumanian political leaders in and out of government were alarmed by these acts because they called into question the very foundation of collective security, and the half-hearted responses of France and Britain provided little reassurance.

Rumanian governments consistently promoted regional alliances as a means of preserving the Versailles settlement. They took a leading role in the formation of the Little Entente and the Balkan Entente, through which they sought to ally themselves with Poland, Czechoslovakia, Yugoslavia, and Greece to thwart the revisionist ambitions of Germany, Hungary, and Bulgaria. The Rumanians welcomed the support of France for these alliances, but they rejected a French plan for a Danubian confederation put forward at the signing of the Treaty of Trianon as impinging upon Rumanian sovereignty. Throughout the interwar period the Rumanians were wary of schemes for federation sponsored by the great powers, preferring that the diplomatic initiative remain in the hands of local powers.

The Rumanian government was eager to include Poland in an alliance of five, but Polish leaders had special concerns which precluded such a commitment. A territorial dispute with Czechoslovakia, in particular, impeded Poland's adherence to an East European alliance system. Repeated Rumanian efforts to mediate failed. But Poland and Rumania concluded an alliance of their own, because of concern about the security of their new frontiers with the Soviet Union. The Czechoslovak government approved, for it hoped eventually to draw Poland into a more general East European alliance. The most important article of the Polish–Rumanian treaty, which was signed on 3 March 1921, provided for common defence against a Soviet attack. It was renewed in 1926 and 1931, but the commitment of both sides was less than whole-hearted. Poland was interested in an understanding with Hungary and for that reason did not recognize the validity of the Treaty of Trianon, which had ceded Transylvania to Rumania, while Rumania was not prepared to come to the aid of Poland, if such action was contrary to her own best interests.

The Little Entente was created out of the need felt by Rumania, Czechoslovakia, and Yugoslavia to provide for their own security, as their doubts about the effectiveness of the guarantees contained in the treaties of Trianon and Neuilly grew. They had little interest in a Danubian federation. First of all, they saw it as a limitation on their independence, but they also realized that a federation, to be effective, would have to include Austria and Hungary, and they feared that by giving them equal status, they would be encouraging a resurgence of Austro-Hungarian domination of the region. Their own Entente consisted of three bilateral agreements—Yugoslavia and Czechoslovakia (signed on 14 August 1920), Rumania and Czechoslovakia (23 April 1921), and Rumania and Yugoslavia (7 June 1921), each of which obliged the signatories to come to her partner's defence in case of an unprovoked attack from Hungary. The Rumanian-Yugoslav treaty was also aimed at Bulgaria. Rumania continued efforts to bring Poland into the Little Entente, but even after Czechoslovakia and Poland had reached an accord over the disputed territory of Teschen in 1924, relations between them remained cool. Poland was interested in closer co-operation with the three allies as an additional guarantee for her eastern frontier, but Czechoslovakia had no wish to be drawn into a conflict with the Soviet Union.

The defensive character of the Little Entente was manifested by its consistent support of disarmament and international agreements to outlaw war as a means of settling disputes. The members of the Entente singly and as a group also participated in attempts between 1928 and 1933 to arrive at a definition of aggression. They showed their determination to maintain the status quo by opposing all forms of territorial revision—the restoration of the Habsburgs, the idea of *Mitteleuropa*, and the Anschluss.

Rumania and the other members of the Entente were also wary of attempts by the great powers, even their Western friends, to make decisions for the region without considering the wishes of the nations there. One of the main reasons for the creation of the Entente in the first place had been to show the great powers that the nations of Central Europe could manage their own affairs and would no longer tolerate being merely the object of bargaining by others. Thus, they opposed the Locarno Pact of 1925 as a French concession to Germany, since it ignored the frontiers of Eastern Europe. Their reaction to the so-called Pact of Four in 1933 was similar.[5] Put forward by Mussolini, it proposed that the

---

[5] Dinu Giurescu, 'La Diplomatie roumaine et le pacte des Quatre (1933)', *Revue roumaine d'histoire*, 8/1 (1969), 77-102.

'four Western powers'—Britain, France, Germany, and Italy—should form themselves into a 'European Directorate' for the purpose of defining a 'common political line' on European problems, including a revision of the peace treaties. The members of the Little Entente questioned the notion that the great powers could dispose of Eastern European problems without consulting them and flatly rejected any changes in existing frontiers. Nicolae Titulescu, the Rumanian Foreign Minister and perhaps the only Rumanian political figure in the inter-war period regarded in Western capitals as being of European stature, undertook at the behest of the Permanent Council of the Entente a mission to London and Paris to persuade the two Western democracies not to play the 'revisionist game' of Germany and Italy. His arguments seem to have had some effect, particularly in Paris. In any case, Mussolini's project was stillborn, as the French government, recognizing the dangers it presented to its own position in Central and South-eastern Europe, rejected it.

Despite occasional modest successes, the Little Entente failed to bring about the cohesion necessary for either concerted diplomatic action or the co-ordination of its members' economic interests. At a meeting of Entente Foreign Ministers in 1932 and 1933 Titulescu expressed anxiety at the absence of strong links among the three allies and urged his colleagues to find ways of facilitating common action on the critical issues of the day.[6] As a result of intensive work by Titulescu, Eduard Beneš of Czechoslovakia, and Bogoljub Jevtić of Yugoslavia the so-called Pact of Organization of the Little Entente was drawn up and approved on 16 February 1933. It provided for the transformation of the existing loose alliance into a united community with its own distinct legal personality. It stipulated that henceforth every political treaty and every economic agreement having political significance entered into by a member of the community would need the unanimous approval of all three partners to be binding. The chief motivation behind the Pact was a growing sense of unease at the course international relations were taking. In urging ratification of the treaty in the Rumanian parliament in March 1933, Titulescu warned that such acts of collective security were crucial at a time of international instability. But the Pact had no effect on the course of international relations and did not appreciably enhance co-operation among its signatories.

<hr />

[6] Nicolae Titulescu, *Discursuri* (Bucharest, 1967), 388–92.

Nor did the Pact improve the economic fortunes of the three allies. Its proponents hoped that provisions for co-ordinating their economies would eventually lead to the economic union of Central Europe. But formidable obstacles to economic co-operation could not be overcome. At the root of the problem were the divergent interests of an industrialized Czechoslovakia, on the one hand, and the still largely agrarian Rumania and Yugoslavia, on the other. All three countries tended to remain isolated from one another in their own national economies and made little progress in expanding trade with one another. Czechoslovakia and Yugoslavia accounted for only a small share of Rumania's foreign trade. Czechoslovakia sent manufactured goods to Rumania, but, because of strong opposition from Czech agrarian interests, her markets were generally closed to Rumanian agricultural products. Trade between Rumania and Yugoslavia was negligible for just the opposite reason: their economies were similar, and they even competed with each other for foreign markets. As Germany's diplomatic and economic activity in the region intensified in the latter 1930s, the trade of all three countries turned in that direction.

The Balkan Entente represented an extension into South-eastern Europe of the principles of regional security embodied in the Little Entente. The treaty establishing the alliance, which was signed by representatives of Rumania, Yugoslavia, Greece, and Turkey on 9 February 1934, declared it to be purely defensive, but it was clearly directed at Bulgaria, the main revisionist state in the region. The Balkan Entente provided for permanent political co-operation among its members, but failed, as the Little Entente had, to create a united front on vital international issues.

All the efforts by successive Rumanian governments in the 1920s and 1930s to assure the inviolability of their country's new frontiers to the north and east, in the end, proved unsuccessful. They could not assuage the differences between themselves and their two main revisionist neighbours—Hungary and the Soviet Union, neither of which could be reconciled to the loss of territory at the end of the war.

The problem of Transylvania stood in the way of any significant *rapprochement* between Hungary and Rumania. Successive Hungarian governments throughout the inter-war period never ceased to hope for the return of a territory they regarded as an integral part of historical Hungary, and no Rumanian government would contemplate the slightest concession that might diminish its sovereignty over the province. Typical of the disputes between the countries in the 1920s was that occasioned by the protest of over 500 Hungarian landlords in Transylvania against the expropriation of their estates under the provisions of the Rumanian agrarian reform. Granted the right by the Treaty of Trianon to opt for either Rumanian or Hungarian citizenship, they chose the latter and, supported by the Hungarian government, they argued that expropriation was a violation of the peace treaty. The case was heard by various international bodies, including the Council of the League of Nations in 1923, until finally at the Hague Conference on reparations in 1930 the issue was finally settled, largely to the satisfaction of Rumania.[7]

The bone of contention between Rumania and the Soviet Union was Bessarabia. Its reincorporation into Rumania in 1918 had precipitated a break in relations and was to remain the chief obstacle to their resumption until 1934. The two sides negotiated intermittently until 1924, when discussions in Vienna between Rumanian and Soviet delegations broke down. Neither side showed any inclination to resume the dialogue until 1929, when Rumania adhered to the Moscow Protocol, an instrument proposed by the Soviet Union to bring the Kellogg–Briand Pact into force sooner than stipulated. Poland played the role of intermediary in obtaining an invitation for Rumania to send a delegation to Moscow for the signing on 9 February. The Rumanian government was clearly interested in gaining Soviet recognition of Bessarabia's new status, but Soviet officials insisted that the signing of the protocol, by which both countries renounced war as a means of settling disputes, did not signify a change of Soviet policy.[8]

The resumption of direct contacts in Moscow did not lead immediately to new negotiations, as both sides stuck to their original positions on Bessarabia. Maniu, the Rumanian Prime Minister, made normal relations dependent upon the Soviet Union's recognition of the Dniester River as the boundary between the two countries, while Maxim Litvinov, the Soviet Foreign Minister, just as firmly rejected such a condition. The lack of significant trade between the two countries offered no economic incentive for an agreement. But pressure from other quarters eventually caused both sides to soften their intransigence. In 1931 the countries which Rumania counted as her most important allies—France and

[7] Nicolae Iordache, *La Petite Entente* (Geneva, 1977), 59–67.
[8] I. M. Kopanskii and I. E. Levit, *Sovetsko-rumynskie otnosheniia (1929–1934)* (Moscow, 1971), 12–15, 24–5, 41–2.

Poland—signified their readiness to negotiate treaties with the Soviet Union and urged Rumania to do the same. But discussions between Rumanian and Soviet delegations in Riga in January 1932 foundered once again on Bessarabia. Poland, which had initially made her own agreement with the Soviet Union contingent upon the outcome of the Riga meeting, decided, none the less, to proceed with the signing of a non-aggression pact with the Soviet Union on 25 July 1932, and France warned that she could not delay indefinitely her own normalization of relations with the Soviet Union.

Rumanian–Soviet talks resumed in September 1932 in Geneva. Within a short time the draft of a treaty had been agreed to, but the Rumanian government objected to ambiguous language regarding 'existing matters in dispute', that is, Bessarabia. Its hesitation reflected serious differences within the cabinet and among politicians generally about how far the *rapprochement* with the Soviet Union should go. Even those politicians who were committed to a normalization of relations refused to budge on Bessarabia. Nicolae Titulescu, who in 1932 was Rumania's minister to Great Britain and her permanent representative to the League of Nations, was eager to include the Soviet Union in a general system of collective security in Eastern Europe. He also favoured a non-aggression pact between Rumania and the Soviet Union, but made it contingent upon the latter's recognition of Bessarabia as Rumanian territory. When such a guarantee was not forthcoming the Rumanian government formally rejected the treaty negotiated in Geneva.

Contacts between the two countries, none the less, became more frequent. The signing on 3 July 1933 of the Treaty of London defining the aggressor in international disputes put Rumania and the Soviet Union on the same side. It brought an improvement in relations because a number of Rumanian politicians interpreted the Soviet Union's adherence to the treaty as a tacit recognition of Rumania's possession of Bessarabia. The Little Entente also encouraged a *rapprochement* by passing a resolution in January 1934 suggesting that the time had finally come for the establishment of diplomatic relations between all three countries of the alliance and the Soviet Union. Czechoslovakia exerted particular pressure on Rumania. Eduard Beneš, the Foreign Minister, thought that an understanding between Rumania and the Soviet Union was essential if an Eastern European security pact was ever to become a reality. The example of France in seeking a pact with the Soviet

Union to maintain the international status quo was a powerful incentive to many Rumanians, like Titulescu, who relied on France as the chief guarantor of the Versailles system, to pursue a similar accommodation with the Soviet Union. In Geneva on 9 June 1934 under the auspices of the Little Entente Litvinov, Beneš, and Titulescu exchanged letters establishing regular diplomatic relations. They made no specific reference to Bessarabia.

The Rumanian government still lacked the guarantee of its eastern frontier that had been the main object of its negotiations with the Soviet Union. Under the direction of Titulescu, now Foreign Minister, it sought to conclude a mutual assistance pact with the Soviet Union as one of a network of such agreements in Eastern Europe. The signing of mutual assistance treaties with the Soviet Union by France and Czechoslovakia in May 1935 spurred Rumania's interest in a similar agreement. These treaties also enhanced Rumania's strategic importance. Because of Poland's hostility to both Czechoslovakia and the Soviet Union, it was doubtful that she would allow Soviet troops to cross her territory to come to the aid of Czechoslovakia. Thus, if the Czechoslovak–Soviet pact was to have any meaning, the land bridge across Rumania had to be secured. There was a note of urgency in Titulescu's efforts to conclude a pact with the Soviet Union, for he was certain that eventually Hitler and Stalin would set aside their ideological differences and reach an understanding of their own, in which case a mutual assistance treaty with Rumania would have no value for the Soviet Union.

After lengthy negotiations Titulescu and Litvinov agreed on the general outlines of a treaty. Like the French and Czechoslovak treaties with the Soviet Union, it provided for mutual aid within the framework of the League of Nations, but unlike them, it was directed against every aggressor, not just Germany. Yet the two parties stipulated that they would be required to fulfil their obligations only if France took action. On 21 July 1936 at Montreux Titulescu and Litvinov initialled the agreement article by article, and the formal signing was scheduled for September. But on 29 August Titulescu, whose efforts at a *rapprochement* with the Soviet Union had made powerful enemies for him on the right and whose ambition and international successes had aroused the king's animosity, was abruptly removed from office in a cabinet reshuffle.[9] The Soviet government took the dismissal of Titulescu as

[9] G. Buzatu (ed.), *Titulescu şi strategia pacii* (Iaşi, 1982), 275–304.

a sign that Rumanian foreign policy had changed course and declared the understanding of 21 July null and void.[10] In the deteriorating international situation of the latter 1930s neither side made a serious attempt to revive the treaty.

GERMANY

The dismissal of Titulescu as Foreign Minister was symbolic of a subtle shift in Rumania's foreign policy in favour of Germany. The overall objective remained the same—security—but now King Carol and others thought it necessary to broaden the base of support for their country's territorial integrity. The king and the majority of Rumanian politicians and intellectuals would have preferred to continue the traditional alliance with France and Britain. The relationship with France was not merely political; it grew out of the Rumanians' perception of a general community of interests between the two countries, of mutual comprehension and even affection, feelings that were entirely absent in contacts with Germany. But the failure of France and Britain to stand up to Germany's assault on the Versailles system had caused even the staunchest of Western sympathizers to reconsider the system of alliances they had been building since the end of the war. The unsettled relationship with the Soviet Union increased the anxiety with which they re-examined their foreign policy. Both the supporters and the opponents of Carol had an almost irrational fear of the Soviet Union. For them, she was Rumania's hereditary enemy, always present, always a threat to her existence. Germany in the mid-1930s did not seem as dangerous.

Until this time Rumania's relations with Germany had not gone beyond the usual diplomatic forms. The war, especially the rigours of the occupation, had represented a sharp break in the pre-1914 tradition of respect for German economic and military power and appreciation of her cultural achievements, and Rumanian opinion in fact never fully recovered. The world economic depression led to somewhat closer economic relations, but Rumanian leaders, including Carol, were wary of Germany's penetration of the country's economy. Politically, Rumania continued to be a pillar of the system of collective security in Eastern

[10] A. A. Sheviakov, *Sovetsko-rumynskie otnosheniia i problema evropeiskoi bezopasnosti, 1932–1939* (Moscow, 1977), 153–8, 170–208.

Europe, which France sponsored and Germany opposed. The German Foreign Ministry recognized how unpromising the terrain was in Bucharest. It advised the new minister to Rumania, Wilhelm Fabricius, in April 1936 that he could expect to gain little politically and should, instead, concentrate on improving economic relations between the two countries.

A major impediment to close political and economic ties with Germany was intervention by Nazi Party officials in internal Rumanian political affairs, which put Carol on his guard. As early as 1935 the Foreign Policy Office of the Nazi Party began to cultivate relations with Octavian Goga and Alexandru Cuza and made contact with Alexandru Vaida and Gheorghe Brătianu with the immediate objective of forcing Titulescu out as Foreign Minister and of uniting Goga's supporters and the Iron Guard. The Foreign Ministry and Fabricius, however, opposed such actions as counter-productive. Rather than risk offending national sensibilities, they preferred to let closer political relations develop 'naturally' out of increased commercial and financial contacts.[11] Both events, in fact, occurred, but in reverse order. Carol's resistance to German economic penetration gradually weakened as political dependence on Germany grew in response to crucial changes in international relations.

Rumanian foreign policy, as formulated by Carol and Prime Minister Tătărescu, was now marked by intensive efforts to strengthen the country's defences against mounting German pressure. They strove to reinforce the bloc of neutral states in Eastern Europe as a means of maintaining good relations with both Germany and the Soviet Union, but were careful to avoid offending the former. The difficulties inherent in such a balancing act were evident in the government's efforts, on the one hand, to reinforce the military alliance with Poland, which was directed against the Soviet Union, and, on the other hand, to avoid weakening ties to the Little Entente, especially Czechoslovakia, which sought closer relations with the Soviet Union. When Jozef Beck, the Polish Foreign Minister, visited Bucharest in April 1937 he proposed that Rumania create a new Entente with Yugoslavia, Hungary, and Bulgaria, which would act in concert with Germany. The advantage for Rumania, he suggested, would be Hitler's consent to moderate Hungary's territorial claims on Transylvania. The Rumanian Foreign Minister, Victor Antonescu,

---

[11] Andreas Hillgruber, *Hitler, König Carol und Marschall Antonescu* (Wiesbaden, 1954), 11–12.

favoured the plan, but Carol and Tătărescu were reluctant to risk Rumania's traditional ties to Czechoslovakia and, above all, to France by such a drastic about-face. In any case, they were anxious to preserve their freedom of action.

The Sudeten crisis in the spring and summer of 1938 narrowed the choices available to Rumanian leaders. Carol and his ministers in the newly proclaimed royal dictatorship were now more anxious than ever not to offend Germany. The immediate issue, as they saw it, was whether to come to the aid of Czechoslovakia. Convinced that the initiative in international relations had passed to Germany, they decided that any action they might take in the absence of forceful leadership by France would merely jeopardize the territorial integrity of their own country. Consequently, at a meeting of Foreign Ministers of the Little Entente on 4–5 May the Rumanians, along with the Yugoslavs, took no action to support their ally. None the less, a week later at the League of Nations in Geneva the Rumanian foreign minister, Nicolae Petrescu-Comnen, agreed with his French counterpart, Georges Bonnet, that Germany's aggressive behaviour posed a grave threat to the security of all her neighbours. Nor did Petrescu-Comnen have any doubt about Germany's intention to gain control of Rumania's raw materials. But he opposed the passage of a Soviet army across Rumania to aid Czechoslovakia out of fear of provoking Germany and turning his country into a battlefield. At the same time Carol informed Beneš, now the President of Czechoslovakia, that Rumania could not afford to become involved in a conflict between Germany and Czechoslovakia. Nor did he or other Rumanian leaders seriously contemplate joining forces with the Soviet Union. Rather, they continued to hope that France would be shaken out of her 'inertia', and they looked increasingly to Britain to thwart German ambitions for supremacy on the continent.

As the crisis over the Sudetenland deepened Rumanian officials stood firm against allowing Soviet troops on Rumanian soil. But they agreed to close their eyes to overflights by Soviet aircraft, a formula the Soviet government declared unacceptable. On 27 September 1938, two days before the signing of the Munich agreement, Petrescu-Comnen informed Fabricius that Rumania wanted no conflict with Germany and would do everything possible to remain neutral. He was at pains to point out that Rumania was not bound by the pact of the Little Entente to intervene on behalf of Czechoslovakia unless Hungary attacked.

In Bucharest the Munich agreement of 29 September confirmed the view shared by a broad spectrum of political opinion from Carol to Maniu and Constantin Brătianu that closer relations with Germany had become imperative in order to secure the country's frontiers against Hungarian and Soviet revisionism.[12] But there was no headlong rush into the German camp. Carol still hoped that Britain would somehow become a counterweight to Germany in South-eastern Europe. He had great respect for Britain's economic power and thought that she would eventually be victorious in any new war. In mid-November he visited London and Paris with the aim of obtaining some type of commitment to support Rumania's independent stance against Germany, but he came away with nothing substantive. The attitude of the British government was especially disappointing. Prime Minister Chamberlain agreed to send a trade delegation to Bucharest, but was evasive on the question of increased British purchases of Rumanian oil and wheat and credits to enable Rumania to buy British military equipment. He even suggested that 'natural forces' might give Germany a preponderance in the economy of South-eastern Europe.[13]

The meagre results of his efforts in London and Paris persuaded Carol to abandon his reserve about meeting Hitler, and on 24 November the two men had a long conversation at the Berghof. Carol was anxious to obtain a promise from Hitler of German support against Soviet and Hungarian territorial claims on Rumania. He assured his host that Rumania was anti-Russian and that he would never allow Soviet troops to cross Rumanian territory, and he asked pointedly what stand Germany would take in the event of war between Rumania and Hungary. Hitler's response was not at all reassuring. He said little about the Soviet Union and thought that a Rumanian-Hungarian conflict was not of direct concern to Germany and would not, therefore, require her intervention.

Carol's main concern in foreign affairs in the months following his meeting with Hitler was to avoid a binding commitment to any of the power groups. To perform this delicate feat he brought in Grigore Gafencu (1892–1957), a leader of the National Peasant Party and pro-Western, as Foreign Minister. Gafencu attempted to adapt the alliances to which Rumania already belonged to the

[12] Rumania's reaction to the Czechoslovak crisis is analysed in detail in Viorica Moisuc, *Diplomaţia României şi problema apărării suveranităţii şi independenţei naţionale în perioada martie 1938–mai 1940* (Bucharest, 1971), 45–105.
[13] Paul D. Quinlan, *Clash over Romania* (Los Angeles, 1977), 36–8.

new circumstances, but to no avail. Most disappointing for him was his inability to persuade Beck to resist further German advances or to co-operate with the Balkan Entente. Gafencu also turned to the West in search of guarantees of Rumanian security. Hitler's destruction of Czechoslovakia in March 1939, which caused a stiffening of the Western powers' position toward Germany, offered him new hope of success.

From the spring of 1939 until the conclusion of the Nazi-Soviet pact on 23 August 1939 Rumania was under mounting pressure from Germany to expand economic ties between the two countries and to shun any security bloc unfriendly to Germany. Such demands were not incompatible with Carol's own policy, as set forth in Gafencu's memorandum on foreign policy of 15 April 1939. In it the Foreign Minister urged that Rumania maintain a neutral stance between Germany and the Western powers, but seek guarantees of her security from both. He recognized the threat posed by both Germany and the Soviet Union to the territorial integrity and independence of the country and hoped to play the one off against the other. But, if a choice had to be made, he clearly preferred Germany to the Soviet Union and recommended that no action be taken in international relations that would provoke Germany. Hitler's intense hatred of 'Bolshevism' thus precluded Rumanian adherence to any alliance system to which the Soviet Union was a party.

A measure of Germany's growing influence in Rumania, and in South-eastern Europe generally, was the economic treaty concluded between the two countries on 23 March 1939. Valid for five years, it provided for a close linking of the two countries' economies through co-ordinated planning and joint companies. Both sides agreed that their common economic plan would give special attention to Rumania's needs and capabilities, Germany pledging to supply capital and industrial goods to improve the Rumanian economy. The main task of the joint companies was thus to develop Rumania's mineral resources—copper, chromium, manganese, and especially oil. Until now oil had played only a secondary role in German trade with Rumania, because of the difficulties of transporting it to Germany and its price, which was above that of the world market. The intensified German interest in Rumanian oil was linked to preparations for war and the need to become independent of overseas supplies, which could be cut off by a British blockade. For the same reasons Germany wished to make certain of a regular supply of Rumanian agricultural products. Rumania also stood to benefit from the treaty. Besides help in developing her economy, she had found in Germany a supplier of modern military equipment and a reliable purchaser of large quantities of grain at better prices than anyone else was prepared to pay. As an economic document the treaty was generally welcomed by Rumanian politicians and economists, although a few, like Virgil Madgearu, expressed fear about the 'colonialization' of Rumania's economy. But Carol's decision to sign the treaty was based less upon economic considerations than a perceived need to placate Germany and gain time to work out accords with Britain and France.

After Germany's occupation of what remained of Czechoslovakia on 15 March 1939 Britain and France became more active in trying to block further German expansion in Eastern Europe. Their attention was directed toward Poland, which appeared to be Hitler's next victim, and, with somewhat less urgency, Rumania. The new Rumanian minister to Britain, Viorel Tilea, tried to impress upon the Foreign Office the need for immediate British aid for his country by reporting two days after the entrance of German troops into Prague that Germany had given Rumania an ultimatum in the form of drastic economic demands. Although there had, in fact, been no ultimatum—Tilea had simply been overzealous in carrying out his charge from Carol to do everything possible to obtain British support for Rumania's neutrality—British diplomats in Bucharest warned that action was imperative, since Rumania could not continue to resist German pressure alone.[14]

At first, Chamberlain and Foreign Secretary Halifax proposed a four-power bloc composed of Britain, France, Poland, and the Soviet Union to oppose aggression in Eastern Europe and thus stiffen Rumania's resistance to Germany. But neither Poland nor Rumania wished to be associated with the Soviet Union. Nor could Halifax persuade either country to come to the aid of the other if attacked, even if Britain and France joined in the effort. Finally, on 31 March, the British and French governments, believing Poland to be in imminent danger, pledged themselves to defend Poland's independence against any aggression. In the meantime, the Rumanian government had been seeking similar guarantees for itself. In the latter part of March it had urged

---

[14] On the 'Tilea affair', see Gheorghe Buzatu, *Din istoria secretă a celui de-al doilea război mondial*, i (Bucharest, 1988), 10–27.

Britain and France to announce publicly that they would not tolerate further boundary changes in Eastern Europe and would come to the aid of every country engaged in defending its independence. But the Rumanian government stipulated that such a guarantee should be seen as a spontaneous act, not one requested by Rumania, out of fear that Germany would thus be provoked into taking drastic reprisals. On 13 April after complicated negotiations, Britain and France promised all possible aid to Rumania in resisting any threat to her independence. Despite the limited nature of the British and French guarantees—they referred to Rumania's independence, not her territorial integrity—political circles in Bucharest welcomed them as a sign that the Western powers had at last abandoned the policy of appeasement. The guarantee to Rumania was reinforced by the Anglo-Turkish agreement of 12 May, whereby the two countries promised to support one another in case of war or aggression in the Mediterranean region. Article 3 provided that Turkey would assist Britain and France if they came to the aid of Rumania.

Rumanian foreign policy throughout the summer of 1939 continued to aim at maintaining a balance between the two principal threats to her security—Germany and the Soviet Union. Besides cultivating the Western powers, Gafencu sought to activitate the Balkan Entente. In June in talks with Turkish leaders in Ankara he promoted the idea of close military co-operation between Turkey and Poland. But he remained circumspect, refusing to join with Turkey and the Soviet Union in a Black Sea pact on the grounds that such action would tilt Rumania too far to one side and give offence to Germany. Carol took the same position during his visit to Ankara on 11 August. He was convinced that the German military build-up in Silesia was directed not against Poland but at Rumania in order to gain control of her oil fields. He and Turkish officials agreed that the attitude of Britain and France was the 'essential factor' in their ability to resist and decided to call immediately on both countries to honour their guarantees in case of aggression. But Carol refused to consider a security pact with the Soviet Union because of suspicions about the latter's intentions toward Bessarabia and fears about Germany's reaction.[15]

The non-aggression pact of 23 August between Germany and the Soviet Union came as a shock to Rumanian leaders, for they had based their foreign policy upon the deep-seated hostility be-

[15] Eliza Campus, Înţelegerea Balcanică (Bucharest, 1972), 307, 313–14.

tween Nazism and Communism. They now felt more insecure than ever before, and although they did not know the details of the secret protocol, by which Germany recognized the Soviet Union's special interest in Bessarabia, the very existence of the treaty had undone their strategy of balance between the two powers. A measure of the Rumanian government's desperation was its offer to Hungary on 24 August of a non-aggression pact, a proposal which was immediately rejected; its note to Poland on the 25th that if war broke out between her and Germany, Rumania would remain neutral; and Gafencu's assurances to the German minister on the 27th that the cultivation of strong ties with Germany would be the most important object of future Rumanian policy and that deliveries of oil, grain, and other raw materials would continue even if war broke out. Carol and his ministers had thus accepted the obvious: the foreign policy of the 1920s and early 1930s, which was based upon a system of interlocking alliances supported by France and adherence to international agreements promoting collective security, could no longer defend Rumania's frontiers.

During the month that Poland was overrun by German and Soviet armies Rumania remained neutral. Carol formally proclaimed neutrality on 6 September. When Soviet troops invaded Poland on 17 September the Polish government did not request aid from Rumania, as provided for in the treaty of 1921, for it was apparent that Rumania could not fulfil her obligations.

Rumanian leaders were now convinced that the greatest danger to their country's territorial integrity came from the Soviet Union. A declaration of neutrality sent to the Soviet government on 21 September did nothing to allay their anxiety over the future of Bessarabia, and the Rumanian government appealed to Britain to extend her guarantees against aggression to include the Soviet Union. But the British War Cabinet rejected the idea on the 29th on the grounds that such action could have no effect and might widen the war by bringing Britain and the Soviet Union into conflict. Soviet diplomats raised the question of Bessarabia officially for the first time on 5 December when a deputy Foreign Minister mentioned to the French ambassador in Moscow that Odessa had become a 'dead port' because it had been deprived of its agricultural hinterland, Bessarabia. In early December when Gafencu asked the German minister how his government stood on the question, the reply was that if war on the Western front became 'more difficult', Germany would be unable to prevent the Soviet

Union from carrying out 'certain plans'.[16] But the Soviet Union postponed action on Bessarabia, because of the war with Finland and a wait-and-see attitude toward events in the West. Finally, in the spring of 1940, after peace had been concluded with Finland, the Soviet government declared Bessarabia to be an 'unresolved question' and, accusing Rumania of provoking border incidents, began to concentrate troops along the Dniester.

The events on the Western front in the spring of 1940 brought a drastic change in Rumanian foreign policy. German victories in the Low Countries and northern France in May convinced Carol that the Allied cause was lost, and on 29 May he decided that only one course of action remained—to rely upon Germany to protect the country's territorial integrity. Tătărescu, the Prime Minister since 24 November 1939, agreed, but Gafencu, who favoured a continuation of the policy of neutrality, resigned and was replaced by the pro-German economist Ion Gigurtu. The immediate consequence of this change of direction was the signing of a so-called 'oil treaty' with Germany, which committed Rumania to deliver a fixed quantity of oil to Germany at autumn 1939 prices in return for military equipment. The Rumanians had resisted granting Germany such an important stake in this vital national resource as long as any hope of an Allied victory had remained.

The wooing of Germany could not save Bessarabia. On 23 June the Soviet Foreign Minister Molotov informed the German ambassador of the Soviet Union's intention to demand the 'return' of the province and the 'transfer' of Bukovina. On the 25th the German Foreign Minister Ribbentrop replied that his government did not object, since the proposal was in accord with their treaty of 23 August 1939, in which Germany had expressed her 'disinterest' in Bessarabia. But he raised several points. The demand for Bukovina struck him as a 'new issue', since it had not previously been the object of German-Soviet negotiations. He reminded Molotov that it had been a province of the Austrian Crown and was densely populated by Germans, whose welfare was of particular concern to Germany. He also noted that Germany had a vital interest in the economic resources of the other Rumanian provinces and did not want them to become battlegrounds. In response to German concerns Molotov announced that the Soviet Union would limit its claims to Bukovina to the northern half.

[16] Grigore Gafencu, *Prelude to the Russian Campaign* (London, 1945), 257; Alexander Cretzianu, 'The Soviet Ultimatum to Roumania (26 June 1940)', *Journal of Central European Affairs*, 9/4 (1950), 397–9.

Assured of German support, Molotov handed Soviet demands for the cession of Bessarabia and northern Bukovina to the Rumanian minister, Gheorghe Davidescu, on 26 June. He resorted to the Soviet version of history to justify his government's claims. He accused Rumania of having taken advantage of Russia's military weakness in 1918 to seize Bessarabia, thereby destroying a century-old union between this province, which, he claimed, was inhabited mainly by Ukrainians, and the Ukraine, an act, he insisted, which the Soviet Union had never recognized. As for northern Bukovina, he again raised the issue of its supposed Ukrainian ethnic and cultural character, but he deemed the transfer of this territory to the Soviet Union all the more justified because it would serve as 'modest compensation' for all the losses suffered by the Soviet Union and the inhabitants of Bessarabia during the twenty-two years of Rumanian rule. In conclusion Molotov gave the Rumanian government twenty-four hours to make a satisfactory reply. Davidescu made a valiant attempt to explain Rumania's ethnic and historical rights to Bessarabia. He pointed out that the majority of the population was Rumanian and that the union of Bessarabia with Rumania in 1918 had been carried out with the enthusiastic support of the majority of the population and had thus righted a historic wrong committed in 1812 when Russia annexed the territory from the Ottoman Empire. As for Bukovina, he showed how Austria had taken it from Moldavia in 1774 and how it had never been under Russian administration. But it was all to no purpose; Molotov would not budge. Carol, who was caught by surprise by the Soviet ultimatum, immediately sought German support. But none was forthcoming because Hitler had already assured the Soviet Union of his acquiescence in the annexation of Bessarabia and northern Bukovina. Instead, Fabricius and other German officials urged Carol and his ministers to avoid war and accede to Soviet demands. Similar advice came from Italy, Turkey, and several Balkan states. On the 27th the pressure mounted when the Hungarian and Bulgarian governments signified their intention to press forward immediately with their own territorial claims against Rumania, by force if necessary. At a meeting of the Crown Council on the same day Carol expressed his determination to resist the Soviet ultimatum, but he was supported by only eleven of its twenty-six members. At its second meeting that evening only six voted to reject the ultimatum. The majority were swayed by the advice from abroad to yield and by the gloomy report from the chief of the army general staff that the army could not survive an all-out attack from the Soviet Union. But the government played for time and proposed negotiations with the Soviet Union, a ploy Molotov summarily rejected. He gave the Rumanian government until two o'clock in the afternoon of the 28th to accept the ultimatum, which now included the requirement that Rumanian military forces be evacuated and the territories be transferred to the Soviet Union within four days of that date. Carol and the majority of his advisors saw no acceptable alternative and yielded.[17] On the 28th Soviet troops began to occupy the ceded territories, an operation that was completed by 3 July. Rumania had thus lost 44,422 square kilometres of territory and 3,200,000 inhabitants in Bessarabia and 5,396 square kilometres and 500,000 inhabitants in northern Bukovina.

Carol now spared no effort to ingratiate himself with Hitler in a desperate attempt to deflect the territorial demands of Hungary and Bulgaria. On 1 July the Rumanian government renounced the British guarantees of April 1939, and on the 4th Carol brought in a new, pro-German cabinet. The majority of its members came from Goga's and Cuza's old National Christian Party: Gigurtu was Prime Minister, and Mihail Manoilescu, the advocate of corporatism, Foreign Minister. Three members of the Iron Guard also received cabinet posts. Horia Sima, who had succeeded the slain Codreanu as the leader of the Guard, took over the Ministry of Cults, but he was removed after only four days because of his extreme political demands. Carol rejected proposals from the National Peasants and Liberals for a broad-based unity government because Germany would have interpreted it as a return to the old foreign policy of neutrality. On the day it took office the government declared its wish to adhere to the Rome–Berlin Axis, and on 11 July it announced Rumania's withdrawal from the League of Nations.

While these events were taking place, Carol sought a German guarantee of Rumania's existing frontiers and the sending of a military mission to Bucharest to establish close co-operation between the armies of the two countries. But on 15 July Hitler replied that he could consider these requests only after the border questions with Hungary and Bulgaria had been resolved. He had thus changed his earlier policy of maintaining the status quo

---

[17] Hillgruber, *Hitler*, 72–4. For a Soviet version of the 'peaceful solution' of the Bessarabian question, see B. M. Kolker and I. E. Levit, *Vneshniaia politika Rumynii i rumynsko-sovetskie otnosheniia (sentiabr' 1939–iiun' 1941)* (Moscow, 1971), 82–112.

in South-eastern Europe, probably in order to thwart Soviet attempts to gain influence in Hungary and particularly Bulgaria by supporting their territorial demands on Rumania. Carol had no choice but to accede to Hitler's wishes.

Negotiations began on 19 August with Bulgaria over the strip of southern Dobrudja which Rumania had acquired in the Treaty of Bucharest in 1913 and were concluded quickly. The Treaty of Craiova of 7 September restored the frontier of 1912 between the two countries. Rumania thus gave up 7,412 square kilometres of territory and approximately 360,000 inhabitants. The treaty also mandated an exchange of population; some 65,000 Bulgarians from north of the new frontier and 110,000 Rumanians from the south were to be relocated.[18] Rumanian public opinion could accept the loss of southern Dobrudja with a certain equanimity, since it had displayed little emotional attachment to an area perceived as peripheral.

While the settlement with Bulgaria was being worked out Rumania was engaged in far more momentous negotiations with Hungary over the future of Transylvania, a province which Rumanian public opinion regarded as the cradle of the nation. Pressure from Berlin and Rome in July to reach a quick, peaceful settlement with Hungary induced Carol to establish direct contact with the Hungarian government. Negotiations between the two sides began at Turnu-Severin on 16 August, but agreement proved impossible. The Hungarian government saw the issue as one of territory and aimed at acquiring a large section of Transylvania, including the districts in the very heart of Greater Rumania. The Rumanian government, on the other hand, proposed an exchange of population to be followed by slight modifications of the frontier to accommodate those Magyars who might choose to emigrate to Hungary. The two points of view could not be reconciled and were terminated on 24 August.

Meanwhile, tension mounted along the Rumanian border with both Hungary and the Soviet Union. In the latter half of August the Soviet Union massed large numbers of troops along the Prut River, and Hungary moved twenty-three divisions to districts close to its frontier with Rumania. Facing them were twenty-two Rumanian divisions in Moldavia and southern Bukovina and eight in Transylvania. As the concentration of troops continued, hostilities and even a Soviet occupation of the Rumanian oil fields

---

[18] Dimitrie Gherasim, *Schimbul de populaţie între state* (Bucharest, 1943), 93–115.

seemed a distinct possibility to Hitler. On 26 August he took action. He moved troops in occupied Poland closer to Rumania and instructed Ribbentrop to invite the Foreign Ministers of Hungary, Rumania, and Italy to Vienna for 'consultations' on the future of Transylvania. He was determined to settle the boundary dispute with all possible haste in order to avoid war in the east and to protect vital sources of raw materials in the south-east.

Hitler reserved to himself the final decision about Transylvania's new frontiers. He combined two proposals, which German experts had prepared, an act which awarded Hungary more territory than either had provided. In delineating the new boundaries, Hitler had both strategic and economic ends in mind. He thought it necessary both to satisfy Hungary and to avoid crippling Rumania, whose value to the German war effort he never ceased to acknowledge. Yet, he apparently saw the importance of keeping both countries dissatisfied as a means of ensuring their co-operation in the German new order in Europe. Thus, he thought Hungary would support Germany in hopes of gaining more of Transylvania, and Rumania would do the same in order to get back lost territory. Moreover, the new frontier in Transylvania, which reached almost to Braşov, offered substantial protection to the Rumanian oil fields by bringing German troops (with the co-operation of Hungary) within a few hours of them.

The consultations over Transylvania in Vienna were limited simply to the efforts of the German and Italian Foreign Ministers to persuade the Hungarian and Rumanian delegations to accept Hitler's decision. Only the Rumanians resisted. Mihail Manoilescu, the Foreign Minister, who had brought along a number of specialists, was anxious to argue his country's case in detail, but, instead, he was presented with Hitler's offer of 'arbitration' and given the choice of either accepting it or facing war with Hungary supported by the Axis.[19] Yet Ribbentrop also promised that in exchange for accepting Hitler's solution, Rumania would receive a German military guarantee of all her frontiers, an offer which Ribbentrop characterized as 'exceptional', not only because it had not been made to any other country, but because it would represent the cornerstone of Germany's new policy in the East. Manoilescu, shaken, asked for time to consult with the king. In the early morning of 30 August the Crown Council in Bucharest

[19] Mihail Manoilescu, *Dictatul de la Viena: Memorii iulie-august 1940* (Bucharest, 1991), 183–237.

debated the choices before it, without knowing precisely how much of Transylvania would be lost. Maniu, Brătianu, and others urged a rejection of Hitler's 'arbitration', but Carol and the majority decided that acceptance, together with German guarantees for the new frontiers, was the only way of preventing the destruction of the country.

In Vienna on 30 August Hitler's decision was formally read. Only then did the Rumanian delegation learn the full extent of their country's losses. Hungary was awarded a large salient carved out of northern Transylvania beginning from Oradea in the south and Maramureş in the north and encompassing Cluj and districts along the western slopes of the Carpathians extending to the vicinity of Braşov. Rumania was thus deprived of 42,243 square kilometres of territory and approximately 2,600,000 inhabitants, roughly 50 per cent of them Rumanians and 37 per cent Magyars and Szeklers. In return Rumania received a German guarantee of the inviolability of her frontiers. But it signified a loss of her independence in foreign affairs and the subordination of her economy to the German war effort.

As a result of the cessions of territory to the Soviet Union, Hungary, and Bulgaria, the Rumania which had come into being at the end of the First World War lost a third of her territory (99,790 square kilometres) and of her population (6,161,317). Carol's kingship could not survive the national catastrophe.

11

The Second World War,
1940–1944

DICTATORSHIP

The cession of Bessarabia and northern Bukovina at the end of June 1940, added to the undisguised aversion of the National Peasant and Liberal parties to the royal dictatorship and the homicidal tendencies of the Iron Guard toward the royal person, obliged Carol, whose prestige had reached its nadir, to turn to General Ion Antonescu as the one person capable of controlling the dangerous situation. The choice of Antonescu was not an easy one, for the dedicated career officer had made no secret either of his contempt for Carol or of his own ambition.

Born in 1882, Antonescu carried on the military traditions of his family, serving as a major in the First World War and then as military attaché in Paris in 1922 and London in 1923. As Chief of the General Staff in 1934, he clashed with Carol over many issues, but particularly galling to him was the power of the palace camarilla, which he held responsible for corruption in the army and in the country as a whole. Carol sought to end the confrontation by banishing Antonescu to a divisional command, but, because of his honesty and efficiency, his standing within the officer corps remained undiminished. It was during this period that Antonescu cultivated relations with the political right, notably the Iron Guard and Octavian Goga. He had numerous meetings with Codreanu, who promised to do what he could to bring Antonescu to power, and when Goga became Prime Minister in December 1937 he prevailed upon Carol to accept Antonescu as Minister of National Defence. A shared belief in authoritarian rule suggested a long-term collaboration with the king, but when Carol decided to take strong measures against the Guard after the proclamation of the royal dictatorship Antonescu protested and resigned. He remained in retirement for almost two years.

Antonescu returned to centre stage in the summer of 1940. At the beginning of July at an audience with Carol he bluntly criticized the king for having yielded territory to the Soviet Union. He also demanded a mandate to form a new, authoritarian government, which would have deprived the monarch of most of his powers. Carol's response was to order Antonescu's arrest and internment in the monastery of Bistriţa in Oltenia. His friends alerted German diplomats in Bucharest to the possibility that he might suffer the same fate as Codreanu. When the German minister, Fabricius, expressed concern to Prime Minister Gigurtu that any untoward incident involving Antonescu might be misinterpreted in Germany at a time when their two countries were drawing closer together, he received assurances that the general was in absolutely no danger. Yet, despite their solicitude, the Germans knew very little about Antonescu. Although he was thus not yet an important factor in their plans for Rumania, Fabricius saw the value of intervening on his behalf because he remembered that Antonescu had once expressed his willingness to co-operate with Germany.

Circumstances soon forced the king to give Antonescu the mandate he had sought. Carol chose him to form a government in order to save himself. He wanted to use Antonescu's connections with the Iron Guard to bring about a reconciliation between its leaders and the throne, his good relations with the National Peasants and Liberals to neutralize their opposition to the royal dictatorship, and his close contacts with members of the German legation in Bucharest to demonstrate Rumania's firm attachment to Hitler's new order in Europe and ensure German support for her king and her political independence. But Carol made a grave miscalculation. He did not grasp the extent of Antonescu's ambition or the depth of his hatred for Carol. Nor did he know that German officials now looked with favour on an Antonescu dictatorship and that Antonescu and Maniu had agreed at a secret meeting on 1 September to co-operate in bringing about Carol's abdication.

Antonescu accepted support from the Germans and the major political parties without in the least modifying his own conception of what the future Rumania should be like. He was, and remained, a nationalist whose goal was the creation of a prosperous, strong ethnic state, a respected middle-sized power carrying out its international responsibilities at the regional level in harmony with the broader European state system. He was also an authoritarian who was convinced, given the level of Rumania's political and economic development and the dangers that threatened from without, that he could achieve his ends only if he assumed absolute control of the nation's destiny. It is not surprising, therefore, that he and Maniu could discover no firm basis for co-operation after Carol had departed.

Antonescu, the authoritarian, had no intention of accepting political and economic vassalage to Germany. To begin with, he was not pro-German. Like the majority of Rumanian officers, he was pro-French and pro-English. In December 1937 he had, in fact, made his participation in Goga's government conditional upon the avoidance of close links with Germany and had favoured Rumania's joining in any Western effort to prevent Hitler from destroying Czechoslovakia. Goga finally won him over by arguing that a Goga government would reassure Germany of Rumania's good intentions and that Antonescu's presence in the cabinet would at the same time serve as a guarantee to France and Britain that Rumanian troops would never take the field against them. Antonescu felt an obligation to the Germans because of their intervention on his behalf during the summer and even admitted that he owed his life to them. But he was not a sentimentalist. When he finally decided to throw in his lot with Germany he did so because he was convinced that the salvation of the country required such a course. His feelings toward the West remained the same, but the international situation had changed drastically. Greatly affected by recent events—the defeat of France, the expulsion of Britain from the continent, and the aggressive behaviour of the Soviet Union against her small neighbours—he was now certain that Germany was going to win the war. Consequently, in the summer he laid the foundations of his political alliance with Germany in a series of conversations with German legation officials. An arrangement with Antonescu was eminently satisfactory to the Germans. Although an instrument of German policy lay readily at hand in the Iron Guard, many German officials doubted its effectiveness, because of its lack of capable men and a clear programme. Antonescu, on the other hand, offered those guarantees of order and stability they judged essential for the furtherance of the German war effort.[1]

Antonescu's accession to power came in the wake of the political crisis brought on by Carol's acceptance of Hitler's decision on Transylvania on 30 August, the so-called Vienna Award. As soon

---

[1] A. Simion, *Regimul politic din România in perioada septembrie 1940–ianuarie 1941* (Cluj-Napoca, 1976), 20–1.

as its terms became known in Rumania a strong reaction from the public, the army, and all political groupings threatened to dissolve the country in violence and chaos. On 3 September the Iron Guard took to the streets of Bucharest and several other cities, weapons in hand, in an attempt to seize power. Although the police and gendarmes quickly suppressed the uprising, the violence heightened public tension and uncertainty. A distinct possibility existed that individual army commanders in Transylvania would not withdraw their troops from the territories ceded to Hungary, but would oppose the entrance of Hungarian forces into the province, which was due to begin on 5 September. At first, public indignation had been directed at the Axis powers, but it quickly turned against Carol, who was universally condemned for his failure to resist. The Gigurtu government, Carol's chosen instrument, proved utterly incapable of dealing with the situation. Aware of German support for the Guard and Antonescu, Carol on the fourth invited Antonescu to form a new cabinet and gave him complete freedom to choose his ministers.

During the next two days Antonescu was in continuous contact with Fabricius, whose advice appears to have been decisive. He urged Antonescu to assume dictatorial powers as the only means of avoiding anarchy. But he made German support conditional upon Antonescu's willingness to carry out the terms of the Vienna Award, to receive a German military mission, and to enter into close economic relations with Germany. These terms were acceptable to Antonescu, and Fabricius informed Berlin that he had found the man who would establish a strong, efficient government capable of carrying out German wishes.

Certain of German support, Antonescu went to the palace on the evening of 4 September with a demand that the king grant him full authority to govern the country. After consulting his advisers early the next day Carol signed decrees suspending the constitution, dissolving parliament, and granting Antonescu unlimited powers. As events were to show, these acts sealed Carol's own fate and opened the way for the establishment of a military dictatorship and German ascendancy in Rumanian political and economic life.

As Antonescu continued negotiations with other political leaders on the fifth it became evident that a solution to the political crisis would be impossible as long as Carol remained on the throne. Maniu, speaking for himself and Constantin Brătianu, declared that he would support no government formed under Carol's auspices and urged his abdication. The Iron Guard took advantage of the king's weakened position to resume violent street demonstrations, which reinforced Antonescu's pressure on Carol. At a late night audience on the fifth, Antonescu flatly demanded that the king abdicate and leave the country. Carol hesitated, but finally yielded to an ultimatum from Antonescu to the effect that unless he abdicated immediately his own life would be in jeopardy and the country would dissolve in civil war and face occupation by 'a foreign power'. On 6 September Carol renounced the throne in favour of his 19-year-old son, Michael, and left the country on the following day.

Lack of support from Germany was decisive in persuading Carol to abdicate. All his efforts to curry favour with Berlin since the conclusion of the economic treaty of March 1939 had been futile because the royal dictatorship had in the end proved itself bankrupt and, hence, of no use to the Germans in pursuing their aims in Rumania and South-eastern Europe. It was obvious to German representatives in Bucharest that Carol and the palace camarilla had made themselves odious to all levels of society and could not prevail against the overwhelming pressure of the opposition. But the Germans also realized that the great majority of Carol's opponents were anti-German, and they thus concluded that a complete change of regime was imperative.

At this moment of crisis for the dynasty Antonescu apparently considered abolishing the monarchy. But he took no action because of opposition from the major political parties to such a drastic structural change. Maniu and Brătianu, while welcoming Carol's departure, publicly called for the preservation of a constitutional monarchy. Antonescu was also afraid that the peasants, who had been brought up to revere the king, would resort to violence if he moved against the monarchy. But he was unwilling to endure the tutelage of a new Carol and therefore decided to achieve his ends by reducing the new king to the status of a purely ceremonial figure, while he himself exercised the real power.

On 6 September, the day of his accession to the throne, Michael issued a decree giving Antonescu full powers as the Leader of the Rumanian State (Conducătorul Statului Român). But it contained an important provision absent from the similar decree signed by his father on the previous day: the king *appointed* the Minister President. The difference went unnoticed at the time, but four years later these few words provided the legal justification for Michael's dismissal of Antonescu and the appointment of a new head of government. Under the circumstances prevailing in the autumn of 1940, Antonescu may be excused for having ignored the point.

Armed with his sweeping mandate from the king, Antonescu set about forming a government. He would have preferred one of national union composed of all parties, especially the National Peasants, the Liberals, and including the Iron Guard as a mass movement. The leaders of the first two had supported him during the crisis because they believed him to be the one person capable of establishing a working relationship with Germany that would not require the total subordination of the country to Hitler's war aims. But the sympathy of Maniu and Brătianu always lay with the Western democracies, which, they were certain, would eventually win the war. At the same time they were realistic enough to recognize that the prevailing international situation required a temporary accommodation with Germany in order to preserve the Rumanian state. Consequently, they decided to give all possible aid to Antonescu, even allowing members of their parties to take posts in the new cabinet. They were anxious to have capable, experienced men in positions of responsibility in order to counteract the influence of the Guardists and make up for their incompetence, but neither Maniu nor Brătianu nor other leaders of their parties were themselves willing to take part in a dictatorship.[2] Maniu, who was the principal spokesman of Rumanian democracy, intended to establish an opposition and keep his forces intact until the end of the war, when, he was convinced, the victory of the Western Allies would make it possible for the democratic parties to return to power. Antonescu knew of Maniu's plans, but he did not try to counteract them. He himself had no wish to sever all links with Britain, for he was certain that she would continue to play an important role in international affairs, even if Germany dominated the continent, and he thus thought that Maniu's opposition group and its relations with the West would prove valuable later on. But he had no sympathy whatever for Maniu's long-term plan to re-establish a parliamentary regime, for he had only contempt for the traditional Rumanian political system. There were other reasons, too, why a broad coalition government failed to materialize. On the one hand, the Iron Guard, upon whom Antonescu was relying to mobilize

[2] I. Scurtu, *Din viaţa politică a României, 1926–1947* (Bucharest, 1983), 436–8.

popular support, demanded the formation of a 'legionary government' or at least one in which it would control the important ministries, and, on the other hand, German officials, to whom Antonescu owed so much, objected strenuously to the participation of pro-Allied politicians.

To bring the political crisis to an end Antonescu decided upon a government composed of Guard leaders in a majority of the ministries, army officers in the Ministry of National Defence, and a few non-party specialists in the economic ministries. But Antonescu proved to be a hard bargainer in negotiations with the Guard between 6 and 14 September over the precise composition of the cabinet. At his first meeting with Horia Sima shortly after Carol's abdication, Antonescu promised to co-operate fully with the Guard, but he also made it clear that he would resist any attempt by Sima to place his party above the government. Antonescu could barely conceal his contempt for Sima and the other Guardist negotiators, whom he regarded as incompetents.

A cabinet was finally agreed to on 15 September. Antonescu assumed the presidency of the Council of Ministers and became Minister of National Defence, while the Iron Guard became the dominant political force in the new government. Horia Sima was vice-president of the Council, and Guardists held five ministries, including Interior, Foreign Affairs, and Education and Cults. The Guard also controlled the entire press and propaganda service, the majority of the permanent secretaries and directors in the ministries, and forty-five out of forty-six of the *judeţ* prefectures. Mihai Antonescu (1904–46), a professor of law at the University of Bucharest and a close friend of the General, but no relation, was Minister of Justice, while non-party experts were appointed to the Ministry of the National Economy and its departments. The announcement of the new cabinet was accompanied by the proclamation of Rumania as a 'National Legionary State', in which the only political movement allowed to function was the Iron Guard.

Antonescu had not waited for the government to be constituted formally before proceeding to refashion Rumanian political life to his own liking. His immediate aims were to assure order, to eliminate all vestiges of the Carolist dictatorship, to institutionalize his ascendancy over the king, and to enhance his popularity among all classes of the population. Decree followed decree with dizzying rapidity, as he replaced the old political system with a radically different form, which he himself later described as a 'national totalitarian state'.[3] He made one point absolutely clear: he had no use for parliaments and political parties. His participation in various governments in the 1930s had reinforced his disgust for the practices of Rumanian democracy, which he considered inherently defective and unsalvageable. Underlying its failure, he thought, was its cultivation of 'liberty', which placed the interests of individuals above those of collectivities and the state. He thus made no room for political parties in his new order. His earlier proposal for a national unity government had simply been a device to enable him to draw upon the experience of certain members of the National Peasant and Liberal parties, and his sharing of power with the Iron Guard was, for him, an unavoidable, but strictly temporary, expedient.

In foreign affairs Antonescu's most pressing concern was to consolidate the alliance with Germany. The success of that endeavour required the fulfilment of the terms of the Vienna Award, which, however distasteful to him personally, he was determined to carry out with dispatch. He also began to lay the foundations of Rumania's new role in a German-dominated South-eastern Europe by reinforcing military and economic links to Germany. He thus repeated an earlier call for the sending of a German military mission and began negotiations for a new Rumanian–German economic pact.

The alacrity with which Berlin responded to Antonescu's overtures suggests how important Rumania had become in German strategic planning in South-eastern Europe. Because of the failure of the Italian invasion of Greece, Hitler had decided that a German relief expedition would be necessary and that it would have to go through Rumania and Bulgaria. But Rumania's role in the East was not to be limited solely to that of a staging area and a supplier of raw materials. Worsening relations with the Soviet Union had persuaded Hitler to accelerate planning for the settlement of German–Soviet differences by military means. In the event of war, he planned to assign to Rumania the key role of southern anchor of the German eastern front.

The first German troops arrived in Rumania on 10 October 1940 following discussions between Antonescu and representatives of the German high command in mid-September. Their ostensible purpose was to train and reorganize the Rumanian army, but German officials also expected them to carry out their 'real' tasks—

---

[3] Simion, *Regimul politic*, 47–65.

to protect the Rumanian oil fields from attack by a third power and to prepare both German and Rumanian forces for war with the Soviet Union, if that occurred, but German commanders were instructed to conceal these objectives from the Rumanians. By the middle of November there were some 23,000 German troops in Rumania, and their number increased dramatically in the next two months as a military confrontation in the Balkans drew nearer following the occupation of Crete and some of the Aegean islands by the British army at the end of October and the collapse of the Italian invasion of Greece in November and December. Hitler and his military commanders had now to reckon with the possibility that British bases in the Aegean and mainland Greece would bring their bombers within range of the Rumanian oil fields. On 4 November Hitler instructed the army high command to prepare a plan of operations for an attack on Greece. Its main task was to increase as rapidly as possible the number of German divisions in southern Rumania.

In order to assure himself of full Rumanian co-operation Hitler invited Antonescu to Berlin on 21–4 November. The official reason for the visit was to complete Rumania's adherence to the German–Italian–Japanese Pact, which Antonescu, in fact, signed on the 23rd. Far more important, however, were the conversations between Hitler and Antonescu on the 22nd, which decisively influenced the subsequent course of German–Rumanian relations. Antonescu made a favourable impression on Hitler as someone he could trust, a conviction that endured until Antonescu's downfall in August 1944. Antonescu insisted in a two-hour exposition of Rumania's aspirations and of his own plans for co-operation with Germany that the Vienna Award be revised, even though he had been informed that the subject would be distasteful to Hitler. In reply, Hitler made no promises, declaring simply that after the war the situation would not be the same as it had been, but Antonescu took this statement as a commitment to alter the terms of the Award.[4] From then on and throughout the war with the Soviet Union he had Transylvania constantly in mind, and he was convinced that close co-operation with Germany was the only way to ensure its return. He also raised economic questions, requesting aid to develop Rumanian industry and communications, which he promised to put at the disposal of Germany. He also

---

[4] A. Hillgruber, *Hitler, König Carol und Marschall Antonescu* (Wiesbaden, 1954), 114.

promised to fight side-by-side with the Axis. Impressed, Hitler declared Rumania's economic prosperity, because of her valuable raw materials, to be in Germany's own best interest, and he expressed his readiness to enter into long-term commercial agreements. He also informed Antonescu about plans to intervene in the Italian–Greek conflict and requested his help in facilitating the undertaking, which, he promised, would not involve Rumania in war. Hitler came away from the meeting confident that Antonescu was the ideal person to head the Rumanian state.

Shortly after Antonescu's trip to Berlin, on 4 December, the two countries signed an economic agreement which geared Rumania's economy to the German war effort. Although it provided numerous benefits for the Rumanian economy through extensive German credits at reasonable interest rates and deliveries of agricultural machinery and chemical fertilizers, the main objective of German negotiators had been to strengthen those branches of Rumanian industry and agriculture that would mesh with German economic development. The Germans reserved a place for Rumania as a producer of agricultural products and other raw materials in the new economic order they were planning, and, hence, they were little interested in developing Rumanian industries, except those which could contribute directly to the war effort. Nor were they willing to leave the growth and management of the Rumanian economy solely in Rumanian hands. The treaty stipulated that Germany would send agricultural, industrial, and other specialists to 'assist' Rumanian enterprises and government ministries. The hundreds of Germans who thus descended upon Bucharest and other cities gained a significant influence over key branches of the Rumanian economy.

While Antonescu had thus achieved his main goal in foreign policy—close co-operation with Germany—his political alliance at home with the Iron Guard had failed to bring about the civil tranquillity and economic progress he desired. The Guardists had proved to be incompetent and unreliable partners, who, it was obvious, did not share Antonescu's vision of the new Rumania.

In the autumn of 1940 the Guard had assumed the responsibility for organizing the totalitarian state. It sought to rally the mass of the population behind the ideals of the national legionary regime and restore its own popularity by resorting to those means which had proved so effective before 1938. It organized public ceremonies of all kinds, many of which took on a quasi-religious character, and it rapidly expanded the number of its publications in an effort to inundate cities and villages with its message. *Cuvântul*, Nae Ionescu's newspaper which reappeared on 14 October, became the central organ of the movement. It was seconded by numerous other newspapers published throughout the country, along with calendars, books, and brochures of every description.

This massive propaganda effort was directed at every social class and professional group, but the Guard directed its main attention at the urban working class. It promised to limit the power of factory-owners and to raise salaries and improve working conditions, and it established legionary retail stores in certain workers quarters and legionary restaurants in many large industrial enterprises. To bring masses of workers into the legionary movement Guard leaders reorganized and intensified their workers organization, Corpul Muncitoresc Legionar (The Legionary Worker Corps), which had been founded in 1936. All these activities had considerable success. Hardly an enterprise existed without a Guardist labour organization. The social categories in which the Guard showed the greatest interest were the recently urbanized workers, apprentices, and trade-school students, many of whom seemed especially responsive to its propaganda. Similar appeals were made to the peasantry, but on a more modest scale than before 1938, and to intellectuals and state employees. The Guard also attracted numerous participants to its public demonstrations from among elementary and secondary schoolteachers, but many were simply following instructions from the Minister of Education, the legionary Traian Brăileanu. Priests provided a relatively large contingent of supporters. Many were impressed by the religious orientation of the Guard and hoped to improve their own economic status with its help. The Guard also gave special attention to university students. It controlled the major student centres throughout the country, and the leading student organization, Uniunea Națională a Studenților Români Creștini (The National Union of Christian Rumanian Students) was obliged to have as its president a legionary commander.[5] Moreover, Antonescu had given the Guard the general responsibility for 'organizing and guiding' the youth of the national legionary state, which enabled it to adapt the entire educational system to the needs and spirit

---

[5] The efforts of the Iron Guard to gain support are described in Simion, *Regimul politic*, 71–5, 87–92. For the composition of Guard membership after 1938, see A. Heinen, Die Legion 'Erzengel Michael' in Rumänien (Munich, 1986), 453–8.

of the legionary movement and to enroll the great majority of elementary and secondary school students in legionary 'brotherhoods of the cross'.

Despite the opportunity it thus had to influence and coerce the public, the Guard succeeded only temporarily in regaining the popularity it had enjoyed before the installation of Carol's dictatorship. In the autumn of 1940 it brought out large crowds for its ceremonies and marches, notably on 6 October in Bucharest to celebrate the first month of the legionary state and on 8 November in Iaşi to observe the day of the Archangel Michael, the patron saint of the Guard. But by January 1941 it had lost most of the political capital it had accumulated. The main cause was its failure to live up to its promises. Its support of workers, for example, proved to be completely worthless because the dictatorship had deprived them of the most elementary trade union rights. Legislation forbade strikes under the most severe penalties and dissolved existing unions (*bresle*), which were not replaced by any other kind of professional organization. Salaries, it is true, increased, and the minimum wage was introduced, but the cost of living rose more rapidly than income. The Guard had also made much of its intention to establish a new social order in which the bourgeoisie would be eliminated and economic exploitation would thus disappear. But in practice the Guard fostered harmony between workers and factory-owners and sought to introduce legionaries into the bourgeoisie in order to refashion it into a class fully conscious of its duties in the legionary state.

The ambitions of Guard leaders were boundless. Behind the scenes they sought to gain control of the police and the army, institutions which had previously been impervious to Guard influence. In Bucharest and other cities the police forces were now thoroughly infiltrated by legionaries. In addition, on Horia Sima's initiative, a separate force, the legionary police, was formed to be used by Guard leaders against opponents of the regime. Its members were recruited from among the least desirable elements of society and had no professional training. With the army, however, the Guard had little success. The officer corps had always been hostile to the legionary movement, because it represented disorder, criminality, and subordination to Germany. Only in the lower ranks did the Guard gain a few adherents. Antonescu himself took drastic action to prevent the 'legionary spirit' from gaining a foothold in the army. On 29 November he informed the Council of Ministers that military discipline would be maintained in the army at all cost, and on 5 December he issued a decree imposing severe penalties for 'rebellion' and 'insubordination', including death for instigators and leaders of such actions.

Antonescu's measures were undoubtedly a response to the atrocities committed by legionary death squads in the final week of November. Among the victims were Nicolae Iorga and Virgil Madgearu, who were taken from their homes and shot, and a number of former government ministers and other officials, who were among sixty-four prisoners killed in a Guardist rampage at Jilava prison, near Bucharest.[6]

The Guard applied similar methods to its management of the country's economy. The anarchy it inflicted could not have come at a worse time. The events of the preceding year had thoroughly undone the economic recovery of the late 1930s. The mobilization of troops, which had deprived agriculture of manpower, combined with the loss of rich agricultural regions in the ceded territories reduced the autumn harvest of 1940 to about 30 per cent of normal. The consequences were a shortage of food and inflation. Many industries were also adversely affected by the redrawing of the country's boundaries, for some lost raw materials and others their markets. The influx of refugees from Transylvania and other ceded territories, whose number reached 300,000, strained both private resources and the state budget.

The Guard succeeded in gaining control of key economic agencies. The Ministry of National Economy, which had responsibility for overall economic planning and co-ordination, fell under its direction. All measures undertaken by the Ministry, consequently, bore the stamp of legionary ideology and practice. It soon became evident that the chief aim of the Guardists was not to revive the economy, but to gain control of it. The totalitarian nature of the regime allowed them to proceed unhindered. On 5 October they obtained the promulgation of a decree which created commissioners of Rumanianization (*comisari de românizare*), who could be appointed to any enterprise judged essential to the economic welfare of the country. The commissioners were invariably legionaries and had, in effect, unlimited control over the factories and businesses to which they were assigned. But none possessed the knowledge or experience to run a complex (or simple) industrial or commercial enterprise, and, as a result, the arbitrary

---

[6] The official description of these gruesome events is *Asasinatele dela Jilava, Snagov, şi Strejnicul* (Bucharest, 1941).

measures they took brought production in many places to a standstill. In other places they allowed the owners to operate as before
in return for handsome salaries and other benefits for themselves.
Particularly destructive were the efforts of the commissioners to
autochthonize the economy. The main victims were Jews, but
Rumanians also suffered, as businesses of all kinds were taken
over or simply pillaged. The cumulative effect of this management
style was to bring the economy of the country to the verge of
collapse.

The Guard's drive for power severely strained its relations with
Antonescu. The decree of 14 September creating the new regime
had in theory established a partnership between them. It designated
Antonescu as the 'Leader' of the national legionary state and Sima
as 'Commander of the Legionary Movement', and placed them on
an equal footing. In the beginning, in September and October, the
two men frequently exchanged public compliments. Sima referred
to Antonescu's 'wisdom' and to the Guard's 'gratitude' to him for
bringing it to power, and on behalf of the legionary movement
he swore fidelity to him. Antonescu, in turn, urged his 'dear
comrades' to close ranks around him. But neither trusted the
other, and behind the façade of unity they were engaged in a
feverish struggle for control of the administrative and security
apparatus.

The conflict between Antonescu and the Guard had to do with
fundamental differences about the form which the totalitarian state
should take and how it should be administered. Sima demanded
that the country be governed in accordance with the 'legionary
spirit', by which he meant that the government should be formed
entirely of legionaries and that drastic measures should be taken to
terminate political activity by all other groups. On 28 October
he went so far as to accuse Antonescu of violating the decree
establishing the national legionary state by allowing the National
Peasant and Liberal parties to function. Such political diversity, he
warned, was contrary to the principles of the totalitarian state. He
also found fault with the prevailing economic organization of the
country and demanded a complete overhaul, or, as he called it,
an 'economic revolution'. He wanted to apply German national
socialist principles to Rumania in order to bring every aspect of
economic life under centralized control. In a letter to Antonescu
on 16 October he warned that the country faced 'bankruptcy'
unless the current liberal economic structure was immediately dis-
mantled and a new economic system compatible with the national

legionary political order was introduced. But Antonescu had no intention of allowing the state or the economy to be run by legionaries. By October he had accumulated overwhelming evidence of their perfidy and incompetence, which merely reinforced his earlier convictions about the Guard's inability to govern. He agreed with Sima's dire predictions about the country's economic future, but he laid the blame for imminent bankruptcy on Sima's own cohorts. Yet, his duel with Sima went beyond questions of efficient administration and coherent economic policy. It was about power, for Antonescu sought supreme command of the legionary movement for himself and its subordination to his own vision of a disciplined, orderly Rumania.

Relations between Antonescu and the Guard reached the breaking-point after the murders carried out by legionary death squads in November. At a meeting of the Council of Ministers on the 27th Antonescu demanded that the government and the legionary movement issue a joint statement to the public condemning what had taken place. But, instead, the Guardist ministers excused the killings, and when Antonescu tried to replace the legionary chief of police of Bucharest with a military officer, the Guard prepared for armed resistance. Although Antonescu seemed ready then to settle accounts with his rivals, he decided to wait until the Guard had discredited itself completely in the eyes of public opinion. Sima also held back because he realized that the Guard was ill prepared for a showdown with the army. A compromise was therefore patched together which left a legionary as chief of police of Bucharest, but provided for the public condemnation of the November murders. None the less, both sides regarded the arrangement as merely a truce.

Antonescu had strong support for his stand against the Guard. The army was solidly behind him, and even the leaders of the National Peasant and Liberal parties, though opposed to dictatorship in any form, found themselves siding with Antonescu when confronted with the lawlessness and violence of the Guard. In a letter of 4 December Maniu warned Antonescu that the chaos into which the Guard had plunged the country threatened its very existence, for he had no doubt that the 'military instructors' (a reference to the large German military mission) could very quickly become an army of occupation in order to ensure Rumania's co-operation in Germany's grand design for Eastern Europe. He therefore urged Antonescu to re-establish order as soon as possible and to ensure the lives and property of all citizens by bringing to justice the perpetrators of the November murders and other crimes.[7]

The conflict between Antonescu and the Guard indeed attracted the attention of German officials in Berlin and their representatives in Rumania. Although Hitler had been favourably impressed by Antonescu, he had made no final choice between him and the Iron Guard. The leaders of the Nazi Party apparatus, particularly the SS, supported the Guard as the organization best qualified to carry out Hitler's designs for Rumania, while the Foreign Ministry and its man in Bucharest, Fabricius, and the army high command considered the Guard by itself incapable of managing the government and economy of this important ally. At first, the tide in Berlin seemed to favour the Guard, for Fabricius, whose reports from Bucharest had favoured Antonescu at the expense of the Guard, was recalled on 13 December and replaced by an SA officer, Manfred von Killinger.

As the strained relations between Antonescu and Sima headed inexorably toward a final break Antonescu requested a meeting with Hitler to discuss 'matters relating to the defence of Rumania' and to obtain Hitler's 'advice' concerning internal problems. Such a meeting was important for Hitler, too. On 13 December he had signed an order setting in motion the planning of 'Operation Maritza', the campaign against Greece, and was anxious to have Antonescu's full co-operation. In the course of a long discussion on 14 January 1941 at the Berghof Antonescu expressed his willingness to participate in the projected German campaign south of the Danube, if necessary, and to join Germany in a common defence of Eastern Europe against a possible Soviet attack. He expressed the hope that in the new Europe that Hitler was building he would accord Rumania her 'natural role' as a regional power. Then Antonescu came to the main purpose of his trip. He accused the Iron Guard of having brought the country to the brink of anarchy and proposed that he take over sole leadership of the national legionary state. He suggested two ways of doing this: the removal of the legionaries from all positions of authority and the establishment of a military dictatorship, or the 'reorganization' of the Guard with him in control of it. At first, Hitler was evasive. He explained how some years before he himself had faced a similar challenge from within his own party and had been obliged to liquidate such elements, and he suggested that Antonescu

[7] 23 august 1944: Documente, i (Bucharest, 1984), 157–60.

might have to do the same. Later, just before Antonescu's departure for home, Hitler assured him that he was 'the only man capable of guiding the destinies of Rumania'.[8] This short conversation dispelled Antonescu's final doubts about Hitler's position in his struggle for power with the Guard.

Antonescu returned to Bucharest on the evening of 14 January determined to eliminate the Iron Guard. For their part, Sima and other Guard leaders were feverishly preparing for armed conflict. At a meeting on 16 January in Bucharest they agreed that the 'divorce' between the Guard and Antonescu had become irremediable. On the 19th similar meetings were held in major cities throughout the country, at which legionaries from Bucharest conveyed instructions for co-ordinating an uprising against Antonescu. In the meantime, Antonescu had set in motion a purge of the Guard. He ordered the dismissal of all legionary commissioners of Rumanianization on the 18th and the removal of the legionary Minister of the Interior and other security officials on the 20th. On the same day armed legionaries occupied police headquarters, administrative offices, and communication centres in a number of provincial cities. In Bucharest legionaries barricaded themselves in various public buildings and refused to hand over the headquarters of the security forces and the police to Antonescu's new appointees. They also blocked off sections of the city where they concentrated men and arms for a final showdown with Antonescu. These actions marked the beginnings of the legionary rebellion.[9]

Antonescu had the full support of the army and did not doubt the favourable outcome of a clash between it and the Guard. But rather than take action at once, he waited for the legionaries to commit acts that would discredit them in the eyes of the populace and German officials. When on the 21st he appeared to give in to legionary demands for a withdrawal of the army to its barracks and a change of personnel in the government, Sima took his action as a sign of weakness and demanded Antonescu's 'retirement' and the formation of a 'pure' legionary government.

Both sides sought German support, for they were aware of the immense stake Germany had in the outcome of their struggle. Antonescu was in regular contact with the German legation in Bucharest and through it on 22 January he received approval from

---

[8] Hillgruber, *Hitler*, 117–19.
[9] A detailed account of the Iron Guard's uprising is in Simion, *Regimul politic*, 244–72.

Hitler to 're-establish order'. Legation personnel had kept Hitler and other high officials in Berlin informed of events and had expressed their own support for Antonescu as the person best able to further German aims in Rumania. Most important was their assurance that the army was fully behind him. They dismissed Sima and the legionaries as utterly incapable of governing. The legionaries were also active. On 20 January Sima visited General Erik Hansen, the chief of the German military mission in Rumania, to obtain the support of the German army in Rumania, which now numbered about 170,000 men. But by this time the decision had already been made in Berlin that the German army would support Antonescu, and on the 21st Hansen issued a directive to that effect.

On the 22nd Antonescu decided to crush the rebellion. Under the direction of General Constantin Sănătescu, whom he had installed as the military commander of Bucharest on the previous day, the army proceeded to retake the important public buildings held by the legionaries. By evening the issue had been decided. Sima and other Guard leaders vainly sought the intervention of Hansen and other German officials, but they advised surrender, promising only that they would seek permission from Antonescu for Guard leaders to go to Germany. They thought it necessary to preserve the Guard in some form as a means of putting pressure on Antonescu if in the future he decided to act contrary to the interests of Germany. On the 23rd the legionary rank-and-file surrendered, but the chief of the German secret service in Rumania on his own authority arranged for Guard leaders to be spirited out of the country to Germany. Moreover, Killinger, the new German minister to Rumania, who arrived in Bucharest on the 24th, had instructions to persuade Antonescu to revive his political alliance with the Guard.

All Antonescu's actions following the suppression of the rebellion showed clearly that he had no intention of restoring the Guard to a position of authority, for he excluded its members from the new government. He tried again, as in the previous September, to interest the leaders of the National Peasant and other parties in forming a national unity government, but failed. Maniu's position had not changed. He refused to join a government which disdained parliamentary practices and prohibited normal party activities, a conviction strengthened now by his perception of it as subordinated to Germany. The cabinet which Antonescu introduced on 27 January was thus composed mainly of military officers, whose primary task was to assure public order and efficient administration. With his team in place he proceeded to lay the foundations of his brand of authoritarianism. On 5 February he decreed severe punishment for anyone who disturbed public order. Although he intended specifically to discourage a resurgence of legionary activities, his decree touched every aspect of political and public life. In effect, it prohibited the establishment of any kind of organization, political, religious, or cultural, which did not have government approval, and forbade public gatherings, however small and random, as subversive. During February a round-up of persons implicated in the legionary rebellion resulted in the arrest of over 9,000. Some 3,000, among them 218 priests, were tried before military courts, 1,842 of them drawing sentences of a few months to life in prison. These measures culminated in the formal abolition of the national legionary state on 14 February and a sweeping prohibition against political activity of any kind. In June the military tribunal of the capital convicted the main leaders of the Guard in absentia of 'rebellion' and sentenced them to varying terms in prison from life (Horia Sima and nine others) to five years. It also sentenced to death twenty legionaries responsible for the murders committed in November 1940. In a national plebiscite on 2–5 March, 99.9 per cent of those voting approved Antonescu's measures. Although this figure appears exaggerated, there can be no doubt that at this moment the great majority of Rumanian voters and members of the old-line parties supported Antonescu against the Iron Guard. But Maniu and Brătianu, while welcoming the removal of the Guard from power and the restoration of order, were not prepared to acquiesce in dictatorship. They insisted that Antonescu restore parliamentary government and allow political parties to resume their activities.

The regime which Antonescu instituted on 27 January 1941 cannot be classified as fascist.[10] A more apt description would be military dictatorship. Unlike Hitler's Germany and Mussolini's Italy, it lacked an ideology and was not supported by a mass political party. Instead of a philosophical justification for its existence, Antonescu made order and security, which he deemed indispensable for the progress of every society, the reason for being of his regime. As we have seen, he had no use for political

[10] The nature of the Antonescu regime is discussed in A. Simion, *Preliminarii politico-diplomatice ale insurecţiei române din august 1944* (Cluj-Napoca, 1979), 14–28, 130–5, and Mihai Fătu, *Contribuţii la studierea regimului politic din România (septembrie 1940–august 1944)* (Bucharest, 1984), 57–132.

parties and politicians and had, in effect, banned both. He often declared his disdain for 'speeches, applause, and parades' and denounced the 'hypocrisy' inherent in copying foreign institutions. His purpose, rather, was 'to build the nation' in order to enable it to withstand all the dangers that were certain to come its way. He thus relied upon neither the masses nor the politicians. In their place his instruments were the army and the security apparatus, which he expected to provide direction and suppress dissent. When, in one of their early meetings, Antonescu described his ideal regime to Hitler the latter observed that he had, in effect, defined a police state. 'If you wish', Antonescu replied, 'but the police and the army must be strong enough to impose order at all costs because order is the minimum requirement for the progress of a people'.

After the suppression of the legionary uprising and the establishment of his military dictatorship Antonescu drew even closer to Germany. When he proclaimed his new government he was at pains to point out that Rumania stood side-by-side with the Axis as 'an act of conscience' rather than from political calculation. Although such words may be dismissed as simply a rhetorical flourish, they none the less accurately measure the depth of his commitment to the new German political and economic order in Europe. He demonstrated his allegiance by supporting the German campaigns in the Balkans in March and April and by joining wholeheartedly in the invasion of the Soviet Union in June.

Rumania was not directly involved in the campaign against Greece. The bulk of German troops left Rumania on 2 March 1940 crossing the Danube into Bulgaria. When the pro-Axis government of Yugoslavia was overthrown on 27 March Hitler added that country to his list of military objectives. But he did not demand the participation of Rumania in the campaign, as he did Hungary and Bulgaria, mainly because he counted on Rumania to provide cover against a possible Soviet attack. Antonescu, who was informed of these plans on 5 April, initially declared that Rumania had always maintained friendly relations with Yugoslavia and had no demands to make on her, and, hence, would not participate in the campaign. But he objected to the German plan to use Hungarian troops in the Yugoslav Banat and refused to move Rumanian troops to the east of Timişoara, as the Germans requested, in order to facilitate communications between German and Hungarian forces. He warned that if the latter entered the Yugoslav Banat he would send in the Rumanian army to force them out, a threat which persuaded the German high command to place this territory under German administration. Antonescu changed his mind about seeking Yugoslav territory in late April after he heard about German and Italian plans for the division of the conquered country. In order to balance the acquisitions made by Hungary and Bulgaria he requested the cession of the Yugoslav Banat to Rumania and the establishment of an independent Macedonia with political autonomy for the Rumanians settled in the Timok and Vardar valleys. But he got neither, as Hitler had other plans for these territories.

In the meantime, preparations for the attack on the Soviet Union proceeded, and toward the end of March Hitler made the final decision for war. He and German army commanders foresaw only a limited role for the Rumanian army because they had serious doubts about its capacity to carry out independent offensive actions. They were far more concerned about protecting the Rumanian oil fields from a Soviet attack and entrusted their defence to the head of the German air force mission in Rumania. As they saw the situation, Rumanian oil supplies would become critical once the war began because shipments from the Soviet Union, Germany's other major supplier, would obviously cease. On 12 June in Munich Hitler informed Antonescu of his plan to attack the Soviet Union. Antonescu's response was to promise the full military and economic participation of his country in the campaign.

WAR AGAINST THE SOVIET UNION

On 22 June 1941, a few hours after the German invasion of the Soviet Union had begun, King Michael and Antonescu proclaimed the beginning of a 'holy war' to free Bessarabia and northern Bukovina from Soviet occupation. This war enjoyed the over-whelming support of the Rumanian populace, which saw it as a means of removing the Russian threat to their country's existence once and for all. Political leaders and the public had full confidence in the military superiority of Germany and expected a short, victorious campaign.

Antonescu committed the bulk of his army to the campaign— twelve infantry divisions, an armoured division, six special brig-ades, and 672 airplanes, including 219 bombers and 146 fighters. Of these, six infantry divisions, three brigades of mountain troops, three brigades of cavalry, and other smaller units were placed directly under the commander of the German 11th Army. The most serious deficiencies of the Rumanian army, which became evident as it drove more deeply into Soviet territory, were the lack of artillery, inadequate supplies of munitions, and too few tanks and other motorized vehicles. In 1940 Antonescu had planned to reorganize the army by reducing its size and enhancing its mobility and fire power. But Rumanian industry could not produce the necessary equipment, and German leaders preferred to create new German armoured divisions rather than supply the Rumanian army with tanks and motorized vehicles. To strengthen his army, therefore, Antonescu had no alternative but to increase the number of infantry divisions.

At the beginning of the Russian campaign Rumanian and German forces in Moldavia were concentrated in three army groups: in the north, the Rumanian Third Army; in the centre, the German 11th Army, the largest; and in the south, the Rumanian Fourth Army. Together, they formed the so-called Antonescu Army Group, over which Antonescu himself had supreme command, seconded by a general staff composed of German officers. Initially, the principal mission of this group was to cover the right flank of the German South Army Group in occupied Poland.

The general offensive on the Rumanian front got underway only on 2 July because it had been much further east than the base from which the South Army Group had begun operations. By mid-July Rumanian and German forces had reached the upper and middle Dniester River. In the south the Rumanian Fourth Army was joined by units from Dobrudja, which crossed the Danube on the 21st, and by the 26th they had reached the lower Dniester. Thus, within a month of the beginning of hostilities the primary Rumanian military objectives—the liberation of Bessarabia and northern Bukovina—had been achieved. But Antonescu had already decided to send Rumanian troops across the Dniester. He was certain that a German victory would come in the foreseeable future and he intended, as he wrote to Hitler on 30 July, to fight alongside Germany until they had achieved their final goal of destroying the Soviet Union. On 17 July Rumanian troops made their first crossing of the Dniester, and by the beginning of August the territory between the Dniester and the Bug rivers had been cleared of Soviet forces, except for Odessa.

Hitler and Antonescu met at the headquarters of the South Army

Group on 6 August to discuss the future role of the Rumanian army in the war. Their decisions committed Rumania still further to the German war effort. They agreed that the Rumanian army would occupy and provide security for the territory between the Dniester and the Dnieper rivers and that certain army units, notably cavalry brigades and mountain troops, would be used east of the Dnieper.

Hitler and Antonescu also agreed that the territory between the Dniester and the Bug, now called Transnistria, would come under Rumanian civil administration. The convention signed at Tighina on 30 August, which formalized the arrangement, was concerned mainly with the allocation of agricultural and other products of the region and with the transportation facilities, which were placed temporarily under German control. It also required the Rumanian civil governor, 'in the interests of the common war effort', to follow instructions issued by the German army command. But this agreement did not grant Rumania permanent possession of Transnistria.[11] Such an omission may reflect fundamental differences between Hitler and Antonescu. The former seemed willing to give Transnistria to Rumania, but only on condition that Antonescu give up all claims to northern Transylvania. Antonescu, on the other hand, adamantly opposed any concessions on Transylvania, for he regarded it as part of the ancestral home of the Rumanians, territory which, he insisted, they had inherited from the Daco-Romans. For the next three years the recovery of all the territory ceded to Hungary in 1940 never ceased to preoccupy him.

The capture of Odessa, the last Soviet foothold in Transnistria, was assigned to the Rumanian Fourth Army. Antonescu had underestimated the strength of the Soviet defences and had refused German offers of assistance. The first general assault on the city on 18 August revealed the enormity of the task that lay before the Rumanians. They would need a massive concentration of artillery, air support, and tanks, none of which they possessed. Odessa finally fell on 16 October, after the German 11th Army had occupied the Crimea and surrounded Sevastopol, the main supply base for Odessa. But by then the bulk of the Soviet defenders had been evacuated by sea. The two-month siege had taken a frightful toll on the Rumanian army: as many as 70,000 dead and wounded. The bulk of the crippled Fourth Army had to be withdrawn

[11] Hillgruber, *Hitler*, 138–42.

to Rumania, leaving only two divisions to provide security for Transnistria. Thus, the Rumanian contribution in manpower to the campaign on the eastern front during the winter of 1941–2 was much reduced. Only five to six divisions took part in the fighting, mainly in the Crimea as part of the German 11th Army.

In the meantime, Rumania's relations with Great Britain and the United States deteriorated. Under pressure from the Soviet Union the British government sent an ultimatum to the Rumanian government on 30 November 1941 demanding the withdrawal of its army back across the Dniester by 5 December. When this did not happen, Britain declared war on 7 December. Rumania, obliged by Germany and Italy to honour her commitments under the terms of the Tripartite Pact, which Antonescu had signed in November 1940, declared war on the United States on 12 December. The United States did not get around to responding with its own declaration of war until 5 June 1942. Antonescu and the majority of Rumanian politicians were reluctant partners in Germany's war against the Western Allies. Antonescu's reported statement to a group of journalists on 12 December suggested his own lack of enthusiasm: 'I am the ally of the Reich against Russia; I am neutral between Great Britain and Germany; and I am for the Americans against the Japanese.'[12]

When Hitler and Antonescu met at Rastenburg, Hitler's headquarters on the eastern front, on 11 February 1942 they were certain that the Soviet Union had been defeated and would be unable to mount a serious counter-offensive, because of the enormous losses in men and equipment it had sustained in the first year of the war.[13] Antonescu repeated his pledge to commit large Rumanian forces to the coming spring offensive, but he set as a condition that Germany provide his army with modern equipment. He also requested that Hungary and Bulgaria make similar commitments to the eastern front. He had been angered by Ribbentrop's declaration in Budapest on 8 January 1942 that the Hungarian–Rumanian border problem had been permanently settled by the Vienna Award. Antonescu reminded Hitler that Rumania had entered the war not to revise the Versailles settlement but to fight against the Slavs. It struck him as foolish, therefore, to fight against the Slavs in the east and to allow those in the

---

[12] Gheorghe Barbul, *Mémorial Antonesco, le IIIe homme de l'Axe*, i (Paris, 1951), 141.

[13] Simion, *Preliminarii*, 167–78.

south (the Bulgarians), along with the Magyars, to strengthen themselves. He warned again that Rumania would never give up her claims to all of Transylvania, but he promised not to press these demands until the end of the war. His goal, he explained, was to re-establish Greater Rumania as a bastion against both the Slavs and the Magyars. Hitler remained non-commital, but later he instructed all German officials to exercise the utmost discretion in dealing with Hungary and Rumania, since both would be called upon to make 'additional sacrifices' for the war effort.

Large numbers of Rumanian troops took part in the massive German offensive in southern Russia and the Caucasus in the summer of 1942. Some eight divisions were engaged in operations east of the Sea of Azov, but the bulk of Rumanian forces took part in the drive to the Volga. They were assigned positions on the northern and southern flanks of the German spearhead. It was here that Soviet forces made a decisive breakthrough in their great winter offensive, which began on 19 November. By the end of December they had completed the encirclement of the German Sixth Army at Stalingrad. Rumanian units had fought well, but, lacking sufficient armour and artillery, they were ill prepared to deal with the Soviet assault. The Rumanians sustained staggering losses: the better part of eighteen divisions, or two-thirds of their forces on the eastern front, were destroyed.[14]

The disaster at Stalingrad and, especially, the question of responsibility for it—German or Rumanian—led to a severe strain in the alliance. But Hitler and Antonescu put recriminations behind them and sought to redefine Rumania's future role in the war when they met on 10–12 January 1943. They were concerned primarily with the reconstitution of the Rumanian army and decided to form nineteen new divisions, to be equipped by Germany. But, aware that this task could not be completed before the spring of 1944, they agreed that Rumania's military contribution would for the time being be limited to the eight existing divisions in the Caucasus and the Crimea.

Despite these agreements and talk of final victory, the disaster at Stalingrad had a decisive influence on Rumanian policy. It convinced Antonescu that Germany did not possess the military strength to defeat the Soviet Union and that other means had to

---

[14] Hillgruber, *Hitler*, 150–2; Platon Chirnoagă, *Istoria politică și militară a răsboiului României contra Rusiei Sovietice (22 iunie 1941–23 august 1944)* (Madrid, 1965), 203–35.

be found to protect the country from being overrun by the Red Army. He turned to the West. In the spring of 1943 he authorized Mihai Antonescu, since June 1941 deputy Minister-President, to initiate contacts with the Western Allies.

As the war continued and casualties mounted and the sacrifices demanded of the civilian population increased, the military dictatorship tightened its control over the home front. Order and obedience were its watchwords. Antonescu himself exercised absolute power, which was based upon three decrees promulgated in early September 1940. In the first, that of 5 September, Carol had granted Antonescu 'full powers to lead the Rumanian state', but none the less had reserved several important royal prerogatives: the conclusion of treaties, the modification of organic laws, and the appointment of ministers. But with Carol's abdication came a drastic reduction of the king's powers. Decrees of 6 and 8 September, signed by Michael, created a new political institution— the Leader (Conducător) of the Rumanian State—who monopolized legislative and executive power. He had the authority to initiate and promulgate all laws and to modify those already in force; to appoint and dismiss any state functionary, including ministers; and to conclude treaties, declare war, and make peace.[15]

Antonescu was thus responsible to no one for his actions in either domestic or foreign affairs. He dispensed with parliament. A substitute to which he had recourse in order to give his regime legitimacy—Adunarea Obştească Plebiscitară a Naţiunii Române (The General Plebiscitary Assembly of the Rumanian Nation)— was a sham. It had no power and was, in fact, used only twice, first, on 2−5 March 1941 for the purpose of registering public approval of the way Antonescu had governed (2,960,298 in favour, 2,996 opposed), and, then, for the same purpose, on 9 November 1941, two days after celebrations in Bucharest marking what was then thought to be the end of the Rumanian army's military campaign (3,446,889 in favour, 68 opposed). Although the results of these plebiscites no doubt accurately reflected the general public mood, they were by no means democratic because public meetings and discussions and any other means of expressing approval or disapproval of the regime had been proscribed. Nor did the Council of Ministers serve as a check on Antonescu's powers.

---

[15] An analysis of the powers exercised by Antonescu and his ministers is contained in Paul Negulescu and George Alexianu, *Tratat de drept public*, i (Bucharest, 1942), 315−90.

Although it met regularly, it was not a forum for the discussion of broad policy issues and for the making of collective decisions. Rather, its meetings consisted of reports by ministers on the activities and problems of their respective departments and Antonescu's approval or disapproval. Although the decisions reached at these meetings were attributed to the Council of Ministers, they in fact represented Antonescu's point of view. On questions of major importance—internal security, for example—not even the whole Council met; Antonescu simply consulted those ministers who were directly concerned with the matter at hand.

Authoritarian principles of government were extended to every level of administration. The prefects were the unchallenged masters of local government. They were appointed by the Conducător and were responsible solely to him. In October 1942 their already substantial powers were expanded to give them control over every branch of administration and its personnel in their jurisdictions. The citizenry was deprived of any voice in the selection of local officials, as the Minister of the Interior appointed the mayors of cities, and the prefect those of rural localities. Elected local councils were abolished and replaced by bodies composed of administrative officials and, beginning in October 1942, by representatives of industry, commerce, and the professions appointed by the prefects and other local officials. As a consequence of these measures, a sense of responsibility to the local population disappeared, and local initiative all but ceased.

The spirit which guided the dictatorship is evident from the numerous decree-laws intended to discourage all opposition. The foundation of the repressive legal system was the decree-law of 6 February 1941, which prescribed the death penalty or long prison terms for broad categories of acts which the authorities deemed threats to the existence and the interests of the state. An effective instrument of repression was the concentration camp, in which persons judged 'undesirable' could be interned with few formalities; the recommendation of the Minister of the Interior was usually sufficient to deprive a person of his liberty. During the dictatorship some 5,000 persons were thus interned, two-thirds of them for political offences.

The Communist Party was a particular object of the regime's attention. The decree of 6 February stipulated that when persons who were found guilty of its provisions were members of the Communist Party, the punishments were to be doubled. Beginning in March 1941 the Ministry of the Interior undertook a systematic campaign to destroy the party's organizational structure by imprisoning its leaders and chief activists. The great majority of those arrested were interned in concentration camps. Their numbers included most of the so-called 'native' leadership of the party which emerged after the war, that is, those Communists who stayed in Rumania in the inter-war years and were ethnic Rumanians, as opposed to those who resided in the Soviet Union, many of whom belonged to the Jewish and other minorities. By December 1942 their number had reached 1,905. Yet, while party activity largely ceased, its leaders were able to maintain a semblance of organization behind prison walls.

Organized opposition by the major pre-war political parties was also impossible, but Maniu and Brătianu regularly made known their views in blunt letters to Antonescu. Their criticism ranged from domestic politics to foreign affairs. They thought that after the suppression of the Iron Guard's rebellion in January 1941 their own and other parties would be able to resume normal activities and participate once again in governing the country. But Antonescu's resort to plebiscites and his draconian legislation against any form of dissent quickly dispelled their hopes for a revival of the parliamentary system. They therefore refused to take part in the plebiscites or join the cabinet on the grounds that neither reflected the 'true sentiments' of the country. Before the German invasion of the Soviet Union Maniu and Brătianu warned Antonescu against linking Rumania too closely with Germany out of fear that such a policy would deprive the country of every semblance of independence and might endanger its very existence. Instead, they recommended a policy of balance between Britain and Germany. They supported Antonescu's decision to join Germany in the war against the Soviet Union in order to recover Bessarabia and northern Bukovina, but they urged him not to send Rumanian troops beyond the Dniester. As Maniu pointed out in a letter of 18 July, to do otherwise would be to sacrifice Rumanian soldiers for foreign goals at a time when the army should be saved for the defence of Rumanian interests. Antonescu replied to all these attacks on his policies in long, often harsh letters of his own. Although he was angered by Maniu's and Brătianu's criticisms and accused them of 'disloyalty', he took no action against them.

The Antonescu dictatorship treated the economy the same way it did political parties and public administration. Control and regimentation were the order of the day. Characteristic was the decree of 18 February 1941, which provided for the 'militarization' of both state-run and private enterprises whenever the 'higher interests' of the state required it. This process brought both management and employees under the general direction and discipline of military officers. Another decree, of 10 March 1941, subjected the rural population to obligatory labour service, granting the Ministry of Agriculture and communal agricultural committees almost unlimited power to requisition labour and co-ordinate production. On 15 May these provisions were extended to all adults. Henceforth, persons who were capable of working, but were not employed productively, could thus be 'mobilized' to work for the 'public good'. The number of individuals affected was small at first, but these laws, which were promulgated before Rumania's entrance into the war, clearly reveal the spirit of a totalitarian regime: the subordination of individual rights and interests to the all-encompassing needs of the state. The war against the Soviet Union intensified the demands on and regimentation of the working population.[16] The decree-law of 2 October 1941 set the tone of labour legislation throughout the war. Its primary aim was to increase the production of both military and civilian goods by requiring greater output from the work-force. Much of the labour legislation enacted in the 1920s and 1930s to improve working conditions was thus, in effect, abrogated. The new work week was increased from 56 to 60 hours and might, under extreme circumstances, be raised to a maximum of 72 hours, but provision was made for overtime pay. Restrictions on the employment of young people and women were relaxed, allowing boys at 16 and women at 18 to be hired full time. The government discouraged all independent trade-union activity and used an extensive network of labour inspectors to resolve workers' grievances before they turned into open confrontations with management or the state.

Agriculture was at the centre of the regime's economic planning. This concern reflected in part the primary role Germany had assigned to Rumania as a supplier of foodstuffs in the war against the Soviet Union. But it also corresponded to Antonescu's view that Rumania was essentially an agricultural country and, hence, that its economic development ought to be based upon 'existing realities'. His plans, which he set forth in a proclamation on 6

---

[16] Dumitru Tuțu, 'Regimul forței de muncă în România în anii războiului hitlerist 1941–1944', *Revista de istorie*, 34/12 (1981), 2199–213.

November 1941, represented yet another attempt to solve the long-standing problems of Rumanian agriculture. He proposed to increase production and improve the standard of living of the rural population by organizing the peasant's labour more rationally, by providing him with proper tools, and by increasing the availability of credit through a network of village banks.

Antonescu was especially concerned about the fragmentation of peasant holdings, which, like so many of his predecessors, he judged a fundamental cause of low productivity and rural poverty. His solution was to consolidate small and scattered fields and strips into economically viable holdings of 10–15 hectares. He intended to accomplish his goal by promoting the interests of the 'agricultural middle class', which he, like many agrarianists, regarded as the backbone of the nation. Nor did he make any secret of his willingness to let those peasants who lacked the middle-class work ethic swell the ranks of the agricultural proletariat. The main instruments for carrying out his design were new agricultural associations (obştii săteşti). An appropriate decree was issued in June 1942 which encouraged peasants with adjoining holdings to combine them in the interest of efficiency and profitability. The association thus formed was empowered to buy equipment, buy or lease land, and obtain credit on favourable terms. Yet, despite these inducements, the results of the programme were disappointing. By the summer of 1943 there were only 203 associations composed of 6,400 members and covering an area of 38,000 hectares.

The regime resorted to numerous other means, all tried before, of solving the problems of agriculture. It promoted co-operatives, which were to serve as agencies for carrying out a variety of government measures. As their number rose from 3,649 to 5,463 between 1940 and 1943 they became the chief recipients of the tractors and other machinery imported by the state and served as the major conduits of agricultural credit and the providers of specified quantities of foodstuffs to the state. The regime also sought to re-equip agriculture. It subsidized the importation of large quantities of machinery and tools. For example, the number of tractors in use rose from 3,296 in December 1940 to 8,250 in the autumn of 1943. Crop diversification was encouraged. The amount of land given over to textile and industrial crops expanded steadily, as land sown in flax, hemp, and cotton increased from 60,436 hectares in 1939 to 146,039 hectares in 1943, and plantings of sugar beets and soybeans were expanded to 80,053 hectares and 23,068 hectares, respectively, in 1943. Plans were made to establish agricultural processing plants at eight designated centres in order to stimulate the production of industrial and garden crops and thus offer peasants a source of income other than the raising of wheat and corn.[17]

All these measures, however, failed to alter the fundamental structure of agriculture. The main crops continued to be grains, especially wheat and corn, and large numbers of small, inefficient holdings stymied attempts to rationalize production. Grain production, in fact, declined from the levels it had reached in 1939 after the recovery from the depression of the early 1930s. The cause lay mainly in the demands of war, which took large numbers of men and horses from the land. Tractors and other types of equipment could not make up for their absence because the only practical sources of power on smallholdings, still the characteristic production unit, were men and horses.

Efforts to spur industrial production were only partially successful. Food processing fell below the level of 1939, and there were continuous shortages of staple goods, caused mainly by the extraordinary draining of resources by the war. Textile manufacturing was also down significantly from 1939 levels. Although the amount of coal mined remained about stationary during the war, the pumping of crude oil declined from 6,240,000 tons in 1939 to roughly 5,350,000 tons in 1943. The bright spots were the metallurgical and chemical industries. The latter had been of minor importance, but beginning in 1942 it made rapid progress, becoming the only Rumanian industry to produce goods for export.

The Rumanian economy between 1941 and 1944 developed under unrelenting German pressure to increase the production of raw materials needed for the war effort and was subject to equally persistent German attempts to gain control of key Rumanian industries. But German officials at all levels discovered to their chagrin that Antonescu was little inclined to make wholesale economic concessions to Germany. He was much influenced by Liberal economic and banking circles, which had by no means abandoned the policy of 'prin noi însine' and sought desperately

[17] For the organization and development of agriculture under the Antonescu regime, see *Trei ani de guvernare, 6 septemvrie 1940–6 septemvrie 1943* (Bucharest, 1943), 85–98, 128–9, 131–3, and Fătu, *Contribuţii*, 236–58.

to maintain Rumanian control over economic resources and development.

The German drive to monopolize crucial sectors of the Rumanian economy began in earnest in 1941. The legal pretext was a protocol signed in Berlin on 4 December 1940 which provided for co-operation between the two countries to carry out a ten-year plan to revitalize the Rumanian economy. Germany was primarily interested in Rumanian oil, and in time she gained outright control of a number of former Western companies and even a 50 per cent share in Astra Română, the largest Rumanian-owned oil company. A co-ordinating agency, 'Petrol Continental', was founded in Berlin on 27 March 1941 to develop and supervise all German petroleum interests in Rumania. German economic planners were also anxious to increase oil production and sought to have the mining law of 1937 amended to make possible a massive exploration for new sources with the full participation of foreigners, that is, Germans. German capital was also directed toward the Rumanian metallurgical industry, notably the Malaxa Works, where the goal was to obtain a 50 per cent share of the stock. The Germans also manifested keen interest in Rumanian grains. Through their control of major international trading companies they nearly monopolized commerce in wheat and a number of other commodities.

Antonescu tried in various ways to limit German penetration of the Rumanian economy. A decree of 17 July 1942 reduced the amount of foreign capital in the oil industry in favour of Rumanian capital and gave special concessions to those firms in which ethnic Rumanians had at least a 75 per cent share. Antonescu also increased the participation of the Rumanian state in a number of enterprises, especially in the metallurgical industry. As early as 28 January 1941, a few days after the suppression of the legionary uprising, he signed a decree giving the state 50 per cent of the stock in the Malaxa Works, and then on 18 February he completed the acquisition of the remaining 50 per cent. A decree of 3 December 1941 provided that ethnic Rumanians have at least 60 per cent of the capital in the Reşiţa iron and steel works. To prevent the 'Germanization' of the Rumanian grain trade Antonescu declared it a state monopoly on 17 December 1941.

None of these measures of economic self-defence were entirely effective, particularly after the beginning of the war against the Soviet Union, because by then the Rumanian economy had become too closely bound up with that of Germany to operate independently. For example, certain raw materials essential for Rumanian industry such as coke and iron ore could be imported only from Germany, and Germany, because of the British naval blockade, was the chief customer for Rumanian agricultural products. The massive German military presence was a mixed blessing. On the one hand, Germany was the principal supplier of equipment for the Rumanian army, but the enormous purchases of foodstuffs and other supplies for the German army at the front adversely affected the financial stability of the country. As early as the autumn of 1941 Rumanian leaders were complaining that the huge quantities of goods bought and the high prices paid by German purchasing agents had brought on severe inflation and had, consequently, weakened the country's currency, undermined its tax structure, and turned the annual budget 'upside down'. These problems were the subject of almost continuous negotiations, but by 1944 they had still not been resolved.

The 'Jewish question', as it had been called since the second half of the nineteenth century, was the most serious minority problem to confront the Antonescu regime. Strong national feeling and tactical foreign-policy goals rather than doctrinaire anti-Semitism determined attempts to 'solve' it. The Jewish population, which numbered 722,000, or 4 per cent of the total population in 1930, had risen to about 800,000 in 1940. After the cession of territory to the Soviet Union and Hungary the number of Jews in the remaining two-thirds of Greater Rumania fell to 315,000, but rose again to about 375,000 when Bessarabia and northern Bukovina were recovered in the summer of 1941.

As Rumania drew closer to Germany in the summer of 1940 the situation of the Jews steadily deteriorated. Directly related to Rumania's realignment in foreign policy in May and June 1940 were the decisions of the Gigurtu cabinet on 9 July to remove all Jews from the civil service and on 8 August to redefine the legal position of the Jews, action which effectively deprived them of political and civil rights.

Dramatic changes in the status of the Jews occurred after the establishment of the national legionary state. Both Antonescu and the Iron Guard were anxious to Rumanianize the economy. The Guard, as we have seen, had no coherent plan, but used the occasion to give free rein to their violent brand of anti-Semitism. For Antonescu, on the other hand, Rumanianization was the means to a greater end—the creation of a strong, self-reliant native middle class, which would form the political and social backbone of the country. The idea had by no means originated with him. Ştefan Zeletin had made an eloquent plea for the Rumanianization of the economy and the strengthening of the ethnic Rumanian bourgeoisie in *Burghezia română*. Behind the Liberal Party's determination in the inter-war period 'to do it ourselves' was the same thought. But now Antonescu had the power to act. In September 1940 he decided that the time had come to remove Jews and foreigners from the country's economic structure and replace them with ethnic Rumanians. A series of decrees expropriated Jewish-owned rural property (4 October 1940), forests (17 November), river transport (4 December), and urban property (28 March 1941). The latter expropriation proved to be extremely complex, for it included shares in companies where it was often difficult to identify individual stockholders. As this broad programme got underway it quickly became evident that the Germanization rather than the Rumanianization of capital and the means of production was taking place. Owners of property and stocks were selling out in desperation to anyone who would buy, and Germans proved to be one of the few groups who in the autumn of 1940 could feel secure from arbitrary expropriations by the legionary commissioners of Rumanianization. The general economic breakdown which their activities threatened to bring about led Antonescu, as we have noted, to abolish these offices on 18 January 1941. From this time on Rumanianization became more methodical and orderly. Characteristic of the new approach was the gradual implementation of the decree of 16 November 1940 concerning the Rumanianization of the personnel in private business, industry, and other, non-profit organizations, which were all required to replace their Jewish employees with ethnic Rumanians by 31 December 1941. Official statistics showed that the number of Jews in these enterprises was gradually reduced from 28,225 in November 1940 to 16,292 by the deadline and then to 6,506 on 1 March 1943. But more credible are secret reports, which estimated the number of Jewish employees at over 21,000 in the spring of 1943. They remained in place because they were essential to the efficient operation of their respective enterprises. Elsewhere in the economy, too, Rumanianization seems to have made only modest progress. For example, the number of commercial enterprises owned by Jews and foreigners declined only from 53,919 (38.3 per cent) in September 1940 to 41,640 (28.1 per cent) as of 1 June 1943.

Measures taken against Jews before the attack on the Soviet

Union were primarily economic, except for the violent acts committed by legionaries against individuals. But after 22 June 1941 official policy assumed more ominous forms.[18] A decree of 14 July 1941, which reiterated the contents of earlier laws excluding Jews from military service, made Jewish males between 18 and 50 liable for labour service individually or in groups at the discretion of the army general staff. Those with university degrees, active or retired officers, doctors, and technicians were excused from manual labour, but could be mobilized to perform their specialities whenever needed. In 1943, 101,334 such persons were registered, of which 44,234 performed some kind of manual work, usually in labour battalions, and 21,078 were 'requisitioned' for white collar jobs in industry and commerce.

The deportation of Jews began after the recovery of northern Bukovina and Bessarabia. Large numbers, perhaps as many as 130,000, had already fled these provinces for the Soviet Union as Rumanian and German armies advanced. The killing of at least 4,000 Jews in Iaşi and during their deportation to Wallachia on 28–30 June by German and Rumanian troops confirmed the wisdom of such flight. As soon as the Rumanian army had secured Transnistria Rumanian authorities began to deport the mass of Jews from Bessarabia and northern Bukovina as far to the east as possible. The Treaty of Tighina of 30 August 1941, which recognized the Rumanian civil administration of Transnistria, specified that the Jews sent there be held in concentration camps and be used as a labour corps. Perhaps as many as 100,000 Jews were deported to Transnistria between 1941 and 1943, and, because of unspeakable conditions, thousands died. Thousands more Jews perished in numerous other atrocities.

The Antonescu regime, however, did not participate in the mass deportation of Jews which had been organized by Nazi officials as part of Hitler's plan for a 'final solution' of the Jewish problem in Europe. At first, it showed an interest in the project and agreed that beginning in September 1942 Jews fit for labour could be rounded up and sent to Lublin from the *judeţe* of Arad and Timişoara in the Banat and Turda in Transylvania. The deportations appear to have begun on schedule, but soon afterwards, in December 1942, they were halted, as the government changed

---

[18] On Rumanian government policy toward the Jews, see Hillgruber, *Hitler*, 236–46. A grimmer account is Radu Ioanid, *The Sword of the Archangel* (Boulder, Colo., 1990), 199–230.

its policy toward the Jews, primarily in response to the deteriorating military situation on the eastern front after the battle of Stalingrad and as attempts were undertaken to reach an accommodation with the Western Allies.[19] Evidence of a new Jewish policy was Antonescu's proposal in December 1942 to organize the emigration of 80,000 Rumanian Jews to Palestine. But such a plan could not be carried out, among other reasons, because of German fear of upsetting potential Arab allies in the Middle East. By the summer of 1944 Antonescu had decided to carry out the plan independent of German wishes, but by then the collapse of his own regime was at hand.

Besides the war on the eastern front, the most urgent foreign policy issue for the Rumanian government between 1941 and 1943 was the recovery of northern Transylvania. Both Antonescu and Hungarian leaders sought German support for their respective claims, but they received little satisfaction. Although Hitler was anxious to prevent the undisguised enmity between his two allies from interfering with their contributions to the desperate military situation in the east, he was not at all averse to playing one off against the other in order to obtain greater commitments of troops and supplies for the front.

Far from settling matters, the Vienna Award had exacerbated relations between Rumania and Hungary. It did not solve the nationality problem by separating all Magyars from all Rumanians. Some 1,150,000 to 1,300,000 Rumanians, or 48 per cent to over 50 per cent of the population of the ceded territory, depending upon whose statistics are used, remained north of the new frontier, while about 500,000 Magyars (other Hungarian estimates go as high as 800,000, Rumanian as low as 363,000) continued to reside in the south. The restrictions on political activities, impediments to education and culture in the national language, and ethnic discrimination in economic life imposed by both governments added to the bitterness.

Throughout the war the two governments failed utterly to resolve their differences. The most serious attempt at a *rapprochement* came in the first six months of 1943. The main incentive for both sides was the realization that Germany had lost the war and that, consequently, they must find a way out of the conflict before their countries became battlegrounds. Both sought to ward off the

[19] Ezra Mendelsohn, *The Jews of East Central Europe between the World Wars* (Bloomington, Ind., 1983), 210–11.

catastrophe of a Soviet occupation by placing themselves under the protection of the Western Allies. The initiative throughout the negotiations lay with Mihai Antonescu. The thought was never far from his mind that Hungary might try to seize the rest of Transylvania while the bulk of the Rumanian army was concentrated on the eastern front. Following Ion Antonescu's proposal on 6 January for talks between the two countries delicate negotiations, pursued in spite of Hitler's warnings to both sides that he knew what was afoot, led to a meeting between Miklós Bánffy, a former Hungarian Foreign Minister, and George Mironescu, a former Rumanian prime minister, in Bucharest on 9 June. Their discussions got off to a bad start. Mironescu denounced the continued occupation of Rumanian territory with a population of 1,400,000 Rumanians by Hungary as intolerable, and Bánffy bluntly countered that he had not come to discuss territory, since his government considered the matter of northern Transylvania settled. None the less, the Rumanians seemed willing to accept Bánffy's proposal that the two countries abandon the Axis at the same time, but they rejected his second point that the status quo in Transylvania be maintained until after the war, when the great powers would render a final decision. It seemed to the Rumanians that the Hungarian government intended to hold on to northern Transylvania at all cost in the hope that the Allies could be persuaded to endorse their possession of it. The Rumanian delegation and Iuliu Maniu, whom Bánffy met on 23 June, made it clear that they would never recognize the legality of the Vienna Award. Unable to find a compromise, the two sides broke off negotiations and allowed events to take their course.[20]

DEFEAT

The disaster at Stalingrad was a critical turning-point in relations between Rumania and Germany. Convinced that Germany could not now win the war, Antonescu bent all his efforts toward protecting Rumania from the 'great danger' to the east. That, after all, had been his primary motive in going to war against the Soviet Union. Thus, despite increasing strains with Germany as Soviet forces moved relentlessly westward, his policy displayed a

---

[20] Simion, *Preliminarii*, 296–307; Dániel Csatári, *Dans la tourmente: Les relations hungaro-roumaines de 1940 à 1945* (Budapest, 1974), 220–4.

remarkable continuity. He maintained the alliance with Germany and supplied her with men and *matériel* as usual for her war effort, but at the same time he undertook to gain understanding for Rumania's 'difficult position' from the Western Allies.

Tension between Rumania and Germany in the immediate aftermath of Stalingrad was evident at the meeting between Antonescu and Hitler at Rastenburg on 10–12 January 1943. Economic matters proved the most troublesome.[21] German officials complained that Rumania was not carrying out her obligations to deliver adequate supplies of oil, citing a decline from 3.9 to 3.3 million tons and a rise of 25 per cent in Rumanian consumption. Mihai Antonescu, who was the principal Rumanian negotiator on economic questions, raised the matter of German payments for oil and foodstuffs, which he judged insufficient to prevent a collapse of the Rumanian economy. To bolster the Rumanian currency and control inflation he demanded payment in gold. The impasse was broken by Hitler, who was obliged by Germany's desperate economic situation to make concessions to the Rumanians. The protocol signed on 11 January obliged Germany to deliver enough military equipment to reconstitute the Rumanian army at a level of nineteen divisions by February 1944 in return for half-payment immediately (in the form of oil and foodstuffs) and a promise to settle the account at no interest after the war. Germany also agreed to turn over 30 tons of gold to the National Bank of Rumania and to facilitate the Bank's acquisition of convertible currency. For her part, Rumania undertook to raise the amount of oil delivered to Germany and Italy in 1943 to 4 million tons by opening new fields and by drastically curtailing domestic consumption, and to pay 1,000 million lei for the maintenance of German forces stationed in the country.

Hitler and Antonescu met again three months later on 12–13 April at Klessheim. It was not a happy occasion. The urgent need for men and oil manifested by his hosts reinforced Antonescu's conviction that the war in the east had been lost. Furthermore, the discussions of grand strategy were punctuated by Hitler's accusations of treason against both Mihai Antonescu, who had not made the trip, and Iuliu Maniu, because of their efforts to establish contact with the Western Allies. Antonescu stoutly defended his right-hand man, but, feeling the need to placate Hitler, he agreed to give him a 'vacation' to recover from 'overwork'. Antonescu

---

[21] Simion, *Preliminarii*, 242–50.

dismissed Maniu's activities as unimportant and declined to have him arrested. But, in fact, he approved of both men's initiatives, and he urged Hitler to end the war against the Western powers as soon as possible in order to direct all available resources against the Soviet Union. But his arguments had not the slightest effect, and he found himself repeating earlier assurances that Rumania would stand with Germany to the end.

None the less, Antonescu encouraged his second in command Mihai to pursue contacts with the Western Allies and to call their attention to the danger which the Soviet Union posed for all of Europe, not just the East. Both Antonescus (and the overwhelming majority of Rumanian politicians and the public) had never regarded Britain and the United States as enemies.

Mihai Antonescu approached Italy first.[22] In the autumn of 1942 he had frequent conversations with the Italian minister, Renato Bova Scoppa, about a common Italian–Rumanian approach to the Western Allies for a separate peace. In January 1943 Bova Scoppa presented Antonescu's ideas to Foreign Minister Ciano, who was also convinced that the war was lost. When Ciano broached the subject with Mussolini, he was rebuffed. In May, after his diplomatic vacation, Antonescu pursued his Italian initiative, urging upon Bova Scoppa the formation of a 'Mediterranean Entente' led by Italy and Rumania as a means of asserting independence from Germany. Antonescu thought that Hitler was so obsessed by the Russians that he would sacrifice everything in his vain attempt to defeat them. On 1 July, during a visit to Italy, he discussed with Mussolini his plan for Italy to begin negotiations with Britain and the United States for a separate peace. This time Mussolini showed interest, but suggested waiting until the military situation in the Mediterranean had improved. After Mussolini's overthrow on 25 July Antonescu tried to interest the new Italian government in his plan, but it preferred to act alone and concluded an armistice with the Allies on 3 September.

Between the summer of 1943 and the spring of 1944 German armies were steadily pushed back to the frontiers of Rumania. The most important operation in which Rumanian troops were engaged was the defence of the Crimea, where seven divisions, retreating from the Kuban bridgehead, took up positions alongside five German divisions. These forces were cut off from the German Sixth Army in the Ukraine at the end of October 1943, and in the

---

[22] Renato Bova Scoppa, *Colloqui con due dittatori* (Rome, 1949), 69–118.

following April a Soviet offensive to retake the Crimea began. Overwhelmed by superior Soviet manpower and weaponry, the last German and Rumanian forces were evacuated from Sevastopol on 10–13 May. Approximately 150,000 of the some 230,000 troops engaged in the battle of the Crimea were evacuated, mainly by sea to the Rumanian ports of Constanţa and Sulina. By this time the battlelines had already reached Rumanian territory, Soviet troops having crossed the Prut in April.

By the spring of 1944 other political elements in Rumania had joined the effort to extricate the country from the war. The key figure was Iuliu Maniu, who was widely recognized as the leader of the democratic opposition to the Antonescu dictatorship. Between November 1942 and March 1943 he had sent a stream of messages to the British government through a variety of channels, including Swiss and Turkish diplomats, in which he explained Rumania's role in the war and her aspirations. He insisted that public opinion in Rumania had opposed continuing the war against the Soviet Union beyond the Dniester and now sought only to defend the territorial integrity of the country, including northern Transylvania. He claimed that the Rumanians cherished the same ideals as the 'Anglo-Saxon powers', but they could not act in accordance with their true convictions because their country was effectively occupied by the German army. He rejected Allied suggestions that military action be taken against the Axis as a means of hastening Rumania's withdrawal from the war by pointing out that in the absence of the Rumanian army, which was at the front, the Germans had the military force necessary to overturn the Antonescu government and bring back a legionary regime, a situation that would bring an end to all democratic opposition. None the less, he knew that the public 'mood' was ready for action favourable to the Allied cause and had no doubt that the Rumanian army could also be won over, but, he claimed, everyone was holding back until the British and American governments had guaranteed the country's territorial integrity.[23] It was evident in all these communications that Maniu, like Mihai Antonescu and Rumanian politicians generally, considered the Soviet Union the chief threat to the independence of Rumania and saw in the West their only hope of avoiding a catastrophe.

[23] P. D. Quinlan, *Clash over Romania* (Los Angeles, 1977), 82–5; Direcţia Generală a Arhivelor Statului, *23 august 1944: Documente*, i (Bucharest, 1984), 526–8: Note of the Rumanian Special Intelligence Office, 20 April 1943.

The initial response from Britain was disheartening. In January 1943 the Foreign Office informed Maniu that the boundaries of post-war Rumania would be drawn in accordance with the Atlantic Charter and Britain's recognition of the Soviet Union's security interests along her western frontier. The implication was clear that Rumania could not hope to deal solely with the Western Allies, but would also have to reach an accommodation with the Soviet Union. But on another vital territorial question—northern Transylvania—the Foreign Office expressed the opinion that after the war the Vienna Award would be annulled and the region returned to Rumania. In March 1943, in response to urgent messages from Maniu, British representatives in Istanbul informed him that the British and American governments appreciated Rumania's special position, but could make no commitments before they had reached an understanding about Rumania with the Soviet Union. None the less, the note continued, the British and American ambassadors in Moscow had been instructed to broach the subject of Rumania's withdrawal from the war with the Soviet government, and Maniu would be informed of the results of these conversations in due course.

The Soviet government at first showed only moderate interest in treating with the democratic opposition in Rumania. When the British ambassador in Moscow, Sir Archibald Clark-Kerr, offered to put Soviet authorities in contact with Maniu, Molotov replied that such action would be premature, but he suggested that the British pursue this opening, since Maniu and his supporters were the only serious opposition in Rumania. But Maniu himself showed no interest in dealing with the Soviet Union unless the Western Allies were prepared to guarantee that Rumania would not fall under Soviet domination. In August 1943 he repeated his willingness to negotiate with Britain and the United States but not with 'Russia'.

Maniu and Constantin Brătianu made no secret of their opposition to Antonescu's continuation of the war at Germany's side. In three letters to him in the spring and summer of 1943 they vigorously protested against the 'folly' of sending additional Rumanian troops across the Dniester to fight 'Germany's war'.[24] They called attention to the fact that Rumania had serious matters

---

[24] Simion, *Preliminarii*, 311–14: the letters were dated 20 April, 10 July, and 12 August 1943; *23 august 1944: Documente*, i 555–6: Note of the Rumanian Special Intelligence Office, 15 July 1943.

of her own to resolve with Hungary. Instead of dispatching the last reserves of young men to be 'ground up' in battles far from home, they urged a husbanding of human resources to defend the country's ethnic boundaries. Maniu and Brătianu also denounced the 'hostile attitude' which the Antonescu regime had taken toward the 'great Anglo-American democracies . . . our natural allies', whose help had been decisive in the creation of Greater Rumania. They concluded this series of letters on 12 August with an appeal on behalf of the entire nation to stop the fighting and withdraw the army to the country's frontiers in order to avoid further 'grave prejudice' to national interests.

Antonescu's reply suggests how little inclined he was to change course.[25] His tone was harsh. He reminded Maniu and Brătianu of the grave circumstances in which the country had found itself when he assumed power in 1940 and, accusing them of partial responsibility for that 'tragic situation', he denied them any right to speak on behalf of the broad public or the army. He rejected out of hand their key demand that he leave the war and bring the troops home, warning that drastic counter-measures by the Germans would lead to the destruction of the army and the subjugation of the country. His admission of almost total dependence upon Germany thus bore out Maniu's argument to the Allies about Rumania's special circumstances. If challenged, Antonescu warned, Germany would simply take Rumanian oil and grain, instead of paying for it, and would give southern Transylvania to Hungary and Dobrudja to Bulgaria. Despite his attacks on the two political leaders and his knowledge that Maniu was in contact with the British, Antonescu made no move to arrest them. In effect, he assured them of his protection, which allowed Maniu to continue his activities.

Both Maniu and Mihai Antonescu now made indirect contacts with the Soviet government, but their main purpose was to test the latter's attitude toward Rumania rather than to negotiate, since they still hoped to surrender to the Western Allies. Maniu solicited the help of Eduard Beneš, the head of the Czechoslovak government in exile in London, to present Rumania's case to the Soviet government. Beneš held talks with Molotov and Stalin in Moscow between 14 and 18 December 1943, during which the latter apparently agreed to hold the Antonescu regime rather than the Rumanian people responsible for the attack on the Soviet

[25] Simion, *Preliminarii*, 316–19.

Union and to favour Rumania over Hungary in solving the Transylvanian problem.

The other Rumanian channel to Moscow went through Stockholm, where the Rumanian minister, Frederic Nanu, held talks between December 1943 and January 1944 with officials from the Soviet legation over the interest expressed by 'certain circles' in Rumania (evidently, Mihai Antonescu) to negotiate a withdrawal from the war.[26] In February Nanu informed Bucharest that the Soviet government had promised to respect Rumania's sovereignty and independence and to help in recovering Transylvania if she left the war, but Mihai Antonescu did not reply, for he thought it safer for Rumania to deal with the West. He was pursuing talks in Madrid with the American ambassador to Spain and was encouraged to think that they might lead to a separate peace with the Western Allies. At the same time he even contemplated allowing the democratic opposition to take over peace negotiations in the hope that Maniu and his associates could gain better terms than the Antonescu dictatorship.[27]

By this time Maniu and Ion Antonescu were already engaged in a new peace initiative with Britain and the United States. At the end of 1943 the Western Allies had accepted Maniu's proposal that a representative of the opposition be sent to negotiate directly with the Western powers. Maniu and his associates agreed on Prince Barbu Ştirbey, who had headed a transition cabinet for a few weeks in 1927, as their intermediary and in February 1944 dispatched him to Cairo, the headquarters of the Allied Middle East command.[28] At his first meeting with representatives of the three allies on 17 March he declared that all elements in Rumania—the government, the king, and the opposition—wanted to change sides. He was certain that Antonescu was ready to take such action because he knew that the war was lost, but he also thought that Maniu could organize a *coup d'etat*, if the Allies wished, on condition that the country's independence and territorial rights be respected and that she be recognized as a co-belligerent. When asked what he meant by territorial rights he specified the return of northern Transylvania and the settlement of

[26] F. C. Nano, 'The First Soviet Double Cross', *Journal of Central European Affairs*, 12/3 (1952), 236–58.

[27] Ibid. 245.

[28] A well-documented survey of the negotiations may be found in Gheorghe Buzatu, *Din istoria secretă a celui de-al doilea război mondial*, i (Bucharest, 1988), 245–82.

Bessarabia's future by a plebiscite. The three Allied representatives made no commitments, but they made it clear that the primary condition for any agreement was unconditional surrender.

An intensive examination of the 'Rumanian question', as it came to be called, was now undertaken in the three Allied capitals. Molotov accorded little importance to Ştirbey's declarations because now he doubted that Maniu really opposed Antonescu and that Antonescu had any intention of leaving the war. American and British diplomats, on the other hand, were inclined to follow up Ştirbey's initiative and were willing to assure the maintenance of Rumania's independence and to examine carefully the question of her post-war boundaries (a plebiscite for the territory between the Prut and the Dniester seemed reasonable, but Transylvania was too complex a matter for immediate comment), but neither the State Department nor the Foreign Office was prepared to move until 'the Russians' had made their views known.

In the meantime, the rapid approach of Soviet armies and the German army's occupation of Hungary on 19 March had thoroughly alarmed political circles in Bucharest. On 21 March Mihai Antonescu dispatched an urgent message to Ştirbey in Cairo via the Rumanian minister in Ankara asking to know the Allied reaction to the events in Hungary and whether Rumania could count on Allied political and military support in the event of a similar German move against Rumania. The reply came on the 22nd from General Henry M. Wilson, commander of Allied forces in the Mediterranean, who, because of the shortness of time, did not consult his American and Soviet colleagues. He minced no words. He instructed the Rumanian government to capitulate immediately and to offer no resistance to the advancing Soviet armies. He warned that Rumania now had a final opportunity to contribute to the defeat of Germany and that the peace terms imposed upon her would in large measure be determined by her own efforts on behalf of the Allied cause.[29] A week later Wilson sent another message to Mihai Antonescu in which he added to the conditions already set down the need for direct contacts between Antonescu and the Soviet high command to arrange co-operation between Rumanian and Soviet armies against the Germans. On 2 April Wilson wrote to Maniu, setting down the

---

[29] *Foreign Relations of the United States* (henceforth, *FRUS*), *1944* (Washington, DC, 1966), 154–5: US Ambassador to the Yugoslav Government in Exile to Secretary of State, 24 Mar. 1944.

same conditions for an armistice and urging the immediate over-throw of the Antonescu regime on the grounds that it would never break with Germany of its own accord.[30] Neither Antonescu nor Maniu replied because Wilson's proposals lacked any of the guarantees they thought essential to preserve the Rumanian state. But now they could have no illusions about a separate peace with Britain and the United States or about the major role the Soviet Union was to play in determining Rumania's future.

Ion Antonescu continued to co-operate with Germany, despite the mounting evidence of military catastrophe, because, as he had explained earlier to Maniu, he saw no other viable alternative. Although he wished at all cost to avoid the subjugation of the country by the Soviet Union, he faced the more immediate threat of a German-legionary regime, which, he was certain, would complete the destruction of the country's political and economic superstructure and leave her to the mercy of 'others'. Such a danger was by no means imaginary, for on 26 January 1944 Hitler had ordered planning to begin for the occupation of Rumania ('Margarethe II') in the event of an anti-German coup. But the tension in Rumanian-German relations was eased by a new economic agreement on 9 February and, especially, by Antonescu's renewed pledges of support at a meeting with Hitler on 28 February. On that day, in fact, Hitler, his confidence in Antonescu apparently restored, ordered planning for 'Margarethe II' discontinued.

Antonescu met with Hitler again on 23–4 March. Their main concern was how to martial all the available manpower and *matériel* for 'total war', in Hitler's phrase, against the Soviet Union. Antonescu again signified his willingness to co-operate, but he set two conditions: German guarantees against a Hungarian move into southern Transylvania and additional German equipment for the Rumanian army. Hitler promptly replied that the first condition had been met by the German army's occupation of Hungary and that he had already given instructions to the high command to increase the flow of armaments to Rumania. But Hitler realized that promises alone could not secure Rumania's loyalty. He therefore informed Antonescu that Germany no longer recognized the validity of the Vienna Award and promised that he would soon order Hungarian troops to evacuate northern Transylvania. Antonescu made no comment, but when he pro-

---

[30] Alexandre Cretzianu, *The Lost Opportunity* (London, 1957), 131–3.

posed that 200,000 Rumanian refugees in southern Transylvania be permitted to return home, Hitler did not reply.

On the same occasion Mihai Antonescu and Ribbentrop discussed the possibility of a separate peace with the Western powers. Antonescu thought that a compromise could be worked out between Britain and Germany, but Ribbentrop rejected the notion as 'utopian' and even 'dangerous', because of the effect rumours of such peace overtures would have on the morale of German and Rumanian troops. For the same reasons he also objected to Ştirbey's mission to Cairo, about which, to Antonescu's surprise, he had detailed information.

The negotiations between Ştirbey and the Allies in Cairo reached a critical juncture in April. The Soviet Union took a more active role as its armies reached the Prut. To hasten a Rumanian capitulation Molotov announced on 2 April that the Soviet Union did not seek to acquire any Rumanian territory or change the country's social order.[31] On the 12th the Soviet representative in Cairo presented Ştirbey with his country's minimum conditions for an armistice, which had been worked out in consultation with the British and American governments. Communicated also to Ion Antonescu and Maniu via Ankara, they called for a complete break with Germany and a common struggle of Rumanian and Allied armies against Germany; the re-establishment of the Russo-Rumanian frontier as of 22 June 1941; the payment of reparations to the Soviet Union; the liberation of all Allied war prisoners; the unhindered movement of the Red Army on Rumanian territory; and the nullification of the Vienna Award and Soviet support for the return of northern Transylvania to Rumania.

The reaction in Bucharest was mixed. Maniu responded on 19 April with counter-proposals. Obviously putting little faith in Soviet promises to respect Rumanian sovereignty, he accepted the proposal for an armistice, but urged that no foreign (by which he meant, Soviet) troops should be permitted to enter the country unless invited to do so. Anxious to avoid a Soviet occupation, he had already requested the Allied Middle East command to send two airborne divisions to Rumania. On 21 April the Allies rejected further negotiations and demanded a clear acceptance or rejection of the armistice terms. After several further attempts to soften the Allied ultimatum had failed, Maniu on 10 June reluctantly accepted an armistice on the basis of the six points of 12 April.

---

[31] *FRUS, 1944,* iv. 165–6: The Soviet Embassy to the Department of State.

But even now, rather than contact the Russians directly, he preferred to work through Cairo in order to make certain that Britain and the United States were full partners in any agreement.

The Antonescu government flatly rejected the Allied terms on 15 May. The Antonescus interpreted them as a capitulation to the Soviet Union and had no doubt that such action endangered the very existence of the country. They also hoped that a favourable turn in the war might yet bring Western troops to Rumania and, therefore, they intended to wait as long as possible before committing themselves. This tactic seems to have guided Mihai Antonescu's negotiations with Soviet diplomats in Stockholm. They had been revived at the end of May, but Nanu received instructions on 11 June not to commit himself too deeply, 'lest other possibilities be compromised'. 'Other possibilities' referred to Mihai Antonescu's attempts to conclude an armistice with Britain and the United States.

Political groups in Rumania opposed to the war and to the Antonescu dictatorship grew increasingly bold in the spring of 1944. The need for co-ordination led the National Peasant, Liberal, Social Democratic, and Communist parties to create the National Democratic Bloc (Blocul Naţional Democratic) in early June. It declared its objectives to be the immediate conclusion of an armistice with the Allies; the withdrawal from the Axis and all-out support for the Allied war effort; and the abolition of the Antonescu dictatorship and its replacement by a democratic regime. The Bloc also made it clear that its members, while agreeing to work together to achieve immediate goals, intended to maintain their ideological and political distinctiveness. As was evident in the negotiations between Maniu and Communist representatives to create a common front against Antonescu, which had begun in the autumn of 1943, neither side trusted the other. Maniu hesitated to enter into any accord with the Communists until he had obtained guarantees of Rumania's pre-1940 territorial integrity and could be certain that no Soviet-sponsored Communist government would be formed on Rumanian territory as the Red Army advanced.[32]

Maniu dispatched a special emissary to Cairo with news of the formation of the National Democratic Bloc. He also informed

[32] *23 august 1944: Documente*, ii (Bucharest, 1984), 283–7: Notes of the Rumanian Special Intelligence Office, 7 and 9 June 1944, and pp. 293–8: Secret note of the Ministry of Internal Affairs, 14 June 1944.

the Allies that the Bloc intended to overthrow the Antonescu dictatorship and that he himself would form a government, whose immediate task would be to declare an armistice and carry out Allied terms. To assure success he requested three Allied airborne brigades and air attacks on strategic military targets in Hungary and Bulgaria to prevent the Germans from reinforcing their positions in Rumania. He appeared resigned to co-operating with Soviet forces by promising that the Rumanian general in command of the Iaşi front would arrange for their rapid march through the country to Bucharest. This message was delivered on 29 June, but Maniu received no reply, even though he made repeated enquiries, the last on 19 August.

The reason for Allied silence became apparent later. Important decisions affecting the political development of Rumania had already been made by the time Maniu's message reached Cairo. In mid-May 1944 the British and Soviet governments agreed to divide South-eastern Europe into military operational zones. The British, who had taken the initiative, proposed that Greece be in theirs and Rumania in the Soviet zone. They then asked the American government if it could accept the plan. But before an answer was received, Churchill on 8 June proposed that Bulgaria be added to the Soviet zone and Yugoslavia to the British. On 12 June Roosevelt, with some reluctance, approved the arrangement. None of the parties intended it as a final delineation of spheres of influence, but the subsequent course of events none the less consigned Rumania to the Soviet zone.

A final meeting between Hitler and Antonescu took place on 5 August at Rastenburg. As usual, they covered a wide range of topics, particularly the military situation on the eastern front (Hitler promised new, well-equipped German divisions) and Rumanian-German economic problems (no decisions were reached), but the central issue for Hitler now was whether Rumania and Antonescu himself would stand by Germany 'to the end'. Antonescu responded by posing three questions: could Germany hold the southern front against a major Soviet offensive? Could Germany put an end to Allied air raids on Rumanian refineries and transportation facilities, which had begun in early April? And what action would Germany take, if Turkey opened the Straits to Allied warships? Hitler did not reply, and the discussion drifted to secondary matters. The two dictators parted, having resolved nothing. In Bucharest Antonescu took no action to sever Rumania's ties to Germany. He still hoped to persuade the Western powers to protect Rumania from a Soviet advance into Europe. He thought that the West would see that its own best interests were at stake, for he had come to view the war against the Soviet Union as a struggle to preserve European civilization.

The massive Soviet offensive on the Rumanian front began on 20 August. The Red Army broke through defensive positions in a number of places. The situation around Iaşi was especially critical. The resistance of German forces was far more intensive than that of Rumanian units, many of which simply fell apart. On the 22nd Antonescu visited field headquarters and immediately recognized the gravity of the situation. If Soviet troops broke through the Focşani–Galaţi defence line between the Carpathians and the Danube in southern Moldavia, then he was certain that Rumania's fate would be sealed 'for all time'. Reports of Soviet advances all along the front convinced him at last that no hope of stemming the tide remained. He returned quickly to Bucharest to inform the king.

The rapid pace of events, particularly the collapse at the front, had surprised the democratic opposition. Although discussions had been going on within the National Democratic Bloc about the form and personnel of a new government and about military aspects of the projected coup, as late as 20 August no date for the overthrow of Antonescu had been set. The Soviet offensive made a decision imperative. Maniu and Brătianu in close co-operation with King Michael, who were the principal organizers of the coup,[33] agreed on 26 August as the date to strike, but when they learned that Antonescu would leave for the front on the 24th, they moved the date up to 23 August. On that afternoon the king invited Antonescu to the palace. When he refused to accept an immediate armistice the king ordered his arrest along with that of Mihai Antonescu, who had accompanied him. Other close associates of Antonescu were summoned to the palace for a supposed meeting of the Crown Council and were also arrested. Thereupon, the king, exercising his constitutional prerogative, appointed General Constantin Sănătescu (1885–1947), one of the army commanders who had helped to plan the National

---

[33] Rumanian historiography before 1989 accorded the Rumanian Communist Party the paramount role in organizing and carrying out the overthrow of the Antonescu regime. One of the last such desciptions published before the overthrow of the Communist regime in December 1989 is contained in Comisia Română de Istorie Militară, *România în anii celui de-al doilea război mondial*, ii (Bucharest, 1989), 61–79.

Democratic Bloc's overthrow of Antonescu, as prime minister. He in turn appointed by decree the members of his government. Composed mainly of military men, it also included Maniu, Brătianu, Constantin Titel Petrescu, head of the Social Democratic Party, and Lucreţiu Pătrăşcanu, of the Communist Party, as ministers without portfolio whose job it would be to provide the new government with political direction as representatives of the National Democratic Bloc. At 10 o'clock in the evening of 23 August the king broadcast a proclamation to the nation announcing a break of diplomatic relations with Germany and an armistice with the United Nations. He declared that Rumania had joined forces with the Allies against the Axis and would mobilize all her forces to liberate northern Transylvania. Sănătescu instructed the Rumanian emissaries in Cairo to accept an armistice on the basis of the Allied terms of 12 April.

German diplomatic and military representatives in Rumania were caught off guard by the dramatic turn of events. Although a number of officers, including General Hans Friessner, the commander of German armies on the Rumanian front, urged an immediate evacuation of all German forces from Rumania to territory controlled by Hungarian troops, where a new defence line could be established, Hitler ordered him to occupy Bucharest and set up a new government headed by a pro-German general. The effort failed. German commanders had too few troops available to overcome an army and a people determined to change course. By 28 August Rumanian troops had eliminated the German military threat to Bucharest and by the 31st German forces were in retreat throughout the country. On that day the Red Army occupied Bucharest. A new era in Rumanian history was about to begin.

12
The Transition, 1944–1947

The institutions and the spirit that had guided their country's evolution since the middle of the nineteenth century had brought Rumanians closer to Europe. In politics parliamentary government had served as their model, even if practice had sometimes fallen short of the ideal; the economy, slowly but no less deliberately, had moved toward a Western capitalist-entrepreneurial and market-oriented system; the social structure had gradually assumed a Western pattern, as manifested by the predominance of the middle class in inter-war political and economic life; and the majority of intellectuals and politicians had not wavered in their belief that they were a part of Europe. The process of nation-building itself—the creation of Greater Rumania and its defence—was a quintessentially European phenomenon.

This Rumania was replaced by another beginning in 1944. After the overthrow of the Antonescu dictatorship the country's course of development took an abrupt turn away from Europe toward the East. Occupation by the Soviet army and the rapid elevation of the Communist Party to power by Soviet authorities led to the dismantling of existing structures and the submergence of intellectual and spiritual affinities to the West in an alien ethos. In politics an unprecedented authoritarianism replaced a century-long experiment in parliametary democracy; in economic life rigid central planning and direction replaced the loose mix of private enterprise and state co-ordination; and in matters of the mind and the spirit intellectuals were obliged to harness their talents to the creation of a 'new society'.

THE PROVISIONAL GOVERNMENT

The most pressing task of the Sănătescu government was to stabilize its relations with the Allies, in the first instance, with the Soviet Union. The Red Army was pouring into Rumania, and Soviet commanders were treating the country as conquered territory and showing no inclination to deal directly with the government in Bucharest, which they understandably took to be the enemy. Urged on by Iuliu Maniu and Constantin Brătianu, who were anxious to curtail the interference of Soviet officers in civil matters and to set aside zones free of Red Army occupation, Sănătescu bent all his efforts to concluding a formal armistice agreement as quickly as possible. The Soviet government was unusually receptive to the idea because it was eager to assure its lines of communication with the front in Transylvania and Hungary to the north and the Balkans to the south and to bring Rumanian manpower and supplies fully into play. On 27 August Molotov informed the American and British ambassadors in Moscow that he was ready to negotiate directly with Rumanian representatives. On the 29th a Rumanian delegation headed by the Communist Lucreţiu Pătrăşcanu and including Ghiţa Popp, the secretary-general of the National Peasant Party, representing Maniu, and Barbu Ştirbey, who flew home from Cairo to join the delegation, left for Moscow.

The draft of an armistice, drawn up by Soviet officials, was communicated to the American and British governments on 31 August. It was evident to them that the Soviet Union regarded Rumania as a conquered country. They objected particularly to the provision that the Soviet High Command in Rumania would alone supervise the fulfilment of the terms of the armistice. Under British and American urging Molotov modified his position slightly. He agreed to the creation of an Allied Control Commission for Rumania, which would include American and British representatives, but he made it clear that the Soviet High Command would reserve to itself all the important decisions concerning Rumania. He also implied that Western representatives would not be allowed to deal directly with the Rumanian government, but would have to go through Soviet authorities.[1]

The Rumanian delegation received the draft on 10 September and made strenuous efforts to soften its terms. They were anxious particularly to gain recognition of Rumania as a co-belligerent in the war against Germany, to set precise limits on the period of Soviet occupation, to accord Rumanian authorities greater latitude in internal administration, particularly in security and police matters, and to secure an Allied commitment to return all of Transylvania to Rumania. Molotov, who served as general

---

[1] *Foreign Relations of the United States* (henceforth, *FRUS*), *1944*, iv (Washington, DC, 1966), 223: Averell Harriman to Secretary of State, 6 Sept. 1944.

chairman of the three Allied delegations, allowed the Rumanians to present their case at some length, but he refused to be drawn into a discussion of the armistice terms, and when it seemed to him that enough time had been spent on one point he brusquely moved on to the next. Whenever the Rumanians objected to arbitrary procedures he bluntly reminded them that they had fought alongside the Germans until the summer of 1944 and had left the war only then because they were faced by a crushing defeat. He rejected out of hand any modification of the existing Soviet military control of Rumania.[2]

The armistice was signed on 12 September and in the main simply expanded upon the conditions set forth during the negotiations in Cairo. It required the Rumanian government to join in the Allied war effort with at least twelve fully equipped infantry divisions and to allow the free movement of Allied forces on its territory and to provide money and supplies regularly in support of Allied military operations against Germany and Hungary. Rumania also assumed the burden of paying reparations amounting to 300 million dollars to the Soviet Union for losses during military operations on its territory and to return all goods removed from its territory. The one bright spot for Rumania was the abrogation of the Vienna Award and the return of northern Transylvania to her, though the final disposition of the territory was reserved to the general peace conference after the war.

The Rumanian delegation left Moscow feeling that their country had, all things considered, been treated lightly. But at home the leaders of the democratic political parties were deeply worried about how Soviet occupation authorities would interpret and carry out the terms of the armistice. Their concerns were shared by Averell Harriman, the American ambassador in Moscow, who had participated in the armistice negotiations and had conferred with members of the Rumanian delegation. He had no doubt that the armistice had given the Soviet Union complete political and economic control of Rumania, at least until the conclusion of a final peace treaty.

The campaign against remaining German and Hungarian forces north and east of the Carpathians was the primary Soviet concern in the autumn of 1944. Rumanian troops, numbering about 385,000, were brought together for the campaign with remarkable swiftness and with no significant defections from within the officer

---

[2] Ibid. iv. 232, 235: Harriman to Secretary of State, 14 and 15 Sept. 1944.

corps, much to the surprise of German commanders, who had counted upon continued Rumanian military support to stem the Red Army advance. The prospect of recovering northern Transylvania, which appealed to the army's national feeling, and the relative forebearance of Soviet commanders in dealing with Rumanian units made possible the rapid transition from ally to enemy of the Germans. An initial German and Hungarian advance into southern Transylvania in the first two weeks of September, which was designed to secure the passes in the Carpathians, was halted, and a major offensive by Soviet and Rumanian armies began on 20 September. The enemy was unable to hold its defence line along the Mureş River, which was pierced in the Banat on 5 October. With the route into the great Hungarian plain now open, a general German and Hungarian retreat from Transylvania ensued, and by 25 October all pre-war Rumanian territory had been retaken. Rumanian losses in the battle for Transylvania had been substantial—some 50,000 dead and wounded.

Despite co-operation on the battlefield, the Sănătescu government and Soviet occupation authorities were continually at odds with one another. Since the Red Army occupied large areas of the country, which were designated 'military operations zones', and since Soviet army commanders appointed local officials on their own authority, the Rumanian government found it almost impossible to establish a regular administration and carry out its policies outside Bucharest. Both the central ministries in the capital and the provincial bureaucracy had to endure continuous Soviet interference in the conduct of their affairs. For example, in early October the Soviet chairman of the Allied Control Commission handed the government a list of forty-seven persons, including the sitting ministers of National Economy and of Education, whom he denounced as 'war criminals' and whose immediate arrest he demanded. Later, on 13 October, when a demonstration organized by the National Peasant Party in Bucharest led to street fighting with Communists he denounced the event as anti-Soviet and forbade another demonstration scheduled for the 15th. He closed *Universul*, the large-circulation and pro-Western daily, for the same reason. Although the ban on the demonstration was lifted and *Universul* was allowed to resume publication a few days later, these incidents were an ominous foretaste of what was in store for the democratic political forces in Rumania. The contempt of Soviet authorities for Rumania and her institutions was made manifest by Andrei Vyshinsky, the Soviet deputy Foreign

Minister, whose diplomatic style during his stay in Bucharest in November to oversee the fulfilment of the armistice terms was characterized by Rumanian officials as 'negotiation by ultimatum'. Reparations had become a particularly touchy issue. The Russians were engaged in the wholesale removal of 'war booty', especially industrial and railway equipment and vehicles of all kinds, and were lax in accounting for what they were carrying off. The method of evaluating reparations was also in dispute. The Rumanian government insisted that their value be based upon current world prices, but Soviet authorities preferred 1938 as the base year for calculating their amount because the sum which Rumania owed would thus be increased threefold. Vyshinsky served notice on the Rumanians to accept the Soviet position within two days or he would refuse to discuss any other aspect of the armistice.[3] The Sănătescu government had no choice but to yield.

In confronting the Soviet Union, the Rumanian government stood practically alone. The Western Allies, in effect, had yielded the initiative in Rumanian affairs to the Soviet Union as a result of Churchill's so-called percentages agreement with Stalin in October. On that occasion he had offered the Soviet Union a 90 per cent say in Rumania in return for a 90 per cent say for Britain in Greece and fifty-fifty sharing in Yugoslavia. It made no difference that the United States was not a party to the agreement or that Roosevelt insisted upon retaining full freedom of action in the region. In the end, the massive presence of Soviet occupation authorities determined the direction that Rumanian political development was to take. Striking evidence of Soviet predominance was the impotence of the Allied Control Commission. As late as the end of November it had not yet been formally constituted. The Soviet High Command simply issued instructions to the Rumanian government in its name. The Western powers thus shared responsibility for the consequences of these acts, but had no part in formulating them. The Soviet chairman regarded the Control Commission as an instrument for carrying out Soviet policy and treated his Western colleagues merely as observers.[4] Yet, the American and British governments chose not to make an issue of the Commission as long as the war against Germany was in full swing.

[3] Ibid. iv. 269: Berry, US representative in Rumania, to Secretary of State, 29 Nov. 1944.
[4] Ibid. iv. 275–7: Berry to Secretary of State, 4 Dec. 1944.

In Rumanian domestic politics September and October were a period of mobilization by the major parties. All had suffered a disruption of their normal activities under the dictatorships of Carol and Antonescu and now, after six years, they bent all their efforts at re-establishing national and local organizations and increasing membership. In the process the coalition which had carried out the overthrow of Antonescu on 23 August, the National Democratic Bloc, disintegrated under the strain of competing political ambitions.

Of the four parties composing the Bloc, the Communist Party was the weakest. During the war its membership had been reduced to perhaps 1,000, and the majority of its leaders before the August coup had been in gaol. In the waning days of the Antonescu dictatorship a number of them, notably Gheorghe Gheorghiu-Dej, who had been imprisoned since 1933, because of his role in a strike of railway workers, escaped from gaol or were released. They were joined by other Rumanian Communists who had spent many years in Moscow, among them Ana Pauker, who now arrived in Bucharest in the wake of the Red Army. As the local Communists and the so-called 'Muscovites' strove to revive the party they benefited enormously from the presence of Soviet occupation authorities and the diplomatic support of Moscow. Within a week of the overthrow of Antonescu the Central Committee of the Rumanian Communist Party declared its intention to transform the National Democratic Bloc into a mass organization and called upon workers to organize their own political committees under the aegis of the Bloc. The Bloc proved useful to the Communists as a political umbrella as long as their own party was weak and disorganized. But they made it clear that they no longer regarded the Bloc as a suitable instrument for achieving their objectives. Yet they said nothing about changing the economic and social structure of the country. Instead, they stressed the need for all 'democratic' forces to work together to win the war and to 'cleanse' the country of the 'residue' of fascism.[5] As a show of solidarity with their partners in the Bloc they joined in a mass anti-fascist demonstration on 6 September, the fourth anniversary of the installation of the Antonescu-legionary regime. But this event proved to be the last important public expression of unity by the partners in the Bloc.

[5] Mihai Fătu, *Alianţe politice ale Partidului Comunist Român, 1944–1947* (Cluj-Napoca, 1979), 121–5.

Communist leaders spent the next month devising a new plan of action and laying the foundations of a new political front more attuned to their objectives than the Bloc. The programme which they drafted was not yet an expression of exclusively Communist goals, but was couched in sufficiently broad terms to attract support from almost all strata of society. Its main purpose was to serve as the manifesto of a new coalition of parties and groups on the left committed to immediate, far-reaching economic and social change. The Communists put enormous pressure on the Social Democratic Party to join the coalition in order to increase their own influence over the working-class movement. Their eagerness to co-operate on such a broad scale reflected their party's continued organizational weakness and lack of mass support.

The National Peasant and Liberal parties, which came to be known during the period as the 'historical parties', were also hard at work reviving their organizations in Bucharest and the provinces. Within a week of Antonescu's overthrow, on 31 August, Maniu dispatched a circular letter to all National Peasant Party organizations outlining the procedures for a resumption of activity. He urged leaders at all levels—*judeţ*, city, and village—to bring their cadres and membership up to full strength as quickly as possible, but he temporarily excluded those party members who had joined Carol II's Front of National Renaissance or Party of the Nation without permission. Six weeks later, on 16 October, he and Ion Mihalache announced the new party programme. In almost all respects it remained faithful to old Peasantist economic and sociological theses and the idea of the peasant state elaborated in the inter-war period. It dealt at length with the special character of rural property, which, it insisted, must belong to those who worked it.[6] Mihalache reiterated all these principles a few weeks later when he declared that the party would uphold the rights of private property and had no intention of upsetting the prevailing social structure of the village. In all these pronouncements it was evident that the economic and social model which he and his party had in mind was the medium-sized holding which Peasantists had traditionally regarded as characteristic of the modern agricultures of Western Europe and hoped would allow an enterprising, public-spirited peasant middle class to develop and prosper in Rumania, too. The 'family holding' thus remained their ideal economic unit, which they defined as a maximum of 100 hectares and which, in

[6] Mihai Fătu, *Sfîrşit fără glorie* (Bucharest, 1972), 127–9.

their view, a typical family with, perhaps, hired seasonal labour could cultivate profitably. To achieve their objective they approved the expropriation of the remaining large properties. They also restated their faith in co-operatives as the most appropriate form of economic organization for the peasantry. Even the old Peasantist reservations about industrialization continued to figure in the party programme. It emphasized the benefits of 'peasant industry' as a means of providing employment for the excess rural population, but it said little about encouraging large-scale industries, as Virgil Madgearu had proposed in 1940, except to advocate the nationalization of those already in existence. The National Peasants thus continued to see the country's destiny linked closely to agriculture, but they had no doubt that the best means of restoring the country's economic health lay in re-establishing as quickly as possible commercial and financial relations with the West. As for urban workers, the National Peasants promised to support their right to form unions in order to defend their professional interests, but they opposed the direct involvement of worker's organizations in politics. As Mihalache pointed out, labour unions tended toward a 'dictatorship' in public life, and he left no doubt that a dictatorship of the proletariat, in particular, was completely at odds with his own party's respect for democracy and for freedom of thought and expression. With the Communists clearly in mind he denied that the general welfare could be secured through the abolition of individual liberties.[7]

Unlike the National Peasants, the Liberals found themselves in considerable disarray in the autumn of 1944. Many of the party's organizations in the provinces were leaderless and a prey to factionalism. The situation in Bucharest was hardly better. Constantin Brătianu, who had been president of the party since 1933, was less vigorous than Maniu and Mihalache in restoring the party machinery. Although he sent out directives to local party organizations urging intensified activity, no general meeting of *judeţ* leaders to formulate party policy seems to have taken place. Nor was a comprehensive programme, like that of the National Peasant Party, drawn up. Rather, Brătianu and other leaders issued a general statement that the party would remain faithful to its traditional principles and would defend the political and civil rights of all citizens. On economic development they gave priority

[7] Ion Mihalache, *Lămurirea programului Partidului Naţional-Ţărănesc* (Bucharest, 1944), 21–4.

to industrialization. In so far as they concerned themselves with agriculture, they recommended land reform, but urged that it be limited to those regions where land was abundant and rejected expropriation or other measures that would disrupt production at such a critical time.

The most damaging internal problem confronting the Liberal Party was the rift between the regular organization and the Tătărescu faction, which harked back to Carol II's reign. It impeded the revival of the party's fortunes, especially in Muntenia, where neither faction could gain the upper hand. Various attempts at a reconciliation failed. A deep personal antipathy separated the Brătianu family from Tătărescu. It was caused primarily by the latter's ill-concealed political ambitions and readiness to sacrifice principle for power, as he had demonstrated during Carol's reign, but in the months following the coup differences over policy and tactics drove the two sides still farther apart. By the middle of December Tătărescu had made the break complete by forming a dissident National Liberal Party (Partid Naţional-Liberal). On 19 December he announced his programme. It associated the new party with the 'left', a term, he explained, which meant that it would serve the interests of the 'producing classes'—peasants, urban workers, small and middle bourgeois of the cities and villages, and intellectuals. To the mass of the peasants he offered land, to be made available to them in various ways, including the expropriation of large properties, and to the urban workers he promised numerous social and economic benefits, notably a minimum wage and a more equitable distribution of national income in order to prevent a few persons from becoming 'super-rich' at the expense of the labouring masses. By such appeals Tătărescu hoped to position himself between the two historical parties in the centre and the Communists on the extreme left. His strategy was the same in foreign policy. Exhibiting unusual pre-science, he urged the conclusion of a treaty of mutual assistance and 'permanent friendship' with the Soviet Union, but he also left the doors open for the resumption of Rumania's traditional ties with the West.[8]

By mid-October the new political coalition promoted by the Communist Party had taken form as the National Democratic Front (Front Naţional Democrat). Besides the Communists, it was composed of the Social Democratic Party; the Ploughmen's

[8] Fătu, *Sfîrşit*, 137–40.

Front; the Union of Patriots (Uniunea Patrioţilor), which had been formed in 1942 mainly by leftist intellectuals opposed to the Antonescu dictatorship and favouring a separate peace with the Allies; the Patriotic Defence (Apărarea Patriotică), a mass organization founded in 1940 on the initiative of the Communist Party; and the Union of Hungarian Workers of Rumania (Romániai Magyar Dolgozók Szövetsége), a leftist political organization founded in 1934 in Tîrgu Mureş. The programme of the Front avoided the rhetoric of social revolution. It was designed to appeal broadly to democratic organizations and individuals who were unwilling to return to the social system and politics of the interwar years. In foreign policy the Front advocated the mobilization of all human and material resources to pursue the war against Germany and to put an end to the policy of hostility toward the Soviet Union. At home it stood for the creation of a new political system based upon the broadest possible extension of civil rights and political freedoms, including a new electoral law granting the franchise to all citizens over 18 years of age. It appealed especially to the poorer strata of the peasantry, by calling for an extensive land reform and the granting of land to peasants who had none or very little, and sought support among the small urban and rural producers of goods by promising credit on easy terms.

The National Democratic Front formally came into being on 12 October. On the same day it invited the National Peasant and Liberal parties to join, but Maniu and Brătianu flatly refused. Two days later Pătrăşcanu and Titel Petrescu informed them that their respective parties were leaving the National Democratic Bloc, an act which brought an end to the coalition that had overthrown the Antonescu dictatorship and the uneasy political truce it had sponsored.

For the time being the Front remained a loosely knit coalition, as the Social Democrats and the Ploughmen's Front, its two main components besides the Communists, maintained their independence. The Social Democrats, for example, favoured the nationalization of the means of production, an end to all forms of economic exploitation, and the creation of a society based upon the equality of all its members, but they were determined to achieve these goals through democratic and peaceful means. The Ploughmen's Front showed considerable vitality, and at least in the autumn of 1944 and the following spring it was able to expand its organization in the provinces rapidly.

The formation of the National Democratic Front precipitated a crisis within the Sănătescu government. It had never received more than token support from the Communists, who regarded it, correctly, as an instrument of the two historical parties and the king. They kept up a constant attack on the government in their press and at public rallies, which increased in intensity in September and early October. On 16 October the Communists and the Social Democrats left the government, and on the 18th the national council of the Front urged the formation of a new government with Petru Groza, the head of the Ploughmen's Front, as prime minister. The National Peasants and Liberals rejected the idea, but on 4 November the cabinet was reorganized. The National Peasants and Liberals had ten seats in the cabinet, and the Front seven, with Groza as vice-premier, Gheorghiu-Dej, the head of the Communist Party, as Minister of Communications, and Pătrăşcanu as Minister of Justice. The Front's formal representation in the cabinet suggests its own growing strength and particularly its support by the Soviet Union, which was mainly responsible for its successful challenge of the Sănătescu government. Although the Communists, in particular, had thus made significant gains and had, in effect, become a government party, they continued to attack the government. They sought to remove Nicolae Penescu, the Minister of the Interior and a leader of the National Peasant Party, who had made no secret of his anti-Soviet and anti-Communist feelings. He had aroused their ire by creating a special section of his ministry to monitor Communist activities and by preventing Communists and their allies from replacing prefects and mayors who opposed them with their own men. Sănătescu, increasingly frustrated by his inability to govern the country in the face of Communist obstruction and Soviet interference, and isolated from his own supporters (including Maniu, who thought he had not been tough enough in dealing with the Communists), resigned on 2 December.

A new government, little changed from its predecessor, took office on 6 December. It was headed by General Nicolae Rădescu, who was noted for his bluntness of speech, a characteristic which had landed him in a concentration camp during the war when he denounced the German occupation of Rumania.

Of all the problems the new government inherited from Sănătescu, none caused greater anxiety to the historical parties and the defenders of Greater Rumania than the fate of northern Transylvania. They realized that the territory had still to be won for Rumania, despite the reassuring language of the armistice convention. It was apparent from both that document and the actual state of things after the expulsion of German and Hungarian troops at the end of October that the Soviet Union would have a decisive role to play in the final disposition of the region. Northern Transylvania was now the scene of a bitter confrontation between leftists allied with the Communist-led National Democratic Front in Bucharest and the supporters of the National Peasant and Liberal parties. The advantage lay with the former because the territory was under Soviet military administration. Under its auspices a National Democratic Front for northern Transylvania, composed of both Rumanian and Hungarian leftist political elements, was formed to provide a civil administration until a final disposition of the territory could be made. The executive committee of the Front entertained serious hopes of creating an autonomous northern Transylvania. Its members sought in this way to assure the triumph of socialism and to guarantee full civil and political equality for all citizens, regardless of nationality, goals they thought unattainable in a Rumania governed by one or more of the historical political parties. In the middle of February 1945 it proceeded to organize a provisional administration with eleven commissions, or ministries, to handle such matters as finances, justice, and education.[9] But this brief experiment in autonomy came abruptly to an end when Stalin on 9 March, following the installation of a government representing the National Democratic Front and headed by Petru Groza on 6 March, assigned northern Transylvania to Rumania. The executive committee of the Front in northern Transylvania had no choice but to acquiesce. Yet, in welcoming the formation of the Groza government, it also proclaimed its attachment to a 'democratic Transylvania in a free and democratic Rumania'.

The immediate problem for Rădescu and his supporters was the survival of his government. For a time the Communists softened their opposition, but in the middle of January 1945 Gheorghiu-Dej and Ana Pauker made a trip to Moscow for talks with Soviet party leaders. The latter may have decided that the time had come to take advantage of the percentages agreement with Churchill. British intervention against the Communists and their supporters in Greece in December 1944, Soviet leaders may have reasoned, justified their giving Rumanian Communists the go-ahead to in-

---

[9] D. Csatári, *Dans la tourmente: Les relations hungaro-roumaines de 1940 à 1945* (Budapest, 1974), 380–3.

stall their own government in Bucharest. In any case, this meeting proved fateful for Rumania, for Gheorghiu-Dej and company were assured of the support they needed in their drive to seize power.[10] After the delegation returned home the National Democratic Front—in fact, the Communists—initiated a systematic campaign to replace the Rădescu government with one of their own. On 29 January the Front demanded the installation of a 'truly democratic government', the removal of 'fascists' from the civil service, and the 'cleansing' of the army of 'reactionary and fascist elements' and its reorganization in a 'democratic spirit'. The Communists used the terms 'democratic' and 'fascist' in a special sense. The former referred to themselves and their supporters and was meant to distinguish them from the National Peasants and Liberals; 'fascist' was, in effect, a sweeping accusation against everyone who opposed the new 'democratic forces'. There were many persons in government at the national and local level and in the army who had served in the royal and Antonescu dictatorships, but the majority were hardly fascists. Moreover, the Communists themselves had opened party membership to the most heterogeneous elements in an effort to create a mass organization as quickly as possible. As for its economic objectives, the Front appeared relatively moderate. To be sure, it demanded immediate land reform, to be carried out by the expropriation of all individual holdings of over 50 hectares. But it spared the property of churches and monasteries and of the royal house, undoubtedly to avoid alienating the clergy and large segments of the population, especially the peasantry, who were attached to church and king. Nor did the Front speak of the nationalization of the means of production or the dictatorship of the proletariat. The Communists displayed a certain moderation in economic matters in order to attract dissident factions of the National Peasant and Liberal parties and social reformers in general at a time when their own party was weak and they stood in the minority.

Since the previous autumn the Communists had been zealously recruiting new party members. Anxious to increase their numbers, they welcomed all comers. Besides urban workers, they took in peasants, businessmen, professional people, secret police, and Iron Guardists—anyone, in fact, who could be useful in their struggle to dislodge the historical parties. The Communists also pursued negotiations with National Peasant and Liberal dissidents. In

[10] P. D. Quinlan, *Clash over Romania* (Los Angeles, 1977), 120.

February 1945 Anton Alexandrescu, of the National Peasant Party, who advocated more rapid social change than Maniu and Mihalache and sought a greater voice for himself in party affairs, joined the National Democratic Front, but took only a few party functionaries with him. More serious was the Communists' wooing of Gheorghe Tătărescu, who was ready to accept certain radical economic reforms and advocated friendly relations with the Soviet Union as the key element in Rumania's foreign policy. He had no intention of contributing to the destruction of the existing social order, but since the Communists seemed willing to co-operate with other parties, he thought it possible to make a mutually beneficial accommodation with them and to assure himself of a leading role in post-war politics.

The Communists combined their recruitment drives and their negotiations with dissident National Peasant and Liberal groups with an increasingly virulent campaign against the historical parties and Maniu and Brătianu personally, whom they denounced as fascists. They had the full support of Soviet authorities and of Andrei Vyshinsky, who arrived in Bucharest in the middle of February to co-ordinate the drive for power, or, as Rumanian observers put it, 'to prepare for future events'.[11] When Rădescu resisted the pressure of Rumanian Communists and Soviet officials to accept the new order, they turned their fire against him. Soviet occupation authorities also imposed drastic reductions of the Rumanian police, gendarmes, and army, action which deprived Rădescu of the forces he needed to maintain order and resist the violence of his opponents.

The struggle for power reached a climax on 24 February when a demonstration organized by the National Democratic Front moved toward the Ministry of the Interior. Shots were fired—by whom is uncertain—and several persons were killed. Rădescu publicly accused Ana Pauker and other Communists of responsibility for the incident and of attempting to overthrow the government. The Communists and Soviet authorities, in turn, blamed the Rădescu government, branding it 'fascist', and Soviet officials summoned Rădescu himself to the headquarters of the Allied Control Commission to explain his accusations against Communist leaders. This summons was the prelude to direct interference in the constitutional process by Vyshinsky. At an audience

---

[11] *FRUS, 1945*, v (Washington, DC, 1967), 470–1: Berry to Secretary of State, 19 Feb. 1945.

with the king on 28 February he insisted that the Rădescu government be replaced immediately by a Front government headed by
Petru Groza. When the king replied that he would have to await
the outcome of consultations with party leaders, Vyshinsky gave
him two hours to dismiss Rădescu and name his successor.[12] The
implication was clear that Vyshinsky, who was acting on precise
instructions from Moscow, would use whatever means were
necessary to install a pro-Soviet government. At the same time
the Communists appeared ready to seize power behind the façade
of a mass demonstration of the Front or by even more direct
means. Vyshinsky let it be known that unless the king accepted a
Groza government he could not be responsible for the maintenance
of Rumania as an independent state, a threat which appears to
have been decisive in resolving the crisis. A message from Groza
to the king was more reassuring: Soviet officials had promised him
a substantial improvement in Soviet—Rumanian relations upon the
formation of a Front government, including an easing of the
armistice terms and a return of northern Transylvania. For a time
the king considered abdicating, but Maniu and Brătianu persuaded
him not to desert the country. Lacking any promise of significant
Western help, the king could no longer resist Soviet pressure and
announced the formation of a government headed by Groza on 6
March. The new regime was thus imposed by the Soviet Union.
The Front did not have widespread support. Although it could
bring out large crowds for demonstrations in Bucharest and the
Communists had at their disposal squads of armed men, these
forces would have been no match for the Rumanian army, if
Rădescu had been able to use it. But Soviet military commanders
had taken the precaution of moving Rumanian army units away
from Bucharest and the surrounding area in order to forestall
resistance by the government to a Communist coup.

The Soviet Union moved decisively to secure its position in
Rumania sooner than elsewhere in Eastern Europe because, as in
the time of the tsars, Rumania was the gateway to the Balkans and
the Straits. The Declaration on Liberated Europe, which the Soviet
Union along with the United States and Great Britain had adhered
to at Yalta on 12 February 1945, just weeks before the appointment
of Groza as Prime Minister, played no part in determining Soviet
policy toward Rumania. The notion of broadly representative and
democratic governments established through free elections and

---

[12] Ibid. v. 487: Berry to Secretary of State, 28 Feb. 1945.

responsive to the will of their citizens, which the Declaration called for, ran counter to Soviet theory and practice and, if applied in this particular case, would have prevented the installation of a friendly and docile government in Bucharest. The antipathy which the majority of Rumanians felt toward the Soviet Union and their desire to maintain traditional ties to the West made the prospects of a freely elected pro-Soviet regime coming to power extremely remote. Rumanian Communist leaders, aware of their party's unpopularity, also had no wish to leave the choice of government to the electorate.

The Western Allies, confronted by the open Soviet challenge to the armistice agreement with Rumania, did little else but protest, action which could have no effect on the course of events. Since the war was still going on and broader issues of the general European settlement had yet to be settled and the final assault on Japan mounted, the American and British governments felt obliged to restrain their criticism of Soviet behaviour.

American and British inaction raised doubts among pro-Western Rumanian politicians about the wisdom of further resistance to Soviet pressure. By December 1944 Maniu had become convinced that the Soviet Union was intent upon 'communizing' Rumania and worried that the Western powers would be satisfied merely to observe the process. At the time of the armistice he had thought that the United States and Britain would preserve an independent Rumania, but now, he asked their representatives, did they prefer that his country become a part of the Soviet Union? If so, he was certain that he could arrange better terms than the Rumanian Communists. [13]

THE STRUGGLE FOR POWER

The government headed by Petru Groza was a minority government. Imposed by the Soviet Union, it did not represent the will of the majority of Rumanians, who were anti-Russian and anti-Communist. No members of the two largest parties—the National Peasants and the Liberals—sat in the cabinet, where Communists held key posts, including the Ministry of the Interior. Although Gheorghe Tătărescu, the dissident Liberal, was foreign minister, and Anton Alexandrescu, the dissident National Peasant, was

[13] Ibid. *1944*, iv. 279: Berry to Secretary of State, 9 Dec. 1944.

Minister of Co-operatives, they represented only small factions of their respective parties.

To compensate for its lack of support in the country at large the new government took a variety of measures to fortify itself and cripple the opposition. Most important were sweeping changes in local administration introduced by the Ministry of the Interior in May 1945. Communist prefects were appointed and Communist-dominated councils with extensive powers were created in every *judeţ*. The latter were composed of one member from each of the parties represented in the government and thus effectively excluded the National Peasants and Liberals. The absence of parties which had traditionally wielded decisive influence in local affairs facilitated the work of the new councils. Designed as executors of central government policies, they were empowered to consider 'all important questions of the day'—economic reconstruction, administrative reform, public order, and the 'democratization of the state apparatus'—and had the responsibility for mobilizing support for these policies among the local population. Similar bodies were installed in cities and villages. The Groza government also sponsored local 'vigilance committees', which took over the duties of the police and gendarmerie in many places and, like the political councils, served as instruments of its policies. In the countryside the government encouraged newly formed peasant committees to expropriate and distribute land from large estates, and in urban centres it spurred workers' committees to wrest control of factories and other businesses from their owners, even though such organizations had no legal authority to act. All these administrative bodies and *ad hoc* committees had as their ultimate objective the undermining of existing political and economic structures as a means of smoothing the way for the advent of the new order.

The government, or, more accurately, the Communist Party, relentlessly extended its influence among all parties and groups represented in the Front. Communist leaders gave particular attention to a strengthening of ties with the Social Democratic Party within the framework of the United Workers' Front (Frontul Unic Muncitoresc), which a few Communists and Social Democrats had created in April 1944 as part of a general mobilization of the opposition to Antonescu. Now, in May and June 1945 the Communists spared no effort to consolidate their control of the Workers' Front and use it to gain dominance over the Social Democratic Party and the entire working-class movement. But

Constantin Titel Petrescu, the leader of the Social Democrats, and other party officials rejected the embrace of the Communists. In the first place, they stood for a genuinely representative, democratic political system, which, it was apparent, the Communists had no intention of creating, and, second, they considered themselves the true representatives of the working class and refused to sacrifice their individuality or their programme by subordinating themselves to the Communist Party. Rather, in the spring and summer of 1945 they made strenuous efforts to attract the mass of workers to their party and to organize them in socialist labour unions. Only the small left wing of the party, gathered around Lothar Rădăceanu, the Minister of Labour in the Groza cabinet, called for close co-operation with the Communists.

Communist leaders were also disappointed in their dealings with the other parties in the government. Although the Tătărescu Liberals had shown a willingness to accept state co-ordination of the economy, they stopped short of endorsing the Communist economic programme. At their first party congress on 1 July they reaffirmed their commitment to the maintenance of private property and private capital as the most effective means of promoting the economic recovery of the country and social progress in general. Tătărescu himself made it clear that the main reason for his party's existence was to find ways of integrating the middle class into the new political and economic structures of the country.[14] The final break between the Liberal Party and the Tătărescu faction occurred when the congress adopted a separate programme and appropriated the name, National Liberal Party. The leaders of the Ploughmen's Front also seemed intent upon maintaining the separate identity of their party as the representative of the poorer peasantry. At its first congress, held on 24–7 June, the delegates, the majority of whom were peasants (an event worthy of notice in itself), expressed their gratitude to the Communist Party and the urban working class for their support of peasant interests, but then they proceeded to approve a programme which would strengthen the individual smallholder and fulfil some of the goals of the Peasantists—the reinvigoration of the village co-operatives, the granting of credit on easy terms, the creation of industries specializing in the processing of agricultural products, and the improvement of agricultural education.[15]

[14] Fătu, *Sfîrşit*, 244–6.
[15] G. Micle, *Răscoala pământului* (Bucharest, 1945), 395–457.

The National Peasants and the Brătianu Liberals continued to offer the main opposition to the Groza government and the Communists. Maniu had by now established himself as the leader of all those who sought to create a genuine parliamentary democracy on the Western model and to protect the country from Soviet domination. But he himself was not optimistic about the future. In June he had concluded that Rumania was no longer a sovereign state because the government consisted almost entirely of persons willing to do the bidding of the Soviet Union and because proposed economic agreements between the two countries would ensure the Soviet Union's control of Rumania's industries and would, in effect, 'communize' the entire economic structure of the country. His own efforts to mobilize the opposition were continually thwarted by the government. For example, he was refused permission to hold conferences of provincial National Peasant leaders on the grounds that his party was not represented in the government and, thus, could not be recognized as a bona fide political party. None the less, he was prepared to risk a confrontation with Groza and the Communists by recommending to the king that he dismiss the government as unrepresentative and, hence, in violation of the armistice and of subsequent Allied agreements. But he made any such risky initiative dependent upon American and British support, which, in the end, he failed to receive. American officials made it clear to him that the policy of the United States was based upon the armistice and the Declaration on Liberated Europe and that it would intervene in Rumanian affairs only to the extent necessary to ensure the carrying out of the provisions of these two agreements. They expressed the wish that all important political groups be represented in the government and that the Rumanian people themselves exercise the right to choose their own form of government, but they urged Maniu to avoid any action which might impede a settlement of the 'Rumanian question' jointly by the three Allied powers.[16]

The defeat of Germany in May brought an end to Rumania's four-year ordeal of war. Her contributions to the campaigns in Hungary and Czechoslovakia had been substantial. Some eleven Rumanian army divisions had taken part in the so-called Budapest Operation in central and northern Hungary from the end of October 1944 to the middle of January 1945, sustaining 11,000 killed and wounded. From December 1944 to May 1945 nearly

---

[16] *FRUS, 1945*, v. 525–6: Acting Secretary of State to Berry, 29 Mar. 1945.

250,000 Rumanian troops had been in the very centre of the drive through Slovakia and Moravia into Bohemia, advancing to within 80 kilometres of Prague until ordered to halt on 12 May. These forces, too, had suffered heavy losses: 70,000 killed and wounded, or about 30 per cent of those engaged in the campaign.

Peace in Europe, however, did not bring a settlement of the impasse between the Western Allies and the Soviet Union over Rumania. At the Potsdam Conference (17 July—2 August 1945) the Americans and British denied the legitimacy of the Groza government on the grounds that it did not represent the will of the majority of the Rumanian people. When the American delegation pointed out that the Yalta declaration on the future of Eastern Europe had been ignored in Rumania, Stalin complained about high-handed British action in Greece. He also insisted that a friendly Rumania was vital to the security of the Soviet Union because she had served as a bridgehead for aggression from Europe. In later discussions Stalin categorically rejected the idea of free elections in Rumania because they would most certainly bring to power an anti-Soviet government.

Although the West and the Soviet Union reached no decisions about Rumania at Potsdam, the firmness of the United States and Britain in withholding recognition of the Groza government encouraged the opposition parties to try to force it from office. National Peasant and Liberal leaders, now supported by Titel Petrescu and the majority of the Social Democrats, decided to ask the king to replace the Groza government by one composed of their three parties and the Communists, a move which would, in effect, revive the coalition which had organized the overthrow of Antonescu. The procedure which the king now followed in the middle of August was to consult the leaders of the four parties on the advisability of a change of government. Maniu, Brătianu, and Titel Petrescu favoured the change; Groza, understandably, did not. The king decided to follow the advice of the former. Citing both the Potsdam declaration, which had made a genuinely democratic government a condition for the conclusion of a final peace treaty with Rumania and her admittance to the United Nations, and the refusal of the United States and Great Britain to recognize the existing government as democratic, the king asked Groza to resign on 21 August. He refused and was backed by the Soviet occupation authorities, who brought extreme pressure to bear on the king. The Soviet chairman of the Allied Control Commission, who never deviated from the instructions he received

from Moscow, threatened Michael with a break in relations between Rumania and the Soviet Union and the arrest of his advisers
who had 'set him on an anti-Soviet course'.[17] Groza's refusal to
return his mandate at the request of the king was a clear violation
of the Constitution of 1923, which was recognized as the fundamental law, at least by the king and the historical parties, because
it gave the monarch the power to appoint and dismiss ministers.
Unable to take more forceful action, the king decided to treat
Groza's cabinet as merely a *de facto* government. He refused to
sign any bills or decrees, except those necessary for carrying on
the day-to-day affairs of the state, and disassociated himself from
all the other activities of the government.

The London Conference (11 September–3 October 1945) failed
to assuage East–West differences in general or resolve the constitutional impasse in Rumania in particular. Among the many issues
defying solution was the definition of the term 'democratic' as applied to the new governments in Eastern Europe. The Americans
and British interpreted it as referring to their own representative
political system, whereas Molotov equated it with Communist
and pro-Soviet regimes. Molotov also had difficulty understanding
how the Americans and British could, at one moment, agree that
the Soviet Union was entitled to have friendly governments on its
western borders and then, the next moment, demand free elections in Rumania, when the result would surely be a government
hostile to the Soviet Union.

In the autumn of 1945 the Communist Party and its allies grew
stronger as the political struggle in Rumania intensified. Communist leaders turned their attention to creating a disciplined
party, and on 16 October they convoked the first national party
conference. The delegates elected a Central Committee and a
Politburo, composed of Gheorghiu-Dej as secretary-general, and
Ana Pauker and Teohari Georgescu, the Minister of the Interior,
as secretaries. These three and several colleagues were, in effect, to
rule Rumania until 1952. Pauker seems to have played the leading
role at the conference. Lucrețiu Pătrășcanu, the Minister of Justice,
who enjoyed wide support among party intellectuals, was, surprisingly, not elected to high party office. Although he was committed to the Communist programme and during the next two
years apparently raised no objections to the methods which the

[17] Ibid. v. 585: Melbourne, acting US representative in Rumania, to Secretary
of State, 22 Aug. 1945.

party used to eliminate the opposition and solidify its control of the country, he seems to have been suspect to his colleagues and particularly to the Soviet party, perhaps because he was inclined to lead rather than follow.

In the principal address delivered at the conference Gheorghiu-Dej set forth the immediate and long-term objectives of the party. He concentrated on the economic transformation of the country and proposed to accomplish it through a sustained programme of industrialization which would emphasize heavy industry and the creation of new sources of power, particularly electrification. Although he rejected the notion of Rumania as a pre-eminently agricultural country whose recovery must be based upon 'existing realities', that is, an increase in the production of crops and animals and the export of grains, he could by no means ignore the countryside. But agriculture was clearly to be subordinated to the development of industry. Gheorghiu-Dej assigned to the villages the primary task of supplying food and raw materials for the growing urban industrial centres. He recommended the completion of agrarian reform, the creation of special stations where peasants could rent tractors and other machinery, and the expansion of rural credit. But he said nothing about collectivization, which was the ultimate aim of Communist agricultural policy, because to have done so would have alienated the majority of peasants at a time when the struggle for power had not yet been won. But he made no secret of the role to be played by the state. As the instrument of the Communist Party he assigned to it the organization and the direction of the economy, a responsibility which was incorporated into all subsequent government economic legislation.[18]

During the autumn of 1945 the Communists intensified their efforts to force the Social Democratic Party to join the common workers' front. But they had little success. Relations between the two parties had rapidly deteriorated after the August confrontation between the king and Groza because Titel Petrescu and the majority of socialist leaders supported a constitutional, parliamentary regime. Despite threats against him and his supporters, whom the Communists branded as 'traitors', they persisted in their demand, set forth in a declaration of the party's central committee on 28 September, for a government fulfilling the conditions laid down by the United States and Britain at the Potsdam Conference and guaranteeing political and civil liberties. Although

---

[18] Gheorghe Gheorghiu-Dej, *Articole şi cuvîntări* (Bucharest, 1955), 62–79.

they remained in the government, at their general conference on 1–3 December Titel Petrescu and his supporters, who commanded a majority, decided to run a separate list of candidates in the coming parliamentary elections and to seek support for their own programme, rather than risk a loss of their identity and influence among the workers in an electoral alliance with the Communists.[19]

The Tătărescu Liberals were also displaying a persistent and disconcerting independence. At their general conference on 16 December they expressed little interest in an alliance with the Communists. They insisted that elections be held soon in order to replace the 'provisional' Groza government with a 'definitive and democratic' political system. As for the economy, they continued to recommend state supervision of large-scale private enterprises in order to harmonize their operations with the 'general interest', but they would not yield on the matter of private ownership. Groza himself finally had to acknowledge the existence of 'strains' within the old National Democratic Front and complained in a speech to *județ* prefects on 17 December that the government's authority had been weakened because 'certain parties' sought 'illusory successes' through independent action.

The Communists always regarded the National Peasants and the Liberals as their most dangerous adversaries, and, consequently, they made their existence increasingly grim. They subjected National Peasant and Liberal leaders to continual harassment at public meetings and vitriolic attacks in the Communist press and effectively prevented them from carrying on normal political activity. The Communists and their supporters forcibly disbanded National Peasant and Liberal political clubs in Bucharest and in the provinces, gaoled their organizers, broke up their public meetings, and closed their newspapers.

The West and the Soviet Union worked out a plan to resolve the political impasse in Rumania at their conference in Moscow on 16–26 December 1945. The Soviet Union agreed to the inclusion of one National Peasant and one Liberal minister genuinely representative of their respective parties in the government, which would then set the date for early elections and would guarantee all democratic parties complete freedom of association, assembly, and the press. In return, the United States and Great Britain

[19] Fătu, *Alianţe*, 235–9; *FRUS, 1945*, v. 593–4: Melbourne to Secretary of State, 24 Aug. 1945.

promised to recognize the new government. Finally, a committee made up of Averell Harriman, Archibald Clark Kerr, the British ambassador to the Soviet Union, and Vyshinsky was to go to Bucharest to discuss with King Michael and Groza the most appropriate way of carrying out these provisions.

The three-power delegation arrived in Bucharest at the end of December. On 2 January 1946 they met with Groza, who assured them that his government unconditionally accepted the Moscow formula and would ask the historical parties which of their members should be included in the government. On the same day Harriman met Maniu, Mihalache, and Brătianu, all three of whom doubted that free elections could take place as long as the Communists controlled the ministries of the Interior and Justice, but they agreed, none the less, to seek the support of the king and to try to obtain concessions from the government. Harriman did not think they would succeed, for he was certain that Vyshinsky had instructed the government to make no concessions whatever. When the three-power commission met with Groza on 4 January to discuss National Peasant and Liberal members to be included in the government he rejected Mihalache and Constantin Brătianu, the nephew of the Liberal Party leader. Harriman thought that Groza would have accepted them, had it not been for instructions from Vyshinsky not to. Moscow was obviously anxious to keep out of the cabinet any National Peasant or Liberal who was a prominent political figure or had a popular following.[20] Finally, the National Peasant, Emil Hațieganu, and the Liberal, Mihai Romniceanu, both long-time members of their parties, but not of the front rank, were found acceptable and took their places in the cabinet as ministers of state without portfolio. Groza agreed to hold elections without delay, and on 4 February the United States and Britain recognized his government.

This settlement represented a sharp defeat for the Rumanian historical parties and the West. The new cabinet was by no means representative of the will of the majority of Rumanians and continued to be dominated by the Communists and their Soviet mentors. Western recognition of it before the holding of elections was a tactical blunder, for the United States and Britain had given up the one effective means at their disposal of pressuring the Groza government to abide by the Moscow decisions. As events

[20] *FRUS, 1946*, vi (Washington, DC, 1969), 555–9: Harriman to Secretary of State, 2, 3, and 6 Jan. 1946.

were to show, neither the government nor the Soviet Union had any intention of allowing free elections, which, they rightly feared, would have swept the historical parties into power. They showed their true colours a few days after the granting of American and British recognition. The Politburo of the Rumanian Communist Party rejected as unacceptable the note of the American government of 5 February setting forth the procedures for free elections and urging that they be held in the coming April or May, while Tătărescu, the Foreign Minister, acting for the government, made no reply, but simply acknowledged receipt of the note. Clearly, the Communists were uncertain of their ability to control the outcome of any free and general consultation with the electorate. Thus, the elections, which were to have been held 'soon', were postponed until November.

Political activity during 1946 was focused on preparations for the elections. By this time almost all political forces had coalesced into two large opposing coalitions—the Communists and their supporters, on the one side, and the National Peasants and the Liberals, led by Maniu, the chief representative of the democratic, pro-Western forces, on the other. For a time after the American and British recognition of Groza there was a lull in the Communist campaign of intimidation against the opposition, but by April and May it was again in full swing.

The Communist Party was active on many fronts. Its drive, begun in the autumn of 1944, to bring public institutions under its control was unrelenting. It gave special attention to the army, for it doubted the political reliability of the officer corps. The Groza government thus retired or dismissed large numbers of officers, replacing them with more congenial elements, and it introduced special units into the army, whose task was to carry out the political 're-education' of officers and men alike. By the spring of 1946 the Communists had fashioned the army into an instrument for carrying out their policies. They also established an effective control over the newspaper press. They continually harassed opposition newspapers and shut down many of them through censorship, control of often scarce newsprint, domination of the printers' union, which often refused to print National Peasant and Liberal newspapers, and strong-arm tactics against editorial staffs and distributors. At the beginning of 1946, as a result of the Moscow agreement, the National Peasant *Dreptatea* (Justice) in Bucharest and *Patria* (The Fatherland) in Cluj and the Liberal *Liberalul* in Bucharest were allowed to resume publication, but they again soon ran foul of the authorities: *Patria* had to close, but *Dreptatea* and *Liberalul* held out until the summer of 1947.

The Groza government's harassment of the opposition press was symptomatic of its attitude toward cultural and intellectual life in general. Lucreţiu Pătrăşcanu assumed the role of the government's spokesman on these matters. In a speech to a conference of secondary schoolteachers in Bucharest in October 1945 he urged his listeners to join wholeheartedly in the work of creating a new culture which would be national in form and socialist in content and would offer the broad masses of the population every opportunity to participate in it. But he also issued a warning: all this activity must be 'progressive'; there was no place for literary and philosophical works that were out of step with the goal of the Communist Party to build a new society, and he cited the works of Lucian Blaga as a prime example of a 'negative factor' in Rumanian literature and philosophy. He thus gave voice to the principle underlying the Communist attitude toward culture: it must serve social ends and could not be allowed to evolve through the natural play of individual talent and the free exchange of ideas. In another public pronouncement in December Pătrăşcanu addressed himself directly to the intellectuals. He displayed contempt for the inter-war intellectual, whose 'lack of principles' and 'cheap opportunism' he attributed to the society in which they lived. Now, he admonished, they were at a crossroads: they must not look back to the past for the route to take, but must grasp the opportunity offered them by the Communist Party to build the 'new democratic Rumania'. He made an ominous comparison with Russian intellectuals in 1917: those who understood what was happening 'aligned themselves' with the great events of their time and accomplished important tasks: the others were 'run over by history'.[21]

The Groza government began to set up the institutional superstructure of cultural conformity within weeks of assuming office. On 23 March 1945 it founded the Ministry of Propaganda, which was responsible for the dissemination of all cultural, artistic, and scientific information and exercised the powers of censorship over the press and all other publications. A month later a Ministry of Arts came into being endowed with broad powers over all aspects

---

[21] Lucreţiu Pătrăşcanu, 'Democraţie şi naţionalism', in *Pentru democratizarea învăţământului* (Bucharest, 1946), 175–6, 180–1: Lucreţiu Pătrăşcanu, *Scrieri, articole, cuvîntări, 1944–1947* (Bucharest, 1983), 119–29.

of artistic and literary activity. Religion was also subject to increased state regulation. On 12 May the Department of Cults was established for the purpose of supervising all denominations and their various institutions and foundations, including theological seminaries. The new ministry had the power to control the financial affairs of both central church bodies and parishes and to approve the establishment of new parishes and new clerical positions. These provisions were but the beginning of a process by which the Orthodox Church would relinquish what had remained of its role in public affairs in the inter-war years and would be reduced administratively to a government department.

Yet, despite the pressure to promote Communist social and political goals and the evident trend toward conformity, cultural and literary life, at least in 1945 and 1946, retained much of its inter-war effervescence. Its individualism and aesthetics found expression, for example, in the romantic and anarchic verse of Constant Tonegaru (1919–52). In his volume of verse, *Plantaţii* (1945; Plantations), he was absorbed by his own feelings and perceptions of the world around him and he protested against the social and political conditioning to which he had been subjected. He was simply not interested in politics and the great social issues of the day. He was a celebrator of Bohemia who advocated the absolute freedom of the artist to create and to communicate in a language that suited him. Consequently, his verse had to be deciphered, to be read over and over in order to grasp its meaning. But another kind of poetry was also coming to the fore, one that was socially relevant. At its best it was represented by *Un om aşteaptă răsăritul* (1946; A Man Awaits the East) by Mihai Beniuc (b. 1907), which expressed the poet's aspiration toward the ideal of collective life. The theme was a common one, but Beniuc treated it with an authentic and refined poetic temperament, which distinguished his work from what the critic Vladimir Streinu characterized early in 1947 as the 'massive mediocrity' of an 'artificial generation of social and political poets'.[22]

During this period reviews once again assumed a leading role in literary life. Older ones, like *Viaţa românească*, which had been suspended in the autumn of 1940 after the installation of the National Legionary State, resumed publication in November 1944. Although Mihai Ralea in the first issue urged writers to create a

---

[22] Vladimir Streinu, 'Poezia socială şi aventura "criticii funcţionale"', *Revista fundaţiilor regale*, 14/2 (1947), 118.

new 'humanitarian light' in place of old obscurantist dogmas, he reasserted the review's commitment to its traditional goals. It was able to maintain a balance between pre-war aesthetic and cultural values and the new emphasis upon the social role of literature and thought as long as the Communist Party had to contend with a significant political opposition. The weekly *Contemporanul* (The Contemporary), which began publication in September 1946, represented the new trends in literary and intellectual life. It campaigned on behalf of the 'new literature', one that was socially committed to the building of a new society. Writers and critics who would rise to prominence in the 1950s and 1960s monopolized its pages, particularly beginning in the latter half of 1947. A striking novelty in all the literary and cultural reviews of the period was the increased attention given to Soviet literature and literary ideology, subjects that had been virtually absent from Rumanian publications in the inter-war period, except for leftist reviews. Now, the Soviet presence gradually overwhelmed the traditional Western sources which had nourished Rumanian intellectuals since the early decades of the nineteenth century. In the process of the Sovietization and the proletarianization of Rumanian literary and cultural life the creativity represented by a Constant Tonegaru was overwhelmed by a literature often bereft of aesthetic value and intended to promote the social and political goals of the moment.

The Groza government made strenuous efforts to change the composition of the bureaucracy. It rapidly expanded the programme, begun in the autumn of 1944, of purging all those civil servants and officials who had served in government and the military between 1 September 1940 and 23 August 1944. It issued a sweeping decree-law on 29 March 1945 which threatened with dismissal all such persons currently employed in the central government, *judeţ*, commune or any other body, including even scientific and professional organizations, whose budgets were subject to government approval. In practice this law was applied to every area of public life and was continually reinforced by additional legislation. For example, a decree of 11 April 1945 simply abolished the association of plastic artists and another on 31 July 1945 'cleansed' the association of architects, because of their 'anti-democratic spirit' and 'reactionary restrictions' on the admission of new members. Those dismissed were replaced by persons often of lesser talent, but who were deemed reliable by the Communist Party and were chosen from among its own members and members of allied parties, labour unions, and peasant organizations.

The Groza government accelerated the prosecution of persons accused of war crimes and responsibility for the disaster which had overtaken the country. Earlier legislation, of 21 January 1945, had already defined 'war criminal' and 'war profiteer' and had set up the legal machinery to deal with them. But on 21 April the new government promulgated a law which considerably broadened the above definitions and established new judicial bodies, notably people's tribunals, where the usual legal procedures could be ignored, in order to speed up prosecutions.[23] Arrests began at once of former ministers and other high officials in the Antonescu dictatorship and of former prefects, police officials, and functionaries of all kinds. By the end of May the number of arrests had reached 4,000.

The most spectacular of the war crimes trials was that of Ion and Mihai Antonescu. The proceedings began on 4 May 1946. The outcome was never in doubt, for both the judges and the defence lawyers, who had been appointed by the government, knew what was expected of them. The prosecutors also took the opportunity to implicate Maniu and Brătianu in the activities of the two Antonescus by citing occasional instances when they were all in agreement, while ignoring the harsh criticism which Maniu and Brătianu had made of Ion Antonescu's wartime domestic and foreign policies. These attacks did not diminish the standing of either in democratic opinion, but they were a foretaste of what they could expect in the coming election campaign, because of their implacable opposition to the new order and its submissiveness to the Soviet Union. Ion Antonescu maintained his dignity throughout the trial and, when his turn to testify came, he accepted full responsibility for his actions. Mihai Antonescu, however, had been broken by the experiences of his detention. On 17 May the court found them guilty and sentenced them to death. Both were shot at Jilava prison on 1 June.

While these events were taking place the Communist Party was intensifying its efforts to create a single electoral bloc of parties composing the National Democratic Front. Its primary concern was to enter the elections at the head of a unified working-class movement. Perhaps its greatest success was gaining control of the

---

[23] Venera Teodorescu, 'Activitatea legislativă a primului guvern revoluționar democratic (martie 1945–octombrie 1946)', *Studii și materiale de istorie contemporană*, 3 (1978), 107–12.

Social Democratic Party, a process which provides a characteristic example of the means it used to weaken and divide the opposition. By the beginning of 1946 the Communists had placed their supporters and some secret party members in sufficient numbers in positions of authority to be able to take over the party machinery. At the Social Democratic Party congress on 10 March 1946 they commanded the allegiance of a majority of the delegates. Titel Petrescu's motion to run a separate list of candidates in the coming elections was defeated in favour of a proposal to join the Communist Party in an electoral cartel.[24] Titel Petrescu and his supporters thereupon left the congress and formed the Independent Social Democratic Party (Partidul Social-Democrat Independent), which allied itself with the National Peasant and Liberal parties. All the other members of the National Democratic Front and the Tătărescu Liberals fell easily into line.

The Communist Party on 17 May announced the formation of the Bloc of Democratic Parties (Blocul Partidelor Democrate), which would present a single list of candidates in the elections representing the Communist Party, the Social Democratic Party, the Tătărescu Liberals, the Ploughmen's Front, and smaller groups like Anton Alexandrescu's Peasant Party. The first four parties were to be represented equally on the list, the others in proportion to their size. All retained their distinct ideologies, but accepted a common electoral platform: guarantees of democratic liberties to all citizens, respect for individual private property, an improvement in the standard of living of the mass of the population, the development of heavy industry as the basis of a general economic recovery, the mechanization and rationalization of agriculture, a progressive income tax, and a state take-over of the National Bank. Such an all-encompassing social and economic platform was certain to have wide appeal, but a dutiful promise of friendship and co-operation with the Soviet Union turned many prospective supporters away.

As a prelude to the election campaign the government promulgated a crucial decree-law on 13 July 1946. Although it extended the right to vote to all citizens over 21, including women for the first time, other provisions offered the government ample opportunity to influence the outcome of the election in its favour. The law allowed the government to appoint its own functionaries

---

[24] Gheorghe Țuțui, *Evoluția Partidului Social-Democrat din România de la frontul unic la partidul unic (mai 1944–februarie 1948)* (Bucharest, 1979), 113–18.

as the heads of all electoral boards, which, among other tasks had the responsibility of registering voters. The law also permitted voting in government offices, factories, and other institutions, where pressure could easily be exerted, and it disenfranchised numerous, vaguely defined categories of persons, such as those who were guilty of 'crimes against the people' or had had 'positions of responsibility' during the Antonescu dictatorship. In order to undermine the strength of moderate and middle-class elements, who were openly anti-Communist, the law changed the traditional structure of parliament by abolishing the Senate, which in the past had usually served conservative interests. The National Peasant and Liberal members of the cabinet strenuously objected to the law, and Maniu and Brătianu urged the king not to sign it and thus break with the government once and for all. Their aim was to provoke an international crisis which would force the United States and Britain to intervene, even if their action led to a Soviet occupation of Rumania. Maniu thought that this was the only way to prevent the fraudulent election of a Communist-dominated parliament, which would seal the fate of the country. But the king was certain that such rash action would end all hope of turning the tide, whereas if he remained in the field, there was always a chance that something would happen to change democratic fortunes.[25] Pătrăşcanu, speaking for the dominant Communist element in the government, offered the king a few minor concessions, but he refused to go further, because, he said, to do so would be to hand the country over to the historical parties. In the end, the king signed the decrees, but the conflict between two opposing political and social philosophies only deepened.

In the middle of October the government set 19 November as the date for the elections, but, in fact, the campaign had been underway since August. Both the Communist-dominated Bloc of Democratic Parties and the National Peasants, who led the opposition, considered the elections the decisive battle in the struggle for power. The Central Committee of the Communist Party had placed the Ministry of the Interior, headed by the Communist Teohari Georgescu, in charge of arranging the elections. It was his task to force magistrates throughout the country, who had responsibility for interpreting the electoral law, to follow directives from the Ministry, that is, from the Communist Party.

---

[25] *FRUS, 1946*, vi. 614–16: Berry to Secretary of State, 11 July 1946.

Leading Communists were dispatched to all parts of the country to take personal charge of the election campaign. A formidable administrative apparatus had thus been mobilized to promote the candidates of the Bloc and, especially, to prevent the opposition from mounting an effective campaign. Police and other officials interfered with the circulation of opposition newspapers and pamphlets and, together with specially formed squads of Communists and their sympathizers, they broke up National Peasant and Liberal meetings. They were also diligent in keeping large numbers of opposition voters off the registration lists, and in rural areas, where the National Peasants were especially strong, they had polling places moved far from centres of population in order to make it difficult for peasants to vote. As election day drew near the police and the gendarmerie were reinforced by large numbers of Communist auxiliaries, who had been recruited 'to maintain order'. Protests from the opposition to the government and Soviet officials on the Allied Control Commission were ignored. Gheorghiu-Dej made no secret of Communist Party intentions. At the height of the election campaign he informed members of the American mission in Bucharest that the election was a battle in which the enemy, the historical parties, had to be defeated, and he freely admitted that the government was taking advantage of every 'weakness' of the opposition in order to win. He also confided that Soviet authorities expected the Rumanian government to win.[26]

The opposition was by no means impotent and fought back with all the resources, however limited, at its command. The bluntness of their attacks on the government and its supporters in the press is striking. The National Peasant *Dreptatea* in the summer and autumn of 1946, for example, gave as good as it got, despite censorship and all the other impediments its editors faced. The paper carried numerous articles pointing out the abuses committed by the censors and demanding freedom of the press. It was critical of governmental policies all down the line, but none more so than the campaign to purge the bureaucracy of 'collaborators' of the old regime. It took particular delight in noting such prominent exceptions to the general opprobrium as Gheorghe Tătărescu, and

[26] Ibid. 632–4, 638, 643–4, 648–9: Melbourne and Berry to Secretary of State, 12 and 23 Sept. 19 and 26 Oct. 1946. The tactics used against the National Peasant opposition are graphically described by an American journalist who accompanied Ion Mihalache on an election tour in Moldavia in the spring of 1946: Reuben Markham, *Rumania under the Soviet Yoke* (Boston, 1949), 272–91, 303–13.

the National Democratic Front was often the butt of devastating humour in the best traditions of Rumanian journalism. The opposition press in general kept up a constant barrage on the government and the Bloc, accusing them of systematically subverting the electoral process.

The balloting on 19 November took place in an atmosphere of extreme tension. The government was expected to announce the results on the 20th, but for reasons which it could not satisfactorily explain there was a delay of forty-eight hours. Only on the 22nd did it finally publish the figures. These showed an overwhelming victory for the Bloc with some 70 per cent of the votes and 349 seats in the new Assembly to 32 for the National Peasants and 33 for the other non-Bloc parties. But there are strong indications that just the opposite took place on election day. Various independent sources suggest that the National Peasants were on their way to a landslide victory with about 70 per cent of the vote, an expression of faith in the most democratic of all Rumanian political parties, and, no less, a manifestation of strong national feeling. It appears that when Communist leaders realized the extent of their impending defeat they had the reporting of returns suspended as of noon on 20 November and sent instructions to all prefects to 'revise' the figures in order to show a victory for the Bloc. Ana Pauker and other Communists appear to have consulted Moscow and to have received the go-ahead to falsify the election results.[27] Hence, the unusual delay in reporting the vote.

Immediately after the official announcement of the results Maniu and Brătianu declared that they would not recognize the elections as valid and called upon all their supporters to oppose the 'dictatorship', a term they henceforth regularly applied to the government on the grounds that it was a minority regime kept in power by force. They also decided to boycott the new Assembly and to seek the help of the United States and Britain in annulling the elections and scheduling new ones. At the end of November Maniu tried to persuade both governments to use the Moscow agreements of the previous December as a means of reversing Rumania's slide into a Communist dictatorship dominated by the Soviet Union. Although the United States and Britain denounced the elections as unrepresentative of the will of the Rumanian people and held the Groza government responsible for reneging

---

[27] *FRUS, 1946*, vi. 663–5, 668–9: Berry to Secretary of State, 27 Nov. and 3 Dec. 1946.

on its promises about free elections, neither was prepared to go further in support of those whom they had earlier encouraged to oppose Soviet and Communist pressure. The elections represented the end of the attempts by the three wartime allies to resolve the Rumanian question together. Henceforth, Western influence on the course of events in Rumania for all intents and purposes ceased.

The negotiations for a final peace with Rumania, which had begun in Paris in August 1946, were brought to a conclusion early in the new year. Tătărescu, with Gheorghiu-Dej and Pătrăşcanu at his side, led the Rumanian delegation. They sought, unsuccessfully, to obtain recognition of co-belligerency status and to move the official date of Rumania's entry into the war back from 12 September to 23 August 1944 in the hope of lightening the burden of reparations. But, in general, the Rumanian delegation did not contest any issues of vital concern to the Soviet Union. For example, although the pre-1940 frontier between Rumania and Hungary was restored on the grounds that it had been altered under threat of force, Tătărescu and company did not object to the Soviet annexation of Bessarabia and northern Bukovina. Nor did they bring up the Treaty of Craiova of 1940 with its loss of southern Dobrudja to Bulgaria, now a close Soviet ally. Rumanian diplomats who had taken refuge in the West, among them Grigore Gafencu, who had settled in Switzerland shortly after the invasion of the Soviet Union in 1941, were active in Paris. They tried to represent the national interests of Greater Rumania and repeatedly showed Western diplomats how the behaviour of the official delegation was dictated by the Soviet Union, but they had no influence on the course of events.

The peace treaty was signed on 10 February 1947. A number of decisions, which had already been made in the armistice agreement in 1944 covering such matters as boundaries and war indemnities were incorporated into the new document. Noteworthy was the provision under which the Western powers formally renounced their claims to German and Italian assets in Rumania, which later were to form the Soviet share of various joint Soviet-Rumanian companies, the so-called Sovroms. The Soviet Union agreed to withdraw its army from Rumania within three months after the treaty came into force, except for those units that were necessary to maintain communications with Soviet occupation forces in Austria (large Soviet ground and air forces, in fact, were stationed in Rumania until 1958). In Article 3 the Rumanian government bound itself to protect the fundamental rights of all citizens, including freedom of speech and of the press, of association, and of assembly, but, as events again were to show, it had not the least intention of abiding by such pledges.

A new Rumanian government was formed on 1 December 1946. Although the ministries were divided more or less equally among the partners in the Bloc of Democratic Parties, the Communist Party held the key positions of Prime Minister (Groza), Interior (Georgescu), Justice (Pătrăşcanu), and Communications (Gheorghiu-Dej). To these must be added the ministries of Education, Labour and Social Insurance, Mines and Oil, and Arts, which were headed by the leftist Social Democrats allied with the Communists. The Communist Party kept up the appearances of a coalition government by allotting four portfolios—Foreign Affairs, Finance, Public Works, and Religion—to the Tătărescu Liberals. Tătărescu himself, besides remaining as Foreign Minister, also became Vice-President of the Council of Ministers. These changes were not simply a cabinet shuffle, but marked a further step in the consolidation of power by the Communist Party.

The contest between the Communist Party and the historical parties was also being played out in economic life. The National Peasants and Liberals stood for the maintenance of private property and private initiative with the state serving merely to encourage and to regulate, whereas the Communists sought to give the state, that is, themselves, the power to plan and direct every significant facet of the economy, although for tactical reasons they stopped short of advocating the immediate nationalization of the means of production and the collectivization of agriculture. As with politics, so, too, the economic struggle proved unequal, as the Communist Party, guided by Moscow and assisted by Soviet occupation authorities, gained the initiative in agriculture and industry.

The revival of the economy after the severe strains of three years of war against the Soviet Union and while the military effort continued on the Allied side and reparations payments to the Soviet Union were begun proved a daunting task in the autumn of 1944 and the spring of 1945. In agriculture the production of both foodstuffs and industrial crops had declined precipitously, and as late as 1946 it had attained a level of only 60 per cent of the annual average in the latter 1930s. The recovery was hindered, first, by the drought and subsequent failure of the corn crop in 1946, which caused a severe famine in the following winter and spring, and then by massive deliveries of agricultural products to the Soviet Union, a decrease in the number of draft animals, and, to a lesser extent, the dislocations caused by the land reform initiated in 1945. Industry and the transportation system were in an equally grim condition. The output of the oil and metallurgical industries had also suffered enormously. In 1944 the production of crude oil had fallen to 3.5 million tons from 6.6 million tons in 1938, and refining and cracking capacity had been reduced by over 80 per cent, because of Allied bombing. The major steel works in 1944 were operating at less than 50 per cent of capacity. Light industry and food-processing were in a similar condition, because of the lack of raw materials and the destruction and disorganization of the transportation system.

An additional burden for the Rumanian economy to bear was the overwhelming presence of the Soviet Union. Reparations payments, which included foodstuffs and raw materials of all kinds, war booty, particularly industrial equipment, and the obligation to supply Soviet armies in the field with all manner of goods drained the country of critically needed resources for its own economic recovery. Soviet authorities made their requisitions without taking into account Rumania's capacity to provide them. At the same time the Soviet government was intent upon monopolizing Rumanian production and foreign trade in the postwar era through a series of long-term economic treaties. The most far-reaching of these in its implications for the future political as well as economic development of the country was signed on 8 May 1945 in Moscow. It provided for the establishment of joint Soviet–Rumanian companies, the Sovroms, which in theory were partnerships of equals intended to ensure a mutually beneficial economic relationship, but in practice became instruments of Soviet exploitation of Rumania's economic resources.[28] Sovroms were established for every significant branch of the Rumanian economy, and those of most importance to the Soviet Union— Sovrompetrol and Sovromtransport—began to operate at once. The Rumanian investment in such enterprises was disproportionate to the benefits received and the control exercised. To create Sovrompetrol, for example, the Rumanian government put up Rumanian firms and natural resources, whereas the Soviet side

[28] Ion Alexandrescu, *Economia României în primii ani postbelici (1945–1947)* (Bucharest, 1986), 214–17.

put up confiscated German and Italian companies and seized equipment, not capital and resources of its own. Direction and management were in the hands of Soviet officials. The Sovroms benefited from every possible advantage, such as exemptions from taxation and restrictive regulations, while British, American, and Dutch companies had to operate under the most adverse conditions, designed by the government to drive them out of business. One fateful consequence of the massive Soviet economic penetration of Rumania was the severance by 1947 of her traditional ties to the West, an isolation far more complete than that during Ottoman suzerainty in the eighteenth century.

From the moment the Sănătescu government was installed in August 1944 agriculture was its main economic preoccupation. There was, first of all, the immediate need to supply the armies in the field and the home front with food and other necessities, but as politicians of all parties struggled to solve these practical problems and to devise a plan for the long-term reorganization of agriculture, political advantage and ideology were never absent from their thinking.

Of all the programmes for agrarian reform, the one put forward by the Communist Party was the most radical. It called for the immediate confiscation of all landlord property above 50 hectares and the distribution of the land to peasants who had none or very little. National Peasant Party leaders also advocated reform, but they were more cautious. They were worried that the rapid, wholesale expropriation of estates and the distribution of land in lots of 5 hectares or less would lower production and encourage the new peasant landholders to plant corn to satisfy their own needs, thereby strengthening one-crop agriculture, which had proved such a formidable obstacle to progress in the past. For the time being, moderation prevailed, as the National Peasants persuaded the Rădescu government to investigate the condition of agriculture before embarking upon reform. In February 1945 the National Peasant Party published a comprehensive plan of agrarian reform, which in essence revived the Peasantist theories of the inter-war period. It stood forth as the defender of the small, independent peasant producer as the 'foundation' of the Rumanian state and insisted that the peasantry be recognized as its leading class.

Agricultural policy, however, was in the hands of others. Two weeks after the Groza government had assumed office, on

20 March 1945, it issued a decree-law on agrarian reform.[29] It provided for the expropriation of all privately owned estates over 50 hectares and, unlike the reform of 1921, it treated all the holdings of a landowner as a single estate and offered no compensation. As a result, large landlord property finally ceased to exist. Numerous other categories of landowners, notably those designated as war criminals and those who had collaborated directly with German authorities in Rumania or who had volunteered for service in the German army, suffered the full confiscation of their property. These provisions were applied indiscriminately to the Saxons in Transylvania and the Swabians in the Banat and thus caused the destruction of many of their communities. Yet, other properties escaped expropriation altogether. Foremost among them were the holdings of monasteries, churches, rural co-operatives, and cultural and charitable organizations. The Communist members of the government urged that these properties be exempted in order not to turn the peasantry, the clergy, and numerous intellectuals against the government at a time when the struggle for power was in full swing. The confiscation of all equipment and draft animals on the expropriated estates was a significant aspect of the reform, for they were used to stock the new centres for renting agricultural machinery to peasants established in every *judeţ*. These centres represented a crucial step toward the later collectivization of agriculture, although the government proponents of reform were careful to avoid all mention of collectivization, for fear of alienating the peasantry. In order to convince the naturally sceptical peasants of its commitment to uphold private property the government required payment for the land to the state. The sum was small and did not constitute a financial burden for the individual peasant. It was, none the less, important because the Communist Party, aware of the peasants' long struggle to obtain land, used it to prove to them that their possession of the land was definitive.

The reform, which was carried out with relative dispatch and was completed by the spring of 1948, did not significantly change the structure of agriculture. Although 917,777 peasants received land, thus sharing in the 1,109,562 hectares that were distributed

---

[29] On the Groza government's agrarian measures between 1945 and 1947, see Mihail Rusenescu, 'Date privind politica agrară a României (martie 1945–februarie 1949)', *Studii şi materiale de istorie contemporană*, 3 (1978), 80–96, and Traian Udrea, 'Caracterul şi consecinţele social-economice ale aplicării reformei agrare din 1945', *Revista de istorie*, 42/3(1989), 233–46.

to landless peasants and smallholders (out of 1,468,946 hectares expropriated), only modest shifts in the various categories of landholding occurred. The main beneficiaries of the reform were the agricultural proletariat and the poor peasants, as 400,000 new holdings were created and 500,000 smallholdings received additional land. But the percentage of peasant holdings of 1–3 hectares remained almost the same (35.1 per cent in 1941; 36.1 per cent in 1948), while those between 3 and 5 hectares increased slightly (18.1 per cent in 1941; 22.6 per cent in 1948). The most significant change occurred in holdings of under 1 hectare (23.3 per cent in 1941; 17.5 per cent in 1948). Yet, the amount of land each peasant received was so small that his economic and social status hardly changed. Holdings remained as fragmented as before, as the government showed no interest in combining scattered strips; grain production generally grew at the expense of other crops, as the government gave relatively little attention to the intensification and diversification of agriculture; and the raising of animals declined, mainly, it seems, as a result of the break-up of the large estates. Nor did the government make a special effort to promote the co-operative movement. Even though it established the National Co-operative Institute in 1945, it limited the organization's activity mainly to supervising the collection of grain. The government's agricultural policy after the agrarian reform seems to have been one of expectancy, and, in fact, dramatic changes in the organization of agriculture did not occur until after the Communist Party had eliminated the opposition and had secured a monopoly of political power.

The Groza government, in any case, gave its primary attention to industry. It followed closely the principles and strategy which Gheorghiu-Dej outlined at the national conference of the Communist Party in October 1945. There he made both the immediate economic recovery of the country and its long-term progress directly dependent upon its ability to industrialize as rapidly as possible. He also assigned the decisive role in this process to the state, which would integrate the entire industrial capacity of the country, both state-run and private, into a unified whole and would, therefore, allocate raw materials, regulate the sale and prices of goods, and control the investment of capital. By the autumn of 1945 the Groza government had already established the primacy of the state in industry through a stream of decree-laws regulating railways, mining and oil production, prices, and salaries. This legislative activity intensified in 1946 as the Communist Party extended its influence throughout the economy.[30] Its control of economic and financial affairs was virtually complete when on 1 December 1946 Gheorghiu-Dej, the Secretary-General of the party, assumed direction of the newly created Ministry of National Economy, the all-powerful planning and co-ordinating body, whose primary function was to mobilize the entire resources of the country to carry out Communist economic policy. Despite all this attention, and the channelling of scarce investment capital into industry, the latter's recovery was slow and uneven. Nevertheless, by the second half of 1947 the production of coal had reached 96.3 per cent of the 1938 level, pig iron 85.7 per cent, and steel 79.5 per cent, but petroleum lagged behind at 58.8 per cent.

THE FINAL YEAR OF MODERN RUMANIA

Dominant in internal political life since the reorganization of the government on 1 December 1946 and freed of any effective Western intervention by the Paris peace treaty, the Communist Party set about in earnest to eliminate what remained of the opposition. In March and again in May 1947 the Ministry of the Interior carried out mass arrests of opposition politicians, including Social Democrats, and of intellectuals and workers, perhaps 2,000 persons in all, and held them in prison or sent them to concentration camps recently built for this purpose. These waves of arrests represented only the beginning of what was to follow in the next four or five years. Evidence suggests that Soviet authorities in Rumania were deeply involved in this campaign and may even have initiated the action on direct instructions from Moscow. The Soviet Communist Party held the Groza government itself responsible for the continuing strong opposition, accusing it of having allowed too much freedom. The Soviet political presence in Rumania was already massive. Besides the personnel of the government ministries and joint Soviet-Rumanian companies and civilians attached to the Soviet army, there were large numbers of secret police, who had been sent to 'advise' the Rumanian government and Communist Party on political control and other security problems.

---

[30] Ilie Puia, 'Politica industrială a puterii revoluţionar democratice în perioada refacerii economice (decembrie 1946–decembrie 1947)', *Studii şi materiale de istorie contemporană*, 3 (1978), 60–72.

In the middle of March 1947 Maniu, Brătianu, and Titel Petrescu appealed for American intervention to put an end to a situation, which, they claimed, no modern regime, not even the Antonescu dictatorship, had ever imposed on the country and which openly violated the Yalta, Potsdam, and Moscow agreements. Maniu proposed the overthrow of the Groza government as the only solution, and, although he did not suggest revolution, he feared that the carrying out of his plan would cause much bloodshed. To be successful, he insisted that he needed the support of the people, the king, and the Western powers. He had the first two: the people had already spoken in the recent elections, and the king was willing, but he himself was reluctant to move without knowing the attitude of the American and British governments.[31] American officials in Bucharest assured him that the United States supported the efforts of democratic forces in Rumania to establish a truly representative, parliamentary system, as called for in the Yalta Declaration. But they also pointed out that the ability of their government to influence the course of events was severely limited, an assessment borne out fully by subsequent events. Protests in June by the United States that arbitrary arrests and imprisonments were contrary to great-power agreements and Article 3 of the peace treaty, according to which the Rumanian government guaranteed fundamental civil liberties for all its citizens, fell on deaf ears. Foreign Minister Tătărescu replied to the protest on 12 July by accusing the United States of unwarranted interference in the internal affairs of his country.

While its direct assault on the opposition was taking place, the Communist Party was busy redefining its relationship with its two main partners in the government, the Ploughmen's Front and the splinter Social Democrats. By the beginning of 1947 Communist leaders had come to regard both organizations as permanent allies, and as such they were determined to bring their policies into conformity with Communist objectives. They gave particular attention to the membership of the Ploughmen's Front, which they planned to use as the means of extending Communist influence among the masses of peasants and of undermining the popularity of the National Peasant Party. The Central Committee of the Communist Party decided on 9 January 1947 to 'improve' the social composition of the Ploughmen's Front by removing

---

[31] *FRUS, 1947*, v (Washington, DC, 1972), 477: Berry to Secretary of State, 13 Mar. 1947.

'bourgeois elements', a term which referred to those who sought to maintain the independence of the party and who accused Groza and others of too close collaboration with the Communists. The Politburo of the Communist Party and the executive committee of the Ploughmen's Front, composed mainly of Communist supporters, decided at a joint meeting in February to transform the Front from an organization representing all the peasantry into a 'revolutionary party', that is, one which would represent the poorer strata, the so-called 'working peasantry', and co-operate fully with the Communist Party in carrying out its political and economic agenda. By the summer the 'reorganization' of the Ploughmen's Front had been completed.[32]

The Communist Party attempted to strengthen its position in the countryside in various ways. As a necessary prelude to the carrying out of its programme for agriculture it began intensive propaganda and organizational work in the villages in January 1947. According to its own figures, the party at this time had some 9,000 cells and 215,000 members (37.5 per cent of the total party membership) in rural areas. Since the social composition of these organizations was now thought to be too heterogeneous, it decided to redress the balance in favour of 'proletarian elements' by concentrating on the recruitment of poorer peasants, who were judged to be more amenable to party influence and more useful in undermining support for the National Peasants and Liberals than their well-to-do neighbours. To co-ordinate this work party leaders established a special peasant section of the Central Committee. By the end of the year it could report that the number of cells had increased to 11,613 and their membership to 308,000. The party also directed its attention to agricultural labourers, including seasonal workers from the upland regions and industrial workers who continued to live in the village. It assigned the task of setting up 'agricultural unions' to the Communist-dominated General Confederation of Labour (Confederaţia Generală a Muncii). The Confederation overcame the stiff resistance of the National Peasant Party and by December 1947 had enrolled some 100,000 members, all considered 'reliable', in their new rural labour organizations.

During the first half of 1947 the Communist Party moved to

---

[32] G. I. Ioniţa and G. Ţuţui, *Frontul Plugarilor (1933–1953)* (Bucharest, 1970), 238–52.

tighten still further its control of every branch of the economy.[33] Central planning and direction were the order of the day, and all the measures it took turned out to be merely preparatory to the nationalization of industry and the collectivization of agriculture. On 5 April a new Ministry of Industry and Commerce, combining the attributes of the Ministry of National Economy and numerous other state agencies, assumed broad powers to collect and distribute industrial and agricultural consumer goods, allocate raw materials to industry, regulate investment in private and state-run enterprises, and control credit. At the local administrative and plant level so-called industrial offices were created on 10 June to co-ordinate all aspects of production by groups of industries, such as cloth, non-ferrous metals, and chemicals. By 1 December 1947 fourteen offices had been established encompassing 730 enterprises, which together represented approximately 80 per cent of the country's productive capacity. The same trends were apparent in agriculture. The Assembly enacted a law on 6 June imposing strict controls on the private sale of land and granting the state priority in the purchase of land. The government justified the law as necessary to prevent both the reconstitution of large estates and the continued fragmentation of smallholdings, but all the land which it acquired was used to expand the system of state farms. Another typical law, enacted on 2 July, imposed limitations on the sale of agricultural produce by private peasants through a tax in kind. The new tax was, in effect, a forced delivery of crops to the state, which could allocate them as it saw fit. In financial matters, too, the trend was toward increased state control. Decisive for the development of the entire economy was the nationalization of the private, Liberal stronghold, Banca Naţională a României on 20 December 1946. The Communist Party now had at its disposal one of the country's most important economic levers, which would enable it to direct the entire financial system toward the achievement of its economic goals. Yet, the most serious immediate financial problem was runaway inflation. The cost-of-living index had risen steadily during the war from 100 in August 1939 to 944 in August 1944, but by April 1947 it was 440,869 and reached 525,688 in July. The government seemed satisfied for a time to let inflation run its course in order to weaken the economic power of its opponents. But on 15 August

[33] Maria Curteanu, *Sectorul de stat în România anilor 1944–1947* (Bucharest, 1974), 123–52.

it announced a drastic currency reform, which it had prepared in secret. The reform struck hardest at the middle classes, who lost enormous amounts of savings, but workers and peasants, though allowed to exchange more old lei for the new currency, also suffered.

The transformation of the Rumanian domestic economy in accordance with the Soviet model was accompanied by the integration of that economy into the Soviet bloc and a consequent economic isolation from the West. A comprehensive commercial treaty signed in Moscow in February 1947 covering exchanges of goods and payments laid the foundation for regular Rumanian–Soviet economic relations. Foreign trade figures suggest the degree to which Rumania's economy had been integrated into that of the Soviet bloc. By the end of 1947 70 per cent of her imports came from and 90 per cent of her exports went to Eastern Europe and the Soviet Union. The figures for the Soviet Union alone are striking—48 per cent of Rumania's imports and 50.1 per cent of her exports—when account is taken of the low level of Rumanian trade with the Soviet Union during the inter-war period and with Imperial Russia in the nineteenth century. Needless to say, Rumania was among the missing at the Marshall Plan conference, which opened in Paris on 12 July.

The Communists now judged the time ripe for a frontal assault on the National Peasant Party. Ever since the coup of 23 August they had regarded Maniu as their principal enemy, but, because of his immense prestige throughout the country, they had been afraid to touch him and had had to be satisfied with press attacks. But in July 1947 a pretext for stronger action finally presented itself. Maniu and other National Peasants had been in contact with exiles about setting up a democratic government in exile in the West as the true representative of the Rumanian nation as the only practical way left of challenging the Soviet-sponsored Groza government. On 14 July Ion Mihalache and several colleagues were arrested by security police at an improvised airport near Bucharest as they were preparing to fly to the West. On the same day the police searched party headquarters and the homes of party leaders. On the 19th Maniu, who was accused of complicity in the flight of his colleagues, was arrested; the authorities closed *Dreptatea*, and the Assembly lifted the parliamentary immunity of National Peasant deputies. A week later the executive committee of the Bloc of Democratic Parties proposed the dissolution of the National Peasant Party on the grounds that its entire activity constituted crimes against the security of the state, and on 30 July a pliant Assembly dutifully passed the necessary legislation.

The trial of Maniu, Mihalache, and other National Peasant leaders, including those living abroad, among them, Grigore Gafencu, began before a military court on 29 October. Its purpose was to complete the Communist seizure of power by clearing away the last of the opposition. The trial was also another skirmish in the uneven contest between East and West over Rumania, as the Soviet Union sought to destroy the influence of Western democracy by eliminating its foremost representatives in Rumania from public life.

The main accusation against Maniu and his colleagues was treason, specifically, that they had 'conspired' with secret service agents at the American and British legations in Bucharest to overthrow the Groza government. In accounting for his actions, Maniu pointed out that he had been engaged in a struggle to restore free elections, political liberties, and fundamental human rights, and declared that he was determined to use every means available to achieve these ends. He admitted that he had had frequent contacts with American and British representatives, but he insisted that the discussion of domestic and international questions was one of the duties of every statesman. The dignity which he displayed throughout the hostile and unfair proceedings added to his reputation for probity and courage. But the verdict was never in doubt. On 11 November the court sentenced Maniu and Mihalache to life imprisonment and the other defendants to terms of from five years to life in prison. Maniu died in prison in 1953, Mihalache in 1963.

The spirit in which the trial had been conducted was captured in a speech concerning the reorganization of justice made by Pătrăşcanu in the Assembly on 28 November, a few weeks after the verdicts had been pronounced. He rejected the notion that justice in the new Rumania should be impartial or independent of the executive power. Instead, he argued, the primary task of the judicial system at a time of momentous changes in society was to provide the Communist Party with the necessary help in carrying out its economic and political programme. Freely acknowledging the enormous debt which he and his colleagues owed to Soviet law, which served them as a model, he emphasized that the principle which would henceforth guide Rumanian justice would be class consciousness. He promised to make the courts amenable to direction by the Communist Party through newly appointed people's judges (*asesori populari*), who would serve three-month terms alongside career judges, whom they would, moreover, outnumber two to one. Pătrăşcanu made it clear that these nonprofessional judges need not have a knowledge of law codes and cases because they would render decisions according to their own 'minds and consciences' and would never forget their duty to serve the interests of the workers and peasants who chose them.[34]

In their drive to absorb the socialists into a single workers' party the Communists brought the Independent Socialist Party and its leader Titel Petrescu under sustained attack in the autumn of 1947. The Independent Socialists had become anathema to the Communists not only because they were committed to parliamentary democracy but also because they provided a rallying point for other socialists who opposed fusion with the Communist Party. Yet the tide against the socialists was overwhelming, and the Social Democratic Party was eventually 'united' with the Communist Party at a joint congress on 21–3 February 1948 to form the Rumanian Workers' Party. Titel Petrescu's party was dispersed through the intimidation and arrest of its activists, and he himself was arrested in May 1948 an imprisoned without trial.

The reckoning also finally came for Tătărescu and his faction, the only significant political group in the government not yet controlled by the Communist Party. As long as the Communists had thought it necessary to keep up the appearances of a coalition government and as long as Tătărescu proved useful in dealing with the Western powers as Foreign Minister, they kept him on, but their incompatibility had been evident for some time. Tătărescu had not abandoned the Liberal commitment to private enterprise and the maintenance of a middle class in economic life. In agriculture he urged the formation of a prosperous middle-sized peasantry with holdings of 10–30 hectares as a force for order and stability and proposed the expansion of co-operatives free from government control, while in industry he opposed any role for the state beyond general supervision and co-ordination. On 24 May he presented a general critique of the Groza government's activities in which he attacked the very foundations upon which the new regime was based and demanded major changes in its economic and political policies. The response was not long in coming. He became the object of unceasing attacks from Communist leaders and the press, but he was able to cling to

[34] Pătrăşcanu, *Scrieri, articole, cuvîntări, 1944–1947*, 217–18, 221–3.

office because he was still useful. The Maniu trial proved his undoing. When a number of high officials in the Foreign Ministry were implicated in the activities of the regime's opponents Tătărescu's enemies in the Assembly accused him of negligence and pushed through a vote of no confidence against him on 5 November. He resigned on the following day and was replaced by Ana Pauker, but he escaped the fate of Maniu and Mihalache. In December the Liberal parliamentary deputies adopted a new party programme in which they promised close collaboration with the Communist Party in building a new society based upon 'social property'. In January 1948 Petre Bejan, a minor political figure, formally replaced Tătărescu as head of the party, but by this time the Liberal faction no longer counted in the political life of the country.

As the Communists moved inexorably toward a monopoly of political power the monarchy had become an anomaly. Fearful that this last vestige of the old political order might yet serve as a centre of opposition to the new society, the Communist Party took the final, logical step in assuring its domination of the country when it forced the king to abdicate on 30 December 1947. Its proclamation of the Rumanian People's Republic on the same day was the culmination of its campaign to seize power. At one level its action marked the subordination of the country to the Soviet political and economic model at home and to Soviet aims in international relations. At a deeper level it served notice that the modern era of Rumanian history, which had begun with the loosening of ties to the East and the opening to the West, had come to an end.

BIBLIOGRAPHICAL ESSAY

BIBLIOGRAPHIES

The standard bibliography for Rumaian history is the comprehensive *Bibliografia istorică a României*, i (1944–69), iv (1969–74), v (1974–9), vi (1979–84), vii (1984–9) (Bucharest, 1970–90). Under the same title two volumes on the nineteenth century have so far appeared: vols. ii and iii (Bucharest, 1972–4). Also valuable for the historian is *Bibliografia românească modernă, 1831–1918*, 3 vols. (Bucharest, 1984–9), a repertory of Rumanian publications on all subjects that has reached the letter 'Q'. *Publicațiile periodice românești*, i (1820–1906) and ii (1907–18, and supplement, 1790–1906) (Bucharest, 1913–69), is an exhaustive annotated listing of periodicals published in Rumania in all languages and in foreign countries in Rumanian. Several specialized bibliographies are also useful: *Independența României: Bibliografie* (Bucharest, 1979) and a shortened version in English, *The Independence of Romania: Selected Bibliography* (Bucharest, 1980), both extensively annotated; *România în primul război mondial: Contribuții bibliografice* (Bucharest, 1975), on all aspects of Rumania's participation in the First World War: and *Contribuții bibliografice privind Unirea Transilvaniei cu România* (Bucharest, 1969), covering the Rumanian national movement in Hungary from the latter decades of dualism to 1918. Surprisingly, there is no comprehensive bibliography of the Communist movement in Rumania, but Titu Georgescu and Mircea Ioanid, *Presa PCR și a organizațiilor sale de masă, 1921–1944* (Bucharest, 1963) provides valuable data about the national and local Communist press in Rumanian, Hungarian, and German.

1. INDEPENDENCE, 1866–1881

A comprehensive, balanced introduction to the decade preceding the proclamation of Rumania's independence is Lothar Maier, *Rumänien auf dem Weg zur Unabhängigkeitserklärung 1866–1877* (Munich, 1989). Nicolae Iorga, *Histoire des Roumains et de la romanité orientale*, x (Bucharest, 1945), is rich in ideas about the period. A penetrating analysis of political tendencies and early efforts at organizing parties is Apostol Stan, *Grupări și curente politice în România între unire și independență, 1859–1877* (Bucharest, 1979). Useful for the evolution of conservative thought is Anastasie

Iordache, *Originile conservatorismului politic din România, 1821–1882* (Bucharest, 1987).

Prince Charles is one of many political figures of the period who await their biographer. An attempt at a monographic treatment was made by Mihail Polihroniade and Alexandru-Christian Tell, *Domnia lui Carol I,* i (1866–77) (Bucharest, 1937). Of the published sources on Charles, fundamental are the memoirs of his physician, *Aus dem Leben König Karls von Rumänien,* 4 vols. (Stuttgart, 1894–1900), which cover the period 1866–81. They may be supplemented by an ample collection of speeches, papers, and diplomatic documents arranged chronologically by Démètre Sturdza, *Charles Ier, Roi de Roumanie. Chronique, actes, documents, 1866–1877,* 2 vols. (Bucharest, 1899–1904). The moderate Liberal, Mihail Kogălniceanu, has probably received the most attention since the Second World War. Virgil Ionescu, *Mihail Kogălniceanu: Contribuții la cunoașterea vieții, activității și concepțiilor sale* (Bucharest, 1963), is a general survey of his career. The same author examines Kogălniceanu's commitment to social and economic change in *Opera lui Mihail Kogălniceanu sub raportul faptei și gîndirii social-economice* (Craiova, 1979). An exhaustive edition of his speeches, Mihail Kogălniceanu, *Opere,* iv: *Oratorie II* (1864–78), 4 parts (Bucharest, 1977–82), is a primary source for his political ideas. A selection of diplomatic correspondence and other papers, Mihail Kogălniceanu, *Documente diplomatice* (Bucharest, 1972), provides an introduction to his foreign policy. Sympathetic studies of radical liberalism focus on C. A. Rosetti. Vasile Netea, *C. A. Rosetti* (Bucharest, 1970), is a general overview of his career, and Marin Bucur, *C. A. Rosetti: mesianism și donquijotism revoluționar* (Bucharest, 1970), emphasizes the romantic and visionary aspects of his political thought and activities. The most important politician of all in the late 1870s and 1880s, Ion C. Brătianu, has been badly neglected. The last survey of his career, by Constant Răutu, *Ion C. Brătianu: Omul, timpurile, opera (1821–1891)* (Turnu-Severin, 1940), contains much information, but is uncritical. Two collections of sources provide a starting-point for a reconsideration of his policies and practices: Ion C. Brătianu, *Discursuri, scrieri, acte și documente,* ii: *23 aprilie 1876–30 aprilie 1877* (Bucharest, 1912), which covers the policies of the so-called government of Mazar-pasha and the Liberal government that followed, and Ion C. Brătianu, *Acte și cuvântări,* i–v (Bucharest, 1930–5), a comprehensive collection of documents illuminating not only Brătianu's own activities but also the political and economic situation in Rumania in general between 1866 and 1880.

Rumania as an object of great-power interest and as a player in international relations in her own right between the 1860s and independence has been the subject of several solid accounts. Nicolae Corivan, *Relațiile diplomatice ale României de la 1859 la 1877* (Bucharest, 1984), and Gheorghe Cliveti, *România și puterile garante, 1856–1878* (Iași, 1988), treat Rumania as a European problem and deftly interweave the foreign-policy aims of all parties involved with the vicissitudes of Rumanian domestic politics.

Evgenii Chertan, *Velikie derzhavy i formirovanie rumynskogo nezavisimogo gosudarstva* (Kishinev, 1980), brings to these problems an extensive bibliography of Russian secondary works and the fruits of his own researches in Russian archives. A comprehensive, up-to-date monograph on Charles's foreign policy is one of many tasks awaiting historians. For an overview recourse must be had to Nicolae Iorga, *Politica externă a Regelui Carol I*, 2nd edn. (Bucharest, 1923), a series of lectures given at the University of Bucharest, which is full of ideas, but shows its age and stops with the Treaty of Berlin in 1878. It may be supplemented by Iorga's edition of sources covering the same period, *Correspondance diplomatique roumaine sous le Roi Charles Ier (1866–1880)*, 2nd edn. (Bucharest, 1938).

Russo-Rumanian relations during the Eastern crisis of 1875–8 occupy a central place in every work on the period. Among specialized studies, Barbara Jelavich, *Russia and the Formation of the Romanian National State, 1821–1878* (Cambridge, 1984), provides a balanced perspective. The Russian point of view is ably argued by Mikhail Zalyshkin, *Vneshniaia politika Rumynii i rumyno-russkie otnosheniia, 1875–1878* (Moscow, 1974), who draws upon a variety of Russian and Rumanian sources. Gheorghe I. Brătianu, *Le Problème des frontières russo-roumaines pendant la guerre de 1877–1878 et au Congrès de Berlin* (Bucharest, 1928), investigates the emotional dispute over Bessarabia with relative detachment. The correspondance of the Rumanian representative in St Petersburg illuminates the policies of both Rumania and Russia: Radu Rosetti (ed.), *Corespondenţa Generalului Iancu Ghica, 2 aprilie 1877–8 aprilie 1878* (Bucharest, 1930).

Publications on the War for Independence are extensive and growing. Two massive collections of sources are indispensable: *Documente privind istoria României: Războiul pentru independenţă*, 10 vols. (Bucharest, 1952–5), covers almost every conceivable subject; *Independenţa României: Documente*, 4 vols. (Bucharest, 1977–8), serves as a supplement, focusing on foreign diplomatic correspondence and providing generous excerpts from the domestic and foreign press. A number of monographs are concerned with the events of 1877–8. Nicolae Ciachir, *Războiul pentru independenţa României în contextul european* (Bucharest, 1977), and N. Adăniloaie, *Independenţa naţională a României* (Bucharest, 1986), emphasize diplomatic aspects. Perhaps the best short account of military operations is Constantin Căzănişteanu and Mihail E. Ionescu, *Războiul neatîrnării României, 1877–1878* (Bucharest, 1977). Its patriotic tone is evident in the more extensive account contained in *Istoria militară a poporului român*, iv (Bucharest, 1987). Nicolae Iorga, *Războiul pentru independenţa României* (Bucharest, 1927), deals with matters that could only be hinted at in recent historiography.

2. MODELS OF DEVELOPMENT

Ilie Bădescu, *Sincronism european şi cultura critică românească* (Bucharest, 1984), an exposition of the processes by which Rumanians came into contact with and adapted Western European culture in the nineteenth century, provides a stimulating and controversial introduction to Rumanian thought of the period. Ion Ungureanu, *Idealuri sociale şi realităţi naţionale* (Bucharest, 1988), traces the main currents of Rumanian sociological thought between 1848 and 1918. Valuable discussions of social thought in the latter half of the nineteenth century are contained in general histories of philosophy and literature. The authors of *Istoria filozofiei româneşti*, vols. i, 2nd edn. (Bucharest, 1985) and ii, part 1 (Bucharest, 1980), cover diverse topics in detail, but the ideological spirit of the times sometimes obtrudes. Basil Munteano, *Panorama de la littérature roumaine contemporaine* (Paris, 1938), relates literary creativity to changing aesthetic and ideological currents. Constantin Ciopraga, *Literatura română între 1900 şi 1918* (Iaşi, 1970), does the same, in greater detail, for a period he perceives as a distinct epoch in Rumanian literature and criticism.

The writing on Junimea is enormous. Perhaps the best introduction to the multiple interests and activities of its members, written from a sociological perspective, is Z. Ornea, *Junimea şi junimismul* (Bucharest, 1975). Tudor Vianu, *La Société littéraire Junimea* (Bucharest, 1968), describes the aesthetic and literary heritage of the society. Its contributions to the development of Rumanian historiography as a craft and history as a state of mind is the focus of Alexandru Zub, *Junimea: Implicaţii istoriografice* (Iaşi, 1976). The memoirs of the Junimists offer unique insights into the thought and spirit of the times. Among the best are Iacob Negruzzi, *Amintiri din 'Junimea'*, in I. Negruzzi, *Scrieri*, ii (Bucharest, 1983), and Gheorghe Panu, *Amintirile de la 'Junimea'*, 2 vols. (Bucharest, 1908–10). On the society's principal organ and the cultural activities of its editors there is Pompiliu Marcea, *'Convorbiri Literare' şi spiritul critic* (Bucharest, 1972). As the principal creator of Junimism Titu Maiorescu has been the subject of continuous examination and polemics. The classic study of his life and career is Eugen Lovinescu. *T. Maiorescu*, 2 vols. (Bucharest, 1940). The same author has described Maiorescu's relations with other Junimists in *T. Maiorescu şi contemporanii lui*, 2 vols. (Bucharest, 1943–4). After a period of neglect following the Second World War a critical yet understanding reconsideration of Maiorescu's contributions to Rumanian intellectual life has taken place. Among the essays meriting attention are Nicolae Manolescu, *Contradicţia lui Maiorescu*, 2nd edn. (Bucharest, 1973), and Simion Ghiţa, *Titu Maiorescu: Filozof şi teoretician al culturii* (Bucharest, 1974). Maiorescu's own diary and correspondence are indispensable: Titu Maiorescu, *Jurnal şi epistolar*, 9 vols. (Bucharest, 1975–89), which cover the years 1855 to 1879. On the second generation of Junimists there is Corina Hrişca, *Constantin Rădulescu-Motru, filosof al culturii* (Cluj-Napoca, 1987), and an anthology, Constantin Rădulescu-Motru, *Personalismul energetic şi alte scrieri* (Bucharest, 1984).

The agrarianist currents at the turn of the century are well represented in the scholarly literature. Z. Ornea's *Sămănătorismul*, 2nd edn. (Bucharest, 1971) is comprehensive and critical. Although there is no monograph about Nicolae Iorga's contribution to the movement, the collection of articles he published in *Sămănătorul*, N. Iorga, *O luptă literară*, 2 vols. (Bucharest, 1979), amply reveals his thoughts about the nature of Rumanian society. Z. Ornea, *Poporanismul* (Bucharest, 1972), is the standard work on Rumanian Populism. It may be supplemented by Valeriu Ciobanu, *Poporanismul: Geneză, evoluție, ideologie* (Bucharest, 1946), which places Rumanian Populism within a broad European, especially Russian, context. Stefania Mihăilescu, *Poporanismul și mișcarea socialistă din România* (Bucharest, 1988), elucidates the classic confrontation between Poporanism and Social Democracy. Z. Ornea's *Viața lui C. Stere*, i (Bucharest, 1989), offers a comprehensive intellectual portrait up to the First World War, whereas Ioan Căpreanu, *Eseul unei restituiri: C. Stere* (Iași, 1988), treats Stere as a leader of the Rumanians' struggle for social and national emancipation. C. Stere, *Scrieri* (Bucharest, 1979), a generous selection of articles on literature, politics, and social questions drawn mainly from *Viața românească* before the First World War, reveals the breadth of their author's intellectual culture and social commitment.

The leading theorist of pre-war Rumanian social democracy has been the subject of two first-rate biographies. Damian Hurezeanu, *C. Dobrogeanu-Gherea: Studiu social-istoric* (Bucharest, 1973), focuses on the evolution of Gherea's thought and his application of socialist doctrine to Rumanian economic and social conditions. Z. Ornea, *Viața lui C. Dobrogeanu-Gherea* (Bucharest, 1982), covers similar ground, but in his hands Gherea's career appears richer and more varied.

On economic thought two works survey the period as a whole. The studies edited by Nicolae Ivanciu, *Din gîndirea economică progresistă românească* (Bucharest, 1968), examines some of the major figures, but leaves out others, who perhaps were not judged progressive enough. Broader in scope is Costin Murgescu, *Mersul ideilor economice la români*, 2 vols. (Bucharest, 1987–90), who follows key trends up to the Second World War. Eugen Demetrescu, *Liberalismul economic în dezvoltarea României moderne* (Bucharest, 1940), is a rigorous guide to liberal economic thought in the nineteenth century. Victor Slăvescu's massive studies of the nineteenth-century economists, which contain ample selections from their writings, are fundamental and constitute a history of economic thought of the period: *Vieața și opera economistului Nicolae Suțu, 1798–1871* (Bucharest, 1941); *Vieața și opera economistului Alexandru D. Moruzi, 1815–1878* (Bucharest, 1941); *Vieața și opera economistului Dionisie Pop Marțian, 1829–1865*, 2 vols. (Bucharest, 1943–4); and *Ion Strat, economist, financiar, diplomat, 1836–1879*, 2 vols. (Bucharest, 1946). Similar in scope and importance is P. S. Aurelian, *Opere economice* (Bucharest, 1967). Ion Ionescu de la Brad awaits an up-to-date monograph, but Gheorghe Bogdan-Duică, *Vieața și opera întâiului țărănist român, Ion Ionescu de la Brad (1818–1891)* (Craiova, 1922), is a useful introduction. On Ion Ghica there are his writings on the history and prospects of the Rumanian economy, *Scrieri economice*, 3 vols. (Bucharest, 1937).

3. THE REIGN OF KING CHARLES, 1881–1914

There is no monograph on the politics of the period as a whole, but the following taken together provide an adequate survey of parties, governments, and their respective policies between independence and the First World War: Paraschiva Cîncea, *Viaţa politică din România în primul deceniu al independenţei de stat* (Bucharest, 1974); Traian Lungu, *Viaţa politică în România la sfîrşitul secolului al XIX-lea (1888–1899)* (Bucharest, 1967); Mircea Iosa and Traian Lungu, *Viaţa politică în România, 1899–1910* (Bucharest, 1977); and Anastasie Iordache, *Viaţa politică în România, 1910–1914* (Bucharest, 1972). Still valuable for its first-hand insights into the art of politics is Titu Maiorescu's *Istoria contemporană a României (1866–1900)* (Bucharest, 1925). On the changing fortunes of the Conservative Party Ion Bulei, *Sistemul politic al României moderne: Partidul Conservator* (Bucharest, 1987), is critical and thorough. Corneliu Mateescu describes politics in a minor key in G. *Panu şi radicalismul românesc la sfîrşitul secolului al XIX-lea* (Bucharest, 1987). The role of the peasants in public affairs and the attempts to bring them into the political mainstream are traced by Romus Dima, *Organizarea politică a ţărănimii (sfîrşitul sec. XIX–începutul sec. XX)* (Bucharest, 1985).

Of all the political parties of the time, the socialists received the most attention after the Second World War, but much of what was published shows the marks of ideological constraints. None the less, *Condiţiile istorice ale apariţiei şi dezvoltării clasei muncitoare din România: Făurirea şi afirmarea partidului său politic (1821–1893)* (Bucharest, 1984), the work of many authors, provides a useful survey of the socialist movement down to the founding of the Social Democratic Workers Party. N. Copoiu, *Refacerea P.S.D. din România, 1900–1910* (Bucharest, 1966), covers the period of crisis in Rumanian socialism. Mariana Hausleitner, *Die Nationale Frage in der rumänischen Arbeiterbewegung vor 1924* (Berlin, 1988), elucidates one of the thorniest problems to confront Rumanian socialists. Among older works, I. C. Atanasiu's *Pagini din istoria contimporană a României, 1881–1916, i: Mişcarea socialistă, 1881–1900* (Bucharest, 1932), contains valuable information, but is not a history of the movement. Constantin Titel-Petrescu's *Socialismul în România* (Bucharest, 1945) is not history either, but it retains its value as a corrective to the treatment of the socialist movement in Communist historiography. The studies of Constantin Dobrogeanu-Gherea by Hurezeanu and Ornea have already been mentioned. Gherea's own writings, *Opere complete*, 8 vols. (Bucharest, 1976–83), are a faithful record of his intellectual journey and of the ideological vicissitudes of Rumanian socialism. Two massive collections of sources are indispensable, even though their contents have been carefully selected to conform to the Communist Party's policies at the time of publication. *Documente din istoria mişcării muncitoreşti din România*, 6 vols. (Bucharest, 1966–75), covering the period 1821–1924, contains party manifestos and propaganda tracts, the minutes of party congresses, and excerpts from the party press. *Presa muncitorească şi socialistă din România*, 6 vols. (Bucharest, 1964–73), contains often generous selections from the radical socialist and trade union press, and the introductions to the major newspapers and reviews make up for the absence of a narrative history of the socialist press. There is nothing comparable to these two collections for the other political parties.

For analyses of the principles and structures underlying the political system older treatises on constitutional and administrative law are indispensable. C. Dissescu, *Cursul de drept public român*, 3 vols. (Bucharest, 1890–2), is a comprehensive contemporary exposition interwoven with the author's commentary. Paul Negulescu, *Tratat de drept administrativ român*, i (Bucharest, 1906), is detailed and authoritative; and Paul Negulescu and George Alexianu, *Tratat de drept public*, ii (Bucharest, 1943), provides an update reflecting contemporary political changes. A recent survey, *Istoria dreptului românesc*, ii, part 2 (Bucharest, 1987), offers instructive comparisons with pre-Communist treatments of constitutional theory and practice. On the functioning of parliament two works are fundamental: George D. Nicolescu, *Parlamentul român, 1866–1901* (Bucharest, 1903), which contains excerpts from parliamentary debates and biographical sketches of its members, and *Istoria parlamentului şi a vieţii parlamentare din România pînă la 1918* (Bucharest, 1883), which examines the programmes drawn up by successive governments and how they fared in the Chamber of Deputies and the Senate. The best account of relations between church and state is in Mircea Păcurariu, *Istoria Bisericii Ortodoxe Române*, iii (Bucharest, 1981).

The leading politicians of the period have received relatively little attention since the Second World War, and, thus, recourse must be had to pre-1940 publications. In the absence of a monograph on Ion C. Brătianu's tenure as Prime Minister, there is Frédéric Damé, *J. C. Bratiano: L'Ère nouvelle—la dictature (1883–1885)* (Bucharest, 1886), a series of newspaper editorials hostile to Brătianu's brand of Liberalism, and Ion C. Brătianu, *Acte şi cuvântări*, v–vii (1879–82) (Bucharest, 1934–9). No biography of Ion I. C. Brătianu exists, but an important source for his ideas has been published: *Discursurile lui Ion I. C. Brătianu*, 2 vols. (1895–1909) (Bucharest, 1933). On his brother there is the admiring *Vieaţa şi opera lui Vintilă I. C. Brătianu* (Bucharest, 1936) by friends and associates. Of greater value is Vintilă I. C. Brătianu, *Scrieri şi cuvântări*, 3 vols. (1899–1914) (Bucharest, 1937–40), which provides firsthand evidence of his political and economic ideas and at the same time elucidates the aims and policies of the Liberal Party. Apostol Stan's *Vasile Boerescu (1830–83)* (Bucharest, 1974), about the Foreign Minister in both Conservative and Liberal governments, tells us much about political life immediately after the War for Independence. It may be supplemented by B. Boerescu, *Discursuri politice*, ii (1874–83) (Bucharest, 1910). Of the great Conservatives, Petre P. Carp alone has been the subject of a firstrate political study: C. Gane, *P. P. Carp şi locul său în istoria politică a*

Ţării, 2 vols. (Bucharest, 1936–7). Besides a comprehensive analysis of Carp's political career, it offers a corrective to much of the writing about the politics of the time produced during the Communist era. Carp the Junimist politician reveals himself in Petre P. Carp, *Discursuri*, i: *1868–1888* (Bucharest, 1907). The various shades of political conservatism may be compared in Nicolae Filipescu, *Discursuri politice*, 2 vols. (1888–1907) (Bucharest, 1912–15); Titu Maiorescu, *Discursuri parlamentare*, 5 vols. (1866–99) (Bucharest, 1897–1915); and Take Ionescu, *Discursuri politice*, 4 vols. (1886–1900) (Bucharest, 1897–1904). The most complete study of the latter's political career remains the uncritical biography by C. Xeni, *Take Ionescu* (Bucharest, 1932). Alexandru Marghiloman's *Note politice*, i (1897–1915) (Bucharest, 1927) is full of information about behind-the-scenes politics. Şerban Orăscu's *Spiru Haret* (Bucharest, 1976) is a brief account of social and cultural liberalism.

A history of Rumania's foreign relations during King Charles's reign has yet to be written, but relations with the Central Powers have received ample attention. The survey by Gheorghe Căzan and Şerban Rădulescu-Zoner, *România şi Tripla Alianţă, 1878–1914* (Bucharest, 1979), serves as an introduction to the main lines of Rumania's foreign policy between the War for Independence and the First World War. Ernst Ebel, *Rumänien und die Mittelmächte* (Berlin, 1939), remains indispensable for the same period, based as it is on a thorough investigation of Austrian and German published diplomatic sources. Uta Bindreiter, *Die diplomatischen und wirtschaftlichen Beziehungen zwischen Österreich-Ungarn und Rumänien 1875–88* (Vienna, 1976), pursues the connection between trade, politics, and nationalism in explaining the vicissitudes of Rumania's relations with the Dual Monarchy, and Şerban Rădulescu-Zoner, *Dunărea, Marea Neagră şi Puterile Centrale* (Cluj-Napoca, 1982), examines one of the most difficult issues between them—navigation on the Danube. Of the relatively few studies of Rumania's relations with the Entente, Vasile Vesa's *România şi Franţa la începutul secolului al XX-lea, 1900–1916* (Cluj-Napoca, 1975) traces the political and strategic considerations behind Rumania's co-operation with France and Russia.

4. SOCIETY AND THE ECONOMY

Much remains to be done on social structure and the day-to-day life and mentalities of the inhabitants of both the countryside and the towns and cities. The focus of attention has been the economic condition of the peasants and their relations with landlords. The modest village mono graphs compiled before the First World War, the forerunners of those masterpieces of the genre produced in the inter-war period, suggest those aspects of peasant life that have been neglected. See e.g. A. V. Gîdei, *Monografia comunei rurale Bragadiru-Bulgar din judeţul Ilfov, plasa Sabaru* (Bucharest, 1904); Ion T. Ghica (ed.), *Monografiile comunelor rurale din judeţul Vlaşca*, i (Bucharest, 1904); and Stan Tuţescu and S. Danilescu,

Monografia satului 'Catanele' din judeţul Doljiu (Craiova, 1908). On the housing, clothing, and diet of the peasantry, there is N. Manolescu, *Igiena ţăranilor români* (Bucharest, 1895). Valuable information on the nineteenth century is contained in Henri H. Stahl, *Contribuţii la studiul satelor devălmaşe romîneşti*, i (Bucharest, 1959), and Valer Butură, *Etno grafia poporului român* (Cluj-Napoca, 1978). Social histories of the large and medium landowning classes have yet to be written. The bourgeoisie has been the subject of two classic studies of their role in Rumanian society: Ştefan Zeletin, *Burghezia română: Origina şi rolul ei istoric* (Bucharest, 1925), and Mihail Manoilescu, *Rostul şi destinul burgheziei româneşti* (Bucharest, 1942). But detailed investigations of this particular period of their ascendancy are needed. As for the urban proletariat, N. N. Constantinescu (ed.), *Din istoricul formării şi dezvoltării clasei muncitoare din Romînia pînă la primul război mondial* (Bucharest, 1959), offers a broad, if one-sided, description of working and living conditions.

The literature on the largest minority in pre-1914 Rumania is abundant, but offers no middle ground. Examples of hostility to the Jews are Verax (Radu Rosetti), *La Roumanie et les Juifs* (Bucharest, 1903), and Anastase N. Hâciu, *Evreii în Ţările Româneşti* (Bucharest, 1943). Carol Iancu, *Les Juifs en Roumanie, 1866–1919, de l'exclusion à l'émancipation* (Aix-en-Provence, 1978), makes a strong indictment of the anti-Semitism of the period.

Of the main branches of the economy, agriculture has received by far the most attention. M.-G. Obédénaire, *La Roumanie économique* (Paris, 1876), contains a many-sided description of the condition of agriculture in the 1860s and early 1870s, intended in the first instance to acquaint Western Europe with Rumania. Constantin Corbu, *Ţărănimea din România între 1864 şi 1888* (Bucharest, 1970), is mainly concerned with the peasants' resistance to prevailing agrarian relations. One of their main grievances was the harsh system of agricultural contracts, which has been exhaustively studied by G. Cristea, *Contribuţii la istoria problemei agrare în România: Învoielile agricole (1866–1882)* (Bucharest, 1977). C. Jormescu and I. Popa-Burcă, *Harta agronomică a României* (Bucharest, 1907), is an indispensable handbook of statistics, maps, and descriptions of every facet of agriculture. Radu Rosetti has edited a series of fundamental sources on the agrarian problem, *Acte şi legiuiri privitoare la chestia ţărănească*, series 2, 8 vols. (Ploeşti, 1907–8), which cover such matters as the sale of state lands and rural credit. A good guide to property relations after 1864 based on ample statistical data is G. D. Creangă, *Grundbesitzverteilung und Bauernfrage in Rumänien* (Leipzig, 1907). G. Ionescu-Şişeşti, *Rumäniens bäuerliche Landwirtschaft* (Bucharest, 1912), contains a many-sided investigation of small-scale, peasant agriculture.

Peasant violence has received considerable attention. Its causes in 1888 and the reaction of the government and politicians are amply covered by Constantin Corbu, *Răscoala ţăranilor de la 1888* (Bucharest, 1978), and N. Adăniloaie, *Răscoala ţăranilor din 1888* (Bucharest, 1988). The former views the uprising as a sign of growing class contradictions in the village, while the latter focuses on the specifically agrarian causes and character of the violence. A collection of sources, *Răscoala ţăranilor din 1888* (Bucharest, 1950), contains reports of local authorities and other official documents. The massive peasant uprising of 1907 has been treated as a watershed in agrarian relations. A thought-provoking analysis of the background to it is Philip G. Eidelberg, *The Great Rumanian Peasant Revolt of 1907* (Leiden, 1974), which is based on an exhaustive search of the relevant archives and contemporary publications. Radu Rosetti conducted a careful and still valuable investigation of the long-term economic and social causes of the uprising: *Pentru ce s-au răsculat ţăranii* (Bucharest, 1908). A prominent contemporary who supported peasant rights to land and to a voice in determining their future was Vasile M. Kogălniceanu, whose *Chestiunea ţărănească* (Bucharest, 1906), is both an analysis of the problem and a programme of reform. The most comprehensive account of the uprising is the collective work, *Marea răscoală a ţăranilor din 1907* (Bucharest, 1967). It is superior in coverage to the revised, shortened edition published under the same title in 1987. The historian has at his disposal a massive collection of local and central government papers, *Documente privind marea răscoală a ţăranilor din 1907*, 5 vols. (Bucharest, 1977–87), which covers the conditions preceding the uprising and the course of the violence by geographical regions. An earlier collection, *Răscoala ţăranilor din 1907*, 3 vols. (Bucharest, 1948–9), is less systematic and thorough in its presentation of primary sources.

A useful general guide to agricultural conditions after 1907 is Vasile Liveanu (ed.), *Relaţii agrare şi mişcări ţărăneşti in România, 1908–1921* (Bucharest, 1967). G. D. Creangă, *Consideraţiuni generale asupra reformelor agrare şi asupra exproprierii* (Bucharest, 1913), is a succinct evaluation of agrarian legislation. Constantin Garoflid, *Problema agrară şi deslegarea ei* (Bucharest, 1908), proposed solutions to the agrarian crisis that would preserve the great estates. The two editions of George Maior's *România agricolă*, published in Bucharest before (1895) and after (1911) the uprising are a measure of its effect on public attitudes toward the peasant and agriculture.

No comprehensive, up-to-date history of industry for the period exists, but N. P. Arcadian, *Industrializarea României*, 2nd edn. (Bucharest, 1936), surveys the main branches of industry, including urban artisans and peasant household crafts, before the First World War. The solid monograph by G. Zane, *L'Industrie roumaine au cours de la séconde moitié du XIXe siècle* (Bucharest, 1973), provides a foundation for further research. An essential source of information on the status of industry at the turn of the century is the extensive *Ancheta industrială din 1901–1902*, 2 vols. (Bucharest, 1904). The oil industry has received more attention that other branches. Constantin M. Boncu, *Contribuţii la istoria petrolului românesc* (Bucharest, 1971), minutely traces its development to the end of the nineteenth century. T. C. Aslan, *Studiu asupra monopolurilor în România* (Bucharest,

1906), should be consulted on state control of the postal service and the salt, tobacco, and other industries. The organization and general state of artisan co-operatives are described in Vasile M. Ioachim, *Cooperativele orăşeneşti în România* (Bucharest, 1915), and Tudor Pamfilie, *Industria casnică la români* (Bucharest, 1910), examines various aspects of household production. A good account of railway construction is C. Botez, D. Urma, and I. Saizu, *Epopeea feroviară românească* (Bucharest, 1977).

The banking system and government financial policies are thoroughly examined by Victor Slăvescu, *Istoricul Băncii Naţionale a României (1880– 1924)* (Bucharest, 1925). Combining a detailed narrative and an abundant selection of sources, C. I. Băicoianu, *Istoria politicei noastre monetare şi a Băncii Naţionale, 1880–1914*, 2 vols. and supplements (Bucharest, 1932–9), covers the same subjects. Mircea V. Pienescu, *Spiru C. Haret şi începuturile mişcării băncilor populare, 1898–1903* (Bucharest, 1933), traces the early growth of local co-operative banks. On money and monetary policy the standard work is Costin C. Kiriţescu, *Sistemul bănesc al leului şi precursorii lui*, i and ii (Bucharest, 1964–7). Still valuable for government tariff policies by an advocate of protectionism is Corneliu G. Antonescu, *Die rumänische Handelspolitik von 1875–1910* (Munich, 1915).

5. THE RUMANIANS OUTSIDE RUMANIA

Two recent histories of Transylvania offer contrasting views of Rumanian political and social development during the dualist period. *Din istoria Transilvaniei*, ii, 2nd edn. (Bucharest, 1963), emphasizes the importance of the Rumanians in Transylvanian affairs, while *Erdély története*, iii (Budapest, 1986), treats the principality within a Hungarian context and tends therefore to diminish the role of the Rumanians.

A dominant theme has been the nationality problem. Ştefan Pascu, *Făurirea statului naţional unitar român*, i (Bucharest, 1983), analyses the progress of the Rumanians toward the attainment of a preordained goal of union with the Kingdom of Rumania. Keith Hitchins, *Studies on Romanian National Consciousness* (Milan, 1983), covers such matters as the relationship between socialism and the national movement. Şerban Polverejan and Nicolae Cordoş, *Mişcarea memorandistă în documente (1885– 1897)* (Cluj-Napoca, 1973), presents a succinct account of the Memo- randum period. On the attempts at co-operation by the nationalities to defend their interests against German and Magyar predominance, Lucian Boia, *Relationships between Romanians, Czechs and Slovaks, 1848–1914* (Bucharest, 1977), is an authoritative guide. Liviu Maior, *Mişcarea naţională românească din Transilvania, 1900–1914* (Cluj-Napoca, 1986), describes the activist policies of the Rumanian National Party. Rumanian political movements are analysed from the standpoint of the Hungarian govern- ment by Veritas (Antal Huszár), *A magyarországi románok* (Budapest, 1908), which contains detailed information on Rumanian churches, schools, and economic activities. Recent historiography has given much attention to the Orthodox Church as a defender of the Rumanian nation against the assimilationist policies of the Hungarian government. Of particular value are the well-documented studies by Mircea Păcurariu, *Politica statului ungar față de Biserica românească din Transilvania în perioada dualismului, 1867–1918* (Sibiu, 1986), which covers measures against the church and school and the attempt at Magyarization through the Uniate Church, and Antonie Plămădeală, *Lupta împotriva deznaționalizării Românilor din Transilvania în timpul dualismului austro-ungar* (Sibiu, 1986), which focuses on the critical years of Metropolitan Miron Romanul's incumbency (1874–98). Indispensable are two extensive collections of sources: Teodor V. Păcățian, *Cartea de aur sau luptele politice-naționale ale românilor de sub coroana ungară,* 8 vols. (Sibiu, 1904–15), which contains a rich sampling of materials centring on the activities of the Rumanian National Party, and Gábor G. Kemény, *Iratok a nemzetiségi kérdés történetéhez Magyarországon a dualizmus korában,* 5 vols. (1867–1913) (Budapest, 1952–71), a general work on the nationality problem in Hungary which gives ample attention to the Rumanians and draws upon archival and published sources, especially the press.

There are few scholarly biographies of leading Rumanian political figures. On the long-time president of the Rumanian National Party, Ioan Georgescu, *Dr. Ioan Rațiu* (Sibiu, 1928), is out of date. It may be supplemented by the introduction in Keith Hitchins and Liviu Maior, *Corespondența lui Ioan Rațiu cu George Barițiu (1861–1892)* (Cluj, 1970). George Cipăianu, *Vincențiu Babeș* (Timişoara, 1980) and Mihail P. Dan and George Cipăianu, *Corespondența lui Vincențiu Babeș,* 2 vols. (Cluj-Napoca, 1976–83), reveal the political thinking and goals of the pre-Memorandum generation of politicians. On the Tribunists, a good introduction is D. Vatamaniuc, *Ioan Slavici şi lumea prin care a trecut* (Bucharest, 1968). Lucian Boia, *Eugen Brote, 1850–1912* (Bucharest, 1974) investigates the new approach to the nationality problem taken by the young generation of political leaders. Brote himself produced a characteristic statement of his generation's aims, *Die rumänische Frage in Siebenbürgen und Ungarn* (Berlin, 1895), a history of the nationality conflict between Rumanians and Magyars accompanied by supporting documents. Essential for an understanding of the new activism which led to negotiations between the Rumanian National Party and István Tisza are the memoirs and correspondence of Ioan Mihu, *Spicuiri din gândurile mele* (Sibiu, 1938). Vasile Goldiş occupies a place apart from the majority of the leaders of the Rumanian National Party, because of his close contacts with Magyar intellectuals and his advanced social thought. There is a solid biography by Gheorghe Şora, *Vasile Goldiş* (Timişoara, 1980), and an ample selection of writings, Vasile Goldiş, *Scrieri social-politice şi literare* (Timişoara, 1976).

The economic aspects of the national movement are summarized in Toader Ionescu, *Idei şi orientări în publicistica economică românească (1890–1918)* (Cluj-Napoca, 1985). Nicolae N. Petra, *Băncile româneşti din Ardeal şi Banat* (Sibiu, 1936), and Mihai D. Drecin, *Banca Albina din Sibiu* (Cluj-

Napoca, 1982), cover the multiple activities of Rumanian banks. On the connection between international relations and the Rumanian question in Hungary Teodor Pavel, *Mişcarea Românilor pentru unitate naţională şi diplomaţia Puterilor Centrale*, 2 vols. (Timişoara, 1979–82), is a valuable introduction.

The scholarly literature on the Rumanians of Bukovina is, with a few exceptions, out of date. Little has been published by Rumanian historians since the end of the Second World War. For a brief survey recourse must be had to the slender volume by Nicolae Iorga, *Histoire des Roumains de Bucovine à partir de l'annexion autrichienne (1775–1914)* (Jassy, 1917). On social structure there are three indispensable works by Ilie E. Torouţiu, which reflect the national anxieties of Rumanian intellectuals before the First World War: *Românii şi clasa intelectuală din Bucovina* (Cernăuţi, 1911); *Românii şi clasa de mijloc din Bucovina* (Cernăuţi, 1912); and *Poporaţia şi clasele sociale din Bucovina* (Bucharest, 1916). Cultural and intellectual life have been sorely neglected. The only general monograph on the Orthodox Church, Ion Nistor, *Istoria Bisericii din Bucovina* (Bucharest, 1916), is devoted mainly to its role as a Rumanian national institution and the struggle against the Ruthenians. Constantin Loghin, *Istoria literaturii române din Bucovina, 1775–1918* (Cernăuţi, 1926), the only work of its kind, describes cultural institutions and literary currents as well as writers and their work. Though concerned with a limited area, I. V. Goraş, *Învăţămîntul românesc în ţinutul Sucevei, 1775–1918* (Bucharest, 1975), is a good introduction to the problems of Rumanian schools in the province as a whole.

No satisfactory history of the Rumanian national movement in Bukovina has as yet been written, but Erich Prokopowitsch, *Die rumänische Nationalbewegung in der Bukowina und der Dako-romanismus* (Graz, 1965), is a useful guide to its main aspects. On the national consciousness of Rumanian university students in Bukovina, Teodor Bălan, *Procesul Arboroasei, 1875–1878* (Cernăuţi, 1937), is enlightening. The same author's *Suprimarea mişcărilor naţionale din Bucovina pe timpul războiului mondial, 1914–1918* (Cernăuţi, 1923), describes numerous individual cases of opposition to Austrian rule. Much of the writing on the nationality question in the province is polemical. The arguments and tone are suggested in *Rutenisarea Bucovinei şi causele desnaţionalisării poporului român*, de un Bucovinean (Bucharest, 1904), and Ion Nistor, *Românii şi Rutenii în Bucovina* (Bucharest, 1915).

The scholarly literature on Rumanian social, cultural, and political development in Bessarabia is sparse and out-of-date. Of the older surveys by Rumanians, Ion Nistor, *Istoria Basarabiei* (Cernăuţi, 1923), provides essential information, while P. Cazacu, *Moldova dintre Prut şi Nistru, 1812–1918* (Iaşi, n.d.), focuses on social classes and institutions. An old, in some ways classic, description of the province by Zamfir C. Arbure, *Basarabia în secolul XIX* (Bucharest, 1899), is still useful. From a Soviet perspective, *Istoriia Moldavskoi SSR*, i (Kishinev, 1965), emphasizes the economic and social integration of Bessarabia into the Russian Empire and has little to say about a distinct Rumanian national identity. On such matters Ştefan Ciobanu, *Cultura românească în Basarabia sub stăpînirea rusă* (Chişinău, 1923), suggests the true dimensions of Russification, and Nicolae Popovschi, *Istoria Bisericii din Basarabia în veacul al XIX-lea subt Ruşi* (Chişinău, 1931), describes the contest between the Russian and Moldavian clergies for dominance of the Orthodox Church in Bessarabia.

Solid work has been done on the economic development of Bessarabia. Indispensable is I. S. Grosul and I. G. Budak, *Ocherki istorii narodnogo khoziaistva Bessarabii (1861–1905)* (Kishinev, 1972), which emphasizes the growth of capitalist relations in industry and agriculture. D. E. Shemiakov, *Ocherki ekonomicheskoi istorii Bessarabii epokhi imperializma* (Kishinev, 1980), is a comprehensive survey of the economy between 1900 and 1914, and V. I. Zhukov, *Goroda Bessarabii, 1861–1900* (Kishinev, 1975), traces the processes of urbanization and stresses the economic and social importance of cities.

6. THE FIRST WORLD WAR

The best one-volume history of Rumania during the First World War is Victor Atanasiu, *et al.*, *România în primul război mondial* (Bucharest, 1979), which devotes ample space to economic and political developments as well as military campaigns. Another general account, V. N. Vinogradov, *Rumyniia v gody pervoi mirovoi voiny* (Moscow, 1969), draws extensively upon Russian archival materials and displays little sympathy for Rumania. Rumania's relations with the Entente and the Central Powers before her entrance into the war are described in Constantin Nuţu, *România în anii neutralităţii, 1914–1916* (Bucharest, 1972). Ema Nastovici, *România şi Puterile Centrale în anii 1914–1916* (Bucharest, 1979), examines the links between international diplomacy and domestic politics. Memoirs and other contemporary writings have a special importance in the absence of a history of politics of the period. Fundamental, because of their detail and the wide political contacts of their author, are the memoirs of Alexandru Marghiloman, *Note politice*, i–iv (Bucharest, 1927), which cover the years 1914–19. Valuable also for the atmosphere of the time are Nicolae Iorga's *Războiul nostru în note zilnice*, 3 vols. (Craiova, 1921–3), a collection of newspaper articles published between 1914 and 1918, and his *Memorii*, i–ii (Bucharest, 1931), daily notes on men and events in 1917 and 1918. Ion I. C. Brătianu, *Discursurile*, iv (1913–18) (Bucharest, 1940), is essential reading for an understanding of the policies of Rumania's most important wartime politician.

The literature on the military campaigns of 1916–18 is voluminous. *România în războiul mondial 1916–1919*, 4 vols. text, 4 vols. annexes (Bucharest, 1934–46), published under the auspices of the Ministry of National Defence, was to have been the official history, but was never completed and brings events only to December 1916. It is more sober and impartial than the bulk of writings on Rumania's part in the war. A popular account in the heroic tradition is Constantin Kirițescu, *Istoria războiului pentru întregirea României, 1916–1919*, 3 vols., 2nd edn. (Bucharest, 1925), which exercised enormous influence on the inter-war generation. Recent collective histories of military operations carry on the tradition: *România în anii primului război mondial*, 2 vols. (Bucharest, 1987), and *Istoria militară a poporului român*, v (Bucharest, 1988). The fullest account of political, economic, and social conditions in Rumania under German and Austro-Hungarian occupation is Emil Răcilă, *Contribuții privind lupta Românilor pentru apărarea patriei în primul război mondial, 1916–1918* (Bucharest, 1981).

Although an up-to-date, comprehensive history of the formation of Greater Rumania is lacking, the process may be followed in monographs on the several provinces which united with the Old Kingdom. Ştefan Pascu, *Făurirea statului național unitar român, 1918*, ii (Bucharest, 1983), examines the crucial events of 1918 in Transylvania. The most detailed description of Rumanian nationalist strivings in Bessarabia in 1917 and 1918 remains Cazacu, *Moldova dintre Prut și Nistru, 1812–1918*. It may be supplemented by Ştefan Ciobanu, *Unirea Basarabiei: Studiu și documente* (Bucharest, 1929), which contains an ample selection of sources. Similar in content on Bukovina is Ion Nistor, *Unirea Bucovinei cu România, 28 noiembrie 1918: Studiu și documente* (Bucharest, 1928). On the decisive encounters at the Paris Peace Conference Gheorghe I. Brătianu, *Acțiunea politică și militară a României în 1919* (Bucharest, 1940), uses family papers to explain the role of Ion I. C. Brătianu. The latter is also the dominant figure in Sherman D. Spector, *Rumania at the Paris Peace Conference* (New York, 1962), a study of great power–small power diplomatic confrontations.

7. THE GREAT DEBATE

A judicious introduction to the social thought of the inter-war period is Z. Ornea, *Tradiționalism și modernitate în deceniul al treilea* (Bucharest, 1980), which represents a thorough reading of all the main currents of ideas, but clearly displays sympathy for the rationalism of the Europeanists. Ovid S. Crohmălniceanu, *Literatura română între cele două războaie mondiale*, i (Bucharest, 1972), deals with similar issues of national character and paths of development from the perspective of literature. Useful also, though certain ideological constraints are evident, is the survey of philosophical thought of the inter-war period in *Istoria filozofiei românești*, ii (Bucharest, 1980).

The ideas of the Europeanists are apparent in studies of the Rumanian bourgeoisie already cited. Of the numerous studies on Eugen Lovinescu, Eugen Simion, *E. Lovinescu: Scepticul mintuit* (Bucharest, 1971), treats his Europeanism as an expression of his aesthetic values, while Florin Mihăilescu, *E. Lovinescu și antinomiile criticii* (Bucharest, 1972), places him in the context of Rumanian criticism between Junimism and modernism.

The most ample introduction to the traditionalism of the period is D. Micu, *'Gîndirea' și gîndirismul* (Bucharest, 1975), which is manifestly hostile to all its currents. Until an impartial monograph appears Crainic's thought is best approached through volumes of his essays, notably: *Puncte cardinale în haos* (Bucharest, 1936), an elaboration of the antinomy between East and West; *Ortodoxie și etnocrație* (Bucharest, 1940), a defence of Orthodox spirituality as the foundation of the new Rumanian ethnic state; and *Nostalgia paradisului*, 2nd edn. (Bucharest, 1942), a proclamation of the primacy of religious faith in society. For Nae Ionescu's social thought the best source remains his *Roza vînturilor* (Bucharest, 1937), a collection of articles which appeared originally in his newspaper *Cuvîntul*. The memoir by Mircea Vulcănescu, *Nae Ionescu, așa cum l-am cunoscut* (Bucharest, 1992), is indispensable. The critical writing on Lucian Blaga is abundant. An early synthesis of his thought by Ovidiu Drimba, *Filosofia lui Blaga* (Bucharest, 1944), retains its value as an introduction. Among recent studies, Ion Mihail Popescu, *O perspectivă românească asupra teoriei culturii și valorilor* (Bucharest, 1980), is a penetrating discussion of his philosophy of culture. A many-sided approach to his thought on culture, ethnicity, and related questions is the collection of essays edited by Dumitru Ghișe, Angela Botez, and Victor Botez, *Lucian Blaga—cunoaștere și creație* (Bucharest, 1987). Mac Linscott Ricketts, *Mircea Eliade: The Romanian Roots, 1907–1945*, 2 vols. (Boulder, Colo., 1988), is a thoughtful guide to the intellectual life of the inter-war period, especially the aspirations of the young generation.

The critical analysis of Peasantism by Z. Ornea, *Țărănismul: Studiu sociologic* (Bucharest, 1969), offers valuable insights into Rumanian thought generally about the third way of economic and social development. The collective work, *Profesorul Virgil Madgearu* (Bucharest, 1987), contains a number of solid studies on the chief theoretician of Peasantism. The best source for Madgearu's ideas remains his own works: *Țărănismul* (Bucharest, 1921), a discussion mainly of the political goals of Peasantism, and *Agrarianism. Capitalism. Imperialism* (Bucharest, 1936), an elaboration of the theory of peasant agriculture.

8. SOCIETY AND THE ECONOMY, 1919–1940

The starting-point for an assessment of population problems in the inter-war period is Sabin Manuila and D. C. Georgescu, *Populația României* (Bucharest, 1937), a systematic analysis of the most recent statistics. The rural population has been a special concern of demographers and sociologists. Sabin Manuila, *Structure et évolution de la population rurale* (Bucharest, 1940), is a comprehensive introduction. An indispensable guide to the study of every aspect of rural life is D. Șandru, *Populația rurală a României între cele două războaie mondiale* (Iași, 1980). Equally important is the massive tenth-anniversary issue (1825 pp.) of *Revista de igienă socială* (Bucharest), Jan.–June 1940, whose articles range from culture to sanitation and diet in the village. The numerous village monographs produced by teams of investigators under the auspices of Dimitrie Gusti's Institute of Social Sciences in Bucharest offer a unique introduction to Rumanian rural society. Notable among them are: H. H. Stahl (ed.), *Nerej: Un village d'une région archaique*, 3 vols. (Bucharest, 1939); Anton Golopenţia and D. C. Georgescu (eds.), *60 sate româneşti*, 5 vols. (Bucharest, 1941–3); and five studies by various authors under the general title, *Drăguş: Un sat din Ţara Oltului (Făgăraş)* (Bucharest, 1944–5). Ernest Bernea, *Civilizaţia română sătească* (Bucharest, 1944), attempts to delineate the spiritual and material boundaries of the village.

On economic development during the inter-war period Virgil Madgearu, *Evoluţia economiei româneşti după războiul mondial* (Bucharest, 1940), is thorough and balanced. More technical, but full of information, is G. M. Dobrovici, *Evoluţia economică şi financiară a României în perioada 1934–1943* (Bucharest, 1943). The economic objectives of the Liberals are analysed by Ioan Saizu, *Politica economică a României între 1922 şi 1928* (Bucharest, 1981). I. Puia, *Relaţiile economice externe ale României în perioada interbelică* (Bucharest, 1982), describes Rumania's foreign trade policies and their effects on internal economic development. Ioan Saizu, *Modernizarea României contemporane (perioda interbelică)* (Bucharest, 1991), surveys diverse strategies of economic development.

Much has been written about the accomplishments and shortcomings of post-war agrarian reform. Mitiţă Constantinescu, *L'Évolution de la propriété rurale et la réforme agraire en Roumanie* (Bucharest, 1925), places these matters in a broad historical context. David Mitrany, *The Land and the Peasant in Rumania* (London, 1930), is the most detailed account of agrarian reform in English and, despite its age, remains a fundamental source of information. The most comprehensive modern treatment, with the omission of Bessarabia and the virtual omission of Bukovina, is D. Şandru, *Reforma agrară din 1921 în România* (Bucharest, 1975). The persistent and multiple deficiencies of agriculture after the reforms are discussed by Vasile Bozga, *Criza agrară în România dintre cele două războaie mondiale* (Bucharest, 1975). D. Şandru, *Creditul agricol în România, 1918–1944* (Bucharest, 1985), investigates one of the critical needs of both large and small agricultural producers. Of the voluminous literature on the cooperative movement, the assessment by a Danish specialist, M. Gormsen, is refreshing for its candour and reveals the serious gap between Peasantist theory and reality: Ion Mihalache, M. Gormsen, and Ion Răducanu, *Problema cooperaţiei române* (Bucharest, 1940).

On industry Arcadian, *Industrializarea României*, provides a useful overview, and Marcela Felicia Iovanelli, *Industria românească, 1934–1938* (Bucharest, 1975), describes its recovery after the great depression. Maurice Pearton, *Oil and the Romanian State* (Oxford, 1971), describes the expansion of the oil industry against the background of nationalist economic policy and foreign exploitation. The predominance of foreign capital and corporations in a number of key industries is subjected to critical scrutiny in Gheorghe Buzatu, *România şi trusturile petroliere internaţionale pînă la 1929* (Iaşi, 1981), and Constanţa Bogdan and Adrian Platon, *Capitalul străin în societăţile anonime din România în perioada interbelică* (Bucharest, 1981). Urbanization and its effects on the social life and psychology of the urban working classes have received relatively little attention. Constantin C. Giurescu, *Istoria Bucureştiilor* (Bucharest, 1966), which traces the economic and social development of the capital, suggests the many possibilities for investigation.

9. POLITICS, 1919–1940

Many works on the political system of the inter-war period dwell on the disparity between principles and practices. In this spirit, A. G. Savu, *Sistemul partidelor politice din România, 1919–1940* (Bucharest, 1976), evaluates the motive force provided by competing political parties, and Matei Dogan, *Analiza statistică a 'democraţiei parlamentare' din România* (Bucharest, 1946), minutely examines its unrepresentative character. Diverse opinions about political institutions and their proper functions were published by the Rumanian Social Institute in Bucharest in connection with the drafting of a new constitution in 1923, *Noua constituţie a României şi nouile constituţii europene* (Bucharest, 1923). The nature of the new constitution and its influence on political practices have been analysed by Eufrosina Popescu, *Din istoria politică a României: Constituţia din 1923* (Bucharest, 1983), and Angela Banciu, *Rolul Constituţiei din 1923 în consolidarea unităţii naţionale* (Bucharest, 1988). Paul Negulescu and George Alexianu, *Tratat de drept public*, 2 vols. (Bucharest, 1942–3), and Erast Diti Tarangul, *Tratat de drept administrativ român* (Cernăuţi, 1944) provide systematic dissections of the theoretical foundations and the functions of political institutions.

A good overview of the programmes and ideologies of the main political parties and currents, including contributions by Madgearu, Manoilescu, and Iorga, is contained in *Doctrinele partidelor politice* (Bucharest, 1923), published by the Rumanian Social Institute. The parties on the extreme right and left have received more attention than those in the centre. The standard work on the Iron Guard is Armin Heinen, *Die Legion 'Erzengel Michael' in Rumänien* (Munich, 1986), a comprehensive analysis of its social structure and political organization. A one-sided condemnation, Mihai Fătu and Ion Spălăţelu, *Garda de Fier: Organizaţia teroristă de tip fascist* (Bucharest, 1971), is typical of post-war historiography. Still useful for its appreciation of the spirit of the Guard is Eugen Weber, 'Romania', in Hans Rogger and Eugen Weber (eds.), *The European Right* (Berkeley, Calif., 1965), 501–74. The anti-Semitism and extreme nationalism practiced by Alexandru C. Cuza and Octavian Goga are condemned by Gheorghe T. Pop, *Caracterul antinaţional şi antipopular al activităţii Partidului Naţional Creştin* (Cluj-Napoca, 1978). On the left, Social Democracy still awaits a scholarly monograph. Titel-Petrescu's *Socialismul în România*, the only general survey, is a compilation of diverse pieces of information rather than a connected history. On the Ploughmen's Front, G. Micle, *Răscoala pământului* (Bucharest, 1945), gives some idea of the aspirations of the rank-and-file, and G. I. Ioniță and G. Țuțui, *Frontul Plugarilor* (Bucharest, 1970), judges the activities of the Front mainly in terms of its support of the Communist Party. Despite all the attention which the Communist Party has received, no thorough, reliable general history exists. The majority of publications exaggerate the importance of the party or accommodate facts to ideological concerns. The following are among the most informative and are extensively documented: Marin C. Stănescu, *Mișcarea muncitorească din România în anii 1921–1924* (Bucharest, 1971) and *Mișcarea muncitorească din România în anii 1924–1928* (Bucharest, 1981). As for other parties, those representing the peasants are the subject of several critical monographs. Pamfil Șeicaru, *Istoria Partidelor Național, Țărănist, și Național-Țărănist*, ii (Madrid, 1963), is an overview of inter-war politics by a leading journalist of the right, and Ioan Scurtu, *Viața politică a României, 1918–1926* (Bucharest, 1975), describes the origins and aims of the Peasant Party. The same author's *Din viața politică a României, 1926–1947* (Bucharest, 1983), traces the rise and destruction of the National Peasant Party. Klaus P. Beer, *Zur Entwicklung des Parteien- und Parlamentssystem in Rumänien 1928–1933*, 2 vols. (Frankfurt am Main, 1983), chronicles the hopes and frustrations of National Peasant governments during the watershed period of Rumanian democracy.

The best general survey of political life in the inter-war period remains Henry L. Roberts, *Rumania: Political Problems of an Agrarian State* (New Haven, Conn., 1951), which analyses the relationship between economic development, foreign policy, and party politics. Mircea Mușat and Ion Ardeleanu, *România după Marea Unire*, ii, parts 1 and 2 (Bucharest, 1986–8), describes in detail the ideologies and social structure of political parties and the domestic policies of governments between 1918 and 1940.

Numerous monographs cover distinct segments of inter-war political developments. Mircea Mușat and Ion Ardeleanu, *Viața politică în România, 1918–1921*, 2nd edn. (Bucharest, 1976), is primarily an analysis of the social bases and programmes of the main political parties in the immediate, unsettled post-war years. Mihail Rusenescu and Ioan Saizu, *Viața politică în România, 1922-1928* (Bucharest, 1979), and Marin Nedelea, *Aspecte ale vieții politice din România în anii 1922–1926* (Bucharest, 1987), are concerned with the policies of the National Liberal Party and the challenge to its predominance posed by the National Peasants and other opposition parties. Florea Nedelcu, *De la restaurație la dictatura regală* (Cluj-Napoca, 1981), traces the steady decline of parliamentary institutions under Carol II down to 1938. A. G. Savu, *Dictatura regală* (Bucharest, 1970), is a many-sided analysis of Carol's dictatorship and the causes of his downfall. Since 1989 the memoirs of key political figures have begun to be published. Especially valuable for the light they shed on inter-war politics are Armand Călinescu, *Însemnări politice, 1916–1939* (Bucharest, 1990), and Grigore Gafencu, *Însemnări politice, 1929–1939* (Bucharest, 1991).

10. FOREIGN POLICY, 1919—1940

The contrast in Rumania's fortunes in international relations between the 1920s, when hopes for the maintenance of the Versailles system were strong, and the 1930s, when revisionism and appeasement shattered these hopes, is the main theme of Viorica Moisuc, *Premisele izolării politice a României, 1919–1940* (Bucharest, 1991). Efforts by successive Rumanian governments to create an international shield to protect the gains made at Versailles are chronicled by Eliza Campus, *Mica Înţelegere* (Bucharest, 1968). Covering the same subjects but more even-handed in judging the motives of the various parties, is Nicolae Iordache, *La Petite Entente et l'Europe* (Geneva, 1977). Eliza Campus, *Înţelegere Balcanică* (Bucharest, 1972), has much to say about Rumania's participation in the Balkan Entente, but often does not carry its analyses far enough. On Rumania's participation in the League of Nations, Petre Bărbulescu, *România la Societatea Naţiunilor* (Bucharest, 1975), is concerned mainly with international attempts to ensure peace and security, while Mihai Iacobescu, *România şi Societatea Naţiunilor, 1919–1929* (Bucharest, 1988), is broader in scope, covering such questions as the protection of minorities and humanitarian and intellectual co-operation. Emilian Bold, *De la Versailles la Lausanne (1919–1932)* (Iaşi, 1976), investigates the disagreements over reparations which soured relations between Rumania and her wartime allies. The principal Rumanian architect of collective security, Nicolae Titulescu, has received more attention than any other Rumanian statesman of the period. Valuable, though admiring, are Ion M. Oprea, *Nicolae Titulescu* (Bucharest, 1966), the fullest biography to date, and the collection of essays covering every facet of Titulescu's career edited by Gheorghe Buzatu, *Titulescu şi strategia păcii* (Iaşi, 1982). Of Titulescu's own writings, perhaps the most valuable selection in Nicolae Titulescu, *Documente diplomatice* (Bucharest, 1967).

The most extensive and reliable survey of Rumania's relations with Germany in the 1930s is Andreas Hillgruber, *Hitler, König Carol und Marschall Antonescu* (Wiesbaden, 1954). Rumania's increasingly desperate efforts to fend off hostile large and small neighbours are described in Viorica Moisuc, *Diplomaţia României şi problema apărării suveranităţii şi independenţei naţionale în perioada martie 1938–mai 1940* (Bucharest, 1971), and Ioan Talpeş, *Diplomaţie şi apărare, 1933–1939* (Bucharest, 1988). On relations with the Soviet Union no middle, scholarly ground has yet been achieved. The bulk of the writing has been done by Soviet historians, who leave no doubt about where justice on the Bessarabian and other matters in dispute lie. Typical of this point of view is B. M. Kolker and I. E. Levit, *Vneshniaia politika Rumynii i rumyno-sovetskie otnosheniia (sentiabr' 1939–iiun' 1941)* (Moscow, 1971). A broader view of relations between the two countries based upon the extensive use of Soviet archives is A. A. Sheviakov, *Sovetsko-rumynskie otnosheniia i problema evropeiskoi bezopasnosti, 1932–1939* (Moscow, 1977). Only since 1989 have Rumanian historians been able to present their own case fully. The first major Rumanian work on the Bessarabian question in the inter-war period to appear since the end of the Second World War is Valeriu Florin Dobrinescu, *Bătălia pentru Basarabia* (Iaşi, 1991), which draws extensively upon Western archival materials. As for relations with the West, Britain's economic interest in Rumania and reluctance to enter into political engagements are analysed by Valeriu Florin Dobrinescu, *Relaţii româno-engleze (1914–1933)* (Iaşi, 1986), and David Britton Funderburk, *Politica Marii Britanii faţă de România (1938–1940)* (Bucharest, 1983), explains why British policy changed after the Munich crisis. The ultimate failure of Rumania's policy of balance between competing great powers is revealed in the memoirs of Rumania's Foreign Minister in the summer of 1940: Mihail Manoilescu, *Dictatul de la Viena: Memorii, iulie–august 1940* (Bucharest, 1991).

11. THE SECOND WORLD WAR, 1940–1944

On Rumania during the Second World War Hillgruber's work cited above is indispensable, especially for economic and political relations with Germany. The most detailed account of Rumania's participation in the war against the Soviet Union is Platon Chirnoagă, *Istoria politică şi militară a războiului României contra Rusiei sovietice, 22 iunie 1941–23 august 1944* (Madrid, 1965). A. Simion, *Regimul politic din România în perioada septembrie 1940–ianuarie 1941* (Cluj-Napoca, 1976), examines the Antonescu–Iron Guard partnership and its break-up. The official account of the Guard's attempt to seize power is *Pe marginea prăpastiei, 21–23 ianuarie 1941*, 2 vols. (Bucharest, 1942). Mihai Fătu, *Contribuţii la studierea regimului politic din România (septembrie 1940–august 1944)* (Bucharest, 1984), analyses the ideology and the labour, agrarian, and education policies of the Antonescu regime and concludes that it bore the characteristic features of a fascist dictatorship. *Trei ani de guvernare, 6 septembrie 1940–6 septembrie 1943* (Bucharest, 1943), the Antonescu government's own estimate of its economic and social accomplishments, provides insight into the nature of the dictatorship. The fullest account of the treatment of the Jews in wartime Rumania is Matatias Carp, *Cartea neagră*, 3 vols. (Bucharest, 1946–8). Since 1989 a spate of works on Antonescu has appeared, all intended to rehabilitate him as a national hero. Useful for an understanding of his policies and long-term goals is the anthology of writings by and about him edited by Gheorghe Buzatu, *Mareşalul Antonescu în faţa istoriei*, 2 vols. (Iaşi, 1990).

The most detailed account of Rumania's slide toward defeat and of efforts by both the Antonescu government and the opposition to make peace with the Western Allies is A. Simion, *Preliminarii politico-diplomatice ale insurecţiei române din august 1944* (Cluj-Napoca, 1979). Valuable information on Rumania's relations with the Allies is contained in Gheorghe Buzatu, *Din istoria secretă a celui de-al doilea război mondial*, i (Bucharest, 1988). The same author has edited a series of studies on the internal political and international conditions leading to the overthrow of the

Antonescu regime, *Actul de la 23 august 1944 în context internațional* (Bucharest, 1984). A highly selective but important collection of documents on the events of 1944 is available in *23 august 1944: Documente*, ii (Bucharest, 1984).

12. THE TRANSITION, 1944—1947

There are many gaps in the historiography of the years between Antonescu's overthrow and the proclamation of the Rumanian People's Republic. No scholarly monograph exists on the period as a whole, and specialized works are often of uneven quality. In contrast to the paucity of works on the Rumanian army's three years on the Russian front, an abundant literature exists on its contributions to the final defeat of Nazi Germany. The most recent account is in *România în anii celui de-al doilea război mondial*, iii (Bucharest, 1989). On the international settlement between the Allies and Rumania Ștefan Lache and Gheorghe Țuțui, *România și conferința de pace de la Paris din 1946* (Cluj-Napoca, 1978), is highly selective. More reliable is Valeriu Florin Dobrinescu, *România și organizarea postbelică a lumii (1945–1947)* (Bucharest, 1988). A useful guide to the disputes between the Western Allies and the Soviet Union over the future of Rumania is Paul D. Quinlan, *Clash over Romania* (Los Angeles, 1977).

Rumanian works on internal political and economic development have placed the Communist Party in the most favourable light possible. Mihai Fătu, *Alianțe politice ale Partidului Comunist Român, 1944–1947* (Cluj-Napoca, 1979), and Gheorghe Țuțui, *Evoluția Partidului Social-Democrat din România de la frontul unic la partidul unic (mai 1944–februarie 1948)* (Bucharest, 1979), emphasize the inevitability and the progressive nature of the one-party system. Mihai Fătu, *Sfîrșit fără glorie* (Bucharest, 1972), describes the disappearance of the National Peasant and National Liberal parties and attributes the cause to their own wilful obstruction of the new, progressive order of things. By contrast, Reuben H. Markham, *Rumania under the Soviet Yoke* (Boston, Mass., 1949), offers first-hand evidence that the responsibility for the destruction of the political opposition lay with the Communist Party and Soviet occupation authorities. A useful survey of economic development is Ion Alexandru, *Economia României în primii ani postbelici (1945–1947)* (Bucharest, 1986). Maria Curteanu, *Sectorul de stat în România anilor 1944–1947* (Bucharest, 1974), traces the growing centralized control and direction of the economy.

INDEX